Desiring Arabs

Desiring Arabs

JOSEPH A. MASSAD

The University of Chicago Press   Chicago and London

The University of Chicago Press, Chicago 60637
The University of Chicago Press, Ltd., London
© 2007 by The University of Chicago
All rights reserved. Published 2007
Paperback edition 2008
Printed in the United States of America

17 16 15 14 13 12 11 10 09 08   4 5 6 7 8

ISBN-13: 978-0-226-50958-7 (cloth)
ISBN-13: 978-0-226-50959-4 (paper)
ISBN-10: 0-226-50958-3 (cloth)
ISBN-10: 0-226-50959-1 (paper)

An earlier version of chapter 3 was published in the journal *Public
Culture* (Spring 2002).

Library of Congress Cataloging-in-Publication Data

Massad, Joseph Andoni, 1963–
    Desiring Arabs / Joseph A. Massad.
      p. cm.
    Includes bibliographical references and index.
    ISBN-13: 978-0-226-50958-7 (cloth : alk. paper)
    ISBN-10: 0-226-50958-3 (cloth : alk. paper)
    1. Civilization, Arab.   2. Arabs—Sexual behavior.   3. Arab
countries—Foreign public opinion, Western.   I Title.
    DS36.77.M38   2007
    306.70917'4927—dc22   2006039690

⊗ The paper used in this publication meets the minimum
requirements of the American National Standard for Information
Sciences—Permanence of Paper for Printed Library Materials, ANSI
Z39.48-1992.

To the memory of

MAGDA AL-NOWAIHI AND EDWARD W. SAID

Contents

Acknowledgments

This book was supposed to be an intellectual history of the modern Arab world revolving around the question of culture, heritage, and modernity. At the time, I began to think about it, and I presented an initial paper on the subject at the annual conference of the Middle East Studies Association, I did not think that the question of desire would become so essential to it. The book would soon take a different turn altogether.

In fact, the question of sexual desire did not come about due to an initial scholarly interest in the subject matter but rather out of political frustration with the nature of Western political discourse on and journalistic representations of the sexual desires of Arabs. Since I arrived in the United States in pursuit of university education in the early 1980s, I argued with many Westerners and a few Arabs who reproduced the discourse of sexual identities as "universals" and upheld their "right" to defend such identities wherever they were repressed. I disagreed vehemently. When I chose the scholarly route, I came to understand identities as discursive effects, and therefore opted not to publish anything about the subject in order not to contribute to the problem by inciting more discourse about it. Mervat Hatem and Neville Hoad, friends and scholars, began to push me since the early 1990s to articulate my ideas in writing, as the analysis and political views I espoused were not being represented at all, and the discourse was expanding relentlessly. My contribution, I hoped, while admittedly inciting more discourse in the Western academy, could at least introduce a necessary criticism to which most remained blind, and could shift the object of discourse from sexual desire onto how discourse about sex is incited and how it relates to concepts like civilization and culture. With much trepidation and uncertainty, I accepted in 1999 a generous invitation from Elizabeth Povinelli, who at the time was teaching at the University of Chicago, to a conference she was organizing titled "Hatred: Confronting the Other" scheduled to take place in February 2000. This provided the opportunity to write and present a first draft of what would become chapter 3. A longer version of the paper would soon be published in the journal *Public Culture*. In light of this, I gradually began to think about the modern intellectual history of the representation of Arab sexual desires. While there were sporadic studies about Western and Orientalist representations, there was nothing about Arab representations. The project became clearer in my mind, and I set out to write it. I thank Mervat, Neville, and Beth for making this book possible.

I began my research in earnest during my sabbatical year 2002–3, which I spent in the United Kingdom at the University of London's School of Oriental and African Studies (SOAS). I am indebted to the late Edward Said and Colin Bundy for arranging my affiliation with SOAS. SOAS and London were the perfect place to be, away from America's jingoism after 9/11 and its more intense anti-Arab and anti-Muslim hatred. I was sustained by the intellectual and political energies of many people affiliated with SOAS, including a great group of undergraduate and graduate students: Awad Joumaa, Khaled Ziada, Afaf Udwan, Reem Botmeh, Samia Botmeh, Omar Waraich, Wafa' Qubbaj, and Nick Denes provided excellent conversations, great food, and the perfect pub companionship. Sarah Stewart was the kindest office companion.

At Columbia, my students in three seminars, "Turath and Modernity," "The Politics of Desire," and "Studying Gender and Sexuality in the Arab world," were excellent interlocutors. Mu'nis al-Hojairi, Hala Al-Hoshan, Alexis (Ali) Wick, Dina Ramadan, Nader Uthman, Nadia Guessous, Lana Kammourieh, Elizabeth Holt, Zachary Wales, Karim Tartoussieh, Claire Panetta, Sandy Choi, Megan Patrick, Linda Sayed, and Jung Min Seo read voraciously. Their complaints about the amount of reading they had to do did not however detract from their enthusiasm. I thank them all for their serious engagement.

I was invited to give lectures based on the book at a number of universities. I thank Elizabeth Povinelli for inviting me to the University of Chicago where I gave the inaugural lecture relating to this book. I also thank Chandan Reddy for inviting me to the University of Washington in Seattle, Eugene Rogan for inviting me to Saint Antony's College at

Oxford University, Robert Young and Rajeswari Sunderrajan for inviting me to Wadham College at Oxford, Yasir Suleiman for inviting me to the University of Edinburgh, Wenchen Ouyang for inviting me to SOAS, Robert Vitalis for inviting me to the University of Pennsylvania, Samir Khalaf and Eugene Rogan for inviting to the American University of Beirut, Wael Hallaq and Michelle Hartman for inviting me to McGill University and Dana Sajdi for arranging it, Ann Lesch and Martina Reiker for inviting me to the American University in Cairo, and Mazhar Al-Zo'by and Khaldoun Samman for inviting me to Macalester College. I also would like to express my appreciation to the Middle East Institute and the Department of Middle East and Asian Languages and Cultures and the University Seminars at Columbia University for their help in the publication of this book. Some of the ideas presented in the book have benefited from discussions in the Columbia University Arabic Seminar. I thank my colleague George Saliba for inviting me to address the seminar.

The book was written in three cities, London, Amman, and New York. In London, the friendship, love, and support of Islah Jad, who was also spending a couple of years in the city, were indispensable. I am not sure what I would have done without her. Making and eating sushi together is one of my fondest memories. Ahdaf Soueif provided much-needed warmth and political solidarity. The companionship of Islah and Ahdaf and that of the SOAS students made London a most pleasant place to be.

In Amman, I received incalculable support from my mother and sisters. My mother complained that I did not have enough time to converse with her and is therefore the happiest that the book is finally done. My father, who was not inclined to things academic, but was excited and proud that I was finishing another book, did not live to see it published. He died of lung cancer in February 2005. My only consolation is that he lived to see my first book published. He would always ask me for more copies to give to his friends. Without the intellectual engagement, friendship, and bibliographic advice of Muhammad Ayyub and Hasan Abu-Haniyyah, Amman would have been much less engaging intellectually. Our conversations at Muhammad's bookstore and over tea and narguileh were (and are) a most sustaining ritual. In New York, the great loving company of Ali Razki and Susan Scott-Kerr provided regularly over the greatest and most delicious meals made the city livable, even at the grimmest moments. If they ever leave New York, they must pack me away with them.

I asked and received advice and help from many colleagues and scholars who responded to my queries with much generosity. Anton Shammas, Talal Asad, Philip Khoury, Carole Bardenstein, Khaled Fahmy,

Ahmad Dallal, Jamil Dakwar, Yousry Nasrallah, Tayeb El-Hibri, and Mona El-Ghobashi gave excellent suggestions of books, newspaper articles, and other reading material that I needed to consider. Yasin Nourani alerted me early on in my research to a passage he remembered in Salamah Musa's autobiography, which opened a Pandora's box, of which he was not aware. My good friend Nour Barakat shared his knowledge of films, popular culture, and literature. Khaled El-Rouayheb shared with me parts of his excellent to-be-published manuscript on the Ottoman period. My colleague Muhsin Al-Musawi was most generous with my incessant queries. His encyclopedic knowledge of Arabic literature meant that he always had the answers and then some. Janaki Bakhle provided much-needed help on publishing matters. Kamal Boullata and Lily Farhoud are walking encyclopedias of modern Arab art. They answered all my questions and provided much advice on Arab Orientalist painting. Mary Murrell was most generous with her time and publishing knowledge. I am eternally grateful for her help and support. I thank them all for being great exemplars of collegiality.

Many friends and colleagues also read portions and gave me excellent feedback. I thank Samia Mehrez, Elias Khoury, and Noha Radwan for indulging me at a time when their schedules were full. Their scholarly feedback and suggestions, packaged with loving friendship, have ensured that this is a much better book. My departmental chair and friend Hamid Dabashi gave much support, on a personal and departmental level. Without his efforts, writing this book would have proven a much more difficult task. I am grateful to all of them.

I have argued time and again with As'ad AbuKhalil about many of the issues raised in this book. It is testament to his generous spirit and open mind that he came to change his mind about many aspects of the arguments presented. As'ad takes political and scholarly (though not personal) criticism in the most open of ways. Even though he comes in for hard-hitting criticism in chapter 3, he never balked in his support of the book. As'ad is one of the most principled and courageous people I have ever met. Our constant arguments about politics sustain our friendship, as does his fierce loyalty. His support of me when insidious forces of repression targeted me was crucial to my sanity. He read two chapters of the book and gave valuable suggestions.

Without the love and support of Fayez Samara and Neville Hoad, this book would not have been written at all. Fayez's generosity, hospitality, and care went beyond all bounds. A consistent supporter of my academic pursuits, Fayez made it impossible for me not to write and finish the book. He read and listened to many portions of it with excitement and expectation and made crucial suggestions. His trust in me and his much-expressed pride mean the world to me. Neville Hoad is everything that a friend should be and much, much more. Neville read the whole manuscript at least twice (and listened to many portions on the phone a myriad of times), giving me the most insightful and critical suggestions. Our work, which overlaps politically and theoretically, has strengthened our friendship since the first year of graduate school. His loving and indefatigable support during the direst period of my life made going through it much less difficult. The love that he and Fayez provided carried me and this project through. I am eternally in their debt.

The two people that I most wanted to read this book, my friend and mentor Edward W. Said and my close friend and colleague Magda Al-Nowaihi, passed away before it was completed. Magda read one chapter and portions of another before she died in 2002. I have missed her every day since. In writing this book, I longed for her brilliant mind, which contained the greatest corpus of knowledge about Arabic literature, and her critical engagement, which, I am certain, would have improved this book immeasurably. I wrote it imagining her looking over my shoulder. Her loss, expected as it was after a long battle with cancer, remains unfathomable to me. Her courage in facing life was only matched by her courage in facing death.

Not only was Edward a mentor, a friend, and a colleague, he was also a surrogate father to me. When I came down with a serious illness in the summer of 2002, he worried about me as only a parent would. While I was in London, Edward spent two months in Cambridge, during which I saw him often. He would visit London throughout the remainder of the academic year, just as I would come to New York on several occasions to give lectures. This ensured that we saw each other every month after he left Cambridge. I would see him almost daily when he visited London, just as I did when I visited New York. This was the last year of Edward's life and the most intimate year that I had had with him since meeting him thirteen years earlier. We met again in London in May 2003 and in Beirut in late June and early July of 2003 and were planning to meet in Seville in August. While I was in Madrid in August, I could not catch up with him in Seville, as he was already quite ill and was not sure he would go till the last minute. It was from Seville that he then proceeded to Portugal for his last trip overseas.

Edward read drafts of three chapters of the book and gave me needed criticisms. It was not entirely clear to me then what he thought of the project. When I came to Columbia to participate in the conference celebrating the twenty-fifth anniversary of *Orientalism* in April 2003, he asked me if I would be interested in publishing the book in his Harvard University Press (HUP) series. I was in disbelief of this unexpected praise. I prepared a proposal quickly and sent it to him and then forwarded it to the HUP editor. The HUP board approved the contract for the book several months later, in September—two weeks before Edward's death. I had been back from my sabbatical by then and saw Edward much more weakened than he had been in early July in Beirut. He called me on his cellular phone from the car while on his way home from yet another chemotherapy treatment at the hospital. "Any word from Harvard?" he asked. I told him that I had just heard half an hour earlier. He was thrilled. I was ecstatic.

Unfortunately, a few weeks before production was set to begin, the HUP editor and I realized that we had differing visions for the book, and we parted ways. I approached Douglas Mitchell at the University of Chicago Press with the project. Douglas's enthusiasm for this book gave me much relief and renewed my excitement. I am honored and lucky that he gave me the opportunity to work with him. Douglas is all that an editor should be and then some. His commitment to scholarship, professionalism, respect, and sensitivity to authors is rare in an increasingly commercialized academic publishing industry. I will always be grateful for his support. Maia Rigas copyedited the manuscript with a light hand. I thank her for her efforts.

The memory and images of Magda and Edward remained before me throughout the process of writing. Had they lived, they would have enriched this book significantly. I can only hope that they would have approved of the final product. It is to their memory that *Desiring Arabs* is dedicated.

Introduction

In his classic *The Marriage of Cadmus and Harmony,* Roberto Calasso observes that "to a considerable extent classical morality [in the Western tradition] developed around reflections on the nature of men's love for boys."[1] *Desiring Arabs* will venture to show that modern and contemporary Arab historiography developed to a considerable extent around the repudiation not only of men's love for boys but also of all sexual desires it identified as part of the Arab past and which the European present condemns and sometimes champions.

An intellectual and scholarly battle has raged since the nineteenth century in the shadow of the political, economic, and military conquests that colonial Europe unleashed on what came to be called the "Arab world." This battle was fought over modern European concepts that defined the colonial conquest, namely, "culture" and "civilization"; how these related to the modern significance of the past of the Arabs; how the latter compared to the present of Europe, and the weight that this excavated Arab past would register on the modern European scales of civilizations and cultures. This battle was not unrelated to the political, economic, and military battles being fought; on the contrary, it was in large measure constitutive of them. As Orientalism assumed a central place in the colonial campaign, its pretensions encompassed defining who the subject people to be colonized were, what their past was, the content of

---

1. Roberto Calasso, *The Marriage of Cadmus and Harmony,* translated from the Italian by Tim Parks (London: Vintage, 1994), 84.

1

their culture, and how they measured up to the civilizational, cultural, and racial hierarchies that colonial thought had disseminated.

These pretensions would not stand unchallenged for long. Intellectuals and scholars from around the colonized "Arab world," itself a colonial appellation, would soon engage the Orientalists in historical excavations of their own. Their archeological efforts would delve not only into the medieval manuscripts and treatises that would soon constitute the canonical archive of the Arab past (now defined as "heritage") for both the Western Orientalists and the Arab writers, but also, and on occasion, of Orientalist archeology itself.

British literary scholar Raymond Williams excavated the modern English term "culture" as having emerged in the eighteenth century and certainly by the early nineteenth as different from its earlier meaning of plant cultivation and its more-recent meaning of the upbringing of children to something that defined class, education, and specific forms of knowledge. The importance of Williams's work on "culture" is his historicization of its emergence as a *category* in terms of which modern scholars study "a people," itself a modern invention, as well as its emergence as an *object* of study for imperial anthropology and archeology, wherein *culture* refers to material production, to imperial historiography, and more recently to cultural studies, wherein the term refers to signifying and symbolic systems of production. For Williams, however, scholars must relate these two notions of culture rather than posit them as contrasting with one another.[2] To be less abstract, kinship ties, religious institutions, marriage and divorce rituals, burials, specific forms of nationalism, laws and rules, forms of societal and economic organization, and styles of political engagement and governmental regulation cannot be studied separate from the overall socioeconomic system within which they exist any more than poetry, songs, and music, oral and written traditions, myths and superstitions, cinema and theater, religious beliefs, gender roles, sexual roles, and indeed sexual desire itself can be studied in isolation from the institutions within which they are enveloped and the overall socioeconomic system that makes them possible.

It is not that culture is simply a subset of other forces any more than it is their organizing principle. Rather, culture as a *category* of modern thought proves to be dynamic and interdependent with existing systems of thought just as culture as an *object* of study proves to be dynamic and

2. Raymond Williams, *Keywords: A Vocabulary of Culture and Society*, rev. ed. (New York: Oxford University Press, 1983), 87–93. See also Raymond Williams, *Culture and Society, 1780–1950* (New York: Columbia University Press, 1983), introduction, xiii–xx.

interdependent with existing socioeconomic and political systems that define it and are defined by it. Williams demonstrated the organic link between "culture" and "civilization": "Like culture . . . with which it has had a long and still difficult interaction, [civilization] referred originally to a process, and in some contexts this sense still survives." He located the modern meaning of *civilization* in English as having emerged in the 1830s. Its use in the plural would come about in the 1860s, when it would be contrasted with barbarism and savagery.[3] Such a historicized notion of culture and civilization was, however, mostly absent from Orientalist scholarship as well as from Arab nationalist scholarship (some Arab Marxist works excepted). Instead, culture and civilization were posited as reified and timeless essences that were separate and separable from the economy, politics, and social and power relations, which they constituted.[4] Thus culture and civilization were both categories in terms of which one thought *and* objects of thought and scholarship to be investigated and studied. Although Williams does not relate the historical process of this transformation to colonialism, the timing of the emergence of the new meanings of "culture" and "civilization" and their use in plural forms is hardly coincidental.

As civilization was the operative evaluative criterion, two antinomies would determine the representation and self-representation of the history and culture of the Arabs. German scholar Reinhard Schulze has argued that the binaries of decadence/renaissance and tradition/modernity would govern all such representations as "the basis of a concept of cultural history which, of course, reflected the [European] political interpretation of historical development current in the nineteenth century."[5] The way this temporal epistemology was institutionalized has much to do with colonialism and its Orientalist correlate, for it was Europeans who "discovered" the decadence of the Arabs. Indeed, to legitimize his invasion of Egypt in 1798, Napoleon worried that the country had been driven to barbarism and decay by the Turks and that it was the duty of France to liberate its population.[6] His view, however, was not shared by

3. Williams, *Keywords*, 57–60.
4. Edward Said maintains that "the Orientalists—from Renan to Goldziher to Macdonald to von Guenbaum, Gibb, and Bernard Lewis—saw Islam, for example, as a 'cultural synthesis' . . . that could be studied apart from the economics, sociology, and politics of Islamic peoples," in Edward W. Said, *Orientalism* (New York: Vintage, 1978), 105.
5. Reinhard Schulze, "Mass Culture and Islamic Cultural Production in the Nineteenth-Century Middle East," in *Mass Culture, Popular Culture, and Social Life in the Middle East,* ed. Georg Stauth and Sami Zubaida (Boulder: Westview Press, 1987), 189.
6. See Niqula al-Turk, *Dhikr Tamalluk Jumhur al-Faransawiyyah al-Aqtar al-Misriyyah wa al-Bilad al-Shamiyyah* [A Chronicle of the French Republic's Occupation of the Lands of Egypt and Syria] (Beirut: Dar al-Farabi, 1990), 30–31. His book was written at the conclusion of the Napoleonic cam-

Egyptians. The Egyptian chronicler of the Napoleonic invasion, 'Abd al-Rahman al-Jabarti (1754–1826), was impressed with the scientific interests of the French but described their mores in scandalous terms:

Their women do not cover themselves and have no modesty; they do not care whether they uncover their private parts. Whenever a Frenchman has to perform an act of nature he does so wherever he happens to be, even in full view of people, and he goes away as he is, without washing his private parts after defecation. If he is a man of taste and refinement he wipes himself with whatever he finds, even with a paper with writing on it, otherwise he remains as he is. They have intercourse with any woman who pleases them and vice versa. Sometimes one of their women goes into a barber's shop, and invites him to shave her pubic hair. If he wishes he can take his fee in kind.[7]

The invading French instead saw themselves as carrying the banner of the Enlightenment. Since Islam was seen as the cause of decadence,

Islam was not to be evaluated as a theology, but as a culture, in the sense employed by Herder, Kant, or Schiller. As culture was used as a synonym for humanity, reason and freedom, the European spectators of the Orient had to define Islam as "un-culture" . . . So, the missionary aim was no longer Christianization, but modernization. The tradition/modernity dichotomy was born. For the Europeans, the birth date could be said to coincide with the date of the French embankment in Alexandria in Egypt, the 1st July, 1798.[8]

Through colonial policies, which set out to modernize the barbarians, "the Islamic world also obtained a culture" for Europeans, even though it synchronically retained much tradition or "un-culture." But as Schulze explains, "as the concept of culture was gradually generalized in Europe, thus leading to an analytic, universal concept, Islamic tradition was also associated with a culture. The essence of the partition between traditional decadence and modern renaissance, however, did not change. Thus the European worldview served to determine Islamic identity."[9]

---

paign and was first published in France in 1839. See also 'Abd al-Rahman al-Jabarti, *Tarikh Muddat al-Faransis bi-Misr, Muharram-Rajab 1213 H.,* translated in a bilingual edition as *Al-Jabarti's Chronicle of the First Seven Months of the French Occupation of Egypt,* edited and translated by S. Moreh (Leiden: E. J. Brill, 1975), 8–9. Al-Jabarti's book was written during the French occupation.

7. Al-Jabarti, *Tarikh Muddat al-Faransis bi-Misr,* 12. I have modified the editor's translation. For an overview of how Arab intellectuals saw the French invaders, see Ibrahim Abu-Lughod, *Arab Rediscovery of Europe: A Study in Cultural Encounters* (Princeton: Princeton University Press, 1963), 20–27.

8. Schulze, "Mass Culture and Islamic Cultural Production," 190.

9. Ibid., 191. For an engagement with the question of decadence, see J. J. Saunders, "The Problem of Islamic Decadence," *Journal of World History* 7, no. 3 (1963): 701–20. See also the proceedings of a conference on the subject held at Bordeaux in 1956, *Classicisme et déclin culturel dans l'histoire de*

It was in this colonial context that Arab intellectuals and scholars were unearthing evidence that would contradict, question, and interrogate the Orientalist claims and conclusions that produced Arab "civilization" and "culture" and placed them low on the European civilizational scale. Arab intellectuals would employ a number of strategies in response, including explaining away certain "cultural" phenomena identified as uncomplimentary either as unrepresentative of the "civilization" of the Arabs or as foreign imports that corrupted a pure Arab "culture"; or as universal, in that they existed among Arabs as they did or do among Europeans and others.

The most successful pedagogy that Orientalism and the colonial encounter would bequeath to these Arab intellectuals was not, however, the production of a nationalist historiographical response, although that was indeed part of it, but an epistemological affinity that would inform all their archeological efforts. These Arab writers would approach the topic at hand by adopting and failing to question these recently invented European notions of "civilization" and "culture" and their commensurate insertion in a social Darwinist idiom of "evolution," "progress," "advancement," "development," "degeneration," and most important, "decadence" and "renaissance." Thus Arab intellectuals

accepted the thesis that the eighteenth century had been decadent and used it to legitimate their own culture production (renaissance [*nahda, nahdah*]). *Nahda* required a concept of cultural decadence, for how else was the claim of cultural renewal to be justified? . . . In addition, the concept of contemporary renaissance required the discovery of a "classical" period in the distant past that might be rejuvenated in the present. Analogous to European concepts of renaissance, Islamic intellectuals in the nineteenth century fell back upon a "Golden Age" of Islam. But even here, the European Orientalists provided precious assistance by explaining to them what the classical Islamic period was, and how it was to be understood and assessed historically.[10]

Schulze argues that colonialism's destruction of the existing Arab intelligentsia and its main scholarly material, namely, hand-copied manuscripts, was carried out through the introduction in 1821 of printing presses and the book form (this was not only the case with the new printing press in Cairo but also in Aleppo, Beirut, and Jerusalem). Books would create a new intellectual reading public that would consider the

l'Islam; actes du symposium international d'histoire de la civilisation musulmane, Bordeaux 25–29 juin 1956, ed. R. Brunschvig and G. E. von Grunebaum (Paris: Besson, Chantemerle, 1957).

10. Schulze, "Mass Culture and Islamic Cultural Production," 191–92.

previous generation as arrested in its dependence on medieval manuscripts and that judged the book form as the measure of civilized modernity. The consumption of books, including new "classics" of Arab and Islamic history, which initially was almost exclusive to the Orientalists and European universities that purchased most of the copies printed in Egypt (the al-Azhar University would also become an important buyer), would soon affect the local market. With the new educational scholarships dispatching young Arabs to Europe and the introduction of European educational systems of instruction in Arab countries, a new book-reading public would soon emerge. Thus, "Culture which had been produced prior to 1821, a year which can be defined as a 'break' in Egyptian cultural history, no longer had the same value as culture emanating from the post-1821 period. As the pre-1821 culture, could not be 'measured' by the standards of European culture, the eighteenth century had to be seen as a period of decline, as part of universal Islamic decadence."[11]

In adopting this Weltanschauung, Arab intellectuals also internalized the epistemology by which Europeans came to judge civilizations and cultures along the vector of something called "sex," as well as its later derivative, "sexuality," and the overall systematization of culture through the statistical concept of "norms," often corresponding to the "natural" and its "deviant" opposite. The linking of sex and civilization can perhaps be traced to Genesis, when sex gave birth to the exile from Eden and subsequent earthly "civilization." The emergence of sex as one of the main axes by which civilization and barbarism can be classified is, however, a thoroughly modern phenomenon. This is how French philosopher Michel Foucault defined sexuality:

The term itself did not appear until the beginning of the nineteenth century . . . The use of the word was established in connection with other phenomena: the development of diverse fields of knowledge . . . the establishment of a set of rules and norms—in part traditional, in part modern—which found support in religious, judicial, pedagogical and medical institutions; and changes in the way individuals were led to assign meaning and value to their conduct, their duties, their pleasures, their feelings and sensations, their dreams. In short, it was a matter of seeing how an "experience" came to be constituted in modern Western societies, an experience that caused individuals to recognize themselves as subjects of "sexuality," which was accessible to very diverse fields of knowledge and linked to a system of rules and constraints. What I planned [to write], therefore, was a history of the experience of sexual-

11. Ibid., 198.

ity, where experience is understood as the correlation between fields of knowledge, types of normativity, and forms of subjectivity in a particular culture.[12]

Like Williams, Foucault was not attentive to the links of these modern concepts to the colonial project. My point here is not that Williams and Foucault failed to historicize how these concepts were applied to the colonies, but rather—and as Edward Said has argued in *Orientalism* and in *Culture and Imperialism*—that these concepts were themselves products of the colonial experience. In her seminal book on the subject of race and desire in the colonies, Ann Laura Stoler argues that "a wider imperial context resituates the work of racial thinking in the making of European bourgeois identity in a number of specific ways." She traces "how certain colonial prefigurings contest and force a reconceptualizing of Foucault's sexual history of the Occident and, more generally, a rethinking of the historiographic conventions that have bracketed histories of 'the West.'" Stoler observed that "what is striking is how consistently Foucault's own framing of the European bourgeois order has been exempt from the very sorts of criticism that his insistence on the fused regimes of knowledge/ power would seem to encourage and allow. Why have we been so willing to accept his history of a nineteenth-century sexual order that systematically excludes and/or subsumes the fact of colonialism within it?"[13]

Edward Said's work engaged precisely how the production of European knowledge, especially of the anthropological variety in the nineteenth century, was linked to colonial authority and the imperial project. In the same vein and more specifically, Kobena Mercer has argued that "historically, the European construction of sexuality coincides with the epoch of imperialism and the two inter-connect."[14] Building on Said's analysis and in line with Mercer's assertion, Stoler demonstrates that students of empire have an important addition to make to Foucault's analysis of the objects of the discourse on sexuality, which he listed as the masturbating child, the "hysterical woman," the Malthusian couple, and the perverse adult. Stoler adds:

Did any of these figures exist as objects of knowledge and discourse in the nineteenth century without a racially erotic counterpoint, without a reference to the libidinal en-

12. Michel Foucault, *The History of Sexuality*, vol. 2, *The Use of Pleasure* (New York: Vintage, 1984), 3–4.

13. Ann Laura Stoler, *Race and the Education of Desire: Foucault's History of Sexuality and the Colonial Order of Things* (Durham: Duke University Press, 1995), 5–6.

14. See Kobena Mercer and Isaac Julien, "Race, Sexual Politics, and Black Masculinity: A Dossier," in *Male Order: Unwrapping Masculinity*, ed. Rowena Chapman and Jonathan Rutherford (London: Lawrence & Wishart, 1988), 106.

ergies of the savage, the primitive, the colonized—reference points of difference, critique, and desire? At one level, these are clearly contrapuntal as well as indexical referents, serving to bolster Europe's bourgeois society and to underscore what might befall it in moral decline. But they were not that alone. The sexual discourse of empire and of the biopolitic state in Europe were mutually constitutive: their "targets" were broadly imperial, their regimes of power synthetically bound . . . In short-circuiting empire, Foucault's history of European sexuality misses key sites in the production of that discourse, discounts the practices that racialized bodies, and thus elides a field of knowledge that provided the contrasts for what a "healthy, vigorous, bourgeois body" was all about.[15]

While Orientalists were exploring the sexual practices and desires of medieval Arabs, Western anthropologists were exploring the contemporary sexual lives and practices not only of Arabs but also of the natives of Africa, Asia, Australia, and the Americas. It was within the context of what was called "ethnopornography" that Arab readers began to read Orientalist accounts.[16] Influenced by such readings, and especially by the Orientalist judgment that Arab culture had "degraded" to an age of "decadence" under the Ottomans, most Arab writers since the middle of the nineteenth century were overcome with a sense of crisis concerning the Arab present, its "culture," its "language," its political and economic order, its "traditions," its views of its own "heritage," even "Islam" itself, in short, a malady that afflicted the whole of Arab Islamic "civilization." The diagnosis would echo Orientalist judgment of the Arabs, including "backwardness," "decadence," "moral decline," "irrationality," and most of all, "degeneration," resulting from centuries of Ottoman rule characterized by stasis at best or retardation of things Arab (and sometimes Muslim) at worst. This understanding of Ottoman rule would become one of the main mobilizing factors in the emergence of the nascent anti-Ottoman Arab nationalism. As early as 1859, Butrus al-Bustani (1819–83), one of the central first-generation intellectuals of the Arab "renaissance," described the present of the Arabs as one of "decadence," existing as it did in a "fallen state."[17] This understanding of the history of the present is not particular to Arab culture during the age of empire, as not only did the colonized more generally express much concern over what had led to their colonial subjection, but also,

15. Stoler, *Race and the Education of Desire,* 6–7.
16. On ethnopornography, see Elizabeth Povinelli, *The Cunning of Recognition: Indigenous Alterities and the Making of Australian Multiculturalism* (Durham: Duke University Press, 2002), chap. 2.
17. Butrus al-Bustani, "Khutbah fi Adab al-'Arab" [A Speech on the Literature of the Arabs], Beirut, 15 February 1859, reproduced in Majid Fakhri, *Al-Harakat al-Fikriyyah wa Ruwwaduha al-Lubnaniyyun fi 'Asr al-Nahdah, 1800–1922* [The Intellectual Movements and Their Lebanese Pioneers in the Age of the Renaissance, 1800–1922] (Beirut: Dar al-Nahar Lil-Nashr, 1992), 175, 181.

by the twentieth century and in the interwar years, European colonial culture worried about itself. Orientalists themselves would espouse this sentiment. As Said remarked: "Both the Orientalist and the non-Orientalist begin with the sense that Western culture is passing through an important phase, whose main feature is the crisis imposed on it by such threats as barbarism, narrow technical concerns, moral aridity, strident nationalism, and so forth."[18]

Sex was always an important feature of Orientalist fantasy and scholarship. Said explained how Orientalists described the Orient "as feminine, its riches as fertile, its main symbols the sensual woman, the harem, and the despotic—but curiously attractive—ruler."[19] He noted that many an Orientalist writer like Edward W. Lane and Gustave Flaubert showed much interest during their Egyptian sojourn in *ʿalmahs* and *khawals*, dancing girls and boys, respectively.[20] In reading Flaubert, who in his novels "associates the Orient with the escapism of sexual fantasy," Said asserted: "Why the Orient seems still to suggest not only fecundity but sexual promise (and threat), untiring sensuality, unlimited desire, deep generative energies, is something on which one could speculate: it is not the province of my analysis here, alas, despite its frequently noted appearance. Nevertheless, one must acknowledge its importance as something eliciting complex responses, sometimes even a frightening self-discovery, in the Orientalists, and Flaubert was an interesting case in point." In fact, Said did venture a speculation.

The [Orientalist representational] repertoire is familiar, not so much because it reminds us of Flaubert's own voyages in and obsession with the Orient, but because, once again, the association is clearly made between the Orient and the freedom of licentious sex. We may as well recognize that for nineteenth-century Europe, with its increasing *embourgeoisiment,* sex had been institutionalized to a very considerable degree. On the one hand, there was no such thing as "free" sex, and on the other, sex in society entailed a web of legal, moral, even political and economic obligations of a detailed and certainly encumbering sort. Just as the various colonial possessions . . . were useful as places to send wayward sons, superfluous populations of delinquents, poor people, and other undesirables, so the Orient was a place where one could look for sexual experience unobtainable in Europe. Virtually no European writer who wrote on or traveled to the Orient in the period after 1800 exempted himself or herself from this quest: Flaubert, Nerval, "Dirty Dick" Burton, and Lane are only the most notable.[21]

18. Said, *Orientalism,* 258.
19. Edward W. Said, "Orientalism Reconsidered," *Cultural Critique* 1 (Fall 1985): 103.
20. Said, *Orientalism,* 186.
21. Ibid., 190, 188, 190.

Richard F. Burton ("Dirty Dick") was exceptional among these, how-ever, in his attempt to theorize the sexual question, especially among men. In his 1885–86 translation of *The Arabian Nights,* Burton included a now-infamous "Terminal Essay," in which he discussed such matters under the heading "Pornography." After offering a spirited defense to his readers for including sexual words that might be regarded as offensive, Burton adds, in reference to male homosexuality, that "there is another element in The Nights and that is one of absolute obscenity utterly repugnant to English readers, even the least prudish. It is chiefly con-nected with what our neighbors call *Le vice contre nature*—as if anything can be contrary to nature which includes all things. Upon this subject I must offer details, as it does not enter into my plan to ignore any theme which is interesting to the Orientalist and the Anthropologist."[22]

Burton spoke of the existence of what he called the "'Sotadic Zone,'" a reference to the third-century B.C. Greek-Egyptian poet Sotades, who wrote homoerotic poetry. Here the emphasis is geographical and clima-tological, if not topographical, bound as it is by latitudinal lines: it is decidedly "not racial." The Sotadic Zone encompasses not only Arab countries in Africa from "Morocco to Egypt," extending eastward to in-clude "Asia Minor, Mesopotamia and Chaldea, Afghanistan, Sind, the Punjab and Kashmir," as well as China, Japan, Turkistan, the South Sea Islands, and the New World, but also includes "meridional France, the Iberian Peninsula, Italy and Greece."[23] Inside the Sotadic zone "the Vice is popular and endemic, held at the worst to be a mere peccadillo, whilst the races to the North and South of the limits here defined practise it only sporadically amid the opprobrium of their fellows who, as a rule, are physically incapable of performing the operation and look upon it with the liveliest disgust."[24] Burton is one of the few nineteenth-century thinkers who did not deploy a racialist or evolutionary schema to ex-plain the other. As Neville Hoad has argued, "as problematic as Burton's refutation of evolution is, it represents an attempt to think the other-ness of sexual norms in terms that do not subsume the other into the self in the narrating of identity."[25]

Burton's own participation in this vice during his travels notwithstand-ing, the trend of European sex tourists did not stop in the nineteenth

22. Richard F. Burton, "Terminal Essay," in *The Book of the Thousand Nights and a Night: A Plain and Literal Translation of the Arab Nights Entertainments,* translated and annotated by Richard F. Bur-ton (London: Burton Club, 1886), vol. 10, 177.

23. Ibid., vol. 10, 179.

24. Ibid.

25. Neville Hoad, "Arrested Development; or, The Queerness of Savages," *Postcolonial Studies: Culture, Politics, Economy* 3, no. 2 (2000): 138.

century but continued in the twentieth century.[26] As Said explains, "in the twentieth century one thinks of Gide, Conrad, Maugham, and dozens of others. What they looked for often—correctly, I think—was a different type of sexuality, perhaps more libertine and less guilt-ridden; but even that quest, if repeated by enough people, could (and did) become as regulated and uniform as learning itself. In time 'Oriental sex' was as standard a commodity as any other available in the mass culture, with the result that readers and writers could have it if they wished without necessarily going to the Orient."[27] André Gide's 1902 novel *L'immoraliste* is the prominent example of the new Western fiction of homosexual self-discovery in the Orient. Joseph Boone called it "paradigmatic" of the genre.[28] But if Burton was a universalist on questions of desire and resisted racial theories in favor of climatological ones,[29] the mainstream Orientalist and anthropologist (as well as the nineteenth-century sexologist[30]) would deploy race and social Darwinism as central elements of analysis. In this vein, Said maintained: "Along with other people variously designated as backward, degenerate, uncivilized, and retarded, the Orientals were viewed in a framework constructed out of biological determinism and moral-political admonishment. The Oriental was thus linked to elements in Western society (delinquents, the insane, women, the poor) having in common an identity best described as lamentably alien."[31] Said could have easily added the "sexual deviant" to his list.

In this regard, it is most instructive to review an important debate between French Orientalist Ernest Renan and the Muslim Perso-Afghan

26. A comprehensive survey of the European literature on the sexuality of non-Europeans from the Enlightenment to World War I is Rudi Bleys, *The Geography of Perversion: Male-to-Male Sexual Behaviour outside the West and the Ethnographic Imagination, 1750–1918* (New York: New York University Press, 1995).

27. Said, *Orientalism*, 190.

28. Joseph Boone, "Vacation Cruises; or, The Homoerotics of Orientalism," *PMLA* 110 (1995): 101. See also Edward W. Said's discussion of the novel in his *Culture and Imperialism* (New York: Alfred Knopf, 1993), 192–93.

29. Joseph Boone, in an otherwise excellent survey of Orientalist writings on same-sex contact between Arab and Muslim men, inaccurately characterizes Burton's theory as a "stereotype of Eastern perversity," when in fact Burton was a universalist and at the outset included European countries south of "N. Lat. 43" in his "Sotadic Zone." Not only did Burton never "set the West off-limits" of the "Sotadic Zones," he had listed European countries first before moving to Africa, Asia, and the Americas and was not "forced to confirm *Le vice*'s growing presence" in London, Berlin, and Paris. In those modern cases of the "vice's" appearance outside the Sotadic Zone, he included not only northern European countries but also sub-Saharan Africa. Burton explained that "outside the Sotadic Zone . . . Le Vice is sporadic, not endemic." If anything, while Burton's theory encompasses much of the globe, those excluded are not only northern Europeans but also sub-Saharan Africans, even Bedouin Arabs who are said to be "wholly pure of Le Vice." See Burton, "Terminal Essay," 179, 212; and Boone, "Vacation Cruises; Or, the Homoerotics of Orientalism," 91, 93.

30. See Hoad, "Arrested Development."

31. Said, *Orientalism*, 207.

thinker Jamal al-Din al-Afghani (1838–97). Al-Afghani's ideas would have a prominent role to play in the late nineteenth-century phase of the Arab "renaissance," as it was his disciples, especially Muhammad ʿAbduh (1849–1905), who sought to reform Islam by regulating its doctrine and ridding it of all that was seen as superstition and myth ("innovation") in favor of its "reasonable" and rational message. Al-Afghani lived in Egypt in the 1870s and wrote and lectured in Arabic. It is true that he had a pan-Islamic project in mind, which in the course of the Arab *Nahdah* would become more focused by Arab intellectuals into a pan-Arab project, but this demographic and territorial contraction from a religious base to an ethnolinguistic one was not at the expense of al-Afghani's guiding epistemology; on the contrary, it would use it to its fullest. This is not to say that Arab intellectuals had to draw solely on Orientalist tradition. As Talal Asad explains, ʿAbduh, among others, drew on existing Islamic tradition, even when he disagreed with some of it, to effect a reform whose ideological lineaments were European. Thus even though the medieval ibn Taymiyyah and the eighteenth-century Muhammad bin ʿAbd al-Wahhab's strict and literal interpretation of the Qurʾan stripped Sufism of religious legitimacy, the project of modern religious reformers banished (parts of) it in accordance with modernist European ideas while remaining within a certain strand of tradition.[32]

In a lecture that he gave at the Sorbonne in March 1883 on "Islamism and Science," Renan argued that Islam as a religion and the Arabs as a people had always been hostile to science and philosophy and that any Arab and Islamic achievement in these fields were brought about despite Islam and from mostly non-Arab and non-Muslim populations conquered by Islam and the Arabs. Once the Arabs reestablished control and Islam strengthened itself, these achievements were crushed and the true spirit of both was made manifest, namely, their "hatred of science."[33] Here the question of the "decadence of states governed by Islam, and

32. For an important critique of part of Schulze's thesis as it related to Muhammad ʿAbduh, see Talal Asad, *Formations of the Secular: Christianity, Islam, Modernity* (Stanford: Stanford University Press, 2003), 221–22. ʿAbduh refers in his writings to ibn Taymiyyah, for example, as "the most knowledgeable of people and the most jealous among them for his religion" and as "Shaykh al-Islam" and refers to his books, including *al-Siyasah al-Sharʿiyyah*. ʿAbduh also refers to Muhammad ʿAbd al-Wahhab in his writings, and describes the Wahhabites as following a "good religious school, if it were not for its extremism and excess." See Muhammad ʿAbduh, *Al-Aʿmal al-Kamilah lil-Imam Muhmmad ʿAbduh* [The Complete Works of Imam Muhammad ʿAbduh], edited and collected by Muhammad ʿImarah (Beirut: al-Muʾassassah al-ʿArabiyyah lil-Dirasat wa al-Nashr, 1972–74), vol. 3, 341, vol. 4, 527, vol. 5, 236, vol. 1, 727, vol. 3, 537, respectively.

33. Ernest Renan, "Islamism and Science," reproduced in *Orientalism: Early Sources*, vol. 1, *Readings in Orientalism*, ed. Bryan S. Turner (London: Routledge, 2000), 210. Renan's lecture was delivered on 29 March 1883.

the intellectual nullity of the races that hold, from that religion alone, their culture and their education," were observable by Europeans as "the inferiority of Mohammedan countries."[34] The only exception to these Islamicized and Arabized races, Renan maintained, were the Persians, who retained their "genius."[35]

Al-Afghani's response shared many of Renan's conclusions regarding the present (late nineteenth-century) state of Muslim countries as well as the "responsibility" of the "Muslim religion" for "why Arab civiliza-tion . . . suddenly became extinguished . . . and why the Arab world still remains buried in profound darkness."[36] He universalized religious re-pression of science by comparing Islam's record to Christianity's, there-fore doing away with the exceptionalism with which Renan wanted to endow Islam. Where he disagreed with Renan, however, was on the ra-cialist premises Renan had employed to castigate Arabs as inimical to science and philosophy. Even though he opposed Darwin's theory of evolution in the biological realm, Al-Afghani deployed social Darwinism as the basis of his refutation of Renan.[37] He explained the evolutionary basis of all societies wherein religion, and not "pure reason," emerges in their barbaric state as a transitional phase to civilization. Al-Afghani's universalism was central: "It is by this religious education, whether it be Muslim, Christian, or pagan, that all nations have emerged from barba-rism and marched toward a more advanced civilization."[38] If the "Mus-lim religion" had become an "obstacle to the development of sciences," this was a mere evolutionary phase that would one day "disappear."[39] The motor for the evolutionary change in Europe, al-Afghani had sur-mised, after François Guizot "who wrote *L'Historie de la civilisation*," was the Protestant Reformation.[40] Understanding that the Muslim religion was in the childhood stage compared to the adulthood in which Chris-

34. Ibid., vol. 1, 200.

35. Ibid.

36. Jamal al-Din al-Afghani, "Answer of Jamal al-Din al-Afghani to Renan," first appeared in the *Journal Des Débats*, May 18, 1883. It is reproduced in A. M. Goichon, ed. and trans., *Réfutation des matérialistes* (Paris: Paul Geuthner, 1942), 184; and in Nikki Keddie, *An Islamic Response to Im-perialism: Political and Religious Writings of Sayyid Jamal ad-Din al-Afghani* (Berkeley: University of California Press, 1983), 187.

37. On his arguments against biological Darwinism, see Jamal al-Din al-Afghani, *Al-Radd 'ala al-Dahriyyin* [Response to the Materialists], translated from the Persian by Muhammad 'Abduh (Cairo: Al-Salam al-'Alamiyyah lil-Tab' wa al-Nashr wa al-Tawzi', 1983).

38. "Answer of Jamal al-Din al-Afghani to Renan," in Goichon, *Réfutation des matérialistes*, 177; and Keddie, *Islamic Response to Imperialism*, 183.

39. Goichon, *Réfutation des matérialistes*, 177; and Keddie, *Islamic Response to Imperialism*, 183.

40. He cites Guizot in his *Réfutation des matérialistes*, see Goichon, *Réfutation des matérialistes*, 165. See also al-Afghani, *Al-Radd 'ala al-Dahriyyin*, 101. Guizot's book had been translated into Ara-bic in 1877.

tianity found itself in the nineteenth century, al-Afghani asked Renan for patience:

The Christian religion . . . has emerged from the first period [of its evolution]; thenceforth free and independent, it seems to advance rapidly on the road of progress and science, whereas Muslim society has not yet freed itself from the tutelage of religion. Realizing, however, that the Christian religion preceded the Muslim religion in the world by many centuries, I cannot keep from hoping that Muhammadan society will succeed someday in breaking its bonds and marching resolutely in the path of civilization after the manner of Western society, for which the Christian faith, despite its rigors and intolerance, was not at all an invincible obstacle. No, I cannot admit that this hope be denied to Islam. I plead here with M. Renan not the cause of the Muslim religion, but that of several hundreds of millions of men, who would thus be condemned to live in barbarism and ignorance.[41]

While al-Afghani's response to Renan (unlike his other writings) was not published in Arabic, his social Darwinism was shared by most Arab intellectuals of the period. Indeed in the second half of the 1870s, social Darwinism would be heavily debated on the pages of the Arabic journal *Al-Muqtataf,* and commentaries on Darwin's work (by Ludwig Büchner, for example) would be translated by Lebanese intellectual Shibli Shumayyil (1853–1917) and debated in the 1880s, even though Darwin's *Origin of the Species* itself would not appear in Arabic translation until 1918.[42] The concern over what might have led to the Arab "decline" increased the intensity of the ongoing intellectual battle between Arab writers engaged in producing *the* account of the Arab "cultural" past (and in the process repressing many other possible readings) and Orientalists engaged in a similar task. The scope and the terms of this ongoing

41. "Answer of Jamal al-Din al-Afghani to Renan," in Goichon, *Réfutation des matérialistes,* 177–78; Keddie, *Islamic Response to Imperialism,* 183.
42. For the history of Darwinism and social Darwinism in the late nineteenth-century and early twentieth-century Arab world, see Adel A. Ziadat, *Western Science in the Arab World: The Impact of Darwinism, 1860–1930* (New York: St. Martin's Press, 1986). The first five chapters of Darwin's *The Origin of Species* were translated by Egyptian Isma'il Mazhar and published in 1918 under the title *Asl al-Anwaʿ wa Nushuʾuha bi al-Intikhab al-Tabiʿ i wa Hifz al-Sufuf al-Ghalibah fi al-Tanahur ʿala al-Baqaʾ* [Origin of the Species and Its Emergence through Natural Selection and the Preservation of Dominant Classes in the Struggle for Survival] (Cairo: Dar al-ʿAsr lil-Tabʿ wa al-Nashr, 1928). Mazhar added four more chapters to the 1928 edition. Shibli Shumayyil would publish a number of commentaries on Darwinism in the 1880s and is viewed as the earliest Arab thinker who engaged with the subject and applied Darwinism beyond biology. He continued to write on the subject after the new century set in. See, for example, Shibli Shumayyil, *Falsafat al-Nushuʾ wa al-Irtiqaʾ* [The Philosophy of Evolution and Ascent] (Cairo: Matbaʿat al-Muqtataf, 1910).

battle, since the late nineteenth century to the present, continued to be civilizational in nature. They have rarely been epistemological. The fight therefore has never been about the conceptual tools to be used in the archeological and hermeneutical effort but rather about historical accuracy, the nature of the evidence to be examined, and the kinds of judgment that can, or should, be derived from it. A related moral system that Arab intellectuals also adopted, given its links to social Darwinism, was what was largely perceived as Victorianism. Victorian notions of appropriate and shameful sexual behavior and its civilizational dimensions would rank high in the thinking of these Arab intellectuals, not least because such notions were the basis for judgment not only of non-Europeans but also of late *European* Romantic art, literature, and poetry constituting the "Decadent Movement," which was often condemned as "degenerate," especially on account of its sexually explicit motifs, including sadism, incest, sodomy, and lesbianism, and identified as "barbaric" and "primitive" in sensibility.[43] Thus, Orientalist depiction of Arab sexual desires as of a different qualitative and quantitative order signifying radical alterity would be countered by vigorous assimilationism on the part of the Arab historians who insisted that Arab sexual desires were not all that different from those of Europeans. Indeed, evidence would be produced to demonstrate that when medieval or modern desires of Arabs did deviate from Victorian ethics they were and are condemned by the hegemonic Arab ethical system. In that Arab intellectuals resembled their counterparts elsewhere in the colonized world. As Abdul R. JanMohamed explains, third world peoples and metropolitan minorities are caught between two positions: "on the one hand, there is a desire to define one's ethnic and cultural uniqueness against the pressures of the majority culture and on the other hand an equally strong, if not stronger, urge to abandon that uniqueness in order to conform to the hegemonic pressures of the [white] liberal humanistic culture."[44] He adds that

43. On Romantic decadence in literature and art, see Mario Praz's classic, *The Romantic Agony*, translated by Angus Davidson, 2nd ed. (Oxford: Oxford University Press, 1970). See also Max Nordau, *Degeneration* (New York: Howard Fertig, 1968). Praz explicitly identifies Gabriele D'Annunzio, one of the main figures of the Decadent movement who hails from southern Italy, as "a barbarian and at the same time a 'Decadent,' and there is lacking in him the temperate zone which, in the present period of culture, is labeled 'humanity,'" in Praz, *Romantic Agony*, 401. On the association of Oscar Wilde with primitivism and barbarism, see Neville Hoad, "Wild(e) Men and Savages: The Homosexual and the Primitive in Darwin, Wilde, and Freud" (Ph.D. diss., Columbia University, 1998). It is hardly incidental that D'Annunzio was not considered a civilized Tuscan on account of his Abruzzian origins while Wilde was but a mere Irishman.

44. Abdul R. JanMohamed, "Humanism and Minority Literature: Toward a Definition of Counter-Hegemonic Discourse," *Boundary 2* 12–13 (1984): 289.

historically, this anxiety to be included is far stronger than the need to stress the difference. The traditional narcissism of a dominant white culture—that is, the culture's ability only to recognize man in its own image and its refusal to recognize the substantial validity of any alterity—puts enormous pressure on Blacks and other minorities to recreate themselves and their culture as approximate versions of the Western humanist tradition, as images that [white] "humanism" will recognize and understand.[45]

This assimilationist project is most pronounced in contemporary debates among Arab intellectuals on the question of modernity and heritage (turath). I will digress upon this debate briefly in order to contextualize how the question of desire and civilization inhabits a developmentalist temporal schema whose telos is assimilation into Europe. It is here that the European concept of culture as category *and* object of thought is most persistent.

The Time of the Arabs

Ever since Arab intellectuals and politicians, echoing European Orientalists, coded the Napoleonic invasion of Egypt in 1798 as the inaugural "shock" or "trauma" that "woke" them up, "alerted" them, or "spurred" and "goaded" them from their "torpor" and long "sleep," ushering them into a world wherein the "challenge" of the West had to be faced, the task they set themselves was to meet this challenge by "catching up" with Europe.[46] Perhaps Shakib Arsalan's infamous question, "Why have Muslims regressed [been delayed] and why have others progressed?" which he posed in 1906, encapsulates this dilemma whose resolution is still sought today.[47] The dyad around which these debates have revolved consists of *turath* (heritage) and modernity/ contemporariness. Should one be abandoned in favor of the other, or should they be combined in a variety of permutations that can ensure the sought-after "progress"? The answers provided in the last century and a half have varied in simplicity and complexity but, all in all, have, according to those who posited them, "failed" to achieve their stated goal: namely, "progress" and "advancement." As a result, these questions have not disappeared.

45. Ibid., 290.
46. The theme of waking up after long sleep itself echoes post-Enlightenment representations of the European Renaissance as a waking up from torpor.
47. Shakib Arsalan, *Limadha Taʾakhkhara al-Muslimun wa Limadha Taqaddama Ghayruhum* [Why Were the Arabs Delayed and Why Did Others Advance] (Beirut: Al-Hayat, 1975). For an important analysis of these dilemmas in Arab intellectual production, see Abdallah Laroui's classic, *L'idéologie arabe contemporaine* (Paris: François Maspero, 1967).

They continue to reinscribe themselves in Arab intellectual, cultural, and political debates in the present moment. The contemporary Arab intellectual, cultural, and political theater is teaming with individuals and groups who claim to provide answers to this seemingly intractable dilemma. In the forthcoming pages, I will limit my discussion to the contemporary intellectual debates on the role of *turath* and modernity, or more specifically, the role of *turath in* modernity in order to demonstrate the continuing influence of Orientalist and colonial taxonomies on Arab intellectual production.

The term *turath* refers today to the civilizational documents of knowledge, culture, and intellect that are said to have been passed down from the Arabs of the past to the Arabs of the present. It constitutes the living compendium of the past in the present. It is in a sense a time traveler. Yet despite its strong associations with a certain past, *turath* is a *modern* Arabic term that did not exist as such in the past. When the term was used until the late nineteenth century, it referred to financial inheritance or legacy.[48] *Turath* as a concept is then first and foremost a product of twentieth-century modernity, where, or more precisely, *when* it is located as an epistemological anchor of the present in the past. We will see below how the question of including and excluding certain sexual desires from *turath* will be crucial to this archival operation.

Whereas the concepts of *turath* and modernity are underlain by strong temporal principles, time *and* space seem to define the stated goals of those who want to resolve the relationship between them: namely, the achievement of "taqaddum" (meaning progress, advancement, or more accurately "in frontness"), and its corollary, the repudiation of "takhalluf" (meaning "backwardness" or more accurately "behindness"). Like their English equivalents, these notions posit an *other* in front of whom or behind whom one is located in time and space. Since the onset of colonialism, the other for the "Arab" collective psyche, as it has been for the rest of Asia and Africa, has been and continues to be the "West."

Although the contemporary discourse on the relationship between *turath* and modernity is punctuated with European Enlightenment terms

---

48. For premodern dictionaries, see Muhammad bin Mukarram ibn Manzur, *Lisan al-'Arab* (Beirut: Dar Sadir, 1990), vol. 2, 200–1, where *turath* is used as the inheritance of money or of a family name. There is no entry for *turath* in al-Fayruzabadi, *Al-Qamus Al-Muhit*, see the recent edition (ed. Dar Ihya' al-Turath al-'Arabi [Beirut, 1997]). Even the nineteenth-century dictionary *Muhit al-Muhit*, which was compiled by Butrus al-Bustani and published in 1870, explains *Turath* as financial inheritance from the father, see Butrus al-Bustani, *Muhit al-Muhit, Qamus Mutawwal Lil-Lughah al-'Arabiyyah* (Beirut: Maktabat Lubnan Nashirun, 1987), 964. On the history of the use of the term "turath," see Muhammad 'Abid al-Jabiri, *Al-Turath wa al-Hadathah, Dirasat wa Munaqashat* [Heritage and Modernity: Studies and Debates] (Beirut: Markaz Dirasat al-Wihdah al-'Arabiyyah, 1991), 21–24.

like "reason," "rationality," "science," "scientificity," "secularism," "light," and "darkness," I will focus my discussion on the centrality of certain temporal notions that this discourse deploys, such as regression, lag, backwardness, evolution, evolutionary stages, stages of development, progress, advancement, retardation, and delay. Time, as we will see, is used both as metaphor and as a marker. But what is the importance of time, its movements and dis*place*ments in this discourse? What epistemological or theoretical notions lay the foundations for this specific use of time in it?

It was in the wake of the 1967 Arab-Israeli War that new answers and explorations of *turath* and modernity posed themselves. Ranging from liberals and Marxists to nationalists and Islamists, this debate is characterized by what Syrian literary critic Jurj Tarabishi has termed the "trauma" of defeat. The Islamist tracts continue unabated to offer an Islamist view of Islam as *the turath* to which Arabs and Muslims must "return." On the secular side of the debate, it was Moroccan philosopher Abdallah Laroui who stressed in 1974 the necessity of a historicist method that insists on the acceptance by Arab intellectuals of their and their society's "cultural retardation."[49] In his classic critique of contemporary Arab ideology (published in 1967 before the June defeat) and its insistence on a fictional historical continuity between the Arab past and the Arab present, Laroui believed that only when the Arab nationalist state (in reference to the republican nationalist regimes) becomes "l'état industrialisé" will the Arabs be able to write a positivist history of their past replacing their "ideological history." This complete correspondence and quasi-deterministic relationship between economy and culture is further clarified in Laroui's statement that when the aim of industrialization

is achieved, the modern history of the Arabs—the era of colonialism, the era of liberalism, the era of industrialization—will be so important that it will be able to furnish a substantive object to the positivist methods of history. The Arabs will then be in possession of [historical] material comparable to that which Westerners have used at least since the seventeenth century, and they will have to manipulate it in the same way as Westerners have done.[50]

He adds confidently that "this calm and unemotional method of rereading history is still far from our gates. Here we will only be able to delineate the conditions that will allow it one day to develop among us."[51]

49. Abdallah Laroui, *The Crisis of the Arab Intellectual: Traditionalism or Historicism?* (Berkeley: University of California Press, 1974). See especially his introduction, 1–10.
50. Laroui, *L'idéologie arabe contemporaine*, 106.
51. Ibid., 107.

Positing the Western historical trajectory as the only course to reach the telos of modernity, Laroui, while providing a scathing critique of Arabic literary production since the *Nahdah*, wonders "whence does this situation come, a situation that offers few opportunities for the creative liberty of Arab authors? Why are we not able to understand [our] structural retardation and its simultaneous reflection-complement, namely, superstructural retardation?" He answers his own query by affirming, albeit ambivalently, that

perhaps this depends, in the end, on the dimensions of this retardation? The larger this retardation, the more impossible its compensation on all levels . . . For the essential difference between [Ahmad] Shawqi [a modernizing Egyptian poet] and Pushkin, the real reason for their unequal value, is perhaps the result of the fact that the former lived in an epoch when the West was still young and conscious and having later—at the moment when the latter awoke to the world—lost its liberty, sincerity, and conscience; and that after it had lost them and had lost the dialectic as well as the secret of expression, it made us lose them on the same occasion.[52]

Laroui's philosophical approach and the evolutionary thesis of his project are everywhere in evidence today. As for the grand Marxist critiques of the 1970s elaborated by Lebanese Husayn Muruwwah[53] and Syrian Tayyib Tizini,[54] they were to be replaced by a new "epistemological" approach championed by newcomer Moroccan philosopher Muhammad ʿAbid al-Jabiri, whose 1980 introductory critique in *Nahnu wa al-Turath* (We and *Turath*)[55] culminated in his four-volume *Naqd al-ʿAql al-ʿArabi* (Critique of Arab Reason) in the mid- to late 1980s (vol. 4 was published in 2001), where he offered a reassessment of *turath* based on what he calls a "contemporary" reading of it rather than a "turathist" one. Al-Jabiri's project has elicited rich and multifaceted debates in Arabic magazines, journals, and newspapers as well as in whole books dedicated to responding to him. Other contributors to this debate include Syrian intellectual ʿAziz al-ʿAzmah, Egyptian philosopher Hasan Hanafi, Lebanese writer ʿAli Harb, Syrian political scientist Burhan Ghalyun, and Jurj Tarabishi, to name but a few.

52. Ibid., 208–9.

53. Husayn Muruwwah, *Al-Nazaʿat al-Madiyyah fi al-Falsafah al-ʿArabiyyah al-Islamiyyah* [Materialist Tendencies in Arab-Islamic Philosophy], 2 vols. (Beirut: Dar al-Farabi, 1979).

54. Tayyib Tizini, *Min al-Turath ila al-Thawrah* [From Heritage to Revolution], 2nd ed. (Beirut: Dar ibn Khaldun, 1978).

55. Muhammad ʿAbid al-Jabiri, *Nahnu wa al-Turath, Qiraʾat Muʿasirah fi Turathina al-Falsafi* [We and Heritage: Contemporary Readings in Our Philosophical Heritage], 6th ed. (Beirut: al-Markaz al-Thaqafi al-ʿArabi, 1993). The book was first published in 1980.

One quickly discerns the absence of any discussion of the economic in these debates. Whereas Arab *revolutionary* thought before 1967, like its counterparts elsewhere in the third world, saw the lack of economic development, as well as the systematic underdevelopment of the third world by the West, as the main cause of its "backwardness" and lack of "progress," following the 1967 defeat the cultural encroaches into these debates as the main cause of Arab "backwardness." It is also in the realm of the cultural that a solution to the puzzle of "progress" can be found. By then, the limited experiments of "Arab socialism" were showing their failures and the new élites were abandoning any meaningful notion of socialism in favor of capitalist ventures. While the trend of dependency theory, especially the Samir Amin school, was popular among some in the 1970s, quickly, the question of the economic was bracketed if not abandoned altogether in favor of the cultural. One of the few voices opposing such a bracketing was that of Lebanese communist thinker Mahdi 'Amil.[56]

The two terms that make a ubiquitous appearance in these debates on *turath* and modernity are *takhalluf* (retardation) and *nukus*. *Nukus,* which means regression, like its English counterpart also has the spatial significance of recoil or retreat. As we will see, these temporal notions are everywhere deployed both by al-Jabiri and his critics. Jurj Tarabishi's psychoanalytic approach is one of the more sophisticated critiques within these debates. Like the thinkers he criticizes, Tarabishi is unable to exit from a colonial evolutionary schema whose origins is primitive infantilism, disease, and backwardness and whose telos is adulthood, health, and progress. It is in this vein that Tarabishi concludes that post-1967 Arab intellectuals suffer from a group neurosis characterized by regression or *nuqusiyyah*. The defeat of 1967 "uncovered" Arab political, economic, technological, and cultural "lateness" or "delay" ["ta'akhkhur"].[57] Tarabishi contrasts the erstwhile Arab intelligentsia, who until 1967 constituted an element of "renaissance" and "progress," with the post-1967 intelligentsia, who in its majority positioned itself "inside the equation of backwardness."[58] Whereas Egyptian bellelettrist Taha Husayn had called on the Arabs to accept modern civilization smiling and not frowning, many Arab intellectuals today, Tarabishi tells us, face it "frowning," an

---

56. Mahdi 'Amil, *Azmat al-Hadarah al-'Arabiyyah Am Azmat al-Burjuwaziyyat al-'Arabiyyah*, fourth printing [The Crisis of Arab Civilization; or, The Crisis of the Arab Bourgeoisies] (Beirut: Dar al-Farabi, 1985). The book was first published in 1974.

57. Jurj Tarabishi, *Al-Muthaqqafun al-'Arab wa al-Turath: Al-Tahlil al-Nafsi Li-'Usab Jama'i* [Arab Intellectuals and Heritage: A Psychoanalysis of Collective Neurosis] (London: Riyad al-Rayyis, 1991), 22.

58. Ibid., 11.

attitude that constitutes a "retreat" or "apostasy" [riddah] to be described as a "psychological epidemic."[59] If this neurotic discourse ever becomes the discourse of authority in the Arab world, Tarabishi fears, it would guarantee for all Arabs a future of "darkness," one that would not tolerate any "enlightened" people in its ranks. As neurosis is by definition an expression of a struggle, according to Tarabishi, there are two battling forces in the Arab psyche: the force that emphasizes the past and pushes toward regression and another one that pushes toward resistance, convalescence and progress. Tarabishi's project is to direct attention to this unconscious neurotic mechanism in the hope that better opportunities will arise for the elements of health to reassert themselves and defeat illness.[60] Tarabishi's diagnosis of neurosis is itself implicated in an evolutionary narrative. In strict Freudian terms, neurosis is figured in developmental terms: it is the fixation on a moment in infantile sexuality that precludes a person from fully entering responsible adulthood. Tarabishi, however, is undeterred. The 1967 War and the trauma it caused have "arrested the development" of these intellectuals if not canceled it out altogether ["ilgha' al-numuw"].[61] The so-called "regression" of the Arabs is described by him in almost voluntarist terms as taking the form of a "boycott" or even a "strike" ("idrab") against "development"![62]

Unlike al-Jabiri, who dismisses all modern Arab intellectual production since the *Nahdah* through the present as a discourse that is incapable of understanding reality "rationally," Tarabishi believes that the relationship between modern Arab thought, which reacted to the Napoleonic shock, and contemporary Arab thought, which reacted to the June 1967 shock, is not a relationship of continuity and repetition as al-Jabiri claims but rather one of a break and regression. Whereas al-Jabiri believes that contemporary Arab thought retreats to the nineteenth century and reproduces the same analytical mechanisms of the *Nahdah,* Tarabishi believes that contemporary Arab thought does not regress to the *Nahdah,* but rather is regressing "from it."[63] While, according to Tarabishi, it is understandable that contemporary intellectuals pose the same questions of the *Nahdah*—questions that are still unresolved—the answers they provide are not more "advanced" than the *Nahdah's* answers, rather, they are more "backward."[64] It was not Arab thought that "developed" and "evolved" after the 1967 trauma, rather it was the "germ" of neurosis and disease that was lodged in the consciousness of the Arabs

---

59. Ibid. Also see 61.
60. Ibid., 12.
61. Ibid., 19.

62. Ibid., 31.
63. Ibid., 21, 52.
64. Ibid., 21.

that has "developed and evolved destroying the defenses of health."[65] Here, it seems that it is Tarabishi who is "regressing" to a colonial medical discourse that once labeled the Ottoman Empire "the sick man." It is unclear if Tarabishi recommends to the contemporary Arab world the same measures taken to "nurse" the Ottomans back to "health."

Unlike al-Jabiri then who thinks this "disease" transcends the history of the Arabs as having always existed, infecting their thought, nay their very "reason," Tarabishi insists on "historicizing" it, "periodizing" it, and "specifying" it.[66] His conclusion is that regression as the symptom of this neurosis is in fact the *time* of neurosis, that regression is "the time of contemporary Arab discourse."[67] The existence of *al-Salafiyyah* (or ancestrism, in reference to Islamist thought) as a current of Arab thought is indicative of this disease. For *al-Salafiyyah* is nothing but "progress through going backward."[68]

Tarabishi still believes in the stages of modernization. For him, the reason why the age of revolution failed in the Arab world is not the outcome of economic or political failures, it is rather a result of its attempt to skip the stage of a "philosophical" revolution in Arab thought without even undergoing a theological revolution. This is precisely why, in its attempt to burn several stages by skipping them, "Arab Revolutionary Reason," Tarabishi tell us, ended up burning itself. Karl Marx described this general process:

One nation can and should learn from others. And even when a society has got upon the right track for the discovery of the natural laws of its movement . . . it can neither clear by bold leaps, nor remove by legal enactments, the obstacles offered by the successive phases of its normal development. But it can shorten and lessen the birth-pangs.[69]

Echoing Marx without citing him, Tarabishi concludes that "in the matter of Reason, stages cannot be burned, although it might be possible to abbreviate and compress them temporarily in light of the historical experience of those who were ahead in civilizational take-off."[70] He proceeds to say that from this phased "perspective of stages, the task of a theological revolution is still listed on the work schedule of Arab Reason,

65. Ibid.
66. Ibid.
67. Ibid., 71.
68. Ibid., 76.
69. Karl Marx, preface to the first German edition, *Capital*, vol. 1, *A Critical Analysis of Capitalist Production*, ed. Frederick Engels (New York: International Publishers, 1967), 10.
70. Jurj Tarabishi, *Masa'ir al-Falsafah Bayna al-Masihiyyah wa al-Islam* [Philosophy's Destinies between Christianity and Islam] (Beirut: Dar al-Saqi, 1998), 125.

a revolution that is all the more needed today given the 'rising' of or 'retreat' to fundamentalism that the Arab world is witnessing."[71]

As for al-Jabiri, he states that "as soon as the 1967 defeat took place, [contemporary] Arab discourse began to regress backward not in order to fortify itself in positions fortified by the spirit of revolutionary realism . . . but rather to rely on the ruins of the past, reliving the dream of the renaissance amidst the nightmare of defeat."[72] Al-Jabiri here is invoking another temporal problem; a dream, for psychoanalysis, is nothing but wish fulfillment, a denial of sorts. It is a reaction-formation to time but one that remains outside it.

Al-Jabiri defines *turath* as "all that is present in us or with us from the past, whether our past or the past of others, whether it is [a] recent or distant [past]."[73] This critic of "Arab Reason" further states that Arab thought beginning with the *Nahdah* and through the present has been characterized not by its "evolution" but rather by its lack of evolution; it is therefore a static system of thought doomed to repeat itself—simply marking time. He asserts that "there has been no real evolution in any of the issues raised by the renaissance [Nahdah]" and that therefore "modern and contemporary Arab discourse have not registered any progress of significance on any of its issues."[74] Based on these sweeping statements, al-Jabiri concluded in 1982 that "the time of modern and contemporary Arab thought is a dead time, or one that *can be treated as a dead time*."[75] By 1984, his conclusion was amended: it was no longer modern and contemporary Arab thought that has a dead time, it is "'Arab culture,' as it is the frame of reference of Arab reason . . . [which has] a 'unitary time' [zaman wahid], since the time it was formed through the present, [it is] a static time lived by the Arab of today the same way it was lived by his ancestors in past centuries."[76] For "the time of Arab culture . . . has remained the same since the age of recording, ruminating over itself, and vacillating within the same 'moment' until it ended in stasis . . . in 'being frozen in tradition' in all arenas."[77] The time of Arab Reason is further described as moving "inside a closed circle" thus becoming

71. Ibid.

72. Muhammad ʿAbid al-Jabiri, *Al-Khitab al-ʿArabi al-Muʿasir, Dirasah Tahliliyyah Naqdiyyah* [Contemporary Arab Discourse: A Critical and Analytic Study], fifth printing (Beirut: Markaz Dirasat al-Wihdah al-ʿArabiyyah, 1994), 37.

73. Al-Jabiri, *Al-Turath wa al-Hadathah*, 45.

74. Al-Jabiri, *Al-Khitab al-ʿArabi al-Muʿasir*, 194.

75. Ibid., emphasis in the original.

76. Muhammad ʿAbid al-Jabiri, *Takwin al-ʿAql al-ʿArabi*, vol. 1 of *Naqd al-ʿAql al-ʿArabi* [The Formation of Arab Reason, vol. 1 of The Critique of Arab Reason] (Beirut: Markaz Dirasat al-Wihdah al-ʿArabiyyah, 1984), 70.

77. Al-Jabiri, *Takwin al-ʿAql al-ʿArabi*, 334.

"a repeated or iterated time . . . a dead time," a time that "looks more like the living dead."[78] This is so because the Arabs, in the presence of a powerful other, had a defensive reaction, one characterized by their "heading toward the past" and maintaining strong "posterior positions" to defend themselves.[79]

Al-Jabiri's project is to oppose a "turathist view of turath" through founding a "contemporary ['Asriyyah] view of *turath.*" In doing so "we" will avoid a "*turathist* view of the present."[80] This will enable the emergence of the "complete historical independence of the Arab self," which is freed from *turathist* and European authority and therefore inaugurate a temporal movement toward modernity, which for al-Jabiri is both "the Renaissance and the Enlightenment and the transcendence of both . . . [through] rationality and democracy . . . for if we do not practice rationality in our *turath* and if we do not expose to scandal the origins of despotism and its manifestations in this *turath,* we shall not succeed in establishing a modernity that is particular to us, a modernity in which we should plunge and through which we can enter contemporary "universal" modernity as actors and not simply as reactors."[81] For the Arabs, Renaissance, Enlightenment, and modernity "do not constitute successive stages with the latter succeeding the former, but for us it is interconnected and interwoven and synchronous within the current stage whose beginnings go back a hundred years."[82] In this, al-Jabiri follows in Tarabishi's footsteps with regard to the compression and abbreviation of evolutionary stages.

'Aziz al-'Azmah, another important participant in these debates, is quite clear on the social Darwinist basis of the concept of time on which many Arab intellectuals have relied. He analyzes the Spencerist influ-

78. Al-Jabiri, *Takwin al-'Aql al-'Arabi,* 342. For a critique of al-Jabiri's notion of time, see 'Ali Harb, *Mudakhalat, Mabahith Naqdiyyah Hawla A'mal: Muhammad 'Abid al-Jabiri, Husayn Muruwwah, Hisham Ju'ayt, 'Abd al-Salam bin 'Abid al-'Ali, Sa'id bin Sa'id* [Interventions: Critical Studies on the World of Muhammad 'Abid al-Jabiri, Husayn Muruwwah, Hisham Ju'ayt, 'Abd al-Salam bin 'Abid al-'Ali, Sa'id bin Sa'id] (Beirut: Dar al-Hadathah, 1985), 37–43.

79. Muhammad 'Abid al-Jabiri, "Ishkaliyyat al-Asalah wa al-Mu'asarah fi al-Fikr al-'Arabi al-Hadith wa al-Mu'asir: Sira' Tabaqi am Mushkil Thaqafi?" [The Problematic of Authenticity and Contemporariness in Modern and Contemporary Arab Thought: A Class Struggle or a Cultural Problem?'], in *Al-Turath wa Tahadiyyat al-'Asr fi al-Watan al-'Arabi (al-Asalah wa al-Mu'asarah),* Buhuth wa Munaqashat al-Nadwah al-Fikriyyah allati Nazzamaha Markaz Dirasat al-Wihdah al-'Arabiyyah (Beirut: Markaz Dirasat al-Wihdah al-'Arabiyyah, 1985), 40.

80. Al-Jabiri, *Al-Turath wa al-Hadathah,* 50.

81. Ibid., 17.

82. Ibid., 16. Al-Jabiri adds that in assessing current "universal" thought "it is possible, nay imperative, to make a distinction in it only between what serves progress and heads in the direction of the evolution of history, and what serves the exploitative present and the hegemony of imperialism or of racialist nationalism. This is the only measure of choice from contemporary culture and from past cultures," ibid., 40.

ence on Arab evolutionist thinking since the Arab renaissance,[83] and which continues today in both Islamist and "eclectic" thought ("Taw-fiqi," in reference to the currents that try to reconcile aspects of *turath* with modernity). Much of Arab thought then, according to al-ʿAzmah, is based on a revivalist impulse underwritten by an evolutionary narrative. Yet, this very perceptive critic of the social Darwinism of these epistemologies cannot resist reinscribing it in his own. Thus, although al-ʿAzmah is clear that the predominance of the current conflation between Islam and Arab nationalism, or at least the commitment to *turath* and nationalism on the part of the Arab right and left is itself a response to globalization,[84] he still asserts that espousing this position will not guarantee our "movement to the level of civilized nations. For we live in a world that is on the verge of the twenty-first century; capitalism— the unifying system of the modern world—has entered a stage wherein the possibility of juxtaposing distant times, and the synchronicity of distant places has advanced . . ."[85] The interconnections of the world can no longer allow for separation: "There is no absolute East and no absolute West; and there is no complete separation between those territories, states or nations that are completely backward and those that are completely advanced." In a world in which communism has been defeated and exposed to the "savagery" of world capitalism, "if some of us continue to establish a politics and a nationalism that are based on nostalgia, on looking for a despot to rescue us, and if our political thinking was limited to imagining the idols of the past, praising and reveling in them," then, this would lead to "preventing us from being elevated [al-irtiqaʾ] . . . to the level of advanced nations."[86] The only way we can be "elevated" is if "we" give up this illusory thinking and replace it with "work and precise thinking" and if "we" sober up from our addiction to "the pleasure in our [Arab] self" or to "the concept of the one homogeneous self" and "replace it with a consciousness of the complexity of our society, its differences, and its temporalities." He finally declares that "we will not be able to ascend unless we sacrifice the pleasure of escaping backwards and the nostalgia for what has passed . . ."[87] The "re-

---

83. ʿAziz al-ʿAzmah, *Al-Asalah Aw Siyasat al-Hurub min al-Waqiʿ* [Authenticity; or, The Politics of Flight from Reality] (Beirut: Dar al-Saqi, 1992), 39–52.

84. ʿAziz al-ʿAzmah, "al-Turath wa al-ʿAwlamah" [Heritage and Globalization], in *Dunya al-Din fi Hadir al-ʿArab* [The World of Religion in the Present of the Arabs] (Beirut: Dar al-Taliʿah, 1996), especially 46–47.

85. Ibid., 10.

86. Ibid., 10–11.

87. Ibid., 11.

gressive" currents characterizing much of Arab thought since the 1970s, according to al-ʿAzmah, "promise us a return to backwardness."[88]

The Syrian Marxist Yasin al-Hafiz goes even further by dividing the Arab world into different time zones. As such, these "regressive" trends in Arab thought are not only the product of relatively modern Arabs who are regressing reactively as a result of the 1967 defeat, it is also a result of the recent domination of the less-backward Arabs by the more backward Arabs: "Finally came the turn of the Bedouin traditionalist ideology which instead of being carried on the back of camels, is being carried on the back of petroleum barrels: the non-petrol Arab peoples, who are remarkably less backward than the petrol peoples, are being subjected to an ideological and cultural, not to mention political, pressure and invasion, from the latter."[89] Again, culture is the operative cause for backwardness, albeit a culture *backed* by capital. Hafiz, however, is not the first Arab thinker who subdivided the Arab world into different temporal regions. Palestinian George Antonius had already done so in his 1937 classic *The Arab Awakening*. In his discussion of the provisions of the Sykes-Picot Agreement, which created the borders of the eastern part of the Arab world, Antonius identified the "faults" of the agreement by glancing at the map:

The population inhabiting [Syria, Iraq, and the desert regions between them] is made up of Arabic-speaking communities who had reached different stages of development, those occupying . . . the coastal regions of the Mediterranean seaboard and the lower basins of the Tigris and the Euphrates . . . being intellectually more advanced and politically more developed than those, mainly nomadic, who lived in inland regions.[90]

Antonius marvels at the "absurdity" of the provisions of the Sykes-Picot Agreement, which would place Syria and Iraq under foreign administration while the inland regions, "whose population lagged far behind in point of political experience and maturity," would form independent Arab states: "It was like putting the adults to school and sending the pupils of the elementary classes out into the world."[91]

Antonius aside, these current culturalist debates are about political development and evolution whose desired telos is Western democracy. But even that might prove impossible. Jurj Tarabishi insists that the

---

88. Ibid., 16.
89. Yasin al-Hafiz, *Al-Hazimah wa al-Aydiyulujiyyah al-Mahzumah* [Defeat and the Defeated Ideology] (Beirut: Maʿhad al-Inmaʾ al-ʿArabi, 1990), 143. The book was originally published in 1979.
90. George Antonius, *The Arab Awakening* (New York: Capricorn Books, 1965), 248.
91. Ibid., 249.

prerequisite to Western-style democracy is the development of a democratic "culture," which he finds now lacking in the Arab world. Tarabishi's litmus test of a "democratic culture" among Arab intellectuals is whether they would accept a "Muslim Luther" or an "Arab Voltaire." If Arab intellectuals cannot accept such a personage in their midst, how could the Arab masses? "Can we accept another Salman Rushdie in our midst?" he asks.[92] Tarabishi is not being very original. His call for a Muslim Luther is a nineteenth-century one, first suggested, as we saw earlier, by Jamal al-Din al-Afghani, who fancied himself a Muslim Luther.[93] In insisting on an epistemology of evolutionary stages, Tarabishi recommends that the Arab world institute limited procedural democracy following in the footsteps of nineteenth-century Europe. He realizes that what he is recommending is a "democratic heresy." This does not mean that suffrage (which is universal among the adult population in those Arab countries that have formal democratic procedures—including Kuwait more recently) should be limited to the propertied classes or to men, as this would discriminate against women and the poor. Suffrage, Tarabishi proposes, should be limited to the literate in order to defeat the Islamists who promise to destroy democracy once democratically elected and who will do so through their populist discourse, which appeals to the increasing number of illiterate citizens in the Arab world. This, it would seem, would not discriminate against women and the poor, who by sheer coincidence happen to swell the illiterate ranks of the Arab world as they do the rest of the third world![94]

These are culturalist debates that allow no place for the economy or capital. The reasons why Europe "modernized" are found in an immanent cultural realm, as are the reasons for why the Arabs "have not." What we discern in the above examples is a central temporal schema whereby the Arabs are currently "late," "delayed," and "behind." They are late in their movement toward modernity, seen as the time of "democracy," and are located behind "Europe" and its American extension, seen as the site of "democracy." The reasons for this distressing temporal and spatial location are cultural in origins, and the only way to transcend them is by transcending them culturally. What is needed, then, is a culturalist schema that can accelerate the stage of development of

92. Jurj Tarabishi, *Fi Thaqafat al-Dimuqratiyyah* [On Democratic Culture] (Beirut: Dar al-Tali'ah, 1998), 18.

93. See Jamal al-Din al-Afghani, *The Truth about the Neicheri Sect and an Explanation of the Neicheris,* in *An Islamic Response to Imperialism: Political and Religious Writings of Sayyid Jamal ad-Din al-Afghani,* ed. Nikki Keddie (Berkeley: University of California Press, 1968), 171.

94. Tarabishi, *Fi Thaqafat,* 25.

the Arabs to one that is contemporaneous with Europe and a schema that locates them adjacent to, rather than trailing behind, Europe. These ideas are not much unlike those espoused by American neoconservatives and the policies of the administration of George W. Bush toward Arab (and Muslim) countries.

When capital enters the picture in these debates, it does so as a subsidiary of culture or one that is parallel to it. Mahdi ʿAmil, being one of the few intellectuals who saw a role for capital in all this, asserts that what such intellectuals postulate is an "evolutionary crisis, a crisis of transition from the past to the present or rather the transition *of* the past to the present." Time in such a discourse, insisted ʿAmil, is "but the movement of this essence called Arab civilization."[95] For ʿAmil, who was criticizing the premise of a 1974 conference in Kuwait on the "crisis of Arab civilization," the so-called "backwardness" of Arab society of which the participants spoke is based on a central problematic: for them, the "backwardness" of the present is a result of the insistence of the past to remain within it. ʿAmil counters that it is the present, not the past, which is culpable, as the present causes the past to remain within it, not vice versa.[96] For him, the crisis was not one faced by Arab "civilization" but by the Arab bourgeoisies.

Perhaps, these contemporary intellectuals are heeding the historicist advice given to them almost three decades ago by Abdallah Laroui:

To understand the historical process is to understand both oneself and others in a temporal perspective; it is to conceive of tested and effective courses of action. To the extent that Arab intellectuals . . . have a non-evolutionary conception of reality, so will all collective action in the Arab milieu be deprived of a constant and definite orientation; and so will politics, in the noble sense of the word, be reduced to the level of short-sighted maneuvering subservient to egotistical interests.[97]

All the same, these temporal notions are being deployed, like the theories that postulated them in the first place, without providing a narrative history of international capital. Instead, there is now a new and hegemonic practice that has pervaded contemporary Arab intellectual discourse as well as other intellectual discourses across the globe: recoding capitalism as "civilizing mission" ("taqaddum" and "tamaddun"),

---

95. ʿAmil, *Azmat al-Hadarah al-ʿArabiyyah Am Azmat al-Burjuwaziyyat al-ʿArabiyyah*, 22–23.
96. Ibid., 43–65.
97. Laroui, *Crisis of the Arab Intellectual*, ix.

otherwise known as imperialism, or as "development" ("tatawwur" or "tanmiyyah"), otherwise known as neocolonialism, or finally as "democracy," otherwise known as globalization.[98] Whereas in the age of high imperialism, "progress" for most Arab intellectuals meant "renaissance," or *Nahdah,* and in the neocolonial period it meant "revolution," today, in the age of globalization, "progress" for many among them means Western-style "democracy." Note that only in the final phase do Arab intellectuals espouse the same vocabulary espoused by the ideologues of the globalization of capital.

What is unchanging then in Arab debates today is not the "regressive" nature of Arab intellectual discourse nor of *turath* or its influence on Arab culture—as both *turath* and its influence, as we will see in the course of this book, have been subjected to myriad interpretations since the Arab "Renaissance" through revolutionary nationalism and Marxist thinking and the current "epistemological" debates. What remains constant then is a commitment to an evolutionary temporal schema that recognizes change only within the dyad of *turath* and modernity. Contra al-Jabiri and in line with Theodor Adorno and Max Horheimer's view of Enlightenment as myth, what is needed—not only for Arab intellectuals but especially for their European counterparts—is a view of *turath* and modernity that is located outside this dualism, one that is not subject to their temporal peregrinations.[99]

European and Arab Desires

One of the consequences of accepting Orientalist taxonomies and judgment of Arab cultural production during the Ottoman period as "decadent" is the almost total neglect of that period of Arab history by *Nah-*

---

98. See Gayatri Chakravorty Spivak, *A Critique of Post-Colonial Reason: Towards a History of the Vanishing Present* (Cambridge: Harvard University Press, 1999), 354.

99. Here Abdallah Laroui's 1974 words are still worth citing:

One could maintain that any hermeneutic tending to relativize Western culture is an indirect result of the infringement of extra-European cultures on the consciousness of Europe. But as yet, apart from circumstantial writings, we can accredit to no great name of the extra-European world any radical critique of the fundamental European ideology: rationalism applied to nature, man, and history . . . Yet between Europe and non-Europe there is a conflict, open or concealed. Will this conflict one day give rise to such a critique? If this should happen, we can at least be sure that Europeans and non-Europeans together will assist in its formulation.

Laroui, *Crisis of the Arab Intellectual,* 126. On Enlightenment as myth, see Max Horkheimer and Theodor Adorno, *The Dialectic of Enlightenment* (New York: Continuum, 1972).

dah and post-*Nahdah* Arab scholarship. This neglect extends to Arabic poetry produced in the period. Khaled El-Rouayheb, who has completed a recent study on the subject, notes that

anyone approaching this period in the history of Arabic poetry is confronted with a remarkable dearth of secondary studies. This lack of interest stands in stark contrast to the abundance of extant poetry . . . What seems to have been lacking so far is not source-material but modern scholarly interest. This lack of interest presumably derives from the apparently still influential assumption that there was not much interesting or original Arabic poetry produced between 1500 and 1800. From the nineteenth century onwards, historians of Arabic literature have tended to dismiss the period between 1500 and 1800 as one of cultural stagnation or decadence (*inhitat*). However, it is still difficult to see how such an assessment can be justified in the absence of any serious study of the poetic output of the period.[100]

El-Rouayheb cites the few and rare existing summaries of the poetry of the period and notes that the authors of these few studies "give their readers the impression that the love poetry of the period usually portrayed a female beloved." In contrast, El-Rouayheb's study found that "the portrayed beloved was often, and perhaps most often, a male youth," and not a woman.[101]

El-Rouayheb maintains that "much if not most of the extant love poetry of the period is pederastic in tone, portraying an adult male poet's passionate love for a teenage boy."[102] This does not mean that what we know today as "homosexuality" was widespread, as many Orientalist observers usually affirm. El-Rouayheb is careful in his assessment that "Arabic-Islamic culture on the eve of modernity lacked the concept of 'homosexuality,' and that writings from this period do not evince the same attitude towards all aspects of what we would be inclined to call homosexuality today."[103] Indeed, as the evidence that El-Rouayheb suggests, there are no indications in the literature of the period that anyone thought that those men who either wrote love poems to youthful boys or those who had sexual intercourse with men, whether active or passive, were exclusively "homosexual." No commentator thought their desires for men or boys excluded desires for women. It is important to

---

100. Khaled El-Rouayheb, "The Love of Boys in Arabic Poetry of the Early Ottoman Period, 1500–1800," *Middle Eastern Literatures* 8, no.1 (2005): 3.

101. Ibid., 4.

102. Khaled El-Rouayheb, *Before Homosexuality in the Arab-Islamic World, 1500–1800* (Chicago: University of Chicago Press, 2005), 1.

103. Ibid.

insist that not only did the concept of homosexuality itself not exist but also that if exclusive "homosexual" male desire as such existed at all, it was not the main topic of discourse. What was discussed was the "love of boys" and "sodomy," neither of which indicated any exclusivity and at best gestured towards a hierarchy of preferences that was deployed in a certain period (youth), and changed in others (adulthood or old age). It should be emphasized here that those who wrote love poetry to youthful boys did not necessarily practice sodomy. In fact, there are many indications that the pious religious scholars who would observe the accepted interpretation that Islam prohibited sodomy did not commit the act but saw no contradiction between the prohibition on sodomy and falling in love with youthful boys. Such infatuation and the poetry that expressed it did not always, or even often, as El-Rouayheb demonstrates, seek sexual consummation, which was not seen as the telos of the expressed desires. Distinctions were indeed made between sodomy, which was prohibited theologically, and expressing love for youthful boys, which did not carry such prohibitions.

Egyptian educator and author Rifaʿah al-Tahtawi—the imam for a number of scholars dispatched by Egypt's ruler Muhammad ʿAli to learn the sciences of the French and acquire their knowledge (he was imposed on the educational mission by al-Azhar's educational establishment)— wrote a chronicle of his travels, which lasted from 1826 until 1830. In his description of his sojourn in France, al-Tahtawi commented on the habits and traits of the French in a protoanthropological fashion. He had undertaken the writing of his book on the advice of his friends and relatives, especially his mentor Shaykh Hasan al-ʿAttar (1766–1835), "who adores hearing about wondrous news and reading about strange traditions [athar]." Al-ʿAttar, who incidentally wrote love poetry about youthful boys, urged al-Tahtawi to write an account of his travels so that "it can remain as a guide for traveling to [France] for those seeking travel, especially so, as since the beginning of time until now, there has never appeared in the Arabic language anything about the history of the city of Paris . . . or about its conditions or the condition of its inhabitants."[104] In this important book, which he titled *Takhlis al-Ibriz fi Talkhis Bariz* (The Extrication of Gold in Summarizing Paris) and which he pub-

104. Rifaʿah al-Tahtawi, *Takhlis al-Ibriz fi Talkhis Bariz Aw Al-Diwan al-Nafis bi-Iwan Bariz* [The Extrication of Gold in Summarizing Paris, or the Valuable Collection in the Drawing Room of Paris], in *Al-Aʿmal al-Kamilah of Rifaʿah al-Tahtawi*, ed. Muhammad ʿImarah (Beirut: al-Muʾassassah al-ʿArabiyyah lil-Dirasat wa al-Nashr, 1973), vol. 2, 10–11. The book was originally published in 1834 and was based on al-Tahtawi's travels to France in 1826. The book was republished in 1849 and again in 1905.

lished in 1834 in Cairo, al-Tahtawi offered comparisons of the best and worst traits of the French with regards to sociosexual habits with those of Egypt and the Arabs. Echoing some of al-Jabarti's observations, he began by stating that among the traits of the French was "their spending money on the needs of the soul and on satanic desires, their play and games, as they are extremely extravagant. Their men are also slaves to their women and under their command, whether they are pretty or not . . . The Franks also do not suspect the worst in their women, although [the latter's] lapses are many, as a man among them, even from their nobility, when his wife's debauchery [fujur] is proved to him, he leaves her altogether, and separates from her forever."[105] However, this is not to say that al-Tahtawi found everything reprehensible in Paris:

One of the better things among their traits, which truly resemble the traits of Bedouins ['Arab], is their lack of predilection for the love of male juveniles or for writing rhapsodies for them, as this is one thing that is never mentioned among them and which their natures and morality reject. And, one of the better attributes of their language and poetry is its refusal of the flirtation of one kind with the same kind [jins], for it is not allowed in the French language for a man to say, "I have fallen for a male juvenile ['ashiqtu ghulaman]," as this is considered abhorrent speech . . . which is why if one of them translated one of our books, he would twist the words to say, "I have fallen for a youthful girl," or he would get rid of the sentence altogether, as they see in this a corruption of morals, and they are right, as one of the two kinds [of people] has in those who are not of his kind a characteristic to which he is inclined just like the attraction of a magnet to iron, for example, or that of electricity to attract objects, and the like, as, if the same kind united, this characteristic would disappear, and it [this kind] would have departed from the natural state. For them, this would be one of the worst abominations [fawahish], so much that they have rarely mentioned it openly in their books but rather eschew it as much as possible, and one never hears conversation about it in the first place.[106]

105. Ibid., 78.

106. Ibid. Note how his use of the term "jins," which would acquire the meaning "sex" in the twentieth century, means "kind." He never uses it to designate sexual relations or coitus. It is actually used to refer to the French popular militia as the "alkhafar al-jinsi" (207). Also, he uses the plural of jins, "ajnas" in a conventional way when referring to different ethnic groupings (256). Note also that when he speaks of "desire and progeny" in his later book *Al-Murshid al-Amin Lil-Banat wa al-Banin* [The Safe Guide to Girls and Boys], he never uses the word *jins* to designate males and females but simply addresses the permitted pleasure within their marital relationship and desire for reproduction. See his *Al-Murshid al-Amin Lil-Banat wa al-Banin* [The Safe Guide to Girls and Boys], in *Al-A'mal al-Kamilah of Rifa'ah al-Tahtawi*, ed. Muhammad 'Imarah (Beirut: al-Mu'assassah al-'Arabiyyah lil-Dirasat wa al-Nashr, 1973), vol. 2, 318. This book was first published in 1873, the year of al-Tahtawi's death. Similarly, Butrus al-Bustani, in his 1852 speech on the education of women, used the term *jins* also in the sense of kind, when he referred to women (but not to men), see his "Khitab fi Ta'lim

Still, however, the question of women's infidelity nagged at him:

Among their worse traits: the dearth of chastity among many of their women, as already mentioned, and the lack of jealousy among their men compared to the jealousy of Muslim men . . . how is this so when adultery [zina] for them is a vice and a shame but not a primary sin/guilt [dhunub], especially with regards to the unmarried man . . . Generally speaking, this city, like the rest of France's cities and the rest of the great countries of the Franks [Europeans], is charged with abominations [fawahish], innovations [bida'], and perdition [dalalat], although the city of Paris is the wisest city of the entire world and the home of world-based [barraniyyah] science and is the French Athens.[107]

This does not mean that the French have no sense of sexual honor (" 'ird") as Arabs do: "It should not be thought of them that they have no sexual honor because of their lack of jealousy of their women, as sexual honor appears in this context more than in any other. As even though they might lack jealousy, once they know of anything suspicious about their women, they become the most evil of people to them [the women], to themselves, and to those who have betrayed them with their women. The thing is that they simply err in handing over leadership to women [in their interactions with them]."[108]

On the question of public nudity, France seemed to be slightly "safer" as far as hiding people's genitals from the eyes of onlookers was concerned, specifically in its public baths, but the French bath experience proved less "pleasurable" than the Egyptian: "Public baths in Paris are diverse, and in fact are cleaner than Egypt's baths, although Egypt's baths are more beneficial and better built, and are better in general. The bathhouse in Paris has a number of private spaces in each of which there is a copper tub big enough for one person only, and in others there may be two tubs, but they do not have one general tub as in Egypt. But this is a safer habit as far as the pudenda [al-'awrah] are concerned, as there is no way a person can look at the pudenda of his companion. Even the private spaces that contain two tubs have a curtain separating them. There is no pleasure, however, in going into these tubs as there is in going into the baths [of Egypt], as one never perspires in them, for there is only heat inside the tub, but never in the private space around it, although one

---

al-Nisa'" [Speech on the Education of Women] (Beirut: A'mal al-Jam'iyyah al-Suriyyah, 1852), reproduced in Fakhri, *Al-Harakat al-Fikriyyah*, 183–97. This indicates a sort of transitional period before *jins* would acquire its modern meaning of designating both two kinds of humans *and* coitus between them. On the etymology of the word "jins" as sex, see chapter 3.
107. Al-Tahtawi, *Takhlis al-Ibriz fi Talkhis Bariz Aw Al-Diwan al-Nafis bi-Iwan Baris*, 78–79.
108. Ibid., 257.

could order a steam bath which they would prepare for him, but at extra cost than the usual."[109] Al-Tahtawi is careful to provide a class angle in assessing women's chastity. He clearly observed the difference between bourgeois sexual mores and those of the aristocracy and the poor. He observes that "chastity captures the hearts" of the "women of the middle classes, except for the women of the nobility and of the riffraff."[110]

Many of al-Tahtawi's views are echoed by the Moroccan traveler Muhammad bin ʿAbdullah al-Saffar, who undertook a short visit (lasting a mere fifty days) to France, and especially Paris, in the winter of 1845–1846.[111] Al-Saffar does make a passing reference to al-Tahtawi's account, from which he seemed to borrow many details.[112] While al-Saffar seemed more impressed with many aspects of Paris and had a higher opinion than al-Tahtawi of Parisian women, he was appalled at the Parisian practice (which he also remarked in Marseilles[113]) of urinating in the streets, against walls and corners, even though there existed public cubicles for urination,[114] and was disgusted at the free flow of urine in the streets of Paris (reminiscent of al-Jabarti's remarks about the personal hygiene and toilet habits of the French).[115] Regarding sexual desire, al-Saffar, like al-Tahtawi, did remark with surprise that

for them, only flirtation, rhapsody, and courtship with women exist, for they are not inclined toward young men [ghilman] and juveniles, as for them this is a great shame and merits punishment, even though it be with mutual consent. This is contrary to the way they regard loving women and intercourse [khilwah] with them. For if they both consent to it, no one interferes with them.[116]

Khaled El-Rouayheb remarks that al-Tahtawi's views "should clearly be considered against the background of the kind of love poetry written in Egypt in Tahtawi's own time. The poetry of the prominent eighteenth- and early nineteenth-century Egyptian poets . . . was overwhelmingly pederastic." He adds that as

109. Ibid., 127.
110. Ibid., 258.
111. Al-Shaykh Muhammad bin ʿAbdullah al-Saffar, *Al-Rihlah al-Titwaniyyah ila al-Diyar al-Firansiyyah 1845–1846* [The Tetouanite Journey to the Country of the French, 1845–1846], ed. Umm Salma (Titwan: Matbaʿat al-Haddad Yusuf Ikhwan, 1995). He stayed in Paris proper from 28 December 1845 until 16 February 1846. See ibid., 107.
112. Ibid., 57.
113. Ibid., 37.
114. Ibid., 69.
115. Ibid., 94.
116. Ibid., 95.

indicated by Tahtawi's remarks, European Arabists in the early nineteenth century disapproved of this theme in Arabic love-poetry, and sought to conceal its very existence. At around the same time as Tahtawi was in Paris, the great British Arabist Edward Lane was in Egypt, collecting material for his seminal *An Account of the Manners and Customs of the Modern Egyptians.* Lane, who also produced a heavily bowdlerized version of *The Arabian Nights,* clearly considered pederasty to be an unmentionable vice, and had nothing to say about the phenomenon in his *Account.*[117]

Some Arab poets continued to write love poetry for youthful boys during the nineteenth century.[118] The last one to do so was perhaps Hafiz Ibrahim (1872–1932), who in 1906 wrote at least one poem about a young handsome soldier, singing his praises and wishing he would add his sword to those defending Egypt against the British. The poem did not contain any expression of sexual desire.[119] Most remarkable about the transformation of Arabic literature since the late nineteenth century is that *ghazal* poetry for youthful boys or men disappeared completely as a poetic genre or subgenre, as no major or minor poet (except for a few marginal poets), wrote verses expressing erotic love toward young or old men in twentieth-century Arabic poetry.[120]

Indeed, within a few decades of al-Tahtawi's and al-Saffar's accounts, not only would surprise at the sexual desires of Europeans and frank discussion of the desires of Arabs dissipate among Arab writers, but these bewildered views themselves would become surprising to later generations of the Arab intelligentsia. The explicit and frank discussions of matters sexual by nineteenth-century Lebanese writer Ahmad Faris al-Shidyaq (who himself complained that medieval Arab men's practices of polygamy and taking concubines was one of the reasons for the destruction of the medieval Arabs, as it did the Greeks, the Persians, and

117. El-Rouayheb, "The Love of Boys," 16.

118. El-Rouyheb, *Before Homosexuality,* 157.

119. See Hafiz Ibrahim, *Diwan Hafiz Ibrahim* [The Collection of the Poetry of Hafiz Ibrahim], ed. Ahmad Amin, Ahmad al-Zayn, and Ibrahim al-Abyari (Beirut: Muhammd Amin Damaj, 1969), part 1, 247–48.

120. The rare exception is Iraqi professor of Arabic literature ʿAbd al-Razzaq Muhyi al-Din (1910–83), who also wrote and published poems in Iraqi and Lebanese newspapers. Muhyi al-Din wrote a poem in 1932 which he published in Lebanon titled "Kurrat al-Sallah aw ʿala Lawhat al-Sabburah" [Basketball; or, On the Chalkboard), which expresses the erotic love and yearning of a male teacher towards one of his male students. The poem, which was included in his posthumously published collection of poetry, is identified by the editor as having been written by Muhyi al-Din "on behalf" of a teacher friend of his. See ʿAbd al-Razzaq Muhyi al-Din, *Diwan al-Qasaʾid* [Collected Poems], ed. Dr. Muhammad Husayn ʿAli al-Saghir (Amman: Dar Usamah lil-Nashr wa al-Tawziʿ, 2000), 51–53. Muhyi al-Din's poem partakes of an Arabic poetic tradition of expressing a teacher's erotic love to a male student that still flourished in Ottoman times. See El-Rouayheb, *Before Homosexuality,* 34–36.

the Romans[121]), for example, would soon be condemned by fin-de-siè-cle literary historians. Major *turath* compiler and historian Jurji Zaydan had the following to say in 1902 about Shidyaq's 1855 magnum opus *Al-Saq ʿala al-Saq* (One Leg over Another), in his biography of famous nineteenth-century personages:

We cannot proceed beyond our description of the book of the *Fariyaq* [One Leg over Another] before mentioning something that we had hoped God would spare us looking into, namely, that he [Shidyaq] had mentioned in that book terms and expressions intended to express bawdiness [mujun] but went beyond its limits so much so that no man of letters could recite it without wishing that it had not occurred to our Shaykh and that he had not included it in his book in order to steer the pens of writers away from what would cause a young man, not to mention a virgin [girl], to blush [khajal].[122]

Half a century later, the bewilderment would be of a different order altogether. If Zaydan waxed Victorian about the use of sexual expressions in printed matter, Tawfiq al-Tawil, a mid-twentieth-century historian of Sufism in Egypt, questioned in his 1946 book about the subject the very credibility of earlier accounts of desire altogether: "There is no better indication of the spread of sexual deviance among those people [Sufis] than the amazement of Rifaʿah al-Tahtawi when he traveled to France that he did not find this illness widespread among its people, as if its being widespread was the natural thing, and that it was unnatural that it was not widespread among the people."[123] But if al-Tawil expressed horror that al-Tahtawi thought "sexual deviance" was not an "illness," that he expected it would be widespread, and that this would be the "natural thing," half a century later al-Tawil's view would become so dominant that Jurj Tarabishi, in a Western liberal moment of exasperation on matters sexual, would measure the "failure" of contemporary Arab "civilization" to advance by its levels of sexual tolerance, as Arab

121. Ahmad Faris al-Shidyaq, *Kanz al-Ragha'ib fi Muntakhabat al-Jawa'ib* [The Treasure of Wishes in the Selection of Articles from *Jawa'ib* magazine] (Istanbul, 1871–72), part 1, 90, cited by Majid Fakhri, *Al-Harakat al-Fikriyyah*, 81–82.

122. *Tarajim Mashahir al-Sharq fi al-Qarn al-Tasiʿ ʿAshar* [The Biographies of Famous People of the Orient in the Nineteenth Century] (Cairo: Al-Hilal, 1910), vol. 2, 90. This was the second edition of the book which was first published in 1910.

123. Tawfiq al-Tawil, *Al-Tasawwuf fi Misr ibban al-ʿAsr al-ʿUthmani* [Sufism in Egypt during the Ottoman Age] (Cairo: Al-Hay'ah al-Misriyyah al-ʿAmah lil-Kitab, 1988), 157. The book was first published in 1946 by Maktabat al-Adab in Alexandria. I would like to thank Khaled al-Rouayheb for bringing this to my attention.

"backwardness" for him is marked by the denial of "democracy in sexual relations (and here I am limiting myself to heterosexual [ghayriyyah] relationships without venturing to address homosexual [mithliyyah] ones)."[124] Tarabishi's views, as will become clear, are commensurate not with the prevailing ideas in the contemporary Arab world but with those prevailing in the contemporary West.

Orientalism and Sexual Rights

It is in the realm of the emergent agenda of sexual rights that made its appearance in the United States and other Western countries in the late 1960s and began to be internationalized in the 1980s and 1990s that talk of sexual practices in the rest of the world, including the Arab world, would be introduced to the international human rights agenda and would be coupled with notions of "civilized" and "uncivilized" behavior. This *incitement to discourse* on sexual rights outside the United States and Western Europe necessitated that human rights organizations and advocates incorporate existing anthropological knowledge of the non-Western world.[125] This was central for the purpose of constructing the human subjects—or, more precisely, objects—of human rights discourse (see chapter 3). In the course of such "international" human rights activism, two prime victims of human rights violations in Arab countries emerged and/or were created: women and "homosexuals." While the premodern West attacked the world of Islam's alleged sexual licentiousness, the modern West attacks its alleged *repression* of sexual freedoms. The horror of "honor" crimes taking the life of a quarter of all women murdered in Jordan, for example, would take a life of its own with special reports on American television networks and popular books by alleged native informants. Yet no special television programs on U.S. networks investigated the fact that at least one-third of all women murdered in the United States are murdered by their boyfriends or husbands.[126] Nor were these comparisons made when exhibiting real and imaginary Arab "honor" crimes for television viewers.

124. See Tarabishi, *Fi Thaqafat,* 18.
125. On incitement to discourse, see Michel Foucault, *The History of Sexuality,* vol. 1, *An Introduction,* trans. Robert Hurley (New York: Vintage Books, 1980), 17–35.
126. See "Violence against Women: A National Crime Victimization Survey Report," U.S. Department of Justice, Washington, D.C., January 1994, and *Violence by Intimates: Analysis of Data on Crimes by Current or Former Spouses, Boyfriends, and Girlfriends* (publication NCJ167237), ed. Lawrence Greenfeld et al. (Washington, DC: U.S. Department of Justice, Office of Justice Programs, Bureau of Justice Statistics, 1988), and available at http://www.ojp.usdoj.gov/bjs.

If Orientalists and anthropologists depicted the sexual practices of Arabs with keen interest in the sexual desires of Arab men, many Western writers and tourists as mentioned above would travel to Arab countries to fulfill their desires for Arabs. As I will discuss in chapter 3, gay tourism to Morocco and Egypt, as well as the large number of gay men in the diplomatic corps of Western embassies, in the local offices of Western newspapers, and on the staffs of Western NGOs stationed in the Arab world, has continued that tradition. The history of that tourism is itself instructive of how the issue of "culture" and colonial and neocolonial power interact. Joseph Boone remarked in the case of Morocco that

given the reality of the homosexual persecution that drove a number of Europeans and Americans to settle in Tangier, I do not mean to undervalue the degree to which these enclaves created self-affirming communities impossible elsewhere or to overlook the degree to which these expatriate colonies, however privileged in their trappings, sometimes allowed for the emergence of desires and practices that resisted the dominant Western erotology of romantic coupling. But the "sanctuary of non-interference" that [William S.] Burroughs applauds depended on certain historical and economic factors of Western colonialism that perpetuated degrees of exploitation potentially as objectionable as the experience of marginalization and harassment that sent these Western voyagers abroad in the first place.[127]

Boone adds that "in those narratives where the occidental traveler, by virtue of his homosexuality, is *already* the other, we have seen how the presumed *equivalence* of Eastern homosexuality and occidental personal liberation may disguise the specter of colonial privilege and exploitation encoded in the hierarchy of white man/brown boy."[128] It is in this context of continued Western sex tourism and increasing anthropological attention to same-sex practice among men in the Arab world that Western human rights groups began to pay special attention to the violation of the "rights" of "homosexuals" in Arab countries.

Gayatri Chakravorty Spivak has recently noted that the "idea of human rights . . . may carry within itself the agenda of a kind of social Darwinism—the fittest must shoulder the burden of righting the wrongs of the unfit—and the possibility of an alibi. Only a 'kind of' social Darwinism, of course. Just as 'the white man's burden,' undertaking to civilize and develop, was only 'a kind of' oppression. It would be silly to footnote the scholarship that has been written to show that the latter

127. Boone, "Vacation Cruises; or, The Homoerotics of Orientalism," 99–100.
128. Ibid., 104.

may have been an alibi for economic, military, and political intervention."[129] As I will demonstrate in chapter 3, the goal can also be and often is one of ethical and epistemic normalization. Spivak is clear that "colonialism was committed to the education of a certain class. It was interested in the seemingly permanent operation of an altered normality. Paradoxically human rights and 'development' work today cannot claim this self-empowerment that high colonialism could. Yet, some of the best products of high colonialism, descendants of the colonial middle class, become human rights advocates in the countries of the South."[130] As the examples of chapter 3 will show, the collusion between middle- and upper-class native informants and diasporic members of the national group in question on the one side, and the Western human rights groups and organizations on the other, makes it clear that it is not only a Eurocentric culture that is being universalized, but a culture that has important class attributes and therefore serious consequences for those unfit to defend themselves. Spivak explains that "the work of righting wrongs is shared above a class line that to some extent and unevenly cuts across race and the North-South divide."[131] This native middle class, "although physically based in the South . . . is generally also out of touch with the mindset—a combination of episteme and ethical discourse—of the rural poor below the NGO level. To be able to present a project that will draw aid from the North, for example, to understand and state a problem intelligibly and persuasively for the taste of the North, is itself proof of a sort of epistemic discontinuity with the ill-educated rural poor. (And the sort of education we are thinking of is not to make the rural poor capable of drafting NGO grant proposals!)"[132] I would add that Spivak's conclusions about the rural poor apply also in large measure to the urban poor, even though the latter may get more NGO "attention" from international and local agents of human rights organizations, especially when the issue has to do with "sexual rights."

Yet, despite the class, race, and colonial position of the fittest human rights activists who defend the unfit victims of violations, the allure of righting wrongs persists even among careful scholars and attentive advocates against identity oppression. Thus, Judith Butler, an otherwise exemplary scholar in her attention to detail, pushes for a universalizing

129. Gayatri Chakravorty Spivak, "Righting Wrongs," *South Atlantic Quarterly* 103, nos. 2–3 (Spring–Summer 2004): 524.
130. Ibid.
131. Ibid., 525.
132. Ibid., 527.

of sexual rights: "One of the central tasks of lesbian and gay international rights is to assert in clear and public terms the reality of homosexuality, not as an inner truth, not as a sexual practice, but as one of the definite features of the social world in its very intelligibility . . . Indeed the task of international lesbian and gay politics is no less than a remaking of reality, a reconstituting of the human, and a brokering of the question, what is and is not livable?"[133] Butler's concern is that contemporary human subjectivity in constituted through a repudiation of what is lesbian and gay, which are therefore banished beyond the perimeter of the human. While this may be arguably true in certain Western contexts, it has no bearing on contexts in which lesbianness and gayness, let alone homosexuality as configured in the normalized West, are not the other against whom the self is constituted. In calling for the internationalization of Western sexual ontology, Butler is risking another subjective repudiation, a banishing of another *other*, in the formation of the Western human that is inclusive of the homosexual, namely, those cultural formations whose ontological structure is not based on the hetero-homo binary. The universalist moment here is the assimilationist moment which guarantees that the sexual subjectivity of the Western purveyors of international lesbian and gay politics itself is universal while its racial/national/class constitution is carried out through a repudiation of the subjectivities of those unfit to defend themselves by the fittest subjectivity of all.

Butler understands the implications of international human rights work but seems to believe in the beneficial consequences of its universalization: "International human rights is always in the process of subjecting the human to redefinition and renegotiation. It mobilizes the human in the service of rights, but also rewrites the human and rearticulates the human when it comes up against the cultural limits of its working conception of the human, as it does and must."[134] Butler expresses much concern about imperialism while at the same time she correctly rejects cultural relativism as effective or desirable resistance: "An anti-imperialist or, minimally, nonimperialist conception of international human rights must call into question what is meant by the human and learn from the various ways and means by which it is defined across cultural venues. This means that local conceptions of what is human or, indeed, of what the basic conditions and needs of a human life are, must be subjected to reinterpretation, since there are historical and cultural

133. Judith Butler, *Undoing Gender* (New York: Routledge, 2004), 29–30.
134. Ibid., 33.

circumstances in which the human is defined differently."[135] In place of the imperialist and the reductively relativist view, Butler insists that "we are compelled to speak of the human, and of the international, and to find out in particular how human rights do and do not work."[136] I am not persuaded by this argument. Butler is admirably attentive to the different configurations of including and excluding the category of woman, which has been institutionalized as a universal category at the expense of the differing local formations and legal standings of the term, informed by racial, geographic, and class positionings inter alia. Including the categories of gay and lesbian as if they were analogous to the universalized category "woman," however, is even more problematic. The categories gay and lesbian are not universal at all and can only be universalized by the epistemic, ethical, and political violence unleashed on the rest of the world by the very international human rights advocates whose aim is to defend the very people their intervention is creating. In doing so, the human rights advocates are not bringing about the inclusion of the homosexual in a new and redefined human subjectivity, but in fact are bringing about her and his exclusion from this redefined subjectivity altogether while simultaneously destroying existing subjectivities organized around other sets of binaries, including sexual ones. While subjectivities in many non-Western contexts do not include heterosexuality and exclude homosexuality, as that very binarism is not part of their ontological structure, what the incitement and intervention of international human rights activism achieves is the replication of the very Euro-American human subjectivity its advocates challenge at home. The new and redefined universal human subjectivity that they are proselytizing to the rest of the world is not that of including the homosexual but that of instituting the very binary (an assimilationist move that facilitates the tabulation of "data" in the databases of the human rights industry) which will exclude the homosexual that it created in the first place, and all that is carried out in the name of "liberation" from oppressive cultures and laws. Here, Diana Fuss's intervention is most apt:

Is it really possible to speak of "homosexuality," or for that matter "heterosexuality" or "bisexuality," as universal, global formations? Can one generalize from the particular forms sexuality takes under Western capitalism to sexuality *as such*? What kinds of colonializations do such translations perform on "other" traditions of sexual difference?[137]

135. Ibid., 37.
136. Ibid.
137. Diana Fuss, *Identification Papers* (London: Routledge, 1995), 159.

Talal Asad insists that the dominant view of cultures as "fragmented" and interdependent, "as critics never tire of reminding us," is not sufficient:

Cultures are also *unequally displaced practices*. Whether cultural displacement is a means of ensuring political domination or merely its effect, whether it is a necessary stage in the growth of a universal humanity or an instance of cultural takeover, is not the point here. What I want to stress is that cultures may be conceived not only in visual terms ("clearly bounded," "interlaced," "fragmented," and so forth) but also in terms of the temporalities of power by which—rightly or wrongly—*practices* constituting particular forms of life are displaced, outlawed, and penalized, and by which conditions are created for the cultivation of different kinds of human.[138]

The exercise of political power to repress, if not destroy, existing non-Western subjectivities and produce new ones that accord with Western conceptions "often presents itself as a force of redeeming 'humanity' from 'traditional cultures.'"[139] My point here is not to argue in favor of non-Western nativism and of some blissful existence prior to the epistemic, ethical, and political violence unleashed on the non-West, as facile critics would have it, but an argument against a *Western nativism* armed with a Rousseauian zeal intent on forcing people into "freedom," indeed a Western nativism that considers assimilating the world into its own norms as ipso facto "liberation" and "progress" and a step toward universalizing a superior notion of the human.

There is nothing liberatory about Western human subjectivity including gays and lesbians when it does so by forcibly including those non-Europeans who are not gays or lesbians while excluding them as unfit to define or defend themselves. I am not merely suggesting a Derridian insistence that a binary division is always already transhistorical and exists and is constituted at the level of metaphysical ontology, as Derrida did in his famous critique of Foucault's historicizing the banishment of madness and the constitution of reason,[140] but that the historical changes brought to bear on Western ontology always already reinscribe the binary by banishing those unfit to occupy it. While I am sympathetic to the political project of an all-encompassing utopian inclusivity, I am less sanguine about its feasibility and more worried about its cruelty.

138. Asad, *Formations of the Secular,* 153–54.
139. Ibid., 154.
140. See Jacques Derrida, "Cogito and the History of Madness," in Derrida, *Writing and Difference* (Chicago: University of Chicago Press, 1978), 31–63.

Take the example of one sexual rights missionary writing on Lebanon. He accuses those Lebanese men who refuse to identify as "gay" and answer Western questions about their alleged gayness by insisting that "I'm not like that" as "self-hating" or even as expressing "homosexual homophobia."[141] This missionary even marshals Freud's authority to define those unfit to define themselves as having a "split in the ego": "This repudiation functions as the foundations [sic] of defense and is part of an individual protection mechanism that Freudian psychoanalysis calls 'disavowal of difference.'"[142] Such vulgar Freudianism notwithstanding, the author, a German-Algerian studying anthropology in the United States, wants to insist that despite the absence of a gay community in Lebanon, there is a dearth of "gay" spaces in the country! He does, however, cite a demonstration by "a half dozen individuals" in Beirut against the U.S. invasion of Iraq in March 2003 "underneath the rainbow flag" as evidence of the existence of some "gays," failing to mention that he, as a missionary, was one of the main (if not the main) organizers of the demonstration, which probably also included other members of international gay brigades, and which he is now citing as evidence of indigenous gay activism.[143]

In the course of defending universal human rights in non-European countries and cultures, many anthropological treatises would be marshaled for the effort. Increasingly, however, anthropological studies about "Arab sexuality" are used not only to defend the sexual and human "rights" of Arabs by Western benefactors and their local representatives, but also, by the U.S. military and war planners, to *violate* them. The primary study used for this latter effort was Orientalist Raphael Patai's *The Arab Mind,* first published in 1973. Patai explains how while Western societies suffer from guilt because their individuals have a conscience, Arab societies suffer mainly from "shame." Patai was hardly original, as he seemed to have borrowed his thesis from Ruth Benedict's now infamous book on Japan, *The Chrysanthemum and the Sword,* in which,

141. Sofian Merabet, "Disavowed Homosexualities in Beirut," *Middle East Report* 230 (Spring 2004): 33.

142. Ibid.

143. Ibid., 32. On the demonstration, see "Mithliyyun Rafaʿu Aʿlamahum wa Sharaku" [Homosexuals Raised Their Flags and Participated], *Al-Nahar,* 16 March 2003. I have interviewed a number of journalists and activists in Beirut in December 2003 about the demonstration, all of whom maintained that it was Mr. Merabet who organized the demonstration and was the force behind it. On a related event of transnational organizing producing a grassroots constituency that identifies as "gay," see Neville Hoad's discussion of the Zambian organization, LEGATRA, whose leader claimed that there existed "ten thousand" gays and lesbians in Zambia while a local human rights NGO claimed the existence of half a million gays and lesbians in the country. In the end, "more than 20 gays and lesbians joined LEGATRA," in Hoad, "Between the White Man's Burden and the White Man's Disease: Tracking Lesbian and Gay Human Rights in Southern Africa," *GLQ* 5, no. 4 (1999): 572–73.

as part of her work for the U.S. government's Office of War Information, she studied the diaries of captured and dead Japanese soldiers and watched Japanese films to come to the conclusion that Japanese culture was a "shame" culture as opposed to the "guilt" culture of Europeans.[144] In line with Benedict, whose book he did not cite, Patai concluded that "one of the important differences between the Arab and the Western personality is that in the Arab culture, shame is more pronounced than guilt."[145] While sex is identified as "a prime mental preoccupation in the Arab world," it is also revealed as "repressed" and carrying a "taboo" in Arab culture.[146] This explains a hierarchy of shameful behavior that Patai attributes to Arabs. For example, he claims that "masturbation among the Arabs is condemned more severely than in the United States" and that "masturbation is far more shameful than visiting prostitutes."[147] He also informs his readers that "in most parts of the Arab world, homosexual activity or any indication of homosexual leanings, as with all other expressions of sexuality, is never given any publicity."[148] Basing his argument on a study conducted by Western anthropologists in the 1950s among Arab university students, which concluded that the "active homosexual role in particular is thought of by the Arab students as compatible with virile masculinity," Patai explains that the "the role of the passive homosexual is considered extremely degrading and shameful because it casts the man or youth into a submissive, feminine role."[149] Patai's approach, as Edward Said had noted, is commensurate with traditional Orientalism, which defines the "relation between the Middle East and the West . . . as sexual . . . the male scholar wins the prize by bursting open, penetrating through the Gordian knot."[150] Patai, however, on occasion had to restrain himself from such pleasures. He tells readers that "as far as the traditional Arab sex mores can be observed without *penetrating* into the secrets of the bedchamber, the impression is gained that they are the product of severe repressions."[151]

Following the revelations of American systematic physical and sexual torture of Iraqi prisoners at the Abu Ghraib prison, veteran American journalist Seymour Hersh revealed that the view that "Arabs are particularly

144. Ruth Benedict, *The Chrysanthemum and the Sword: Patterns of Japanese Culture* (Boston: Houghton Mifflin Company, 1946).
145. Raphael Patai, *The Arab Mind* (New York: Charles Scribner's Sons, 1976), 106.
146. Ibid., 118.
147. Ibid., 134, 135.
148. Ibid., 135.
149. Ibid., 134–35.
150. Said, *Orientalism,* 309.
151. Patai, *Arab Mind,* 128.

vulnerable to sexual humiliation became a talking point among pro-war Washington conservatives in the months before the March, 2003, invasion of Iraq." According to Hersh, America's neocons learned of such a "vulnerability" from Patai's *The Arab Mind*. Hersh quoted his source that the book, was "the bible of the neocons on Arab behavior." Hersh's source asserts that in the discussions of the neocons, two themes emerged: "One, that Arabs only understand force and, two, that the biggest weakness of Arabs is shame and humiliation." Hersh continues his revelations:

The government consultant said that there may have been a serious goal, in the beginning, behind the sexual humiliation and the posed photographs. It was thought that some prisoners would do anything—including spying on their associates—to avoid dissemination of the shameful photos to family and friends. The government consultant said, 'I was told that the purpose of the photographs was to create an army of informants, people you could insert back in the population.' The idea was that they would be motivated by fear of exposure, and gather information about pending insurgency action, the consultant said. If so, it wasn't effective; the insurgency continued to grow.[152]

Such torture is emblematic of imperial cultures not only at present but also historically. Here is one such report:

The types of torture employed are varied. They include beatings with fists and [stomping] with boots . . . as well as using canes for beating and flogging to death. They also included . . . the penetration of the rectums of the victims with canes, and then moving the cane left and right, and to the front and back. They also included pressing on the testicles with the hands and squeezing them until the victim loses consciousness from the pain and until they [the testicles] get so swollen that the victim would not be able to walk or move except by carrying his legs one at a time . . . They also included the starving of dogs and then provoking them and pushing them to devour his flesh and to eat off his thighs. It also included urinating on the faces of victims . . . [Another form of torture included the soldiers'] sodomizing them, as it seems that this was done to a number of people.[153]

This report, which describes in almost identical terms what the Iraqi prisoners experienced, was written in August 1938 describing how British and Zionist Jewish soldiers treated revolutionary Palestinians during

152. See Seymour M. Hersh, "The Gray Zone," *New Yorker*, 24 May 2004.
153. The report is reproduced in Akram Zuʿaytar, ed., *Watha'iq al-Harakah al-Wataniyyah al-Filastiniyyah, 1918–1939* [The Documents of the Palestinian National Movement, 1918–1939] (Beirut: Mu'assassat al-Dirasat al-Filastiniyyah, 1979), 493–94.

the 1930s Palestinian Anti-Colonial Revolt. The author of the report, Subhi Al-Khadra, was a Palestinian political prisoner detained in the Acre prison. He came to know of the torture of these prisoners, which had taken place in Jerusalem, because the prisoners were relocated later to his prison in Acre, and told him of their experiences and showed him the physical signs of torture on their bodies. This is how he described the motivation of the British torturers:

This was not an investigation in which forceful methods are used. No. It was a vengeance and a release of the most savage and barbaric of instincts and of the concentrated spirit of hatred that these rednecks feel towards Muslims and Arabs. They mean to torture for the sake of torture and to satisfy their appetite for vengeance, not for the sake of an investigation nor to expose crimes.[154]

Khadra's report was published in the Arabic press and sent to British members of parliament.

The mixture of sex and violence in an American (or European) imperial setting characterized by racism and absolute power is a uniform occurrence. Just over a decade and a half ago, during the "first" Gulf War of 1990–91, American fighter and bomber pilots would spend hours watching pornographic films to get themselves in the right mood for the massive bombing they carried out in Iraq.[155] In the more recent Iraqi context, the U.S. military understood well that American male sexual prowess, usually reserved for American women, should be put to military use in imperial conquests. In such a strategy, Iraqis are posited by American supermasculine fighter and bomber pilots as women and feminized men to be penetrated by the missiles and bombs ejected from American warplanes. By feminizing the enemy as the object of penetration (real and imagined), American imperial military culture supermasculinizes not only its own male soldiers, but also its female soldiers who can partake of the feminization of Iraqi men. Thus, both male and female American (and British) soldiers can participate in sodomizing Iraqi soldiers with chemical lights, beat them, urinate on them, force them to perform homosexual acts (while hurling racial and sexual epithets at them), unleash dogs on them, and kill them. Such practices clearly demonstrate that white American male sexuality exhibits certain sadistic attributes in the presence of nonwhite men (and women) over whom white (and sometimes Black) Americans (and Brits) have government-sanctioned racialized power.

154. Ibid., 493.
155. *Washington Post,* 26 January 1991.

The sexual dynamic that insistently characterizes imperial relations, whether of violating or defending human rights, are therefore informed by the same type of subjectivity. Indeed the very same discourse that calls for the "liberation" of Arabs from dictators and "defends" them against human rights violations is what allows both imperial ventures and human rights activism. Even the data on the Arabs necessary for imperial conquest and human rights activism derives from the same anthropological and Orientalist sources. The epistemic collusion is total, even though the political implications are articulated differently. Thus it would seem that Orientalist fascination with the sexual desires and lives of Arabs has led Westerners over the last two centuries to seek them out as an outlet for frustrated Western desires or to condemn and flinch from even discussing such uncivilized sexual practices—or, more recently, to participate in them. This participation involves ironically giving Arabs the "pleasure" they are said to enjoy by Orientalism through sexual torture or by assimilating them into the "liberatory" agenda of Western sexual minorities. What all these responses do is consolidate the civilizational epistémè that informs Western views of the Arabs, and what they *do not do* is question the superiority of the Western notion of the human. No wonder Arab intellectuals since the Arab "Renaissance" had little choice but to engage this very question that links their sexual desires to their civilizational worth.

Hegemony and Dominance

At the end of the nineteenth century, the emergent Arab intelligentsia began to write the "civilizational" history of the Arabs, a project that was part and parcel of the rising anti-Ottoman Arab nationalism. In the process, they would begin to engage the sexual question in ways not studied by previous generations but in line with Orientalist engagement. How did this transformation in the representation of Arab sexual desires occur? What intellectual and literary strategies brought about a new sexual epistemology? How did tolerance and intolerance of sexual desires and practices become the measure of backwardness and progress, of renaissance and decadence?

This book will chart this intellectual journey from the end of the nineteenth century to the beginning of the twenty-first. Edward Said's *Orientalism* showed how Orientalism created the Oriental and how it shaped and still shapes the views that Westerners hold about Arabs since the European Enlightenment. *Orientalism* generated an important body of scholarship about various kinds of Orientalist representations of Arabs and Muslims in Europe but, unfortunately, little if any scholarship was produced in its wake about Orientalist representations in the Arab world, whether in Arabic or in European languages.[156] *Desiring Arabs* aims to fill this gap by showing the influence and impact that Orientalism has had in shaping the Arabs' own perceptions of themselves and each other since the Arab Renaissance to the present. I will look not only at how history is constructed and negotiated and how Arab heritage comes to be defined and represented but also at the modern projects that this effort serves. The debates are rich in detail and contain differing political and ideological views. Participants will come from across the Arab world. Philosophers, psychoanalysts, feminists, literary critics, novelists, playwrights, political scientists, sociologists, communist activists, journalists, university professors, lay historians will all produce what will become the hegemonic understanding of Arab culture and its past achievements. These debates will be interrupted and informed by many political and economic changes that Arab countries would undergo over the course of the twentieth century. An epistemological break would take place in the early 1980s that would polarize this ongoing debate. I will analyze the factors that brought this about and examine the literature produced in its wake and how it differs from the literature preceding it. In the final two chapters, I will also undertake a detailed examination of the role of Arabic fiction in the representation of Arab sexual desires. Ultimately, the book examines how the hegemony of Western ideas functioned for much of the century on the Arab intellectual scene and how the rise of sexual identity politics in the West and international human rights activism would come to define in the 1980s not only Arab nationalist responses, but also and especially Islamist ones, and what implications these would have for the sexual desires and practices of contemporary Arabs.

Once this hegemony about things sexual was established among the élite and the intelligentsia, it began to seek to dominate the population at large. I will demonstrate that what the Western assimilationists, and their unwitting Islamist epistemic allies, want to do is to extend this hegemony to the rest of the population so that their sexual practices, identities, and most of all, desires would accord with the hegemonic Western

156. This is not to say that there are not a number of works in Arabic dealing with the history of Arab responses to and engagement with Orientalist scholarship; indeed there are many. See, for example, Muhsin Jasim al-Musawi, *Al-Istishraq fi al-Fikr al-ʿArabi* [Orientalism in Arab Thought] (Beirut: Al-Muʾassasah al-ʿArabiyyah lil-Dirasat wa al-Nashr, 1993).

views.[157] This book will chronicle how this intellectual epistémè, while hegemonic in intellectual and elite circles, has failed to become hegemonic among the population and how assiduous efforts are appealing to the state to employ its juridical and coercive abilities to render this sexual ontology—which is hegemonic in the West—dominant in the interstices of Arab societies and psyches in order to break down the resistance of these desiring Arabs. My concern about the productive and repressive functions of this epistemological hegemony builds on my earlier work on Jewish and Palestinian identities in the context of Zionist and Palestinian histories and broadens the national focus of my *Colonial Effects,* which analyzed the construction of national identities in a colonial and postcolonial setting.[158] While my investigation of the institutions of law and the military in *Colonial Effects* was most appropriate for colonial and postcolonial forms of sovereignty, this book engages the permutations that imperial power assumes in an age of unrestrained globalization.

Desiring Arabs traces the history of the unfolding of the concepts of culture and civilization in the contemporary Arab world. It is decidedly *not* a history of "Arab sexuality," whatever that is, but an intellectual history of the representation of the sexual desires of Arabs in and about the Arab world and how it came to be linked to civilizational worth. To do so, and given the lack of any prior scholarship about the subject, I undertook to create a modern archive of Arab writings about sex and desire first and then to analyze this archive in relation to Orientalist, imperialist, and nationalist epistemologies. Western social Darwinists, who include modernization and development theorists and their kindred spirits (UN agencies, human rights organizations and activists, NGOs, the IMF, the World Bank, the U.S. State Department, etc.), would see the possible "advance" of the Arab world (as well as the rest of the "underdeveloped" world) toward a Western-defined and sponsored modernity as part of a historical teleology wherein non-Europeans who are still at the stage of European childhood will eventually replicate European "progress" toward modern forms of organization, sociality, economics, politics, and sexual desires. What is emerging in the Arab (and the rest of the third) world is not some universal schema of the march of history but rather the imposition of these Western modes by different forceful

157. See Ranajit Guha, *Dominance without Hegemony: History and Power in Colonial India* (Cambridge: Harvard University Press, 1997).

158. On Palestinian and Jewish identities, see Joseph Massad, *The Persistence of the Palestinian Question: Essays on Zionism and the Palestinians* (New York: Routledge, 2006), and on national identity in the case of Jordan, see Joseph Massad, *Colonial Effects: The Making of National Identity in Jordan* (New York: Columbia University Press, 2001).

means and their adoption by third world elites, thus foreclosing and re-pressing myriad ways of movement and change and ensuring that only one way for transformation is made possible. In the process much state and societal repression has ensued, and more is still to come. This en-sures the success of the Western theorists' universal civilizational teleol-ogies and unwittingly guarantees for them the production of a Western-defined outcome to the future of "humanity."

In addition to the introduction and the conclusion, the book is di-vided into six chapters. Chapters 1 and 2 provide a detailed intellectual history of how modern Arabs sought to write the history of Arab civiliza-tion and culture from the pre-Islamic period to the present and how this civilizational project was implicated in the kinds of sexual desires and practices Arabs and Muslims were said to have enjoyed. The debates over the status of the medieval poet Abu Nuwas in Arab heritage are discussed in detail, especially so as I see them as emblematic of the "civilizational" anxiety felt by the modern historians.

Chapters 3 and 4 chronicle the kinds of Western interventions brought about by universalizers of Western sexual identities and how Arab intel-lectuals as well as Arab states reacted to such interventions. Chapter 4 will discuss how the Western-incited discourse on sexual identities elicited a strong Islamist response (theological, medical, criminological, social, inter alia) which interrupted the mostly secular debates that had existed until then, and demonstrates how the Islamists and the Western assimi-lationists end up as allies imposing a new shared sexual epistemology.

Chapters 5 and 6 engage modern Arabic fiction and its representa-tions of the contemporary sexual desires of Arabs. Several seminal nov-els, some short stories, and one major play are analyzed in detail to demonstrate the effect of the different kinds of discourses on sexual de-sire that came to bear on the modern Arab world. While some of these novels have already been translated to English, I will cite the Arabic edi-tions throughout and use my own translations unless otherwise noted. I have found most of the English translations not particularly helpful to my analyses.

ONE

Anxiety in Civilization

Since the Arab "renaissance" emerged in the mid-nineteenth century, thousands of medieval manuscripts dating back to the seventh through the fourteenth centuries have been published in the Arab world, in addition to scores of studies and analyses of that period of Arab history. European Orientalist scholarship, as discussed in the introduction, showed initial interest in these texts and began to publish them and comment on them in European languages. The emergent Arab intelligentsia in the nineteenth century took upon itself the revival and modernization of the Arabic language, which was seen to have also "degraded" under Ottoman repression. This intellectual trend combined with (some would say, produced) a nascent Arab nationalism opposed to Ottoman rule that appeared during the last decades of the century and took upon itself the task of uncovering the cultural heritage of the Arabs of yesteryear as a foundation for the Arabs of the present.

This revival ranged from studies in the literary production of the past, to theological and jurisprudential studies, to historical, scientific, and sociological treatises. The emergent intelligentsia sought the past of the Arabs as a basis for their modern future by repudiating the more recent traditions that developed under Ottoman rule, seen through the eyes of the emergent nationalism as foreign and "degraded" in character. It was by repudiating the more recent past and by reviving the ancient past that the Arabs of the present could chart their project for modern life. These intellectual trends are reminiscent of European modernity, which sought to adopt "its" ancient Greco-Roman heritage and repudiate its Christian Middle Ages. The "revival" of this ancient past is evident in treatises written on politics, economics, and religion, as it is in treatises written on women's liberation and society at large.[1] To the casual observer, with few notable exceptions, there was little in these voluminous accounts dedicated to the sexual life of the ancient Arabs or to the place of sex in what increasingly came to be known as a coherent category called "Islam." In fact, important debates on sex and desire did exist, but rarely on their own. They were mostly embedded in discussions of literature and *turath* more generally. There seems to be little familiarity in the Arabic or English secondary literature of these debates, much less any examination of them.

While predominant Orientalist representations of the modern Arab world and Islam portray them as constituted by a repressive sexual ideology and an even more repressive sexual culture that revels in the oppression of women and bans any discussion of sex, this chapter and the next will discuss a century-long rich Arab intellectual debate about sex in the past of the Arabs and its implications for the present. The debate has many nuances and ideological turns, is rich in argument and material, and has engaged some of the important intellectual minds of the modern Arab world. The aim of these chapters is both to retrieve from scholarly obscurity an archive of modern writings on the classical history of the Arabs that made use of medieval documents to paint a picture of the life of the ancients, their cultural production, desires, and sexual practices, and also to explore the way that these writings were deployed in the creation of a viable tradition for Arab modernity.

Intellectuals writing about the sexual life of the medieval Arab world, as we will see, would come from different disciplines, different parts of the Arab world, and different ideological backgrounds. They found medieval documents useful for many different political and intellectual projects within which they would deploy their discussions of sex and desire. Whether liberal educators, historians committed to sexual liberation, Arab nationalists, radical secularists, psychoanalytic literary critics, Marxists, feminists, or Islamists, they would all believe that there were lessons to be learned from the sexual history of the Arabs of the past. Common to all of them is a commitment to a civilizational inheritance

---

1. See, for example, Qasim Amin, *Tahrir al-Mar'ah* [The Liberation of Women], originally published in 1899, and republished in *Qasim Amin, al-A'mal al-Kamilah,* ed. Dr. Muhammad 'Imarah (Cairo: Dar al-Shuruq, 1989), 385–86, where he gives examples of women's liberation in the early Islamic era to illustrate it as a precedent to be emulated by modern Muslims. Examples abound in his writings and those of his contemporaries.

whose content must be uncovered. Much of the analysis employed in the debate is fully informed by late nineteenth-century European notions of civilization and culture and subsidiary concepts like progress, regression, evolution, degeneration, decadence, renaissance, ascent, decline, as well as the statistical language of norms and deviations. In the debates that follow, we will see how these notions are introduced as a hermeneutical grid to *interpret and produce turath,* which functions as both a repository of civilizational documents *and* a moral code. For some of our authors, these two aspects of *turath* may be separable while to others they may not be. The question that arises for many of them, however, is whether Arab civilization itself can survive the rupture between the two meanings of *turath* in the modern period.

Early Beginnings

At the end of the nineteenth century and in the context of a declining Ottoman Empire and surging Turkish nationalism, the Arab Renaissance was in full swing, accompanied with the early stirrings of anti-Ottoman Arab nationalism. The new renaissance of Arab knowledge production involved an increased acquaintance with European Orientalist thought and the construction of the Arab within it. In the course of writing classical and medieval Arab history, these modern historians encountered an ancient Arab society with different sexual mores and practices that were difficult to assimilate into a modern Arab nationalist project informed by European notions of progress and modernization and a Victorian sexual ethic. Some of the important questions being theorized dealt with new concepts that did not exist before and that were being deployed in the excavation of history. In addition to *tamaddun* and *hadarah* (both words mean "civilization"; *tamaddun* was coined first but was later frequently replaced by *hadarah*) and *turath* (heritage), there were other related European concepts that informed these endeavors and that proliferated, including *thaqafah* (culture), *inhilal* (degeneration), *inhitat* (decadence or degradation), *taqaddum* (progress), *ta'akhkhur* (backwardness), *jins* (sex), and *shudhudh* (deviance), among others. What was at stake in this historical excavation was the safeguarding of the heritage of Arab civilization for future generations. The use of European notions on which to base these efforts at excavating Arab-Islamic national heritage did not seem contradictory or problematic to our authors. Rather, they were seen as neutral scientific tools and concepts that could be fully integrated into their modernist project.

The first modern comprehensive history of Arabic literature from the pre-Islamic period to the early twentieth century was written by the famed German Orientalist Carl Brockelmann (1868–1956). Brockelmann published the first volume of his *Geschichte der arabischen Litteratur* in 1898 (the second in 1902) and the last one in 1948. These volumes would be translated to Arabic in the early 1960s, with more volumes published in the 1970s. The entire collection would be reprinted and republished in 1993 in Cairo.[2] Brockelmann's Herculean efforts, however, were supplemented by other Orientalist scholars who did not have his erudition, including the earlier work of F. F. Arbuthnot's *Arabic Authors* (1890), and later works like Clement Huart's *Literature Arabe* (1902), Italo Pizzi's *Litteratura Araba* (1903), or Reynold A. Nicholson's *A Literary History of the Arabs* (1907). Adam Mez's important study *Die Renaissance des Islams* found by his bedside upon his death in 1917 was only published posthumously in 1922. All of these books would rely on the already published volumes by Brockelmann. In fact Brockelmann himself would republish his books updated with appendices and citing works by Orientalist and Arab scholars published in the interim.

In these important surveys, Orientalist scholars addressed not only the literary writings of the Arabs but also described their sexual desires and the way these were expressed in poetry and prose, as well as the national origins of such desires and practices. In his entry on the poet Abu Nuwas, for example, Brockelmann wrote of the poet's "bawdy" (mujun) poetry but did not specify the love of boys.[3] Nicholson commented that "the scenes of luxurious dissipation and refined debauchery which [the bawdy poets] describe show us, indeed, that Persian culture was not an unalloyed blessing to the Arabs any more than the arts of Greece to the Romans."[4] Mez would dedicate a chapter to the "Manners and Morals" of the medieval Arabs, addressing the "pervasive" nature of pederasty among poets from the fourth to the tenth century A.H. (tenth to sixteenth century A.D.), as well as in "circles high and low."[5] H. A. R. Gibb,

2. See Karl Brukilman, *Tarikh al-Adab al-'Arabi* (History of Arabic Literature), 10 vols. (Cairo: al-Hay'ah al-Misriyyah lil-Kitab, 1993). The translation was supervised by the book's Arabic editor, Mahmud Fahmi al-Hijazi. For the history of the book's translation into Arabic, see the introduction of Muhyi al-Din Sabir (vol. 1, 5–9).

3. Ibid., vol. 1, parts 1–2, 348. He also likened Abu Nuwas to the title character in Carl Maria von Weber's *Singspiel* opera *Abu Hassan* (first performed in 1811), ibid., 349. The Abu Hassan character is adapted from the stories of Abu Dulaymah, cited by the eleventh-century al-Khatib al-Baghdadi in his *Tarikh Baghdad* [History of Baghdad] (Beirut: Dar al-Kitab al-'Arabi, 1966), vol. 8, 493, although others suggest that the Abu Hassan story comes from vulgarized versions of the *Arabian Nights*.

4. Reynold A. Nicholson, *A Literary History of the Arabs* (Cambridge: Cambridge University Press, 1966), 295–96. The book was originally published in 1907.

5. Adam Mez, *The Renaissance of Islam*, translated by Salahuddun Khuda Bakhsh and D. S. Mar-

whose book on Arabic literature appeared in 1926, would liken the Abbasid poet Abu Nuwas to Heine: "He is at his happiest in his wine songs, but his elegies, love poems, and satires, though often containing much both in subject and sentiment that offends our taste, are little inferior."[6]

In this vein, a number of classical and medieval political and literary figures and events were to cause as much anxiety to modern Arabs as they had to European Orientalists before them. Upon encountering historical material about the sexual life of the Abbasid period, the question of civilization and *turath* became immediately intertwined with sexual morality. Thus any and all attempts to recover the Abbasid period, generally considered the golden age of Arab-Islamic civilization and knowledge production, had to confront the sexual question, read under the sign of morality. The Abbasid poet Abu Nuwas became particularly a focus, if not a cause, of such anxiety, on account of his explicit poetry that detailed sexual desires and practices deemed immoral. The gaze of Arab historians was squarely fixed on European judgment of their *civilization,* as that modern European concept was always posited in a comparative framework. European thinkers imagined the non-European world either in developmentalist terms, as representing an earlier stage of Europe, the childhood of Europe itself, which European colonialism would shepherd to adult maturity, thus duplicating if not replicating and reproducing Europe on a global scale, or as representing a radical alterity that can only be bridged, if at all, by a comprehensive overhauling of these "civilizations" by, or their utter subjugation to, European supremacy. Arab thinkers, like anticolonial thinkers elsewhere, overcome by a narcissistic injury inflicted by either of these judgments, and intent on building a new national project, begged to differ.

Their efforts coincided with the fledgling European colonial presence in the Arab world—the French had colonized Algeria in 1830 and the British occupied Egypt in 1882. It was with this background that the following exchange between two writers, one Arab (Egyptian), one French, offers a useful introduction into the complex deployment of sexuality in negotiations around questions of religious and, increasingly, national and cultural identity—in short, about civilizational stature. In 1894, an unknown Qasim Amin wrote his first book *Les Égyptiens,*[7] in French, in

---

goliouth (Patna: Jubilee Printing and Publishing House, 1937), 359. The German original written in 1917 was published in Heidelberg in 1922.

6. H. A. R. Gibb, *Arabic Literature: An Introduction* (London: Oxford University Press, 1926), 42.

7. Qasim Amin, *Les Égyptiens, Réponse à M. le duc d'Harcourt* (Cairo: Jules Barbier, 1894). The Arabic translation was published in 1975 and reprinted in the collected works of Amin in 'Imarah, *Qasim Amin*. Citations are from the Arabic translation.

response to an Orientalist account written by one M. Le Duc D'Harcourt about Egypt and Islam. Amin was scandalized by D'Harcourt's claim that

Islam encourages pleasures and enjoyment of all that we harbor in our hearts of emotions and yearnings, except for gluttony and voraciousness. He [D'Harcourt] spoke aplenty of lust, obscenity, and degeneration without ever telling us where he saw such things. While we know that an Oriental who visits Europe for the first time returns from it, undoubtedly enchanted by the different types of beauty that such a mighty civilization diffuses across its lands, such admiration, however, is always mixed with a sense of repulsion that the conditions of degenerating morals, degeneration, and perdition are widespread everywhere—just as when a European visits a Muslim country, often complains of a lack in entertainment venues.[8]

If this were not enough to convince his French readers, a horrified Amin unequivocally asserted to his European audience that "what is incredible is that [a Muslim man] does not see in sexual pleasure but a silly satisfaction of one of the bodily needs, so much so that all the tricks of love that ingenious [European] lovers innovated and of which Occidentals are enamored, have no effect on the souls of chaste Muslims. As I have reached this critical point, I should complete the picture by stating that even the most debauched Muslim man would never surrender to obscenity completely; he rather maintains an amount of bashfulness that always saves him from sinking to the bottom."[9] This is to be contrasted with men in Europe, as "there is a large number of men who have no concerns but the enjoyment of everything in all manners. Indeed, some of them boast about how much they have seen and done, so much so that there is no longer anything that can excite their emotions. In addition to these bored men, there are those who are pleasure-mad who do not get satiated, in addition to the depraved and the debauched as well as those women who no longer desire to continue to perform the task of bearing children and prefer to shine in society."[10] Amin's defensive posture against Orientalist representations of Arab and Muslim sexual desires is not unlike that of many European women writers from Mary Wollstonecraft onward, who took up defensive postures against the claims that women had larger sexual appetites than men and reversed the charge in an attempt to fend off sexist attacks.[11]

8. Qasim Amin, *Al-Misriyyun,* in *Qasim Amin, al-A'mal al-Kamilah,* ed. Muhammad 'Imarah (1899; Cairo: Dar al-Shuruq, 1989), 274.
9. Ibid.
10. Ibid., 275.
11. See Mary Wollstonecraft, *A Vindication of the Rights of Woman* (New York: Dover, 1996). Her

Amin moved on to publish the first major treatise in Arabic calling for women's liberation in 1899. Reversing Orientalist generalizations and applying them to Europeans, however, would become one of the most effective weapons used by Arab and Muslim writers in response to continuing Orientalist accounts throughout the twentieth century. But unlike Amin's discussion of the sexual desires and conduct of contemporary Arabs and Muslims, the next century would witness a debate not necessarily about the sexual life of contemporary Arabs (although occasionally it would), but mainly about the sexual life of the ancient Arabs. Clearly, the discussion of the past had many implications for the present of which our writers were conscious. Still, while d'Harcourt failed to incite discourse about the sexual life of modern Arabs, Amin's response in French notwithstanding, a century would pass before a new incitement would interrupt the flow of debates about the sexual life of the ancient Arabs and shift it to a discussion of the sexual life of moderns. The new inciters, as we will see in chapter 3, would be a group of Western missionaries and their local followers attempting to disseminate their message of sexual identities, and a surging Islamism intent on constricting social and sexual life.

Pedagogy of the Repressed

Qasim Amin's reaction did not dictate subsequent discussions of sex in modern Arab intellectual history. The ensuing debates centered on a number of themes, paramount among which were the pedagogical role that the past would play in the present, the role of the aesthetic versus the role of religious and social morality, and the nature of audiences and readerships of belles lettres. The debate would encompass questions about what aspects of the past should be emulated and what lessons learned. Just as important, the debate would address questions about what aspects of the past should be condemned or discussed at all and which aspects never to be emulated. The implication of these questions was *civilizational* in scale, as what was included in the archive of Arab heritage would reflect immediately on the stature of Arab civilization. The initiation of the Arabic reading public to these debates would begin through the pathbreaking books of the important Lebanese writer and publisher Jurji Zaydan. Zaydan (1861–1914), a central figure of the Arab

book was first published in 1787. See also Mary Poovey's important examination of Wollstonecraft's thought, *The Proper Lady and the Woman Writer: Ideology as Style in the Works of Mary Wollstonecraft, Mary Shelley, and Jane Austen* (Chicago: University of Chicago Press, 1984), 48–81.

Renaissance (he belonged to the second generation of *Nahdah* thinkers), not only wrote literary history but also many popular novels that were fictionalized yet well-researched accounts about life in the classical epoch. Zaydan had started his university education in 1881 as a medical student at the Syrian Protestant College in Beirut, which was founded by New York State in 1866. The college was rechartered in 1920 as the American University of Beirut. In 1882, Zaydan was dismissed from the college for leading a student strike protesting the dismissal of one of his professors, one Professor Edwin Lewis, for referring to the works of Charles Darwin in a commencement speech (delivered on 19 July 1882), which was seen as contradicting the goals of the Protestant mission to which the American administrators of the college, in Beirut and in the United States, were committed.[12] Darwinism, or at least its social interpretation, would have a deep impact on Zaydan's thought and work.[13]

In his magisterial five-volume history of Islamic "civilization" (tamaddun), Zaydan cited certain sexual desires disapprovingly, although he never saw them but as marginal to the course of that history. He affirmed that

one of the ugliest forms of that debauchery [tahattuk] during this process of civilization was the flirtation [taghazzul] with youthful boys and their being taken as slave boys. This had appeared especially in the days of [the Abbasid caliph] al-Amin [r. A.D. 809–13], and increased with the increase of Turkish and Roman youthful boys since the days of [the caliph] al-Muʿtasim [r. A.D. 833–42], and they included those who became slaves through being taken prisoner [of war], and those who were bought. People then rushed to own them as they did to own concubines . . . and the love of youthful boys became widespread among the state elite in Egypt, and poets wrote *ghazal* [erotic love] poetry to them so much that women became jealous and opted to look like boys in their dress and mannerisms to capture the hearts of men.[14]

12. Jurji Zaydan, *Mudhakkarat Jurji Zaydan* [The Memoirs of Jurji Zaydan], ed. Salah al-Din al-Munajjid (Beirut: Dar al-Kitab al-Jadid, 1968), 66–95. On this incident, see Shafiq Jiha, *Darwin wa Azmat 1882 bi al-Daʾirah al-Tibiyyah wa Awwal Thawrah Tulabiyyah fi al-ʿAlam al-ʿArabi bi al-Kulliyyah al-Suriyyah al-Injiliyyah (Al-An: Al-Jamiʿah al-Amrikiyyah fi Bayrut)* [Darwin and the Crisis of 1882 in the Medical Department and the First Student Revolt in the Arab World in the Syrian Protestant College (Now, The American University of Beirut)] (n.p.: n.p., 1991).

13. Indeed, Zaydan would publish a biographical profile of Darwin in his magazine *Al-Hilal* a decade later. See "Sharls Darwin," *Al-Hilal* 1 October 1894, 81–88. On Zaydan's other social Darwinist writings, see Adel A. Ziadat, *Western Science in the Arab World: The Impact of Darwinism, 1860–1930* (New York: St. Martin's Press, 1986), 57–58.

14. Jurji Zaydan, *Tarikh al-Tamaddun al-Islami* [History of Islamic Civilization] (Cairo: Matbaʿat al-Hilal, 1906), vol. 5, 130.

Zaydan's comments however did not generate much debate, as they remained incidental to his historiography. Indeed, in his historical novel, *Al-Amin and al-Ma'mun*, he hardly mentioned the infamous sexual life of the caliph al-Amin except for a cursory note that he "would overdo buying eunuchs [khisyan] from the far reaches of the country and spend on their purchase fortunes so that they could be with him in his private quarters day and night and so that they could oversee his food and drink."[15] It was in an earlier historical novel that Zaydan provided more details about al-Amin. In his *Al-'Abbasah Ukht al-Rashid*,[16] Zaydan described how a number of people seeking to unseat al-Amin provided him with sexual temptations to distract him. Zaydan, who described al-Amin as a "courageous" and "muscular" young man who would wrestle with lions,[17] and as an "articulate" man of letters, lamented his predilection for "excess" in whimsy as well as for slave girls and boys.[18] Zaydan credited al-Amin with being the first in Islamic history to arrange for youthful boys and eunuchs to put on singing and dancing shows resembling those performed by singing girls.[19] In his novel, he described with meticulous detail one of the parties thrown by al-Amin at his palace before he assumed the throne, one to which the famed Abbasid poet Abu Nuwas had been invited. The love of boys shared by al-Amin and Abu Nuwas is evident throughout the florid descriptions peppering Zaydan's account.[20] It is important to note that in his account of Amin's desires for boys, Zaydan did not think it important to mention that the caliph was married and had two sons. Such information was superfluous to Zaydan, as it was immaterial to Amin's predilection for youthful boys.

It was in his book on Arabic literary history that Zaydan expanded slightly on his account. Even though earlier chapters of the book had been serialized in Zaydan's magazine *Al-Hilal* in 1894 and 1895,[21] four years before Brockelmann's book was published, Zaydan would make use

15. Jurji Zaydan, *Al-Amin wa al-Ma'mun*, 2nd rev. ed. (1907; Cairo: Matba'at al-Hilal, 1911), 137.

16. Jurji Zaydan, *Al-'Abbasah Ukht al-Rashid* [Al-'Abbasah, the Sister of al-Rashid], 2nd. rev. ed. (1906; Cairo: Matba'at al-Hilal, 1911).

17. The incident with the lion is often cited in medieval sources. See, for example, al-Hafiz Jalal al-Din al-Suyuti (d. A.D. 911), *Tarikh al-Khulafa'* [The History of the Caliphs] (Beirut: Dar al-Kutub al-'Ilmiyyah, 1988), 238.

18. Zaydan, *Al-'Abbasah Ukht al-Rashid*, 64–65.

19. Ibid., 70.

20. Ibid., 70–78.

21. Readers called on Zaydan to publish his chapters in book form as early as December 1894, which he promised to on the pages of *Al-Hilal*. However, its publication would have to wait seventeen years. See his note to the reader, "Tarikh Adab al-Lughah al-'Arabiyyah" [The History of the Literature of the Arabic Language], *Al-Hilal*, 15 December 1894, 295.

of Brockelamann when he later published his *Al-Hilal* chapters in a multivolume book in 1911–14.[22] In his book, he mentioned *ghazal* (erotic love) poetry for youthful boys as well as poetry praising wine, which he combined together as manifestations of the "vice" that prevailed in Abbasid society. What made this "vice" more strongly present in these poets was "their closeness to [the caliph] Muhammad al-Amin, who owned many youthful boys, who [in turn] became a temptation [fitnah] to his poets . . . As for Abu Nuwas, in his collected poetry [diwan], there is a section that they call 'ghazal in the masculine' that includes 1,000 couplets, which we are content [only] to refer to in order to steer the reader clear from [tanzihan] having to read them."[23] In the earlier *Al-Hilal* version of the chapter, Zaydan had only praise for Abu Nuwas.[24] Indeed, first-generation Renaissance intellectual Butrus al-Bustani (1819–1883), a Lebanese polymath, wrote glowingly of Abu Nuwas in his four-page entry on the poet in his 1877 Arab encyclopedia, *Da'irat al-Ma'arif.*[25] Al-Bustani discussed at length the poet's love affair with the concubine Jinan and the poems he wrote to her, but made no reference to Abu Nuwas's *ghazal* poetry for young men. In 1911, however, while eager to teach modern Arabs about the history of Islamic civilization, Zaydan clearly understood that modern readers should be steered in certain directions and away from others. Unlike al-Bustani, Zaydan wanted his readers to know that poems of "ghazal in the masculine" did exist, but he made sure that they did not read them. Selectivity of historical material was clearly a conscious methodological strategy for him.

If Qasim Amin was scandalized by Orientalist judgment of the alleged contemporary licentiousness of the Arabs, and Jurji Zaydan sought to steer his readers away from the actual licentiousness he discerned in medieval Arab society, Taha Husayn was to see such licentiousness as a crucial factor in the development of Arabic poetry in the early Abbasid period (A.D. 750–945). The lectures and writings of Husayn (1889–1973), the Egyptian literary educator and the doyen of Arabic belles lettres in

22. Shawqi Dayf, "Taqdim al-Kitab" [introduction to the book], in Jurji Zaydan, *Tarikh Adab al-Lughah al-'Arabiyyah* (Cairo: Dar al-Hilal, 1956), vol. 1, 7. The four volumes were originally published in Egypt starting in 1911 and through 1914.

23. Zaydan, *Tarikh Adab al-Lughah al-'Arabiyyah*, vol. 2, 51.

24. See his "Tarikh Adab al-Lughah al-'Arabiyyah, min Aqdam Azmaniha ila al-An: Al-Nahdah al-'Arabiyyah fi 'Asr al-'Abbasiyyin" [The History of the Literature of the Arabic Language since Its Earliest Times Until Now: The Arab Renaissance in the Abbasid Era], *Al-Hilal*, 15 August 1894, 739–40. Another article about Abu Nuwas, most likely written by Zaydan, was published in *Al-Hilal* in 1897 and also lacked any moralizing about the poet. See "Abu Nuwas," *Al-Hilal*, 1 May 1897, 642–48.

25. See Butrus al-Bustani, *Da'irat al-Ma'arif, Encyclopedie Arabe, wa huwa qamus 'am li-kul fann wa matlab* [The Compendium of Knowledge: Arab Encyclopedia, Which Is a General Dictionary of Every Art and Question], vol. 2 (Beirut: Matba'at al-Ma'arif, 1877).

much of the twentieth century, would precipitate important debates that are still with us to this day.

Husayn, who grew up under British occupation, studied in France and returned to British-occupied Egypt to teach. He belonged to the first generation that imbibed the knowledge and literature produced by the Arab Renaissance as well as the then recently constituted Western canon. He was to use such training to expand substantially on the *Nahdah's* achievement. In his *Hadith al-Arbi'a'*,[26] a compilation of weekly lectures that were also published in the early 1920s in the Egyptian newspaper *Al-Siyasah,* Husayn was generally descriptive and rarely moralized about the lifestyle of the Abbasid poets he studied. If anything, in response to his detractors who wrote to express their objections to his representation of the Abbasid period as an era of "doubt, frivolity, and bawdiness,"[27] and who worried that he, as a pedagogue, was corrupting the youth, Husayn countered that

we did not create Abu Nuwas and his companions and we did not inspire their whimsy and *mujun* [a term designating licentiousness and openness about illicit sexual desires and practices, otherwise described as bawdiness], and we did not dispatch them to frivolity and the pursuit of pleasure but we found them thus. Therefore, we found ourselves before two choices, to be ignorant of them or to know them, and we chose the latter, as courage in the study of history is better than cowardice . . . and we know that there is no danger to the minds and morals of people posed by these literary pursuits, as people were not waiting for Abu Nuwas and his companions to learn whimsy, nor have people been waiting for these chapters [to be written] to learn frivolity, as there exists in the circumstances of the life we are leading temptations for whimsy and incitement to frivolity that are stronger and more eloquent than the whimsy of Abu Nuwas.[28]

While the present's pedagogical role as far as whimsy and *mujun* (bawdiness) were concerned was self-evident to Husayn, the past could still teach moderns other things. Husayn was so focused on his interest in literary and poetic development that he asserted unequivocally that in light of the prevailing lifestyle during the Abbasid period, "morals lost . . . and literature [adab] gained."[29] This is a remarkable assertion in light of the history of the term *adab* in Arabic. While during *jahiliyyah* and the early Islamic period, *adab* referred to the moral dimensions

26. Taha Husayn, *Hadith al-Arbi'a'* [Wednesday Talk], vol. 1 (Cairo: al-Matba'ah al-Tijariyyah al-Kubra, 1925).

27. Ibid., book zayn.

28. Ibid., book ha.

29. Ibid., 39. The article from which this quote is taken was published originally in *Al-Siyasah,* January 10, 1923.

61

of personal conduct, it was to acquire two other meanings during the Umayyad period, namely, its reference to the proper education and up-bringing that private tutors provided to the children of the elite of society. These *mu'addibun* (conduct or etiquette tutors) were distinguished from teachers, who did not command the same respect. It was later, in the third and fourth century of the Islamic calendar (tenth and eleventh centuries A.D.) that *adab* came to be associated with poets and what we would today call literature, while still maintaining an affiliation with its etymological origins and its association with morality and good conduct.[30] Such etymology was well known to Husayn's contemporaries, like the Egyptian literary historian Mustafa Sadiq al-Rafiʿi, who provided a history of the term and the association of literature with moral conduct.[31] For Husayn to split *adab*'s two meanings into competing rather than complementing notions was indeed innovation, not only in linguistic terms but also and especially in epistemological ones.

Unlike his detractors, Husayn clearly saw the dichotomy (and competition) between morality and literature as productive and not necessarily as a cause for alarm. In his book *Adib* (Belletrist), Husayn tells the story of a dear anonymous friend (to whom he had dedicated the book), who is torn between a licentious and debauched life of whimsy and his quest for academic knowledge, a moral dilemma that costs him his sanity.[32] *Adib*, which consists mostly of the texts of letters from this friend, ends with Husayn receiving a suitcase of papers belonging to the now insti-tutionalized friend. When Husayn finally opened it years later he found "great literature, sad and honest, of which our language has no equal in what our modernist writers have produced." It was agony over morality that produced this great literature. While *Adib* was an introduction of this literary genius to the public, Husayn wondered, "Will circumstances of Egyptian literary life permit the publication of this oeuvre one day?"[33]

Husayn seemed to privilege literature over morals in his excavation of civilization without providing a clear explanation as to why such privi-leging was necessary. It may be possible here to read the significance of

30. For a history of the term *adab,* see Mustafa Sadiq al-Rafiʿi, *Tarikh Adab al-ʿArab* [The History of the Literature of the Arabs] (Beirut: Dar al-Kitab al-ʿArabi, 1974), vol. 1, 31–43. The book was originally published in 1911.

31. See ibid.

32. Taha Husayn, *Adib* [Belletrist] (Cairo: Dar al-Maʿarif, 1930).

33. Ibid., 178. There is a controversy on whether the friend in *Adib* is Husayn's alter ego or a real person. There is evidence to support both theories, although apparently Husayn claimed the friend as real and named him in an interview towards the end of his life. See Mustafa ʿAbd al-Ghani, *Al-Mufakkir wa al-Amir, Taha Husayn wa al-Sultah fi Misr, 1919–1973* [*The Thinker and the Prince:* Taha Husayn and Political Authority in Egypt, 1919–1973] (Cairo-Al-Hayʾah al-Misriyyah al-ʿAmmah lil-Kitab, 1997), 463–69.

literature for Husayn as not just tolerance for sexual indulgences or a route to courage in understanding one's history, or even as just sublimation, but also as a recoding and a recording of societal energies in an aesthetic realm, which would then justify its privileging. This, for him, would be an important legacy of Arab-Islamic civilization that should benefit modern Arabs.

When Husayn discussed the emergence of a new form of *ghazal* poetry, describing the love of youthful boys in the Abbasid period, he matter-of-factly stated that this was the specific "legacy of Abbasid civilization, a legacy that was founded by Persian civilization [hadarah] when it mixed with the Arabs or when the Arabs moved to it [the Persian empire] and spread their authority over Baghdad."[34] Indeed, Husayn, who was much less defensive than Qasim Amin, hastened to explain to his readers that there was nothing peculiar about the opulence and licentiousness of the Abbasid period, as "this is not exclusive to the Arabs or the Abbasids or to Baghdad, for the Greeks had known it, as had the Romans and the Europeans, and so had Athens, Rome, and Paris . . . it is sufficient for one to read Pericles, Augustine, and Louis XIV to understand the epoch of al-Rashid, al-Amin, and al-Ma'mun."[35] If many Orientalist thinkers posited the life of modern Arabs as reminiscent of the European past in developmentalist terms, Husayn posited the earlier and later history of Europe (and France in particular) as reminiscent of the earlier history of the Arabs. Orientalist representations of the Arabs are ever present in the minds of most modern Arab writers. Thus, for Husayn, if the Orientalist claims of a Muslim Arab exceptionalism are to be rejected, then no Muslim Arab particularism could be tolerated either, at least as far as sexual life and mores were concerned. Husayn's universalism here registers an ethical resistance to the very act of excavating a particular national culture or civilization, in which he himself was engaged, by transforming it into a collective interchangeable heritage for humanity. Thus, while recognizing civilizational specificities in certain areas, he was equally interested in asserting a noncivilizational, universal, shared culture across the globe. In so doing, he rejects the two European theses on non-European civilizations, namely, developmentalism and radical alterity, simultaneously, assuring his readers of an equal place for Arab civilization with Europe with whom it shares a human heritage coevally. This move safeguards Arab civilization against both Orientalist attacks and attacks by Arab purists.[36]

34. Husayn, *Hadith al-Arbiʿaʾ*, 39.
35. Ibid., 44.
36. This rejection of Arab exceptionalism is also manifest in his study of pre-Islamic poetry and his claim that not only the medieval Arabs, but also the classical Greeks and Romans had invented

Husayn's liberal thought was not appreciated by all his readers, as some of them continued to protest his "corruption of the youth." His response was predicated on an antiessentialist notion of morals, of which he provided a historical account. He explained to his audience that the morals of today were not the morals of yesteryear and that if some of his detractors were scandalized by what he wrote, his current morals did not permit him to cite for them what many prominent Islamic figures had said in the early history of Islam, and how the explicitness of what they said was appreciated by many, including the Prophet Muhammad himself: "Yes, morals prevent us from publishing this now because the epoch has changed, and lifestyles have evolved, but there are things that we can publish without assailing morals and without endangering them."[37] Indeed, in splitting morals from literature, Husayn seems to hold morals as the dynamic and changing feature of societies but not the aesthetic value of literature itself, which he holds constant throughout. For him, the quantitative (one might even say economic) dialectic of loss and gain between morals and literature, however, remains operative in the present as it had been in the past.

Husayn characterized earlier Islamic periods and our "righteous ancestors" (al-salaf al-salih) as "more open and welcoming and more tolerant, listening to that which was serious and that which was humorous; indeed, they themselves were serious, and they were humorous."[38] In staging this public debate, Husayn and his critics were inaugurating an important theme that would be used often after them, namely, using the example of the past as a pedagogical model for the present. But, while Husayn and his critics agreed that the past should play a pedagogical role for the present, they disagreed on *which* history of the past should be uncovered and *which* history should be the pedagogical tool for the youth.

This disagreement would inform much of Husayn's later approach, as his discussion of the poet Abu Nuwas reveals. He proceeded with his weekly lectures and his columns in *Al-Siyasah* to deal with the literary production of Abu Nuwas without equivocation, although with more defensiveness. His praise of Abu Nuwas was such that he insisted that the latter's erotic love poems (ghazal) for youthful boys were of a higher quality than the best *ghazal* poems written for women by poets as highly

---

poetry and history in their writings. In this sense, Husayn's own endeavor to uncover the roots of pre-Islamic Arabic poetry was part of this universal research agenda, which employed the "Cartesian" method. See Taha Husayn, *Fi al-Shiʿr al-Jahili* [On Jailiyyah Poetry] (1926; Cairo: Dar al-Nahr lil-Nashr wa al-Tawziʿ, 1996), 81–84.

37. Husayn, *Hadith al-Arbiʿaʾ*, 52.
38. Ibid.

acclaimed as the earlier Umayyad poet ʿUmar ibn Abi Rabiʿah. In fact, Abu Nuwas's poetry was so good, asserted Husayn, that he "forces you when you read his *ghazal* for youthful boys to admire such *ghazal* despite what it contains of what is incompatible with one's constitution [tabʿ], morals, or religion."[39] Here, Husayn's commitment to an appreciation of the aesthetic clearly outweighed whatever concerns he had about societal or religious morality. For Husayn, this very well might be the value of literature as that medium that allows identification with human subjects radically different from oneself. In this vein, literature could be seen as imaginative self-extension, which itself is an aesthetic and a moral value, a form and practice of pedagogy, rather than a content to be taught.

Husayn worried that pedagogy could corrupt history, which begged the question of appropriate audience and readership. To address this conundrum, he opted not to discuss Abu Nuwas's poetry about youthful boys in a lecture or a newspaper article, for fear of its pedagogical implications, "but rather only in a specialized book about Abu Nuwas, to be read by specialists and where the public's hand could not reach except through coincidence and after much effort."[40] Such a solution, it seems, averted pedagogical anarchy and the imparting of desires to the youth that they should not get from literature. It also registers Husayn's ambivalence about his earlier splitting away the moral dimension of *adab*. Husayn concluded that in his whole discussion of Abu Nuwas, he had selected poetry that was respectful of "people's morals in this day and age as well as their inclinations, and the need of the youth for pure and innocent speech."[41] He even went so far as to state that "Abu Nuwas is a dangerous poet and we do not advise reading him except to a specialized group of people who can read him and evaluate him without being influenced [by him] and without imitating him."[42] Clearly, a defensive Husayn seemed, at least in the case of Abu Nuwas, to have come much closer to his opponents' views about which of the different histories of the past should have a pedagogical role in the present and which histories should not. He also seemed increasingly less invested in splitting the two notions of *adab*, aesthetics and good conduct, as he had done earlier, by reinscribing them in the case of Abu Nuwas, albeit with an important twist. Abu Nuwas's poetry, it seemed, was to be relished by few, but not emulated by many. If morality was a universal concern, the aesthetic, Husayn seemed to posit, was solely a concern for the intellectual elite. Within the mobilization of *turath* as the core of civilization,

---

39. Ibid., 137.
40. Ibid., 127.

41. Ibid., 156.
42. Ibid., 157.

on the matters of aesthetics and of certain kinds of sex, different kinds of publics were being imagined. By positing this strategy, Husayn resolved the conundrum—the pedagogical and the aesthetic could be separated along the lines of the publics consuming them.

This is an interesting resolution in light of Taha Husayn's personal experience in his youth with what he termed "Nuwasite" classmates when he studied at al-Azhar University prior to his departure to France. In his autobiography, *Al-Ayyam* (The Days), Husayn recounted how the literary student lived a life of

contentment and resentment elicited by reading various books, wherein he would think like the ancients whose writings he was reading, and would feel the way they felt, and would conduct himself with people the way they did. These young men insisted on reading and learning by heart *jahiliyyah* poetry as well as Islamic and Abbasid poetry. They also insisted on reading the biographies of poets, writers, and language scholars. As a result, they lived the life of those people in the depths of their hearts, as they could not live it in their real lives, since circumstances stood between them and what they desired of it. They were readers of the poetry of Abu Nuwas and his companions and they read ʿUdhri love poetry also. They enjoyed love poetry [ghazal] as much as those poets had . . . and they created for themselves ideals of beauty to which they wrote love poetry and rhapsodies. The conservatives among them could only conjure their ideals entirely for their lifestyles barred them from ever meeting prostitutes. The renewers were more fortunate, as it was not prohibited for them to encounter beautiful faces inside and outside al-Azhar, and to take objects of beauty for their love poetry that were not conjured up by fantasy, but rather were offered by life itself. There was among these young men those who adopted the school of Jamil and Kuthayyir [ʿUdhri Platonic poets], and therefore absolute deprivation was their lot. Others followed the school of Abu Nuwas and his companions, which made them experience deprivation much less and made their share of bliss more. For one, among them, would meet those with beautiful faces, speak to them and listen to them speak, be infatuated with them, compose poetry for them, and go as far as he could with his poetry so much that his infatuation and poetry would entangle him and his classmates in a little or a lot of evil. The third one of these was a Nuwasite in his taste in poetry and desire. How fast he would become familiar with those who had beautiful faces, become close to them and meet them![43]

Indeed, this fellow's story was quite entertaining to his friends and his classmates alike, so much so that as a prank, some of his friends wrote on

43. Taha Husayn, *Al-Ayyam* [The Days] (Cairo: Dar al-Maʿarif, 1978), vol. 3, 16–18. The first and second volume of Husayn's memoir were published in 1929, and this third one was published much later in 1967. The English translation of the book was titled *The Days*, translated by E. H. Paxton, Hilary Wayment, and Kenneth Cragg (Cairo: American University in Cairo Press, 1997).

the wall a famous couplet that Abu Nuwas had written about Abu ʿUbay-dah Muʿammar bin Muthanna (a ninth-century theologian and chroni-cler and contemporary of Abu Nuwas) accusing him of having been a follower of the people of Lot "ever since you began to have wet dreams until now when you are past sixty" (mundhu ihtalamta wa qad jawazta sittinan).[44] While a young university student, Husayn had encountered those who read and emulated Abu Nuwas; as a scholar, he began to cau-tion against it. It is significant that the above reminiscences were writ-ten under a chapter title "The Effect of the Disappearance of Women."

Husayn had one more reference to same-sex practice when he was at al-Azhar at the age of thirteen (1902), namely, in reference to a young man dubbed "Abu Tartur," who was said to pay periodic nocturnal visits to the apartments of al-Azhar students (who were invariably a few years older than Husayn). The young man would slip into their beds and as-sume the passive position in coitus with them. While Husayn refrained from any graphic description of what actually transpired under the bed covers, he would explain how the young men would have to get up af-terwards and bathe, which was an arduous task in winter for lack of hot water in the apartments. The young men would from time to time speak about Abu Tartur in "quick furtive whispers followed by quick chuckles interrupted by shyness and reserve."[45] Abu Tartur would choose a differ-ent student each time. It is unclear and perhaps unlikely that he visited the young Taha, even though the latter would "reflect" upon what the young men would say about Abu Tartur.[46]

Husayn was to go further in accommodating his critics by adopting their stance in judging the work of a contemporary Egyptian literary critic and professor of literature, who also collected his newspaper articles in a book he titled *The Sources of Tears of Lovers* (Madamiʿ al-ʿUshshaq).[47] Zaki Mubarak (1891–1952), a former student of Husayn, who was also French-educated, had published his articles in the newspaper *Al-Sabah* starting in 1922 to the distress of many religious and conservative read-ers who chastised him and declared him an "atheist and a debaucher"[48]

---

44. Taha Husayn does not actually cite the last line of the couplet due to its licentious nature and keeps it hanging. Indeed most books about Abu ʿUbayda cite the couplet without including the offending line except for Muhsin al-Amin al-Husayni al-ʿAmili, who cites it in its entirety in his *Abu Nuwas, al-Hasan bin Haniʾ al-Hikami al-Sha ʿir al-Mashhur* (Damascus: Matbaʿat al-Itqan, 1947), 87.

45. Taha Husayn, *Al-Ayyam* (1929; Cairo: Dar al-Maʾarif, 1978), vol. 2, 94.

46. Ibid., 97.

47. See Zaki Mubarak, *Madamiʿ al-ʿUshshaq* [The Sources of Tears of Lovers] (Beirut: Dar al-Jil, 1993), first published in 1924. Literally, the title means "the lachrymal canals of lovers," i.e., "the eyes of lovers."

48. Ibid., 12.

who corrupts the youth.[49] Mubarak stated at the outset that any "seduction" (fitnah) that his book would place in the hearts of "the youth and
the elderly" is his sole responsibility, and that those readers "who seek
safety should desist immediately from reading this talk."[50]

The book is a collection of poetry culled from the ancient and recent
past in which poets spoke of crying and of shedding tears over a number of situations involving their loved ones (although not exclusively
so, as Mubarak cited lachrymal poetry of nostalgia as well). Mubarak
wrote a confrontational introduction challenging his critics and sign-
ing it as "the atheist and debaucher, in accordance with their claims."[51]
The book included a chapter on lachrymal poetry written by women for
their women lovers,[52] where Mubarak lamented the dearth of women's
lachrymal poetry of desire toward male lovers. He began the chapter
comparing this type of poetry with "what had transpired in Berlin of
the love of Mrs. Klein to Mrs. Repp! And what they had committed for
the sake of this strange love!!" Mubarak, echoing Husayn, proceeded to
express his regret that he could not delve in this topic in a newspaper,
as people "prefer ignorance in the interest of decorum!"[53] He cited the
Prophet as having prohibited *suhaq* (sapphism) just as the Qur'an had
prohibited adultery. He then proceeded to echo Taha Husayn's rejection
of the Orientalist claims of the exceptionalism of Arabo-Muslim civilization by rejecting the flip side of the argument also, namely, the exceptionalism of European civilization, as anyone who knows

the literature of the French finds in the confessions of women strange and marvelous
things that devils could not match! And, Arabic literature is full of similar marvels,
as people are the same in every country and in every generation; so do not believe
that excess in bawdiness is an innovation invented by the women of Berlin! As far
as I am concerned, the error of reformers in the Orient is their ignorance of the de-

49. Ibid., 10.
50. Ibid., 9.
51. Ibid. 12.
52. Ibid., 62–65.
53. Ibid., 62. In another of his books, Mubarak made several references to Abu Nuwas's love of
young men and to a "dangerous" social "habit" in the Baghdad of Abu Nuwas, which consisted
of dressing concubines in the apparel of young men. He even linked this interest in masculinized
women to the modern young women of Europe, "who wear the clothes of young men. If this
were not a recent innovation, it was then a remnant of the whimsy of the ancient inhabitants of
Baghdad." Anticipating the objections of some readers for his inclusion of Abu Nuwas poems that
describe how both the sodomite and the adulterer prefer masculinized women, Mubarak explains
that "the transmitter of infidelity is not an infidel himself, and the transmitter of debauchery is not
debauched himself," in Zaki Mubarak, *Al-Muwazanah bayna al-Shu'ara'* [Comparing Poets] (Cairo:
Dar al-Katib al-'Arabi lil-Tiba'ah wa al-Nashr, 1968), 403–4. The book was first published in 1926 in
Cairo by Matba'at al-Muqtataf.

tails of human life, and their neglect of the principal foundation of reform—which is the diagnosis of the disease before the prescription of medicine, [through] the issuance by many of them of commands about things that one cannot issue commands about and the issuance of prohibitions of things that cannot be prohibited; what is catastrophic is that the reformers themselves are hypocrites! . . . Have we not characterized Western belles lettres as excessive is describing women? We have made that into a bad thing that is unforgivable, when, in my opinion, it is a good thing, as it is incumbent on every reformer to strengthen what exists between men and women of natural inclinations so that we would not complain about women's infatuation with women, and men's love of youthful boys! Read this and think about it before you give us a headache with your calls for virtue from whence you do not know![54]

While Europe and the Arab world are not exceptional, Mubarak waxed ironic against his critics by claiming that certain aspects of Europe could prove pedagogical for these "hypocritical" Arab civilizational reformers—at least by strengthening Arab "natural' desires about which these reformers seemed concerned. Having called on his critics to strengthen "natural" desires between men and women aside, Mubarak proceeded to identify women's poetry for women as expressing a desire that is considered a "curiosity" within the classification of desires.[55] His book also made cursory reference to lachrymal poetry written for boys.

Once the book was published, Taha Husayn wrote a short note about it "deploring" it as "very dangerous." Husayn asserted that the book "had a literary value that is not without danger," as he was displeased with what he described as the author's "flattery of his own sentiments and the sentiments of his readers to the point of excess. His chapters, as a result, came out less as scholarly and literary research and more as research that rouses emotions and incites passions."[56] His reservations notwithstanding, Husayn felt that he also needed to "praise" the book. But as with his remarks about the appropriate audience of Abu Nuwas's poetry and the pedagogical mission that he would set for "scholarly" research, Husayn's ambivalence about Mubarak further demonstrated the former's selective adherence to societal morality in the context of debates on the value of the aesthetic and its relation to sexual transgression. Husayn and Mubarak would become the bitterest enemies and would attack each other in the press for years to come.[57]

54. Ibid., 62.
55. Ibid., 64.
56. Husayn, *Hadith al-Arbi'a'* (Cairo: al-Matba'ah al-Tijariyyah al-Kubra, 1925), vol. 3, 65.
57. On the battle between them, see Samih Kurayyim, *Taha Husayn fi Ma'arikihi al-Adabiyyah*

Husayn wrote during an innovative decade that began with daring liberal intellectual experiments that conservative elements in society attempted to kill at birth. ʿAli ʿAbd al-Raziq's important book on Islam and governance, published in 1925, caused an uproar, and its author was put on trial.[58] This fate would befall Taha Husayn's own upcoming heretical book on pre-Islamic *jahiliyyah* poetry, which he published in 1926.[59] Conservatives feared the liberal impulse of these thinkers due to the fact of the British occupation, which they feared might corrupt the minds of Egyptians with hostile European ideas about Arab and Muslim history and civilization. The fact that Husayn, for example, held an official university position and was seen as close to the regime and the British occupation did not mitigate the hostility of critics, especially so as Husayn belonged to the party of the Liberal Constitutionalists (Hizb al-Ahrar al-Dusturiyyin), which competed with the anti-British Wafd, the party of the Egyptian national hero Saʿd Zaghlul. For now, however, despite his manifest concessions, Husayn was not silenced; but his detractors were increasingly successful in making him more defensive about his sacrilegious thesis concerning the Abbasid period, namely, that it was a period of "doubt, bawdiness and an era of temptations and atheism with regards to familiar morals, inherited habits, and religion too."[60] He set out not only to prove his thesis but also to demonstrate to his audience that although the poets he studied were all practitioners of these attributes, people admired and approved of them in that era. He continued to insist on the important value of the aesthetic in the lives of people, including religious folks. One attack on him criticized him for publishing such writings during the holy month of Ramadan. In response, Husayn insisted on historical accuracy and the role of the past as pedagogy. He also stressed the importance of aesthetic pleasure:

no matter how much we deny the appearance of doubt and *mujun* [bawdiness] and similar traits in that era and its taking over the souls of the enlightened of that period, it will not stop that era from being an era of doubt and *mujun* that conquered the minds of the majority of the enlightened of its people, including many scholars of

wa al-Fikriyyah [Taha Husayn in His Literary and Intellectual Battles] (Cairo: Kitab al-Idhaʿah wa al-Tilifizyun, 1974), 323–27.

58. ʿAli ʿAbd al-Raziq, *Al-Islam wa-Usul al-Hukm: Bahth fi al-Khilafah wa al-Hukumah* [Islam and the Bases of Governance: An Inquiry into Succession and Government in Islam] (Cairo: Matbaʿat Misr, 1925).

59. Husayn, *Fi al-Shiʿr al-Jahili*.

60. Husayn, *Hadith*, vol. 3, 184. He restated his thesis in his article about the poet Mutiʿ bin Iyyas, published in *Al-Siyasah*, April 9, 1924, which corresponded to the Islamic calendar date of Ramadan 5, 1342.

jurisprudence [fuqaha²] and theology [kalam] . . . [People] will then say to me: What benefit is it to us to know that this was an era of doubt or an era of certitude, and what would harm us if we remained ignorant of this? I am not certain that I have a reasonable answer to this. What possible reasonable answer could one give to those who ask one about the benefit of knowledge and the harm of ignorance? They will say . . . why are you telling us about them during the month of fasting . . . ? . . . Could you not have postponed this until people finished fasting . . . ? . . . Perhaps I chose to talk about these charming people and their stories in order to make things easier on those who are fasting and to lighten their fasting pains. Is there any sin or crime in this?[61]

Husayn provided pedagogical examples from the early Islamic era of people addressing similar issues during the month of Ramadan without embarrassment. He concluded:

Why are we embarrassed today? Is this embarrassment itself not an example of weakness, the softness of belief, and the confusion of certitude? The true believer, the true religious person who is loyal in his devotion and in his worship worries not about his faith, his religion, his asceticism, and his worship from the poetry of Muti' [bin Iyyas] and Muti''s companions. He who fears this poetry is he who feels himself weak and wants to avoid and eschew those things that caused and tempted its writing.[62]

As the intensity of the attacks on him continued, the importance of the aesthetic experience receded for Husayn in the interest of the pedagogical one.[63] The objective of Husayn's studies, he would insist, was pedagogical, based as they were on "scholarly ['ilmiyyan, also meaning "scientific"] research, as we do not seek to please and entertain people with it, but to benefit others and ourselves."[64] All the same, Husayn remained optimistic throughout. As late as 1937 when he published what many consider his magnum opus, Mustaqbal al-Thaqafah fi Misr (The Future of Culture in Egypt), Husayn was clear that there was a societal consensus on the preservation of the works of Abu Nuwas, Bashshar bin Burd, and others. While arguing for "rejoining" European civilization, of which he considered Egypt an integral part, Husayn insisted that "we inherited the poetry of Bashshar and Abu Nuwas and their cohorts as we inherited the jurisprudence of the imams and the theology [kalam] of the theologians and the asceticism of ascetics. What is strange is that

61. Ibid., 186.
62. Ibid., 186–87.
63. For a discussion and a reproduction of the articles attacking Husayn in *Al-Siyasah*, see Kurayyim, *Taha Husayn*, 133–46.
64. Husayn, *Hadith*, vol. 3, 187.

we are benefiting from all that we inherited from our ancestors and that it would not occur to anyone of the ultraconservatives that the study of Bashshar or Abu Nuwas be banned, nor to request of the authorities to burn what we have inherited of the legacy of the philosophers, *zanadiqah* [those who adhere to *zandaqah,* whose meaning indicates a number of things including atheism, adopting Persian Manicheanism, and other irreligious thinking[65]], and *mujjan* [bawdy people] of whom religion does not approve . . . Indeed if someone were to call for the enactment of a law mandating the burning of the poetry of Abu Nuwas, Bashshar, and Hammad and their cohorts, the men of religion themselves would rush to denounce this ugly call and would be the most condemnatory among people of anyone who would call for such action."[66]

Husayn provided ample reason for the emergence of this peculiar mode of living under the Abbasids, including the life of luxury and the existence of a class of aristocratic Arabs who were barred from politics under the Umayyads (who ruled from A.D. 661 to 750)—which led them in turn to be self-preoccupied—as well as the influence of Persians. Although he insisted that this frivolity had "an Arab coloring that distinguishes it,"[67] there was more to it than that: "But were I to want to provide a literary diagnosis to this *zandaqah,* I would say that it is a type of anger at the Arabs, their traditions and morals, and their conservatism and religion especially. It is a type of this kind of anger coupled with a fondness for the life of the Persians and their traditions, pleasures, and culture."[68] While Husayn's explanation was not necessarily situated within a nationalist grid of argumentation, this anti-Arab impulse that he discerned, especially in the works of Abu Nuwas, would serve as a major argument by later purists to cleanse Arab history and civilization of the latter's "debauchery."

For now, however, attempts were underway to eliminate evidence of sodomy or love of youthful boys altogether in reprinted books of *turath,* especially stories highlighted by Orientalists as significant. Thus, in the course of summarizing the occurrence of pederasty in the *Arabian Nights,* Richard F. Burton classified it into three categories: "the second is the grimmest and most earnest phase of the perversion, for instance where

---

65. "Zandaqah" is most likely derived from the name of the Zoroastrian book of commentary "Zend" or "Zand" in Persian. Hence, it initially must have referred to Zoroastrianism.

66. Taha Husayn, *Mustaqbal al-Thaqafah fi Misr* [The Future of Culture in Egypt] (1937; Cairo: Dar al-Maʿarif, 1993), 46.

67. Husayn, *Hadith,* 198.

68. Husayn, *Hadith,* 199.

[the poet] Abu Nowas [*sic*] debauches the three youths."[69] While the 1836 Arabic edition of *A Thousand and One Nights* (and other editions) that preceded Burton's declaration included the story of Abu Nuwas and the three youths, the reprinted edition of 1930 opted to eliminate it (and a few others) altogether.[70] Similarly, while the collected poetry of Abu Nuwas published in 1898 and republished in 1905 included his poetry of love for youthful boys,[71] the 1937 edition would exclude most of them. When the editor of the 1937 collection addresses the "bawdiness" of Abu Nuwas, he does so only in relation to women.[72] These censorious developments were very much part of the project of emphasizing the pedagogical role that the past was supposed to play in the present by eliminating features that did not accord with modern (read European) normativity. This role remained a fulcrum around which many historically based arguments and historical research itself, continued to revolve.

In this vein, let me turn to one such endeavor, namely, the work of Taha Husayn's associate, the Egyptian literary historian Ahmad Amin (1886–1954). In the late 1920s, Ahmad Amin (no relation to Qasim) began a project of writing the early literary and intellectual history of Arab society after Islam. Amin was an al-Azhar graduate who later studied to be a Shariʿah judge. He learned English from private British tutors in Cairo and was fond of reading Orientalist studies of Islam as well as Darwin and Spencer, about whom he lectured at the Shariʿah law college where he taught in 1918.[73] In 1926, Taha Husayn, who was dean of the college of literature at the university, hired him as a lecturer in Arabic

69. Richard F. Burton, "Terminal Essay," in *The Book of the Thousand Nights and a Night, A Plain and Literal Translation of the Arab Nights Entertainments*, translated and annotated by Richard F. Burton (London: Burton Club, 1886), vol. 10, 217.

70. Muhammad Quttah al-ʿAdawi, ed., *Alf Laylah wa Laylah* [A Thousand and One Nights] (Beirut: Dar Sadir, n.d.), vol. 1, 562–64. This edition is an exact replica of the original Bulaq edition published in Cairo in A.H. 1252 (A.D. 1836). The story is included in the 1884 edition. See also *Alf Laylah wa Laylah* (Cairo: al-Matbaʿah al-Saʿidiyya wa Maktabatuha, A.H. 1348/A.D. 1930), vol. 2, 317, cited in El-Rouayheb, *Before Homosexuality*, 158, 160.

71. Mahmud Afandi Wasif, *Diwan Abi Nuwas* [The Collected Poetry of Abu Nuwas] (Cairo: Iskandar Asaf, Al-Matbaʿah al-ʿUmumiyyah bi-Misr, 1898). This collection included a large section of Abu Nuwas's *ghazal* in the feminine, 359–401, followed by another large section on his *ghazal* in the masculine, 402–36.

72. See Mahmud Kamil Farid, ed., *Diwan Abi Nuwas, Tarikhuhu, Raʾy al-Shuʿaraʾ fih, Nawadiruhu, Shiʿruhu* [The Collected Poetry of Abu Nuwas: His History, the Poets' Evaluation of Him, His Anecdotes, and His Poetry] (Cairo: Al-Maktabah al-Tijariyyah al-Kubra, 1937). For the few instances when Abu Nuwas's poems of *ghazal* in the masculine are included, see 116, 132–33. See also the editor's introduction, 3–78.

73. See Ahmad Amin, *Hayati* [My Life] (Cairo: Lajnat al-Taʾlif wa al-Tarjamah wa al-Nashr, 1950), 166–67.

literature.[74] Amin would later travel to Europe to attend and lecture at conferences on Orientalism. He was forced by the prominent Orientalist D. S. Margoliouth (1858–1940) to translate his lecture to English, as most of the Orientalists in attendance did not understand Arabic![75] The influence of Darwin's and Spencer's evolutionist thought would be felt in Amin's works even at the titular level, for the titles of his most famous books (which became classics) would be *The Dawn of Islam, The Forenoon of Islam,* and *The Noon of Islam.*

Like Taha Husayn, Amin began with a nonmoralist approach that became more moralistic when the civilizational question arose. In his *Duha al-Islam* (The Forenoon of Islam), published in 1933, Amin noted in passing how when the Abbasid caliph al-Amin assumed power in A.D. 809, "whimsy increased manyfold, and no matter what investigative historians might say about the [fact that a] large amount of such reports were written during the period of [the caliph] al-Ma'mun [who killed his half-brother al-Amin in A.D. 813 and replaced him] for the purpose of defaming al-Amin's reputation, downgrading his status, and justifying what was done to him, [al-Amin's] inclination toward excess of whimsy, drink, and youthful boys was such that it cannot be denied."[76] In his description of the Abbasid period, he dedicated sections about the debate on wine and its prohibition or permissibility in Islam, about *zandaqah,* of which a number of prominent people were accused, about slavery, and about singing girls, as examples of the "life of whimsy" in this period.[77] In his analysis of the Abbasid period and the transformation of the culture of the Islamic empire from an Arabian Peninsula–based culture to a multicultural imperial culture, Amin, like the Orientalist Nicholson before him, cited Persian culture as principally influential in this period on the styles of whimsy and opulence, especially in the poetry of both Arab and Persian poets, like Muti' bin Iyyas (an Arab poet whose father came from Palestine) and Abu Nuwas. These two poets produced "lewd literature that does not shy away from fooling around with youthful boys and does not desist from any debauchery. Even though it excelled in its artistic aspects, noble taste would [still] not find it palatable."[78] If it were not for the influence of the Persians in the Abbasid period and the Umayyad dynasty had continued, Amin wrote, "you would not have

74. Ibid., 208.
75. Ibid., 265.
76. Ahmad Amin, *Duha al-Islam* [The Forenoon of Islam] (Cairo: Matba'at Lajnat al-Ta'lif wa al-Tarjamah wa al-Nashr, 1933), vol. 1, 120.
77. Ibid., 81–168.
78. Ibid., 193.

seen rhapsodies for youthful boys, nor this torrential river of singing girls, and you would not have seen abundant luxury and opulence."[79] Clearly, the civilizational question was on Amin's mind, as here his interest lay in safeguarding a pure Arab civilization whose erotic practices were not offensive to his modern criteria (the Victorian origins of which he seemed oblivious to) were it not for Persian influence, which so far he only cited and did not condemn.

By 1945, Amin had a moralistic judgment to share with his readers. In his *Zuhr al-Islam* (The Noon of Islam), Amin described literary production of the Abbasid period as representative of social life, both its opulent and poverty-stricken aspects. He discussed how the literary figures of the period themselves partook of the "decadence of morals."[80] His judgment of much of literary production in this period was that it was "like the opulent social life [that predominated], form without spirit."[81] He described the poetry that praised the singing girls as an example, but "the biggest calamity was that the echo of what befell society of the love of youthful boys appeared in literature."[82] This was the result of "slavery in social life and the reflection of its image in literature, as the literature of the period was filled with the description of singing girls, white and black concubines, and youthful boys, so much so that we cannot find a single poet who did not write poetry in this genre."[83] While Amin claimed that Abu Nuwas was initially alone in this genre, when this epoch arrived, "most of the poets engaged in it."[84] What was peculiar for Amin regarding this period related to what he considered "a strange phenomenon," namely, "that high-ranking people, such as ministers and judges, were not embarrassed in speaking abundantly about these issues, which indicates that public opinion's abhorrence of such things had become tempered."[85] In addition to noting the permissiveness of popular culture, Amin discerned a general "degeneration" in this period, as he cited other types of poetry that used "common" idioms and spoke of "bawdy" things about women and wine and personal sexual escapades, which was "the clearest indication of the level of moral de-

---

79. Ibid., 194. Amin also mentions how medieval Arab Christian monasteries, as medieval books had recorded, were a place for both asceticism and whimsy, as many poets have written "rhapsodies for the youthful girls and boys" who resided therein, see ibid., 369.

80. Ahmad Amin, *Zuhr al-Islam* [The Noon of Islam] (Cairo: Matba'at Lajnat al-Ta'lif wa al-Tarjamah wa al-Nashr, 1945), vol. 1, 132–33.

81. Ibid., 134.

82. Ibid., 138.

83. Ibid., 136

84. Ibid., 139.

85. Ibid., 140.

generation reached by this society."[86] For Amin, the task was to rescue the Abbasid era for Arab-Islamic civilization by ridding its legacy of such degeneration, or at least by explaining it away as an uninheritable trait that did not pass to later periods of Arab history. If anything, it would seem that through a self-cleansing mechanism, Arab-Islamic civilization discovered the problem later and corrected it.

Taha Husayn introduced Amin's *Duha al-Islam,* affirming its peda-gogical attributes—"the life of [ancient] Muslims from now on will no longer be as it was before, obscure and confused, about which literary historians write through approximation, not investigation . . . That epoch has now passed, as Ahmad Amin has dropped a heavy curtain separating it from those who will write literary history [in the future]."[87] For Husayn, it was not only the past history of Muslim Arabs that had a pedagogical role to play but also the very act of excavating it, as the latter was an important feature of modern civilization to which Husayn was strongly committed. His effusive praise of Amin's achievement was such that he ended his introduction to the book with the assertion, "Let this serious, fertile and productive life . . . which Ahmad Amin lives be a beneficial lesson, and a good example for those who want to live in Egypt the life of scholars."[88]

Abu Nuwas as Civilizational Anxiety

Modern discussions of the revolutionary import of Abu Nuwas contin-ued after Taha Husayn's inaugural columns in the early 1920s. While no one ever denied the poetic and artistic importance of Abu Nuwas as a modernizer of Arabic poetry, it was a difficult task squaring his promi-nent presence in the history of Arabic poetry with his artistic commit-ments to write about his erotic desires and practices. In his magiste-rial textbook for secondary schools, *Tarikh al-Adab al-ʿArabi,*[89] which he published in 1923, Egyptian literary critic Ahmad Hasan al-Zayyat (1885–1968) acknowledged the poetic genius of Abu Nuwas but had a differing assessment of his "transporting *ghazal* from a description of the feminine to a description of the masculine." Al-Zayyat asserted that "it is

86. Ibid., 141.
87. Ibid., book ta.
88. Ibid., book lam.
89. Ahmad Hasan al-Zayyat, *Tarikh al-Adab al-ʿArabi, lil-Madaris al-Thanawiyyah wa al-ʿUlya* [The History of Arabic Literature for Secondary and High Schools] (1923; Beirut: Dar al-Thaqafah, 1978).

doubtless that this style that this debauched poet had legitimized was a crime against literature and a disgrace to the history of Arabic poetry."[90]

'Abbas Mustafa 'Ammar, an Egyptian professor at Teachers College (Madrasat al-Mu'allimin al-'Ulya), was the first to write a monograph on Abu Nuwas.[91] His book, published in 1929–1930, sought to arbitrate between the modernist critics and the traditionalists who were beholden to the classical assessments of Arabic literature. While condemning the "traditionalists," he engaged the modernists critically.[92] 'Ammar cited Orientalist scholarship, including that of Nicholson, as well as the work of Taha Husayn,[93] and cited the opposition by "reactionaries" to previous research on the poet in a clear reference to the debate over Taha Husayn's work.[94] 'Ammar reproduced Husayn's judgment of the morals of the Abbasid period as "decadent" and "degraded," and apologized for not being able to reproduce all the relevant medieval texts in his study on account of contemporary "conventions and morals."[95] His interest was in studying the "aesthetic" value of Abu Nuwas, which he admitted could not be given justice due to the "many constraints that lie before us, which will prevent us from even suggesting, let alone, declaring" what is currently considered immoral.[96]

'Ammar addressed the different medieval accounts about Abu Nuwas's paternity and concluded that the poet must not have had an Arab father, let alone any known father, effectively accusing Abu Nuwas's Persian mother of being a prostitute.[97] The book examined the poetic and aesthetic innovations that Abu Nuwas inaugurated and critically evaluated medieval judgment of his poetry, nuancing it by being more selective about the aesthetic value of certain poems compared to others. Before moving to study Abu Nuwas's poetry, 'Ammar's approach was to contextualize Abu Nuwas in the Abbasid "environment" that produced him, thus generalizing his morals as part of the "decadence" of Abbasid society at large. He dedicated the last section of the book to Abu Nuwas's *ghazal* in the masculine and delved into his love affair and poetry with the concubine Jinan, to whom Abu Nuwas had written many *ghazal*

---

90. Ibid., 310.
91. 'Abbas Mustafa 'Ammar, *Abu Nuwas, Hayatuhu wa Shi'ruhu* [Abu Nuwas, His Life and Poetry] (Cairo: Matba'at Wadi al-Muluk, 1929–30).
92. Ibid., 1–9.
93. Ibid., 6, 28.
94. Ibid., 9.
95. Ibid., 11.
96. Ibid., 12.
97. Ibid., 12–15, 20–23.

poems, noting however that Abu Nuwas possessed a hierarchy of sexual object choices, beginning with youthful boys and then followed by women.[98] This, 'Ammar insisted, in no way rendered Abu Nuwas's love for Jinan any less sincere.[99]

The year 1933 proved an auspicious year for Abu Nuwas studies, as treatments of him appeared in Arabic and English. The English study was written by William Harold Ingrams (1897–1973), a British colonial official and cultural cross-dresser. Ingrams served in the colonial administration in Zanzibar, Mauritius, the Gold Coast, and most illustriously in Yemen and Hadramawt, where he donned local dress. He wrote much about his travels, including Zanzibar, Hadramawt, and southern Arabia.[100] *Abu Nuwas in Life and in Legend* is a quaint study of the poet's "actual," "apocryphal," and "mythical" life.[101] Ingrams appropriately dedicated the book to the memory of Sir Richard F. Burton, on whom he relied extensively for the "apocryphal" stories about Abu Nuwas in *A Thousand and One Nights.* Ingrams investigated the far reach of myths about Abu Nuwas across the African continent where he is known by variations on his name and is associated with many epigrammatic anecdotes. Ingrams wanted to write his book about Abu Nuwas because "I have found that there is little in the English language or for a matter of fact in any European language about a man who is eminently worth knowing."[102] Indeed it was a labor of love as, "it has afforded me some pleasure and amusement to write this study and I hope it may amuse, if not interest, those who read it."[103] Ingrams had concerns similar to those of Taha Husayn regarding publishing his book on Abu Nuwas. Ingrams had apparently been reluctant to publish the book earlier because "the collection contains tales that cannot be considered suitable for general publication; they are in fact wherever they are read, distinctly pas pour les jeunes filles [*sic*]. I believe the time has past when apology is necessary for printing such matter."[104] While Harold Ingrams interested himself in the libertine life of Abu Nuwas, his wife, Doreen, who accompanied him in his colonial appointments, would become interested in the lives of

98. Ibid., 120.

99. Ibid., 121

100. See W. H. Ingrams, *A Report on the Social, Economic, and Political Condition of the Hadhramaut* (London: H. M. Stationery office, 1937), and his *Zanzibar: Its History and Its People* (London: H. F. & G. Witherby, 1931).

101. W. H. Ingrams, *Abu Nuwas in Life and in Legend* (Port-Louis, Mauritius: Privately published, 1933).

102. Ibid., ii.

103. Ibid.

104. Ibid., ii–iii.

Arab women about whom she would write.[105] Thus between the two of them, they covered the two most exotic issues for Europeans regarding the Arab Orient: women's social position and men's sexual desires.

Harold Ingrams did contextualize Abu Nuwas for his audience through comparisons: "Burton says of Abu Nuwas that he was the Rochester or Piron of his age."[106] While Ingrams agrees with the Rochester comparison, he suggests better ones with French poets other than Piron, including La Fontaine, Villon, and especially Verlaine.[107] Ultimately, for Ingrams, the major rationale for writing a book about Abu Nuwas was that "It is rightly thought today that no study of a people, and one may add, *of a representative of a people*, can be complete unless it includes the good and the bad, the pleasant and the unpleasant."[108] It is this representative status that Abu Nuwas seemed to signify to colonial officials and Orientalists alike that many Arab intellectuals wanted to challenge.

The Arabic book published the same year as Ingrams' was a brief two-volume overview of Abu Nuwas's biography and poetic style by Lebanese literary critic 'Umar Farrukh.[109] Farrukh provided a brief biographical account of the poet, noting that he had surrounded himself with debauchers and "effeminates" (mukhannathin).[110] He provided evidence of Abu Nuwas's marriage and his begetting children and spoke of his death as not being a natural one, implying that he had been murdered by political enemies.[111] Farrukh noted the debate that Taha Husayn's remarks a decade earlier had elicited. He agreed, however, not with Husayn, but rather with al-Zayyat's judgment about Abu Nuwas's *ghazal* in the masculine.[112]

Farrukh, like later authors, would show concern about the question of "natural" versus "unnatural" desires, notions that he and others seemed to borrow wholesale from European psychology and psychoanalysis, as medieval Arab social taxonomy did not *necessarily* designate desires for women and youthful boys by recourse to nature. For example, he

105. See Doreen Ingrams, *The Awakened : Women in Iraq* (London: Third World Centre, 1983).
106. Ingrams, *Abu Nuwas*, iii.
107. Ibid., v–vii.
108. Ibid., emphasis added.
109. See 'Umar Farrukh, *Abu Nuwas, Sha'ir Harun al-Rashid and Muhammad al-Amin, Al-Qism al-Awwal, Dirasah wa Naqd* [Abu Nuwas: The Poet of Harun al-Rashid and Muhammad al-Amin, part 1, Analysis and Criticism] (Beirut: Maktabat al-Kashshaf, 1932), and the second volume subtitled *Mukhtarat min Shi'rihi* (Beirut: Maktabat al-Kashshaf, 1933). The book was republished in 1988 by Dar al-Kitab al-'Arabi. This latest edition of the book was published in one volume and with a new introduction by the author.
110. Farrukh, *Abu Nuwas*, vol. 1, 7.
111. Ibid., 10–11, 14.
112. Ibid., 39.

explained that "when poets wrote erotic poems and rhapsodies to women, no one saw any embarrassment in it—unless the object of the rhapsody was one specific [named] woman—and no criticism would be made, as it is natural [tabi'i] for a man to be attracted to a woman and to find her physical attributes beautiful, but it is unnatural that a similar relation would arise between one man and another. It is from this angle only that this type of *ghazal* [poetry] was innovation [bid'ah], and some people liked to listen to it because it was something to which they had not been accustomed."[113] Farrukh, like Zaydan before him, found no need to include examples of Abu Nuwas's poems that are classified under the headings of bawdiness (*mujun*) and debauchery (tahattuk). His logic for the exclusion was impeccably utilitarian: "I see no advantage in studying this . . . nor in selecting any of these poems."[114]

Other authors concentrated on debauchery (tahattuk) as the important feature of Abu Nuwas's life, thus adhering to period descriptions more closely rather than imposing modern and anachronistic categories. Lebanese Arabic literature professor Butrus al-Bustani (not to be confused with his nineteenth-century namesake) dedicated a chapter to Abu Nuwas's life and poetry in his 1934 study of medieval Arabic poetry.[115] Al-Bustani discussed Abu Nuwas's life (A.D. 762–814) in a matter-of-fact way. He recounted how Abu Nuwas had become "a debaucher as a young boy [tahattaka sabiyyan]" and that he rented himself out for one dinar as a wine carrier for *mujjan* (bawdy) poets on their outings.[116] Al-Bustani only mentioned in passing Abu Nuwas's association with his mentor, Walibah bin al-Hubab, the Kufi poet, who was "charmed" by Abu Nuwas and was impressed by his "intelligence and manners." Bin al-Hubab took Abu Nuwas with him to the city of Kufah (south of Baghdad), where he taught him "poetry and imparted to him his literature, taught him his ethics and manners, and introduced him to his bawdy friends."[117] Al-Bustani paid more attention to Abu Nuwas's association with the caliph al-Amin, "whose morals were degraded in his youth, and his submerging himself in whimsy and depravity was one of the reasons that lost him his kingship."[118] Al-Bustani mostly relied on medieval sources for his study, as the only available modern literature on Abu

113. Ibid., 39–40.
114. Ibid., 40.
115. See Butrus al-Bustani, *Udaba' al-'Arab fi al-A'sur al-'Abasiyyah, hayatuhum, atharuhum, naqd atharihim* [Arabic Belletrists in the Abbasid Epochs, Their Lives, Their Work, and Criticism of Their Work], 3rd ed. (1934; Beirut: Maktabat Sadir, 1947).
116. Ibid., 51–52.
117. Ibid., 52.
118. Ibid., 54.

Nuwas at the time ('Ammar's and Farrukh's modest works excepted) was his collected poetry (diwan), published in a sanitized Arabic edition in Cairo in 1898 and a collection of his more sexually explicit poems published that same year in response.[119] Ibn Manzur's thirteenth-century book about Abu Nuwas's life had also been published in Cairo in 1924, after the publication of Taha Husayn's columns but was subsequently banned by the British Mandate-controlled Egyptian government. There was one more matter-of-fact treatment of Abu Nuwas by Egyptian historian Ahmad Farid al-Rifaʿi, who dedicated a section of a chapter to the poet in his three-volume book on the epoch of the caliph al-Maʾmun. Rifaʿi made reference to the "bawdiness" of Abu Nuwas and to his love affair with the concubine Jinan without moralizing.[120] Besides Rifaʿi's book, Husayn's, 'Ammar's, and Bustani's discussions of Abu Nuwas remained the major references until the 1940s.

Interest in Abu Nuwas continued in the 1940s with the publication of the first modern biography of the poet in 1944 ('Ammar's and Farrukh's studies aside) written by the Egyptian ʿAbd al-Rahman Sidqi.[121] Sidqi discussed Abu Nuwas's life in a detached scholarly manner that avoided sensationalism. In narrating Abu Nuwas's love story with the concubine Jinan (who belonged to someone else), Sidqi introduced the question of desire:

Each sex is pulled to the other sex due to that natural commanding need placed [in us] by [God] . . . This instinct is extremely deep, and extremely general, as it occupies a large place in human interest . . . and our poet, Abu Nuwas, despite his recklessness,

---

119. The *Diwan* was published by Iskandar Asaf. See also Mansur ʿAbd al-Mutaʿali and Husayn Ashraf, eds., *Al-Fukahah wa al-Iʾtinas fi Mujun Abi Nuwas wa baʿd Naqaʾidih maʿ al-Shuʿaraʾ* [Humor and Sociability in the Bawdiness of Abu Nuwas] (Cairo: 1316 [1898]). I should mention here that the article about Abu Nuwas that was published in *Al-Hilal* in 1897 provided a biography of the poet and samples of his poetry. See "Abu Nuwas," *Al-Hilal*, 1 May 1897, 642–48. The article was most probably written by *Al-Hilal* editor Jurji Zaydan. According to the author of the article, he could locate three editions of Abu Nuwas's poetry only, an 1860 Cairo edition, most probably published by Bulaq, an 1861 edition "published in Europe," which is most probably a reference to W. Ahlwardt's *Diwan des Abu Nowas nach der Weiner und Berliner handschrift, mit Benutzung anderer Handschriften herausgegeben*, of which only one volume appeared, *Die Weinlieder* (Greifswald, 1861), and an 1884 Beirut edition published by Jamʿiyyat al-Funun, see *Al-Hilal*, 648. It would seem that none of these editions were available in the 1930s except for the later 1898 Cairo edition, which had not yet been published when the article in *Al-Hilal* first appeared. W. H. Ingrams cited another selection of Abu Nuwas poems translated into German by A. von Kremer (Vienna: n.p., 1855) and a reference to the poet by the Orientalist I. Goldziher in *Abhandlungen zur Arabischen Philologie* (Leyden: 1896), 1, 145 ff. in Ingrams, *Abu Nuwas in Life and Legend*, 87.

120. See Ahmad Farid al-Rifaʿi, *ʿAsr al-Maʾmun* [The Epoch of al-Maʾmun] (Cairo: Matbaʿat Dar al-Kutub al-Misriyyah, 1928), vol. 3, 206–48.

121. See ʿAbd al-Rahman Sidqi, *Abu Nuwas, Qissat Hayatih wa Shiʿruh* [Abu Nuwas: His Life Story and His Poetry] (Cairo: Dar Ihyaʾ al-Kutub al-ʿArabiyyah, 1944).

like the rest of the bawdy depraved men in their whimsy, drinking, and association
with youthful boys [fityan], would not, especially as he became a man, deviate from
the path [yakhruj ʿan] of the victory over emotion and the authority over the soul that
natural love between the sexes commands.[122]

Sidqi, like many of the modern interpreters of Abu Nuwas after him,
was intent on exonerating Abu Nuwas of much of the hyperbole used to
describe his "deviant" lifestyle. His concern for "natural" desires echoed
Farrukh's. I should note here that the term "deviant" in this period,
while increasingly used to describe same-sex male desire, continued to
be more expansive in its reference. Taha Husayn himself used it in 1929
to describe himself and when he cited his own father's reference to him
(Taha) as "shadh" for being a contrarian know-it-all teenager.[123] Nevertheless, Sidqi described Abu Nuwas not as someone who outdid others
in their debauchery, but rather as someone who outdid them merely in
speaking about such things, that his "debauchery was in art" and not
in real life.[124] Sidqi's distinction of artistic debauchery aimed to push
the aesthetic impact of Abu Nuwas to the fore at the expense of the
biographical, which is what Taha Husayn insisted on. In his conclusion, Sidqi endeavored to prove Abu Nuwas's ultimate faith in God and
his reported repentance on his deathbed, thus classifying Abu Nuwas's
behavior not as some kind of pathological deviance but rather as willful
acts of sinful debauchery and bawdiness, which he later repented.[125]

Contemporary reviewers of Sidqi's biography were not always happy
with his choice. The critic Muhammad ʿAbd al-Ghani Hassan reviewed
the book for the scholarly journal *Al-Muqtataf* appreciatively but critically. He was not satisfied with Sidqi's choice of poet for a biographical
study as "we have not yet finished writing about the prominent personalities of jurisprudence, politics, conquest, and thought [fikr] for us to favor writing about people prominent in debauchery and whimsy."[126] But
if Sidqi attempted a straightforward biography of the controversial poet
that expressed certain concerns about natural and unnatural desires,[127] a
mere three years later, he would become more concerned about contextualizing the sexual world in which Abu Nuwas lived.

---

122. Ibid., 69–71.
123. Taha Husayn, *Al-Ayyam* [The Days] (1929; Cairo: Dar al-Maʿarif, 1978), vol. 2, 126, 143.
124. Sidqi, *Abu Nuwas*, 178.
125. Ibid., 178–89.
126. Muhammad ʿAbd al-Ghani Hasan, review, *Al-Muqtataf*, 1 January 1945, 62.
127. I should note here that another book on Abu Nuwas was published in 1947 by Lebanese
Shiite scholar Muhsin al-Amin al-Husayni al-ʿAmili that was more like a large encyclopedia entry on
the poet. See his *Abu Nuwas, al-Hasan bin Haniʾ al-Hikami al-Shaʿir al-Mashhur.*

The new study that Sidqi published in 1947 titled *Alhan al-Han, Abu Nuwas fi Hayatih al-Lahiyyah* (The Melodies of the Tavern: Abu Nuwas in His Whimsical Life),[128] was mostly a study of the different taverns, monasteries, and other places of drinking in the medieval epoch and the importance of wine to poetry. The reason for the historic importance of Abu Nuwas, Sidqi maintains, is not his great skill in poetry, nor his excessive love of wine or his writing about it, for others have comparable attributes: "The secret lies in the personality of Abu Nuwas himself. The man had a lovely spirit, was very likable, full of youthful vitality, with a vigilant perceptiveness of whatever strikes his senses, intensely sociable with those around him, generous in his depths, harmonious in his constitution, with attention to the place of humor and an intent for whimsy."[129] Under the section titled "Infatuation with youthful boys and *ghazal* poetry in the masculine," Sidqi proceeds to investigate Western "scientific" studies of "inversion" (irtikas). He explains that scientific opinion has it that in effeminacy, "the defectiveness may be in the organic functions more so than in the outward appearance or bodily structure, although in some it may very well appear outwardly and cannot be concealed."[130] Abu Nuwas's poetic descriptions of the physique of some of the youthful boys he fancied is marshaled as evidence of such a condition. Sidqi explains also that socially the predilection for youthful boys was introduced to the Arabs by Persians. The source for this was most likely the German Orientalist Adam Mez who, in his book on medieval Arab society, attributed the love of boys among Arabs to Persian origins (see chapter 2).[131] The Arabic translation of Mez's book is listed in Sidqi's bibliography.[132]

Sidqi explains that while Abu Nuwas introduced *ghazal* in the masculine to Arabic poetry, the genre was already known in ancient Greek and Roman literatures and during the European Renaissance. Michelangelo's poem to a beloved friend is cited as evidence as are Shakespeare's sonnets. Sidqi mentions as more recent examples Oscar Wilde and Paul Verlaine, and not neglecting "the new American continent," which "despite the briefness of its literary history, did not exclude those who sang the praises of this love, [mainly] through the pen of its poet Walt Whit-

128. ʿAbd al-Rahman Sidqi, *Alhan al-Han, Abu Nuwas fi Hayatih al-Lahiyyah* [The Melodies of the Tavern: Abu Nuwas in His Whimsical Life] (1947; Cairo: Dar al-Maʿarif al-Misriyyah, 1957).
129. Ibid., 3.
130. Ibid., 275.
131. Adam Mez, *The Renaissance of Islam*, translated from the German by Salahuddin Khuda Bakhsh and D. S. Margoliouth (Patna: Jubilee Printing and Publishing House, 1937), 358.
132. Sidqi, *Alhan al-Han*, 422.

man."[133] He referenced Havelock Ellis about the artistic inclinations among "educated inverts," providing as an example medieval Arab musicians and singers. Sidqi was careful to explain that inclination toward youthful boys did not always elicit a sexual act. He cited the *Symposium* and Platonic love as examples of this. The reason for his digression into the history and medical explanations of "sexual deviance" was to "specify the location of Abu Nuwas in the classes of those with sexual deviance." Listing the three "groupings," those attracted to the other sex exclusively, those attracted to the same sex exclusively, and those attracted to both sexes, he ventured to prove that Abu Nuwas belonged to the exclusive same-sex category.

While Sidqi marshals evidence to support his theory that Abu Nuwas refused to marry, he ignores other evidence that he did marry and begot children. He provides a psychoanalytically influenced summary of the poet's childhood, insisting that his father was an Arab who died while Abu Nuwas was a toddler. Identified as the causes for his sexual predilections are his mother's initial excessive love, which was tempered after she remarried, with traumatic consequences for the child, combined with the nature of society at the time Abu Nuwas was growing up and the widespread practice of the love of youthful boys among its literati.[134] Sidqi discounted Abu Nuwas's love poems for many a concubine as of the wishful variety and that such love was never consummated.[135] Throughout, Sidqi maintained for the most part the objective, albeit sympathetic, tone he deployed in his earlier study, although he would refer to sex with youthful boys occasionally as a "vice" and as "sexual deviance," more generally, and cited Western medicine, that it was an "ailment."[136]

Concern about the "deviant" desires of Abu Nuwas exploded in the 1950s with the publication of two psychoanalytic studies of the poet. In 1953, Egyptian Arabic literature professor Muhammad al-Nuwayhi (1917–80) published a psychoanalytic investigation into the life of Abu Nuwas that can only be compared to Freud's study of Leonardo da Vinci in terms of the breadth and depth of the analysis and al-Nuwayhi's sensitivity to and sympathy for Abu Nuwas and his poetry. After postulating the sexual nature of Abu Nuwas's "fetishistic" relationship to wine (khamr) in the Freudian sense, al-Nuwayhi, who obtained his doctorate in Arabic literature at the University of London's School of Oriental and African Studies (he would later teach at American University in Cairo and as visiting professor at Harvard and Princeton), set out to investi-

133. Ibid., 280.
134. Ibid., 289–91.

135. Ibid., 291–93.
136. Ibid., 273, 277, 283.

gate Abu Nuwas's "sexual deviance." Basing himself on psychoanalysis as well as other European studies in biology, sociology, and culture, al-Nuwayhi, a modernist literary critic who advocated the liberation of women, posited three causes for sexual deviance—physiological, psychological, and social—which could be present in concert or alone in each person "afflicted with this illness." In this, he was echoing Sidqi's analysis. Al-Nuwayhi, like many of our authors, was interested in the link between sexual desires and civilizations. He theorized that sexual deviance was a feature of civilizations at their peak and on the verge of decline, as they get afflicted by "many ethical plagues [afat], including the spread of sexual perversion."[137] In this sense, deviance was not the cause of the decline of Abbasid civilization but an effect of such decline. Al-Nuwayhi's interest in the question of civilization and sexuality was paramount. He provided a brief account of sexual deviance in the history of ancient Egypt, Greece, and modern Europe. He also postulated, following Western sources (including Somerset Maugham and Aldous Huxley, inter alia), that sexual deviance was more frequent in artistic and intellectual circles.[138] He listed Socrates and André Gide as examples, "but we will not speak of people who are alive, as speaking of them is unacceptable."[139]

Delving into the case of Abu Nuwas, al-Nuwayhi pointed to much evidence about Abu Nuwas's "feminine" constitution manifesting in physical delicateness and softness that could indicate physiological causes for his deviance. However, al-Nuwayhi was not convinced by the evidence and launched an investigation into Abu Nuwas's childhood and upbringing (psychological causes) as well as the culture and circumstances of his epoch (social causes), which he considered "sufficient to explain his deviance."[140] Indeed his analysis identified Abu Nuwas's childhood as a departure point. The poet's father died and his mother, who worked to support him, married another man later. For al-Nuwayhi the loss of Abu Nuwas's primacy in the life of his parents, especially that of his mother, was the main childhood factor that contributed to Abu Nuwas's deviance. True to psychoanalysis's overdetermination of causes to any sexual condition, al-Nuwayhi then moved to analyze the society that Abu Nuwas entered in his teenage years. He found it to be a society where sexual deviance was widespread and in whose "claws many men

137. Muhammad al-Nuwayhi, *Nafsiyyat Abi Nuwas* [The Psychology of Abu Nuwas] (1953; Cairo: Dar al-Fikr, 1970), 72.
138. Ibid., 74.
139. Ibid.
140. Ibid., 78.

were caught."[141] He did not, like other authors, attribute sexual deviance to Persian origins, and al-Nuwayhi insisted that such attribution was wrong. He posited the mixture of the many civilizations, cultures, and religions under Islamic tutelage as what had contributed to the rise of sexual deviance on a societal scale. This was especially so as the Islamic empire rose in exponential speed from a desert-based conglomerate of tribes into a world empire in a short time of less than a century, an outcome it was able to achieve due to its mingling of all these civilizations and its learning from them.[142] It is in introducing this cultural/environmental aspect that al-Nuwayhi diversified the causes of deviance, as surely

we cannot claim that all these people were afflicted with the physiological perversion that causes deviance, as such pathological conditions afflict only few individuals. Nor can we discern in their upbringing the same things we discerned in the childhood of Abu Nuwas . . . But we do find the correct explanation if we remember what scholars have said about the moral degeneration [inhilal] that afflicts many civilizations and if we remember what they say about the links between the aesthetic and the sexual affects.[143]

Having specified the exact nature of what binds civilization and sexual affect, al-Nuwayhi then posited the abundance of singing girls and concubines in the Abbasid period as having caused many men to consider sex with them "cheap and vulgar." As a result, "they began to seek other ways to vent their erotic emotions . . . which they did not find in the vulgar concubines . . . and found in boys. What increased the pleasure of this infatuation was its novelty, strangeness, and its unfamiliarity, which had a touch of innovation that the artistic mind appreciates."[144] If many poets and cultural figures at the time followed this new fad, Abu Nuwas's deviance "surpassed all of them in intensity and violence" and "increased the fieriness and exhaustion [tahaluk] of his *ghazal* poetry for youthful boys so much so that he became the greatest known figure in this genre of Arabic poetry."[145] His deviance was such on account of the combination of causes affecting him, namely, his own childhood experience and the social environment surrounding him.

Al-Nuwayhi posited Abu Nuwas's "unresolved" oedipal conflict with his mother as "arrested development"[146] that had been compounded by societal forces that corrupted him further. Thus, while al-Nuwayhi

141. Ibid., 88.
142. Ibid.
143. Ibid., 87.

144. Ibid., 89.
145. Ibid., 90–91.
146. Ibid., 157.

posited deviance as a feature of all civilizations at a certain period of their development or decline, at the level of the individual, he posited it, pace Freud, as marking not decline but arrested development. The shuttling between the individual and the societal in this case is constant across al-Nuwayhi's analysis. Like ʿAmmar before him, he, for example, exonerated Abu Nuwas of the accusation that he had pioneered the love of youthful boys, writing *ghazal* poetry for them, or his infatuation with wine: "Abu Nuwas did not introduce to his epoch any corruption that it did not already possess."[147] His societal sin was to declare his activities openly and to question the hypocrisy of so many pretenders of piety, who in the dark would indulge in the same practices for which they condemned him.[148] Al-Nuywahi wanted to sensitize his readers to the greatness of Abu Nuwas's integrity and his fine sensibility. When Taha Husayn later criticized al-Nuywahi's use of the psychoanalytic method as unjust to Abu Nuwas,[149] he responded in disbelief that anyone would draw such a conclusion from his analysis. Indeed, if previous authors were concerned about Abu Nuwas's bawdiness, by pathologizing him as a "deviant" (in addition to Abu Nuwas's fetishism and sexual deviance, al-Nuwayhi diagnosed him with manic depression in his later years), al-Nuwayhi was able to rescue him for *turath*. He insisted that "my study pulsates with what I feel toward him of sympathy, of asking [others] for compassion [in judging him], and of attempting to convince the reader to adopt a similar attitude towards him."[150] The story of Abu Nuwas that al-Nuwayhi narrated was not a story of a poet with agency who willfully chose a debauched lifestyle but rather a story of civilizational decline that produced a deviant culture of which the poet was a mere effect, if a tragic one.

Within a few months of the publication of al-Nuwayhi's book, another prominent lay historian, literary critic, and prolific Egyptian author published another book psychoanalyzing Abu Nuwas. ʿAbbas Mahmud al-ʿAqqad's *Abu Nuwas, al-Hasan Bin Hani*ʾ[151] launched an in-

---

147. Ibid., 166.

148. Ibid., 168.

149. See Taha Husayn, "Israf," in *Al-Ahram*, 23 May, 1953, republished in *Khisam wa Naqd* [Disputation and Critique], in *Al-Majmuʿah al-Kamilah li-Muʾallafat al-Duktur Taha Husayn* [The Complete Collected Works of Dr. Taha Husayn] (1960; Beirut: Dar al-Kitab al-Lubnani, 1974), vol. 11, part 2, 678–82. Husayn, hostile to psychoanalysis, objected to its use in literary criticism.

150. Muhammad al-Nuwayhi, "Al-Adab bayn al-Fahm wa al-Tadhawwuq" [Literature between Comprehension and Savoring], in al-Nuwayhi, *Nafsiyyat*, 179. Al-Nuwayhi includes a number of responses to critics in the 1970 second edition of the book.

151. ʿAbbas Mahmud al-ʿAqqad, *Abu Nuwas, al-Hasan Bin Hani*ʾ, *Dirasah fi al-Tahlil al-Nafsani wa al-Naqd al-Tarikhi* [A Study in Psychoanalysis and Historical Criticism] (1953; Cairo: Kitab al-Hilal, 1960).

vestigation of the causes of the myths that had always surrounded Abu Nuwas, including his unique fame, down through the ages, even among the "illiterate," the many false stories and poetry attributed to him by medieval authors, and reports about him, not only in Iraq where he resided, but as far as North Africa and Egypt. Al-'Aqqad compared his fame to that of Oscar Wilde—"irrespective of the artistic worth of Oscar Wilde, his fame surpassed his worth considerably" with studies and translations of his works into myriad languages.[152] For al-'Aqqad, the mythology and fame surrounding the personality of Abu Nuwas have covered up and not revealed "the truth of Abu Nuwas," which his book would endeavor to uncover.[153]

Al-'Aqqad (1889–1964), a conservative anti-Communist (and anti-Nazi) whose formal education ended with primary school, was a self-taught intellectual and popularizer of Islamic and Arab histories whose disputes with contemporary Egyptian intellectuals are legendary.[154] In his study of Abu Nuwas, al-'Aqqad posited the poet as having what he called a "paradigmatic personality" (shakhsiyyah namudhajiyyah) that sought the "forbidden fruits" of his times,[155] and thus was afflicted, not with fetishism or sexual deviance, as the latter failed to account for his overall behavior according to al-'Aqqad; rather what Abu Nuwas suffered from was a more generalized deviance, namely, "narcissism," a condition that al-'Aqqad set out to unravel and by which he wanted to demonstrate its comprehensive explanatory power of Abu Nuwas's behavior.[156] Abu Nuwas, insisted al-'Aqqad, was not a "homosexual," as he desired both youthful boys *and* women.[157] Unlike al-Nuwayhi and others who did not trust the genuineness of Abu Nuwas's *ghazal* poetry for women (mostly concubines) and who considered it an affectation compared to his "more" genuine love of boys, al-'Aqqad would not have any of it. Abu Nuwas clearly liked both sexes, and those critics who concluded otherwise forced that conclusion by their initial misunderstanding of the nature of his sexual deviance, which they deemed to mean an ex-

---

152. Ibid., 29. Al-'Aqqad's judgment of Oscar Wilde's fame was not unlike that of Max Nordau, who claimed that "Wilde obtained, by his buffoonery and mummery, a notoriety in the whole Anglo-Saxon world that his poems and dramas would never have acquired for him," in *Degeneration* (New York: Howard Fertig, 1968), 319.

153. Al-'Aqqad, *Abu Nuwas*, 29.

154. For an informative memoir of al-'Aqqad's views and intellectual battles, see Anis Mansur, *Fi Salun al-'Aqqad kanat lana Ayyam* [We Had Many a Day in Al-'Aqqad's Salon] (1983; Cairo: Dar al-Shuruq, 2005).

155. Al-'Aqqad, *Abu Nuwas*, 28–29.

156. Ibid., 35.

157. Ibid., 42.

clusive attraction to members of the same sex.[158] In that, Abu Nuwas, al-ʿAqqad averred, was not unlike Oscar Wilde, who was married and had two children and who was considered an example of "dandyism." In a move that posited modern Europe as reminiscent of the Arab past, Wilde, al-ʿAqqad wrote, "was the modern copy of Abu Nuwas."[159] He diagnosed Wilde with narcissism and specifically with exhibitionism and proceeded to cite Gide's account of Wilde to illustrate the latter's exhibitionism and love of forbidden fruit: "He went to a small town in North Africa that is frequented by seekers of leisure and came out of it telling his friend André Gide: 'My ultimate wish is that I succeeded in corrupting this village.'"[160]

Al-ʿAqqad reviewed modern psychiatry's exposition of the condition of "homosexuality," a term he cited in English, and launched into a review of the literature of endocrinology to explore physiological causes of sexual deviance, not only of the "homosexual" variety but also of the "narcissistic" one. Al-ʿAqqad then discussed with much erudition psychoanalytic and other psychological literature that, like him, criticized Freud's account of narcissism (he seemed to like Karen Horney's account).[161] For al-ʿAqqad, narcissism is the key diagnosis because it included under its umbrella all the symptoms that Abu Nuwas showed, namely, exhibitionism, "autoerotic gratification" (he is said to have reveled in his own looks and would challenge anyone to write better poetry), that he desired women, and desired men both as "actor" and as "reactor." Al-ʿAqqad was quick to point out how psychiatrists had devised different treatments for homosexual "actors" and "reactors," as each had a different set of causes of their conditions.[162]

Al-ʿAqqad concluded, like al-Nuwayhi before him, that Abu Nuwas had some physiological conditions that predisposed him to his "illness": his presumed delicateness, softness, postadolescent abundance of hair (on his head), which he like women and children never lost as most "men do"; and his lisp, a voice with a certain raspiness that developed beyond childhood but fell short of adulthood.[163] It is noteworthy that neither al-Nuwayhi nor al-ʿAqqad considered other evidence of Abu Nuwas's athletic abilities and physical fitness, inferred from a poem about a game of sawalijah (sing. sawlajan) that he played, which was cited by the medieval writer Hamzah al-Isbahani. The game is played on horseback with the players holding a *sawlajan* (a staff with a curved end) used

158. Ibid., 168–69.
159. Ibid., 60.
160. Ibid., 59.

161. Ibid., 86–89.
162. Ibid., 115–16.
163. Ibid., 89–93.

to hit a ball toward the opponent's side—most likely the origin of what would later become polo in Europe. Abu Nuwas is said to have played this game skillfully and would mostly win against his opponents.[164]

Still for al-ʿAqqad, the presumed physiological conditions combined with his childhood upbringing, the social environment, and the epoch in which he lived (al-ʿAqqad provided a historical account of the political and cultural life that Abu Nuwas confronted). While each of these causes was not sufficient to produce all the types of "deviance" that afflicted Abu Nuwas, all of them combined produced his narcissism.[165] Al-ʿAqqad's study, like al-Nuwayhi's, expressed much sympathy and appreciation for Abu Nuwas the person and the poet. In his conclusion, he affirmed the goodness of Abu Nuwas who helped and supported others in need and had no evil proclivities: "His affliction was one of weakness and not that of evil and harm."[166] Al-ʿAqqad concluded by reaffirming the importance of Abu Nuwas's aesthetic contributions as central to any evaluation of the poet. He ended his book by posing a question: "Have the failings of Abu Nuwas increased the amount of vice in this world? [Well,] the amount may vary depending on the appraiser, but all appraisers will agree on the amount of spiritual fortune and eloquence [bayan] that he increased."[167] Aesthetics, in the last instance, do seem to trump morality. Abu Nuwas is thus preserved as part of Arab civilizational legacy.

As in the case of al-Nuwayhi's study, Taha Husayn did not like al-ʿAqqad's book and accused him of placing the poet in an "iron cast." Al-ʿAqqad was not impressed. He waxed sardonic wondering whether his analysis would have been more accurate had he used a "silk cast" instead.[168]

If certain liberal thinkers were to tackle Abu Nuwas psychoanalytically, Arab Marxists would have a different take on both Abu Nuwas and, like many Western Marxists, on the psychoanalytic method itself. Lebanese Marxist Husayn Muruwwah responded to al-Nuwayhi and al-ʿAqqad in less than friendly fashion in a 1965 book of literary essays positing the "realist method" as the proper one to use instead of psychoanalysis.[169] While al-Nuwayhi and al-ʿAqqad published their books within a year of the Egyptian coup d'état that toppled the monarchy

---

164. On the poem that Abu Nuwas wrote on the occasion of winning a game of *sawlajan*, see Mubarak, *Al-Muwazanah bayna al-Shuʿaraʾ*, 349–57. Mubarak cites Hamzah al-Asbahani as his source.

165. Ibid., 116.

166. Ibid., 200.

167. Ibid., 201.

168. The dispute is cited in Mansur, *Fi Salun al-ʿAqqad*, 12.

169. See Husayn Muruwwah, *Dirasat Naqdiyyah, fi Duʾ al-Manhaj al-Waqiʿi* [Critical Studies in the Light of the Realist Method] (Beirut: Maktabat al-Maʿarif, 1965), 231–63.

and declared a revolution, Muruwwah's response would be published a decade after a leftist anticolonial nationalism, inaugurated by the coup-leading Free Egyptian Officers, became hegemonic across the Arab world. While the new discourse saw itself as socialist, it remained fiercely anti-Communist, rendering critiques like Muruwwah's less welcome.

The major objection that Muruwwah posited was the "bourgeois" na-ture of psychoanalysis as a method that ignored social conditions and concentrated on individual experience. He accused al-Nuwayhi of fall-ing in that trap when al-Nuwayhi in fact had accounted for and inte-grated social conditions in his analysis, as he himself would assert in his later response to Muruwwah.[170] Muruwwah also questioned the basis on which al-Nuwayhi could claim that Abu Nuwas's *ghazal* poems for boys were sincere while his poems for women were cold and insincere, at-tempting to prove that indeed Abu Nuwas had strong desires for women for which his attraction for boys was mere substitution.[171] Muruwwah's major point, however, was that the "phenomenon" of Abu Nuwas did not result from processes located in the "unconscious,"[172] but could be better explained as resulting "from existing social relations in the poet's surroundings and in his epoch, that is, from the widespread phenomena of moral degeneration [inhilal] existing in those surroundings then, in addition to the phenomena of dissimulation and hypocrisy prevalent among the ruling groups and the rich who used to commit the ugliest of offences, while pretending to be the protectors of morals and religious laws, leading Abu Nuwas to ridicule them and to challenge their dis-simulation and hypocrisy."[173] Indeed, this was part of the explanation offered by al-Nuwayhi. Muruwwah, however, more attuned to norma-tive judgments than al-Nuwayhi and al-'Aqqad, was insistent that Abu Nuwas was no more "deviant" than the society within which he lived, as "when we describe Abu Nuwas's conduct as deviant, we mean de-viant in relation to absolute moral values—assuming this is the right expression—but were we to attribute the man's conduct to the conduct of the social group with which he came in contact and to whose lives he tied his, whether in Basra, Kufah, or Baghdad, then we would not find his conduct anomalous [shudhudh] from the conduct of that group whose deviations [inhirafat] were abundant then."[174] Thus, unlike stan-

---

170. Al-Nuwayhi's response is included in his 1970 second and expanded edition of his book on Abu Nuwas entitled *Al-Marksiyyah wa 'ilm al-nafs al-hadith* [Marxism and Modern Psychology], in al-Nuwayhi, *Nafsiyyat*, 240.
171. Muruwwah, *Dirasat Naqdiyyah*, 240–45.
172. Ibid., 250.
173. Ibid., 248.
174. Ibid., 257.

dard Arab nationalist narratives that celebrated the glory of the Abbasid period by citing the opulence of the ruling classes, Muruwwah, committed to class analysis, was more interested in debunking civilizational commitments in favor of class analysis that exposed the poverty and oppression of the majority of the people during such glorious periods. The problem with Abu Nuwas, therefore, according to Muruwwah, was not "deviance" but his "defeatism," which manifested in his "immersing himself in sensual pleasures excessively without concerning himself with other matters afflicting his confused society, of many tragedies, concerns, injustices, and corruption."[175]

Where Muruwwah and al-Nuwayhi agreed was in dispelling the accusation made by many nationalist literary historians, Ahmad Amin included, that Abu Nuwas was an anti-Arab "Shuʿubi" (a reference to those who, in the Abbasid period, expressed pro-Persian and anti-Arab chauvinist views), which made it easier for nationalists to expel him outside the perimeter of Arab cultural production. In response, Muruwwah, like al-Nuwayhi, quoted many of Abu Nuwas's poems in which he praised the Arabs and insulted some Persians to counter the verses in which he denigrated Arabs and praised Persians, which are often cited by those who claim him as anti-Arab. Muruwwah also cited the attempt by medieval and modern historians to label any creative figure from the classical period whom they did not like a "Shuʿubi" as doing a disservice to Arab history. In this vein, he cited the question marks placed on the paternal origins of Abu Nuwas, which vacillate between his being an "authentic" Arab or a *mawla* (originating outside the Arabian Peninsula) as not particularly helpful.[176] Thus, despite their differences, Muruwwah and al-Nuwayhi were both committed to preserving Abu Nuwas for *turath.*

If Abu Nuwas caused anxiety to modern Arab intellectuals, he was also a curiosity. His life was so intriguing to modern Arabs that Egyptian poet and journalist Kamil al-Shinnawi wrote a book in 1968 titled *The Confessions of Abu Nuwas,* in which he traveled back in time and interviewed Abu Nuwas about all the rumors and myths surrounding him.[177] Attempting to persuade Abu Nuwas to "confess the truth," al-Shinnawi informed him that a whole slew of "European" men of letters had "confessed," including "Saint Augustine [apparently al-Shinnawi did not know that Augustine was born in Algeria], Jean Jacques Rous-

175. Ibid.
176. Husayn Muruwwah, "Abu Nuwas wa al-Shuʿubiyyah" (1962), in *Turathuna, Kayfa Naʿirifuh* [Our Heritage, How Do We Know It?] (Beirut: Muʾassassat al-Abhath al-ʿArabiyyah, 1985), 263–73.
177. Kamil al-Shinnawi, *Iʿtirafat Abi Nuwas* (Cairo: Dar al-Maʿarif bi-Misr, 1968).

seau, Oscar Wilde, and André Gide . . . they confessed to what had befallen them in their youth . . . about the violations they experienced . . .
they spoke about their sexual deviance!"[178] It is assumed by al-Shinnawi
that Abu Nuwas understood the term (shudhudh) as somehow meaningful despite its anachronism, especially as al-Shinnawi later asked him
about whether he had "natural" or "deviant" love affairs when he lived
in the city of Basra.[179] What is important, however, in this comparison
was the isolation of Abu Nuwas's sexual practices from his Abbasid surroundings, and comparing them to European practices. In this way al-
Shinnawi saved *turath* from being implicated in them.

Al-Shinnawi was fascinated by Abu Nuwas and went to pains to alleviate his readers' presumed anxiety about the latter's compromising his
manhood. When he interrogated (and there is no other word for it) Abu
Nuwas about his relationship with his mentor, the poet Walibah bin al-
Hubab, the fictional Abu Nuwas recited a story of rape wherein Walibah
gave Abu Nuwas the choice of sodomizing him or stabbing him with a
dagger (the book has a pictorial illustration to dramatize the effect). The
fictional Abu Nuwas naturally chose death but was then seduced by the
poetry of Walibah and thus compromised himself.[180] Examining medieval sources, with which al-Shinnawi showed familiarity, this story turns
out never to have taken place. In fact, in ibn Manzur's (A.D. 1232–1311)
book about Abu Nuwas, as is the case in other sources, we learn that
after Abu Nuwas sought out Walibah and met him, Walibah became
enamored of the young Abu Nuwas.

[Abu Nuwas] walked with him. When they arrived at his house, after they drank and
ate, Walibah wanted him. When he disrobed him and saw the beauty of his body, he
could not but kiss him on the anus. Abu Nuwas farted. So he said to him: 'What is
this, sly boy?" He answered: "I did not want the known proverb to be lost and not to
come true, namely: "The penalty for he who kisses the anus is its farts." His admiration and love for him grew further . . . When Abu Nuwas hardened and grew older
and understood his own value and favor, he said: "Oh, what wonder! A brilliant poet
whom Walibah ibn al-Hubab fucks."[181]

178. Ibid., 18–19.
179. Ibid., 49.
180. Ibid., 26.
181. Ibn Manzur, *Akhbar Abi Nuwas, Tarikhuh, Nawadiruh, Shi'ruh, Mujunuh* [The Stories of Abu
Nuwas, His History, His Anecdotes, His Poetry, and His Bawdiness], ed. Muhammad 'Abd al-Rasul
Ibrahim and 'Abbas al-Sharbini (Cairo: Matba'at al-I'timad, 1924), vol. 1, 9. Abu Nuwas's comment
has a modern parallel in Joe Orton's declaration in his diaries about a sexual encounter with a
Moroccan boy: "So we had sex, or at least I lay and allowed him to fuck me, and thought as his

Al-Shinnawi was so intent on redeeming Abu Nuwas's masculinity that he portrayed this shameless poet, whose poetry described in meticulous detail the pleasures he sought and experienced, as being so overtaken with embarrassment when confessing his sin of being the "reactor" in his same-sex contact with Walibah that he bowed his head to avoid looking al-Shinnawi in the face.[182]

Unlike al-ʿAqqad and Muruwwah, but like al-Nuwayhi, al-Shinnawi was convinced of the fakeness of Abu Nuwas's desires for women. He made Abu Nuwas confess that he had never had sex with any woman at all and that all references to his children in his poetry were fake, as he never had any.[183] Yet, al-Shinnawi was nonplussed throughout the interview by any of the revelations of Abu Nuwas, as he was only interested in the details of his life and not in judging him. Perhaps the only time al-Shinnawi's less than liberal views about sex manifested was when he forced this fictional Abu Nuwas to confess to coming back empty-handed from his Egyptian sojourn, having failed to sully the honor of Egypt's youthful boys. Abu Nuwas obliged and told a story of being actually beaten up by beautiful Egyptian boys whom he sought for pleasure on the beach of the Nile River but who defended their honor valiantly.[184] This fictional story contradicts medieval biographical accounts of Abu Nuwas that spoke of his refusal to come near the Nile when he was in Egypt for fear of its formidable crocodiles.[185] Still, al-Shinnawi's fictional account can be partly corroborated by medieval sources. In his book of anecdotes about Abu Nuwas, ibn Manzur cited a story about Abu Nuwas and handsome Egyptian boys, three of whom he had encountered in the marketplace.[186] Abu Nuwas, according to ibn Manzur's account, pretended to be a porter in order to carry their bags. Once at their home, the boys invited him to spend the night at their house. During the night, to al-Shinnawi's certain horror, Abu Nuwas penetrated all three of them anally while they were sleeping. Al-Shinnawi's fictional account was clearly based on a good amount of reading of medieval sources. As he wrote during the heyday of Arab nationalism, al-Shinnawi's doctoring of the story of the Egyptian youthful boys demonstrates that his liberal approach had its limits, and they were clearly nationalist limits.

---

prick shot in and he kissed my neck, back, and shoulders, that it was a most unappetizing position for world-famous artist to be in," Joe Orton, *The Orton Diaries*, ed. John Lahr (New York: Perennial Harper, 1986), 174.

182. Ibid., 28.
183. Ibid., 53.
184. Ibid., 56.
185. On this, see Sidqi, *Abu Nuwas*, 139.
186. See ibn Manzur, *Akhbar Abi Nuwas*, 244–48.

To Emulate or Not to Emulate: That Is the Question

While al-'Aqqad and many others, as we saw, compared Abu Nuwas to Gide and posited Wilde as the "modern Abu Nuwas," Syrian poet and literary critic Adonis, contra these authors, would consider Abu Nuwas as "the Baudelaire of the Arabs," anachronistically rendering Europe, not Arab-Islamic civilization, the reference. The Baudelaire comparison is instructive in a number of other ways. For Adonis, it was not Abu Nuwas's "deviance" that compared to modern European poets and writers like Wilde and Gide, but rather Abu Nuwas's declaration that "my religion is mine," which Adonis identified as a protosecular invocation that is "the cry of the modern world since Baudelaire."[187] In this sense, Adonis posited Abu Nuwas as a "presentist" poet whose sense of time is always of the present: "This is why he fears no punishment but rather commits what would bring punishment about."[188]

Adonis's analysis of Arabic poetry is indeed of a different order than what we have seen so far, focusing on the philosophical and the aesthetic, rather than the sociological and the normative.[189] For Adonis, the poetry of Abu Nuwas and his contemporaries differed from *jahiliyyah* poetry in important regards, as the earlier poetry was characterized by its acceptance and celebration of its culture while the later one questioned it.[190] The new poetry rebelled against the poetic style of its predecessor as well as against the hegemonic social values of its own time. While Adonis explained the change sociologically, through the increase of population and its concentration in the city, which led to social "fracture and perdition," his interests remained philosophical. He explained that as a result of these sociological changes "the movement of true poetry, amidst the abundant inherited rubble, was no longer linked to politics, morals, or predominant public habits, as much as it became linked to the movement of civilizational evolution."[191] Here, it is not

187. Adunis, *Muqaddimah lil-Shi'r al-'Arabi* [Introduction to Arab Poetry] (Beirut: Dar al-'Awda, 1983), 47. The book was originally published in 1971. I should mention here that he compares not only Abu Nuwas to modern French poets but also, for example, the poet Abu Tammam, whom Adonis described as "the Mallarmé of the Arabs," 47.

188. Ibid., 48.

189. His analysis of Abu Nuwas's poetry and import owe much to the analysis of Algerian scholar and professor Jamel Eddine Bencheikh (1930–2005) who wrote about Abu Nuwas and his Bacchic poems in French. See Jamel Bencheikh, "Poésie Bachiques d'Abu Nuwas, Thèmes et Personnages" [Abu Nuwas's Bacchic Poems, Themes and Personalities], in *Bulletin D'Études Orientales* (Damascus) 18 (1963–64): 1–84. See also his entry on Abu Nuwas and Khamriyyat in the *Encyclopedia of Islam* (Leiden: Brill Academic Publishers, 2001).

190. Adunis, *Muqaddimah lil-Shi'r al-'Arabi*, 37.

191. Ibid., 38.

civilization and sexuality that are linked à la al-Nuwayhi, but rather poetry and civilization. Thus, the old poetic formula of the presence of the other and the absence of the I in the poem was reversed in this period of questioning: "Poetry came to be established on the basis of the presence of the I and the absence of the other, that is, on innovativeness and renewal, and estrangement. The poet had become separated, a chasm exists between him and others."[192] Indeed to many poets, especially Abu Nuwas, cynicism (*sukhriyah*) came to replace tragedy so much so that in his poetry, "cynicism became his conception of the world [around him], and [a certain] vision with which he wanted to replace philosophy and morals."[193] Thus, Abu Nuwas's sense of time, as that of the eternal present in which the "salvation of man" is obtainable, informs his "openness . . . to joy, happiness, and pleasure."[194]

What Adonis is interested in is not some sexual "deviance" or nonnormative sexual desires and practices but rather the centrality of wine in a society that prohibits its drinking and its symbolic importance to Abu Nuwas, the poet of the *khamriyyat* (bacchic poems) par excellence.[195] In a celebratory statement of the revolutionary impact of Abu Nuwas's poetry, Adonis asserted:

Abu Nuwas is the poet of sin because he is the poet of liberty. When the gates of liberty close, sin becomes sacred. The Nuwasite refuses to be content except with what is prohibited and its pleasures, as sin provides him with a comfort that he overglorifies, making him no longer accept ordinary sins, but demand the wonderful sins of which he can boast, losing the other sins. Sin, for him, within the life that he was living, is an existential necessity, because it was the symbol of liberty, the symbol of rebellion and salvation.[196]

Thus, unlike Taha Husayn, Adonis feared not the modern emulation of Abu Nuwas; he rather posited the imperative to imitate his revolutionary spirit, what Adonis would call "that living force which moves the world."[197] If Taha Husayn sought the modern meaning of literature as separate from that of morals as a basis for rescuing Abu Nuwas, for Adonis, this separation was itself instantiated by Abu Nuwas himself long before the advent of modernity. For Abu Nuwas, Adonis insisted, "con-

192. Ibid., 39.
193. Ibid., 40. "Sukhriyah" means literally "sarcasm" but also retains and is often better rendered by "cynicism."
194. Ibid., 48.
195. Ibid., 51–52.
196. Ibid., 52.
197. Ibid., 110.

firms the separation of poetry from morals and religion, refusing the solutions of his epoch, declaring new morals, the morals of free action and
free vision: the morals of sin." In this sense "the Nuwassite is a person
who does not face God with the religion of the group, but with his own
religion, his own innocence, and his own sin. Perhaps, from this perspective, [Abu Nuwas] is the most perfect model for modernity in our poetic
heritage."[198] With such a declaration, Adonis overturns the cautious assertions of Taha Husayn, spoken at less turbulent times half a century earlier. Writing after the 1967 Arab-Israeli War and its consequent malaise
across Arab society, Adonis seemed to seek a model for questioning the
hegemonic social values of his own time. For an ardent critic of the Arab
present like Adonis (who often relies on Orientalist axioms), this could
perhaps inaugurate the "evolution of civilization," which he saw Abbasid
poetry as reflecting and bringing about in that past epoch. Adonis's interest in civilizational evolution in the present, which would transcend the
malaise that he discerned, is quite explicit. For this to occur, it was not
poetic style that should be emulated but the poetic élan that characterizes revolutionary change, for the poetic needs of the contemporary period are particular to "us": "It is natural for us, as we are in a civilizational
stage that differs from that of our ancestors, that we have, if we are indeed alive, a particular way of expression, and particular poetic forms."[199]

If Adonis seemed unconcerned with the sexual life of the early Abbasid period, he seemed to credit such eroticism, at least partially, in
his judgment of later Arabic poetry, from the years A.D. 1000 to 1900:
"Arab life contracted during these nine centuries and fell prisoner to the
palaces, gardens, concubines, and related things . . . Poetic legacy itself
crumbled and was reformulated in bits of crafty decorations. Nothing
was added to it. It was simply extended in form by the force of crafty
play and the force of necessity, which life in the city began to impose,
and around the palaces and their environs."[200] The transformation of
poetry from art into a craft arrested the development of poetry so much
so that even "what came to be called 'the epoch of the renaissance' did
not help in exiting to the space of real poetry. On the contrary, as far
as poetry was concerned, it was a continuation of decadence. Indeed, it
was an era of emulation, imitation, and artificiality that the age of decadence [a reference to the centuries of Ottoman rule] looks like a golden
age in comparison with it."[201] Thus, Adonis was not against inventive
emulation as such, as he saw Abu Nuwas as a "model" to be emulated

198. Ibid., 53.
199. Ibid., 109.

200. Ibid., 70.
201. Ibid., 76.

in modernity. It was the emulation of poetry through emptying it of content by extending form that destroyed the potential for revolutionary renewal until the twentieth century. What Adonis sought was the emulation of the revolutionary in poetry, precisely to advance a civilizational leap forward in the present as Abu Nuwas had done to early Abbasid civilization. In this regard Adonis stands alone among those who addressed the import of Abu Nuwas, in placing him solely within the history of Arabic poetry as a force of civilizational "evolution" rather than "arrest" or "decline." His reading of Abu Nuwas as the poet who stands alone against the tribe is informed by Adonis's own identification with the individualism of Western Romantic poets. This aside, Adonis remained seemingly unconcerned with Abu Nuwas's place in the history of Arab sexual desires and practices.

The anxiety that Abu Nuwas caused to modern Arab scholars would not abate after the age of formal colonialism ended and the age of independence set in, as our discussion of al-Shinnawi and Adonis demonstrated. As we will see in the next chapter, however, nationalists would undertake important revisions regarding Abu Nuwas's place in Arab civilization. Still, the important transformation of Abu Nuwas in half a century from someone who might be dangerous to emulate into someone whose emulation is necessary testifies to the varied nature of opinions regarding the future of the Arab world. The fact that these opinions were often informed by the different political conditions within which they were expressed is a clear indication of the dynamic interaction that Arab intellectuals and scholars continued to have with the society in which they lived and worked and with theoretical methods and new sources of knowledge elaborated in the West. The postcolonial debate that was ushered in once the Egyptian "revolution" of 1952 consolidated itself and set itself a clear direction in the late 1950s would provide more impetus to this dynamism.

TWO

Remembrances
of Desires Past

From the turn of the century to the 1950s, Arab scholars
actively excavated and scrutinized what they identified as
past civilizational documents that formed the heritage of
the present and the future. As we saw in the previous chapter, they were assisted in their endeavors by new European
concepts of civilization, culture, decadence, degradation,
degeneration, heritage, sex, and deviance, among others.
As in European scholarship, these concepts would be internalized and institutionalized as solid scholarly concepts
that required little if any questioning. Indeed, even Arab
painters, who on occasion sought to represent the lives of
the medieval Arabs, would do so following the Orientalist
model (see, for example, some of the work of Syrian Tawfiq Tariq, 1875–1940, Lebanese Habib Surur, 1860–1938,
and Lebanese Mustafa Farrukh, 1901–57, inter alia). As we
will see in this chapter, many new innovative ideas and
approaches would be used to shed light on the past, and
all of them without exception would continue to posit the
classical civilization of the Arabs and Islam as a foundation
for the present. They would do so through use of the very
same concepts that entered the lexicon of modern Arab
scholarship from the *Nahdah* to the end of formal European colonialism. The centrality of the notions of civilization and culture, the transformations that these concepts
would continue to undergo following European uses, and
their emergence as the questions that must be addressed
at all costs informed these postcolonial endeavors. While

the national project of formulating a sustainable civilizational present for modern Arabs against (and after) European colonialism intensified after the end of colonial rule and the ushering in of a new postcolonial order, the epistemological underpinnings of European knowledge, which developed in Europe itself in the age of empire and were (and still are) used against the colonized, remained intact. If anything, these concepts would form the cornerstone of all future debates. The defensiveness of many Arab intellectuals against Orientalism and colonial racist ideas about the Arabs was not only the outcome of the scars European colonialism left behind but also on account of its continued efforts to dominate the Arab world, whether by the very same colonial powers whose rule had formally ended but who were still trying to resuscitate it, namely, Britain and France, or by the United States, whose imperial policies in the Arab world picked up where European colonialism left off.

In this vein, history and history writing became the central instrument for recovering civilizational memory for use in the present. This was hardly particular to Arabs, as the discipline of history that they inherited from nineteenth-century Europe had been put to that use more intensely by European and American nationalisms. Indeed, Arab historians, like anticolonial historians across the formerly colonized world, shared the appreciation for history as a discipline that had major implications for cultural survival against the onslaught of colonial European culture. In this chapter, I explore how the history of Arab "civilization" and "Arab" sexual desires was written and what implications were drawn from it for the present. I will begin by analyzing the work of Salah al-Din al-Munajjid, a representative liberal nationalist with a comparative focus, the ideas of ʿAbd al-Latif Shararah, a nativist nationalist interested in the historical relationship of love to sex, and how he differs from the philosophically liberal approach of Sadiq Jalal al-ʿAzm on the subject. I will then move to examine the work of the leading Islamist thinker Sayyid Qutb, and of Salamah Musa, a maverick social Darwinist feminist and socialist, and then proceed to historian of sexuality Abdelwahab Bouhdiba and the feminist approaches of Nawal al-Saʿdawi and Fatima Mernissi. The writings of these various authors share a commonly determined historicity. They represent an anticolonialism that intensified in the postcolonial period during which many of them wrote and a liberatory social approach whose telos included sexual and gender emancipation. Like the authors we encountered in the previous chapter, civilizational concerns would remain paramount in the thought of all these authors.

A History of Sex

Taha Husayn opened up a debate about the sexual life of the ancient Arabs and in the process produced a whole line of argumentation about heritage and civilization, the benefits of knowledge, the importance of the aesthetic, and the nature of morality. He also outlined a comparative grid of a repressive present and an open past. But if Husayn's and later authors' fascination with and anxiety about Abu Nuwas produced a whole discourse about the nature of the medieval Arab society within which he lived, Salah al-Din al-Munajjid's pioneering *Al-Hayah al-Jinsi-yyah 'ind al-'Arab* (The Sexual Life of the Arabs), published in 1958, was the first attempt to give a comprehensive account of sexual desire and sexual practices in Arab society from the pre-Islamic *jahiliyyah* period to the Abbasid dynasty (sixth–thirteenth centuries A.D.).[1] Al-Munajjid, of Syrian origins, was editor of scores of medieval manuscripts and headed the Arab League's Institute of Arab Manuscripts in the 1950s. The Institute, which was founded in 1946 (Ahmad Amin was one of its founders[2]), had as its main goal the collection of medieval Arabic manuscripts, of which it reportedly owns 24,000. It was based on these manuscripts, largely ignored by Orientalists, that he would write a number of works that dealt with certain aspects of desire and sex in the life of the ancient Arabs, including *Al-Zurafa' wa al-Shahhadhun fi Baghdad wa Baris* (Charmers and Beggars in Baghdad and Paris), published in 1946,[3] *Bayn al-Khulafa' wa al-Khula'a' fi al-'Asr al-'Abbasi* (Between the Caliphs and the Debauched in the Abbasid Period) published in 1957,[4] and *Jamal al-Mar'ah 'ind al-'Arab* (Women's Beauty among the Arabs), published in 1957,[5] all preceding *The Sexual Life of the Arabs*. Al-Munajjid, a liberal Arab nationalist, was keen, as we will see, on the need to revolutionize all aspects of social life in the Arab world. His three books served as dress rehearsal for the later book. Indeed, his effort was pioneering not only in an Arab context but also in a Western context, where such explicit sexual histories remained uncommon until the 1970s.

1. Salah al-Din al-Munajjid, *Al-Hayah al-Jinsiyyah 'ind al-'arab, min al-Jahiliyyah ila Awakhir al-Qarn al-Rabi' al-hijri* [The Sexual Life of the Arabs: Since Jahiliyyah until the End of the Fourth Century A.H.] (1958; Beirut: Dar al-Kitab al-Jadid, 1975).

2. Ahmad Amin, *Hayati* [My Life] (Cairo: Lajnat al-Ta'lif wa al-Tarjamah wa al-Nashr, 1950), 309.

3. Salah al-Din al-Munajjid, *Al-Zurafa' wa al-Shahhadhun fi Baghdad wa Baris* [Charmers and Beggars in Baghdad and Paris] (1946; Beirut: Dar al-Kitab al-Jadid, 1969).

4. *Bayna al-Khulafa' wa al-Khula'a' fi al-'Asr al-'Abbasi* [Between the Caliphs and the Debauched in the Abbasid Period] (1957; Beirut: Dar al-Kitab al-Jadid, 1974).

5. Salah al-Din al-Munajjid, *Jamal al-Mar'ah 'ind al-'Arab* [Women's Beauty among the Arabs] (1957; reprint, Beirut: Dar al-Kitab al-Jadid, 1969).

In the 1975 second and expanded edition of *Al-Hayah al-Jinsiyyah,* al-Munajjid included a review of the first edition by Syrian poet and literary critic Shafiq Jabri, which had appeared in 1959, as a forward. In his review, Jabri ventured a "personal opinion" by asserting that "I believe that the reason why our literary figures of old produced such an abundant output [about sexual matters] unequalled in the world, or [at least] one of the reasons for such abundance, is the activeness of their drives [nashat ghara'izihim], as had they suffered from what we call repression of the drives, their hearts would have been blinded and their minds rusted and our literary legacy today would not enjoy what it does of works that have no counterpart elsewhere."[6] Al-Munajjid himself seemed to espouse the cause against sexual repression. In his introduction to the first edition of the book, he justified the need to publish a study like his not only for pedagogical purposes, which he sought, but also for liberatory purposes, namely, sexual liberation. He wanted people no longer to "whisper in the dark" when they spoke of things sexual, and that the sexual drive not be redirected through "twists that lead it to disease." He rather wanted sex to be taught "scientifically" in order to "face up to its problems" and "to orient it in a proper way," as silence and banning "cannot confront sex, this pulsating force moving in our depths, but rather lead to violent repression on the part of our male youths and girls, and repression leads to many sexual complexes that are difficult to resolve and be rid of."[7] In fact, oddly, al-Munajjid saw the contemporary repressive situation as directly linked to the past of the Arabs:

What is strange is that our [male] Arab ancestors were not like we are, and their attitude about sex was one full of liberalism and exuberance. They did not feel embarrassed when speaking about women and about sex or when writing about them. I believe that this very wide [margin of] freedom that they enjoyed is what caused the rigidity that we find today.[8]

Although it is never made clear how this causal relationship is established, al-Munajjid's argument, which drew a direct line of cause and effect between the past and the present, is contradicted by his other theses in his book. For example, his thesis about the discontinuity between the past and the present and the importance of reestablishing this link through historical excavations renders his linking present repression to

6. Shafiq Jabri, foreword, in Al-Munajjid, *Al-Hayah al-Jinsiyyah,* 7.
7. Ibid., 9–10.
8. Ibid., 10.

the past problematic. Indeed, the past for al-Munajjid, as we saw with Taha Husayn, had a pedagogical role to play in the present.

In this vein, al-Munajjid took on the questions of embarrassment and shame. He unequivocally asserted, against those who held "prim" views about sex, that not only did major figures in the history of Islam speak about and address sexual matters openly and with ease but that even the Qur'an had addressed sex openly. Here al-Munajjid is marshalling the authority of religion and science to his cause:

If speaking about [sex] was shameful, the Qur'an would not have mentioned it . . . Therefore it is no shame to speak about sex as we speak of food and drink and other matters of life, and no embarrassment to write about sex scientifically clarifying and explicating its issues. It is high time that sexual education acquire its special place in our general and comprehensive culture, provided that such writings not aim at exciting the drives in our male youths and girls, but rather instruct them and make the drives express themselves in an orderly fashion.[9]

Moreover, al-Munajjid, unlike Jabri's confidence in the unique "activeness" of the drives of the Arabs and more in tune with Taha Husayn's mindful contextualization for the benefit of Orientalists, cautioned against civilizational particularity. He argued against the conclusion that the Arabs are unique in their "pursuit of sexual pleasures," as "the history of the Greeks and the Romans, and of France and England, provide us with many examples about similar pursuits, which indicates that human nature—to a large extent—is one, no matter the difference in time and space."[10]

While al-Munajjid narrated the sexual history of the pre-Islamic *jahiliyyah* and the first century after Islam with little moralizing or judgment except to note the "wild" and active sexual desires of Arab men and women throughout these periods (caused as they were by their "desert" origins, which "was the best environment for the excitement of the drives in the hearts of Arabs"[11]), he suddenly switched to a moralizing tone in concluding his section on the Umayyad period (which ends in the middle of the second century A.H. [eighth century A.D.]) which he contrasted with the succeeding Abbasid period:

While these are examples of the Umayyad caliphs' love of women, as all of them enjoyed women [in accordance with Islamic jurisprudence], and they were not exces-

9. Ibid., 11.
10. Ibid., 12.

11. Ibid., 15.

sive in their pursuit of pleasures, and did not show what was to be shown later by the Abbasid caliphs of debasement, obscenity, and whoring . . . And what was said about them [the Abbasids] as relates to sexual deviance and contemptible things was not said about the Umayyads . . . The drop of fondness for sexual desire that the Umayyads possessed became a vast sea in the case of the Abbasid caliphs.[12]

This relatively mild concern about "sexual deviance" and "contemptible things" had very little resonance in al-Munajjid's earlier works. In his 1946 book about the "charmers" and beggars in Baghdad and Paris,[13] his account of tenth-century Abbasid sexual pleasure and lifestyle is quite playful and borders on the celebratory (as is his account of eighteenth-century Paris with which tenth-century Baghdad is contrasted throughout, in another move that posits modern European history as reminiscent of medieval Arab history). The foreword to the book was written by the literary critic Ahmad Hasan al-Zayyat, whom we encountered in chapter 1 as the purveyor of the judgment that Abu Nuwas's *ghazal* for boys was "a crime against literature and a disgrace to the history of Arabic poetry."[14] Al-Zayyat noted the uniqueness of the work of al-Munajjid, who delved into Arab-Islamic history and literature when other writers had spurned "our literary figures and writers" and concerned themselves with writing only about the West.[15] Al-Zayyat's concern was centered on the question of civilization:

It is our hope that this writer and friend continue unhurried on his path through this ingenious fragrant garden, picking from it, from time to time, the flowers of beauty, art and literature, as an instruction and remembrance to our youth who have almost—as seems evident—forgotten that they had a past that was once new to people, and a civilization that was a light to [other] nations, and a character whose effect remains evident in the science, art, literature, and civilization that the West inherited.[16]

Al-Munajjid himself revels in his description of many aspects of life under the Abbasids, or the period he calls the age of luxury, extending from the year A.H. 158 (A.D. 774) through the fourth century A.H. (tenth century A.D.), when Baghdad "blossomed . . . with felicity, and was the cen-

12. Ibid., 75.
13. Al-Munajjid, *Al-Zurafa' wa al-Shahhadhun.*
14. Ahmad Hasan al-Zayyat, *Tarikh al-Adab al-ʿArabi, lil-Madaris al-Thanawiyyah wa al-ʿUlya* [The History of Arabic Literature for Secondary and High Schools] (1923; Beirut: Dar al-Thaqafah, 1978), 310.
15. Al-Munajjid, *Al-Zurafa' wa al-Shahhadhun,* 6.
16. Ibid., 7.

ter of fine taste, agile thought, sweet play, delicate natures, wide wealth, tender love, and pretty charms."[17] When al-Munajjid delved into what he would later call "sexual deviance and contemptible things," there was no trace of such moralization:

I must note that the erotic love (hawa) of the charmers was divided between youthful boys and singing girls. A group of them were seduced by the delicateness [latafah] of the youthful boys, so they loved them, such as ʿAbdullah bin al-ʿAbbas the poet, and like al-Muʿtazz and al-Muʿtamid, Husayn bin Dahhak, and Abu Nuwas. Another group preferred singing girls to youthful boys "due to the integral nature of their beauty, their wondrous looks" . . . In sum, the charmers celebrated love greatly. Indeed, the philosophy of the charming women [among them] can be summarized in a statement made by one of them: "There is no consultation in love!" Despite the spread of suhaq [sapphism] among some of them and its becoming known, they [also] loved men and they loved each other. Badhl used to say. "I do not see anything more pleasurable than sapphism."[18]

Although many of the charmers held notions of love that were not sexual, a group of them

were taken with sexual pleasure. For them, love became a lustful one, Amour Sensuel [sic], and they fell all over themselves in pursuit of this pleasure in a strange way. A group of them set their bodies loose to experience pleasure. They would not care if they derived pleasure from the back or from the front, whether they were a pleasure to others or others were their pleasure, as long as their bodies experienced pleasure and their senses were graced . . . [sic]. This reminds us of the French writer André Gide.[19]

As late as 1957, one year before Al-Hayah al-Jinsiyyah was published, al-Munajjid seemed still unconcerned with "contemptible things," although he wanted to account for "sexual deviance."[20]

---

17. Ibid., 13.

18. Ibid., 45–46.

19. Ibid., 47. It is interesting to note in this regard that André Gide and Taha Husayn were good friends and that Gide had introduced Husayn to French readers. See Taha Husayn, Le libres des jours, with a preface by André Gide (Paris: Gallimard, 1947).

20. Al-Munajjid's first book about the sexual life of the medieval Arabs, published in 1944, was in fact a playful fictional account based on medieval sources. It told tales of the caliphs and their beloved concubines and singing girls. He introduced his book by affirming that "I only wrote it for the sake of playfulness, and I intended for it to be pleasurable. For this is literature." See Salah al-Din al-Munajjid, Fi Qusur al-Khulafaʾ [In the Palaces of the Caliphs] (Beirut: Dar al-Makshuf, 1944), 7. A year later, he published a book titled Nisaʾ ʿAshiqat [Women in Love] (Damascus: Manshurat Asdiqaʾ al-Kitab, 1945), which told the stories of Western women as depicted in French literature, including the works of Flaubert, Stendhal, Rousseau, and Mme de La Fayette, author of La Princesse de

Al-Munajjid delved diligently into the history of Arab women's sexual desires. He spoke about women's explicit expression of their needs and demands for sexual intercourse during the pre-Islamic *jahiliyyah*.[21] He addressed the practice of sucking on the clitoris and how during the *jahiliyyah*, mothers would let their children suck on their clitoris for pleasure. "This is why some people would be [later] reproached by being called 'clitoris-sucker,' and it would be said: 'You, mother-clitoris-sucker.' This later became an insult and a curse."[22] Al-Munajjid seemed proud that Muslim women in the early Islamic era spoke openly about their sexual needs, citing a poem by a woman whose husband was away on a trip, which expresses her longing for intercourse.[23] Al-Munajjid explained that in this period "women saw themselves as a venue for play, pleasure, and enjoyment. For 'A'ishah [the wife of the Prophet] used to say that 'women are the playthings of men. Let each man make up his plaything as much as he can, for this is better for his desire and more satisfying for his eye.'"[24] Women in the Medina of early Islam were also said to express their preference for "long intercourse and how they felt contempt for he who could not keep up with them, and how they would not have intercourse with him again, even if he offered them the world."[25] He also told the story of the famed singing girl in the Abbasid period, Duqaq, who theorized that women "required intercourse more than men and had etched a statement to that effect on her fan."[26]

In his discussion of boys in the life of the Abbasid caliphs in his book *Bayna al-Khulafa' wa al-Khula'a' fi al-'Asr al-'Abbasi*,[27] al-Munajjid sympathetically narrated love stories between caliphs and youthful boys. In concluding his discussion, however, he attempted to provide a sociological and a civilizational explanation for this phenomenon: "We do not know the reason for this turning away from women to boys. Perhaps, this sexual deviance came as a result of the abundance of women in the palaces, which led to the caliphs' boredom of them and their inclination towards boys. Or maybe this was a result of Persian influence, as they were fond of [youthful boys]."[28]

Cléves. The aim of the book was to spur young Arabs to "return to the classics of Western literature and translate them to Arabic. This is the thing we need most in our nascent literary renaissance [Nahdah]," 8.

21. Al-Munajjid, *Al-Hayah al-Jinsiyyah*, 18–19.
22. Ibid., 23.
23. Ibid., 51.
24. Ibid., 52.
25. Ibid., 59.
26. Ibid., 81.
27. Al-Munajjid, *Bayna al-Khulafa'*, 48–52.
28. Ibid., 52.

The reasons for the "prospering" of sexual life under the Abbasids were threefold, according to al-Munajjid, who was echoing Taha Husayn (without citing him):

First, the readiness of the drives in the souls of the Arabs and their liking sexual pleasure no matter whence it came; second, the influence of Arabized Persians, as they were licentious before Islam, picking pleasure wherever they found it, and having intercourse with their mothers and daughters . . . ; as for the third factor, it was the civilization that Baghdad enjoyed, whose effects were wide scale opulence, vast wealth, absolute freedom, excessive debasement, and the weakening of the influence of religion on the aristocratic and intellectual classes. There were two important sources of sexual pleasures in that era, singing girls [qiyan], and youthful boys [ghilman].[29]

The singing girls and concubines were quite knowledgeable about various sexual matters, as they came from "every corner of the Earth . . . India, Sind, Rome, and the far reaches of Africa." It is their influence that expanded the ways of sexual pleasure that were previously unknown in Baghdad and increased the limited number of known sexual positions dramatically.[30] The singing girls were also innovative, as one of them is said to have "made a lock that she gave to her owner to place on his penis so that he would not approach [other] women."[31] Al-Munajjid contrasted this with the chastity belt that the Crusading Europeans imposed on their women before embarking on their conquest of the Orient, and then humorously mentions a "German physician named Weinheld from the city of Halle," who in the early nineteenth century invented a male chastity belt: "Thus we find that the concubines of Baghdad invented, in pursuit of sexual pleasure, what the West came to know centuries after them."[32] Al-Munajjid also credited the concubines and singing girls with elaborating over sixty different sexual positions. He was so proud of this achievement that he insisted on another civilizational comparison: "This is a number never reached among other nations. During the Renaissance, there were only sixteen sexual positions known in Italy, as represented by Giulio Romano, Michelangelo's apprentice, and were etched by Marcantonio Raimondi."[33]

As for youthful boys, al-Munajjid postulated a reason for their popularity that was to be adopted by writers after him as fact: "Perhaps, the

29. Al-Munajjid, *Al-Hayah al-Jinsiyyah*, 77–78.
30. Ibid., 78–79.
31. Ibid., 84.
32. Ibid.
33. Ibid., 79.

abundance of concubines [jawari] is what caused men to become averse to them, and to like youthful boys [instead]."[34] While Taha Husayn saw the Persians as influential in the development of *ghazal* poetry about youthful boys, al-Munajjid credited them with imparting to the Arabs the erotic love of boys. In this, he was following in the footsteps of Orientalist scholarship and medieval Arab scholars. Adam Mez, for example, claimed that "the real pederasty, according to Muslim tradition, came from Khorasan [in Persia] with the Abbasid army. Even in the third century [A.H.] Afghanistan is noted for it."[35] Mez cited al-Jahiz, who died in A.D. 868, for his claim on Khurasan and al-Thaʿalibi on Afghanistan.[36]

Taha Husayn's note that anti-Arab anger had mobilized the licentiousness of the Abbasid period began to take a strong nationalist turn. Al-Munajjid affirmed that "there is no doubt that Arabized Persians had a big influence in the spread of sodomy [liwat] and the love of youthful boys. For the most famous practitioners of sodomy in the Abbasid period were of Persian origins, especially the poets and the religious scholars [ʿulamaʾ] among them."[37] This civilizational displacement was being made in the heyday of Nasirist Arab nationalism. It was only two years earlier, in 1955, that the imperial powers formed the anti-Soviet Baghdad Pact, which included Iran under the Shah. In insisting that the Soviets were the main enemy, the imperial powers were correctly perceived by Arab nationalists as deflecting attention from Israel, the main enemy of Arab countries at the time. Along with Britain and France, Israel had just invaded Egypt in 1956 following Nasir's nationalization of the Suez Canal Company. The Shah's alliance with Israel against Arab nationalism did not endear him or his country to Arab nationalists. The use of Iran (and royal Arab regimes) by imperial powers to weaken Nasirism might very well have been on the mind of al-Munajjid.

Al-Munajjid would also provide a kind of etiology for *suhaq*: "Women [in the Abbasid period] also took to sexual deviance in deriving plea-

---

34. Ibid.
35. Adam Mez, *The Renaissance of Islam*, translated from the German by Salahuddin Khuda Bakhsh and D. S. Margoliouth (Patna: Jubilee Printing and Publishing House, 1937), 358.
36. The only reference that we have for al-Jahiz's Khurasan claim is found in Gregor Schoeler, ed., *Diwan Abu Nuwas* (Damascus: Dar al-Mada, 2003), vol. 4, 185, a translation of *Der Diwan Des Abu Nuwas*, 4 vols., the first three volumes edited by Ewald Wagner and the fourth by Gregor Schoeler (Wiesbaden: F. Steiner, 1958–). The *Diwan* reproduces most of Hamzah al-Isbahani's medieval recension of Abu Nuwas's poetry, in which al-Isbahani quotes from the now lost fragment of al-Jahiz's *Fi Al-Muʿallimin* [On Schoolmasters]. Other fragments from *Fi al-Muʿallimin*, however, survive. See ʿAbd al-Salam Muhammad Harun, ed., *Rasaʾil al-Jahiz* [The Treatises of al-Jahiz] (Beirut: Dar al-Jil, 1991), vol. 2, part 3, 27–51. I thank Everett Rowson for sharing with me his knowledge about extant and lost manuscripts of al-Jahiz.
37. Al-Munajjid, *Al-Hayah al-Jinsiyyah*, 85.

sure."[38] I should note here that the Arabic word for "lesbianism," "su-haq," is not derived from the root *sin-ha-qaf* (sahaqa), as is commonly believed. It is a postclassical word that was most likely foreign in origin. The tenth-century al-Azhari and the thirteenth-century ibn Manzur tell us as much in their dictionaries without speculating on its origin.[39] The word is most likely derived from the Greek *sapphikos* and like many other words must have entered the language along with other Greek words in the ninth or tenth century in the heyday of the age of translation or even earlier. Al-Munajjid explained that "some of [the women] were inclined toward it for physiological reasons: It was mentioned [in the medieval literature] that if the pharynx of a woman's uterus was long she would be inclined to intercourse; if it was short, she would hate intercourse and would be inclined to *suhaq*. Al-Kindi [the philosopher, A.D. 800–873, known in the West as al-Kindus] mentioned that sapphism is a natural desire that is located between the two labia. Others were inclined toward it for other reasons: virgins feared defloration and nonvirgins feared pregnancy."[40] It is noteworthy that al-Munajjid's explanation for sodomy was cultural while for sapphism physiological and natural. He also addressed masturbation and bestiality as some of the other practices that were found during the Abbasid period, but he did not provide similarly specific explanations of their "origins."

Although he periodically mentioned the sexual excesses of the Abbasid caliphs, including their pursuit of boys, al-Munajjid reserved his harshest judgment for Abu Nuwas, who, according to al-Munajjid, was known to have enjoyed women and boys as well as having derived pleasure "from behind and from the front." Such excesses "illustrate Abu Nuwas's sick and deviant personality which finds all pleasure in wine and in the body."[41] It is important to note in this regard that while Al-Munajjid mentioned the practice of sodomy and sapphism during the time of the Prophet as well as during the Umayyad period, he only characterized them as "sexual deviance" in the context of his discussion of the Abbasid period.[42] In so doing, he safeguarded Islamic civilization against the Persian-derived "deviations" of the Abbasid era.

---

38. Ibid., 89.

39. See Muhammad ibn Ahmad al-Azhari, *Tahdhib al-Lughah*, ed.'Abd al-Karim al-Gharbawi and Muhammad 'Ali al-Najjar (Cairo: al-Dar al-Misriyyah lil-Ta'lif wa al-Tarjamah, 1964), vol. 4, 23; and Muhammad bin Mukarram ibn Manzur, *Lisan al-'Arab* (Beirut: Dar Sadir, 1990), vol. 10, 153. Al-Azhari and ibn al-Manzur assert that the word is of "muwallad" derivation, that is, foreign to Arabic.

40. Al-Munajjid, *Al-Hayah al-Jinsiyyah*, 90.

41. Ibid., 108.

42. See for example his discussion of sapphism and sodomy in early Islam where the term "sexual deviance" is not used; ibid., 20, 21, 58, and 60.

While al-Munajjid seemed mostly unhappy with the Abbasid caliphs who presided over this "moral decadence" (inhitat khuluqi) and the "touting of religion" leading to this "dirty life that exceeded what is reasonable,"[43] he was most distressed about the effects this was to have on modern Arab civilization: "The Abbasid era was sex-crazed. It is unfortunate that the subsequent eras followed its example in this madness, which became one of the reasons for the descent (inhidar) and backwardness that the Arabs and Muslims have reached."[44] This moral judgment stands in stark contradiction, however, with the initial pedagogical purpose of the book about the openness of the past and the repression of the present. It should also be contrasted with al-Munajjid's more tempered, earlier book on the standards for women's beauty in Arab history, where he mentioned in a matter-of-fact way how in the Abbasid period, "due to the influence of the love of youthful boys, [standards of] women's beauty [were] transformed to be in line with the beauty of boys."[45] More important, it seems to create a theoretical conundrum. If, as al-Munajjid theorized earlier, wealth and opulent civilizations are related to the relaxation of sexual morals, then it should follow that barbarism and poverty might strengthen them. It is not clear however how this decadence is a feature of both Abbasid society (high civilization) and contemporary Arab society ("backwardness"). What accounts then for such a contradiction? What accounts for the change and vacillation in al-Munajjid's views? What transformed al-Munajjid's concern for the contemporary state of Arab civilization into a condemnation of classical Arab civilization whose praises he had sung for so long?

Al-Munajjid seemed unresolved about the sexual life of the ancient Arabs. His ambivalence is manifest throughout *Jamal al-Mar'ah*, and his judgmental mood shifts throughout the book. In his discussion of "popular" sex stories cited in the *Wondrous Tales* (Al-Hikayat al-'Ajibah) and *A Thousand and One Nights*, he assured his readers that "these sexual experiences . . . are natural and real and are not woven by fantasy and illusion. They used to happen a thousand years ago and they could hap-

---

43. Ibid., 128.
44. Ibid., 129.
45. Al-Munajjid, *Jamal al-Mar'ah*, 62. On boyish women, or "al-mar'ah al-ghulamiyyah," see the interesting essay by Habib al-Zayyat, "Al-Mar'ah al-Ghulamiyyah fi al-Islam," *Al-Mashriq*, March–April 1956, 153–92. In a rare editorial comment, al-Zayyat, an Arab Orientalist scholar, notes that these women who adopted boyish looks and mannerisms to appeal to boy-lovers would even take on male names. "But one difference remained between the two sexes, which is what betrayed al-Banuqah bint al-Mahdi, the rise of her breasts and their standing on end. Did it ever occur to these smart charmers to be flat [jadda'] without breasts as has occurred to the American boyish women [ghulamiyyat] today?" 172. It is noteworthy that this essay was published posthumously, as it was found in Zayyat's papers after his death.

pen today, in our own era, because they emanate from human nature, despite the deviance we find in some of them."[46] While sapphism and sodomy were cited by him as having existed long before the Abbasid period, what he seemed to have objected to in the Abbasid period was the commercialization of such practices on a grand scale, through the acquisition of slave boys and singing girls and the proliferation of public discourse about such practices in the *ghazal* poetry of the period. Thus his objection seemed less about the practices themselves and more about how they registered themselves in the public sphere. This contrasts sharply with his denunciation of modern repression and his celebration of the openness of the ancients. Al-Munajjid clearly approved of the openness of ancient women and men when it came to their expressed desires for the other sex and disapproved of it when it expressed desires for the same sex.

It would seem that al-Munajjid had an Aristotelian commitment to moderation. What he disliked was excess, whether excess in openness as he found in the Abbasids or excess in repression as he found in modern Arabs. While initially impressed with the openness of the Abbasids, as his earlier books made clear, when he wrote *Al-Hayah al-Jinsiyyah,* he needed to provide a pedagogical evaluation of this historical period and the role it should play in the present, which, for him, made moralizing a necessity.

In this, what had started out with Zaydan and later with Husayn has by the time of al-Munajjid developed into what Raymond Williams would call a "structure of feeling" wherein a kind of excess and deviation from moderation were seen as the reasons that brought down classical Arab civilization after the Abbasids came to power and continued until the present. This is what made the Arabs "weak" and led to their subjection by foreign powers and to the perpetuation of their "decadence." This is not unlike what Williams discerned in the case of English nationalist mythology, namely, that "the transition from a rural to an industrial society is seen as a kind of fall, the true cause and origin of our social suffering and disorder . . . [This myth] is the main source for the structure of feeling which we began by examining: The perpetual retrospect to an 'organic' or 'natural' society."[47] For Williams, structures of feeling are

affective elements of consciousness and relationships: not feeling against thought, but thought as felt and feeling as thought: practical consciousness of a present kind, in a

---

46. Al-Munajjid, *Al-Hayah al-Jinsiyyah,* 138.
47. Raymond Williams, *The Country and the City* (Oxford: Oxford University Press, 1973), 96.

living and interrelating continuity. We are then defining these elements as a "struc-ture": as a set, with specific internal relations, at once interlocking and in tension. Yet we are also defining a social experience which is still *in process,* often not yet recog-nized as social but taken to be private, idiosyncratic, and even isolating, but which in analysis (though rarely otherwise) has its emergent, connecting, and dominant char-acteristics, indeed its specific hierarchies. These are often more recognizable at a later stage, when they have been (as often happens) formalized, classified, and in many cases built into institutions and formations. By that time the case is different; a new structure of feeling will usually already have begun to form, in the true social present.[48]

We will see in the remainder of this book how this structure of feel-ing will inform "secular" and "Islamist" approaches to the question of Arab (or "Islamic" in the case of the Islamists) civilization and culture. The question will not be whether there was deviation from an originary ideal—be it *jahiliyyah* society, early Islamic society, or late Ottoman so-ciety, etc.—to a decadent present, but rather identifying the historical point *when* such deviation actually took place leading to contemporary "decadence."

Nationalism and the Purity of Civilization

Al-Munajjid's concern was to shed light on a chapter of Arab history that had remained obscure and then compare it with a sexually repressive West whose scholars had constantly denounced Arab civilization. He also wanted this glorious and open past Arab civilization to be emulated as a model to rid the present of its own repression. In contrast, a num-ber of literary historians committed to a deeply conservative version of Arab nationalism would attempt to characterize all that they considered unsavory in Arab civilization as a foreign import and assert the purity of all that they found noble. This was indeed a reaction to Orientalist en-deavors to deny that Arab "civilization" had made major contributions to the world. The ability of nationalism to interpellate historical figures a posteriori as "Arab" or "foreign" is matched by its categorical abil-ity to expel from and incorporate desires and practices into "tradition" in a procrustean manner. If this meant that the nationalists must mis-read the historical evidence to produce an ancient Arab civilization in line with modern nationalist criteria, they, like nationalists everywhere, would not shy away from their mission.

48. Raymond Williams, *Marxism and Literature* (Oxford: Oxford University Press, 1977), 132.

Lebanese ʿAbd al-Latif Shararah, an ardent Arab nationalist, was interested in tracing the origins of the ideas of love in Arab civilization to pre-
Islamic times to ascertain which parts of post-Islamic civilization were
"authentically" Arab and which parts the result of foreign influences on
the Islamic empire. Shararah, like Ahmad Amin, Husayn, al-Nuwayhi,
and al-Munajjid, was also concerned about women's position in Arab
civilization; he postulated that women had been more equal to men in
the first *jahiliyyah* (extending for three millennia prior to the fifth century A.D.) than in the second *jahiliyyah* preceding the rise of Islam (sixth
century A.D.).[49] He delved into that early history, citing as examples the
presence of Arab queens in Sabaʾ (Sheba) and in Palmyra, and proceeded
to examine the decline of women in the second *jahiliyyah* and subsequently.[50] While the first decline that Shararah discerned occurred sometime between the first and second *jahiliyyah* and is inexplicable due to
our limited historical knowledge of that period,[51] the second decline,
which took place during the second *jahilliyah,* is blamed on women in
power. Shararah argued that powerful ruling women were so tyrannical,
"violent and strict," due to women's "closeness to daily living, and their
intimacy with sadness and pain, on account of their suffering in love,
in marriage or lack thereof, in pregnancy or lack thereof . . . that once
they ruled over society or within the family, or the State, they would
use violence often against their subjects and cause them suffering . . .
All these factors taken together created in the *jahilliyah* Arabs, gradually and unconsciously, a type of 'resentment' [maqt] of women that
represented an obscure psychological state—very obscure—of rebellion
against women's authority, and it was a concealed authority in their
lives, and which [i.e., the psychological state] became clearer and clearer
with time."[52] As for the exact timing of the decline of women in Arab
history, Shararah admitted that it was difficult to pin down precisely,
although he postulated that it must have begun during the rule of Ze-
nopia, queen of Palmyra.[53] Shararah's main point ultimately was that
when Islam appeared on the scene, women's status had already declined
greatly and that Islam stemmed the tide of this decline by criminalizing many antiwomen practices that had been legitimized in the second

49. For more on Shararah's view on the first and second *jahiliyyahs,* see his *Al-Janib al-Thaqafi
min al-Qawmiyyah al-ʿArabiyyah* [The Cultural Dimension of Arab Nationalism] (Beirut: Dar al-ʿIlm
lil-Malayin, 1961). On his views on women's equality to men in the period of *jahiliyyah,* see his *Falsafat al-Hubb ʿind al-ʿArab* [The Arabs' Philosophy of Love] (Beirut, Dar Maktabat al-Hayah, 1960), 39.
50. Shararah, *Falsafat al-Hubb,* 39–66.
51. Ibid., 40
52. Ibid., 55.
53. Ibid., 57.

jahilliyah, including female infanticide.[54] Indeed, despite the "responsibility" with which Islam endowed men over women and children, this
did not "lose the Arab woman her character, but rather increased her
strength and persistence on a pure spiritual basis, for Islam gave her the
right to self-determination, left her her money to do with as she pleased,
and did not give her husband the slightest authority over her . . ."[55] Shararah would have more to say later as to what befell Arab women under
Abbasid rule.

Shararah's book, *Falsafat al-Hubb ʿind al-ʿArab* (The Arabs' Philosophy
of Love),[56] traced the differences in ideas about love from early Arab
pre-Islamic civilization through the second century following Islam. He
examined Arab ʿUdhri poetry ("ʿUdhri" actually means "virginal" and
is derived from the adjective referring to the pre-Islamic poets who belonged to the tribe of bani ʿUdhra, who happened to compose nonsexual "virginal" poetry) and questioned how some have related it to
Plato's notion of love explicated in the *Symposium* and the *Republic*: "Platonic love is pure philosophical abstraction, while ʿUdhri love is a socio-
historical event that was felt by individual Arab lovers, and that no one
else of other nations felt, . . . and was [as such] an expression of a civilization in one of its evolutionary phases. The former is an idea while the
latter is life, and the difference between idea and life is great."[57] Unlike
Husayn, Mubarak, and al-Munajjid, the nationalist Shararah was committed to an Arab particularism, if not exceptionalism. Shararah was
interested in showing how for the Arabs, love was spiritual and uncontaminated by corporeality, and that the richness of the pre-Islamic Arabic language that gave birth to the Qurʾan and the early Islamic philosophy of love is an effect of a pure Arab culture uncontaminated by foreign
contact: "Pure Arab philosophy that is not contaminated by any Greek,
Persian, Indian, or Roman impurity is based mostly on the language of
the Arabs, and then on their literature, and then on their practical conduct . . ."[58] But if this is so, what then is the nature of Arab-Islamic culture and philosophy since the second century A.H.? Taking Taha Husayn's
remark and al-Munajjid's nationalist observations to their logical conclusion, Shararah's answer was unequivocal:

The Arabs had no hand in the "philosophy" that was adopted by "Islamic" communities beginning in the second half of the second century of the Hegira, especially as

---

54. Ibid., 58.
55. Ibid., 59.
56. Ibid.

57. Ibid., 93.
58. Ibid., 141.

related to social issues and concerns. Rather, it was the hand of Abu Nuwas, Bashshar [bin Burd] and the like who were foreign [dukhala'] to the Arabs, to the Arab spirit, and to Arab thought.[59]

Shararah's horror at the sexual life of the Abbasids and how it "contaminated" the "authentic" approach to love that he saw as having existed in "pure" Arab culture became clearer in his attempt to banish out of classical Arab civilization the love of beardless boys. He cited the tenth-century (fourth century A.H.) essay "Fi mahiyyat al-'ishq" (On the Nature of Erotic Love) written by the brothers al-Safa', Ikhwan al-Safa' (who lived in the Abbasid period) to prove his point.[60] Shararah cited Ikhwan al-Safa' as saying that "they [the Ikhwan] determined that 'it is not in the nature of Arabs to desire intercourse with youthful boys [ghilman] or to love beardless boys [murdan],' and explain this by saying that they [the Arabs] are not part of 'the nations that deal with the sciences and the arts.' Irrespective of the reason they give to explain the nature of the Arabs, this determination of theirs confirms— and they are closer to those epochs than we are—that the corruption of social life that was pervasive during the Abbasid period found its way to people through 'the people of Persia' and other nations that desired beardless boys."[61] Shararah, in fact, doctored the quote from Ikhwan al-Safa', who said no such thing. Ikhwan al-Safa''s words were quite different:

Then, know, that if children and boys forsake the upbringing of their fathers and mothers, they will still need the education of teachers in the sciences and the arts until they reach completion and perfection. It is on account of this that there is in adult men a desire for boys [sibyan] and a love for youthful boys [ghilman], so that this would lead to their literary and moral education [ta'dibihim wa tahdhibihim], and their perfection, in order that they reach their intended goals. This exists in most nations that have a predilection for the sciences, the arts, literature, and mathematics, like the people of Persia, the people of Iraq, the people of Syria, the Romans, and other nations. As for nations that do not dabble with the sciences, the arts, and literature, like the Kurds, Bedouins [al-A'rab], blacks, and Turks, the desire to have intercourse with youthful boys [ghilman] or the love of beardless boys [murdan] is rarely found among them, or in their nature.[62]

59. Ibid., 142.
60. See "Fi mahiyyat al-'ishq," the thirty-seventh treatise of Ikhwan al-Safa' in *Rasa'il Ikhwan al-Safa'* [The Treatises of Ikhwan al-Safa'] (Beirut: Dar Sadir, 1957), vol. 3, 269–86.
61. Shararah, *Falsafat al-Hubb*, 142.
62. Al-Safa', *Rasa'il Ikhwan al-Safa'*, vol. 3, 277.

The assertion of Ikhwan al-Safa' in this paragraph was that people whose predominant life was nomadic did not desire boys, while city dwellers with what would after the nineteenth century be called "civilization" did have these desires, and these included not only the "foreign" Persian element but also Syrian and Iraqi Arabs in whose lands the seats of the Arab-Islamic Umayyad and Abbasid dynasties, respectively, were based. Shararah's confusing the word for Bedouins, A'rab, with the word for Arabs, 'Arab, could have been innocent,[63] but his dropping the peoples of Syria and Iraq from the equation is clearly a deliberate ideological subtraction engineered to produce the "pure Arab" prior to Persian contamination.

If Shararah wanted to render (what he posited as) certain Arab sexual desires foreign in character, he was not alone in his efforts, as Ahmad Taymur Basha could not even locate such desires in the life of the medieval Arabs. In his book on love in medieval Arab culture, Al-Hubb 'ind al-'Arab,[64] Taymur, a well-known Egyptian linguist who died in 1930, quoted extensively from medieval treatises. His book, however, was only published posthumously in 1964. In one section, he wrote that "the people of India agreed with the Arabs in [writing] ghazal for women, unlike the Persians and the Turks, whose ghazal is directed at beardless boys and has no mention of women. For love's sake, they are unjust, as they do not put the thing in its proper place." Taymur proceeded to quote a Qur'anic verse regarding the punishment of the people of Lot.[65] As the rest of his book indicated, Taymur could not have been ignorant of ghazal poetry for youthful boys as he cited all the major medieval treatises that are the main source of information about it, although Abu Nuwas was nowhere to be found in his book. The rest of the book is replete with poetry praising women's beauty and cites stories about unrequited and fulfilled love without religious moralizing of any kind. As the book's editor asserted, Taymur proved in his book that "love is not denied in religion, nor banned in religious law," which clearly does not apply to all love, as far as Taymur was concerned.[66]

Another important conclusion that Shararah drew from this foreign contamination was the diminution in women's stature and women's power in Arab civilization. While the first and second such diminution,

---

63. I should note here that in another book of his, Al-Janib al-Thaqafi, 7, he criticized Western Orientalists for thinking that all Arabs were Bedouins, a view he was not in agreement with.

64. Ahmad Taymur Basha, Al-Hubb 'ind al-'Arab [Love among the Arabs] (1964; Cairo: Dar al-Afaq al-'Arabiyyah, 2000).

65. Ibid., 45.

66. For more on Taymur's other works, see Ahmad al-Tawili, Kutub al-Hubb 'ind al-'Arab [Books about Love among the Arabs] (Beirut: Riyad al-Rayyis lil-Kutub wa al-Nashr, 2001), 127–33.

which took place in the first and second *jahiliyyah*s on the eve of the rise of Islam, as mentioned above, were the result of women's tyrannical authority, the further erosion of Arab women's power under Islam was explained thus:

Arab women lost their struggle with the foreign concubines, and lost their character with time, and so ended all that they possessed of authority in their hands once the caliphate was transferred to [the Abbasid caliph] al-Mutawwakil, who put political power [mulk] in the hands of the Turks (Al-Mutawwakil assumed the caliphate in A.H. 232).[67]

Shararah is being less than original. The idea of the decline of the power of Arab women and their higher status under the Abbasids had already been postulated at the turn of the century by Jurji Zaydan in *Tarikh al-Tamaddun al-Islami*, in which he stated that the preponderance of foreign concubines "led to the degradation of the [Arab] woman and the disappearance of her pride and her independence of mind . . ."[68] This was not all, as far as Shararah was concerned, as "true love disappeared with the disappearance of Arab dominance, and the triumph of the concubines over the caliphs and their palaces, and the dissemination of their ideas and lifestyles in Islamic communities. Then, a new era had dawned, the era of philosophizing and sexual deviance, which started at the hands of Abu Nuwas, and continued until it led to Sufism, then ossification, and then decadence [inhitat]."[69]

Shararah (a secular Shiite Muslim) had almost a Christian obsession with the evil of sensuality and sex that appeared after the *fall* of Arab civilization at the hands of "foreigners." To this view, he juxtaposed a chaste and pure love that he believed had existed in the paradisiacal Arab past before the fall and that guaranteed a higher and more equal stature for women in society. Indeed, he asserted that modern European Romanticism was inherited from those parts of Arab Sufi and love culture that survived the fall, which were transferred to Europe through Arab Andalusia and Arab Sicily, as well as through the Crusaders.[70] But all was lost once philosophy polluted everything as it had done in the Abbasid period. Shararah credited Darwin, Marx, Nietzsche, and Freud with responsibility for the defeat of Romanticism. It was Freud (and others like him) who made the world lose "love," as "Freud was able to redirect

67. Shararah, *Falsafat al-Hubb*, 163–64. For a similar assessment, see also 177.
68. Jurji Zaydan, *Tarikh al-Tamaddun al-Islami* [History of Islamic Civilization] (Cairo: Matbaʻat al-Hilal, 1906), vol. 5, 67.
69. Shararah, *Falsafat al-Hubb*, 131.
70. Ibid., 188.

people towards sex instead of love."[71] For Shararah, Arab identity and culture must be pure and chaste, and such notions that he adopted were not, as far as he was concerned, borrowed from European Victorian and Romantic nationalist thought but rather were constitutive of pure Arab thought itself, of which European Romanticism was but a recent heir.

Shararah's thought, however, was not hegemonic, as other intellectuals had different approaches that included less interest in sexual or national purity. If Shararah's concern was some Platonic ideal of love avant la lettre that predominated in pre-Islamic Arabic literary production, notably ʿUdhri Arabic poetry, secular Syrian philosopher Sadiq Jalal al-ʿAzm's 1968 book on the nature of love for the ʿUdhri poets reached the opposite conclusion. Al-ʿAzm set out to undo the pervasive perception of the ʿUdhri male poets as "virginal" at all and reconstructed them instead as sensual lovers who desired their lovers' bodies and sought sexual pleasure, albeit while avoiding the telos of marriage to their lovers and preferring instead permanent separation as a condition of their desire and love. Al-ʿAzm, who was horrified not by sensuality but by the attempt to cover it up, convincingly demonstrated how these poets did seek sexual union with their female lovers whom they would not, rather than could not, marry (any more than the women, who also did not want to marry them). For al-ʿAzm, what made ʿUdhri love special was precisely that, namely, its opposition to the institution of marriage to one's beloved (as some of the women involved were married to other men whom they did not wish to divorce), and not some incorporeal ideal free from sensuality.[72] This tradition would be passed on centuries later from Arab Andalusia to the troubadours and the new innovations of Provencal courtly love. Love for the ʿUdhri poets could not be sublimated into social reproduction, as they seemed to have experienced it as freedom from society rather than the intimate form that binds the social.

Like ancient writers on the ʿUdhri poets and his contemporaries,[73] Shararah wanted to show virginal Arab love "before" Plato (in the sense

71. Ibid., 194.
72. See Sadiq Jalal al-ʿAzm, Fi al-Hubb wa al-Hubb al-ʿUdhri [On Love and on Virginal Love] (Beirut: Manshurat Nizar Qabbani, 1968), 79–116. Al-ʿAzm also judged his contemporary Arab world as sexually repressive, noting that people who rushed to enjoy books like A Thousand and One Nights did so due to its description of "prohibited love relationships when measured by the pervasive religious and moral values" (69) that the society, in which these readers live, upholds.
73. Shararah's contemporaries who wrote on the issue include Yusuf Khulayf, Al-Hubb al-Mithali ʿind al-ʿArab [Ideal Love among the Arabs] (Cairo: Dar al-Maʿarif, 1961), and Musa Sulayman, Al-Hubb al-ʿUdhri [Virginal Love] (Beirut: Dar al-Thaqafah, 1954), among others. I should note here that an obscure Beirut-research outfit put out a book in 1980 that heavily plagiarized from Shararah (whole paragraphs) and which echoed his puritanical commitments. The book however is not

that Arabic ʿUdhri poetry was composed before Arab civilization had actually discovered Plato and translated him) in order to produce a completely "pure," self-contained Arab civilization. In that, he and his cohort were responding to Orientalist racism that posited every interesting characteristic of Arab culture as a foreign import. Perversely, one might argue that Shararah was doing the same thing by attributing all interesting sexual matters as coming from the outside.

Less defensive Arab philosophers, however, contra the Orientalists, had no issue with showing the importance of Plato's theory of love on Arab civilization without seeing it as taking away from the contributions of Arabs, especially in the field of medieval Arab *ars erotica*. The Egyptian philosopher and priest Jurj Shihatah Qanawati, for example, made a compelling case for Plato's large influence on Arab *ars erotica* in his historical study of how medieval Arab authors, in their own writings about love and sex, used and quoted, agreed and differed with Plato's account of love in the *Symposium* and other books.[74] Whether authors like al-ʿAzm or Qanawati would identify as nationalists or not, they had little concern about questions of "purity" when it came to philosophy or sex.

The nationalist theme, however, was to predominate in some literary circles. The major literary historian Shawqi Dayf had a more ambivalent record on the matter. In his study of the history of Arabic literature, which he published in the mid-1960s and in which he applied class analysis when discussing the economic basis of the Abbasid empire and the opulence in which its caliphs lived, he would still deploy nationalist historiographic criteria in his assessment of what he considered to be less than flattering social phenomena.[75] Paramount among such phenomena was of course the abundance of concubines and singing girls, whose presence caused "moral corruption" and led to the development of lewd "exposed" *ghazal* in which "the dignity of both men and women" was compromised.[76] He cited the many poets who championed such poetry, including Bashshar bin Burd, whose poetry became "a loud proclama-

known and did not form part of the debate on sex. See al-Maktab al-ʿAlami lil-Buhuth, *Al-Hubb ʿind al-ʿArab* [Love among the Arabs] (Beirut: Dar Maktabat al-Hayah, n.d. [1980?]). The same outfit published two other books on unrelated issues that same year.

74. See Jurj Shihatah Qanawati, "Athar al-Maʾdubah aw al-Hubb al-Aflatuni fi al-ʿAlam al-Islami" [The Influence of "The Sympoisum"; or, Platonic Love in the Islamic World], in *Al-Maʾdubah aw fi al-Hubb li-Aflatun* ("The Symposium"; or, On Love by Plato], translated and edited by ʿAli Sami al-Nashshar, Jurj Shihatah Qanawati, and ʿAbbas Ahmad al-Sharbini (Alexandria: Dar al-Kutub al-Jamiʿiyyah, 1970), 323–431.

75. Shawqi Dayf, *Al-ʿAsr al-ʿAbbasi al-Awwal* [The First Abbasid Era] (Cairo: Dar al-Maʿarif 1966). This is the third volume of Dayf's study.

76. Ibid., 72.

tion of the sexual instinct" that Dayf found disgraceful ("yanda lahu jabin al-sharaf wa al-khuluq").[77]

While Ahmad Taymur Basha denied the very existence of *ghazal* poetry written for youthful boys in the Muslim Arab tradition, Dayf had something more sophisticated up his sleeve. He would postulate that such *ghazal* poetry for youthful boys was nothing short of dissimulation to cover up the poets' real love for and debauchery involving *women*. This is how it works: the life of opulence that the Abbasids lived, Dayf affirmed, led these bawdy poets to spread another "despicable ailment," namely, that of desiring beardless youthful boys. He then recited briefly al-Amin's attachment to "eunuchs" and his mother's intervention of dressing up concubines as youthful boys to seduce him. Against this background Dayf cited the medieval poet and critic ibn al-Mu'tazz (A.D. 861–908) who claimed that Abu Nuwas's *ghazal* for boys was a "cover-up" for his "real debauchery with the promiscuous concubines."[78] The conclusion was inescapable: "Perhaps herein lies the secret of why Abu Nuwas would often speak about concubines using the masculine pronoun."[79] In fact, ibn al-Mu'tazz made no mention of such poetic substitution at all. What ibn al-Mu'tazz actually said was that "Abu Nuwas used to mention sodomy [liwat] excessively and boast of it while he was more adulterous [with women] than an ape."[80] Dayf gave unjustified weight to ibn al-Mu'tazz's parenthetical statement when he added that if ibn al-Mu'tazz "was right, then it would be wrong to analyze the psychology of Abu Nuwas based on this deviant ailment, which he pretended to have in order to conceal the truth of his secret thoughts and his bawdy life."[81]

Dayf's undefended conclusion about Abu Nuwas's desires was characteristic of his overall discussion of the poet. Indeed, he suggested multiple strategies to confront the biography of Abu Nuwas. If denying and recoding his *ghazal* poetry for boys as dissimulation and substitution was not persuasive to mitigate this poetry's effect on Arab civilization, then a surer strategy was to expel Abu Nuwas altogether from the domain of Arabness. In this vein, Dayf would insist that Abu Nuwas was born to "a Persian mother and father too," rejecting others' claims that his father was a Damascene Arab without any justification and with questionable

77. Ibid.
78. Ibid., 233.
79. Ibid., 73–74.
80. 'Abdullah ibn al-Mu'tazz, *Tabaqat al-Shu'ara'* [The Ranks of Poets] (Cairo: Dar al-Ma'arif fi Misr, 1956), 309. I should state here that ibn al-Mu'tazz does not mention this in his discussion of Abu Nuwas's poetry, to which he devoted a section in his book (193–217), but while discussing the poet Muhammad bin Hazim al-Bahili.
81. Dayf, *Al-'Asr al-'Abbasi al-Awwal*, 233.

evidence.[82] Although he cited three sources for his claim, Dayf imputed to them things that were not in the original. Ibn al-Muʿtazz, on whom Dayf relied, clearly claimed that Abu Nuwas's father was "from Damascus."[83] Although ibn al-Muʿtazz claimed him as a "mawla" (not originating from the Arabian Peninsula), he never identified him as a "Persian mawla" as Dayf claimed.[84] This also applies to his second source, *Al-Ishtiqaq*, written by the philologist ibn Durayd (A.D. 837–933), in which he identified "al-Jarrah bin ʿAbdillah bin Juʿadah bin Aflah bin al-Harith bin Dawwah, the master of Khurasan," as "the mawla [patron] of Haniʾ, the father of Abu Nuwas," that is, that Haniʾ came from outside the Arabian Peninsula and needed a peninsular Arab Muslim as a patron, which is consistent with his known Damascene origins.[85] Dayf's third source does not fare any better, as the ninth-century Abi Hiffan (died circa A.H. 256) never mentioned this alleged Persianness, although he did identify Abu Nuwas as follows: "Abu ʿAli Hasan bin Haniʾ bin al-Sabbah, the client [mawla] of al-Jarrah bin ʿAbdillah al-Hikami, the ruler [wali] of Khurasan,"[86] and on another occasion stated that Abu Nuwas himself was "the mawla [client] of al-Jarrah bin ʿAbdillah al-Hikami."[87] Dayf did not consult those sources on which others relied and which identified Abu Nuwas's father as a Damascene or as originating in Yemen, as Abu Nuwas himself used to claim. His questioning of Abu Nuwas's paternal national origins notwithstanding, Dayf would attempt to defend Abu Nuwas against accusations that he was an atheist or that he was anti-Arab in the *shuʿubi* tradition.[88]

82. Ibid., 220–21.

83. Ibn al-Muʿtazz, *Tabaqat al-Shuʿaraʾ*, 194.

84. Dayf, *Al-ʿAsr al-ʿAbbasi al-Awwal*, 221.

85. Ibn Durayd, Abu Bakr Muhammad bin al-Hasan, *Al-Ishtiqaq* [Etymology], ed. ʿAbd al-Salam Muhammad Harun (Cairo: Muʾassassat al-Khanji, 1958), 406. Abu Nuwas is said also to have "walaʾ" to al-Jarrah (76).

86. ʿAbdullah bin Ahmad bin Harb al-Mihzami Abi Hiffan, *Akhbar Abi Nuwas* [The News of Abu Nuwas], ed. ʿAbd al-Sattar Ahmad Farraj (Cairo: Maktabat Misr, 1957?), 109.

87. Ibid., 121.

88. Dayf, *Al-ʿAsr al-ʿAbbasi al-Awwal*, 220–37. This view is also repeated by Yusuf Husayn Bakkar, who insists on the Persian origins of the normalization of Abbasid boy love, while acknowledging that the practice, while atypical, did exist before the Abbasids. He names "*ghazal* in the masculine" as a "deviant *ghazal*" not on account of sexual deviance (to which he refers as "inversion" or "homosexuality" following Freud and others), but because "our Arabic literature did not know it in its long history since the *jahiliyyah* until the middle of the second century [A.H.]." His interest was to address all the factors that brought about this "obscene habit, which became widespread in our Arab society since that time and until the present." It seems however that there are major differences between the Abbasid era and the present: "One of the evil misfortunes of that era was how this situation became common, so much so that seeking to seduce youthful boys in the streets became a normal or almost normal thing, to the extent that it could be compared with how young men flirt with young women [on the streets] nowadays." See Yusuf Husayn Bakkar, *Ittijahat al-Ghazal fi al-Qarn al-Thani al-Hijri* [The Directions of Love Poetry in the Second Century A.H.] (Cairo: Dar al-Maʿarif bi-Misr, 1971), 195–265, especially 195, 203.

Dayf's nationalism got the better of him when he discussed other poets accused of "bawdiness and *zandaqah*" and attributed their entire tradition to Persian origins.[89] His condemnation of Walibah bin al-Hubab, Abu Nuwas's mentor, was categorical. Although most medieval sources attest that Walibah was an Arab of the Asad tribe, something doubted by his major detractor at the time, the poet Abu al-'Atahiyyah, pointing to his red hair as evidence of his "Roman" origins, Dayf did not mince words in his description of him: "Walibah was a devil on the prowl [shaytanan maridan], excessive in his bawdiness and depravity and in his deviant *ghazal* for youthful boys, claiming that he belonged to the Asad tribe, when it [the tribe] and all Arabs are innocent of any association with him, his debauchery, or his deviance."[90] It hardly helped Walibah's case that "it was he who trained and corrupted Abu Nuwas, as the narrators claimed."[91] Just as Renaissance and later Enlightenment Europeans were to project all their anxieties onto non-Europeans in the process of inventing Europe as a cohesive civilizational category and setting the stage for all kinds of extremist nationalist ideologies and practices, some modern Arab nationalists wanted to safeguard the "pure" Arab civilization of the past as a basis for the modern Arab nation. Following in the footsteps of the architects of the idea of Europe and modern European nationalists, a number of Arab nationalist writers sought to expel "foreign" elements in the process of cleansing the past, thus setting the stage for the expulsion of all contemporary foreign elements in order to cleanse the present.

Contemporary Sex in Islamist and Secular Frames

If nationalists concerned themselves with revolutionizing the sexual mores and the literary and aesthetic tastes of Arabs, assisted by their peremptory power to include certain historical figures in, or exclude them from, Arab history, some radical religious and secular thinkers of the period were more concerned with how the present was to be lived. They would pay less attention to the sexual life of the ancients. While radical secular trends began to emerge in the late nineteenth century, a radical Islamist trend made itself felt in the 1920s, on account of the collapse of the Ottoman Empire and the end of the caliphate system. Islamism remained a subordinated discourse in the public sphere even though its

---

89. Dayf, *Al-'Asr al-'Abbasi al-Awwal*, 382.
90. Ibid., 383–84.
91. Ibid., 384.

echo continued to exist in muted form. The radical secularists would not fare much better, even though their representatives would have a stronger presence in the public sphere of ideas. While Sayyid Qutb was the most prominent Islamist thinker to emerge from this movement, Salamah Musa would be the most prominent spokesperson for radical secularism. As the following discussion will explain, they both dabbled in civilizational thinking and geographic displacements and accepted as given the cultural divide between East and West. Antiessentialists in many respects, they both saw the possibility of transcending one's cultural makeup. Where they differed was in the value they attached to such transcendence and the direction they wished it to take.

Of the new crop of Islamist thinkers, Sayyid Qutb (1903–1966) stood out as the most compelling. He was the earliest of Islamist writers to tackle the question of contemporary sex in the West. He also tackled questions of literary criticism in Arab history and the present.[92] He was the sole civilian member of the revolutionary council that ruled Egypt after the 1952 Revolution but fell out of favor in 1954 and was subsequently jailed; he was the leading thinker of the Muslim Brothers in Egypt until his execution in 1966 by Nasir's revolutionary regime.[93] In Qutb's writings on literature, he was a most sophisticated critic. He studied medieval Arab schools of literary criticism and modern European schools as well as modern Arab applications of the latter. Affirming the limitations of the historical method in studying literature, Qutb remarked that Taha Husayn's historical approach to questions of the literary had led him to make hasty conclusions. This seemed to him especially the case when Husayn judged the "spirit" of the Abbasid period as "bawdy" based on his study of *mujun* poetry. "Such a judgment," averred Qutb, "would require a study of all the arts of speech during this era, as well as all the arts of thinking in all aspects of life, coupled with a comprehensive study of the historical documents that addressed the entire context [mulabasat] of that era before making a judgment on the spirit of the period like the one that the professor [Husayn] issued."[94] Statements like the ones Husayn made, including his assertions that "the expansion of the influence of the Persians is what created *mujun* and bacchic poetry" and "the abundance of concubines is what caused the spread of the art of singing" are "liable

92. See his sophisticated *Al-Naqd al-Adabi, Usuluh wa Manahijuh* [Literary Criticism, Its Bases and Methods] (1947; Beirut: Dar al-Kutub al-'Arabiyyah., 1965).

93. The Society of the Muslim Brothers was established in Egypt in 1928 by Hasan al-Banna as an antisecular revivalist political movement that advocated a "return" to Islam as the solution to social, economic, and political ills.

94. Ibid., 174.

to be in error due to the certainty of the assertion and to its attributing a literary or social phenomenon to one sole cause. It is rare that a phenomenon would have one cause. It is imperative that we study the whole set of historical, social, political, intellectual, economic, and personal circumstances that suffused such a phenomenon and preceded it."[95] Qutb's insistence on the overdetermination of such phenomena was his point of departure in criticizing the historical method, the artistic method, and the psychological method, which he insisted could only work as an integrated whole when applied to a literary work, as each of them alone would only provide a partial analysis.[96] He demonstrated how in studying Leonardo da Vinci, Freud was careful never to say that psychoanalysis allows us to understand the "nature of artistic production" but rather that he was studying the person in the artist and not the artist in the person.[97]

The preceding discussion aside, some of the more relevant remarks that Qutb made about questions of desire and sex dealt with the contemporary West. While his book on literary criticism was published in 1947, Qutb would face exile for his political activities the following year. In 1948, Egypt's prerevolutionary royal government had unofficially banished Qutb to the United States, where he spent two years before returning to Egypt in 1950. Upon his return, Qutb wrote a number of observations about the United States with special attention to the sexual practices and mores of U.S. society. He had written a manuscript titled "The America That I Saw," which was never published and is believed to be lost. However, a few letters under the same title, which he published in a magazine in 1951, were thorough in their assessment of America. Many of Qutb's other observations about American society appeared in letters and in comments in his other published works. These writings would be resurrected in the 1980s and 1990s by Islamist writers whose concern was not the sexual life of America, as it was for Qutb, but that of the contemporary Arab and Muslim worlds. Indeed, Qutb's writings on America were collected and edited and published in 1986 in Saudi Arabia under the title *America from the Inside*.[98]

Qutb's observations about American sexual mores in the period 1948–1950 would seem incredible to today's readers, as they described a type of sexual behavior that the United States did not witness until the 1960s, and in some cases till the 1990s, if even then. The popular view

95. Ibid., 175.
96. Ibid., 136.
97. Ibid., 135, 217–21.
98. Salah ʿAbd al-Fattah al-Khalidi, ed., *Amrika min al-Dakhil bi-Minzar Sayyid Qutb* [America from the Inside, through the Eyes of Sayyid Qutb] (Jiddah: Dar al-Manarah, 1986).

of America, then propagated by Hollywood, of a country where young women were sexually licentious and available and where premarital and adulterous sex was common if not the norm punctuated Qutb's anthropological observations throughout, as did his views of the alleged tolerance of U.S. society in the late 1940s for homosexual sex among men or women. This is ironic, as this was the period when the rise of U.S. anti-Communism broadened to target homosexuals, who as early as 1947 began to be purged from government jobs. The McCarthyist targeting of American homosexuals, which reached its apogee in 1950, would victimize thousands in government, civilian, and military employment and would trump up hysterical media coverage of the possible national disloyalty of "deviants" and "faggots."[99]

Reversing Western developmentalism and applying it to the United States, Qutb was impressed with what he termed American "primitivism." He was particularly astonished at American appreciation of violence and physical strength and male muscularity, whether manifested in violent sports, actual wars, or as signs of male sexual attractiveness. He described American football, wrestling, and boxing as "bloody and savage" and "animalistic," and how American audiences were taken with the sight of blood and broken bones, which excited them further. This was evidence "of the primitivism of feeling" that they had.[100] Indeed, Americans "are also primitive in their sexual lives, including in their marital and family relations." This is mostly manifest in the primacy of "the body" for them.[101] American women, for example, "know well their physical attributes that attract [men]. They know it in their face, the inviting eye, the thirsty lip, and know it well in [the rest of] the body: a full bosom, a round posterior, shapely thighs, and smooth legs—and they show it all and do not hide any of it; they also know it in their clothing: in the florid colors which awaken the primitive feeling in him, in the tailoring which uncovers the enticing parts of the body."[102] As for what American women like in their male lovers,

the American lad knows well that a broad chest and a flexed muscular arm are what ensure that no woman would reject him and that [such a woman's] fantasies only

---

99. On the persecution of American homosexuals during this period, see John D'Emilio, *Sexual Politics, Sexual Communities: The Making of a Homosexual Minority in the United States, 1940–1970*, 2nd ed. (Chicago: University of Chicago Press, 1998), 42–49.

100. Sayyid Qutb, "Amrika allati Ra'ayt: fi mizan al-qiyam al-insaniyyah," *Al-Risalah*, 959, 19 November 1951. The letter is included in Salah 'Abd al-Fattah al-Khalidi, *Amrika min al-Dakhil bi-minzar Sayyid Qutb*, 104.

101. Ibid., 112.

102. Ibid., 112–13.

acknowledge Cowboys . . . Plainly speaking, a nurse told me at the hospital [where Qutb was being treated for an illness], "I only require in my dream boyfriend that he have strong arms that can squeeze me hard." *Look* magazine polled a number of young women of all ages, educational levels, and income brackets, about what it termed "beefy muscles." The sweeping majority expressed their absolute admiration for young men with beefy muscles"![103]

Throughout Qutb's interests were civilizational. Western civilization failed the test when compared with Islamic civilization. He spoke of the degeneration/dissolution [inhilal] of European societies as a result of the permissiveness [ibahiyyah] among its young men and women, the fate destined for America as well. Moreover, "there were those who would sell America's and Britain's military secrets to their enemies, not because they needed money, but because they were afflicted with sexual deviance, which resulted from the effects of the sexual chaos that predominates in society."[104] While Qutb here seems familiar with the U.S. media and government accusations that homosexuals were potential traitors, he could also be making a direct reference to Guy Burgess, Anthony Blunt, and others, whose homosexuality and espionage for the Soviet Union were the stuff of (what would be called today) Western homophobic propaganda of the early 1950s.

Qutb's concern about the "spread of sexual deviance" in the West was evident in a number of statements he wrote (when discussing Freud's study of da Vinci, Qutb, in contrast, used the term *mithliyyah* (sameness) and not "deviance" to describe da Vinci's sexual desires[105]). He observed that contrary to the widespread notion that "the segregation [ihtijab] of women spreads this deviant abomination in society!" in reality, "witnessing the actual situation" shatters such arguments.

For in Europe and America, there was no longer a single obstacle to total sexual mixing between every male and every female—just like in the world of beasts!—and the rate of this deviant abomination increases, rather than decreases, as a result of mixing! Thus, it is not limited to deviance among men but goes beyond it to deviance among women. He who is not convinced by this evidence must read "Sexual Behavior among Men" and "Sexual Behavior among Women" in the American Kinsey Report.[106]

103. Ibid., 113.
104. Sayyid Qutb, *Fi Zilal al-Qur'an* [In the Shadow of the Qur'an], 25th printing (1952, 1972; Cairo: Dar al-Shuruq, 1996), vol. 2, 636.
105. Qutb, *Al-Naqd al-Adabi*, 219. I should note here that to my knowledge the da Vinci book was not yet translated into Arabic. It would seem that "homosexuality" was rendered "al-mithliyyah al-jinsiyyah" by Qutb himself.
106. Qutb, *Fi Zilal al-Qur'an*, vol. 3, 1316.

Here Qutb was indeed responding to Orientalist views that posited segregation as leading to homosexuality in the Muslim world; he ingeniously reverses the argument and applies it instead to the West. But if we are to accept Qutb's important argument that not segregation but gender mixing is what produces male homosexuality, then would this mean that homosexuality (both male and female) is always a result of an excess of available vaginas? If this is the case, then why would this not be the outcome in Muslim societies as well, wherein Muslim men could marry four wives? Alas, Qutb did not address this contradiction.

Qutb, like many Arab writers after him, Islamist, secular, or feminist, found in the Kinsey Reports a well of anthropological information. As anthropologist of America, Qutb cited the reports again in a different context to provide a background to an incident he witnessed:

Alongside this absolute licentiousness—or because of it—cheap and available normal sexual relations are no longer satisfying sexual inclinations; thus the sexual deviance of being attracted to the other sex, whether in the world of young men or that of young women, became widespread. The Kinsey report on "Sexual Behavior among Men" and "Sexual Behavior among Women" includes precise and amazing statistics about this deviance . . . I remember—insofar as bashfulness and good manners allow—a personal observation in one of Washington's hotels: I was with an Egyptian colleague staying at a hotel—two or three days after we first arrived in the United States. The black elevator operator was quite friendly to us—because we are closer to his [skin] color and because we do not despise colored people. He began to offer his services to us in the field of "entertainment" and mentioned a few "samples" including various "deviancies." During his presentation, he informed us that often there would be two young men or two young women staying in one of the hotel rooms and would ask him to bring them a bottle of Coca Cola without changing their [compromising] positions when he would enter the room! When we showed disgust and amazement and inquired of him, "Were they not embarrassed?" He answered us amazed, in turn, but at our disgust and amazement and our question regarding embarrassment: "Why? They are satisfying their own inclinations and are providing each other with pleasure." . . . I was to find out later—from my many observations—that American society does not deplore a human being's satisfying himself in the manner that he likes, as long as there is no coercion and thus no crime, even in matters that the law—at least on paper—still considers a crime.[107]

It is surprising that Qutb would make such statements when American antihomosexual repression was at one of its highest points. In a

107. Al-Khalidi, *Amrika min al-Dakhil*, 196, cited from *Al-Islam wa Mushkilat al-Hadarah*, 70–71.

later observation, he cited an oft-repeated quote attributed to President John F. Kennedy in which "he said that six of every seven young men in America are not fit for military service due to the moral degeneration in which they live."[108] Indeed, the American "Committee of Fourteen" in charge of the country's moral life "estimated that 90 percent of Americans are afflicted with lethal venereal diseases."[109] Qutb discerned that this early attention to sexual licentiousness and venereal disease was a major concern to American Christians and conservatives. This concern, as we will see in a later chapter, would be internalized and adopted by Islamist writers in the 1980s and 1990s. Indeed, the spread of venereal disease would become the irrefutable proof of what sexual licentiousness leads to and what the role of Islam would be in protecting people and civilization from it. For now, however, Qutb's voice would remain a lonely one. The Islamist mantle would have to wait a few decades before it was picked up by a new generation of Islamists intent on transforming Arab civilization into an Islamist civilization.

The only other Arab thinker in this period to address questions of contemporary sexual practices and the nature of sexual desire with any seriousness was the Egyptian radical secularist, socialist, and feminist Salamah Musa (1887–1958). Occupying the other end of the political spectrum from Qutb, Musa was a prolific writer and journalist who was highly influenced by Fabianism and by the thought of Nietzsche, Darwin, Spencer, Freud, Adler, and Pavlov. His first book in 1910 was about Nietzsche's *überman*.[110] He also wrote about evolution and is in fact credited by some for inventing the Arabic equivalent term "tatawwur."[111] His other interests included eugenics and population control as well as psychology, literature, and music. He wrote dozens of popular books aimed at a general audience, including a number of books aimed at the youth, in which he explored the sexual life and difficulties faced by the young men and women of Egypt and linked these topics to civilizational worth. His books were widely distributed in all major Arab cities, includ-

---

108. Qutb, *Fi Zilal al-Qur'an*, vol. 2, 636. Muhammad 'Ali Qutb (no relation to Sayyid) used the same Kennedy quote in his 1984 book *Al-Hubb wa al-Jins min Manzur Islami* [Love and Sex from an Islamic Perspective] (Cairo: Maktabat al-Qur'an, 1984), 129.

109. Qutb, *Fi Zilal al-Qur'an*, vol. 2, 637.

110. Salamah Musa, *Muqaddimmat al-Subirman* [Introduction to the Superman] (1910; Cairo: Salamah Musa lil-Nashr wa al-Tawzi', 1962).

111. Ghali Shukri, *Salamah Musa wa Azmat al-Damir al-'Arabi* [Salamah Musa and the Crisis of Arab Conscience] (Cairo: Maktab al-Khanji, 1962), 48. Adel Ziadat credits Lebanese intellectual and *Al-Muqtataf* editor Ya'qub Sarruf for inventing the term. See Adel A. Ziadat, *Western Science in the Arab World: The Impact of Darwinism, 1860–1930* (New York: St. Martin's Press, 1986), 48.

ing Cairo, Baghdad, Casablanca, Damascus, and Khartoum.[112] Educated in Britain, Musa was an admirer of Bernard Shaw. A Christian Copt by birth, he was critical of both Islamic and Christian teachings and sought to secularize (read Europeanize) contemporary culture, the Arabic equivalent term for which, "thaqafah," he was also said to have coined.[113]

Musa's interest in contemporary sexual life and romantic liaisons can be traced to his early writings.[114] In 1925, he published a book on love stories from the Arab and Western traditions elaborating on the importance of spiritual love. To him, spiritual love was distinct from sexual desire, which is "instinctual" (gharizi) and was quite different from spiritual love.[115] In a later book, *The Secrets of the Heart,* dedicated to the study of the unconscious, Musa insisted on discussing the "strength of the sexual instinct," especially as people were "shy" and "silent" about talking about it despite its serious consequences: "Madness in our male youths, women fall prey to hysteria, while secret habits arise among some to the point of taking away their reason."[116] He was concerned about the health of society and the possible social ills that could afflict society if it did not take certain precautions. Waxing Aristotelian, he insisted that excess and extremism (ghuluw) were dangerous, as "extremism [in religious worship] is related to another extremism, that of surrendering to one's desires. One of the oddest things that history has proven is that monasticism spread in the Christian world when vices proliferated and people sought to satisfy their desires. It is hardly coincidental that the Mamluks were the builders of the monumental mosques of Cairo even though they led a life full of vice."[117] In a chapter on the prerequisites for genius, Musa adapts Freud's notion of sublimation and its connection to civilization to the Egyptian context:

One of the prerequisites for success and genius is to sublimate sexual energy and divert it to the service of the fine arts. This energy floods over during youth and forces

112. See the last page of his book *Muhawalat Saykulujiyyah* [Endeavors in Psychology] (Cairo: Maktabat al-Khanji, 1953), where the publisher lists all book distributors in the cities where the book is sold.
113. Shukri, *Salamah Musa,* 48.
114. It is significant that intellectual biographies of Musa, whether in Arabic or English, ignored his focus on sexuality. While Shukri noted it only perfunctorily in *Salamah Musa,* Vernon Egger made no mention of it. See Vernon Egger, *A Fabian in Egypt: Salamah Musa and the Rise of the Professional Classes in Egypt, 1909–1939* (London: University Press of America, 1986).
115. Salamah Musa, *Al-Hubb fi al-Tarikh* [Love in History] (Cairo: Salamah Musa lil-Nashr wa al-Tawziʿ, 1946). This is the second edition of the book which was first published in 1925.
116. Salamah Musa, *Asrar al-Nafs* [The Secrets of the Heart] (1927; Cairo: Salamah Musa lil-Nashr wa al-Tawziʿ, n.d.), 17.
117. Ibid., 140.

its owner, whether male or female, toward the other sex with intensity. If mating takes place at that time, the libido will dissipate, and the repressed energy therein will have been released, but if sexual intercourse does not take place, then the repressed energy is diverted to one of two paths: (1) either sexual deviances, such as the secret habit or seeking the unfamiliar; or (2) sublimation toward the service of the fine arts, which resemble loving women.[118]

Musa concluded that "delay in marriage increases genius in a nation, even though it can also cause deviances and illnesses. We can add to this that permission to marry more than one woman decreases genius, because it decreases sublimation, as the sexual instinct finds a natural venue by going from one woman to another."[119]

Musa seemed particularly concerned about what he termed the "secret habit," a rough translation of the English "solitary" or "secret vice" and its effect on the nation's youth and was horrified by what he termed "sexual deviance" in reference to same-sex contact, especially among men.[120] He would revisit both subjects in most of his books. In one of the earliest veiled references to masturbation, Musa stated: "Let us assume that a young man fell into a bad habit that took hold of him. The way to get rid of it is for him to suggest to himself at every chance he has to relax and to instruct himself with a statement whose content is something like: I hate this habit, a . . . habit (here he must mean it), and would continue to repeat it until it is imprinted in his mind as a creed that will take hold of him, filling him with hatred for this habit."[121] Musa postulated that it was sexual segregation that caused "our youth after adolescence to practice the secret habit, for we have exiled them and removed them from reality when we prohibited their mixing with young women [fatayat]. Their sexual desire forced them to surrender to a substitutive imagination."[122] He identified the "secret habit" as one of those "bad habits that retard the development of the personality."[123]

Musa was primarily concerned about the adolescent boy where "we find a natural change in his body and soul. But this young man could succumb to the secret habit and then would practice it excessively at which point his personality would change in a sickly manner as he would start

118. Ibid., 143.

119. Ibid., 145.

120. The most likely person who invented the term "secret habit" for masturbation is Jurji Zaydan. On this, see chapter 5.

121. Musa, *Asrar al-Nafs*, 86.

122. Salamah Musa, *Al-Shakhsiyyah al-Naji'ah* [The Efficient Personality] (1943; Cairo: Salamah Musa lil-Nashr wa al-Tawzi', n.d.), 38.

123. Ibid., 122.

to like solitude and surrender all day and some of the night to genital sexual thoughts, which will take him far from reality, make him neglect his homework, and he would end up being a disappointment at school." To correct the errant path of this young man, Musa proposed sports, cinema, theater, and "to encourage a hobby that he may get attached to, such as taking up one of the arts."[124]

Musa would soon zero in on the most effective treatment and cure for the "secret habit." In 1947, he wrote in his memoir how when he was involved in the 1930s with the YMCA in Cairo (founded in 1922), he would meet with Egyptian youth (not only Christians, but also Muslims and Jews), every Monday to discuss things "family-style."[125] The conversations would touch on

the problems facing the youth, whether cultural, sexual, or familial, which is why the sexual direction would emerge more prominently in these discussions. This is where I found benefit for myself in these conversations. Those youth were "the raw material" through which I was able to study human nature. These young men were between the ages of eighteen and twenty-five. This is why sexual problems were prominent for all of them . . . I would often find one of the young men burdened and exhausted with sexual passion, which he would rid himself of through the secret habit. I would find often that failure in school exams was caused by the immersion in this habit, whose danger increases due to the lack of gender mixing. The isolation of each sex makes people surrender to fantasy to which one commits until [the fantasy] returns, as if one had schizophrenia, that is, the mania characterized by complete surrender to fantasy and absolute separation from reality and society.[126]

Musa's views on sex were consistent with social Darwinism. He would often combine Freudian ideas with behaviorism in elaborating a cure for the secret habit.

I often thought about this complex topic of how a young single man, exhausted by sexual passion, is to entertain himself in our segregated Egyptian society. I still remember a young man of twenty who came to me in humiliation, sometimes implying, other times openly declaring, that he could no longer stand his situation and that he was on the verge of doing something dangerous if he could not rid himself of the secret habit.[127]

124. Ibid., 174–75; see also 160–61.
125. Salamah Musa, *Tarbiyat Salamah Musa* [The Education/Upbringing of Salamah Musa] (Cairo: Mu'assasat al-Khanji, 1962), 172. This is a revised and updated edition of Musa's memoir, which was first published in 1947. The memoir is available in English as *The Education of Salama Musa,* translated by L. O. Schuman (Leiden: Brill, 1961).
126. Ibid., 171–72.
127. Ibid., 172.

The cure that Musa offered to the young man was to take up dancing with girls at dance clubs. At first, the young man was not successful in making the acquaintance of "girls" but was ultimately successful in meeting a few and in finding dance partners.

I saw him two months later, took him aside and asked him how he was doing. He told me, to my great astonishment, that he had learned from dancing how to give up the secret habit. His explanation was incredible. He said that in dancing, there is chivalry, good taste, and beauty, traits that accompany dance and that contradict the humiliation and baseness that exist in the secret habit . . . His words were a beacon for me . . . there are those who benefited from advice to get interested in books and culture, others who would find success in school that would distract them from this habit, but dance was one of the greatest means for a cure, especially in critical cases.[128]

Musa provided other examples of people who contacted him or cases with which he was familiar involving the secret vice. One example he gave was of a young man who had degenerated due to excessive masturbation resulting from strict parents who blocked his social life by forcing him to study all the time. The young man, who was to be the pride and joy of the family, was institutionalized as a result of dissociating from reality, which resulted from his overreliance on fantasy during masturbation as a way to escape his strict living conditions.[129]

At times, Musa seemed to have less categorical views on masturbation. He suggested that practicing the secret habit "once or twice a week was not harmful, and that 99 percent of young men might have done so without harm. It would be harmful for those who practice it this much only if they consider it a low and contemptible habit, or that it weakens his health and destroys it. Harm in such cases results from the perception and not from the habit."[130] In Musa, we see how masturbation had become a full-fledged disease requiring a cure, which is a combination of behavioral modification and voluntary sublimation. Indeed, for Musa, masturbation was one of many "deviances" afflicting urban youth, especially the middle classes. Others included depression, sexual anxiety,

128. Ibid., 173.
129. Salamah Musa, *Dirasat Saykulujiyyah* [Psychological Studies] (1956; Cairo: Salamah Musa Lil Nashr wa al-Tawziʿ, n.d.), 103–10. Another case of masturbation that Musa cited involved a thirty-three-year-old man preparing for his doctorate who sought Musa's help to rid him of his fifteen-year addiction to the "secret habit." Musa recommended to him to mix with women or to go with a friend to dance clubs. Musa insisted that the man should only marry after he rid himself of the "baseness" [khissah] of this habit. See Salamah Musa, *Ahadith ila al-Shabab* [Sayings for the Youth] (1957; Cairo: Salamah Musa lil-Nashr wa al-Tawziʿ, n.d.), 114–18.
130. Musa, *Ahadith ila al-Shabab*, 122. See also Musa, *Muhawalat Saykulujiyyah*, 57.

and the like. He refused to echo Freud that "sex is the sole root of all our activities and problems," as the sole root was none other than the anxious social structure: "In scientific societies, males and females should live together from the moment of birth until death, with no separation of the sexes, as this is the natural way that nature screams forth. A society that opposes nature is a corrupt and putrid [fasid] society. It will not be able to defeat nature, because nature strikes back. What will result from the separation of the sexes are those deviances that have spread in many Oriental societies, nay, it may lead to madness."[131]

Musa became increasingly concerned about "sexual deviance" among men and linked it to "Oriental" societies' social arrangements past and present. He would address its existence in the present, the influence of the past, especially its literary products, and how to combat such an "abomination" quickly. Perhaps his earliest reference to sex among men was in his book *Secrets of the Heart,* where he dealt with it in the context of dreams. In a section on symbolism in dreams, Musa gave a number of examples to illustrate his point, including this one: "A. dreams that he debauched his brother. He recounts the dream with hatred and disgust, as he never desired his brother and he is also distant from this deviant desire. In a simple analysis, meaning after some questions and answers, I found out that he had had a fight with his brother and that he was not able to avenge himself sufficiently. As debauching someone in social conventions is an insult, or even a great perfidy to the person being debauched, A. avenges himself on his brother by debauching him."[132] Although he was well versed in Freud, Musa failed to provide alternative Freudian readings, namely, that the very fight of the two brothers itself was an expression of sexual feelings that they shared for one another. If for Freud, social situations are impelled by sexual feelings, for Musa (and here the influence of Adler is clearest), sexual feelings are simply expressions of social feelings of aggression. In line with this analysis, Musa would insist in a later work that "aggression is the prevalent characteristic of sexual desire. I refer here to desire not love . . . I have found that in many dreams, when a young man gets upset at another man he dreams that he debauched him. Sexual desire here was excited, in its deviant form, by the quarrel and aggression, as it represents both."[133]

In one of his rare references to homosexuality in the West, Musa discussed the life and work of André Gide in a brief article on the occasion

131. Musa, *Muhawalat Saykulujiyyah,* 66–67.
132. Musa, *Asrar al-Nafs,* 48–49.
133. Musa, *Muhawalat Saykulujiyyah,* 163.

of Gide's eightieth birthday and after Gide had received the Nobel Prize for literature. Musa was clear on where he stood on homosexuality in the West. He tells us that in his youth Gide

had met Oscar Wilde and learned wantonness [istihtar] from him, especially sexual wantonness. In this vein, we should listen to what Nietzsche once said: "It would not harm us to read geniuses even though they have some worms in their heads." In his youth he visited Algeria and immersed himself in psychological, mental, and physical enjoyment . . . and in 1936 he visited Russia and studied this young State and found in it what he thought were restrictions on freedom. Here we find that worms were eating away at his head, for he blames the Russians because they restricted freedom by prescribing punishments for sexual deviance . . . This month, an English translation of his book *Journal,* meaning "diaries," in which he expresses his feelings and thoughts, appeared. What is amazing is that these English approved of the two-year imprisonment of Oscar Wilde while they now welcome his disciple who echoes Wilde's very call.[134]

When it came to Egypt and "the Orient," Musa offered a full-scale diagnosis not unlike the one he had offered about masturbation. If for Qutb the excessive mixing of the sexes caused deviance in the West, for Musa, who echoed the Orientalists, it was the separation of the sexes that caused sexual deviance: "If the two sexes are separated, corruption ensues and each of them will think of their own sex excluding the other sex. This is what we call deviance, which is a journalistic, unscientific term, which allows us to avoid using other words that are abominations and which we are too disgusted to mention."[135] To remedy the situation is not easy:

We still need years to render mixing of the sexes prevalent in order to alleviate sexual exhaustion. Through this mingling, both sexual deviance among the male youth and the secret habit will disappear. Sexual deviance is common among Oriental nations due to this existing sexual segregation, and our youth practice the secret habit, despite their disgust at it and their hatred of it, also as a result of this segregation. I do not mean to say that Europe and America do not have these two vices at all, what I rather mean is that the youth there is less immersed in it compared to the youth of the Oriental nations because they mix with the other sex.[136]

134. Salamah Musa, *Tariq al-Majd lil-Shabab* [The Path of Glory for the Youth] (1949; Cairo: Matba'at al-Khanji, 1964), 189–190.
135. Salamah Musa, *Al-Adab Lil-Sha'b* [Literature Is for the People] (Cairo: Salamah Musa Lil-Nashr wa al-Tawzi', 1956), 82.
136. Musa, *Muhawalat Saykulujiyyah,* 47.

Musa cited the case of a seventeen-year-old who wrote him seeking help for his predicament of finding men sexually attractive. He explained that

such feelings are almost natural among all adolescents, including females. It may continue until the age of twenty, namely, that a young man admires another young man of the same age or younger and that a young woman admires another young woman of the same age or younger. Such admiration is of course sexual in its essence, that is, it is deviant. Deviant contact often takes place in these years. . . . But if the environment is good and mixing between the two sexes is permitted then this deviant sexual orientation is redirected toward the other sex and the young man forgets his admiration for other young men as the young woman forgets her admiration for other young women, at which point both revert to their natural state. This is what happens in Europe and America and all other countries that allow the mingling of the sexes in society and in primary and secondary schools and at university.[137]

Musa nuanced his earlier claim regarding the prevalence of same-sex desire in "Oriental" nations by providing a class angle:

Deviance is prevalent in Egypt because of the segregation of the two sexes. Such deviance prevails in cities and is rare in the countryside because in the countryside mixing is available as a result of the necessary work that includes both sexes. This is also the case among the poor classes in the cities where segregation is not total. This is why sexual deviance does not prevail in these classes as it does among the middle class, especially as marriage age is delayed in this class . . . This social situation has another effect. The secret habit in the countryside among both sexes, as is the case among the urban poor, is almost unknown, in contrast with the middle class, where it is endemic.[138]

Musa revisited the matter in a book dedicated to women's rights. He asserted that "we men and women should never separate our sexes from one another, for when we are separated we succumb to ugly sexual deviations . . . This segregation is the reason for sexual deviance, which renders a man into an animal, hideous, contemptible, sick, living a secret life devouring young men, corrupting them and deviating them from their future manhood. There is no cure to this malady except by sexual mingling, so that sexual desire will take its natural course without deviation, and a man will love a woman and not a young man."[139] While in

137. Ibid., 51.
138. Ibid., 52–53.
139. Salamah Musa, *Al-Mar'ah laysat Lu'bat al-Rajul* [Woman Is Not Man's Plaything] (1956; Cairo: Salamah Musa Lil-Nashr wa al-Tawzi', n.d.), 13–14.

his memoir Musa recounted the case of a man who sought his help for an addiction to the secret habit and for whom he had recommended dance as a cure, in his book about women's rights Musa retells another story, that of the seventeen year old (whom he had cited in *Muhawalat*, as discussed above) who had written to him seeking help for his ailment of finding men sexually attractive. He uses this example to generalize about society at large. Musa attributed his "deviance" to living in a sexually segregated society and to the delay in marriage age in "our social milieu." While in America and Europe marriage age is also late, "there is sexual mixing there while here there is separation. There a man mingles with a woman, straightening [tastaqim] his sexual fantasy because she is his aim . . . thus he is normal [sawiyy]. But an Egyptian man only finds young men of his age and thus transfers to them his sexual exploration and fantasizes about their beauty because he does not see anyone else as an aim to his instinct. This is why he is a deviant."[140] Musa seemed to imply here that exclusive attraction to men is the norm among Egyptian men just as exclusive attraction to women is the norm of American and European men. It is unclear how Egyptian men who desire women are able to deviate from the norm and how European and American men who desire men deviate from theirs. His advice to the young man who wrote him was to "beware lest you fall, for you are at the precipice and on the way to sexual deviance. You must transfer your love and admiration to the other sex and meet a young woman and accord her respect and be an honest friend to her. I am confident that this will be difficult for you now because your fantasies do not touch on women at all. But you must practice."[141]

Musa insisted in book after book that mixed dancing was the best cure for all sexually related complexes in Egyptian society, including same-sex desire, for it constituted

the most successful treatment for sexual deviance; a man who dances with a woman takes the correct sexual direction without deviation or swerving, as it is impossible that he would turn to anyone but women in fantasy or reality . . . This is an important benefit to many young men who are so advanced in their bachelorhood that they began to swerve and deviate. In Egypt sexual deviance [inhiraf] is more common than in Europe due to the existing segregation of the sexes . . . and when we bring the deviant young man and prod him to dance with the other sex—and this is not easy—we are

140. Musa, *Al-Mar'ah laysat Lu'bat al-Rajul*, 41. This is the same man whose letter he cited in *Muhawalat*, 40.
141. Musa, *Al-Mar'ah laysat*, 42.

attempting to return him to the correct sexual aim, at which point he would acquire a new personality that enables him to regain his sexual health and dignity together.[142]

Musa explained how Egyptian dancing is retrograde, as it was built on degrading women. He reiterated his call for European mixed dancing as the best mode for social training of the sexes: "Finally, we should mention and never forget that the male dancer will never succumb to deviance because dancing habituates him to orient himself toward women and only women. He orients his sexual look toward its natural object. The same is true for women."[143]

Musa saw the question of contemporary sexual deviance as a continuation of the medieval past and focused his condemnation on the figure of Abu Nuwas as the most debauched in the Arabic canon. In an earlier book, ironically, he seemed perturbed that restrictions were placed on Abu Nuwas's poetry. He had recounted how as a result of what he called the "disease of the Arabic language," identified as "a reactionary classicism": "We read about the [recent] rejection of one of the poems of Abu Nuwas—and he is the great renewer—in a literary contest."[144] He would change his opinion later. In a move reminiscent of Taha Husayn, and in a context of stressing that the youth must buy books to educate themselves, Musa cautioned against "bad books, ones that are terrible, such as the poetry collections of ibn al-Rumi [a medieval poet who also composed sexually explicit poems] and Abu Nuwas. We are embarrassed to leave these books behind for our sons and daughters to read, which is why we should be embarrassed to read them ourselves. Although I believe that the mature man who needs to expand his historical vision needs to read them—but read them for history's sake, not for art's."[145] Thus, Abu Nuwas's poetry should not be enjoyed and appreciated but rather can function as a sort of native informant for historical anthropology.

---

142. Musa, *Dirasat Saykulujiyyah*, 155–56.

143. Musa, *Al-Mar'ah laysat Lu'bat al-Rajul*, 114. In addition to dance, Musa also ventured a few existential pieces of advice. In at least one case, Musa claimed he was able to cure a man, namely, a twenty-five year old whose uncle had "debauched" him for a whole year when he was a young boy of twelve. As an adult, the young man "debauched" (fasaqa) boys and "debauched prostitutes deviantly" (the reference here is to anal sex). The man also hated honest men and was an alcoholic. Musa helped him by suggesting to him that he understand why he does these things, on account of his childhood trauma, and that he stop and "evolve" and seek "elevation" and be "reborn." When later Musa asked the man what most influenced him to be cured, he told him it was the part that he had to be "reborn, to have a new birth." See Musa, *Ahadith ila al-Shabab*, 135–39.

144. Salamah, Musa, *Al-Balaghah al-'Asriyyah wa al-Lughah al-'Arabiyyah* [Contemporary Rhetoric and the Arabic Language] (1945; Cairo: Salamah Musa lil-Nashr wa al-Tawzi', 1964) 82–83.

145. Salamah Musa, *Ahadith ila al-Shabab*, 42–43.

At the outset, Musa identified sexual deviance as the "Nuwasite malady" (al-ʿahah al-nuwasiyyah).[146] The present era, he argued, was not unlike the era in which Abu Nuwas lived: "Perhaps had Abu Nuwas lived in a mixed society wherein he would find women in the market and social situations, in the office [sic], and the shop, would his sexual instinct have swerved and corrupted him as he would corrupt other young men like him? . . . The greatest thing that safeguards society from sexual deviance, which is the most degraded corruption of nature that anyone can imagine, is the mingling of the sexes, and the best exercise for sexual health is dance."[147] In exasperation, Musa issued a call to university professors: "Teach dance to our young men and women so that we can guarantee them good sexual health, so that they can be ready for beautiful love. Create a ballet company for us. Give us pleasure and teach us and correct our instincts so that we will not be Nuwasites."[148] This dread of Nuwasites, however, did not mean that Musa supported Hitler's solution for homosexuals. In discussing eugenic proposals, Musa averred that "some nations understood the value of heredity and made laws to sterilize those lacking in intelligence, meaning imbeciles. Hitler's government went overboard when it sterilized some Nuwasite criminals who debauched boys or those whose repetition of the crime was proven."[149]

His diagnosis that the separation of the sexes caused the "Nuwasite malady" caused a fracas in 1954: "I had to confront the public and the mob with these words of mine."[150] Indeed, Musa was not much liked by his contemporaries with whom he warred in the pages of Egyptian newspapers. His detractors included Taha Husayn, ʿAbbas Mahmud al-ʿAqqad, Kamil al-Shinnawi, and the playwright Tawfiq al-Hakim, among others.[151] He remained unique among prominent Arab thinkers of the

146. Salamah Musa, *Dirasat Saykulujiyyah*, 21.
147. Salamah Musa, *Al-Marʾah laysat Luʿbat al-Rajul*, 115. He would add elsewhere that "this milieu in which Abu Nuwas lived, a milieu where the sexes were segregated, is one we and many nations are still living in. In fact, I can venture to say that there are laws which have been legislated in our country that increase this separation, and naturally increase this Nuwasite deviance . . . We cannot expect a man who remains until the age of thirty without ever having been a colleague or a companion to a woman to be a healthy man. He must succumb to deviance, which includes (1) the deviance of the secret habit, which disintegrates his being and may lead him to neurosis; (2) the deviance of turning to his own sex which may lead him to jail; [and] (3) the deviance of repression, which may lead him to the mental asylum." See Musa, *Al-Adab Lil-Shaʿb*, 82.
148. Musa, *Al-Marʾah laysat Luʿbat al-Rajul*, 117.
149. Salamah Musa, *Ahadith ila al-Shabab*, 75.
150. Salamah Musa, *Al-Adab Lil-Shaʿb*, 185.
151. For a discussion of their views of him and his response, see Musa, *Al-Adab Lil-Shaʿb*, 187–96.

twentieth century in his quest to transform Egyptian (even Arab and Islamic) culture and manners into Europeanness by forsaking all local cultural attributes, including food, dress, and music, which he also sought to transform into European forms. While other intellectuals sought out past "civilizational" achievements as a model to help the present modernize, Musa's adoration of things English and European impelled him to call for the transformation of Egypt into Europe. From this came his concern, nay obsession, with normalizing (and his sense of shame of) Egyptian sexual desires and practices so that they can reflect the European present.

Musa was unhappy with his contemporaries' approach to studying the past and offered a different aesthetic and social reading of it for his presentist approach. He insisted that medieval Arabic literature was beholden to the caliphs and the upper classes and their pleasures and failed to function as a "literature for the people." This did not mean that there was nothing good in this literature but rather that "the best of this [literature] among the ancients cannot include the sodomitic [lutiyyah] poetry that Abu Nuwas composed or the fecal [buraziyyah] poetry that ibn al-Rumi composed."[152] As literature and art, in Musa's estimation, "aim at higher ethics," then "we cannot call the poetry of [Abu Nuwas] beautiful art. For how could sodomy be beautiful?"[153] He added that

a literature that is engagé or committed makes it imperative that we take on social problems. A belletrist [adib] is responsible; and his responsibility is to society and humanity. He should always stand against war, colonialism, exploitation, against the denigration of women, against inequality between the sexes in civil, constitutional, and economic rights, and he must call for justice to the workers and for love between the two sexes . . . This is if he were responsible. Were he to be irresponsible, then he might as well compose poems to [King] Faruq describing him as a "philosopher" and he may say that Abu Nuwas is a great man of letters, and support the tyrants in overthrowing the constitution so that [Kings] Fuʾad or Faruq could rule without parliament, and let the nation go to hell.[154]

Musa identified the literature that modern Arabs and Egyptians inherited as a "feudal" literature. He complained about how "six or seven books by and about Abu Nuwas have already been published—and I

152. Ibid., 11. See also 177 for similar descriptions. Ibn al-Rumi had indeed included many references to excrement and flatulence in his *hijaʾ* (defamatory) poems.
153. Ibid., 12.
154. Ibid., 20–21.

can name them all—all of which are feudal books whose purpose is ephemeral pleasure derived from feudal anecdotes, enjoyable innuendo, drunken fantasy, and deviant desire. Abu Nuwas lived in a feudal society from whose tables he ate and whose ethics and values he echoed. Our writers who have revived his memory in their contemporary writings do not differ from him in their feudal spirit and milieu, which propelled them to write such books. They write in the language of Abu Nuwas and aim to distil the meaning of literature by dictating it."[155] In another diatribe against Abu Nuwas, Musa exclaimed:

Is it possible for us to say that the poetry of Abu Nuwas serves social health? No. It rather serves social illness and renders abomination [fuhsh] and debauchery [fisq] lovable to people . . . The genius of Abu Nuwas cannot be denied by any mature man of letters, but it is the genius of the craft only. As for the genius of an art that aims at life and sees the vision of life and depicts noble ethics and feels human responsibility, none of this can be found in Abu Nuwas. When I read him, I find in his words and meanings a glitter that is the glitter of rottenness growing on decay, or poisonous flowers from which we must protect the young man. His literature is the literature of sexual malady ['ahah], the literature of abomination at which the good and clean man is disgusted despite what it contains of luster and flashes . . . This is why I say that the significance of Abu Nuwas for me is not artistic or literary but social and psychological . . . The social significance is that Abu Nuwas lived in a segregated society that separated the sexes, which led to the corruption of his sexual instinct . . . Some may say that this corruption also exists among nations where the sexes mingle. This is true. But there exists a great difference between a nation whose most intelligent poet specializes in composing two thousand pages of poetry about abomination and deviance and one where one of its poets composes a story or a poetry verse containing such meanings that would be published in secret.[156]

Musa proceeded to explain his focus on Abu Nuwas: "I would not have turned to Abu Nuwas were it not that I wanted to extract the moral for our own society . . . the moral is that our society differs but in degree from the society in which Abu Nuwas lived. What we aim for is social health for the people, which cannot be achieved if we—or more precisely, some of us— continue to call for segregation."[157] The main bogeyman for Egyptian society remained sexual segregation:

Where there is separation, deviance replaces health. The young woman goes to other young women while the young man seeks out young men. This is the ugly social

155. Ibid., 69.
156. Ibid., 81.
157. Ibid., 82–83.

malady that has clung to Oriental societies for the past thousands of years when the segregation of the sexes was common. Abu Nuwas's poetry, in which he glorifies this deviance, is but a reflection of the social situation prevailing in his era as a result of the segregation of the sexes.[158]

What was at stake for Musa in all this was the survival of Egyptian civilization. For him the separation of the sexes caused addiction to the secret habit and sexual deviance in addition to oppressing women, whose equality he sought. True to his Spencerist ideals, Musa summed up his concerns as follows: "We are in a struggle for survival with civilized nations. We must produce like they do. If we prevent women from working, our production will decrease . . . and then we will be defeated in the struggle for survival. We may even become extinct as the Heksos became extinct, as did the Hittites, the Canaanites, the Babylonians, the Medeans, the Nabateans, and dozens of other peoples that did not evolve."[159] To become European, Egyptians must act and be European.

Musa had some allies among Arab intellectuals who were less well known but who wrote in the same vein. One of them was Iraqi sociologist 'Ali al-Wardi, who taught at Baghdad's Teacher's College and dabbled in ideas similar to Musa's. Unlike the pan-Arab popularity of Musa, al-Wardi was only known in Iraq. U.S.-educated, al-Wardi was a staunch secularist and modernist who wrote sensationalist and theoretical books about literature, Islamic history, psychology, and sociology. His ideas provoked many religious and secular conservatives in the Iraq of the 1950s, ruled then by an absolutist Hashemite monarchy (there seems to be no reference to his work outside Iraq). Concerned about sexual relations and desires in the medieval and contemporary Arab world, especially in Iraq, al-Wardi found in Rifa'ah al-Tahtawi's chronicle of his nineteenth-century trip to Paris an opening to discuss sex in contemporary society. In a book that railed against religious preachers and thinkers, inter alia, as nothing less than "the sultans' preachers," al-Wardi castigated al-Tahtawi for criticizing the liberties that French women enjoyed while praising the French "because they are not inclined to sodomy or the love of youthful boys." Al-Wardi insisted that

this Azharite praised the French because they do not love youthful boys and disparaged their women for not covering [sufur] and for mixing with men, and did not

158. Musa, *Ahadith ila al-Shabab,* 89.
159. Musa, *Al-Mar'ah laysat Lu'bat al-Rajul,* 138.

know that the two go together and that one does not exist without the other . . . Our preachers persist in calling for women to cover themselves and be confined, which has resulted in the habit of sexual deviance [al-inhiraf al-Jinsi] in both men and women. Humans [*sic*] are naturally inclined toward women, and women also towards men. If we prevented nature from reaching its object through a straight path, it would be forced to seek it through a deviant route. All evidence has shown that sexual deviance, including sodomy, sapphism, and the like, prevails in a society where women are segregated.[160]

Unlike Tawfiq al-Tawil (who was cited in the introduction) whose objection rested on al-Tahtawi's surprise about the absence of expression of love for youthful boys in French society and al-Tawil's own goal of denying the "natural" occurrence of "sexual deviance," al-Wardi's agenda was more radical. He did not wish to deny the existence of sexual deviance but to insist on its prevalence and wished to offer an explanation for this troubling phenomenon. Al-Wardi's attacks on religious preachers were intense. He added in a footnote that "sexual deviance is widespread among the preachers themselves more than among other communities."[161]

In contrast to the restrictions on "natural" desires in Iraq, the West seemed to acknowledge "natural" desires in Western society. Here al-Wardi seemed to accord mixed dancing a value similar to Musa. Western universities, for example, do not "preach" to their students on matters sexual, rather "they created spaces where their female and male students can mix and dance."[162] Citing Freud on the sexual nature of repression, al-Wardi maintained that "modern societies have begun to eliminate some of the reasons for psychological turmoil when it set women free and elevated their educational and economic levels and allowed them to mix with men and to flirt, dance, and play with them."[163] Al-Wardi concluded that this "intense primness [tazammut] that distinguishes our Oriental civilization consists of the remains of our ancient golden glory. Women then used to be bought and sold. Princes and the rich in those days used to buy concubines and fill their palaces with them . . . and built high walls around them . . . lest a poor man catch a glimpse

160. 'Ali al-Wardi, *Wu''az al-Salatin, Ra'y Sarih fi Tarikh al-Fikr al-Islami fi du' al-Mantiq al-Hadith* [The Sultans' Preachers: An Honest Opinion about the History of Islamic Thought in the Light of Modern Logic] (1954; London: Dar Kufan, 1995), 8.
161. Ibid.
162. Ibid., 9.
163. Ibid., 17.

of them, or even a wink"[164] In reaching such conclusions, al-Wardi cited the Orientalist authority of Adam Mez.[165]

This took al-Wardi back to a familiar theme, namely, medieval Arabic poetry and "sexual deviance" (al-shudhudh al-jinsi). Al-Wardi insisted that such poetry was an expression of the spread of "sexual deviance" in society at large. He maintained that the individual poets should not be criticized for it, as "the defect is not theirs, but that of the society within which they live."[166] As for Abu Nuwas, historians have mentioned that "Abu Nuwas was afflicted with sexual deviance to a large degree, and was in his youth a passive deviant, and in his old age an active deviant. It is also said that he admitted to this without embarrassment or regret. It is clear that this intense deviance of his prompted him to invent *ghazal* in the masculine in Arabic poetry for the first time in history." Al-Wardi added that "it would be correct to say that sexual deviance started to spread among people before the era of Abu Nuwas, but people would not admit to it and would cover it up. None of them dared to say that he was a sodomite who loved youthful boys. Unexpectedly, Abu Nuwas appeared and tore up the curtain yelling at them: 'Why all this hypocrisy, people?'"[167]

Arguing against one of his critics about his thesis that Islamic dress for women (hijab) and gender segregation leads to "sexual deviance," al-Wardi stated that while sexual deviance existed in all societies, it was more prevalent in Arab and Islamic societies. This quantitative difference could be confirmed scientifically, for "sexual deviance has become one of those scientific subjects about which one can no longer exaggerate or joke and is now subject to objective studies and statistics more than personal opinions, which our men of letters are habituated to voice about people."[168] In fact, one could even ascertain empirically the prevalence of "sexual deviance" in Iraqi society. Al-Wardi invited one of his critics, literary historian Dr. ʿAbd al-Razzaq Muhyi al-Din, to "stroll around those areas where the *hijab* is most intense to see the extent which sexual deviance had reached in them. He should also remember how deviance spread among us during the Ottoman era."[169] Modernity,

---

164. Ibid., 9.
165. Ibid., 10.
166. ʿAli al-Wardi, *Usturat al-Adab al-Rafiʿ* [The Legend of Refined Literature] (1957; London: Dar Kufan, 1994), 72.
167. Ibid., 73–74.
168. Ibid., 75.
169. Ibid. Al-Wardi's critics included, in addition to Muhyi al-Din, ʿAbd al-Rida Sadiq's *Sufistaʾiyyah lil-Bayʿ, Manhaj al-Duktur ʿAli al-Wardi wa Tafkiruh* [Sophistry for Sale: The Method and

he hoped, would change all that. Although he did not seem to know that little if any modern Arabic poetry had been written to express love for youthful boys (Muhyi al-Din, in fact, who was not a major poet, had been one of the very few who had written in 1932 a rare poem expressing the erotic love of a male teacher for a youthful boy[170]), al-Wardi was still optimistic about the civilizational future of the Arabs. He predicted: "In the next century, Arabs will not be able to rhapsody [taghazzul] youthful boys given the existence of slender women with deep set black eyes [al-hayfawat wa al-da'jawat] all around them."[171]

Inherited Desires

The 1940s and 1950s introduced daring literary and psychoanalytical methods for the study of the legacy of the ancient Arabs and the sexual lives of contemporaries, while the 1960s institutionalized the nationalist and counternationalist methods. The post-1967 Arab world, in contrast, would desperately look for new paradigms through which to view its history and present. Arab intellectuals residing in the Arab world and in the diaspora, writing in Arabic or in European languages, would attempt to tackle some of these issues employing new methods and approaches ranging from semi-Orientalist to secular feminist accounts. The disenchantment with certain accounts of Arab nationalism and with Arab nationalist regimes following the 1967 war seemed to signal to some that Orientalist methodology and politics could be adopted by Arabs themselves to explain their own society (a phenomenon that would become endemic among Arab intellectuals following the 1990–1991 U.S. invasion of the Arabian Peninsula and intensified further after the U.S. invasion of Iraq in 2003). Abdelwahab Bouhdiba's sophisticated book *Sexualité en Islam*[172] is a hallmark of that period. While Bouhdiba's book had little impact in the Arab world, it would become a seminal reference in the West about "Arab sexuality." The book was published in 1975

Thinking of Dr. 'Ali al-Wardi] (Baghdad: Dar al-Hadith, 1956); Suhayl al-Sayyid Najm al-'Ani, *Hukm al-Muqsitin 'ala Kitab Wu''az al-Salatin* [The Judgment of the Just [of the Book], *The Sultans' Preachers*] (Baghdad; Matba'at al-'Ani, 1954); Murtada al-'Askari, *Ma' al-Duktur al-Wardi fi Kitabihi Wu''az al-Salatin* [With Dr. al-Wardi in His Book *The Sultans' Preachers*] (1955?; Qum: Kulliyat Usul al-Din, 1997). For a discussion of al-Wardi and his critics, see Jacques Berque, *The Arabs: Their History and Future* (New York: Praeger Publishers, 1964), 271, especially on Sadiq's criticisms.

170. See 'Abd al-Razzaq Muhyi al-Din, *Diwan al-Qasa'id* [Collected Poems], ed. Dr. Muhammad Husayn 'Ali al-Saghir (Amman: Dar Usamah lil-Nashr wa al-Tawzi', 2000), 51–53. See also note 120 in the introduction above. Muhyi al-Din would also serve as the union minister with Egypt in 1964.

171. Al-Wardi, *Usturat al-Adab al-Rafi'*, 72.

172. Abdelwahab Bouhdiba, *La sexualité en Islam* (Paris: Presses universitaires de France, 1975).

in French, and its first (poor) Arabic translation would appear only in 1986,[173] with a (not so) "corrected" version (by the same translator) published in 2001.[174] Bouhdiba's main thesis was that the

sexual ethic experienced by Muslims and the vision of the world that underlies it have less and less to do with the generous declarations of the Quran and of Muhammad himself. One can even speak of a degradation, which began at a very early date, of an ideal model. The open sexuality, practiced in joy with a view to the fulfillment of being, gradually gave way to a closed, morose, repressed sexuality.[175]

One is left with the conclusion after reading Bouhdiba's book that the Arabs, through their sexual philosophy and practice, have corrupted a pure and open Islamic doctrine. This is partially related to Renan's views, discussed in the introduction. Unlike authors who were more concerned about the decadence and degradation of morals during the Abbasid period and contemporary repression, Bouhdiba's concern was more the "degradation" of the present and its having moved away from an open Islamic ideal and less its repression of desires. For example, while Islam guaranteed women's rights of inheritance, Bouhdiba showed how in practice Muslim Arab societies limited that right historically: "How far we are from the feminism of the Quran!"[176] Bouhdiba tells us at the outset that

the Islamic model is offered [in his study] as a harmonious synthesis and a permanent adjustment of sexual ecstasy and religious faith. But has this synthesis ever been achieved except in theory? Is it not rather a regulatory harmony, a norm to be attained rather than a practical model?[177]

Yet, the selectiveness of Arab societies' understanding of Islam created the gap between model and practice. While Islam is identified as "feminist," Arab society is "misogynistic."

If misogyny constantly recurs as a leitmotif in Arab culture, it is because it has a meaning. It is evidence for us to break in the quranic harmony. Arab societies drew from

---

173. 'Abd al-Wahhab Bu Hudaybah, *Al-Islam wa al-Jins*, translated by Halah al-'Uri (Cairo: Maktabat Madbuli, 1986).

174. 'Abd al-Wahhab Bu Hudaybah, *Al-Islam wa al-Jins*, translated by Halah al-'Uri (Beirut: Riyad al-Rayyis lil-Kutub wa al-Nashr, 2001). The translation is imprecise in many places, aside from missing citations, quotation marks, etc.

175. See Abdelwahab Boudhiba, *Sexuality in Islam*, translated by Alan Sheridan (London: Routledge and Kegan Paul, 1985), 231.

176. Ibid., 113.

177. Ibid., vii.

Islam not the idea of the complementarity of the sexes, but, on the contrary, that of their hierarchy. Misogyny really is no more than sociological conditioning. The debate about female emancipation thus takes on a striking significance. In any case it cannot mask the fundamental position of the group that intends to maintain its own economic, patriarchal and male base.[178]

One of the principal problems that Bouhdiba discerned in Arab society's corruption of an originary Islam is the "separation of the sexes," due to the deviations that it engendered, so much so that

homosexual relations were relatively encouraged by the Arabo-Muslim societies to the detriment of intersexual relations. In the end, segregation exalted promiscuity. It is difficult for those who have not experienced it to imagine what life under a strict separation of the sexes is like. But it is understandable that homosexuality, so violently condemned by Islam, could be so widely practiced among both men and women. *Mujun* more or less included pederasty and lesbianism . . . The fact that homosexuality was always being condemned proves only one thing: neither the religious nor the social conscience could put an end to practices that were disapproved of by Islamic ethics, but to which in the last resort, society closed its eyes . . . Pederasty and lesbianism were merely consequences, derivatives and compensatory forms created by sexual division and explicitly perceived as second best.[179]

Thus, if Arab society had adhered to originary Islam, heterosexuality would have reigned supreme in Muslim Arab history through the present (clearly Bouhdiba had not read Qutb, whose contrary theory he might have found instructive). The deviation or compensatory forms of sex that resulted from lack of adherence were, and presumably still are, simply coping mechanisms (in addition to homosexuality, he also listed voyeurism, the marrying of cousins, and obscene gestures and words[180]). The oppression of women and the youth would not have pervaded Arab society as it does today were it not for this lack of adherence to the Islamic ideal and the continual degradation away from it. Bouhdiba summarized the result for "us": "as a religion, Islam makes possible a lyrical vision of life, but the Arabo-Muslim societies have almost succeeded in denying this lyricism by refusing it all foundation and by refusing it even to the point of denying self-determination."[181]

Bouhdiba agreed with Shararah's and Zaydan's thesis that Arab women's stature in society was reduced due to the introduction of foreign

178. Ibid., 119.
179. Ibid., 200.
180. Ibid., 210.
181. Ibid., 211.

singing girls and concubines.[182] His agreement though is tempered by the necessary caveat that such a situation pervaded the urban centers but not the countryside, where the wife had no competitor. Bouhdiba was on slippery grounds, however, when he generalized about contemporary Arab society. Throughout the book, he would shuttle between the past and present, discerning only differences between Islam as model and Muslim Arab practice. He did not seem, however, to discern differences between the desires of the Arabs of the past and the Arabs of the present. His general approach was one wherein Arab sexual desires seem to be inherited and passed down the generations. Just as it is for traditional Orientalists, whereby the Qur'an and early Islamic theological texts are to be analyzed to explain modern and contemporary Muslim Arab societies, Bouhdiba (who is critical in his book of Orientalist accounts of Islam) was clear in his methodology that stipulated the timelessness of Islam. There is nothing historical about Islam and Islamic theology at all that was of interest to Bouhdiba in his analysis. He wanted to look at the entire history of Islamic theology, from the seventh century through the present, as it looks at itself, namely, as "Tradition."

So we must not be afraid of the nonhistoricity of Tradition. On the contrary, a rigorous analysis of Islamic culture requires that we situate ourselves at the very heart of that tradition and grasp it as a whole . . . It would, of course, have been highly interesting to carry out a historical and comparative study of the development of this corpus [Qur'an, Hadith, exegesis, and jurisprudence]. One might even have been able to uncover a veritable "archeology" of Islamic views of the world, although neither could nor ought to be my concern. Firstly, too many stages in such a development are missing . . . Secondly, and more importantly, to project historical preoccupations onto Tradition really would have been a sin by anachronism. For Tradition rejects historicity. And what matters in my undertaking is to grasp Tradition as a whole, made up certainly of contributions from different ages, but forming an ethics that claims to be non-temporal. The fact is that, not so long ago, whole generations did not see Tradition in any other way.[183]

Thus, Bouhdiba, never interrogated this "Tradition." Although he would attempt a sociology of medieval Arab societal practice, in terms of socioeconomic issues (slavery, urban-rural divide, economic base of Arab kinship[184]), when it came to the present, the only sociology he was in-

182. Ibid., 106–9.   184. Ibid., 105.
183. Ibid., 3–4.

terested in was in fact an *anthropology* of modern Arabs, whom he saw as consumers of Tradition. In this vein, he self-assuredly stated that

as a result the entire Arabo-Muslim cultural system is centered on the need to identify, analyse, and understand Tradition. Education, politics, the arts, even science are no more than so many ways of learning to conform to this revealed ideal model. It may be, of course, that there are objective explanations to account for this arrested [bloquée] history. But what really matters to us is to observe the extent to which the basic Arabo-Muslim personality was to be indelibly marked by this prior condition; to seek in all things conformity with the past.[185]

What emerges then is not a timeless Islamic theology but in effect a timeless Arab-Muslim society that does not move through time and whose development, in Freudian fashion, has been "arrested." While Bouhdiba ends up providing a sociology of Muslim Arab sexual practice in the medieval period, he does not provide such a sociology of the development of the religious model or its theological development, although most of the writings he analyzes, which came to later constitute Islamic "Tradition," were, except for the Qur'an, not produced at the time of the Prophet but hundreds of years later, precisely in the medieval period he was studying. This is the period when the "repressive" jurisprudence was produced as well as when the sayings and the stories of the Prophet's "openness" about sex in his own personal life and in public statements were invented, cited, recorded, and collected.[186]

Bouhdiba assures his readers that his study "will enable us . . . to understand the nature and profound meaning of the present crisis in love and faith within the Arabo-Muslim societies."[187] His methodology takes an analysis of the past as clarification of the present. After a discussion of Islamic notions of bodily purity and impurity, Bouhdiba suddenly shifted from the theological to the anthropological:

Perhaps more than any others, Muslim societies have produced men and women who are *sick* [malades] with cleanliness . . . This *sick* [maladives] fear and mistrust of uncleanliness in every form and especially the meticulous and excessive attention that one lavishes on one's body in the form of minor purification—all this points directly to anality. Like orality, anality seems to be an essential part of Arabo-Islamic upbringing. [The cleaning of the anus] is, among other things, an eroticization of the [area

185. Ibid., 4.
186. See Ibrahim Fawzi, *Tadwin al-Sunnah* [Recording Sunnah] (London: Riyad al-Rayyis lil-Kutub wa-al-Nashr, 1994).
187. Bouhdiba, *Sexuality*, 5.

near the] anus. One may apply to the fiqh [jurisprudence] Ferenczi's term "morality of the sphincter."[188]

Bouhdiba's investment in medical analogies of health and disease seem comparable to the investment in cleanliness of which he accuses his mythological Muslim societies. In fact, Bouhdiba's personal experience substituted, throughout the book, for ethnographic observation and positivist empiricism. The native informant, as always, is a well of non-falsifiable data.

For Bouhdiba, while the Islamic understanding of sexual desires and the rules surrounding them have been passed down to succeeding generations as intended, the initial Islamic openness about sensuality and sex did not fare so well. Islamic openness was presumably recessive and its correlate ideas were not inheritable, in light of the dominant jurisprudential exegesis that interrupted and reversed them and that were passed down through the generations instead. Bouhdiba's hyperbole and Orientalist analysis would in fact get the best of him. While on one occasion he wrote that "paradoxically, as it may seem, 'Don Juanism' and Islam are not compatible,"[189] he would later show us how Muslims did not follow this "Tradition."

I have already noted that Islam inaugurated a system based on the rotation of women. In fact the system turned all too often into a scarcely disguised Don Juanism. The Prophet may condemn "those who are merely tasters in love" (al-dhaw[w]aqun wal dhaw[w]aqat), but the Arab is a born Don Juan who found his best ally in fiqh [Islamic jurisprudence]. It has been observed that "in Egypt there are many men who have married twenty or thirty women in the space of ten years. Similarly, women who are by no means old have successively married a dozen or more men. I have heard of men who are in the habit of changing wives every month." Again this is a reality of frequent observation.[190]

This typical Orientalist ethnographic comment, which Bouhdiba thought reflected the reality of past and contemporary Arab life, was authorized for Bouhdiba's readers through its attribution by him to the prominent Egyptian literary critic Ghali Shukri.[191] While indeed the quote is found in

188. Ibid., 56, emphasis added. See also Bouhdiba, *Sexualité*, 73.
189. Ibid., 90.
190. Ibid., 224. "C'est encore une réalité d'observation courante," in Bouhdiba, *Sexualité en Islam*, 273.
191. See Ghali Shukri, *Azmat al-Jins fi al-Qissah al-'Arabiyyah* [The Crisis of Sex in the Arab Novel] (Beirut: Dar al-Adab, 1962).

an important book of Shukri's published in 1962, it was not Shukri's own but rather a quote in turn from none other than the early nineteenth-century British Orientalist Edward W. Lane![192] Where the experience of the native informant proved too limited, imperial ethnography was marshaled to the cause, as the two are clearly complementary.[193]

Bouhdiba's comments about contemporary Arab society (he would usually use his native Tunisia for data) are sometimes staggering in their exoticization. For example, he stated that the Arabs have "a special affection for the buttocks" (both a woman's and a youthful boy's).[194] An Islamist critic, who did not deny the affection, ridiculed Bouhdiba by marveling at such unique Arab traits, "as if Marilyn Monroe and Brigitte Bardot were filmed by an X-ray machine, that filmed their skeletons . . . or perhaps they used to shake their hips only for Arabs!"[195] It was Bouhdiba's sociological explanation of the popularity of soft drinks in the Arab world, however, which went beyond the pale of the scholarly:

Indeed systematically, consciously, [the Arab] provokes belching by drinking all sorts of gassy drinks containing magnesium citrate or carbonic gas . . . The froth that bubbles out of a bottle of *gazuza*, the bubbles that twinkle in the glass, symbolize spermatic fecundity. A good *gazuza* sets one dreaming and prepares one for liberation upwards. One cannot but admire the symbolic displacement of the low to the high and from dense liquid into airy gas . . . *Gazuza* is the Islamic equivalent of wine. In its own way it is a water of youth. Refreshing, pleasant, it is valued above all for causing belching . . . undeniably liberation through belching belongs, though in what seems to be a more innocent mode, to the same continuous line of compensatory practices as obscenity.[196]

Bouhdiba's Islamist critic, the Egyptian Muhammad Jalal Kishk, marveled in response: "All this happens to us when we comfort our hearts with a bottle of soft drink . . . ? America must have converted to Islam then as it owns the two largest soft drink companies in the world; nay, Islam itself is spreading with the Coke factories that are opening in Russia and China!"[197] Although Bouhdiba wrote of the varieties of Islams

192. See Shukri, *Azmat al-Jins fi al-Qissah al-'Arabiyyah*, 69.
193. See Bouhdiba, *Sexuality*, 114, for other instances of the complementarity of imperial ethnography with native informant testimony.
194. See Bouhdiba, *Sexuality*, 202.
195. See Muhammad Jalal Kishk, *Khawatir Muslim fi al-Mas'alah al-Jinsiyyah* [A Muslim's Thoughts on the Sexual Question] (1984; Beirut and Cairo: Dar al-Jil and Maktabat al-Turath al-Islami, 1992), 12.
196. Bouhdiba, *Sexuality*, 207–8.
197. Kishk, *Khawatir*, 12.

and Muslim cultures across the Muslim world,[198] such understanding did not stop him from engaging in stereotypical representations that assimilated most of the Muslim world into a quasi monolith. On one occasion, he wrote that "like Turkey and Iran, the Maghreb does not practice female excision but everywhere else in the Muslim world it seems to be universally observed."[199] Like the rest of the data that Bouhdiba provided as a native informant, there was no documentation whatsoever that he relied on beside his own word. In reality, except for Egypt, Sudan, and Somalia, the large majority of Muslim countries do not and never have practiced "female excision." Indeed, in Egypt and Sudan, not only Muslims but the sizeable Christian communities practice it too.

The only change that seems to have occurred in Arab society throughout the ages is the more recent encounter with modernity, which coincided with postcolonial times. It is true that European colonialism ravaged and defeated Muslim Arabs in the nineteenth and twentieth centuries, but formidable as it was, "colonialism was to stop at the threshold of the Arab family, which it respected with good or ill grace."[200] The Islamic faith "was able to raise an effective barrier between itself and the new masters and to undermine any attempt at assimilation."[201] It was the revolt of Arab women more recently (1950s through the 1970s, when his book was published) that constituted the only major change in notions of sex that Bouhdiba discerned in Arab society in thirteen centuries. Women's revolt resulted from the new modernity, but neither seem to have dislodged the Arab man's "will to power."[202]

Thus Bouhdiba's historical analysis was deployed not as analysis of the past but rather as an instrument to explain the present, a repressed present that inherited the desires of the classical civilization but not the originary openness of Islam from which it had deviated to its own detriment. If Shararah wanted to purify Arab civilization from the foreign influences that plagued it after the second century A.H., Bouhdiba seemed to want to purify Islam and modern Arab civilization of all the impurities which infiltrated during the post-Islamic history of the Arabs. His call is indeed a pedagogical one, wherein modern Arabs must abandon their repressive tradition and learn from the openness of early Islam (but not from the West, whose own recent sexual liberation creates more problems than it solves[203]). His use of ancient texts to explain modern society and his focus on modern, not Abbasid, degradation, however,

198. Bouhdiba, *Sexuality*, 104.
199. Ibid., 175.
200. Ibid., 232.
201. Ibid.
202. Ibid., 243.
203. Ibid., 244.

would have adherents, especially, as we will see, in the expanding feminist scholarship of the 1970s and beyond.

Women Feminists and Medieval Sex

Debates about sex in medieval Arab society had been the purview of
literary critics, historians, and philosophers during much of the twentieth century. But women writers, who had been writing about gender
oppression since the nineteenth century, would soon address the importance of sexual history to their project of gender liberation. The debate
on women's rights in society was inaugurated in the mid-nineteenth
century, especially regarding women's education, and was followed by
the women's movement that struggled against the veil and for national
liberation, which extended from the turn of the century though the
1940s (or 1970s in some cases). This was followed by the state feminism
inaugurated by postcolonial regimes in the 1950s and 1960s in countries
like Iraq, Egypt, Syria, Tunisia, and much less so, Algeria, to name the
major ones. The new feminist wave that appeared in the late 1960s and
extended through the early 1980s was influenced by socialist feminism.
Egyptian feminist physician Nawal al-Saʿdawi and, to a lesser degree,
Moroccan feminist academic Fatima Mernissi, were the most influential
representatives of this new debate on women's rights in the Arab world
of the 1970s, although a number of socialist feminist men also wrote on
the topic.[204] While al-Saʿdawi wrote in Arabic and reached large audiences around the Arab world, Mernissi wrote in French and until the
mid-1990s remained relatively unknown to the Arabic reading public.[205]

Both al-Saʿdawi and Mernissi marshaled evidence from pre-Islamic
Arabia and from early Islamic history to draw parallels with the higher

204. Feminist men continued to write during the 1970s on issues related to the equality and
rights of women. See, for example, Buʿali Yasin, *Al-Thaluth al-Muharram, Dirasah fi al-Din, wa al-Jins,
wa al-Siraʿ al-Tabaqi* [The Prohibited Trinity: A Study in Religion, Sex and Class Struggle] (1973; Beirut: Dar al-Kunuz al-Adabiyyah, 1999). See also Yasin al-Hafiz's writings in this period. An earlier pro-
women's rights writer who wrote a book of essays on sex and love was Egyptian Anis Mansur. His
book, which discussed mostly women, love, sex, and marriage in the Western tradition, would be
considered today heterocentric if not heterosexist, as it showed no concern about "deviant" sexual
desires, even though he referred to them sparingly. See Anis Mansur, *Min Awwal Nazrah, Fi al-Jins, wa
al-Hubb wa al-Zawaj* [At First Sight: On Love, Sex, and Marriage] (1966; Cairo: Dar al-Shuruq, 2001).

205. See her pioneering book *Beyond the Veil: Male-Female Dynamics in Modern Muslim Society*
(Cambridge: Schenkman Publishing Company, 1975). The book went through several printings,
and was republished in a revised edition by Indiana University Press in 1987. References to *Beyond
the Veil* in this chapter are to the Indiana University Press revised edition. Except for one book
translated into Arabic early on, in general Mernissi's works began to be translated to Arabic only in
the mid-1990s.

stature that women enjoyed in the past compared to the present. Examples of strong and "active" women from sixth- and seventh-century Arabia were provided and contrasted with the dearth of such women in the present. When sex was discussed in the past of the Arabs, it was in relation to men's and women's jurisprudential sexual rights in marriage and less about social norms and practice. Al-Sa'dawi did invoke the ease with which sexual matters were spoken of in the time of the Prophet and that he was attentive enough to them to caution men about the importance of foreplay and women's orgasm. In terms of foreplay, he instructed Muslim men not "to lie with their women as beasts do, and let a messenger go between you." When asked what kind of messenger that would be, the Prophet answered: "a kiss and words." As for the centrality of women's orgasm, the Prophet stated that a sign of impotence was when "a man approaches his concubine or his wife and achieves his purpose with her before he speaks to her, and before he becomes intimate with her and before sleeping with her, thus obtaining his need from her before she obtains her need from him."[206] The rest of al-Sa'dawi's discussion about sex and Islam in Arab history dealt with the way women were perceived epistemologically in relation to sexual pleasure. Her approach was selective and was in the interest of producing a new revolutionary foundation for sexual relations in the future based on certain progressive aspects in the ancient history of the Arabs, excavated through a Marxist-feminist grid, and combined with modern egalitarian socialist feminist criteria.[207]

Al-Sa'dawi's prolific writings in the 1970s left no stone unturned in the sociology and psychology and the history of gender relations, in the West and in the Arab world. In her discussion of "men and sexual deviance," she provided a history of Greek "sexual deviance," especially Plato's, as one more indication of the misogyny of Greek culture. Michelangelo's sexual deviance was "said to be the reason why in his drawings he magnifies the male organ to a size not found elsewhere in the world of art."[208] Indeed, it was Jean-Jacques Rousseau, through the publication of his confessions, where he spoke of his masturbatory activities, who "opened the way to men who began to compete in publishing their natural/normal

206. Nawal al-Sa'dawi, *Al-Wajh al-'Ari lil Mar'ah al-'Arabiyyah* [The Naked Face of Arab Women], in the collected theoretical works of al-Sa'dawi, *Dirasat 'an al-Mar'ah wa al-Rajul fi al-Mujtama' al-'Arabi* [Studies about Women and Men in Arab Society] (1977; Beirut: al-Mu'assassah al-'Arabiyyah lil Dirasat wa al-Nashr, 1986), 812. On similar views regarding Islam and sexual foreplay, see Yasin, *Al-Thaluth al-Muharram*, 78–79.

207. See, for example, her chapter "Al-Hubb wa al-Jins 'ind al-'Arab," 816–39.

208. Al-Sa'dawi, "Al-Rajul wa al-Shudhudh al-Jinsi" [Man and Sexual Deviance], in *Al-Rajul wa al-Jins* [Man and Sex], originally published in 1977, in *Dirasat*, 558.

and their deviant sexual confessions combined."[209] Al-Sa'dawi's harsh feminist critique of Freud, however, was forgotten when she engaged in Freudian analysis in discussing male "sexual deviance," which she viewed as "arrested development" and as a disease in need of treatment and social understanding (reminiscent of the views of Wilhelm Reich on the matter, which characterized homosexuality as a form of "degeneracy" that deserves understanding and sympathy and that should not be criminalized but eliminated through, inter alia, the inclusion of women in all realms of life, especially in the military[210]). What is interesting in al-Sa'dawi's account of "sexual deviance," however, is that not a word was said about its existence in Arab or Muslim history or present, despite her narrating its "Western" history from the Greeks to the emergent Western gay and lesbian movements (whose literature she cited for evidence).[211] The only time she mentioned anything about medieval Arab sexual relations was in responding to Orientalist scholarship whose representations of the Arab world are "derived" from *A Thousand and One Nights:*

It is doubtless that such images do not represent Arab men and women in our present epoch; indeed, I do not believe it represents the life of men and women in the epoch of Harun al-Rashid [the more famous of Abbasid caliphs]. Perhaps it represents the life of kings and concubines in that period, which is a small sector that does not represent anyway the vast majority of the Arab peoples of these periods. Furthermore, the sexual and nonsexual excesses of kings are known in the East and West, North and South equally.[212]

Unlike al-Sa'dawi, who combined her critique of medieval and modern Arab society and understandings of Islam with a critique of Orientalist representations, thus contextualizing her views for her Arab audience, Fatima Mernissi made no such effort, although she was (and still is) writing to a Western audience (the translation of many of her books in the 1990s to Arabic notwithstanding). Indeed, unlike all our authors—with the exception of Bouhdiba, who excavated the Arab and Muslim past to dispel modern Arab and Western myths about medieval Arab society and deployed that past in a pedagogical program that formed part of their individual ideologies—Mernissi, in classical Orientalist manner, employed seventh- through sixteenth-century Arabic texts to *interpret*

209. Ibid., 559.
210. See Wilhelm Reich, *The Sexual Revolution: Toward a Self-Regulating Character Structure* (New York: Farrar, Straus and Giroux, 1974), 218–21, 278. The book was first published in 1930 as *Die Sexualität im Kulturkampf,* with an expanded second edition in 1936.
211. Al-Sa'dawi, in *Al-Rajul wa al-Jins* [Man and Sex], originally published in 1977 in *Dirasat,* 557–69.
212. Al-Sa'dawi, *Al-Wajh al-'Ari,* 817–18.

and *explain* not medieval but *modern* Arab society. Whether in her first book, *Beyond the Veil,* or in her subsequent work, Mernissi remained committed to this Orientalist methodology.[213]

In *Beyond the Veil,* Mernissi pathologized the Arab world and warned her Western readers "to be careful, when dealing with the Muslim world, not to confuse the symptom, that is, the event (the only dimension the media are interested in), with the diagnosis, that is, the specific combination of forces, tendencies, compromises, and alliances which produce it."[214] "The wonder of the Muslim world," she wrote, "is that people still manage in these apocalyptic, revolutionary times to make sense out of absurd, despotic forces scavenging their lives." She did not wish to "overwhelm" her Western readers with "data," but rather offered them "special illumination" of this wondrous place, which clearly lay in darkness.[215] To explain present male-female relations in such a dark place, Mernissi shuttled between the Qur'an, the medieval jurist al-Ghazali, and contemporary Moroccan folk sayings and maxims on the one hand, and on the other hand, Orientalist scholarship and her anthropological descriptions of women's lives. Time, it seems, had done little to temper the influence of historical texts in the "Muslim world." Mernissi depicted this world as on the verge of modernity, which has revolutionary aspects, and contrasted it with a static view of the "Muslim" past. Indeed, Islam itself was anthropomorphized in the context of her discussion of modern Arab feminist thought, *and* ahistoricized. She asked: "Why does Islam fear *fitna* [discord and temptation]? Why does Islam fear the power of female sexual attraction over men?"[216] This view of "Islam" structures her entire approach.

Related views are echoed by a Moroccan feminist academic writing under what is widely believed to be a pseudonym, Fatnah A. Sabbah. She wrote a book that is most illustrative of how Orientalism informs the method of certain Arab scholars.[217] *Woman in the Muslim Unconscious* examined what Sabbah called the medieval Arab "erotic discourse" and the religious "orthodox discourse." Examining these texts' views of women was taken up by Sabbah not to explore the views of these texts' authors, or the effect of social norms during the times the books were written, or as reflections of particular social realities and discourses, but rather, like Mernissi before her, as eternal truths about Muslim culture and history

213. Fatima Mernissi, *Beyond the Veil: Male-Female Dynamics in Modern Muslim Society,* rev. ed. (Bloomington: Indiana University Press, 1987).

214. Ibid., xiv.

215. Ibid., ix.

216. Ibid., 31.

217. Fatna A. Sabbah, *Woman in the Muslim Unconscious* (New York: Pergamon Press, 1984). The Book was first published in French in 1982 under the title *La femme dans l'inconscient musulman.*

that were as true when these books were written as they are in the present. Indeed, the aim of her book, which had no discussion of the modern Arab world at all, was to answer a particular question:

What are the relationships between the political and sexual spheres in our Muslim society? It is a question that assumes great importance for me, a woman who is living, loving, working, and aspiring to happiness in a Muslim society, not only in the present, but also for the future. What are the policies that our Muslim governments—made up exclusively of persons of the male sex—might adopt in matters concerning sex?[218]

The reason why she thought some of the medieval erotic books were relevant was due to their "popularity" as they are "still very widely consumed in Arab Muslim countries today,"[219] and "are available for a pittance in the streets and bookshops of the old sections of the Muslim cities."[220] In fact, one of the two books she relied upon, namely, *The Perfumed Garden,* was and still is mostly unknown across the Arab and Muslim worlds (although it has been well known in the West since its translation and publication in 1886 in French, in 1905 in German, and in 1927 in English), existing in one commercial and corrupted Moroccan edition unavailable outside Morocco.[221] A scholarly edition was finally published in 1990 by a then London-based Arab publisher, which was banned across the Arab world (see chapter 4).

Aside from the fact that Sabbah's empirical work, like that of Mernissi, is mostly based in Morocco, her premise did not take into account that large sectors of the Arab populations were, then as now, illiterate, or that even among the literate, book buying is not a high consumption practice. This is aside from any analysis of how texts written in medieval times were read and received in their own day and how they are received and read today. The Muslim Arab political psyche is the same, as far as Sabbah was concerned, whether in the medieval period or the present. Time, for the Arabs, does not move. Sabbah's very important "precise question," which her study tried to answer—namely, "How is 'politi-

218. Ibid., 4.
219. Ibid., 11.
220. Ibid., 23.
221. See Jamal Jum'ah, "Al-Irutikiyyah al-'Arabiyyah" [Arab Eroticism] in al-Shaykh al-'Arif Abu 'Abdullah Muhammad bin Abi Bakr bin 'Ali al-Nafzawi, *Al-Rawd al-'Atir fi Nuzhat al-Khatir* [The Perfumed Garden in the Promenade of the Mind], ed. Jamal Jum'ah (London: Riyad al-Rayyis Lil-Kutub wa al-Nashr, 1990), 11. The Moroccan version was republished by an Arab publisher in Germany in 1991 as part of a series of medieval erotica books. See *Al-Rawd al-'Atir fi Nuzhat al-Khatir,* in *Al-Jins 'ind al-'Arab,* vol. 2 (Cologne: Manshurat al-Jamal, 1991). The editors had published an earlier uncorrected edition in 1988.

cal power' in the dependent Muslim societies, given their cultural and economic determinants, going to exploit sexuality as a strategic area in carrying out a chosen social blueprint?"[222]—is never answered or even broached in the body of the book, which analyzes only two manuscripts out of the hundreds of extant manuscripts on erotica and positions them as representative of Arab Muslim history in its entirety. Like Bouhdiba (whom she cites) before her, Sabbah believed that modern Arabs have inherited their notions of sexual pleasure, their very sexual desires, as well as their sexism from the medieval and ancient Arabs.

The same year that *Woman in the Muslim Unconscious* was published in English, Fatima Mernissi edited a short and relatively unknown work written in Arabic on "Love in our Islamic Civilization," her first work to be (presumably) written and published in Arabic.[223] In the introduction, in which quotations from medieval books of *ars erotica* are reproduced, à la Sabbah, Mernissi posed the question: "Are love and sex in our Islamic culture spaces through which the two partners, men and women, possess reason and will? Or are they fields [majalat] wherein one of the partners controls reason and will and thus becomes the only possessor of the authority to choose and decide?"[224] In order to understand this situation in the present, Mernissi sought to answer a number of other questions: "How can we, as responsible individuals love, desire, embrace, be playful, [engage in] dialogue, and be open with a partner who is not allowed to have responsibility, the will to choose, or freedom? What is love in such circumstances? What is sex and what is desire in such relationships?" To find out the answers to these important questions about "our" present, Mernissi, like the pseudonymous Sabbah, posited them "as our point of departure in treating these selected [medieval] texts . . ."[225] In all fairness to her, Mernissi's Orientalist method is deployed when addressing both Arab and Western audiences alike.

Re-membering the Past

The main task confronting most of the authors we discussed in the last two chapters, and who wrote over a span of a century or so, was not only to memorialize a past that had been forgotten, but more importantly to

222. Sabah, *Woman in the Muslim Unconscious,* 13.
223. See Fatimah al-Marnisi, *Al-Hubb fi Hadaratina al-Islamiyyah* (Beirut: al-Dar al-ʿAlamiyyah lil-Tibaʿah wa al-Nashr wa al-Tawziʿ, 1984).
224. Ibid., 13.
225. Ibid., 13–14.

excavate a past "civilization" that was buried and rendered unknown to contemporary Arabs. The project of researching and writing about that past was a project of re-membering it, of piecing it together from extant material, and of evaluating it critically with the aid of modern methods in order to make it the basis for modern Arab civilization, indeed to *invent* it as a civilization. The varied authors seemed interested not only in reproducing how the Arabs of the past considered their own desires and sexual practices, but also, and more centrally, how modern Arabs were to assess these epochs and their desires and practices. The resulting corpus varied from reproducing accounts provided by medieval historians whose works survived the "age of decadence" of the Ottoman period and those excavated by European Orientalists, to evaluating that corpus and framing it within modern criteria of ethical and moral judgments that were alternately nationalist, religious, liberal, Marxist, psychoanalytic, secular, and feminist.

The pedagogical, and hence civilizational, benefits seemed enormous for the majority of our authors. Yet, what moderns were supposed to learn from the ancient Arabs remained obscure, unspecified, and general, especially so as the positive valence assigned to sexual openness in the past was soon transformed into a negative valence or at least judged ambivalently on account of the concern over deviance and excess. What is remarkable in most of the writings we examined, however, is the lack of a utopian project or vision for the future or for the present, although a liberatory vision informs most of the critiques. In fact, what might have appeared as utopic in the past was soon subjected to harsh critique by many of our authors.

Except for Salamah Musa and much less so 'Ali al-Wardi, the very question of the sexual life of the contemporary Arabs was not broached in any detail in this long debate (the quasi-anthropological approach to the contemporary period which peppered the accounts of Bouhdiba and Mernissi and Qutb's anthropology of America notwithstanding). This engagement with the desires of the past can be seen perhaps as a displacement of our modern authors' desire to engage with the desires of the present, which most of them addressed only in general and which they assessed negatively compared to past desires—that is, moderns fare badly in comparison with the ancients. While initially, the past seemed like an excellent civilizational example of freedom to emulate, our authors began to nuance their approach arriving at more ambivalent judgments. Clearly, the inspiration for most of our authors was the liberation of the present from its repression and of learning *some* (and certainly not all) of the civilizational lessons of the past in undertaking this task.

Repudiation of the institutionalization of promiscuous sex with women (as concubines, singing girls, slaves, or even as multiple wives) as well as a repudiation of the normativity of sodomitic (and much less so sapphic) practice for their incompatibility with civilizational ascent, in favor of European-style institutionalization of heterosexual bourgeois monogamous marriage, which marked such ascent, were as large a part of this civilizational project as was learning the openness with which medieval sexual desires were expressed and sexual practices were sought out. But this did not impel the majority of our authors to undertake an overall or a detailed examination of contemporary desires and sexual practices. All of this would change with the onset of the 1980s. As we will see in chapter 3, a new and expanded discourse would be incited. This new discourse would change the terms and concerns of the debate and usher in new players and a new agenda. Unlike the participants in the earlier debates, the protagonists of the new debates would deploy utopic and dystopic concerns in articulating their more rigid views of the past, the present, and the future. The centrality of the notion of civilization, its potential to degenerate and degrade, would remain the fulcrum around which the debates would revolve. The epistemological approach and new ontological concerns, however, would vary quite a bit from the pedagogical concerns discussed thus far.

THREE

Re-Orienting Desire:
The Gay International
and the Arab World

The discussion in chapters 1–2 was mostly confined to intellectual and political developments in the Arab world and how Western trends influenced and informed ongoing debates directly and indirectly. Here, I will turn to developments outside the Arab world, specifically in the United States and Europe, and how they sought deliberately to influence Arab concepts of sexual desire and practice. These developments had been debated in the intellectual field, but some insisted instead that they be squarely placed in the political field of state-society relations. With the rise of the women's movement and the discourse of sexual liberation across Western countries in the late 1960s and especially in the 1970s, the attention of many Westerners came to bear on the sexual question as such, and not only in the West but also and increasingly outside it. The impact of this intervention on the Arab world would be jolting. In this chapter, I will examine these Western interventionist trends and their effects on the contemporary Arab world while in chapter 4 I will examine in detail the Arab intellectual reaction to them.

One of the more compelling issues emerging from within the Western gay movement in the last twenty-five years is the universalization of "gay rights." This project has insinuated itself into the prevailing U.S. discourse on human rights to launch itself on an international scale. Following in the footsteps of the white Western women's movement, which had sought to universalize its issues through imposing its own colonial feminism on the women's movements in non-Western countries—a situation which led to major schisms from the outset (these were apparent at the first UN-sponsored International Women's Year World Conference in Mexico City in 1975 and continuing through the 1980 Copenhagen conference, the 1985 Nairobi conference and the fourth UN conference in Beijing in 1995)[1]—the gay movement sought a similar missionary task. Western male white-dominated organizations (the International Lesbian and Gay Association—ILGA—and the International Gay and Lesbian Human Rights Commission—IGLHRC) sprang up to defend the rights of "gays and lesbians" all over the world and to advocate on their behalf. ILGA, which was founded in 1978 at the height of the Carter administration's human rights campaign against the Soviet Union and third world enemies, asserts that one of its aims is to "create a platform for lesbians, gay men, bisexuals, and transgendered people internationally, in their quest for recognition, equality and liberation, in particular through the world and regional conferences."[2] As for IGLHRC, which was founded in 1991, its mission is to "protect and advance the human rights of all people and communities subject to discrimination or abuse on the basis of sexual orientation, gender identity, or HIV status."[3] It is these missionary tasks, the discourse that produces them, and the organizations that represent them which constitute what I will call the Gay International.

Like the major U.S.- and European-based human rights organizations (Human Rights Watch, Amnesty International) and following the line taken up by white Western women's organizations and publications, the Gay International was to reserve a special place for Muslim countries in its discourse as well as in its advocacy. This Orientalist impulse, borrowed from predominant representations of Arab and Muslim cultures in the United States and in European countries, continues to guide all branches of the human rights community. The Gay International, being

---

1. For information on the discord between European and U.S. women and women from Asia, Africa, and Latin America during these conferences, see, for example, Judy Klemesrud, "Scrappy, Unofficial Women's Parley Sets Pace," *New York Times*, 29 June 1975; Frank Frial, "Women Are Losing Ground, World Parley Is Told," *New York Times*, 15 July 1980; and Georgia Dullea, "Female Circumcision a Topic at UN Parley," *New York Times*, 18 July 1980, and several articles in the *New York Times* covering the Nairobi conference on 19 July 1985.

2. International Lesbian and Gay Association, Constitution, Section C. "Aims and Objectives," Article no. 2 (i), available on the ILGA Web site at http://www.ilga.org.

3. International Gay and Lesbian Human Rights Commission, "Our Mission," available at their Web site, http://www.iglhrc.org.

a relative latecomer to this assimilationist project, has sought to catch up quickly. To do so, supporters of the Gay International's missionary tasks produced two kinds of literature on the Muslim world in order to propagate their cause: an academic literature produced mostly by white male European or American gay scholars "describing" and "explaining" what they call "homosexuality" in Arab and Muslim history to the present;[4] and journalistic accounts of the lives of so-called "gays" and (much less so) "lesbians" in the contemporary Arab and Muslim worlds. The former is intended to unravel the mystery of Islam to a Western audience, while the latter has the unenviable task of informing white male gay sex tourists about the region and to help "liberate" Arab and Muslim "gays and lesbians" from the oppression under which they allegedly live by transforming them from practitioners of same-sex contact into subjects who identify as "homosexual" and "gay." The following remarks may be taken as typical. Lisa Power, co-secretary general of ILGA, states authoritatively that "most Islamic cultures don't take kindly to organized homosexuality, even though male homoeroticism is deep within their cultural roots! . . . most people are too nervous to organize, even in countries with a high level of homosexuality."[5] Robert Bray, public information director for the National Gay and Lesbian Task Force and an officer of ILGA, understands that "cultural differences make the definition and the shading of homosexuality different among peoples . . . But I see the real question as one of sexual freedom; and sexual freedom transcends cultures." While on seemingly sexual escapades in Morocco and southern Spain, Bray states that "at least one guy expressed a longing to just be gay and not have to live within the prescribed sexual behaviors, and he said that there were others like him." Based on this "one guy," Bray confidently concludes that "I believe this longing is universal."[6]

In contradistinction to the liberatory claims made by the Gay International in relation to what it posits as an always already homosexualized population, I will argue that it is the very discourse of the Gay

---

4. The only exception to this poor scholarship is an article by Bruce Dunne, "Homosexuality in the Middle East: An Agenda for Historical Research," *Arab Studies Quarterly* 12, nos. 3–4 (Summer–Fall 1990): 55–82. This article's major weakness lies in the fact that it does not consult a single original Arabic source. Dunne's anthropological impulse, however, gets the best of him in a later article cited below.

5. Quoted in Rex Wockner, "Homosexuality in the Arab and Moslem World," in *Coming Out: an Anthology of International Gay and Lesbian Writings*, ed. Stephen Likosky (New York: Pantheon Books, 1992), 105. This article was reprinted from a number of U.S. gay and lesbian magazines including *Outlines, BLK, The Weekly News* (Miami), and *Capital Gay* (London). Of course no Arab or Iranian could be found to write an article in this "international" anthology, and a white gay American man had to do it instead.

6. Wockner, "Homosexuality," 116.

International, which both produces homosexuals, as well as gays and lesbians, where they do not exist, and represses same-sex desires and practices that refuse to be assimilated into its sexual epistemology.[7] I will show how this discourse assumes prediscursively that homosexuals, gays, and lesbians are a universal category that exists everywhere in the world and, based on this prediscursive axiom, the Gay International sets itself the mission of defending them by demanding that their rights *as* "homosexuals" be granted where they are denied and be respected where they are violated. In doing so, however, the Gay International, as this chapter will show, is producing an effect that is less than liberatory.

The Gay International, through its more illustrious organization, ILGA, launched a new and aggressive universalization campaign in 1994 coinciding with the twenty-fifth anniversary of the Stonewall Uprising. While ILGA achieved official NGO status at the United Nations in 1993 (which it later lost), its international activities continued unabated including "efforts to stop the mass execution of homosexuals in Iran," an unsubstantiated propagandistic claim that was also bandied about by an official of the U.S. State Department.[8] Part of the commemorations of Stonewall was ILGA's convening of its sixteenth "Annual World Conference" from June 23 to July 4, 1994, in New York. Whereas ILGA boasted "delegates" from Western Europe, East Asia, Latin America, Eastern Europe, and the United States, it "was working hard to bring activists from Africa, the Middle East, and the Caribbean."[9] The commemorations included the "International March on the United Nations to Affirm the Human Rights of Lesbian and Gay People," demanding among other things that the General Assembly "proclaim an international Year of the Lesbian and Gay People (possibly 1999)," and the application of the United Nations Declaration on Human Rights to "lesbian, gay, bisexual, drag and transgender people."[10] This aggressive campaign at the United Nations ran throughout the 1990s and into the next decade.

---

7. Because most of this literature deals with male homosexuality, my comments are likewise concerned primarily with that issue.

8. Mark Unger, "Going Global: The Internationalization of the Gay and Lesbian Community," *Metrosource: The Gay Guide to Metropolitan New York* (Summer 1994): 49. See Wockner, "Homosexuality," 107–11, for evidence of the Gay International's collaboration with the U.S. State Department to malign the Iranian government. Citing a U.S. journalist and a U.S. State Department official who investigated the case, Wockner claims that there were mass executions of homosexuals in Iran. Although the official's investigation produced no documentary evidence, the official asserts that the allegation of mass executions was "probably true," 108.

9. Unger, "Going Global," 50. It should be noted that it is not clear whether these delegates were indeed residents of the countries they represented or U.S.–based diaspora members of these regions.

10. See "The Demand of Stonewall 25," in *Metrosource: The Gay Guide to Metropolitan New York* (Summer 1994): 46–47.

Rex Wockner, the author of an acutely othering article on "gays and lesbians" in the Arab world and Iran, which was reprinted in a large number of gay publications in the United States and Britain, wonders in bafflement about Arab and Iranian men who practice both "insertive" same-sex and different-sex contact and refuse the Western identification of gayness: "Is this hypocritical? Or a different world?" he marvels. "Are these 'straight' men really 'gays' who are overdue for liberation? Or are humans by nature bisexual, with Arab and Moslem men better tuned into reality than Westerners? Probably all the above."[11] It is precisely this perceived instability in the desires of Arab and Muslim men that the Gay International seeks to stabilize, as their polymorphousness confounds gay (and straight) sexual epistemology. As I will show below, the assumptions underlying the mission of the Gay International demand that these resistant "Oriental" desires, which exist, according to Wockner, in "oppressive—and in some cases murderous—homelands," be re-*orient*ed to and subjected by the "more enlightened" Occident.[12] I will survey the literature of the Gay International with an eye to the politics of representation it enacts, as well as its stated project of "defending gays and lesbians." Although I will look at different kinds of literature—academic studies, journalistic accounts, human rights and tourism publications—which are governed by different professional demands, political configurations, markets, and audiences, I do not seek to flatten them by erasing these differences, but rather to demonstrate how, despite these manifest differences, a certain ontology and epistemology are taken as axiomatic a priori by *all* of them.

Representing Arab and Muslim Desires

Western gay interest in and representations of sexuality in Arab and Muslim countries, in fact, coincide with the very emergence of Western gay scholarship on sexuality.[13] Although homoerotic and sexual representations of Arab men by Western male writers, as we saw, precede this period (examples include William S. Burroughs, Paul Bowles, T. E. Lawrence, André Gide, Roland Barthes, and Jean Genet, to name the most prominent), these neither constituted a genre nor precipitated a full-fledged discourse among Western gay men about Arab male sexual de-

11. Wockner, "Homosexuality," 115.
12. Wockner, "Homosexuality," 107, 115.
13. For a good survey of some of these writings, see Joseph Boone, "Vacation Cruises; or, The Homoerotics of Orientalism," *PMLA* 110 (1995): 89–107.

sires. They were rather offshoots of standard Orientalist representation of the Arab world. It was John Boswell who inaugurated a debate on Muslim societies in which Western white gay scholars are still engaged. Boswell's romantic and less-than-academic assertions that "most Muslim societies have treated homosexuality with indifference, if not admiration,"[14] was not necessarily a new conclusion, as Western Christian propaganda had for centuries portrayed Muslim societies as immoral and sexually licentious compared to Christian morality. Indeed, as Jeffrey Weeks informs us, "many Western gays, for a long time now, have traveled hopefully to the Muslim world and expected to find sexual paradise."[15] He proceeds to explain, however, that "reality is more complex." Basing himself on the findings of a collection of articles edited by Arno Schmitt and Jehoeda Sofer, Weeks asserts that "the sexual privileges allowed to men [in the Muslim world] are largely at the expense of women" and that "those adult men who do not fit readily into prevailing notions of true manhood . . . are often looked down upon and despised."[16] As Weeks views the present Muslim world as one undergoing change, he concludes that there are two possible outcomes of this change: "Only time will tell whether that culture will approximate more and more to the secularised Western model, or come increasingly under the sway of a new religious militancy. What can be said with some assurance is that it is unlikely to stay the same."[17] The Western model as the only liberatory telos to be applied universally is never interrogated by Weeks.[18]

Indeed, Boswell's romantic descriptions were taken up by Arno Schmitt, who challenges both Boswell's research and conclusions.[19] Contra Boswell's essentialist claims of the timelessness of the categories of homosexuals and gays, Schmitt asserts that in Muslim societies "male-male

14. John Boswell, *Christianity, Social Tolerance, and Homosexuality: Gay People in Western Europe from the Beginning of the Christian Era to the Fourteenth Century* (Chicago: University of Chicago Press, 1980), 194.

15. Jeffrey Weeks, foreword to *Sexuality and Eroticism among Males in Moslem Societies*, ed. Arno Schmitt and Jehoeda Sofer (New York: Harrington Park Press, 1992), x.

16. Weeks, foreword, x.

17. Weeks, foreword, xi.

18. Michael Warner, one of the major queer theorists of the day, is attentive to the issue of the internationalization of white U.S. sexual politics as far as "theoretical languages" are concerned but does not question the internationalization of the epistemologies producing such languages: "As gay activists from non-Western contexts become more and more involved in setting political agendas, and as the rights discourse of internationalism is extended to more and more cultural contexts, Anglo-American queer theorists will have to be more alert to the globalizing—and localizing— tendencies of our theoretical languages," in Michael Warner, ed., *Fear of a Queer Planet: Queer Politics and Social Theory* (Minneapolis: University if Minnesota Press, 1993), xii.

19. See Arno Schmitt, "A Critique of John Boswell's Writings on Muslim Gays," in Schmitt and Sofer, *Sexuality*, 169–78.

sexuality plays an important role. But in these societies there are no 'homosexuals'—there is no word for homosexuality—the concept is completely unfamiliar. There are no heterosexuals either."[20] Schmitt, who is overall more nuanced in his descriptions than Boswell, makes the essentialist claim that the absence of these categories in Muslim societies is itself a phenomenon that is constant across time. Although Boswell was careful to level his judgment about Muslim societies in the classical period (seventh–fourteenth century) of the Islamic era and which coincides with the European medieval period, recent scholars, including Schmitt, tend to extend whatever judgment they have to the whole of Arab Muslim history. Schmitt, like the classic Orientalists who use the seventh-century Qur'an to study Muslims of the twentieth century, insists without any scholarly evidence that "because the behavior of Muslims today can be seen as modification of older behavioral patterns, the study of male-male sexuality in Muslim society should start from the old texts—although most of these reflect the viewpoint of the middle class only. Study of modern texts, conversation, and encounters with them and observations of Arabs, Iranians, Turks help us to understand not only the modern behavior, but the old texts as well."[21] Schmitt's ahistoricism is compounded by the limitations of the audience he imagines. Note how the "us" in his text refers only to Westerners, gay and nongay, but never to Muslims, who must be observed. Indeed, Schmitt's book, which is a collection of mostly Orientalist, if not outright racist, views that he and his contributors bandy about, is aimed, according to him and his coeditor, not only at Western scholars in a variety of disciplines but also at "anybody in contact with Arabs, Turks or Persians—be it a tourist in Moslem countries, a social worker 'in charge' of immigrants, or just as a friend of an immigrant," anybody, that is, who is *not* an Arab, a Turk or a "Persian."[22] One such white gay contributor, on whom the editors rely for information on life in Iran where he had lived before, identifies himself as "a freelance writer now living in New York (and never again in Tehran)."[23] The Orientalist method that Schmitt deploys in this book is one in which Arabs and Muslims can only be objects of European scholarship and never its subjects or audience (his use and inclusion of native informants notwithstanding). Still the Schmitt and Sofer volume has impressed the establishment of the Gay International

20. Arno Schmitt, "Different Approaches to Male-Male Sexuality/Eroticism from Morocco to Uzbekistan," in Schmitt and Sofer, *Sexuality*, 5.

21. Schmitt, "Different Approaches," 20.

22. Schmitt and Sofer, *Sexuality*, xiv.

23. Schmitt and Sofer, *Sexuality*, 194. The author's name is David Reed.

so much that ILGA relies on it as a corrective to its own "research."[24] An example of the "research" conducted by ILGA is its entry on Egypt in *The Second ILGA Pink Book,* where the authors inform us that "Transvestite dancers, 'Khawal's' [*sic*], who dance at feasts are very popular." ILGA's "researchers" seem to confuse the nineteenth-century phenomenon of the *Khawal* with the present.[25] Time, as expected, is never factored in when the topic is Arabs and Muslims.

This timelessness of Muslim Arab sexual culture is noted even by a careful scholar of medieval Muslim societies. Everett Rowson, who acknowledges a puzzling change in Arab sexual categories after the ninth century, concludes, basing himself on Arabic texts written in the eleventh century, that these texts' "concepts can be taken as broadly representative of Middle Eastern societies from the ninth century to the present."[26] Others, like Edward Lacey, defend Islam and Arabs against Western racism insisting that although "Islam possesses its full quota of dogmatism, fanaticism, obscurantism, rigidity and sexism—[it] has always in practice been, and still is (despite the present-day activities of certain bloodthirsty heretics who do not even deserve to be called Muslims), far more acceptant and tolerant of homosexuality, far more receptive, indulgent and permissive toward it . . . than either of the two other great monotheistic religions of the Western world."[27] For Lacey, however, as for Boswell, Schmitt, and Rowson, an antihistoricism is embedded in the heart of their arguments. Using medieval Arabic texts, Lacey affirms what he calls "the constants of human nature, the universal, unvarying qualities of temperament, the unchanged, unchangeable, undying sexual appetites and weaknesses that unite human beings throughout all ages and across all gulfs of religious, cultural and

24. Whereas ILGA's Pink Book, for example, states without explanation that Jordan has laws criminalizing homosexuality, ILGA's Web site corrects the mistake by referring to Schmitt and Sofer, who write in their book that "the Penal Code of 1951 makes no distinction between sexual intercourse by persons of the same sex or persons of different sexes." Schmitt and Sofer, Sexuality, cited on the ILGA Web site; see www.ilga.org/information/legal_survey/middle%20east/jordan.htm. Indeed, this is symptomatic of the shoddy and unprofessional "research" carried out by ILGA. For the Pink Book, see Aart Hendriks, Rob Tielman, and Evert van der Veen, *The Third Pink Book: A Global View of Lesbian and Gay Liberation and Oppression* (Buffalo, N.Y.: Prometheus, 1993), 297.

25. *The Second ILGA Pink Book A Global View of Lesbian and Gay Liberation and Oppression* (Utrecht: Interfacultaire Werkgroep Homostudies, 1988), 189.

26. Everett K. Rowson, "The Categorization of Gender and Sexual Irregularity in Medieval Arabic Vice Lists," in *Body Guards: The Cultural Politics of Gender Ambiguity,* ed. Julia Epstein and Kristina Straub (New York: Routledge, 1991), 72–73.

27. Edward Lacey, "English Translator's Introduction," in Ahmad al-Tifashi, *The Delight of Hearts, or What You Will Not Find in Any Book* (San Francisco: Gay Sunshine Press, 1988), 31. Lacey translated only the five chapters of the book that deal with "homosexual" anecdotes. The chapters were translated from a French translation and not from the Arabic original.

linguistic difference . . . How edifying—and humbling—to realize, for example, that the popular belief that the size of a man's penis may be gauged by the size of his nose was as widespread in those remote times as it is today . . . or that most queens, in the final analysis, preferred, then as now, a thick cock, whatever its length, to a thin one."[28]

Contra Schmitt, As'ad AbuKhalil, a Lebanese political scientist who lives and teaches in the United States, affirms that "homosexual" identities and what he calls "pure homosexuals" have existed in Arab/Islamic civilization.[29] AbuKhalil asserts that the "idea that there were no self-declared lesbians (suhaqiyyat) or gay men is false."[30] His evidence consists of one line that he mistranslates from the famed medieval physician al-Razi as cited by al-Tifashi. While discussing hermaphroditism (al-khinath), which, according to al-Razi, results from the strength and/or weakness of male and/or female sperm, al-Razi also speaks of less extreme outcomes with cases where "you would find masculinized women [nisa' mudhakkarat] as you would find feminized men [rijal mukhannathin] so much so that some of these masculinized women either menstruate less or do not menstruate at all, and some of whom might grow beards, as I have seen weak beards and mustaches on many women . . ."[31] AbuKhalil mistranslates the first part of this line as "You might find males as women and females as men" and lets it hang without the remainder of the line.[32] Throughout his account, AbuKhalil refers to "homosexuals," "gays," "heterosexuals," and "homophobia" as transhistorical identities and phenomena and anachronistically identifies people and practices with them. For example, he cites medieval Arabic books, which "contain collections of poetry and anecdotes by and about gay men and women."[33] Unlike the antihistoricists, however, AbuKhalil believes that changes *have* occurred in the Arab world, but they do not concern identities, which he sees as transhistorically present, but rather "homophobia," which he believes is historically contingent: "The advent of Westernization in the Middle East brought with it various elements of Western ideologies of hostility, like . . . homophobia. This is not to say that there were not antihomosexual . . . elements in Arab/Islamic

28. Lacey, "English Translator's Introduction," 30–31.
29. As'ad AbuKhalil, "A Note on the Study of Homosexuality in the Arab/Islamic Civilization," *Arab Studies Journal* (Fall 1993): 32–34, 48.
30. AbuKhalil, "A Note," 33.
31. Shihab al-Din Ahmad al-Tifashi, *Nuzhat al-Albab Fima La Yuwjad Fi Kitab* (London: Riyad al-Rayyis, 1992), 303.
32. AbuKhalil, "A Note," 33.
33. AbuKhalil, "A Note," 33.

history, but these elements never constituted an ideology of hostility as such."[34] Indeed, AbuKhalil's misreading of the evidence extends to the European scene, which he mentions for contrast, arriving at unsubstantiated conclusions: "The professed homosexual identity among Arabs allowed homosexuals historically a degree of tolerance that was denied for centuries to homosexuals in the West. When homosexuals were hunted down as criminals in much of medieval Europe, homosexuals were rulers and ministers in Islamic countries."[35] This identitarian essentialism characterizes AbuKhalil's entire approach.

Bruce Dunne participates in this academic discourse with his essay "Power and Sexuality in the Middle East."[36] He asserts that "sexual relations in Middle Eastern societies have historically articulated social hierarchies, that is, dominant and subordinate social positions: adult men on top; women, boys and slaves below."[37] Presumably, in non-Middle Eastern societies such hierarchies did not "historically" exist except in the celebrated cases of "Greek and late Roman antiquity," but certainly not in the medieval, let alone the modern, "West." As this situation is contrasted with the "distinction made by modern Western 'sexuality' between sexual and gender identity, that is, between *kinds* of sexual predilections and *degrees* of masculinity and femininity, [which] has until recently, had little resonance in the Middle East"[38]—a judgment that is further illustrated by quotes from Egyptian native informants (a young man and a physician) whom Dunne cites—the conclusion is inescapable: "Western notions of sexuality offer little insight into our contemporary young Egyptian's apparent understanding that sexual behavior conforms to a particular concept of gender."[39] Dunne's approach is to demonstrate how "Middle Eastern" society, *unlike* Western society, is one where non-"egalitarian sexual relations" predominate and where sexuality "conforms to a particular notion of gender." This is the reason why, citing IGLHRC, he affirms that "many homosexuals in Middle East-

34. AbuKhalil, "A Note," 34.
35. AbuKhalil, "A Note," 33.
36. Bruce Dunne, "Power and Sexuality in the Middle East," *Middle East Report* 206 (Spring 1998): 8–11, 37.
37. Dunne, "Power," 8.
38. Ibid. The term "Middle East" is a problematic one due to a number of reasons, not least among them is its imperial pedigree, which locates the area in relation to Europe. Other problems relate to the fact that the Muslim world extends beyond the "Middle East" into Asia and Africa and that the "Middle East" includes non-Arabs and non-Muslims (e.g., residents of the European settler colony of Israel and Armenia). It is not clear if what Dunne and others describe as "Middle Eastern" applies to all these people or not.
39. Dunne, "Power," 9.

ern countries have sought asylum in the West as refugees from official persecution."[40] Thus, he calls for "queering" the "Middle East" to put an end to these conditions.[41] This type of anthropology by Dunne (who incidentally knows no Arabic, as evidenced by the lack of any Arabic sources in his work—his native informants notwithstanding) calls less into question its (and his) conception of the other and more its (and his) conception of its mythical idealized self—one that is incapable of seeing the other except as a projection of all that it is not and that it does not contain, namely, nonegalitarian sexual relations, the oppressive rule of men, "gender-based" sexuality, patriarchy, and so forth. This mythological "West" as reference remains the organizing principle of all such discussions.

A more recent addition to this growing body of literature is Stephen Murray and Will Roscoe's *Islamic Homosexualities*,[42] a title indicative of their limited knowledge of Muslim societies (since "Islamic" is an adjective referring to the religion Islam while "Muslim" refers to people who adhere to it, it is unclear how "Islam," the religion, can have a "homosexuality" let alone "homosexualities"[43]). Murray thinks that Arno Schmitt's claim that Arabs have no conceptions of homosexual persons because (according to Schmitt) "Arabic synonyms for 'to fuck' have no form of reciprocity,"[44] is preposterous, as "I do not know of such a verb in English or any other language. To fuck and be fucked requires more than two persons, or sequential acts, or use of a dildo: human anatomy precludes A's penis being in B's anus while B's penis is in A's."[45] In fact, contra Murray and Schmitt, *both* classical *and* modern Arabic have the verb "tanayaka," which does indicate reciprocity as when two people "yatanayakan" meaning that they are "fucking each other."[46] The language-based errors and mistakes in both Schmitt's and Roscoe and

40. Dunne, "Power," 11

41. Dunne, "Power," 11.

42. Stephen O. Murray and Will Roscoe, eds., *Islamic Homosexualities: Culture, History, and Literature* (New York: New York University Press, 1997).

43. "Islamic" corresponds to "Judaic" as "Muslim" corresponds to "Jewish" or "Jew."

44. Schmitt, "Different Approaches," 10.

45. Stephen O. Murray "The Will not to Know, Islamic Accommodations of Male Homosexuality," in Murray and Roscoe, *Islamic Homosexualities*, 33.

46. Historically, the verb "tanayaka" referred to the eyelids closing on each other, literally fucking each other, as in "tanayakat al-ajfan," or to indicate that people have been overcome with drowsiness, as in "tanayaka al-Qawm." See ibn Manzur, *Lisan al-'Arab*, vol. 10, 502. The verb however was used in the medieval period as it is in the modern period to mean that two people fuck one another. See, for example, the tenth-century classic Abu Faraj 'Ali bin al-Husayn Al-Asfahani, *Kitab al-Aghani* [The Book of Songs], ed. Ihsan 'Abbas, Ibrahim al-Sa'afin and Bakr 'Abbas (Beirut: Dar Sadir, 2002), vol. 21, 63, where the famed ninth-century poetess and singer 'Arib recounts how she and her lover Muhammad bin Hamid were fucking one another, "tanayakna."

Murray's books are too many to list here. Suffice it to say that this is the level that their fight to represent the *true and real* Arab or "Islamic" position on male-male sexuality has reached. Indeed Murray, after a range of quotes from sources or stories dating back to the classical period of Muslim civilization and to contemporary oral reports by Arab native informants, including one "Omar, a cosmopolitan Saudi studying in the United States,"[47] concludes that "with females segregated and tightly controlled, young and/or effeminate males available for sexual penetration are tacitly accepted—and very carefully ignored in Muslim societies, past and present."[48] Indeed, time in the context of the Arab world and Islam is not an agent of change but rather the proof of its lack.

Incitement to Discourse

The advent of colonialism to the Arab and Muslim worlds, its sponsorship of what came to be known later as "modernization" projects, and the proliferation and hegemony of Western cultural products have indeed had their effects. Basim Musallam has shown how such contact from the beginning of the nineteenth century reversed centuries of support that most schools of Islamic jurisprudence had given to women's rights to contraception and abortion, thus assimilating Islam's stance on these questions to the Christian Western position (both Roman Catholic and Protestant).[49] Indeed, as Western cultural encroachment continued, its hegemonic impact was also felt at the level of language. The word "jins," for example, meaning "sex," emerged in Arabic sometime in the earlier part of the twentieth century carrying with it not only its new meanings of a "biological sex" and "national origin," but also its old meanings of "type," "kind," and "ethnolinguistic origin," among others. The word in the sense of "type" and "kind" has existed in Arabic since time immemorial and is derived from the Greek "genos." As late as 1870, its connotation of "sex" had not yet taken place.[50] An unspecific word for sexuality, or "jinsiyyah," which also means "nationality"

---

47. Murray, "The Will," 41.
48. Murray, "The Will," 42.
49. Basim Musallam, *Sex and Society in Islam: Birth Control before the Nineteenth Century* (New York: Cambridge University Press, 1983).
50. Butrus al-Bustani, *Muhit al-Muhit, Qamus Mutawwal Lil-Lughah al-ʿArabiyyah* (Beirut: Maktabat Lubnan Nashirun, 1987), 129. Al-Bustani's dictionary dates from 1870, at which time the word "jins" had still not acquired the meaning of "sex." For medieval dictionaries, which identify jins as "genos," see ibn Manzur, *Lisan al-ʿArab*, vol. 6, 43; and Muhammad bin Yaʿqub Al-Fayruzabadi, *Al-Qamus Al-Muhit* (Beirut: Dar Ihyaʾ al-Turath al-ʿArabi, 1997), vol. 1, 738.

and "citizenship," was coined by translators of the works of Freud in the 1950s (like Mustafa Safwan and Jurj Tarabishi)[51] with a more specific and nonconfusing word coined more recently by Mutaʿ Safadi, one of the two translators of Foucault's *History of Sexuality*.[52] Still the new word "jinsaniyyah" is understood by a few, even among the literati. Words for homo- or heterosexuality were also invented recently as direct translations of the Latin original: "mithliyyah" or sameness in reference to *homo*sexuality, and "ghayriyyah" or differentness in reference to *hetero*sexuality. Arab translators of psychology books (except for translators of Freud who coined the term "mithliyyah"[53]) as well as Arab behavioral psychologists had adopted in midcentury the European expression "sexual deviance," translating it literally as *al-shudhudh al-jinsi*, a coinage that, as we saw in the preceding chapters, remains the most common term used in monographs, the press, and polite company to refer to the Western concept of "homosexuality."[54]

The advent of colonialism and Western capital to the Arab world has transformed most aspects of daily living; however, it has failed to impose a European heterosexual regime on all Arab men, although its efforts were successful in the upper classes and among the increasingly Westernized middle classes. It is among members of these richer segments of society that the Gay International found native informants.[55]

51. See Sighmund Fruyd, *Tafsir al-Ahlam*, translated by Mustafa Safwan (1958; Cairo: Dar al-Maʿarif Bi Misr, 1969), 181, for example; and Sighmund Fruyd, *Thalathat Mabahith Fi Nazariyyat al-Jins*, translated by Jurj Tarabishi (Beirut: Dar al-Taliʿah, 1981).

52. See Mishil Fuku, *Iradat al-Maʿrifah, Al-Juz ʾal-Awwal min Tarikh al-Jinsaniyya*, edited and translated by Mutaʿ Safadi and Jurj Abi Salih (Beirut: Markaz al-Inmaʾ al-Qawmi, 1990).

53. Sighmund Fruyd, *Tafsir al-Ahlam*, translated by Mustafa Safwan, 182, 301, 337, 390, 391, 396, and 400.

54. See chapter 2 above on the biologically essentialist and pathologizing account of homosexuality provided by Nawal al-Saʿdawi in a chapter titled "Al-Rajul wa al-Shudhudh al-Jinsi" in her *Al-Rajul wa al-Jins* (Beirut: Al-Muʾassassah al-ʿArabiyyah lil-Dirasat wa al-Nashr, 1986), 557–69. The book was originally published in 1977. Asʿad AbuKhalil argues that the use of the term "shudhudh jinsi" in the Arab press constitutes oppression of "homosexuals" in the Arab world today. See his "New Arab Ideology? The Rejuvenation of Arab Nationalism," *Middle East Journal* 46, no. 1 (Winter 1992): 35 and 35, fn52, where such use is the only evidence provided by AbuKhalil to support the charge of anti-"homosexual" oppression.

55. One such example is the short essay written by a Jordanian lesbian for a book compiled by IGLHRC. The author uses a silly and wrongly transliterated and Orientalist pseudonym "Akhadar Assfar" [properly transliterated, it would read Akhdar Asfar, meaning Green Yellow], See Akhadar Assfar, "Jordan," in Rachel Rosenbloom, *Unspoken Rules: Sexual Orientation and Women's Human Rights* (New York: Cassell, 1996), 103–4. Although the author is careful to say that her statement "was written to reflect my personal, individual perspective and not to speak on behalf of other lesbians in Jordan" (103), she ends her essay by affirming that "Lesbians in Jordan are without a mention, without recognition, very marginalized . . . YET WE EXIST," 104. Another Tunisian native informant by the name of "Muhammed" provides information to one Francoise Gollain in her "Bisexuality in the Arab World," in *Bisexual Horizons: Politics, Histories, Lives*, ed. Sharon Rose and Chris Stevens (London: Lawrence and Wishart, 1996), 58–61. See the interview conducted by the two gay editors

Although members of these classes who engage in same-sex relations have more recently adopted a Western identity (as part of the package of the adoption of everything Western by the classes to which they belong), they remain a minuscule minority among those men who engage in same-sex relations and who do not identify as "gay" nor express a need for gay politics. This point is conceded by the Gay International whose descriptions of the sexual practices of Arab men, as we saw above, stress the "prevalence" of same-sex contact while acknowledging the dearth of "gay" politics or identification.

It is this minority of native informants and its diaspora members who now staff groups such as the U.S.-based Gay and Lesbian Arabic [sic] Society (GLAS), founded in 1989 by a Palestinian in Washington, D.C. Indeed, as members of the Gay International, this minority is one of the main poles of the campaign to incite discourse on homosexuality in Arab countries. GLAS defines itself as "a networking organization for Gay [sic] and Lesbians of Arab descent or those living in Arab countries. We aim to promote positive images of Gays and Lesbians in Arab communities worldwide. We also provide a support network for our members while fighting for our human rights wherever they are oppressed. We are part of the global Gay and Lesbian movement seeking an end to injustice and discrimination based on sexual orientation."[56] GLAS's newsletter *Ahbab* declares that "since we started this site, we have witnessed the development of a global family of Gay/Lesbian Arabs and friends."[57] For the founder of GLAS and its current outreach director, Ramzi Zakharia, "since the concept of same-sex relations does not exist in the Arab world, being 'Gay' is *still* considered to be sexual behavior . . . Just because you sleep with a member of the same sex does not mean that you are Gay . . . it means that you are engaging in homosexual activity. Once a relationship develops beyond sex (i.e.: [sic] love) this is when the term gay applies."[58] Indeed for Zakharia, the issue of time is crucial. In the Arab world, being gay is "still" considered sexual behavior—the point being that the Arab world has yet to catch up with the liberatory Western model of gayness, a transformation that GLAS seeks to expedite. GLAS's Western sexual epistemology is clearest in its claim to represent those Arab men who practice same-sex contact but do not identify as

---

(one is an Israeli Jew, the other an American Jew) with an Israeli Palestinian man named Walid who identifies as "gay" in *Independence Park: The Lives of Gay Men in Israel,* ed. Amir Sumaka'i Fink and Jacob Press (Stanford: Stanford University Press, 1999), 197–219.

56. See its website and homepage at www.glas.org.

57. See its Web site at http://www.glas.org/ahbab/home.htm.

58. Nur Sati, "Equivocal Lifestyles," *Living Channel,* 30 July 1998, posted on the *Ahbab* newsletter Web site, http://www.glas.org/ahbab/Articles/arabia1.html. Emphasis added.

gay or seek to be involved in gay politics through GLAS or any other organization.[59] In this, these self-identified gay Arab native informants are not unlike many Arab women native informants for Western feminism. As Marnia Lazreg put it, "To what extent [these Arab women native informants] do violence to the women they claim authority to write and speak about is a question that is seldom realized."[60]

The Gay International and this small minority of same-sex practitioners who adopt its discourse have embarked on a project that can only be described as *incitement to discourse*.[61] As same-sex contact between modern men has not been a topic of government or journalistic discourse in the Arab world of the last two centuries (the atypical and exceptional 1950s books and articles by Salamah Musa notwithstanding), the Gay International's campaign since the early 1980s to universalize itself has incited such discourse. The fact that the incited discourse is characterized by negativity toward the mission of the Gay International is immaterial. By inciting discourse on homosexual and gay and lesbian rights and identities, the epistemology, nay, the very ontology of gayness is instituted in such discourse, which could only have two reactions to the claims of universal gayness—support them or oppose them without ever questioning their epistemological underpinnings. Indeed it is exactly these reactions that anchor and strengthen and drive the Gay International's universal agenda. In a world where no one questions its identifications, gay epistemology and ontology can institute themselves safely. The Gay International's fight is therefore not an epistemological one but rather a simple political struggle that divides the world into those who support and those who oppose "gay rights."

The Gay International is aided by two other phenomena accompanying its infiltration of the international public sphere—namely, the spread of AIDS on an international scale and the Western homophobic

59. In an article discussing the gay-bashing of a Pakistani living in Chicago, an otherwise careful observer, Alexander Cockburn (who argues persuasively against hate crimes legislation as a misguided strategy that does not deal with the causes of hate crimes or with the legal inequalities of gays and lesbians in U.S. society) urges the U.S.-based Al-Fatiha Foundation, which he identifies as "an international gay Muslim organization," not to "wast[e] time on hate-crimes issues in Chicago when their Muslim comrades round the world are confronted by forces of intolerance even grimmer than [Chicago] Mayor Daley's Blue Knights . . . Seven Islamic nations prescribe the death penalty for homosexuality" (Cockburn, "Beat the Devil," *Nation*, 21 May 2001, 10). When Al-Fatiha turned its attention to the people who actually created it, Cockburn urges the organization to represent people who never sought its creation, much less its "defense" of their rights.

60. Marnia Lazreg, "Feminism and Difference: The Perils of Writing As a Woman on Women in Algeria," in *Feminist Studies* 14, no. 1 (Spring 1988): 89.

61. I borrow the notion of "incitement to discourse" from Foucault, *The History of Sexuality*, vol. 1, 17–35.

identification of it as the "gay" disease, and the rise of Islamism in the Arab and Muslim worlds during the same period, which demanded a strict order of sexual mores. The Gay International has benefited measurably in its task of inciting discourse by attracting much antigay Islamist and nationalist reactions.[62]

As discussed in the introduction, while the premodern West attacked medieval Islam's alleged sexual licentiousness, the modern West attacks its alleged *repression* of sexual freedoms in the present. Representations of Arab societies in the discourse of the Gay International, which includes the very popular publication *Spartacus,* an "International Gay Guide," range between the horrific and the splendid, the latter on account of the "availability" of Arab men willing to engage in insertive anal intercourse with Western (read white) gay men. In the context of an Arab anticolonial nationalism or the more recent Islamism seeking Western technological modernization while "preserving" its version of cultural or religious "authenticity," the Gay International is *correctly* perceived as part of Western encroachment on Arab and Muslim cultures. The fact that the Gay International resorts to the same organizations (the U.S. State Department, the U.S. Congress, U.S.-based human rights organizations, the American media, inter alia), practices, and discourse that advance U.S. imperial interests is hardly a mitigating circumstance. Indeed, not only the Arab world but also many Muslim countries find themselves in a similar position, as do non-Muslim third world countries.[63] Faisal Alam, the Pakistani American founder of a new Gay International organization for gay and lesbian Muslims, the Al-Fatiha Foundation, explains to his Western audience how Islam is "200 years behind Christianity in terms of progress on gay issues." Alam, not surprisingly (like Robert Bray, quoted above), is a field associate with the National Gay and Lesbian Task Force in Washington, D.C.[64]

---

62. For one of the earlier and measured Islamist responses to Western scholarship on homosexuality in Arabic, see Muhammad Jalal Kishk's engagement with the work of John Boswell in his *Khawatir Muslim fi al-Mas'alah al-Jinsiyyah* [A Muslim's Thoughts on the Sexual Question] (1984; Beirut: Dar al-Jalil, 1992). For a Christian parallel of incitement to discourse, in the case of the Anglican Church, see Neville Hoad, "Homosexuality, Africa, Neoliberalism and the African Church: The Lambeth Conference of African Bishops, 1998," in *Studies on Religion in Africa* 26 (2004): 54–79.

63. On the case of southern African nationalist responses, see Neville Hoad, "Between the White Man's Burden and the White Man's Disease: Tracking Lesbian and Gay Human Rights in Southern Africa," *GLQ* 5, no. 4 (1999): 559–84. On the case of Cuba and the reactions to the Gay International in the context of the cold war, see Lourdes Arguelles and B. Ruby Rich, "Homosexuality, Homophobia, and Revolution: Notes toward an Understanding of the Cuban Lesbian and Gay Male Experience, Part I," in *Signs* (Summer 1984): 683–99, and part 2, *Signs* (Fall 1985): 120–35.

64. David Goldman, "Gay Muslims," *Southern Voice* (Summer 1999), posted on http://www .al-fatiha.org/svoice.html. Alam has become so important in Washington circles that *even the Wash-*

175

The ambivalent gay representation of the Muslim world as a "homosexual paradise" has led some European gay men to convert to Islam. Khalid Duran, a Moroccan social scientist, reports on such occurrences in Britain and Germany: "Such converts are drawn to Islam by the erroneous assumption that Muslims are more tolerant . . ." Indeed it is such beliefs that account for why "Morocco has become a favorite playground for European gay men." As a result, religious circles "are reacting with increasing bitterness to this type of prostitution engendered by tourists from affluent societies. The long-standing indulgence was certainly not rooted in Islam. On the contrary, an Islamic backlash is gaining momentum, despite the abject poverty."[65] Still, the phenomenon Duran discerned in Europe seemed to be reproducing itself in the United States, at least until 9/11. The founder of a new U.S. group called "Queer Jihad" is a white American convert to Islam who goes by the name "Sulayman X."[66]

Duran discusses the result of this touristic assault:

A dispassionate discussion of the human rights of homosexuals is particularly hard to initiate in Muslim societies confronted with a kind of Western homosexual aggression. An instance in point is a representative of a European political foundation who was stationed in North Africa for many years. Extremely extroverted, he projects his homosexuality as a mark of distinction above and beyond his redoubtable academic merits. Such Western extravagances make the task of human rights activists among Muslims very difficult indeed.[67]

Duran understands that gay sex tourism in Morocco incites a discourse that has negative effects. However, he falls in the Western gay epistemological trap that identifies as homosexual only those Arab and Muslim practitioners of same-sex contact who are "passive." Duran describes "active" partners as having "no other homosexual inclinations" or as

---

ington Post featured him in an article. See Emily Wax, "Gay Muslims United in Face of Rejection," *Washington Post,* 3 April 2000.

65. Khalid Duran, "Homosexuality and Islam," in *Homosexuality and World Religions,* ed. Arlene Swidler (Valley Forge, PA: Trinity Press International, 1993), 186.

66. See the site of his group Queer Jihad on the Internet and his own "Confessions of Sulayman X," posted at http://www.well.com/user/queerjhd/confessions.htm. I should note here that Sulayman X's pretensions are made possible within a post–World War II context of African American appropriations of Islam and the appropriation in turn by white U.S. youth culture of African American popular culture. I should also note here that Faisal Alam, the founder of al-Fatiha, met one such convert. He tells the *Washington Post* reporter that his first homosexual encounter was a "relationship with an older male convert to Islam" in the United States where he lives. See "Gay Muslims United in Face of Rejection."

67. Duran, "Homosexuality," 186–87.

suffering from "emergency homosexuality."[68] It is the passive ones who are gay and therefore at risk for human rights violations. Duran notes that Western "gays seeking active partners in North African countries usually do not realize that their local lovers are often motivated by a hostile attitude toward them as citizens of nations that had once been colonial masters. To sodomize a Westerner provides a kind of psychological relief for some people from among the former 'subject races' who now have a chance to take it out on their oppressors. This also holds true of some other African regions; to do it to a white man is like taking revenge, along with having a source of income."[69] By reducing the desire of Moroccan men who are "active" in same-sex contact to the economic, anticolonial, or "emergency" realm, Duran need not account for the different workings of sexual epistemology and sexual desire to which Moroccan men subscribe; sexual desire is simply and conveniently eliminated from his account altogether.

Duran's semianthropological study (vaguely reminiscent of Richard Burton's views on the "Sotadic Zone"), which is punctuated by data that he provides as a native informant, differentiates between what he considers "the more genuine, or genetic type of homosexuality . . . [which is] generally less common among the peoples of the 'Islamic belt' than in Europe" and the more prevalent "emergency" homosexuality he thinks exists in the Arab countries and Iran.[70] Like AbuKhalil, Duran seems to think that the categories of "gay" or "straight" are transhistorical; he writes of "two important historical figures [who are] known to have been gay, Sultan Mehmet Fatih, the Ottoman conqueror of Constantinople (Istanbul), and Sultan Mahmud Ghaznawi, who invaded India from Afghanistan."[71]

Since the early 1980s, in the wake of the Iranian Revolution and the rise of Islamism in the Arab countries and the beginnings of the internationalization of the Western gay movements, a steady, albeit infrequent, discourse about Western "sexual deviance" and later about AIDS became evident in the Arab press. Much of it represented the Western gay and lesbian movements, following Western religious descriptions, as part of the "decadence" and "degradation" of Western sexual mores in general. Still, this limited discourse rarely mentioned "sexual deviance" in Arab

68. Duran, "Homosexuality," 188. Although Duran does not clearly define what he means by "emergency homosexuality," the sense is of men who have sex with men when there are no women available. His notion of "emergency homosexuality" seems related to Freud's notion of "contingent homosexuality." See Sigmund Freud, *Three Essays on the Theory of Sexuality*, trans. James Strachey (New York: Basic Books, 1962), 3.
69. Duran, "Homosexuality," 189.
70. Duran, "Homosexuality," 187–88.
71. Duran, "Homosexuality," 190.

countries and remained infrequent until the 1990s when it became more vociferous, although still infrequent, in response to the crusading efforts of the Gay International.

An example of this is the exchange that took place between the editor of a London-based Arabic newspaper, *al-Hayah,* and a representative of a U.S.-based Arab gay and lesbian group. Railing against Western cable and satellite channels for broadcasting programs containing violence, sexual material, and gay and lesbian weddings, Jihad al-Khazin, then editor-in-chief of the most prestigious Arab daily *Al-Hayah,* referred to gays by the Arabic term "sexual deviants."[72] Al-Khazin's conservative and procensorship argument chastised Arab liberals who fight government control of television and defended Arab governments as the bearers of "the responsibility to protect their societies from the worst aspects of degeneration." Al-Khazin, who often espouses Western conservative opinion on social matters, concluded his tirade by quoting Western sources that "sexual deviants" constitute no more than 1 to 2 percent of Western society. He asserted that "the focus [of television representations] on [a] violence without punishment or pain has led to the spread of violence in society. The danger now [lies in the possibility] that the focus on deviance among women and men, might lead to the acceptance of deviance as a normal, not a deviant, issue, its subsequent spread in the West, and then its reaching us."[73] Incensed by the use of the term "deviant" but not by the procensorship argument, Ramzi Zakharia, the Palestinian American founder of GLAS, wrote a letter to the editor in protest. Zakharia insisted that the term "deviant" "insults me as an Arab who desires people of the same sex as it insults millions like me." Zakharia explained how deviance does not describe people like himself since homosexuality is "genetic" and since his relationship to his sexual partner is based not only on sex but also on love. After issuing a veiled threat to withdraw a number of advertisements that the company for which he works usually places in *Al-Hayah,* Zakharia declared that his group's goals in the Arab world were like those of the feminist movement, namely, to "remove the old and tribalist patriarchal system, which has strangled and continues to strangle our people . . . This system is based on the use of 'traditions' and 'honor' as weapons to repress pluralism in our societies in order to make democracy practically impossible, and to maintain the tribalist mentality whose effects are very clear in the contemporary Arab world."[74] In

72. Jihad al-Khazin, "'Uyun wa Adhan," *Al-Hayah,* 9 February 1996.
73. Al-Khazin, "'Uyun wa Adhan."
74. Ramzi Zakhariyya, "Al-Nizam al-abawi wa aslihatuhu al-qam'iyya," letter to the editor, *Al-Hayah,* 3 March 1996.

response to Zakharia, al-Khazin, whose own concern about "degeneration" is borrowed wholesale from late nineteenth-century European social Darwinism, asserted that he did not intend to insult anyone by his comments but was simply using the Arabic term for homosexuals. The other term that exists, he correctly added, is *mithliyyah* or sameness, a term that is hardly known to most readers.[75] Al-Khazin concluded by asserting that "we" published most of Zakharia's long letter "while registering that the editor-in-chief and *Al-Hayah* are both against sameness [Mithliyyah], or deviance [shudhudh], or whatever the reader would like to call it, for reasons of traditions, religion, and inherited conventions, but without insulting anyone and without coercion, imposition, or oppression and without making a case out of it, as this was not the intention . . . moreover, the editor-in-chief admits his ignorance of this issue more generally as he did not realize that this issue was on the table."[76] Indeed it was not, as al-Khazin's concern was with the spread of "deviance" from the West to the Arab world and not its actual existence in the Arab world, about which he feigned ignorance; and neither the editor of *Al-Hayah* nor *Al-Hayah* itself would have declared their explicit opposition to "sameness" in the Arab world had they not been incited to do so by Mr. Zakharia, who forced such an admission to be issued from his American domicile—an admission that will affect not him but people in the Arab world. Zakharia's letter elicited another response from a Saudi physician in Riyadh who felt it incumbent to assert that the punishment for homosexuals is death and challenging Zakharia's claim of the genetic basis of "sexual deviance," asserting it as a "disease."[77]

Such incitement was not only confined to the pages of *Al-Hayah;* it had exploded in the preceding two years on the pages of many Arabic newspapers. In discussing the UN population conference in Cairo in 1994 and the UN-sponsored World Women's conference in Beijing in 1995, these issues came to the fore as a result of the imposition of the agenda of the Gay International by U.S., Canadian, and European NGOs on the rest of the world. The scandal of distorted translations of texts of

75. I should note here that in the last few years, in their coverage of gay- and lesbian-related news, *al-Hayah* and other Arabic newspapers have begun to employ intermittently the expression *mithliyyah*, indicating a transitional, ambivalent phase in language use between "shudhudh" and "mithliyyah." See, for example, "Mithliyu al-jins ila al-qafas al-dhahabi fi Kanada . . . wa al-baritaniyyun yantazirun al-faraj" [Canada's homosexuals (enter) the golden cage (of marriage) while the(ir) British (counterparts) are still waiting (to follow in their footsteps)], *Al-Hayah*, 13 April 2000, back page.

76. Response of the editor-in-chief (al-Khazin), *Al-Hayah*, 3 March 1996.

77. Dr. ʿAbdullah Bin Hamad, "Al-Shudhudh al-jinsi marad wa laysa amran mafrudan," letter to the editor, *Al-Hayah*, 15 March 1999.

platforms and other resolutions to other languages became a major issue in the preparation of both conferences. It was in this context that Arab columnists began to rail against the "lobby of deviants" in America who want to impose their debauchery on the rest of the world.[78] More recently, it was at the February 1999 population conference in The Hague, "The International Conference on Population and Development—Five Years after Cairo," where this "deviant lobby" showed its less than peaceful face. Intent on applying the Rousseauian formula that those who refuse to obey the "general will" of the Gay International be "forced to do so," indeed "be forced to be free," as Jean-Jacques Rousseau had put it,[79] the conference organizers attempted a repeat performance of 1994 by denying most delegates translations of conference resolutions, as they made them available only in French, English, and Spanish.[80] The resolutions included statements about guaranteeing for the youth the "freedom of [sexual] expression and sexual orientation." The word "orientation" was subsequently translated into Arabic in newspaper coverage as "direction," or "tawajjuh" (which has no idiomatic meaning whatsoever) and explained to the readers as meaning "sexual deviance."[81] It was a Belgian journalist of Muslim Arab origin who, as a correspondent for an Islamist magazine (Al-Mustaqbal al-Islami), alerted the Arab youth delegations to these ambiguous terms and their meanings prompting them to oppose them and to ask that they be removed from the resolutions. As punishment for his efforts, the UN conference coordinator denied him press access to the conference and instructed the UN security guards to take his press card and beat him. He was found by the Dutch police unconscious and handcuffed. They untied him and released him after which he pressed charges against the UN. The journalist, named Bashshar al-Jammali, sent letters to the 187 UN delegations and involved U.S. congressmen and the Dutch police in what became a cause célèbre condemning the machinations of the Gay International. Articles in the Arabic press and interviews with al-Jammali appeared with all the gory details of his beating.[82]

78. See, for example, Zaynab ʿAbd al-ʿAziz, "Kawalis muʾtamar al-marʾah fi bikin," in Al-Shaʿb (Cairo), 7 July 1995, and her "Tafakhur al-shawadh . . . wa muʾtamar al-marʾah," Al-Shaʿb (Cairo), 28 July 1995.

79. Jean-Jacques Rousseau, On the Social Contract, in Rousseau's On the Social Contract, Discourse on the Origin of Inequality and Discourse on Political Economy (Indianapolis: Hackett Publishing Company, 1983), 26.

80. See Danya Amin's report, "Muntada Fi Lahay . . . ," Al-Hayah, Mulhaq al-Shabab, 30 March 1999, 1.

81. Danya Amin, "Muntada Fi Lahay," 1.

82. See Muhammad al-Shaqaʾ, "Hal yasmaʿ Anan anin Bashshar?" Al-Hayah, Mulhaq al-Shabab, 18 May 1999, 20.

Defending Rights

As the twenty-first century dawned, Egyptian authorities began to crack down on Cairo-based locations where Westernized Egyptian gay-identified men and their European and American tourist cohorts congregate. On May 11, 2001, the police raided a discotheque housed in a boat on the Nile in the upper-class neighborhood of Zamalik and arrested 55 people, at least 34 of whom were at the disco at the time of the arrests while the rest were arrested in their homes or on the streets of Cairo. Women and foreign (read European and American) men present at the discotheque were released immediately while three Egyptian men found to be the sons of "prominent" people were released later. The arrested men were alleged to be members of a cult that considers the poet Abu Nuwas their "prophet." This allegation was based on a book, which the authorities claimed they had found at the home of one of the suspects, that elaborates this view and wherein same-sex practitioners are enjoined to go on a pilgrimage to the Dead Sea annually to commemorate the death of the "People of Lot." The men were roughed up and insulted by the police. They were later subjected to physical and psychological torture, including "medical," read rectal, exams to ascertain their "deviance."[83] When interviewed by Human Rights Watch, Dr. Fakhry Saleh, the Egyptian government's director of the Forensic Medical Authority, and his deputy Dr. Ayman Fouda cited the 1857 book of the French forensic doctor August Ambroise Tardieu as their authority for such medical procedures.[84] Tardieu's book, already famous in Europe,

83. For journalistic coverage of the arrests, see Muhammad Salah, "'Abadat al-shaytan yastalhimun qawm Lut" [Satan worshipers receive their inspiration from "the people of Lot"], *Al-Hayah*, 14 May 2001, 7, and *al-Hayah*'s subsequent coverage on the following dates: 15 May 2001, 7; 16 May 2001, 7; 29 June 2001, 5. Note that originally it was reported that fifty-five people had been arrested; by late June the number was reduced to fifty-two—the three upper-class men who were released in the meantime were dropped unceremoniously from the count. See also Muhammad Salah, "'Qawm Lut al-judud' yabkun fi al-jalsah al-ula li-muhakamatihim" ["The new people of Lot" cry at their first trial hearing], *Al-Hayah*, 19 July 2001, 4, for coverage of the first trial hearing; and Bonnie Eslinger and Hossam Bahgat, "Egypt Steps Up Anti-Gay Campaign: 52 Men Face Obscenity Trial," *San Francisco Chronicle*, 19 July 2001, A12. See also Hossam Bahgat, "Explaining Egypt's Targeting of Gays," *Middle East Report*, 23 July 2001 (press information note available online at http://www .merip.org). See also *Al-Hayah*, 16 August 2001, 1, 5, 6; 28 August 2001, 15; 29 August 2001, 6; 30 August 2001, 6. On rectal exams performed on the suspects, see "'Qawm Lut al-judud' al-difaʿ yataʿahhad taqdim wathaʾiq li-tabriʾat al-muttahamin" [The new people of Lot: The defense promises to provide documents to exonerate the suspects], *Al-Hayah*, 5 September 2001, 6. Apparently no exams were made on the penises of the men (for traces of fecal matter, for example) to ascertain if they were "deviant."

84. August Ambroise Tardieu, *Étude médico-légale sur les attentats aux moeurs* [A Medical-Legal Study of Assaults against Morals] (Paris: Bailliére, 1857).

came to be known in Egypt in the late nineteenth century as part of the modernization of medicine in the country.[85]

The official charges brought against these men by the state prosecutor were those of "offending religion" (one of the accused had allegedly written a text that advances a "heretical" interpretation of Islam as a religion that revels in same-sex contact) and of "practicing debauchery"—Egyptian law has no provisions against same-sex practice. Because Egypt has been under emergency regulations since the early 1980s, the men were tried by a special emergency state security court—an indication that the state considers this a national security issue. One person (the alleged author of the "heretical" text) was sentenced to a five-year prison term with hard labor, and his alleged associate received a three-year term. One person received a one-year prison term, and twenty others were found guilty of practicing debauchery and were sentenced to two-year prison terms with hard labor, while the remaining twenty-nine were found innocent of all charges and released. IGLHRC representative Scott Long (misidentified by *al-Hayah* as ILGA's representative or, more precisely, according to *al-Hayah,* "The International Association of Sexual Deviants") was at the trial and spoke with journalists. He condemned the court decisions and asserted that the "government exploits religion in an attempt to oppress the suspects." The court had declared that "Eastern society" as well as all monotheistic religions "condemn deviance [shudhudh] and perversion/delinquency [inhiraf]."[86]

This crackdown followed an increasing visibility of Westernized, Cairo-based, upper- and middle-class Egyptian men who identify as gay and consort with European and American tourists, as well as the related increase in Internet activity among some of these men to arrange for meetings. It should be noted that the police were able to pursue these men mostly through monitoring their Internet correspondence. The most prominent of the Web sites, gayegypt.com, is in English and features tips for European and American gay tourists coming to Egypt.[87] Clearly most Egyptian men who practice same-sex contact neither know

85. See Human Rights Watch, *In a Time of Torture: The Assault on Justice in Egypt's Crackdown on Homosexual Conduct* (New York: Human Rights Watch, 2004), 108–9.

86. See Muhammad Salah, "'Qadiyyat qawm Lut al-judud' fi Misr: al-ashghal al-shaqqah li 23 muttaham wa tabri'at 29" [The "Case of the New People of Lot" in Egypt: Hard labor for 23 suspects and the acquittal of 29], *Al-Hayah,* 15 November 2001, 8.

87. For example, the site has a Web page called "Gay Arabic" in which it states the following: "Welcome to gayegypt.com's gay arabic [*sic*] page—perfect for gay tourists wishing to use a few words in their encounters with Egyptians. Even remembering a few of these phrases will raise eyebrows and enhance your prospects of a profitable holiday." The rest of the Web site acts as a guide to gay tourists visiting Cairo and Egypt more generally and interestingly appropriates Egyptian-born Greek poet Constantine Cavafy as a "gay" poet.

English nor have the wherewithal to afford Internet access, much less know how to use it. This is important in that the police do not seek to, and cannot if they were so inclined, arrest men practicing same-sex contact but rather are pursuing those among them who identify as "gay" on a personal level and who seek to use this identity as a group identification through social and public activities. The campaign of the Gay International misses this important distinction. It is not same-sex sexual practices that are being repressed by the Egyptian police but rather the sociopolitical identification of these practices with the Western identity of gayness and the publicness that these gay-identified men seek.

The arrests prompted a torrent of media collusion with the government, condemning the practice of "deviance" as a new Western imposition—ironically, the hysteria that gripped the Gay International and their local agents only further ignited the rhetoric. IGLHRC was joined by Human Rights Watch and Amnesty International in condemning the arrests and in orchestrating a letter-writing campaign to Egyptian officials.[88] They were joined by GLAS and by Al-Fatiha's now infamous founder Faisal Alam, who not only called for worldwide demonstrations in support of the arrested men but also solicited the signatures of members of the U.S. Congress, recruited by openly gay and anti-Palestinian Massachusetts congressman Barney Frank and by the anti-Arab and anti-Egyptian Tom Lantos to sign a petition threatening a cutoff of U.S. aid to Egypt if the government failed to release the men (both Congressmen are Jewish Americans with strong pro-Israel views—facts that are not considered irrelevant, especially to the Arabic press).[89] Western

88. See also Bahgat, "Explaining Egypt's Targeting of Gays"; and Howard Schneider, "Cultural Struggle Finds Symbol in Gay Cairo: Arrests of 52 Men Reflect Tension between Islamic Traditionalists, Secularists," *Washington Post*, 9 September 2001, A24.

89. A GLAS flyer circulated via e-mail called for the 15 August 2001 demonstration in New York City at the Egyptian consulate. The flyer called on people to "join us for a rally outside the office of the Egyptian Consulate as we send a clear message that Gay Rights are Human Rights and that our tax dollars will not continue to fund the brutal oppression of our brothers and sisters in Egypt or any other Arab country." Al-Fatiha's Faisal Alam issued an Action Alert on 14 August 2001, entitled "International Day of Solidarity and Mourning in Support of 52 Detained Men in Egypt," calling for the 15 August worldwide demonstrations and asserting that "the Egyptian government [should] know that the world will not sit back and watch injustice and oppression take place!" On Alam's call to members of Congress, including Barney Frank, to sign the threatening petition, which many, including Frank, did, see *Al-Hayah*, 15 August 2001, 1, 6. See also the *Washington Post*, 9 September 2001, A24, and *Al-Ahram al-'Arabi*, 25 August 2001 (online version). Alam had already met Frank at least a year earlier when he "presented a copy of the Koran to a group of Jewish gay leaders, including U.S. Representative Barney Frank." See Wax, "Gay Muslims." Lantos's anti-Arab and anti-Egyptian views are noted in *al-Hayah*, "Al-Mithliyyun fi al-'alam yatahaddun li nasrat qawm Lut fi Misr" [Homosexuals in the world (launch a) challenge in solidarity with the "people of Lot" in Egypt], 15 August 2001, 1, 6. His unwavering support of Israel and enmity to Arab countries and the Palestinians is discussed in Janine Zacharia, "Lantos's List," *Jerusalem Post*, 13 April 2001 (online version).

diplomats and the Western press, who are usually silent about most human rights abuses in Egypt as well as the poverty that afflicts the country, flocked to the trial hearings in droves and registered their horror at the proceedings. The reaction of the Egyptian press and the Egyptian government was swift: more vilification campaigns of deviant sex as an imperialist plot followed, as evidenced by the *real* alliances that the Gay International makes with imperialists—Al-Fatiha's activities were seen as particularly egregious. Indeed, the vilification campaign against these men intensified precisely as a result of the actions of the Gay International and the Western politicians whose support it solicited. During the hearings, the prosecution frequently referenced the Gay International's campaign, pledged to defend the "manhood" of Egypt against attempts to "violate" it and wondered what would become of a nation who sits by idly as its "men become like its women" through "deviance."[90] The press and conservative Islamists soon began to call for explicit laws criminalizing same-sex practice.[91] The Gay International and its activities are largely responsible for the intensity of this repressive campaign. Despite the overwhelming evidence that gayness, as a choice, is proving to bring about more repression, not "liberation," and less sexual freedom rather than more for Arab men practicing same-sex contact, the Gay International is undeterred in its missionary campaign. Indeed, more recently, Ramzi Zakharia of GLAS claimed that "we refer to [the Queen Boat raid and trial] as our own Stonewall."[92] Zakharia seems not only to misunderstand the situation in Egypt but also the history of the Stonewall rebellion. The significance of the Stonewall event was not the police raid but rather the reaction it provoked, which mostly consisted of resistance to the arrests and of men and women demonstrating aggressively for their rights to be homosexual and that, as homosexuals, they have the right not to be harassed by the New York police. This inaugural event for the U.S. gay liberation movement and for what came to be known as "gay pride" has little in common with the Queen Boat raid. The reaction of the drag queens at the Stonewall bar was indeed significantly different from the reaction of the men at the Queen Boat discotheque; the latter not only denied being "homosexual" or "gay" but also added that they

90. See Khalid Miri, "Ma'rakah sakhinah bayn al-niyabah wa al-difa' fi qadiyyat al-shawaz" [A heated battle between the prosecution and the defense in the case of the deviants], *Al-Hawadith* (Cairo), 6 September 2001 (online version).

91. See, for example, "Al-Qanun la yu'aqib al-shawaz" [The law does not punish deviants], *Al-Ahram al'Arabi* (Cairo), 25 August 2001, which includes calls for the criminalization of same-sex contact among men in the country.

92. Ramzi Zakharia, radio interview on National Public Radio's "Leonard Lopate Show," WNYC, 14 April 2005

were forced under torture to sign false confessions that they were indeed "deviants." Also, not only did these men not seek publicity for their alleged homosexuality, they resisted the very publicity of the events by the media by covering their faces in order to hide from the cameras and from hysterical public scrutiny. These are hardly manifestations of gay pride or gay liberation.

Reacting to international pressure, the Egyptian government finally relented a year after the initial raid. In May 2002, the government, based on President Mubarak's refusal to ratify the sentences, overturned fifty of the fifty-two verdicts (including innocent and guilty verdicts), explaining that charges of the "habitual practice of debauchery" should have been considered outside the bounds of the State Security Court.[93] Based on this development, 21 of the 23 convicted men were freed except for the two lead defendants who were not included in the decision and remained jailed. Prosecutors opted to retry the twenty-one convicted men in an ordinary court of misdemeanors. The trial opened on July 2, 2002. On March 15, 2003, without allowing the defense to present arguments, the presiding judge reconvicted the men and increased their sentence from two to three years (the maximum under the law).[94] Upon appeal, the judge reduced the sentence to one year (time served). Harassment increased following the Queen Boat case, with police stepping up its surveillance and arrests of people suspected of "debauchery." A report by Human Rights Watch claimed that Egyptian "law enforcement officials read a signal in the Queen Boat case—taking it as an incentive to increasing rigor, or even a route to career advancement."[95]

Indeed, it was not only Egyptian law enforcement officers who would look forward to career advancement in the wake of the Queen Boat case, but so would key members of the Gay International. For his missionary efforts on behalf of IGLHRC and for his monitoring of the Queen Boat trial, Scott Long would soon be rewarded with employment at Human Rights Watch as a director of its newly and specially created program for monitoring worldwide violations of "lesbian, gay, bisexual and transgender rights." Long wrote the organization's report on the Queen Boat trial, *In a Time of Torture: The Assault on Justice in Egypt's Crackdown on Homosexual Conduct,* and reproduced parts of it in the opening article for a special issue of *Middle East Report,* which he wrote, "Sexuality, Suppres-

93. "I'adat muhakamat 50 shakhs fi qadiyyat 'Qawm Lut'" [The Retrial of 50 People in the 'People of Lot' Case], *Al-Hayah,* 23 June 2002, 6.
94. Muhammad Salah, "Raf' al-'uqubah ila Sajn 3 sanawat li 21 min 'Qawm Lut al-Judud'" [Increasing Jail Time to 3 Years for 21 of the "New People of Lot"], *Al-Hayah,* 16 March 2003, 6.
95. Human Rights Watch, *In a Time of Torture,* 49.

sion, and the State" in the Middle East.[96] He would also introduce the report at a public panel in San Francisco convened on the occasion of its release. Long became an instant expert speaking on "gays" in Arab countries on radio shows and at public lectures.[97] At the San Francisco event, Long announced that he had first learned of the arrests in Cairo when an Egyptian gay friend had called him on his cellular phone to inform him of the events (in the article for *Middle East Report,* he claimed that he had learned of them via e-mail messages[98]). As'ad AbuKhalil, who was the discussant on the panel, asked whether persecuted Egyptian Islamists also happened to have the cellular phone numbers of Mr. Long or other U.S. human rights activists. His was a rhetorical question. Indeed, rather than opposing the U.S. State Department's training of Egyptian police in its "Anti-Terrorism Assistance Program," a program in operation since 1983 that is used as the template for finding, arresting, and torturing innocent Islamists, the Human Rights Watch report recommends to the U.S. State Department that it include in its "training programs for Egyptian criminal-justice officials . . . a human rights component that includes issues of sexuality and sexual orientation in a way designed to eliminate prejudice and stigma."[99] The report, perhaps aware of the stigma of being Muslim or Arab in the United States, did not recommend the elimination of the Islamist stigma from the U.S. training program. As corroborated evidence of horrific, yet sadly standard, torture and humiliation proved insufficient exoticization of the situation in Egypt, Long often uses an uncorroborated, incredible story based on a lone report by a man arrested for "debauchery" as evidence of the exotic horror that Egypt constitutes for "homosexuals." The story appeared initially in the 144-page Human Rights Watch report as part of this one man's testimony:

> Once, it's hard to believe this, they brought a class of maybe thirty boys from a school, six or seven years old. They made us lie face down on our stomachs, and the small boys watched the policemen walking on our backs. Then the boys walked on us . . . They told the boys, "This is how faggots [khawalat] end." It was like a school trip.[100]

Long thought this unsubstantiated story was so much more significant (read *othering*) than other corroborated stories of torture that he repro-

---

96. Ibid. See also Scott Long, "The Trials of Culture: Sex and Security in Egypt," *Middle East Report* 230 (Spring 2004): 12–20.

97. His most recent appearance was on National Public Radio on the "Leonard Lopate Show" on WNYC on 14 April 2005 to discuss his expertise on gay Arabs.

98. Scott Long, "The Trials of Culture," 13.

99. Human Rights, Watch, *In a Time of Torture,* 128.

100. Ibid., 71.

duced it in his eight-page article in *Middle East Report*. He reinvokes it regularly at public lectures, including on radio appearances.[101] Like Long, local Egyptians who contacted and helped the Gay International in their efforts during the Queen Boat episode have also been generously rewarded with their own foreign-funded local organizations, such as Hossam Bahgat's "Egyptian Initiative for Personal Rights," founded in 2002, which seeks to defend a number of "personal" rights, including the "sexual and reproductive rights of women and men" and health-related issues, such as "HIV/AIDS."[102]

101. The latest was on the "Leonard Lopate Show," 14 April 2005. Long's polemics are not only directed at the Egyptian authorities but at any one who might question his Gay Internationalist agenda. In an article that is mostly a response to my article on the topic, he mistook my arguments for nativism, claiming that I was a "liberal metropolitan intellectual" who relied in my criticisms on "a distinction between the authentic and the inauthentic." In fact, my article not only exploded nativist notions of the authentic and the inauthentic (as does the rest of my work) but also never deployed such distinctions or used such terms at all to develop its arguments. What Long and the Gay International seem deliberately to refuse to understand is that opposition to their imposition of sexual identities and epistemologies is based on the violence that they perpetrate on the very subjects they seek to liberate, and not on nativist claims of authenticity and foreignness. See Scott Long, "The Trials of Culture," 15. Long was not the only Gay Internationalist offended by my criticisms. For Arno Schmitt's response, see Arno Schmitt, "Gay Rights versus Human Rights: A Response to Joseph Massad," and my reply to him, Joseph Massad, "The Intransigence of Orientalist Desires: A Reply to Arno Schmitt," in *Public Culture* 15 (Fall 2003): 587–594.

Such facile and naïve misunderstandings include Frances Hasso's assertion that "Massad's contention that lesbian and gay identity in Egypt is strictly a product of U.S. and European-based transnational queer organizations is essentializing in defining as impossible such identities among 'authentic' Egyptian men." See Frances S. Hasso, "Problems and Promise in Middle East and North Africa Gender Research," *Feminist Studies* 31, no. 3 (Fall 2005): 669. Invented claims and fabricated quotes about my argument like Hasso's now proliferate within Gay Internationalist literature. For the most recent ill-informed misapprehension of my argument, see Brian Whitaker, *Unspeakable Love: Gay and Lesbian Life in the Middle East* (London: Dar al-Saqi, 2006). His book is strewn with anti-Arab stereotypes that the author is careful to mostly place in the mouths of his anonymous native informants. To justify why he is writing a journalistic book about gays and lesbians in the Middle East while lacking any expertise on the subject, Whitaker claims that he was authorized to do so by a pseudonymous "Egyptian" activist, who upon Whitaker's suggestion that he write a book on the Queen Boat incident, responded to him: "No, . . . *you* should write one" (8). What is "unspeakable," however, in Whitaker's book is not some Arab homosexual love that he is endowing with the gift of speech but rather Whitaker's own European supremacist attitude that is fully informed by social Darwinism. Thus, as Whitaker had determined that it "was clearly time for someone to raise the issue in a serious way" and that his Egyptian native informant allegedly explained to him that "it was difficult for Arabs—at least those living in the region—to do so," he, belonging to the group of fittest humans, took it upon himself to defend those unfit to defend themselves, despite certain "risks" which he decided were "worth taking" (9). Whitaker, like many White European and American Gay Internationalist writers, is so insistent on not questioning his own European supremacist nativism that he apprehends any such questioning on the part of others as nothing short of anti-*European* nativism. Failing to understand my intervention as, among other things, a criticism of European *and* Arab nativism, he reformulates it as one calling for "cultural authenticity" and that it "dismiss[es]" those Arabs who want to adopt gay identity as "unimportant victims of Western influence," and that it posits Western influence on the Arab world in "conspiratorial terms" (207–11). The book is a remarkable example of what ill-informed journalism can produce when inspired by social Darwinism and racialized Eurocentrism.

102. See the organization's Web site, http://www.eipr.org/en/info/about.htm.

By inciting discourse about homosexuals where none existed before, the Gay International is in fact *heterosexualizing* a world that is being forced to be fixed by a Western binary.[103] Because most non-Western societies, including Muslim Arab societies, have not subscribed historically to these categories, their imposition is eliciting less than liberatory outcomes: men who are considered the "passive" or "receptive" parties in male-male sexual contacts are forced to have one object choice and identify as homosexual or gay, just as men who are the "active" partners are also forced to limit their sexual aim to one object choice, either women or men. As most "active" partners see themselves as part of a societal norm, so heterosexuality becomes compulsory given that the alternative, as presented by the Gay International, means becoming marked outside the norm—with all the attendant risks and disadvantages of such a marking.[104] Also, most Arab and Muslim countries that do not have laws against sexual contact between men respond to the Gay International's incitement to discourse by professing antihomosexual stances on a nationalist basis. This is leading to police harass-

103. The most recent campaign has targeted the Palestinian Authority (PA). The campaign started two years after the eruption of the second intifada. Articles published in the U.S. press, written by Israelis or pro-Israel Jewish activists, claimed that Palestinian "gays" are so oppressed that they could only find refuge in "democratic" Israel. Interviews with such "gay refugees" recounted horrid torture by PA elements. Indeed, the effort was inaugurated by U.S. Congressman Barney Frank himself, who used the occasion to praise Israeli "democracy" and the way it has functioned as a refuge for Palestinian gays in a region that oppresses them. See Yossi Klein Halevi, "Refugee Status," *New Republic,* 19–26 August 2002; Davi J. Bernstein, "Gay Palestinians Suffer under Arafat," *Yale Herald,* 13 September 2002; and the remarks of Barney Frank, "Supporting Israel," House of Representatives, 20 May 2002, H2654. Even an American Jewish lesbian activist who supports Palestinian rights joined the fray. Incensed by my article on the Gay International, she described my views as akin to "Stalinist dismissals of demands for the sexual liberation of women and homosexuals as nothing more than a bourgeois aberration." For this distinctly uncharitable response, see Charity Crouse, "Out and Down and Living in Israel," *Gay and Lesbian World Review* 10, no. 3 (May–June 2003). Israeli gay groups were in the forefront of defending these Palestinian men, whom Israeli authorities wanted to deport. See "Death Threat to Palestinian Gays," *British Broadcasting Corporation,* online Report, 6 March 2003; Mazal Mualem, "Groups try to stop expulsion of 3 gay Palestinians," *Ha'Aretz,* 7 March 2003. Concern among pro-Israeli American Jews that gay Americans supported the Palestinian cause resulted in a Zionist offensive that went into full gear to "expose" PA "oppression" of gays. See Daniel Treiman, "Gays Are Divided on Mideast Strife," *Forward,* 23 August 2002. On the status of Palestinian men identified as gay refugees in Israel, see Dan Williams, "Palestinian Gay Runaways Survive on Israel's Streets," *Reuters,* 20 September 2003. An Israeli-produced and -directed documentary film was made about one of them in 2004. The film, titled *Garden* and directed by Adi Barash and Ruthie Shatz, was shown at the Sundance film festival in Utah. It told the story of two Palestinian hustlers who slept with men, one an illegal refugee from the West Bank, the other a Palestinian citizen of Israel. Indeed, there were portrayals in the U.S. press that gay Palestinians and Israelis are a model of coexistence, as "demonstrated" in Jerusalem gay bars, see Orly Halpern, "Isn't That Queer," *In These Times,* 16 August 2002. On patriotic Israeli gay men who serve in the Israeli army, see Danny Kaplan, *Brothers and Others in Arms: The Making of Love and War in Israeli Combat Units* (New York: Harrington Park Press, 2003).

104. On compulsory heterosexuality's coercion of women in the West, see Adrienne Rich's classic, "Compulsory Heterosexuality and Lesbian Existence," *Signs* (Summer 1980): 631–60.

ment in some cases and could lead to antihomosexual legislation. Those countries that already have unenforced laws begin to enforce them.[105] Ironically, this is the very process through which "homosexuality" was invented in the West.

It is not the Gay International or its upper-class supporters in the Arab diaspora who will be persecuted, but rather the poor and nonurban men who practice same-sex contact and who do not *necessarily* identify as homosexual or gay. The so-called passive homosexual whom the Gay International wants to defend against social denigration will find himself in a double bind: first, his sexual desires will be unfulfilled because he will no longer have access to his previously available sexual object choice (i.e., exclusively active partners, as in the interim they will have become heterosexual);[106] and second, he will fall victim to legal and police persecution as well as heightened social denigration as his sexual practice becomes a topic of public discourse that transforms it from a practice into an identity. When the Gay International incites discourse on homosexuality in the non-Western world, it claims that the "liberation" of those it defends lies in the balance. In espousing this liberation project, however, the Gay International is destroying social and sexual configurations of desire in the interest of reproducing a world in its own image, one wherein its sexual categories and desires are safe from being questioned. Because it has solicited and received some support from Arab and Muslim native informants who are mostly located in the United States and who accept its sexual categories and identities, the Gay International's imperialist epistemological task is proceeding

105. The case of the Lebanese vice police's harassment in April 2000 of the managing director of an internet service provider in Beirut for allowing a Web site for "gay" Lebanese to run is one recent example. IGLHRC's intervention on behalf of two people being tried (the internet company's managing editor and a human rights activist) by a military court in connection with the Web site and the campaign it drummed up are exemplary of the incitement to discourse that contributes to even further criminalization and harassment. In one of its campaign mailings, IGLHRC enjoined its supporters to write letters to the Lebanese authorities demanding that they "end discrimination and harassment against gay, lesbian, bisexual, and transgender people in Lebanon." The setting up of the "Gay Lebanon" Web site featuring a buffed blond European man on the first page, itself incited discourse on gay issues in the press. Even human rights activists in the country ran a gay-unfriendly article on the topic. See Nada Iliyya, "Luwat Lubnan wa Suhaquhu Aydan," in *Huriyyat* 20 (Feb. 2000): 39. The Web site itself, whose language, like the corresponding Egyptian Web site, is exclusively English with Arabic making no appearance whatsoever, provides not only cruising tips for Lebanese men who identify as "gay" (and who obviously must be able to read English and must have internet access) but also to foreign visitors (read white Europeans and Americans) who are duly informed in the tradition of Lebanese chauvinism that homosexuality in Lebanon (a country that, unlike many of its neighbors, has colonial French laws from the 1930s criminalizing homosexuality) is "more tolerated" than in other Middle Eastern countries. The Web site address is http://surf.to/gay.lebanon.

106. This is precisely how the desires of the "passive" homosexual are described not only by the Gay International but also and increasingly in Arabic fiction. On this see chapters 5–6.

apace with little opposition from the majority of the sexual beings it wants to "liberate" and whose social and sexual worlds it is destroying in the process. In undertaking this universalizing project, the Gay International ultimately makes itself feel better about a world it forces to share its identifications. Its missionary achievement, however, will be the creation not of a *queer* planet, to use Michael Warner's apt term, but rather a *straight* one.

FOUR

Sin, Crimes, and Disease: Taxonomies of Desires Present

Much of the discourse about sex that took place in the twentieth-century Arab world centered on reconstructions of the medieval sexual life of the Arabs. It posited a peda-gogical role of the past in the present as a model of open-ness or debauchery, prudishness or licentiousness, libera-tion or repression, gender equality or inequality, virginality or sensuality. From the 1980s on, a new discourse emerged that dealt with sexual relations, partially by elaborating the category "sexual deviance," in existence, as we saw, since the 1940s, as a sociological and psychological ailment sym-bolic of decadent societies and applying it not only to the past, but also and more decidedly to the present.

Scholars and intellectuals of the 1970s and early 1980s expanded discourse on sex in the medieval Arab world for a possible sexually liberating pedagogy to benefit the present and future. But the early 1980s saw a veritable explosion of publications of *materia sexualis*. These new publications ranged from books of medieval Arab *ars erotica* to books on love and sex in the medieval Arab world, including ac-counts of "sexual deviance." In addition, a new genre of medical, criminological, and jurisprudential books about sexual "deviance" in general and in contemporary society in particular were published. If Michel Foucault was correct in asserting that unlike other civilizations, Western civiliza-tion was "the only civilization to practice a scientia sexualis,"[1] such a practice had by the 1980s, if not earlier, proliferated to the Arab world like never before. Some of these books seek to put "deviance" in religio-legal terms while others put them in religio-medical terms. Both angles are informed by the resurgent Islamism and its restrictive sexual mores. As discussed in the previous chapter, the rise of Islamism in the Arab world, the incitement to discourse by the Gay International, and the appearance of the AIDS pandemic on a global scale are the main forces behind the emergence of this new discourse.

The rise of Islamism in the late 1970s and its intensified presence in society following the triumph of the Iranian Islamic Revolution brought a resurgence of a discourse on prudishness and purity of morals. If the nationalists harked back to a golden age of Arab civilization whose liberal approach to sexual practices and desires they wanted modern Arabs to learn, the Islamists' interpretation of the early history of Islam aimed to found a modern Muslim society modeled after the Islamists' orthodox vision of early Islamic society from which Umayyad and Abbasid society had "deviated" by forsaking the teachings of Islam. Thus, the importance of the history of the past as a project for the present and future was shared by followers of nationalism and Islamism (as it is used by nationalists and religious fundamentalists around the globe, not least in the contemporary United States). Indeed, what is history's main task in this utilitarian economy if not the struggle to find a usable and emulatable past. Walter Benjamin speaks of how to "articulate the past historically . . . means to seize hold of a memory as it flashes up at a moment of danger."[2] For conservative nationalists and Islamists, history is nothing but a repository of memories that can be galvanized in the face of a perceived danger, whether repression or debauchery, a sort of how-to guide to a glorious future that restores the glories of yesteryear.

The discourse that emerged in much of the twentieth century was peculiar in that, like its European equivalent—as Michel Foucault had discerned[3]— it was preoccupied with how repressed sex was in our present era and how talk of it was restricted and not allowed when what was unfolding was the exact opposite. More and more authors were writing about sex and sexual desire; discussing its history and its different practices; how it related to morality; its relationship to religion, to gender liberation, to intellectual life, to literature, to cultural renaissance and civilizational decline; its nativeness or foreignness, and much more. As

---

1. Foucault, *The History of Sexuality,* vol. 1, 58.
2. See his "Theses on the Philosophy of History," in *Illuminations, Essays and Reflections,* ed. Hannah Arendt (New York: Schocken Books, 1969), 255.
3. See Foucault, *The History of Sexuality,* vol. 1.

discussed in chapter 3, the very term "sex," or *jins*, was invented by the very same discourse that decried its repression. While sexual life might have continued to be socially and legally restricted in a number of ways, a new discourse about sex was being produced and was expanding with each passing decade.

Since the early 1980s however, this discourse about sex took a new turn. The new dominant discourse, unlike the earlier expansive one that addressed questions of sexual and gender liberation in the present by learning the lessons of the past, is concerned with how open sex (and its outward manifestations) had become and the need to restrict its movement and repress its expression in the private and public spheres. The tasks the new Islamist discourse set for itself include restricting the openness of sex and its ability to circulate, controlling its expression, reversing its direction, and punishing the debauchers of the past through retroactive condemnation, and of the present through actual corporeal penalties. The new discourse, as we will see, has suppressed much of the different agendas of the preceding one and is successfully restricting the terms of the debate to Western licentiousness versus adherence to "true" Islam, or in the language of the Gay International, to sexual "rights" versus repression and religious "barbarism."

The earlier discourse sought change and more openness by deploying the excavated Arab culture of the past as a model to build on. Thus it did not threaten but rather strengthened nationalist sensibilities. The new incitement by the Gay International, however, has conjured up the threat of cultural contamination for the new religious nationalists. The appearance of the Gay International on the scene was part and parcel of the heightened European and American presence in post-1967 Arab world. The defeat of 1967, as I discussed in the introduction, was not only a defeat in battle but also a transformative moment of Arab politics and international relations more generally. If the 1967 defeat signaled the death of state-sponsored Arab nationalism, it was also to usher in a new state-sponsored welcome to U.S. and European financial investment in the Arab world, as well as U.S. military deployment across the region, especially in Egypt, which was previously off-limits to the United States. The increased and intensified alliance between a post-Faisal Saudi Arabia and the United States was another manifestation of the increased U.S. presence in the 1970s. This economic and financial "penetration" led to the lifting of subsidies and the increased impoverishment of the poor of Egypt (whose population constitutes one-fourth of the population of the entire Arab world) and the creation of a new comprador class that was enriched overnight. The arrival of the Gay

International on the scene, as we saw in the last chapter, was unfolding in this context of expanding imperialism and was correctly seen as part of it. Its intervention shifted the existing discourse on sex and its concerns from the decadence of the past and its degradation and the need to liberate the present to the decadence and degradation *of the present,* and the need to repress it, *not* to liberate it. In this way the Gay International's intervention has generalized some of Bouhdiba's views in terms of focus. Bouhdiba's argument had it that it was today's deviance that needed to be repressed and policed, not "our" past's.

The new discourse does share many of the contentions present in the previous one, especially as regards the foreign origins of deviance. If those who debated the sexual licentiousness of the past followed the Orientalists in positing Persians (or sometimes Romans) as the originators of the practice, the producers of the new discourse insist on the Westernness of the modern manifestations of sodomy as deviance. It is not sexual liberation or repression as such that are at stake in these raging debates, however, but rather the epistemology and taxonomies of sex, sexual practices, sexual identity, and the scope of sexual desires in relation to national, cultural, and religious identities—in short, to civilization tout court.

If previous authors concerned themselves with debauchery and sometimes with deviance and their relationship to civilizational decline, the current authors obsess about sex differently. Sex, depending on the author, now falls under one or more categories, all of which are related to the impending destruction of society and civilization as we know them. For the Gay International and its adherents, the new relevant categories are sexual identities, sexual rights, as well as the erstwhile goal of sexual liberation (the latter was also sought by the preceding Arab debate), all of which can and must be achieved by exact emulation of the West, whose alleged achievement of these aims marks its very progress, just as the limitations it places on them marks its backwardness. For the Islamists and other social conservatives (just as it is for evangelical Christians and social conservatives in the West), it is not that debauchery and deviance are no longer relevant categories, but that they are made more deadly by being transformed into sins, crimes, and diseases, which together will lead to the spiritual and physical death of society and civilization unless a religious revivalism acts as the cleansing process that eliminates them first. Instead of emulating the West, as the Gay International insists, the Islamists insist that Arabs emulate their Muslim ancestors. The fact that much of Islamist discourse on sex and sexuality is an emulation of Western Christian fundamentalisms and Orientalist constructions of the Arab and Islamic past escapes the notice of both the Islamists and the Gay Internationalists.

Thus, the Gay International and the Islamists both agree that deviance/gayness has much to do with civilization. For the Gay International, transforming sexual practices into identities through the universalizing of gayness and gaining "rights" for those who identify (or more precisely, are identified by the Gay International) with it becomes the mark of an ascending civilization, just as repressing those rights and restricting the circulation of gayness is a mark of backwardness and barbarism. For the Islamists, in turn, it is the spread and tolerance of sexual deviance that mark the decline of civilization, just as repressing, if not eliminating, it will ensure civilization's ascendance. In this, we also see commonality with those thinkers, like al-Nuwayhi, who posited (nonmorally) civilizational decline as a period during which deviance becomes a public affair. If for al-Nuwayhi and others deviance was a feature of civilizational decline in the past, for many Islamist and nationalist thinkers, the very survival of modern Western or Islamic civilization as we know them is what deviance threatens today. Adhering to the very same epistemology of "progress" and "backwardness," the Gay International cannot agree more.

However, this account remains unclear. For if homosexuality leads to civilizational decline, the fear on the part of Islamists is that Islam, as the only component of Arab civilization that survived the medieval decline, will also be destroyed. There is something confused about this fear and about what civilization actually is. For if "Islam" survived the first "decline" under the Abbasids and later the Ottomans, what prevents it from surviving in the age of the Gay International? Clearly, Islamists, as we will see, view the current Western hegemony as chipping away at what they consider as "Islam," and that this "Islam" is the last bastion of resistance against such encroachment. The fact that Western governments, the media, and the Gay International, regularly attack "Islam" as the culprit further confirms such fears and further mobilizes the "resistance." Similarly, the concern of the Gay International that same-sex practitioners can only flourish in a Western-style system contradicts its own historical project, which claims that lifestyles and desires it deems "gay" have flourished in the past of the West, from the Greeks to the Christian Church and, in its Orientalist accounts, in medieval Islam.

In the following, I will examine writings on sex at the moment preceding the epistemological break and immediately succeeding it. This will include the way civilizational thinking is deployed by and against the secularists and by and against Islamists in debates about venereal disease and civilization, crime and civilization, sin and civilization, sexual tolerance and civilization, individual rights and civilization, and more specifically, sexual deviance and civilization. This debate will involve a new generation of writers and thinkers, some well known, others less so. What the debate will demonstrate however is the exponential proliferation of books and commentaries about things sexual and their novel encroachment into the realm of state policy.

Remnants of the Past

As one examines the emergence of the new discourse on sex in the 1980s, one can still discern echoes of the debate that dominated most of the century. The most serious of such continued engagement is perhaps, Jordanian novelist and Marxist-feminist literary critic Ghalib Halasa's book *The World: Matter and Movement*. First published in 1980, it had a strong impact in intellectual circles prompting its author to revise and republish it in 1984.[4] The book offered class analysis of medieval Islamic society and attempted to articulate an explication of the late Umayyad and Abbasid phenomenon of bawdiness or *mujun*. Halasa identified four characteristics common to all those accused of being bawdy or *mujjan* (singular *majin*), namely, having an encyclopedic cultural knowledge, opposition (of hegemonic views) characterized by protest, *zandaqah,* and boasting of the body and its pleasures.[5] He wanted to distinguish between the bawdy person and what societal norms posit as a morally degraded person:

The *mujjan*'s [public] presentation of themselves and of their activities is what provoked the *salafiyyin* and [the ruling] political authority, and not bawdiness [mujun] itself. For, we have not heard that [the caliphs] al-Mahdi, or al-Hadi, or al-Rashid fought the *mujjan* because they drank alcohol or pursued women and youthful boys, as they themselves [the caliphs] used to do the same things, or at least some of them did; rather, they went after them because of their opinions and thoughts. We know that the Abbasid caliphs used to drink alcohol . . . and used to own numerous concubines, and that the caliph al-Amin used to prefer youthful boys, and that he did not

4. Ghalib Halasa, *Al-'Alam, Maddah wa Harakah, Dirasat fi al-Falsafah al-'Arabiyyah al-Islamiyyah* [The World: Matter and Movement; Studies in Arab-Islamic Philosophy] (Beirut: Dar al-Kalimah, 1984).

5. Ibid., 95.

care for women, which bothered his mother. So, she opted to dress concubines in the clothing of youthful boys as a way to pique his interest. We do not know if this woman succeeded in her aim or not.[6]

In a number of ways, Halasa's explanation of the nature of the persecution of *mujjan* parallels the one I offered in the last chapter about the repression of present-day "debauchers" in the Arab world, wherein it is the publicness of socio-sexual identities rather than the sexual acts themselves that elicits repression. Halasa explained the appearance of the phenomenon of the *mujjan* as part and parcel of the rise of a commercial-industrial class that fought the existing feudal-military class (during the Umayyad and later the Abbasid periods) and sought to create a national market. This required ridding society of old parochial ideas of tribalism, ethnocentrism, and the like, ideas that the *mujjan* adopted and expressed in their writings. Thus, Halasa concluded, "we could say that one of the methods for this new capitalist class to express itself was to opt for the destruction of all existing social institutions in order to substitute for them a national market, thus creating one nation. The *mujjan* were the philosophical-artistic expression—to an extent—of this direction, among many, pursued by the new class."[7] Halasa was clear that this was not a conscious alliance or a conspiracy but rather a result of the new dynamism that the new economics created. It certainly was not some mechanical congruence between the commercial class and the *mujjan* intellectuals.[8]

Examples of such *mujjan* include the poets Bashshar bin Burd and Abu Nuwas. Halasa, who identified Abu Nuwas as "belonging to Arab origins" without noting the controversy surrounding his paternal origins,[9] insisted that some of what that poet wrote did not necessarily reflect what he did, but rather that it was intended to provoke his conservative society. Thus,

the majority of the adventures that Abu Nuwas narrated could not be but lies with which he meant to provoke his conservative society, thus appearing as strange and deviant in their view. For when he calls for obtaining physical pleasure with one's neighbor, with elderly men in their eighties, and with male relatives, I believe that all he meant was to disturb the dignity of this conservative society. Indeed, his provocation reaches its apogee when he makes a comparison between drinking alcohol and

6. Ibid., 96.
7. Ibid., 97.

8. Ibid., 97–99.
9. Ibid., 103.

enjoying youthful boys on the one hand and war and beatings on the other . . . preferring debauchery [tahattuk] to heroism in war.[10]

For Halasa, the *mujjan* insisted that life "was worth living" and thus affirmed individual bodily pleasure as central to this life and that it need
not await the paradise of the afterlife.[11] Thus,

differences between the *mujjan* and the opulent classes were not due to lifestyle,
but to two other reasons. First, their lifestyle constituted for the *mujjan* a philosophical stance, or rather their lifestyle was their principal position, meaning that they
did not place a division between their conduct and their adoption of it on the one
hand and their [principled] defense of it. Thus, there was complete harmony between
the conduct and the stance, and declaring both was one of the characteristics of
these *mujjan*. This was at a time when the upper classes were living two different
lives with two different faces . . . Second, the *mujjan* had adopted their conduct as
an expression of a philosophy that they believed . . . while the ruling class had another philosophy and another attitude that made it incumbent upon it to conceal this
lifestyle.[12]

Thus, what Halasa discerned in the poetry of Abu Nuwas, for example, was a call to honesty, to bridge the gap between what was lived and
what was professed. It was a call to expose a ruling class whose hypocrisy
and ethnocentrism served to maintain its control of society. Ultimately,
the poetry of Abu Nuwas and his cohort was a new poetry based on
experience.[13] In a related article, Halasa evaluated the modern Arab renaissance and its major thinkers including Salamah Musa. He considered many of their propositions "laughable" in their "naïveté" about
the Arab past and the European present and excoriated Musa inter alia
for his contempt for the "literature on youthful boys" (adab al-ghilman)
and his cautioning the youth from reading it.[14] Contrary to modern
popular opinion, which believes that "Abbasid authority was fighting
zandaqah and degeneration due to its own religiosity and faith, meaning
that it was carrying its fight out based on a strict moral stance," Halasa
affirms that "its religiosity and faith were mostly mere covers to assert
its control, and to defend its privileges. As for its fighting degeneration
itself, this is belied by the degeneration of this very class itself."[15]

10. Ibid., 103.
11. Ibid., 108–10.
12. Ibid., 111–12.
13. Ibid., 146–50.
14. Ghalib Halasa, "Bu's al-'Aql al-Nahdawi" [The Poverty of Renaissance Reason], in Ghalib
Halasa, *Al-Haribun min al-Hurriyyah* [Fugitives from Freedom] (Damascus: Dar al-Mada, 2001), 219.
15. Halasa, *Al-'Alam, Maddah wa Harakah*, 112.

Halasa's thesis in fact had little to do with the foregoing. As a literary critic, he was most interested in the question of language and aesthetics in the poetry of the *mujjan* and the revolutionary spirit that they introduced to Arabic poetry, which had stagnated in the preceding century (i.e., the first century after the rise of Islam). It is there that Halasa found the economic revolution unfolding in society with its parallel in revolutionary ideas and aesthetics, not to mention the sexual conduct of the *mujjan*.[16] Halasa's approach was interested in explicating the kinds of aesthetics deployed by the hegemonic political system under the Abbasids and those deployed by the opposition, including the *mujjan* poets. In excavating the history of the period, Halasa was neither ashamed nor proud and did not deploy a moralist judgmentalism in evaluating that history despite his obvious biases in favor of the oppressed. Coming at the tail end of a century of excavations and theorization, his serious intervention marked a transition from a rich debate between contending political and philosophical schools of thought to one marked by a strict binary division between intellectual and societal forces. This is not to say that what came in the 1980s and beyond was cut off from the previous debate, but rather that it elided its axioms and concerns in favor of newly formulated concerns that seemed more immediately responsive to Western imperial challenges confronting the Arab world.

Al-Munajjid Revisited

Perhaps the earliest attempt to put Salah al-Din al-Munajjid's pioneering work back on track and preempt the Islamists was Saqr Abu Fakhr's intervention in an article he published in 1981. In "Sex among the Arabs," Abu Fakhr, a Palestinian intellectual living in Beirut, took on the resurgent Islamist discourse and its attempt to rewrite an Arab-Muslim history cleansed of ideological impurities, which edited out details of social life and recast others in ideologically convenient ways.[17] Abu Fakhr was attentive to the fact that most modern Arab writers who work on early and medieval Arab-Muslim civilization have ignored

on purpose, as it seems, a discussion of the sensual and spiritual side of the individual and the group in successive epochs, from the *jahiliyyah* to the Abbasids. And when

16. Ibid., 113–24, 146–65.
17. Saqr Abu Fakhr, "Al-Jins 'ind al-'Arab" [Sex among the Arabs], *Al-Hayah al-Jadidah* (Beirut) 5 (1981), republished in Manshurat al-Jamal, *Al-Jins 'ind al-'Arab* [Sex among the Arabs] (Cologne: Manshurat al-Jamal, 1991), 39–64.

some made reference to this issue, they would do so circumspectly and bashfully, and never exceed talk of the condemnation of the bawdy poets [a usual reference to Abu Nuwas], and about wine and rhapsodic [tashbib] poetry and the like. Indeed, the books of ancient [Arab] heritage were immeasurably more daring in addressing love, sex, and pleasures than those who are today thrusting one another to discover "the enlightened and righteous aspects" of ancient Arab heritage [turath].[18]

Abu Fakhr, like most of our other writers, is also a feminist who was concerned about the status of women in the modern Arab world, which he compared unfavorably to the Arabs of old: "There is a great difference between what Arab women enjoyed in the past and what some are calling for nowadays and what contemporary Arab women used to enjoy."[19] Abu Fakhr was also concerned about contemporary sexual epistemology and taxonomy and how they both differed from those of olden days:

Many of the cases that we consider today as sexual deviance were not considered as such by the Arabs. Having intercourse with youthful boys and having anal intercourse with women, or [vaginal] intercourse during menstruation or in certain stages of pregnancy, all used to be normal things and did not provoke condemnation, although some might have considered it an unpleasant and accursed situation. It should however be reminded that the sexual deviants, of old or more recently, are, in addition to their immense biological causes, victims of instinctual repression and an ignorant upbringing that looks at sex as sin. Treating this phenomenon cannot be carried out through stoning [which some Islamists call for], but rather through correct directed pedagogical bases that considers sex as a vital part of individual activity.[20]

Abu Fakhr seemed to use the term "deviance" to designate not same-sex contact alone but instead a whole range of practices. After citing a case of two young adult Kuwaiti men who kidnapped, raped, and killed two nine-year-old girls in 1981, Abu Fakhr affirmed that "it is certain that cases of sexual deviance, and the sex crimes they generate in some cir-

---

18. Ibid., 41. See also 52–53. A similar view is articulated by ʿAli Harb in his book *Al-Hubb wa al-Fanaʾ, Taʾammulat fi al-Marʾah wa al-ʿIshq wa al-Wujud* [Love and Evanescence: Meditations on Women, Erotic Love, and Existence] (Beirut: Dar al-Manahil, 1990), 79. Harb stated that one "notices the big difference on the discursive level, between the modern and the classical period . . . when discourses flourished about the myriad parts of life, including the discourse on love and sex. Even the discourse on concubines and youthful boys had its share of formation and emergence. He who studies the development of discourses notices that things, between yesterday and today, have indeed taken a path of more restrictions on speech about sex and love."

19. Abu Fakhr, "Al-Jins ʿind al-ʿArab," 46.

20. Ibid., 50.

cumstances, will not cease to appear in a society that is contemptuous of the body and that represses instincts and calls for fake puritanical ideologies."[21] As for sapphism, "its spread had many causes. In addition to the physiopsychological reasons, virgins were concerned about defloration while nonvirgins worried about pregnancy.'"[22] In making female "deviant" sexual desire solely the product of physiopsychological malfunctions and male sexual "deviance" the result of a repressive sociocultural limitations, Abu Fakhr elided any discussion of the causes of "normal" sexual desire as such, which he seemed to naturalize. Abu Fakhr envisioned a sexually open and liberated Arab society, and he believed that familiarity with the sexual history of the Arabs would achieve, or at least, help to achieve that end. Indeed he called for the publication of a number of medieval treatises of erotica that remained in manuscript form at the time (and some to this day), presumably for their pedagogical benefits.[23]

The Islamist Response

If until the 1970s, Islamism was not yet fully resurgent and contributed rarely to the debate about the preceding century, following the Iranian Revolution—which ushered in a phenomenal increase in its popularity— Islamism would have much to contribute. Indeed, the 1980s and 1990s brought forth an expansion of discourse on sexuality in the history of the Arabs and their present from both secular intellectuals, who called for a more "open" and less "repressed" culture, and from Islamists of all colorings, who until then were content defining the moralism of the prevailing discourse in society.

Muhammad Jalal Kishk's important 1984 book, *A Muslim's Thoughts about the Sexual Question,* was the earliest and most sophisticated of such interventions. His book, which was initially banned pending a court case brought against him by other Islamists, was finally permitted distribution. It appeared in three editions (between 1984 and 1992), the last of which included the author's response to his Islamist critics. Unlike Sayyid Qutb's fantastical approach to sexual liberties in the West, Kishk learnedly engaged contemporary Western scholarship, especially the then recent work of John Boswell, about Christianity and Islam in relation to sex, with special attention to homosexuality. In the third,

21. Ibid., 51.
22. Ibid., 61–62.

23. Ibid., 64.

complete edition, the author declared his pedagogical purpose for the book:

The sexual question occupies a large space of a human being's thought and actions and controls to an extent his conduct, nay even his attitudes. If it is a mistake to view humans as sexual phenomena exclusively, as Western philosophers and merchants of sex do, it is a bigger mistake to look at sex as an incidental phenomenon, or as shame . . . as this is not of our religion or of our civilization . . . the sexual question occupies the minds of the youth, but despite this it remains a taboo around which writers circle but never approach, especially the Islamists among them, thus leaving to the enemies of Islam and the enemies of our civilization the opportunity to publish their ideas and plant their poisons in the minds and hearts of our Muslim youth, who no longer follow an Islamic conduct nor are directed by Islamic thought.[24]

Relying on Western sources in his polemical book, Kishk studied the place of sex in Christianity, the Roman Catholic Church, Protestant theology, and Western civilization more generally, and then compared it to sex according to Islamic religious discourse and practice. This allowed him to contrast Islam's openness with the repression of Christian "civilization." He also compared the lower status of women in Christian theology versus their higher status in Islamic theology, especially as related to women's rights to sexual pleasure. Kishk was a liberal interpreter of Islam, rejecting stoning (part of the Jewish scriptures) as un-Qur'anic, and citing Islam, for example, as permissive of masturbation. His discussion of sodomy, however, was of a different order, to which his book paid special attention. He cited John Boswell extensively on the history of homosexuality in the Christian world. Like Qasim Amin a century earlier, Kishk showed how Christian descriptions of the Muslim world were in fact more applicable to Europe itself. After quoting a thirteenth-century European Christian diatribe about the shamelessness of the Muslim Arabs, Kishk stated that

if we changed just the word "Muslims" and replaced it with "Europeans" or "Americans," the text could then be attributed to a Muslim journalist writing on the hippies, punk rockers, or homosexuals in Amsterdam, Piccadilly, or the Village in New York or Santa Monica in California.[25]

24. Muhammad Jalal Kishk, *Khawatir Muslim fi al-Mas'alah al-Jinsiyyah* [A Muslim's Thoughts on the Sexual Question] (Beirut and Cairo: Dar al-Jil and Maktabat al-Turath al-Islami, 1992), 16.
25. Ibid., 168.

Kishk (reminiscent of al-Nuwayhi) advanced his theory that open homo-sexual relations take place in civilizations at their peak of success on the verge of decline, which to him did not mean that sex between men did not occur in other periods. He was clear that it existed in all periods except that openness about it, avowing it by celebrating it, and writing in praise of it only took place at the peak of a civilization.[26] He believed it to be a sign of and a cause of civilizational decline.[27] Moreover, he was clear that Islamic civilization was influenced by the Greeks and Romans as far as the phenomenon of desiring boys was concerned[28] and was quick to point out that what was widespread at the height of Muslim Arab civilization was not sex between two adult men, as is the case in the modern West, but rather between an adult man and a youthful boy.[29] Kishk's tolerance, however, had its limits, as he viewed Abu Nuwas to be emblematic of his civilizational decline theory: "The poetry of Abu Nuwas in its ridicule of religion and chivalry, and the [hedonistic] love of life at its most degenerate [which it expressed] is the prerequisite for achieving civilizational defeat."[30] Abu Nuwas's praise of Persians and defamation of Arabs were hardly mitigating signs in this regard.

Still Kishk's important study of Christian medieval propaganda about Islam and the Arabs and their alleged sodomitic practices and his response to Orientalist representations was not an apologia, as he did not cover up actual same-sex sexual practices in Islamic history or present (the latter was mostly implicit), but rather was interested in integrating it in his civilizational decline theory, which he applied universally.[31] Moreover, unlike conservative Islamists, he demonstrated how neither the Qur'an nor the Prophet had ever devised a punishment for sex between men (let alone between women), despite the Qur'anic condemnation of such practices in the case of the "People of Lot."[32] He also argued that all the sayings attributed to the Prophet about harsh punishment for same-sex practitioners were weak in their sources of transmission as the major compilers of the Prophet's sayings attested.[33] Therefore, while he did not approve of sex between men, he was clear that there was no prescribed punishment for it in Islam. Indeed, Kishk went further by analyzing those parts of the Qur'an that described paradise and

26. Ibid., 133–34.
27. Ibid., 87.
28. Ibid., 127.
29. Ibid., 129.
30. Ibid., 142.
31. Ibid., 111–88.
32. See his last chapter, "Wuldan mukhalladun" [Immortal Boys], 189–214.
33. Ibid., 195–200.

concluded that sex with youthful boys will be the reward for Muslim men who control their desires in this world by not practicing sodomy, that is, sexual desire for youthful boys is normal, just as it is normal, according to Kishk, to desire to steal and transport a "bank safe" into one's home. People do not steal on account of existing laws, while Divine proscription prohibits earthly—but not heavenly—same-sex contact.[34] Kishk's discussion of boys in paradise is an old one, as the debate around this question was part of jurisprudential inquiry in the premodern era.[35]

But if Kishk provided a liberal, sometimes radical, Islamist view of sex in Arab history, present, and future (mainly in paradise), most Islamists who wrote on the subject were less liberal in their interpretations, following instead the example of Qutb. Writing and responding to increased incitement by Western gay groups and activists about alleged oppression of gays and lesbians in the contemporary Arab world,[36] Islamists launched an immediate response. ʿAbd al-Rahman Wasil, an Islamist missionary and evangelist, published a book in 1984, the same year Kishk published his. Wasil's book, however, had a different Islamist view. Titled *The Sexual and Romantic Problems of Young People under the Gaze of Islamic Shariʿah*, it sought to provide a guide to Muslim youth who are taken in by "poisonous" Western ideas and fashions represented by the available Western pornography on the streets of Egyptian cities.[37] Aside from providing brief descriptions of sex in Roman and Greek civilizations and a critique of how the Roman Catholic Church demonized women and sex historically, the book offered itself as a guide to the righteous path through prescriptive explications of how sexual relations look like under the "light" of Shariʿah.

A particular area of concern for Wasil was the Anglican Church's vote to consider "sexual deviance" legitimate in 1957![38] Other concerns deal with contemporary Western society's decadence exemplified by out-of-wedlock pregnancies, American physicians' sexual relations with their patients, wife-swapping clubs, high adultery rate, and female prostitution.[39] Such a "degradation" of social life, contended Wasil, had major

34. Ibid., 114

35. For the premodern debate, see Khaled El-Rouayheb, *Before Homosexuality in the Arab-Islamic World, 1500–1800* (Chicago: University of Chicago Press, 2005), 128–136.

36. El-Rouayheb, *Before Homosexuality*, chap. 3.

37. ʿAbd al-Rahman Wasil, *Mushkilat al-Shabab al-Jinsiyyah wa al-ʿAtifiyyah taht Adwaʾ Al-Shari ʿah al-Islamiyyah* [The Sexual and Romantic Problems of Young People under the Gaze of Islamic Shariʿah] (Cairo: Maktabat Wahbab, 1984), 5.

38. Ibid., 31. This is a remarkable assertion given the fact that the global Anglican Church first placed homosexual issues on its agenda in 1998 at Lambeth.

39. Ibid., 31–36.

physical, psychological, and reproductive effects, not to mention the rise of violence in society.[40] With this situation predominating in Europe and America, Wasil, the missionary, proceeded to present how Islam deals with such problems, and called on Europeans and Americans—who have forsaken Christianity due to its failure to regulate social life properly—to adopt Islam, which provides better solutions to life's problems than the materialist philosophy that has replaced religion.[41] This view of "Islam" as a problem solver, as the cure of all ills, including, as we will see later, of diseases, informs most of the Islamist analysis of both the West and the Muslim world.

Wasil dealt with generalities and particularities. While he addressed the larger questions of what is sexually permissible or impermissible according to Shari'ah, he had time to advise young men and women embarking on marriage not to tell their partners about previous romantic encounters, as this would forever poison their relationships.[42] Under the title "Moral Diseases," to which he dedicated a whole chapter, Wasil listed sexual deviance, adultery/fornication, and masturbation as examples.[43] Sexual deviance is defined as "satisfying desire with the same sex. It is regression and a setback, and is an indication of the deviance of the psyche and the perversion of sentiment. Through it, a human being descends to a status lower than animals, as the animal's instinct rejects such a lowly act."[44] As far as Islam's judgment was concerned, Wasil provided the ubiquitous example of the "People of Lot." He was particularly concerned, however, about the increased publicness of same-sex practitioners, citing newspaper reports of "twenty people representing more than twenty million of professionals and amateurs of sodomy and sapphism [suhaq] went to see the American president Carter in order that he grant them assistance [tashilat]. They declared that they had more hope in him than in others"[45] Sexual deviance also has physical and psychological harms, insisted Wasil, including one wherein

the practitioner of sodomy will no longer be attracted to women . . . inversion . . . weakening of psychological and natural strengths so that the deviant is afflicted with neurological and psychological ailments including sadism, masochism, and fetishism, . . . the effects on the brain as the deviant suffers from a mental imbalance and clear idiocy and absent-mindedness, . . . the loosening of the rectal muscles and their tearing . . . so that the rectum loses its ability to control the release of fecal mat-

40. Ibid., 37–46.
41. Ibid., 47–49.
42. Ibid., 130.

43. See chap. 4, 133–71.
44. Ibid., 135.
45. Ibid.

ter thus rendering the debauched unable to control his own defecation, . . . moral decadence, . . . the destruction of sperm . . . leading to sterility, . . . affliction with typhoid and dysentery, . . . and affliction with the same venereal diseases that infect adulterers.[46]

Such views are hardly original as they hark back to similar assessments in Europe provided by Kraft-Ebing and others at the end of the nineteenth century.[47] Diseases caused by adultery and fornication, according to Wasil, include syphilis and other ailments.[48] Wasil, not unlike the secular Salamah Musa, also targeted masturbation as a "moral disease" and as prohibited by Islam, although he explained that its severity as a sin was far less serious than adultery or sodomy.[49]

The Islamic solution and "cure" to all these problems and diseases, like the Christian solution offered in the West, is (heterosexual) marriage.[50] Failing that, Islamists, had prescribed punishments available to be meted out to the wicked. As early as 1988, an Islamist researcher unearthed an unknown short fifteenth-century treatise titled *Al-Hukm al-Madbut fi Tahrim Fi'l Qawm Lut* (The Exact Ruling in the Prohibition of the Act of the People of Lot) written by a Sufi thinker by the name of al-Ghamri.[51] The modern editor of the text, who insisted that Islam had always prohibited such debauchery, reveled in his preface about God's foresight in prohibiting adultery and sodomy, as the recent AIDS pandemic was one of the diseases that were the outcome of such sexual licentiousness.[52] Al-Ghamri himself, however, had dedicated the last part of the book to reminding his readers that God is most forgiving to those who repent and seek his forgiveness.[53] Many Islamists, in contrast, were proving less forgiving in their writings about the matter. Books with unprecedented titles like *Sexual Relations in Islam,*[54] *Islam and Sex,*[55] and the like, became commonplace. Many (though not all) were influenced by the writings of Sayyid Qutb.

46. Ibid., 143–44.
47. See Richard von Kraft-Ebing, *Psychopathia Sexualis* (London: Velvet Publications, 1997).
48. Wasil, *Mushkilat al-Shab abal-Jinsiyyah,* 150–54.
49. Ibid., 157.
50. Ibid., 163.
51. Shams al-din Muhammad bin 'Umar al-Ghamri al-Wasiti, *Al-Hukm al-Madbut fi Tahrim Fi'l Qawm Lut* [The Exact Ruling in the Prohibition of the Act of the People of Lot], ed. 'Ubayd Allah al-Misri al-Athari (Tanta: Dar al-Sahabah lil-Turath, 1988).
52. Ibid., 18.
53. Ibid., 129–41.
54. Al-Shaykh Marwan Muhammad al-Sha''ar, *Al-'Ilaqat al-Jinsiyyah fi al-Islam* [Sexual Relations in Islam] (Beirut: Dar al-Nafa'is, 1990).
55. Najman Yasin, *Al-Islam wa al-Jins fi al-Qarn al-Awwal al-Hijri* [Islam and Sex in the First Century A.H.] (Beirut: Dar 'Atiyyah Lil-Nashr, 1997).

Venereal Disease: Islam as Cure

In the nineteenth and twentieth centuries, Arab intellectuals were influenced by European science, especially thinkers of evolution and degeneration, psychiatry and psychoanalysis. The new generation of Islamists, additionally, would be highly influenced by Western medicine and the resurgent Christian fundamentalism. In fact, medical interest in sexual matters in the modern Arab world was almost synchronous with the rise of medical knowledge about sexual diseases in nineteenth-century Europe, especially with regards to syphilis (known as da' al-zuhri[56]). Perhaps one of the earliest books that dealt with this matter in detail was a 1922 book by a certain Dr. Fakhri, a specialist in skin and reproductive diseases, titled *Reproductive Diseases: Their Treatment and Preventative Methods*.[57] The book was reviewed in the journal *Al-Muqtataf;* the anonymous editor focused on the book's glossary of English medical terms and the author's concern about Arabization of such terms. Dr. Fakhri's concern is quoted by the reviewer: "While the rest of the world knows [a medical technical term] by one name, we create another for it," thus doing a disservice to Arab medical students who would not be able to learn from European medical books and journals.[58] Syphilis was an important topic in European medical literature at the time and since the nineteenth century was a general concern among Arab authors, hence the interest in this new book. While praising the comprehensiveness of the book, the reviewer condemned those who knew the danger of the disease but who still contracted it through "pursuit of their desires." As early as 1902 an *Al-Muqtataf* reader, a certain M. K. from Cairo, sent a letter to the editors asserting that while some thinkers about civilizations (ba'd al-'imraniyyin) believe that the endemic spread of the "disease of desires [da' al-shahawat] among nations is one of the greatest obstacles that stands against their achieving real progress, others believe that desires in their two varieties, normal ['adiyyah] and abnormal, are the sole incentive for progress, and they use as evidence Europe's current licentiousness, which is banned in other nations, so much so that this has become one of the greatest factors for their enthusiasm in obtaining profits and in bringing about advantages." The latter opinion seems to be an approximation of Freud's later contention in *Civilization*

---

56. The word "al-zuhri" is related to the goddess and planet Venus, "Zuhra"; hence the use of the European etymology of "venereal disease" transforming it into "da' al-zuhri" which came to refer specifically to syphilis.

57. I have not been able to locate a copy of the book in all the library databases that I consulted.

58. See the review of the book in *Al-Muqtataf,* 1 December 1922, 492–93.

and Its Discontents, which was published three decades later, in 1930. The editors responded with much self-righteousness: "If by desires you mean the grave offences [muwbiqat], such as depravity, drunkenness, and profligacy, it would be impossible for those to lead to real elevation because they disease the body, enfeeble the mind, and do away with fortunes; were they to spread in a country, they would corrupt its civilization and destroy its foundations, as happened in the last days of the Roman Empire."[59] This juxtaposition of sexual desires with bodily disease, already extant in Western Christian and secular literature, would not become central to Islamists until the 1980s and 1990s, when it emerged as a central theme in a new genre of religio-medical literature.

One of the earlier Islamist medical books about sexual diseases was Nabil al-Tawil's *Al-Amrad al-Jinsiyyah* (Sexual Diseases). Published in 1971 before the rise in popularity of Islamist ideology, it would be reprinted many times after Islamism became hegemonic in debates about sex and morality.[60] Nabil al-Tawil wrote his book to offset the effects of pornographic books published in the 1960s, which call for "the degeneration of morals, the dissemination of sexual chaos, the spread of disease, and the further weakening of a national body politic already afflicted with a number of illnesses."[61] The organic analogy (common among Western Christian and secular conservatives) wherein the national body is seen as a physical body to which it is actually compared, is quite instructive, as we will see, of how individual disease becomes socialized from an Islamist perspective.

Al-Tawil's book did not aim to analyze this pornographic literature but rather to offer information about sexual diseases resulting from sexual disorder: "If these other books function as the epitome of loosening 'chains of traditions,' as the pornographers call it, I am publishing this [socially] conscious study in an Islamic ethical framework that wants human beings to quench their sexual instincts through clean and polite natural and legitimate methods, and not through a criminal, perverted, disorderly style."[62] Al-Tawil's concern with crime, perversion, and disorder, and their opposites, legality, normality, and order, would dominate the later debate with books dedicated to the subject. For now, however, the book, largely based on Western medical books dealing with venereal diseases, remained a novelty.

59. "Al-Shahawat wa al-Sukr," *Al-Muqtataf,* 1 September 1902, 917.
60. Nabil Subhi al-Tawil, *Al-Amrad al-Jinsiyyah* [Venereal Diseases], 8th ed. (Beirut: Mu'assassat al-Risalah, 1986).
61. He offers these reasons in the introduction to the first 1971 edition, ibid., 5.
62. Ibid., 6.

A newer edition published in 1982 updated the book by discussing a new sexual disease unknown in 1971, namely, herpes genitalis.[63] The author sermonized against calls for Westernization in society, represented both by the cheap pornographic books he criticized and the general 1960s political and cultural modernization and cultural liberalization ushered in by a number of the postcolonial states of the Arab world and called for by postcolonial intellectuals. After providing a glimpse of the spread of venereal diseases in Western countries and their more recent spread in Africa and Asia, al-Tawil sardonically stated: "And then they want us, like apes, to mimic the West in its lifestyle; and if the youth refuses to do this based on science, logic, and health [concerns], not to mention chastity, modesty, and virtuous values, the Westernizers blow their horns with that old broken record accusing this conscious youth of fanaticism, backwardness, zealotry, primness, insularity, extremism, reaction, etc."[64] Al-Tawil provided many Western-documented statistics about the spread of venereal disease, noting that one of the main social culprits for the epidemic was "sexual deviance," by which he meant all sex outside marriage, including premarital heterosexual sex among teenagers, sex with prostitutes, and sex with children.[65] Al-Tawil railed against the Westernizers in Muslim societies:

The calamity of the Muslim world is the presence of many "Westernized" individuals whose number increases day by day and who have Muslim names while their minds are European, whose parents are Muslim while their habits are "Frankish," the religion they inherited in their identification cards is Islam, while their modern mentalities are a mixture of materialist opinions of Westerners—both Western and Eastern [i.e., the materialist opinions derive from Western and Eastern sources]. They may celebrate Muslim religious feasts in their own special way, or some of them may even fast during Ramadan . . . while lesser folks may err and sometimes pray on Friday so as not to offend their families . . . These Westernized people are of the present generation that has been dubbed "the rising generation." They live with us and are still related to us and are the companions of our children and our neighbors' children and the children of our friends, and we shall not give up on them even though they have—by virtue of their ignorance—given up on the values of immortal Islam in their belief, manners, conduct, and interaction.[66]

Al-Tawil was a tolerant social reformer who was also concerned about female prostitutes and illegitimate children and the conditions that lead

63. See author's introduction to the newer edition in ibid., 9–10.
64. Ibid., 18–19.
65. Ibid., 24.
66. Ibid., 103–4.

to their tragic lives. He quoted the Pakistani Islamist thinker and authority Sayyid Abu al-ʿAlaʾ al-Mawdudi (1903–1979), who was Qutb's main inspiration, on the horrible circumstances that surround both groups.[67] As the book was written in the heyday of Arab secularism, its author was defensive in tone throughout. He quoted a certain R. R. Wilcox, who called for abstinence as the only prevention of venereal disease.[68] Indeed, after quoting Western authors about what had befallen Western society by way of disease resulting from sexual licentiousness, he defensively asserted:

> This is also not the claim of a reactionary cleric that cheap newspapers can ridicule with political cartoons and dirty jokes, but rather a presentation of bitter facts about Western society, and sorrow over what has befallen [this] society of degeneration, in the words of Western scientists [themselves] . . . What is odd is that Westerners themselves complain about this, yet they would diligently seek to Westernize Muslim societies and consider anyone who opposes them fanatical, reactionary, backward, and campaign against them and mobilize their faithful students among Westernized Muslims.[69]

Al-Tawil concluded by calling on those in authority to be watchful for what gets published in books and magazines and what gets aired in the electronic media. He called for facilitating early marriage for Muslim men and women by removing social and financial obstacles to it. Finally, al-Tawil called on parents to treat their sons and daughters equally and without sexist discrimination and that they "should not permit their sons to commit [sexual] violations that they would not allow their daughters to commit."[70]

Al-Tawil's efforts were indeed not common in the 1960s and 1970s, as there was not much attention paid by the electronic and print media to venereal diseases. The several reprinting of his book does indicate interest in the topic by Islamist readers, but it also signals the dearth of other writers publishing on the subject, whether Islamist or secular. This situation would change dramatically with the onset of the 1980s when Islamism became increasingly hegemonic in public debates, not only about morality and sexual behavior but also about politics, economics, science, and medicine.

Faʾiz al-Haj's book, *Al-Inhirafat al-Jinsiyyah wa Amraduha* (Sexual Perversions and Their Diseases), published in 1983, was the first Islamist salvo in the war to come. Calm, albeit concerned, in its tone, some of

---

67. Ibid., 108–9.
68. Ibid., 103.

69. Ibid., 120.
70. Ibid., 122–24.

the contentions of al-Haj's book would set the agenda for later discussions.[71] Unlike the defensive al-Tawil, who sought to convince his secular audience of the error of their ways—namely, their blind adoption of the West as a model for the Muslim world—al-Haj sought to elaborate a systematic pedagogical model for what Islamic sexual relations within marriage should look like.[72] He then proceeded to explore the book's central issues: the nature, types, and symptoms of sexual perversions and the attendant venereal diseases that result from them. For al-Haj, perversions include male and female homosexuality, heterosexual adultery, prostitution, narcissism, what he calls "autosexualism," in reference to masturbation, "erotomania," voyeurism, exhibitionism, masochism, and sadism, among others. As for the diseases discussed, they include syphilis and gonorrhea and a few other minor conditions.

The author's discussion of male homosexuality is well informed by citations from Western literature on the topic, both psychiatric (he cited Irving Bieber's psychoanalytic study of male homosexuals published in 1962) and sociological (he cited Laud Humphreys's 1970 book *Tearoom Trade: Impersonal Sex in Public Places*).[73] He explained that homosexual attraction could be "mutual" or one-sided and is sometimes "accompanied by a sort of flirtation [ghazal]—flirtation with youthful boys [ghazal bilghilman]."[74] The author also provided case studies of each perversion in the form of letters written by people "afflicted" with them. While the overall discussion is mostly presented in a detached scientific tone, the author provided a morally inspired judgment of the causes of homosexuality in his conclusion, namely, that it constituted "one of the most dangerous social phenomena [affecting] children, teenagers, and young people."[75] Assigning responsibility for "deviance" and "perversion," al-Haj emphasized that "the causes responsible are upbringing [itself] and those who supervise the upbringing of children, as had they brought them up with a moral compass and provided them with enough love, care, and warmth and supervised their conduct and knew whom they befriended, where they went, and with whom they mixed, the situation of those would not have reached this painful end and [resulted in] this shameful outcome."[76]

71. Faʾiz Muhammad ʿAli al-Haj, *Al-Inhirafat al-Jinsiyyah wa Amraduha* [Sexual Perversions and Their Diseases] (Beirut: Al-Maktab al-Islami, 1983).
72. Ibid., 17–22.
73. Ibid., 28, 30. For the cited books, see Irving Bieber, *Homosexuality: A Psychoanalytic Study* (New York: Basic Books, 1962); and Laud Humphreys, *Tearoom Trade: Impersonal Sex in Public Places* (Chicago: Aldine Pub. Co., 1970).
74. Ibid., 25.
75. Ibid., 37.
76. Ibid.

In addition to presenting social concerns about homosexuality, the author also discussed Islam's "judgment of homosexuality [al-jinsiyyah al-mithliyyah]," namely, the "absolute prohibition" of it. He cited two Qur'anic verses and two sayings of the Prophet to illustrate this. As for the religious punishment for violation of the prohibition, al-Haj correctly asserted that there was no agreement among Islamic scholars. According to the different scholars, the punishment ranged from execution, to stoning (if the person was married, he received the same punishment for heterosexual adultery), to flogging (if he was unmarried, in which case he would receive the same punishment for heterosexual fornication), to censuring the violator as a deterrent.[77] The discussion of heterosexual relations out of wedlock received a stronger moral indictment from al-Haj, both socially and religiously, as indeed they do historically in Islamic jurisprudence. While venereal diseases are not mentioned as resulting from homosexuality, they are listed as a direct outcome of heterosexual sex out of wedlock, whether with prostitutes or not. Moreover, they also lead to other sexual perversions, like sadism, masochism, among others, which adulterous men "would not dare practice with their wives."[78] American studies and indictment of prostitution and sexual licentiousness are presented, as are United Nations (UN) statistics. John F. Kennedy is cited for his concern in 1962 that the immersion in desire of America's youth constituted a "danger to the future of America," as is Nikita Khrushchev's similar concern about "Russia's future" being jeopardized by Soviet youth's respective immersion in sexual desires.[79] Adultery and fornication are seen not as the natural base for the "normative [sawiyyah] human soul" but rather as "aggression against the human instincts of harmony, marriage, sojourn, tranquility, stability, and a prosperous marital life."[80] Thus, it is not only a commitment to classical forms of Islamic practices that are at stake for al-Haj but also aspirations to bourgeois forms of sociality, including the nuclear family and a "prosperous marital life." In this, Islamists seem to be adopting the very same social goals espoused by the nationalists they came to supersede.

AIDS as Divine Punishment

Al-Tawil's and al-Haj's concerns centered on the Westernization of sexual mores in the Arab and Muslim worlds that they feared would lead to

---

77. Ibid., 38.
78. Ibid., 49.

79. Ibid., 49–50.
80. Ibid., 51.

the same social and physiological ills suffered by Western society. In this sense, although the West is seen as powerful and at the peak of its civilization, the price for such an achievement is seen to have been the loss of the West's moral compass, which, to many of our authors, signaled the beginning of its decline.

Since the mid-1980s, a new aggressive campaign would be unleashed by Islamist physicians explicating with an unforgiving religious tone the nature of sexual diseases and the sexual practices that lead to them. Islamist discourse was well established by the mid-1980s as the hegemonic one across the Arab world. Its axioms and morality would be used by proponents and opponents alike. This coincided with the emergence of the new AIDS pandemic, which came to confirm to Islamists, as it had to Western Christian fundamentalists and secular conservatives before them, their worst fears, namely, that licentiousness would lead to nothing short of the death of the body as divine punishment for sinners. Islamists learned well the arguments advanced by Western Christian fundamentalists and framed them in an Islamic worldview.[81]

The most prominent of the Islamist physicians is the prolific Doctor Muhammad 'Ali al-Barr (b. 1939), a naturalized Saudi of Egyptian origins. His book *Al-Amrad al-Jinsiyyah, Asbabuha wa 'Ilajuha* (Venereal Diseases: Their Causes and Their Treatment) was published in 1985. It was updated in 1986 with a much-expanded chapter on AIDS. The book has since become the major Islamist and conservative medical reference book on the subject.[82] Al-Barr's religious approach was apparent from the outset. He began his book with citations from the Qur'an that prohibit adultery and relegate adulterers to eternal suffering. In addition, he quoted the sayings of the Prophet, one of which he found particularly relevant to the topic at hand: "Once an abomination appeared among a people that they would then broadcast, a plague and pains, the likes of which their ancestors had not seen, would spread among them."[83] This quote would be cited and recited numerous times in the book, as it would be in many of the books that followed in al-Barr's footsteps. Religious quotations were followed by more dire quotations from the World Health Organization, former U.S. assistant secretary of health Theodore

<hr>

81. For an Islamist view of Islam's views on sex and love that resembles more Christian than Islamic views, see Muhammad 'Ali Qutb's *Al-Hubb wa al-Jins min Manzur Islami* [Love and Sex from an Islamic Perspective] (Cairo: Maktabat al-Qur'an, 1984). Qutb was also concerned about venereal disease as the effect of licentiousness. See his last chapter, "Akhtar al-inhirafat al-jinsiyyah wa atharuha al-darrah," in *Al-Hubb*, 141–44.

82. Muhammad 'Ali al-Barr, *Al-Amrad al-Jinsiyyah: Asbabuha wa 'Ilajuha* [Venereal Disease, Its Causes and Treatment] (Jiddah: Dar al-Manarah, 1986).

83. Ibid., 5.

Cooper (who held his position from 1975 to 1977), the Merck Manual of Medical Information, and other Western authorities. One Dr. Sheffield was cited for his condemnation of the "media, which calls for and encourages sexual profligacy as if it were a natural biological thing . . . There is an illusory happiness that antibiotics will destroy any venereal disease that might arise as a result of these practices."[84]

In the introduction to the first edition, al-Barr explained that his book "discusses one of the outcomes of *zina* [adultery/fornication] and abominations, namely, the diseases that result from adultery/fornication, sodomy, and from the commission of abominations."[85] He provided a short history of syphilis in the introduction and how it used to be known by most Europeans as the "French disease" on account of its being carried by French soldiers, while the French called it the "Italian disease": "When Western colonialism reached the Arab countries, this disease appeared with them, so the Arabs called it the 'Frankish disease,' a term that is still in use today."[86]

While concerned about what would become of the Arab and Muslim worlds if they continued to adopt Western ways, al-Barr remained confident that for the time being, Arabs could still be saved. In comparison with the dire statistics of AIDS and herpes infections that al-Barr cited for the United States, for example, he quoted one Professor William Bakers, who practiced medicine in the Arab world for twenty years and who affirmed in an article in *Medicine Digest* that "the most chaste [athar] vaginas that I have ever examined were in the Arabian Peninsula," where he examined more than thirty-thousand women, most of whom tested negative for gonorrhea, chlamydia, fungi, and other venereal conditions. The reasons for this clean bill of health, asserted Bakers, were "the rarity of adultery, and the circumcision of the men."[87] Pride in the chastity of Saudi vaginas and the honor that this chastity confers on Saudi men and women aside, it remains unclear why the circumcision of most American men did not figure as a positive health-promoting factor in the case of the United States. Al-Barr most likely assumed that American Christian men were not circumcised and was clearly ignorant of the medical hegemony and its preference for male circumcision in the United States since World War II.

Al-Barr's views of the West are reminiscent of Qutb's in their credulity and propagandistic aims. If Orientalists continue to be scandalized

84. Ibid., 6.
85. Ibid., 16.
86. Ibid., 17.
87. Ibid., 19. The *Medicine Digest* article was published in April 1977, according to al-Barr.

by the Prophet Muhammad's marriage to ʿAʾisha when she was six, a marriage that was consummated when she was postpubertal at the age of nine (one should bear in mind that for centuries after Muhammad and through the Middle Ages, Europeans married their daughters off at a similarly young age), al-Barr was horrified at Westerners who call for sex with children, quoting some (without documentation) saying, "Sex by eight or its [sic] too late."[88] His sensationalist rhetoric was mobilized to further exoticize the United States and the West more generally. No doubt all this was part of the decadence of the West and its degeneration away from civilization. For al-Barr's book aimed to "clarify the West's fake civilization and the extent of decadence that it has reached, so that it would not deceive our youth with its glamour but rather [they] would see it in its reality. This would endow them with a kind of immunity to its temptations, wherein they would take from it its technical sciences in medicine, engineering, and astronomy, among others, while leaving its delinquent [munharifah] philosophies and morals without being affected by them."[89] Al-Barr's book, however, belied this formula of selective borrowing from the West, as he clearly borrowed not only Western medical knowledge but also Western social and ideological criteria— religious, secular, and moral—to reach his conclusions about sex and disease.

In the introduction to the second edition, al-Barr spoke of how "the horror increased so much that AIDS had become the obsession that keeps them [deviants] awake at night . . . and still they remain reckless in their transgressions, calling [others to join them in] their vice and holding tight to their lifestyle."[90] He was horrified at the advice given by Western authors to avoid infection with AIDS: homosexual men limit themselves to one sexual partner, intravenous drug users use clean needles, and "adulterers" limit themselves to one "mistress." Al-Barr clearly shares the same assumptions with many conservative Western authors and politicians who also called for abstinence, but he does not cite them. Nor did he cite Western Christian fundamentalists' and conservatives' condemnation of homosexuality and adultery, views they espoused earlier than he, not to mention the similar rhetoric on AIDS and venereal diseases that they deployed and to which he was clearly indebted.[91] Given al-Barr's project to show a homogeneous decadent West,

---

88. Ibid., 19.
89. Ibid., 21.
90. Ibid., 8.
91. See Patricia L. Jakobi, "Medical Science, Christian Fundamentalism and the Etiology of AIDS," *AIDS and Public Policy Journal* 5, no. 2 (Spring 1990): 89–93.

citing such sources would muddy the waters by showing that there were like-minded Americans who shared the "Islamist" views he espoused. Were he to do so, Islam, as he understood it, might not seem as the only solution to decadence. His conclusion was that "they give their kinds of advice, and we give ours, which are based on a different approach," namely, invocations of the sayings of the Prophet Muhammad against adultery and abominations, which al-Barr listed for his readers.[92]

Al-Barr was clear that the very etymology of the term "sexual diseases," which is the standard term to describe them in Arabic, or "venereal diseases," which is the literary translation of the English equivalent, is erroneous. He explained that it was not sex that caused these diseases but rather "*zina*, sodomy, and other deviant sexual relations, as marriage never leads to any kind of sexual diseases as long as the relationship is exclusive to the two spouses."[93] Therefore, the proper "scientific" term that should be used to refer to these diseases is "the diseases of adultery/fornication and sodomy." However, "no one would dare use this term, especially in the West, as otherwise such a person would be seen as calling people to virtue; what an ugly insult this would be, one that physicians and scientists avoid in the West."[94]

Having lived in Britain, al-Barr provided anthropological information about the nature of sexual debates in British society. He cited the *Daily Mirror*, which in 1970 recounted the story of a young beautiful woman who taught sex education to secondary school students. The teacher was said to have taught her students the practicalities of sex in class by removing her clothes item by item, only "for the reactionary school administration to inform the Ministry of Education on her, who in turn suspended the young teacher and requested of her that she stop teaching her teenage students such exciting lessons." In response, the British press, including the *Daily Mirror*, published the young teacher's picture nude on its front page and "launched a huge campaign against this reactionary school administration and the backwards Ministry of Education for banning this ingenious teacher from continuing to offer these important lessons to her teenage students to teach them about sex." The newspapers are said to have mobilized demonstrations that finally led the school and the ministry to reverse their decision and reinstate the teacher. Thus, "women's liberty and sexual freedom won her her case against the reactionary school administration and the Ministry of Education."[95] Al-Barr concluded by appealing to his readers' sense of

92. Al-Barr, *Al-Amrad*, 9.
93. Ibid., 25.
94. Ibid., 26.
95. Ibid., 26–27.

shock after reading his account of the story: "Do you believe that this took place in a country that claims to be at the peak of civilization, in the name of freedom, progress, and equality, and in a country which is naturally conservative, as they say in Britain?"[96]

Al-Barr's concern was not only about the paralysis of government and school administrations against such societal attacks on his version of religious values but also about the transformation that Western churches were undergoing: "It is doubtless that the Church is keeping up with societal evolution. Many Western churches have allowed fornication, and some have allowed sodomy, and in some churches in the United States, weddings of one man to another are conducted by a minister."[97] What al-Barr marveled about is that "the Church deplores marriage to more than one woman, and considers it bestial and animalistic, as do all Western societies. All Western countries have laws against marriage to more than one wife, banning it completely, while allowing a husband to have as many mistresses and lovers as he would like."[98] Al-Barr provided a list of European kings and church figures (popes, cardinals, priests, and monks) who due to their sexual excesses contracted syphilis and other venereal diseases. This ironic situation was contrasted with westernizing Muslim countries like Turkey, Tunisia, and South Yemen, which banned polygamy, "while their laws allow husbands to have any number of mistresses . . . This is the progressivism and women's liberty which we obtained from the West and whose laws (which it imposed when it colonized us) we maintain."[99]

Al-Barr found the use of "women's liberation" in the press and in media campaigns most objectionable. He quoted an article from the Lebanese daily *Al-Nahar,* whose male author called for women's sexual freedom. The author was quoted to say: "What is women's liberty? Her real liberty is her freedom of sexual relations with the other sex or even her own sex, or both sexes together." A horrified al-Barr concluded: "Yes, this is the freedom that they are demanding for Muslim women, as a huge edifice supported by millions of dollars [funding this propaganda] is set up to get Muslim women to reach this despicable state, where a human being would only be seen as a set of genitalia."[100]

If Western Orientalists chastised the Muslim world for its medieval licentiousness, the Islamist al-Barr reminded his readership of the Greek history of licentiousness, especially pederasty. Al-Barr quoted the *Ency-*

96. Ibid.,
97. Ibid., 32.
98. Ibid., 32.

99. Ibid., 34.
100. Ibid., 35.

clopedia Britannica about how "men's sexual contact with men received much appreciation" among the Greeks, which is why "Greek writings praised sexual deviance . . . As for women's sexual contact with women it only received passing interest, considered an absurdity not worthy of commentary." He further quoted the *Encyclopedia* on how "the habit of sodomy moved from the Greeks to the Persians and Romans; the Jewish view of sodomy contradicted that of the Greeks as the Torah cursed the sodomites and [specified] killing them as punishment . . . a view that was transferred to Christianity, which did not only look upon deviant sexual relations as dirty but also considered healthy [salimah] sexual relations among spouses as also dirty, It also glorified the monastic system."[101]

Al-Barr, like much Western journalistic coverage in the seventies and early eighties, confused Western homosexuality with transsexualism, which he considered "more horrific." He cited newspaper coverage in 1980 of a young Englishman who was "converted into a woman and then married one of the Lords before a British court. Within one year cancer proliferated his body, and he died."[102] Al-Barr, however, seemed to contradict himself in the next paragraph when he assured his readers that these male-to-female sex conversion operations actually "converted women into women," as the patient in question was an "unreal" or false (ghayr haqiqi) hermaphrodite who was assigned the wrong sex at birth and whom physicians now were restoring to the correct sex. But if this was so, and al-Barr was happy with these corrective medical interventions, the basis for his earlier horror at sex conversion is no longer clear.[103] He never advocated, for example, sex conversion operations for all men practicing passive sodomy, which, given his logic, would be the only proper medical corrective to their situation!

Al-Barr was emboldened by the declarations of the new revolutionary regime in Iran, which was said to be executing sodomites. and he chastised the Western press for attacking Iran and a "barbaric Islam" for these executions. Furthermore, if the West was to be horrified by Khomeini's fatwa in 1989 calling for the murder of Salman Rushdie and offering a million-dollar reward, al-Barr shed some light on Western precedents for such fatwas. Al-Barr (who was writing in 1985) cited "the head of the sodomites in Italy" who declared that he would pay "a million dollars to whoever kills Khomeini." A similar million-dollar offer was said to have been made by President Jimmy Carter's mother (who died in 1983).[104]

101. Ibid., 39–40.
102. Ibid. 41
103. Ibid.
104. Ibid., 45. No dates or sources are provided for these claims.

Al-Barr's main interest, however, was to demonstrate the consequences for illicit sex, namely, venereal diseases. Aside from the "really terrifying" scale of the spread of known venereal diseases among "sexual deviants," they seem to be alone in contracting certain other diseases, namely, AIDS. Herpes was another disease that al-Barr mentioned. Such diseases are found in abundance in the "mouths, throats, and esophagi of sexual deviants due to the spread of those deviant practices among them. This is in addition to the affliction of the rectal canal and the digestive system."[105] These statements are punctuated throughout by quotes from the Prophet condemning men who practice sodomy. Other deviant practices are mentioned as well, including child molestation and rape and physical violence against children. This was indicative, according to al-Barr, that "Western societies suffer from a complete breakdown in values."[106]

Al-Barr reviewed world history and how the spread of degeneration afflicted societies in their latter days like the Greeks, and how "adultery and sodomy destroyed their civilizations." Other examples include the Roman and Persian empires, as well as certain periods of Islamic history, especially under brief Qaramite rule in the tenth century.[107] This being said, al-Barr asserted that "human history has not witnessed the terrifying spread of adultery, sodomy, raping of children [nikah al-atfal], and incest as it is witnessing today in the shadow of the miserable Western civilization."[108] It is not made clear here if al-Barr's concern is for the survival of Western civilization tout court which these ailments threaten.

Al-Barr was also aware of Western Christian propaganda against the Prophet, as he referenced it throughout, showing the irony of how what "is truly strange is that those Westerners who are immersed in adultery and sodomy and even sex with animals and incest are the same ones who speak of the Prophet of Islam and the Prophet of mercy and guidance, accusing him of sexualness and lustfulness because he married

105. Ibid., 47–48.
106. Ibid., 59.
107. Ibid., 60.
108. Ibid., 61. Al-Barr is equally condemnatory of Communism, which he asserts allows and calls for adultery, male homosexuality, rape of children, and incest, although he was surprised at how male homosexuality, rape of children, and incest were not widespread in Communist countries—except for adultery, which was particularly endemic in Cuba, "which might be caused by Cuba's location in the Caribbean sea where adultery is widespread in a terrifying way; adultery is also widespread epidemically in North and South America." As this is the case, the inclusion of the Cuban exception, which turned out not to be an exception, seems to have been invoked due to a combination of al-Barr's fervid anti-Communism and European-inspired racism about the sexual mores of the islands of the Caribbean (see 62).

nine women."[109] Al-Barr proceeded to cite the Western press about sexual activity including Amsterdam strip shows of women and dogs having sex, the frequency of rape of daughters by their fathers in the United States, and of course Western male homosexuality: "Do these people deserve a response when they accuse the best of people, Muhammad, may God praise him, that he was sexual because he married nine women?"[110]

Al-Barr's interest was not limited to the medical realm, but extended beyond into the juridical realm. If physicians like him had the task of researching the causes of venereal disease and trying desperately to find a cure (while Islam as cure has been available all along), al-Barr was aware that the medical profession needed juridical help. If medicine unto itself could not control the spread of venereal epidemics, then the law could certainly assist. It is in this context that al-Barr called for the strengthening of Shariʿah laws and the cancellation of positive laws dealing with adultery (which includes prostitution) and sexual contact among men. He viewed existing positive laws as lax and incongruent with Shariʿah, as such laws allow prostitution in some Muslim countries, and those that deal with sexual contact among men, in most Muslim countries, punish it only in the case of rape or forced sex.[111]

Al-Barr correlated the rise in venereal diseases among Muslims with periods "when Muslims deviated from their religion and swerved away from the law of the Lord and held on to the laws of the infidels, which allow adultery, permit whoring, and glorify prostitution and obscenities [khana]."[112] Clearly the present, characterized as a period of deviation, is not so bad compared to the West, as al-Barr cited a 1980 Western study affirming the relatively much lower incidence of venereal diseases in Muslim societies.[113] While few cases of AIDS have occurred in Arab and Muslim countries, al-Barr reminds us that most of them were due to blood transfusion, except for two cases in Tunisia that resulted from the practice of "sexual deviance," in one case with an American tourist.[114]

The only solution to this situation is the adoption of Shariʿah laws and new educational standards that strengthen the Islamic view of life as understood by al-Barr and similar-thinking Islamists. If Western Christian fundamentalists and secular conservatives called for abstinence as

109. Ibid., 76.
110. Ibid., 78.
111. Ibid., 81–92. See also 415.
112. Ibid., 125.
113. Ibid., 125
114. Ibid., 139. Al-Barr cites the London-based Saudi newspaper *Al-Sharq al-Awsat* (January 19, 1986) as the source for the Tunisian cases.

the principal way of combating AIDS and venereal disease as well as unwanted pregnancies, al-Barr insisted on the concept of *ihsan* (safeguarding of oneself) as the "true treatment/cure," and as the only way to put a stop to deviant practices and save Muslim society from sexual epidemics. *Ihsan* for him is an ideological term that he loaded with meaning, including preventive protection (wiqayah), stamina, chastity, freedom, and marriage.[115]

The Saudi context was instrumental not only for the production of literature on venereal disease and its connection to sinful behavior (as it was for the Egyptian-Saudi al-Barr), but also for defining the terms of the discussion. Al-Barr's definitive volume on the subject was not alone for long. In the same year, Jordanian physician 'Abd al-Hamid al-Qudah released his book about the topic. Titled *Al-Amrad al-Jinsiyyah, 'Uqubah Ilahiyyah* [Venereal Diseases, Divine Punishment], the book did not leave its audience long in suspense about its subject matter and its point of view.[116] Al-Qudah, who obtained his doctorate in epidemiology from the University of Manchester in 1982, wrote as an academic expert and as someone acquainted with the West, especially the United Kingdom, where he lived for years. His thesis, as the title indicates, is that God punishes sinners with venereal disease, which kills and torments them. This seems to have been God's practice, both in the past and the present.[117] In this al-Qudah's views are fully consonant with Western Christian fundamentalists, and even with Jewish and Christian scripture.

Al-Qudah's focus was on the twentieth century. He began by citing Sayyid Qutb, who blamed the "liberation of women" for the corruption of nations. He further cited Western historians on how Western governments provided their soldiers with prostitutes during war, which helped to spread disease. His point was that given the smaller number of males relative to females on a global scale, polygyny resolved the question by ensuring that all women have husbands and that none was left without a sexual partner (which ostensibly would do away with prostitution and homosexuality).[118] Al-Qudah presented the problems facing Western society in terms of the weakening of marriage ties and concluded that this led to improper sexual relations: "Such sexual relations, however, are the result of weak-willed, immature, and emotionally imbalanced hu-

---

115. Ibid., 408.

116. 'Abd al-Hamid al-Qudah, *Al-Amrad al-Jinsiyyah, 'Uqubah Ilahiyyah* [Venereal Diseases, Divine Punishment] (London: Medical Publications, 1985).

117. Ibid., 6.

118. See the second chapter of part 1 of his book, 15–24.

man beings. It need not be argued much that it is these types of people who are the transmission tool of venereal diseases . . ."[119]

Al-Qudah's Islamist approach echoed Western Christian fundamentalism in blaming AIDS on homosexuals.[120] Like al-Barr, he was particularly concerned about the existence of civil laws that protected sodomites and their sexual behavior, which are otherwise condemned by monotheistic religions.[121] For al-Qudah, all the laboratories and scientific research that can hardly keep up with the increase in venereal disease could be replaced with the Qur'anic injunction against practices that cause such diseases and with Islam's philosophy of moderation in satisfying one's sexual appetites. Hence following this Qur'anic advice to marry and not to engage in illicit sexual relations would do away with the bane of disease.[122] Al-Qudah followed up with a second book about AIDS specifically. His flare for explicit titles was deployed again, as he titled it *AIDS: The Harvest of Deviance*.[123]

Other books making similar arguments were also published in the same period. They included, for example, Dr. Najib al-Kilani's *The Story of AIDS*.[124] Al-Kilani (1931–1995), an Egyptian, is a major and pioneering contemporary Islamist novelist. Like al-Barr and al-Qudah, he drew parallels between medieval plagues and what the Western media termed the "new plague" in reference to AIDS. He cleverly quoted the Prophet's reference in one of his recorded sayings that previously unknown plagues would hit those who commit abominations.[125] Clearly aware of the Gay International and its missionary campaigns, he ended his book with a condemnation of the gay movement and its demonstrations and marches across the Western world and with those "few deviants in the Islamic world" who popularize its ideas.[126]

Not to be outdone, an Egyptian faculty member of the al-Azhar medical school in Cairo, Muhammad Kamal 'Abd al-'Aziz, also published a book linking medicine and religion titled *Why Has God Prohibited These Things? Pork, Dead Flesh, Blood, Adultery/Fornication* [zina], *Sodomy, Sexual Deviance, and Alcohol* [khamr]: *A Medical View of Qur'anic Prohibitions.*[127]

119. Ibid., 24.
120. Ibid., 96.
121. Ibid., 135.
122. Ibid., 151–59
123. See 'Abd al-Hamid al-Qudah, *Al-Ids, Hasad al-Shudhudh* [AIDS, The Harvest of Deviance] (Beirut: Dar ibn Qudamah lil-Tab' wa al-Nashr, 1986).
124. Dr. Najib Al-Kilani, *Qissat al-Ids* [The Story of AIDS] (Beirut: Mu'assassat al-Risalah, 1986).
125. Ibid., 107.
126. Ibid., 112.
127. Muhammad Kamal 'Abd al-'Aziz, *Limadha Harram Allah Hadhih al-Ashya'? Lahm al-Khanzir, al-Maytah, al-Damm, al-Zina, al-Liwat, al-Shudhudh al-Jinsi, al-Khamr, Nazrah Tibiyyah fi al-*

ʿAbd al-ʿAziz provided medical evidence to support the soundness of the Qurʾanic prohibitions of things that cause disease. He was, however, appalled at the "degeneration" of the West evidenced by the spread of adulterous relations in its societies, and the "collapse of morals," especially in the United States. He cited the Kinsey reports on homosexual relations between men and between women in the United States and then cited the case of Rock Hudson as evidence of the shamelessness of the U.S. media's open coverage of his same-sex relationship.[128]

This new obsession with venereal disease is admittedly not some neurosis that afflicted these Islamist thinkers, rather their concentration on it was a reflection of how much Islamism was a worldly movement that was highly influenced by world events and Western thinking on all subjects. If for Orientalists, it is both the "undemocratic nature" of Islam and its "misogyny," sexual "repression," and "licentious" desires that function as the privileged sites to work through civilizational difference between contemporary Islam and the "West," for many Islamists, sexual mores and practices are selected as the privileged sites for the elaboration of civilizational differences. The question of "democracy" in the West, is actually subsumed by some of them as part and parcel of the sexual "anarchy" reigning there. The concern about gay acceptability in the West (itself based on fictional, uninterrogated Western self-representations), and what it perceived as the audacity of the gay movements in demanding rights not only in the context of Western countries but also by universalizing their claims, are all evident in our authors' accounts. As we saw in the last chapter, such concerns became widespread in the print media with increasing calls to criminalize homosexuality and to set the police loose on it. If God took care of the "People of Lot" by eliminating them, as evidenced in the monotheistic scriptures (a notion long asserted by Englishmen and Spaniards, especially since the Renaissance, and in the context of colonizing the Americas and meting out to "sodomitic" Indians the same punishment God had visited upon Sodom, and in English representations of Arabs and Muslims as sodomites whom God would eventually smite[129]), He (through AIDS), the Islamists, and the police (as we will see below) would take care of the contemporary "People of Lot."

Muharramat al-Qurʾaniyyah [Why Has God Prohibited These Things?] (Cairo: Maktabat al-Qurʾan, 1987).

128. Ibid., 33–34.

129. For a discussion of the centrality of the notion of sodomy as a mechanism of othering used by English writers and politicians against Native Americans and Arabs and Muslims, see Nabil Matar, *Turks, Moors, and Englishmen in the Age of Discovery* (New York: Columbia University Press, 1999), 109–27.

Secular Rebuttals

The explosion of publications about *materia sexualis* in the Arab world, however, did not take place in a vacuum. Since the late 1960s, a similar explosion was taking place in Europe and the United States. Many such books about the history of sex in the West were translated into Arabic and indeed used by many authors, both secular and Islamist. While Saqr Abu Fakhr's essay was published in a magazine, book publications about the topic followed soon after, with more seeing the light in the 1990s coinciding with the 1990 publication of an Arabic translation of Michel Foucault's *History of Sexuality*.[130] Whether secular scholarly books dealing with sex and Islam,[131] or studies about Islam and the body, or even the body more generally, they continued to be put out by publishers.[132] Publishers' interest has been so high that a new Arabic sexual dictionary was also published.[133]

The Syrian publisher and intellectual Riyad al-Rayyis must have been listening to Abu Fakhr's (and al-Munajjid's earlier) advice and thus pioneered in the 1990s the publication of a number of medieval Arab erotica books, some of which had not been published in Arabic in the modern Arab world, or at least not published in scholarly editions. The location of his publishing house in London in the late 1980s and early 1990s (he has since moved to Beirut) helped al-Rayyis circumvent Arab censors who ultimately banned all the erotica books he published anyway. Around the same time, the German-based Arabic publishing house Manshurat al-Jamal also began to publish medieval erotica books, which, however, did not receive the same scholarly editing as al-Rayyis's books.

The first book published by al-Rayyis was the fourteenth-century treatise *The Perfumed Garden* (by al-Nafzawi, d. A.D. 1324) edited by the Denmark-based scholar Jamal Jumʿah.[134] In his introduction to the book, Jumʿah lamented the fact that *The Perfumed Garden* was a book that "is

130. Michel Foucault, Mutaʿ Safadi, trans., *Iradat al-ma rifah, al-juz' al-awwal min tarikh al-jinsaniyya* [The Will to Know, vol. 1, The History of Sexuality] (Beirut: Markaz al-Inma al-Qawmi,1990).

131. See, for example, Najman Yasin, *Al-Islam wa al-Jins*, and Ibrahim Mahmud, *Al-Jins fi al-Qur'an* [Sex in the Qur'an] (Beirut: Riyad al-Rayyis Lil-Kutub wa al-Nashr, 1994)

132. See, for example, Farid al-Zahi, *Al-Jasad wa al-Surah wa al-Muqaddas fi al-Islam* [The Body, the Image and the Sacred in Islam] (Casablanca: Afriqya al-Sharq, 1999), Muna Fayyad, *Fakhkh al-Jasad, Tajalliyyat, Nazawat, wa Asrar* [The Body Trap: Transfigurations, Caprices, and Secrets] (Beirut: Riyad al-Rayyis lil-Kutub wa al-Nashr, 2000), Fu'ad Ishaq Khuri, *Ayduyulujiyyat al-Jasad, Rumuziyyat al-Taharah wa al-Najasah* [The Ideology of the Body] (Beirut: Dar al-Saqi, 1997).

133. ʿAli ʿAbd al-Halim Hamzah, *Al-Qamus al-Jinsi ʿind al-ʿArab* [The Sexual Dictionary of the Arabs] (Beirut: Riyad al-Rayyis lil-Kutub wa al-Nashr, 2002).

134. Al-Nafzawi, al-Shaykh al-ʿArif Abu ʿAbdullah Muhammad bin Abi Bakr bin ʿAli, *Al-Rawd

known to almost every Western reader at a rate equal to the ignorance under which it languishes in Arab cultural circles," although, in his estimation, it is one of the four great books on erotica written in the ancient and medieval worlds—the other three being the *Kamasutra, Anangaranga,* and Ovid's *Ars Amatoria.*[135] In his introduction to another of the erotica books published by Riyad al-Rayyis, Jum'ah addressed the types of sex and marriage arrangements that predominated before Islam in the *jahiliyyah* and that Islam repressed and made illegal. In his discussion of passive male sexual contact with another male, unlike the modern nationalists who attribute all male-male sex to Persian "influences," Jum'ah, was clear that

this primitive sexual mode was known in the Arabian peninsula before Islam, despite the absence of reference to it in *jahiliyyah* poetry, as several of the lords of [the prominent tribe of] Quraysh [to which the Prophet belonged], including Abu Jahl, were accused of it, although I think that this accusation was leveled against him for political and religious reasons, except that the accusation itself confirms that sodomy was widespread in the Qurayshi aristocracy then, in addition to the spread of effeminacy, and the imitation of women.[136]

Unlike Taha Husayn, or al-Munajjid, who reveled in the sexual history of the medieval Arabs under Islam (al-Munajjid's later reservations notwithstanding), Jum'ah was unhappy with that same Islamic history. In his introduction to the collection of "forbidden" poems of Abu Nuwas, Jum'ah began by stating that

It is not new to say that written Arab history is characterized by its unicity, an authoritarian unicity subject to addition, amputation, and change with the changeover of every personalist-tribalist epoch that "history" passed through since the arrival of the Prophet (at which time word-of-mouth oral history began, all the way to [the development of] transmitted written history), to our own present, which is full of amazing varieties of visual and auditory communication media . . . History, our history, rather than being a comprehensive recorded repository of the conduct of the hegemonic power [ruling] over society and the reaction of its opponents, has become documents of accusations, of treachery, and of glorification [takhwin wa tamjid] at

---

al-'Atir fi Nuzhat al-Khatir [The Perfumed Garden in the Promenade of the Mind], ed. Jamal Jum'ah (London: Riyad al-Rayyis Lil-Kutub wa al-Nashr, 1990).

135. Ibid., 11.

136. Jamal Jum'ah, "Al-Irutikiyyah al-'Arabiyyah, al-Sath wa al-qa'" [Arab Eroticism, the Surface and the Bottom] in Shihab al-Din Ahmad al-Tifashi, *Nuzhat al-Albab fima La Yuwjad fi Kitab* [A Promenade of the Hearts in What Does Not Exist in a Book] (London: Riyad al-Rayyis, 1992), 31.

the hands of the Sultans' scribes and the sectarian jurisprudents . . . so much so that historical events pass us in the form of plotted story chapters, wherein reality is erased and acquires color as narrative texts that have a strong formulaic link to *A Thousand and One Nights.*[137]

His description of Abu Nuwas, whom he dubbed "the jurisprudent of the forbidden," as the "poet who has most disquieted the scribes of history,"[138] led him to honor the latter by challenging the restrictive moralism of the post-Islamist Arab world. Yet Jum'ah advised his readers "not to read this book except drunk."[139] Jum'ah ignored the fact however that these poems were not forbidden in any formal sense, as they had been published in a first modern edition in 1898 (which Jum'ah cited) in Cairo in response to the first collected poetry of Abu Nuwas published that same year, and which excluded them. The book was reprinted in Beirut in 1970, something Jum'ah did not seem to know.[140]

Jum'ah's account should be contextualized within the increasing hostility to Abu Nuwas in some literary circles since the 1980s. 'Umar Farrukh (b. 1906), whose 1932 book about Abu Nuwas we discussed in a previous chapter, republished his study with modifications in 1988. Farrukh had noted in the 1932 edition that Abu Nuwas did not invent *ghazal* in the masculine, although "he was the one to popularize it."[141] Although in the earlier edition Farrukh simply concerned himself with the "unnaturalness" of a man's desire for another man, in the later edition he was most concerned with how un-Arab such desires were. In the 1988 edition, Farrukh elaborated on this by providing a genealogy of how such *ghazal* entered Arabic poetry: "If we studied *ghazal* in the masculine, we would find it raised in environments foreign to Arabs and Muslims, as we know well that it had started in taverns [hanat], which were run by none other than the Romans, the Magi Persians, or the Jews. This is an incontestable point. Were you [dear reader] to read

137. Jamal Jum'ah, "Faqih al-Hurumat" [The Jurisprudent of What Is Forbidden], in *Abu Nuwas, al-Nusus al-Muharramah* [Abu Nuwas, the Forbidden Texts] (London: Riyad al-Rayyis, 1994), 21.

138. Ibid., 22. Abu Nuwas wrote a great deal about wine and inebriation, hence Jum'ah's injunction.

139. Ibid., 30.

140. Mansur 'Abd al-Muta'ali and Husayn Ashraf, eds., *Al-Fukahah wa al-I'tinas fi Mujun Abi Nuwas wa ba'd Naqa'idih ma' al-Shu'ara'* [Humor and Sociability in the Bawdiness of Abu Nuwas] (Cairo: 1316 [1898]). The 1970 Beirut edition had no specified publisher and was a mimeographed copy of the 1898 original. The Collected Works were published as *Diwan Abu Nuwas* (Cairo: Iskandar Asaf, 1898).

141. 'Umar Farrukh, *Abu Nuwas, Sha'ir Harun al-Rashid wa Muhammad al-Amin, Al-Qism al-Awwal, Dirasah wa Naqd* (Beirut: Maktabat al-Kashshaf, 1932), 39.

a couplet or two, a stanza or two, which dealt with this matter, I would tell you, along with the English [expression], that 'the exception proves the rule.'"[142] He cited the Torah on the spread of this "abomination [al-fahishah]" among the people of Israel in Sodom and Gomorrah and then quoted the Qur'anic injunction against the People of Lot. He even invoked Edward Gibbons, who indicated that "moral decadence" was one of the reasons for the fall of Rome and Byzantium, and he spoke of this "abomination as existing in Athens and Rome."[143] Farrukh attributed this "abomination" to the Persians, who transmitted it to the Arabs.[144] He worried much about this "disgrace" taking a specifically Arab flavor due to the honesty with which Arabs have studied it. His conclusion was a nationalist one and was well aware of Orientalist judgment:

Ghazal in the masculine is therefore extraneous to Arabic literature and the Arabs themselves. I say this not in defense of Abu Nuwas, as he is—despite Taha Husayn's acknowledgement of his novel aesthetic dimension—a moral disgrace that cannot be covered up. However, the mistake is that of Arab writers. Arab literary historians always make reference to this—which is closer to the truth—while Western literary historians conceal the likes of such disgrace in their literary figures and poets and do not disseminate it, which makes us think—due to our own ignorance—that such as this exists in our literature but is missing in theirs.[145]

Jalil al-'Atiyyah, the other editor of some of the republished sexual manuscripts, was less polemical than Jum'ah with regards to Islamic history tout court, but he did justify his editing of the fourteenth-century text *Tuhfat al-'Arus* by claiming it as an "encyclopedia about Arab women" and "not a depraved text to be read at evening parties or in solitude"[146] or "a cheap book of sexual literature," as he had thought for years until he read a "bad" 1881 Cairo edition of it.[147] His decision to edit it for publication therefore was that it would "enrich the Arabic library," as "it is strange that Westerners have discovered this book be-

---

142. 'Umar Farrukh, *Abu Nuwas, Sha 'ir Harun al-Rashid wa Muhammad al-Amin* (Beirut: Dar al-Kitab al-'Arabi, 1988), 88.

143. Ibid., 89.

144. Ibid., 90.

145. Ibid., 91.

146. See Jalal al-'Atiyyah, "Muqadimmat al-Tahqiq" [introduction], in Muhammad bin Ahmad al-Tijani, *Tuhfat al-'Arus wa Mut'at al-Nufus* [The Gift of the Bride and the Pleasure of the Souls] (London: Riyad al-Rayyis lil-Kutub wa al-Nashr, 1992), 13. Al-'Atiyyah was also the editor of Abu al-Faraj al-Asfahani's *Al-Qiyan* [The Singing Girls] (London: Riyad al-Rayyis lil-Kutub wa al-Nashr, 1989).

147. Ibid., 14.

fore we did! For, it had been translated into French in 1848, and into English and German and other European and Oriental languages [before its publication in Arabic]."[148] 'Atiyyah, however, expressed anger at contemporary "Arab censors" whom he chastised for censoring sexually explicit material.[149] His goal of enriching the Arab library then was more modest, as he saw the publication of such works as having a pedagogical role insofar as they familiarized modern Arabs with their history and not necessarily for the lessons it might impart to them.

'Atiyyah was angry with a general modern Arab approach to medieval sex. His anger was shared by Egyptian dissident journalist and novelist Ibrahim 'Isa, who wrote an angry book specifically responding to the Islamist ban on matters sexual in public debates. He insisted that modern Muslims should be acquainted with the writings not of the average Muslim in medieval times, but particularly writings by Muslim theologians whose faith is above reproach. In his book, *Sex and the Theologians of Islam,* 'Isa summarized the works of al-Nafzawi, ibn Hazm, al-Suyuti, as well as Qur'anic explications by major theologians of the seduction story of the Prophet Yusuf (Joseph) and Zulaikha expounded in the Qur'an itself.[150] 'Isa opined that "the fact that sexual education [al-thaqafah al-jinsiyyah] is missing in the Arab world is the result of the absence of a culture of freedom [thaqafat al-hurriyyah]."[151] The author expressed much indignation about the narrowing of the margin of the debate by some Islamists who consider "ancient books about sex religiously prohibited [haram]" without providing any scriptural evidence to that effect.[152] 'Isa saw his book also as "revising and rehabilitating the status of women in our Arab world."[153]

'Isa was aware that many of the medieval books about desire and sex held women in a lower status than men. 'Isa did not endorse such a sexist view and declared that his interest in these books was "the excitation of mind and thought and the removal of all vacuous taboos that inhibit our brains."[154] His project was presented as a feminist one, as he "discovered how much sex rules the brains of extremists and how women represent an obsession in their lives, which forces them to dedi-

148. Ibid., 13–14.
149. Ibid., 14.
150. Ibrahim 'Isa, *Al-Jins wa 'Ulama' al-Islam, Kalam fi Muharramat al-Tatarruf wa Rijal al-Din* [Sex and the Theologians of Islam, a Discussion of the Taboos of Extremism and about the Men of Religion] (Cairo: Madbuli al-Saghir, 1994).
151. Ibid., 19.
152. Ibid., 21–23.
153. Ibid., 43.
154. Ibid., 44.

cate all their writings, the majority of their religious edicts [fatawa], and most of their sermons and their recorded cassette tapes to [dealing with] women. This contemporary situation in Egypt has produced the most despicable thought and understanding of women, rendering woman a contemptible person, a second-class citizen, and a Muslim who is lacking [in faith]."[155] 'Isa's contempt for these Islamists is matched by his contempt for their alleged funders: "All this is happening in the shadow of a deviance that afflicted whole countries and states who are the first to finance and propagate desert Bedouin thoughts about women, as if the lowering of women's abilities and the raising of the value of their masculinity can function as a covering veil and as a jurisprudential and religious justification for their own drowning in a heated deviance that reflects psychological and social phenomena that have bloody consequences."[156] As we will see in the next two chapters, the allegation that Gulf "Bedouin" Arabs are sexual "deviants" and "sodomites" is an important theme in representing Gulf Arabs in fiction produced in Greater Syria and Egypt since the 1970s.

In contrast to 'Atiyyah's and 'Isa's purely polemical approach, other authors wanted to have a positive engagement with the literature on sex. Syrian author Ibrahim Mahmud is perhaps the most prolific contributor to this approach. His *Al-Mut'ah al-Mahzurah* is the first secular book that deals almost exclusively with the question of sodomy among men and between men and women, otherwise identified as "deviance" or *shudhudh* (the book also includes a short section on bestiality). It is the third of four books that Mahmud wrote on sexual issues. The first two were explorations of the place of sex in the Qur'an and the pleasures of paradise.[157] Mahmud does not necessarily write in an academic mode, although much research and scholarship clearly goes into his work. His writings are often repetitive and full of rhetorical excess. Still, they constitute a new genre of writing on the topic. In this third, albeit repetitive and often incoherent, book,[158] Mahmud sought to study these sexual phenomena in Arab Muslim history without the moral and ethical judgments endemic

---

155. Ibid., 53.
156. Ibid., 54.
157. See his *Al-Jins fi al-Qur'an* (Beirut: Riyad al-Rayyis Lil-Kutub wa al-Nashr, 1994), and his *Jughrafiyyat al-Maladhdhat, al-Jins fi al-Jannah* [The Geography of Pleasures, Sex in Paradise] (Beirut: Riyad al-Rayyis lil-Kutub wa al-Nashr, 1998).
158. An example of such incoherence is the inclusion of a minichapter (chap. 9) in the book about gay pride day in Jerusalem, which includes citations from Daniel Boyarin about Judaism and homosexuality among males. The author offers no comment to link this with the rest of the book and the minichapter has no introduction or conclusion or statement as to why it is relevant to the topic at hand. This is aside from the many incoherent sentences that pepper much of the book. See ibid., 251–53.

to such studies. Indeed, he seemed unfamiliar with much of the modern debate about such matters, except the condemnatory element. Thus he declared that the "rejection" of the historical reality of such phenomena is not "beneficial."[159] The "presence" of sodomy, in its major (male anal penetration of another male) and minor (male anal penetration of a female) varieties, otherwise known as "the major sodomy" (al-liwat al-akbar") and "the minor sodomy," (al-liwat al-asghar), respectively, in the past of the Arabs "is distributed in myriad books: turathist [heritage] books, purely historical books, jurisprudential books, scrapbooks, etc." Thus it cannot be rejected "so as to make history proceed according to the formula of how it should have proceeded but rather requires a different treatment."[160] For Mahmud, this subject needs special treatment "not because it is a matter that is internal to our psychocultural make-up [as Arabs], but because it exists as a culture [thaqafah] unto itself, whose constituents must be researched in addition to [researching] the way that such constituents were formed and crystallized in their own social, historical, anthropological, and intellectual context."[161] Mahmud contrasted his approach with how this "cumulative history of the literature of sodomy in its Arab-Muslim frame" is ignored in modern Arab history

based on an ideological attitude that is currently being directed [by whom?]. Neither the Arabs, nor the Muslims among them especially, nor Muslims more generally, are desirous of listening to whomever might remind them of the presence of sodomy in their history, especially so as this history preserves a sunny and privileged position for them in the past, when Islam was a religion, a culture, and peoples who believed in it or were subjected to its authority . . . and because sodomy is rejected from a predominant moral viewpoint and was banned jurisprudentially on more than one count . . . [in keeping with] a pure image representing global Islam.[162]

Such grandiose claims on the part of Mahmud, however, are inaccurate, as secularists and Islamists have not ignored such writings and such a "presence" but have been negotiating how to fit it into the history of the past and that of the present. The fact that many Islamists were condemnatory of the presence of sodomy in Arab-Muslim history is not analogous to ignoring or neglecting it.

159. Ibrahim Mahmud, *Al-Mutʿah al-Mahzurah, Al-Shudhudh al-Jinsi fi Tarikh al-ʿArab* [The Forbidden Pleasure: Sexual Deviance in the History of the Arabs] (Beirut: Riyad al-Rayyis lil-Kutib wa al-Nashr, 2000), 12.
160. Ibid., 13.
161. Ibid., 13.
162. Ibid., 13.

As we saw, while some Islamists are satisfied with condemnation, they do that in a historicized fashion, acknowledging the presence of sodomy and its condemnation in the past and demanding similar treatment of it in the present. The only people who denied its presence were a few nationalists, while the majority would only go as far as attributing its origins to non-Arabs (following the Orientalist Adam Mez) and not denying its existence in Arab history. What then mobilizes this view that Mahmud holds and which he uses as a starting point for his inquiry? Why is Mahmud claiming to incite a discourse about a topic that has already been part of the discursive framework of historical and literary writing for over a century? And what exactly is missing from the existing archive that he wants to incite?

To begin with, Mahmud insisted that his investigation, which attributes some independent consciousness to sodomy as an object of study, is "a search into the truth of sodomy and how it was, by analyzing its constituent parts, excavating its ground [ardiyyatihi], and the resources that were put at its disposal . . . for the purpose of [developing] an intellectual approach [to look into] its working mechanism in Arab-Muslim history, and how it resisted everything that threatened its existence."[163] In the course of his investigation, Mahmud explicated how the eleventh-century Andalusian lexicographer ibn Sidah (A.D. 1077–1066) viewed the pleasure of the anus in his dictionary, *Al-Mukhassas*. The attention that ibn Sidah lavished on the entry for "anus" in his dictionary did not mean that "we are accusing ibn Sidah of practicing sodomy. For he might have been a sodomite in a specific way, and what he wrote might have been the result of life experience, but it also might not have been that at all. His encyclopedic knowledge of language might have been the result of his observations, without him being [necessarily] a contributor to what was happening with regards to anal pleasure."[164] It is unclear if Mahmud is engaged here in an ambivalent project of outing historical figures, and if so for what political purpose, since, as we will see below, such questions about the nature of the sexual practices and desires of historical figures are posed time and again in the same ambivalent fashion.

Ibrahim dedicated a chapter to "minor sodomy," discussing the jurisprudential views about it and mainly pointing out that the Maliki school is the only one of the four major Sunni jurisprudential schools that per-

163. Ibid., 15.
164. Ibid., 66. Mahmud raises a similar question about whether the thirteenth-century Tunisian author al-Tifashi was a sodomitic missionary of sorts (da'iyah lutiyyan), and concludes that there is no indication that he was. See ibid., 160.

mits it while the rest prohibit it as sinful.¹⁶⁵ Indeed while discussing the views of the fourteenth-century Tunisian jurisprudent al-Tijani on the permissibility of (heterosexual) penile-anal penetration, Mahmud asks, "Was al-Tijani practicing minor sodomy? We do not know that, but even if he were involved in such practices, it is not our right to demand an answer of him about this, as he was legislating for the pleasure of the spirit, and opened up the body to all possible openings."¹⁶⁶ Note that in the case of al-Tijani, the question that seeks to out him with regards to coital practices is not presented as an "accusation," as in the case of ibn Sidah, but as an illegitimate "demand."

Mahmud's outlook is highly influenced by Michel Foucault's volumes on the history of sexuality and contemporary Western views of pleasure. His secularist approach (he occasionally avoids antagonizing Islamists with his measured tone and noncombative approach) however ignores the secular history of sexual debates in the modern Arab world. As he considers sodomy to be "not an exception, but an activity that was practiced deeply, in a friendly climate . . . ," he states that "what is unfortunate is that many, if not the great majority, of those who are interested [in this topic], including researchers among Arab authors (modern and contemporary) played down the importance of this phenomenon, and diluted its effects, despite their referring to it under the category *mujun* (bawdiness), a term that has a taxonomical meaning and one that mobilizes moralism [akhlaqawi istinfari], thus relegating anyone who was part of it to the brink of sin completely."¹⁶⁷ As an example he cited Shawqi Dayf's condemnatory views of Abu Nuwas, while ignoring the long modern genealogy that preceded and succeeded Dayf and that, as we saw in previous chapters, was not always condemnatory of the great poet.¹⁶⁸ He also cited one of the moralizing statements of Ahmad Amin without historicizing it in Amin's own oeuvre, which contained less moralizing observations (as we also saw in a previous chapter). Mahmud unjustifiably claimed that "in light of this ethics, [Amin] refused to deal with what was a historical fact in this regard—as if it did not exist, and as if not mentioning it is sufficient to put a historical end to it."¹⁶⁹ This, however, is inaccurate, as Amin, contrary to Mahmud's claims, did not see sodomy as incidental to Abbasid culture but rather as *representative* of it.

Mahmud went further in his inaccurate generalization about the contemporary Arab world. In fact, it is here where we can discern Mahmud's

165. See chapter 4, "Al-Liwat al-asghar: Mut'at al-dubr al-unthawi al-mahzurah" [Minor Sodomy: The Prohibited Pleasure of the Feminine Anus].
166. Ibid., 99.   168. Ibid., 131, 190.
167. Ibid., 130–31.   169. Ibid., 186.

purpose in pretending to incite a discourse that in fact had already been incited long before him. It is intended to present him as the rare Arab intellectual that shows sympathy to those condemned by society for practicing sodomy. While his sympathy is clearly manifest in his book, in seeking to present it as unique, Mahmud partakes of another discourse, namely, that incited by the Gay International, a discourse that has little to do with intellectual developments in modern Arab history.

Indeed, congruent with the Gay International, Mahmud rushed to impose on the Arab world Lord Alfred Douglas's view of "a love that dare not speak its name." As he spoke correctly of the existence of societal forces (a clear reference to Islamists) that seek to attack real and imagined sodomites for the purpose of declaring the "purity of society," he affirmed the following: "In light of this, we find lectures and panels that convene, or even evening conversations, where such people [sodomites] are cursed . . . Yes, the voice of the sodomite remains pursued inside an ossified collective memory, as a denied voice, that brings shame, and whose conduct remains deplored and provocative of disgust."[170] What is problematic in this imposed Douglasian epistemology is the very notion of subjectivity that it enacts. From our historical overview, we have seen that there was no subject position called "sodomite" which sought to speak, or a "sodomite voice" that was suppressed. If anything, even when Abu Nuwas's poetry had been discussed ad infinitum in myriad books, Kamil al-Shinnawi, as we witnessed above, traveled back in time to allow Abu Nuwas, misidentified as "sodomite" or "deviant," in his subject position, to *speak*, albeit through al-Shinnawi's ventriloquism. This is not to say that societal forces, Islamist and secular, have not been severely judgmental in some cases of same-sex (and different-sex) practices, but simply, that it is an ontological and a logical error (not to speak of an anachronism) to collapse subjects with practices or to conflate sexual desires with identities.

The fact that Mahmud judged most of those medieval figures that he named as "sodomites" in their subject position, and as "misogynists" in the Greek tradition of male homoerotic desire is itself a conclusion derived from analyzing extant poetry and other writings that express such attitudes, albeit not exclusively. But what is problematic, if not utterly inaccurate, is his attempt to assimilate them to and fix them in an exclusive homosexuality that few of them, if any, professed, least of all Abu Nuwas himself.[171] In line with previous authors, which he failed to

170. Ibid., 135.
171. On the misogyny charge, see ibid., 163, for example.

cite, Mahmud claimed that Muslim Arab masculinism professed interest in youthful boys in the Abbasid period "as a masculinist reaction to
the tyranny of the vagina—if the expression permits—. . . especially so
when the palaces of the caliphs, the commanders, and the wealthy were
flooded with concubines of all types and colors who were classified as
commodities; as a result, the inclination towards masculinist homosexual [mithli] love grew as a negative reaction against that phenomenon
mentioned above."[172] Mahmud, like many of our authors, noted that
much of this did not exist when Arabs began to rule the Muslim Empire
but was introduced with the foreign elements that came to rule it. He
quoted Ahmad Amin's citation of Mez that al-Jahiz had claimed that the
infatuation with youthful boys came from non-Arab Khurasan.[173] Yet,
like some but not all of our authors, Mahmud was careful not to endorse
the explanation of sodomy as having foreign origins or as being external
to Muslim Arab culture; rather, he insisted that "sodomy . . . cannot be
explained with what is external, even though external factors might have
played a role in it. There are internal and objective elements that influence its development, its taking roots, its vivification, its intensification,
and its recirculation also."[174] Reviewing the condemnation of sodomy
in the Qur'an and the Hadith to prove that it must have preexisted the
foreign element, Mahmud concluded that "linking sodomy with what is
external does not explain its historical element but is rather a retroactive
justification of a phenomenon that would not have taken root without
social, cultural, and psychological nutrients, especially amidst a human
mixture, of many races and tongues."[175]

Mahmud summarized Muhammad Jalal Kishk's book to his readers,
praising some of his daring conclusions while condemning what he discerned as dictatorial and "threatening" to those readers who disagreed
with Kishk. As example, Mahmud cited Kishk's harsh criticisms of Bouhdiba's book, not as legitimate or insightful but simply as a reflection of
Kishk's "intellectual make-up and that of similar writings that take up
the artifice of Islamist legal texts and add to it an absolute regulatory
value . . . compared to the evil innovation and the polluted imitation
of the differing infidel, wherein he [Kishk] does not discuss as much as
practice defamation of the other and discredits him only for the sake of
discrediting him because the other does not think as he does."[176] Such
stereotypical representation of Islamist thinkers as so bogged down in

172. Ibid., 169.
173. Ibid., 179.
174. Ibid., 180.

175. Ibid., 181–82.
176. Ibid., 201.

ideological posturing can easily find evidence to support it in Kishk's book. What it ignores however is all the evidence that refutes it, as Kishk clearly uncovered much of the absurd Orientalist notions that are strewn about in much of Bouhdiba's book. Mahmud, like the discourse of the Gay International that remains dismissive of these concerns, would not have any of it, as he reserved much of his polemical energy to condemning Kishk.[177]

While many of Mahmud's criticisms of Kishk's arrogant, albeit often humorous, posturing are warranted (including Kishk's condemnation of Abu Nuwas, cited above), Mahmud failed to contextualize Kishk's statements about the West with Western Orientalist views of the Arab and Muslim worlds to which Kishk was responding. Kishk's book, after all, is a personal and ideological book expressing the "thoughts" of the author, as its title indicated, and is not an objective historical study. Yet Mahmud's angry tone could not be contained:

The West does not lack mistakes, or sins, or myriad escapades, on more than one level. However, before others (outside it) discover them, there were those (inside it) who discovered them. The West fears not its "pudenda" although sometimes it tries to cover them up. It recognizes them in a number of ways . . . Can Professor Kishk take on what is in his own society, and in his own Islamic world of murderous mistakes, destructive sins, and practices to which he did not make a single reference, such as sodomy and others, which have a large presence? Did he scrutinize the truth of his explication to what is happening on a civilizational basis? Would this process and its method not lead to an actual impasse in his Arab and Islamic world also?[178]

Mahmud recognized that there was and remains much Orientalist and racist Western propaganda against Islam and that much of that "accuses" Islam of homosexual practices, "but the author's reliance on this, and considering it the truth of Europe, and then reversing the accusation, constitutes a reverse ideological [tamadhhubiyyah] fundamentalism, and one that is proud of itself. For, rendering all the negatives attached to Islam in particular [by Europe] as the identifying marks of Europe [itself], is responding to error with a greater error."[179]

Mahmud's frustration with Kishk was also manifest in the perplexing questions that he posed to him:

How much I wished to find a single reference in his book, a passing one at that, to those who preferred youthful boys to concubines—[not only in the past but also] in

177. Ibid., 194–221.   179. Ibid., 217.
178. Ibid., 216–17.

the present moment—in his Islamic world, which takes place openly—and the moral meaning of this is clear—but I did not find it. Where then is the spirit of scientific research in what this author has written? . . . How much did I also wish to find but one paragraph or a specific reference to the spread of sodomy in the prisons of the Arab and Muslim worlds . . . Seeing what happens in overpopulated neighborhoods (where the downtrodden poor or those nearly so) live in Arab and Muslim cities and the high rates of children that work in the marketplace against their will, engaged in exhausting labor, as well as the physical and psychological woes caused by their work, while they live away from their families, or even are being kept away by their own families to force them to work, including sodomy [*sic,* Mahmud perhaps means prostitution of the sodomitic variety?], as is apparent to anyone who follows social surveys of those people and their movements, and how they are influenced, and pushed towards perversion of all types. All this takes us closer to the lived reality, the truth of sodomy, and the way it circulates![180]

As for sapphism, Mahmud provided a sympathetic portrait of its presence or absence in Greek and Roman texts and in Jewish, Christian, and Islamic scriptures. He mostly dealt with medieval popular writings about it (especially al-Tifashi's book). While Mahmud's feminism was manifest throughout the book in his persistent critique of a masculinist culture that predominated in the Greek and Roman worlds and in the medieval Muslim world as it does today in the West and in the Arab world, his sympathetic approach, like in the case of sodomy, remained deeply heterocentric. Thus, while heterosexuality requires no etiology or explanation, homosexual desire always needs to be explained and its "truth" uncovered. If sodomy has social reasons that result from certain social repression, so, it seems, does sapphism. Therefore, the predominance of sapphic relations during the Abbasid period resulted from an alliance between the free woman (wife) and the enslaved concubine. While the free wife felt abandoned sexually by her husband, who immersed himself in sexual pleasure with concubines and youthful boys, the enslaved concubine felt used and objectified to the point of fostering a "physical complicity" with the free wife, which is "a coerced challenge to the man's authority in reality." Thus, Mahmud concluded, that man's heterosexual rejection of free women and objectification of enslaved concubines *is* the cause of sapphism: "Sapphism remains the child of a marginalized body, and a call of the coerced flesh, a reaction to sexual contempt and a tyrannical sexism that bows before its human presence . . . The consumption of the self-same body—in the case of

180. Ibid., 219.

sapphism—is a warning call of a body that only knows physical repression and neglect [by heterosexual men?—JM] of its pulverized, repressed, and indicted being, before it is even formed!"[181]

Thus sapphism, like sodomy, can only exist as reaction-formation to an unattainable heterosexuality, whose lack of fulfillment, it would seem, resulted in the perversion of (women's) desire, or at least its very deviance from the correct object choice. But herein lies the confusion and contradiction in Mahmud's theory, which is shared by many of our authors, secular or religious, namely, that male homosexuality is caused by an excess of women while female homosexuality is caused by a dearth of men. Are we back here to Aristotelian moderation, wherein it is excess or dearth that causes deviance away from the normal, hence the need for moderation? If this is the case, then Mahmud's homophobia and heterocentrism are all-pervasive, as his solution to the marginalization of homosexuals is to eliminate them along with homosexuality altogether by committing society to a regime of moderation that will ensure a heterosexual outcome in all members. This indeed can be read as Mahmud's theory of desire, if one could be excavated from his book, and/or as an expression of his inconsistent and contradictory views, the axioms of which he shares with the Gay International.

As Mahmud also discussed the case of bestial desires in Greek, Jewish, Christian, and Muslim texts, he was a committed feminist throughout. He noted how in the case of Islam, all jurisprudential schools agree that all sexual relations with animals are prohibited, but they differed on the prescribed punishment. Mahmud, however, was concerned with the sexism with which medieval books dealt with bestiality when it was men rather than women who practiced it. The sexism he discerned in Greek, Roman, Jewish, Christian, and Muslim philosophy and theology governed the book's entire approach. Indeed, the book can be seen as an Irigarayan condemnation of "hom(m)o-sexuality."[182] Here, perhaps, we should reconsider Mahmud's implicit contention that he is the only Arab author who sympathizes with "sodomites" rendered "gay" ontologically and epistemologically in the tradition of the Gay International. If that was his purpose, then he is certainly right, as the bulk of those Arab authors (influenced as they were by Western sexual taxonomies) who showed sympathy with those oppressed because of their sexual desires and practices, from al-Munajjid onward, expressed such sympathy

---

181. Ibid., 312.
182. See Luce Irigaray, *This Sex Which Is Not One,* trans. by Catherine Porter (Ithaca: Cornell University Press, 1985), 171.

from within locally lived configurations of desire (thus resisting their own commitment to Victorian ethics and European social Darwinism), and not from within those imposed by powerful Western forces with arguably imperialist agendas coded as calls for liberation.

Class Revisited

Mahmud, was not the only contributor to these secular rebuttals of Islamists. A number of other Arab authors also made important contributions that did not see the Islamists' puritanical approach unanalytically and as the only relevant element in their philosophy. In *Love and Sex in Fundamentalism and Imperialism,* Syrian author Muhhamad Kamal al-Labwani[183] described Islam's sexual revolution in class terms. Al-Labwani is a Syrian physician, painter, and cultural critic and a major opposition political activist. His book is one of the more sophisticated interventions.[184] For al-Labwani, while "Islam" brought about new ideas about sex and sexual relations, it could not transcend the socioeconomic levels of the society over which it exercised hegemony. Still, to make certain views dominant, al-Labwani contended that the *fuqaha'* conjured up certain readings and interpretations of Qur'anic texts and Prophetic sayings that constituted a coherent system of ideas about matters sexual in the service of the ruling class. These jurisprudents then "stamped with sanctity political decisions that were recently constituted and which serve this class."[185] In responding to possible detractors of his views, al-Labwani insisted that

how is it then that the jurisprudents treated the question of sexual organization with all this attention to precision and literalism while other questions, such as the heredity of [political] authority, which stuck to Islam through the ages, remained neglected and opaque . . . Thus the jurisprudence [fiqh] and ethics that are being offered as representative of true Islam are nothing but obedient servants custom-made for a certain class whose interests they serve. Such a class in Islamic history was either the commercial-military class (among Sunnis) or the agricultural-feudal class (among Shiites).[186]

---

183. Muhhamad Kamal al-Labwani, *Al-Hubb wa al-Jins 'ind al-Salafiyya wa al-Imbiryaliyya* (London: Riyad al-Rayyis, 1994).

184. Al-Labwani was jailed in 2001 for his opposition to the Syrian government's crackdown on dissent.

185. Ibid., 70.

186. Ibid., 70–71.

The struggle that al-Labwani discerned in medieval Islam, following many others before him, was between medieval Mu'tazalite thought, which was philosophically inspired and was inimical to literalism and fundamentalism, and Hanbalite thought, which was deeply conservative and literalist. Thus, modern Islamic fundamentalism

attempts to offer the reading youth, who is looking for an ideology to frame his conduct, the culture of old extinct classes dressed up in the garb of true and authentic Islam; we are hardly surprised, therefore, to find this large amount of very old books, the most recent of which is hundreds of years old, overtaking [today's] book market, [re]published on the best paper with the best leather covers, dominating the windows and shelves of bookstores so much that modern books that discuss existing conditions have little space left for them. Old books have been reprinted and very old questions and problems were revived in the arena of thought while modern and critical questions are neglected.[187]

Al-Labwani did not note the Orientalist role in book production. He understood, however, that the new Islamic fundamentalism, like its counterparts around the world, was responding to the ideas of an imperialist capitalism and the classes it served. If the new imperialist culture is based on the exposure of the body and the excitation of insatiable desires, al-Labwani saw modern fundamentalism as seeking to cover up the body and limit the access points for the fulfillment of excited desires. He subjected imperialist capitalist modernity in the colonies to the same level of analysis that he did fundamentalism:

Modern civilization opened up expansive horizons to an awesome development of desires, and capitalist culture excites in contemporary human beings a terrifying quantity of such desires, so that achieving a balance between the two has become impossible, as most inhabitants of this Earth cannot in theory or practice satisfy a minimum level of their hyperexcited desires. Capitalist cultural policy, or the imperialist ideological sexual technique, is built on the production and reproduction of repression on a large scale at the same time that it claims that it is realizing freedom . . . This huge quantity of repression, not only of the sexual variety but also political, cultural and economic, etc., has before it but a symbolic or substitutive fulfillment; all [this repression] has left is the outer shell as well as its ability to foster complexes and ways to deal with them. Otherwise, [this repression] must follow a path of a dogmatic, complete rejection, which is that of contemporary fundamentalism . . . , itself based on a repression of which it is a result and for which it has a specific technique. It puts

187. Ibid., 72.

[this repression] at the service of another ideology, which in effect rejects the new contradictions, albeit in an ossified form, and rejects the present in toto and all it has fostered, seeking a return to the past where it can hide.[188]

Al-Labwani's point, similar to that of the Frankfurt School theorists, was that the influence of modern capitalist culture was not the production of freedom, no matter how much it claimed it as its goal, but rather more social, political, medical, juridical, and sexual repression and oppression. He believes that the fundamentalist response to imperialist culture is ultimately doomed to failure, as it is a negative defensive response "awaiting a coup de grâce so that it can crumble gradually, becoming form without content . . . What is needed is a positive confrontation, not a negative rejection. Fundamentalism is a popular reaction with wide meanings and contents, but it remains short-sighted, reactive, negative, and disabled."[189]

Al-Labwani opposed equally the fundamentalist approach and that of the Westernizers in the Arab world, as he was not taken in, like Mahmud, with the claims of freedom promised by marketers of Western epistemologies and ontologies of desire. For him, if medieval culture, whose revival is sought by the fundamentalists, is not suitable for the modern Arab world, then neither is modern Western culture any more suitable, as they both are "two sides of the same coin whose basis is the imposition of a culture by force despite the [noncorresponding] infrastructure."[190] Al-Labwani's rich engagement with the conditions of repression and freedom is exceptional among his cohort.

In a different register, radical Egyptian secular physician and writer Khalid Muntasir, a specialist in venereal disease, took upon himself an "objective" approach to "love and the body" in a "romantic study of sex."[191] Parts of Muntasir's book, which is informed by Western psychological, psychiatric, and sociological studies of love, were initially published in the Egyptian weekly *Ruz al-Yusuf*. His book set itself the task of unraveling the "language of the flesh."[192] He explored, among other things, masturbation, sex between men and women, and "sexual deviance." While throughout, the author cautioned the reader not to be offended by the nature of the topic at hand, he was aware that by the time

188. Ibid., 81–82.
189. Ibid., 99.
190. Ibid., 106.
191. Khalid Muntasir, *Al-Hubb wa al-Jasad, Dirasah 'Atifiyyah fi al-Jins* [Love and the Flesh: A Romantic Study of Sex] (Cairo: Dar al-Khayyal, 1996).
192. Ibid., 9–10.

the reader reached the last chapter of the book, in which homosexuality is discussed, "his" patience would have run out. If when discussing masturbation and heterosexual sex, Muntasir begged his reader's forbearance, he understood in turn that what the last chapter would face were "screams of protest . . . that the place of ["deviants"] is not in a book chapter but in a prison cell or a separate room in a leper colony."[193]

Muntasir, who is known for his polemical writings against Islamism, insisted that homosexuality, like other aspects of sex that he studied, merited equal attention, despite its condemnation in the West and the Arab world. He cited the *Journal of Homosexuality* on all the epithets against "sexual deviants" that continue to be in use in the West and the increase of such condemnation after the appearance of AIDS and how some in the West saw the disease as "divine punishment."[194] He also cited the "protest movements" of the last twenty years in Europe and America that called for "ending the condemnation of sexual deviance and demanding its recognition and the decrease if not the elimination of all juridical, social, and moral constraints that result from such condemnation. These protest movements have resulted in the American Psychiatric Association's recognition of deviance and its declaration that it is not a disease requiring treatment."[195] Muntasir provided a brief history from the Greeks to the modern period, citing Plato's *Phaedrus* as unique (and never mentioning, for example, al-Jahiz's *Munazarat al-Jawari wa al-Ghilman*).[196] He also provided an overview of the Western gay movement and the different Western theories as to the "cause" of homosexuality (psychological, biological, psychiatric, social, etc.).[197] His approach was mostly descriptive and sympathetic, and lacked moral judgment. His book is perhaps a unique nonmoralist approach written in a period saturated with secular and religious moral judgment.

One example of secular moralism presented in the guise of class and feminist analysis is Sulayman Huraytani's *Al-Jawari wa al-Qiyan* (Concubines and Singing Girls). Huraytani, a Syrian scholar, attempts to replicate the work of al-Munajjid published four decades earlier, but his book is packaged in a more scholarly manner.[198] This well-researched book

193. Ibid., 169.
194. Ibid., 169.
195. Ibid.
196. Ibid., 173.
197. Ibid., 172–88.
198. Sulayman Huraytani, *Al-Jawari wa al-Qiyan wa Zahirat Intishar Andiyyat wa Manazil al-Muqa-yyinin fi al-Mujtamaʿ al-ʿArabi al-Islami* [Concubines and Singing Girls and the Phenomenon of the Proliferation of Clubs and the Inns of the Owners of Singing-girls in Arab-Muslim Society] (Damascus: Dar al-Hasad, 1997).

is long on description and quotation and short on analysis throughout, except when it comes to things deviant. While the author occasionally registered the sexual oppression of singing girls by a "masculinist" and "patriarchal" class system dominated by an opulent ruling class, he eschewed the question of homosexuality throughout except cursorily. The author was aware, for example, that the widespread sale and ownership of singing girls as well as the "appearance of a group of male effeminates" increased with the increase in fortunes, leading to the "opulent life and the various kinds of debauchery, licentiousness, bawdiness [mujun], and deviant conduct."[199] This seems to have led, like in Ibrahim Mahmud's contradictory theory, to "sexual hunger and the endemic spread of deviant sexual relationships that began to appeal to men in a wide and public way. Thus sodomy spread. . . . and sapphism spread among women, including among the wives and concubines of the caliphs."[200] Al-Huraytani also noted the proliferation of the "boyish woman" as the style of the period in the Abbasid era.[201] He credited the religious scholars or jurisprudents in the employ of the caliphs' courts as responsible for the ideological and jurisprudential facade used to justify or cover up these practices.[202] His conclusion was that these "perverted and possibly deviant practices [that] were performed in some of the private places and [pleasure] gatherings" were

practices that constituted manifestations of the conduct of the large majority of the owners of palaces, the caliphs being in the forefront among them, due to the degree they reached of recklessness, debauchery, perversion, seizing of desires and surrender to the authority of pleasure, while their hands were stained with the blood of the oppressed and the rebellious. These hands, which would sometimes grant thousands and hundreds of thousands of darahim and dinars, would switch between a wine glass and an ablution bowl, just as their lips, which devoured the fortunes of people and the rights of subjects, would switch between the slurping of the saliva of concubines and youthful boys and the recitation of Qur'anic verses in a dualism that reached a peak of political and social hypocrisy of values dressed up in religious garb, in theory and in practice.[203]

Thus, what we see then is on the one hand a crucial class angle (al-Labwani and al-Huraytani) to cultural formations following in the footsteps of Halasa, which has largely been absent in other debates about the

199. Ibid., 88.
200. Ibid.
201. Ibid., 98–101.

202. Ibid., 180.
203. Ibid., 188.

"decadence" of the Abbasids or the "backwardness" of contemporary Arab culture, such as the one discussed in the introduction, and on the other an attempt to familiarize readers (Muntasir) with examples of societies tolerant of "deviance" (the West) in the interest of providing a comprehensive scholarly study for pedagogical purposes.

Debating Incitement

The latest salvo in these debates on sex and desire, however, concerned the very value of republishing medieval erotica and the incitement to discourse it entailed. Saudi secular feminist literary critic ʿAbdullah Muhammad al-Ghadhdhami launched an attack on the publishers and editors of such material, focusing on al-Nafzawi's *Perfumed Garden*. In the second volume of *Woman and Language*,[204] al-Ghadhdhami noted that "at the time that women seek to found a 'feminine charter' that protects their feminine existence from the dominion of masculine culture, another corporeal charter is raising its head again in order to place the feminine body between parenthesis."[205] An example of this new charter is al-Nafzawi's book: "When I mention this book, I am referring to a rich culture that this book represents and that it elicits, namely, man's education about the feminine body."[206]

Al-Ghadhdhami cited the recent activity in the publishing world of reissuing medieval classics dealing with sex and women:

The republishing of these books is not an expression of commercial acumen on the part of a smart publisher; it goes much deeper . . . We should first note that this new movement in publishing takes place among expatriate Arab publishing houses, in Britain and Germany. As people emigrate usually to seek salvation from their chains, the actions of immigrants and their declarations (and publications) are therefore a reflection of this situation of liberation and salvation. Thus, the publication of a book like the *Perfumed Garden* in an elegant edition with scholarly editing, and in an impressive ceremonialism means that the publisher (and the editor) are proud of this book, not as a mark of a past culture but rather because it is "a technical pedagogical book about sex . . . and it is a literary and medical book," as the editor claims. Thus the publisher declares on the back jacket the good news [bushra] that he is presenting us

---

204. ʿAbdallah Muhammad al-Ghadhdhami, *Al-Marʾah wa al-Lughah 2, Thaqafat al-Wahm, Muqarabat hawl al-Marʾah wa al-Jasad wa al-Lughah* [The Culture of Illusion, Approaches to Women, the Body, and Language] (Beirut: Al-Markaz al-Thaqafi al-ʿArabi, 2002).
205. Ibid., 7.
206. Ibid.

with "an exciting and enjoyable book from our heritage that is of benefit to Arabic readers."[207]

Al-Ghadhdhami concluded then that the publication of the *Perfumed Garden* and similar books is

not an innocent activity, nor is it naïve or neutral. It is the result of a cultural and scholarly conviction, meaning that both the editor and the publisher are convinced in the subject matter of the book as a correct scholarly subject and as a serious cultural subject that has credibility . . . This is why the editor ends his introduction with an old and rooted statement: "No one can ridicule [this book] except the stupid ignorant [person] with little knowledge" . . . And these are not adjectives intended only to show contempt for differing opinions, but are also indicative of the absolute self-confidence and trust in the book and its scholarship [on the part of the editor].[208]

As al-Ghadhdhami proceeded to analyze the sexism of the *Perfumed Garden* and what he considered to be its contempt for women, he concluded, noting that the intended reader was male, that

it would not be a problem for someone to say that al-Nafzawi's book is a book that targets the idiotic and stupid masculine reader, and no one would say that it is a technical sex education book, and that it is of benefit to Arabic readers, except if such a person had indeed cancelled out his reason and given himself over to the sorcery of al-Nafzawi, ignoring all personal and human experience with the feminine sex. How then would it be acceptable that women's reason is located between their thighs and that there is great benefit to big dicks—and these two claims are the center of the book . . . Should we then accept the publisher's and editor's celebration of such idiocy, appearing as if they are in agreement with their master, the author [of the book], in strengthening foolishness as part of the nation's culture and in presenting the feminine body and representing it in this lowly manner[?]![209]

Al-Ghadhdhami answers his rhetorical question without equivocation: "This book is a sign of the culture of ignorance, idiocy, and bad intellect and prose. Seeking to make it important or to celebrate it is nothing short of evangelizing ignorance and celebrating foolishness."[210]

Ibrahim Mahmud, expectedly, disagreed with al-Ghadhdhami's hostility to the *Perfumed Garden*, "which dismisses the book in its entirety as bad in content; he is not satisfied, however, with this rejection and

---

207. Ibid., 8.
208. Ibid., 9–10.

209. Ibid., 23.
210. Ibid., 24.

accusation against the book but also criticizes the publisher and editor and all who have contributed to its publication and distribution."[211] In his fourth and most recent book dealing with sexual matters, Mahmud declared that "I do not want to act as . . . the defender of the publisher and the editor, because my most important books have been published and continue to be published by this same publisher, but what I can say is that the attitude of al-Ghadhdhami . . . is not critical, and his criticism is not innocent at all."[212] Mahmud opposed al-Ghadhdhami's conclusions claiming that "my books which [the publisher] publishes are the opposite of what al-Ghadhdhami claims [in the sense that Mahmud's books are feminist and not misogynistic] and they are all banned in his country [Saudi Arabia], which is why I have not found any reference to them in any of his books where he appears as an ally of women."[213] As al-Ghadhdhami claimed that ibn Qayyim al-Jawziyyah's book *Rawdat al-Muhibbin wa Nuzhat al-Mushtaqin* (The Garden of Lovers and the Promenade of Yearners) is a good contrast to al-Nafzawi's book, in terms of the former's nonobjectifying views of women and sex, Mahmud countered that such a choice was indicative of al-Ghadhdhami's partiality toward one of the four Sunni Islamic jurisprudential schools of thought, namely, the Hanbalite school to which ibn Qayyim al-Jawziyyah belonged, and indicative of his hostility to the Malikiyyah school to which al-Nafzawi belonged. It was not "masculinist culture" that al-Nafzawi's book reflected as al-Ghadhdhami claimed, rather, according to Mahmud, it was the intensification of the "efficacy of the body" and the "efficacy of reproduction and the consumption of the flesh" that was sought in al-Nafzawi's book.[214] Mahmud reproduced Moroccan author ʿAbd al-Kabir al-Khatibi's deconstructionist reading of al-Nafzawi against al-Ghadhdhami's deconstruction, delving beyond the immediate meanings that he claims al-Ghadhdhami discerned.

This debate between Mahmud and al-Ghadhdhami is hardly unique to the Arab world. What was at stake in it seems not so unlike the contemporary Western feminist debate about the meaning and value of the pornographic for Western women and feminism—wherein a moralist 1970s U.S. feminism is contrasted with a poststructuralist, amoralist feminism that is not hostile to the body and the pornographic as such. But while these secular arguments were thrown about in the intellec-

---

211. Ibrahim Mahmud, *Al-Shabaq al-Muharram, Antulujya al-Nusus al-Mamnuʿah* [Forbidden Lust: Anthology of Banned Texts] (Beirut: Riyad al-Rayyis, 2002), 63.
212. Ibid., 64.
213. Ibid.
214. Ibid., 65.

tual realm, the material effects of the expansion of discourse on sexual desires and practices would begin to be felt at the level of the police and the law. If "sexual deviance" has been so far discussed as licentious behavior, as a psychiatric or physiological ailment, or as a sin, it would soon be transformed into a crime. This transformation would take place not only indirectly but directly through open calls for state intervention, and indeed through participation by officials from repressive state apparatuses in the ongoing debate through publishing books of their own.

Criminology and Police Work: Islam as Legal Reform

The expansion of discourse about deviance was not an independent phenomenon but emerged in response to the crusading efforts of the Gay International and Western human rights groups who adopted a Gay Internationalist agenda. As we saw in the last chapter, the press coverage of the machinations of the Gay International was extensive and precipitated the publication of a number of books that sought to fight deviance and those who defended it. In the 1980s, the social ramification of AIDS, the Western homophobic propaganda surrounding it, and gay activism combating homophobia were reacted to, as we saw, with the publication of books on venereal disease whose ideas were mostly borrowed from the West. Many of these books called on the state to enact laws to assist them in limiting the spread of AIDS by punishing "deviants," a call that was rarely heeded by the state. By the early 1990s, the emergence of the Gay International in full force precipitated yet stronger calls for criminalizing "sodomy" and "deviance" and punishing their practitioners. This time the state heeded such calls along with its functionaries, some of whom contributed to the literature on deviance. The most interesting of this new literature is that which deals directly with the ability of the state to control "deviants."

Enter criminology as the new player. Debates about sex since the 1980s have not been limited to class, disease, pornography, social disorder, religion, and feminism but have also expanded to sociological phenomena like crime and violence. Interest in sex crimes rose during this period with newspapers and magazines reporting all kinds of sex crimes in society that had not been reported before the 1980s, except in rare cases. Indeed, although an early book dealing with "sex and crime" was published in 1973 dealing mostly with husbands who murder their wives and, to a lesser extent cases of wives murdering their husbands, there was little attention to sex crimes in general.[215] One such book, *Crime and Sex: Qur'anic Manners for the Publication of Crime Stories in the Press*, by Dr. ʿAbd al-Wahhab al-Kahil, published in 1991, dealt with the history of crime in Islamic scripture, namely, the Qur'an.[216] The book cited sex and nonsex crimes, including the murder of Abel by Cain, Moses's accidental killing of an Egyptian, the sex crimes of the People of Lot manifesting in men having sex with one another, and the attempted rape of Joseph, son of Jacob, by Zulaikha, wife of the Egyptian al-ʿAziz.

The author compared how the Qur'anic stories were narrated in a nonsensationalist way and that their goal was to set an example and to sermonize on how people should deal with such crimes. Throughout, al-Kahil, who is Egyptian, compared the Qur'anic stories with sex crime stories from the contemporary Egyptian press, indicating how many of the modern stories are told with much sensationalism and with no pedagogical goal in mind. Instead of teaching people about the horrors of such crimes, they end up, in some cases, teaching people how to commit them.[217] Also, al-Kahil protested the listing of the names of criminals in newspapers, as it created much embarrassment for them and for their families. Revelations in the press of the identities of criminals, he maintained, unless necessitated by their continued danger to society, would leave them no option but to give up on society and persist in their crimes. This foreclosed one of the major options for them, namely, repentance, which would be accepted by God, as stipulated in the Qur'an.[218] Although the author cited many examples of contemporary crimes that contain sexual elements, and although he discussed the People of Lot and their crime of "abomination," he did not cite a single journalistic story about such crimes in the contemporary period, as few, if any, were covered at the time of his writing (1991).

Like other aspects of sex that were now being discussed more openly, the issue of sex crimes was also going to be connected to the issue of "sexual deviance," by both conservative Islamist and secular sociologists alike. A major volume of almost five hundred pages, *Sexual Deviance and Murder Crimes* was published in 1995 by ʿAbd al-Wahid Imam Mursi,

215. See ʿAbd al-Munʿim al-Jiddawi, *Al-Jins wa al-Jarimah* [Sex and Crime] (Cairo: Dar al-Hilal, March 1973).

216. Dr. ʿAbd al-Wahhab al-Kahil, *Al-Jarimah wa al-Jins, Al-Adab al-Qur'aniyyah li-Nashr Qisas al-Jarimah fi al-Sahafah* [Crime and Sex, Qur'anic Manners for the Publication of Crime Stories in the Press] (Cairo: Maktabat al-Turath al-Islami, 1991).

217. Ibid., chap. 1, 16–41.

218. Ibid., 238–39.

an Egyptian police major.[219] Mursi had a clear pedagogical purpose in mind that targeted the youth, as he dedicated the book to his son and daughter as well as to "Egypt's youth, the hope of the present, and the munitions ['uddah] of the future." I will discuss Mursi's book at length not on account of its popularity, which was very limited, but rather for its elaboration on how Egyptian police work and a new dominant moralism should produce strategies of surveillance, which would lead later to the Queen Boat arrests and subsequent harassment.

In the introduction, Mursi expressed his thanks to God for "making marriage the only method for reproduction and the continuation of life," and that Islam is

strict in its punishment of those who might deviate from the specified and planned correct path . . . For the goal that I was careful to ascertain in this modest study is to insist that sexual deviance causes many harms that are not limited to known health problems which everyone knows, except the proud among the deviants, but also other types of harm that lead to the commission of crimes, the ugliest and most horrid of which is murder. Everyone should know that deviance is equally dangerous to the deviant and to society. Indeed following the saying "the released prisoner of today is the prisoner of tomorrow," one could say that "the deviant of today is the murder victim of tomorrow," a statement that we put before today's youth in order that they understand the danger levels of this crime.[220]

Mursi explained that his study, in which he explored deviance in history and in different religions (concentrating on Islam and on Egypt, about which the book offered field research), follows "deviants in places where they congregate and practice."[221] Studying Egyptian society is not to say that deviance "is a problem exclusive to us. On the contrary, it exists in all societies and in fact its occurrence in Egyptian society is much less than in other societies, as Egyptian society is still influenced by its religious and civilizational values, which are considered the main reasons for the relative lower levels of this problem [in Egypt]. Rather, we intended to focus on this problem in Egyptian society as an expression of our wish to purify it from every harm and every impurity."[222] Thus, while al-Barr insisted that Saudi vaginas were the chastest around and were not at risk of venereal disease, Mursi found some, albeit not

219. 'Abd al-Wahid Imam Mursi, *Al-Shudhudh al-Jinsi wa Jara'im al-Qatl* [Sexual Deviance and Crimes of Murder] (Cairo: n.p., 1995).
220. Ibid., 7, 8.
221. Ibid., 10.
222. Ibid., 10.

much, evidence of sexual criminal pollution in Egypt that he sought to eliminate.

Mursi was clear that there is little that is novel about murder crimes or sexual deviance, both of which humanity has known since the dawn of time.[223] For him, as for others we studied, deviance is an expansive notion that covers a number of sexual practices. These include four categories. The first is that "a man have sex with other than woman." This category includes "sodomy, sapphism, bestiality, masturbation."[224] It is unclear how sapphism fits this category, as no man is involved in this activity, yet it is placed under a category of what men practice! The second category prohibits "coitus not in the specified place and not in the specified time and the like." This includes "a man having sex with a woman while she is menstruating, a man having sex with a woman through her anus, and scandalous acts." The author is presumably referring to public exposure. The third category is not named but is invoked as a category "proscribed by monotheistic religions." It includes "adultery/fornication, lying with the dead, pimping, and incest."[225]

The author provided a history of such "crimes" and their prescribed penalty by the law in ancient Babel and Assyria, ancient Egypt, Rome, Persia, China, the medieval Arabs, among others. He also provided an overview of how such crimes were dealt with by primitive religions and the three monotheistic ones. The crimes to which Mursi provided a history are *zina* (adultery/fornication), incest, rape, homosexuality ("al-jinsiyyah al-mithliyyah"), disgracing ("hatk al-'ird")—which usually refers to attempted rape of women or to attempted or actual rape of men—bestiality, necrophilia, and prostitution.[226] Mursi is not a systematic researcher. He would sometimes confuse the evidence that he himself presented about the ancient texts he examined. For example, he cited Hamourabi's Code, which condemned the adultery of married couples and not unmarried ones; yet he presented this as a condemnation of both.[227] Moreover, Mursi provided a history of crimes related to adultery/fornication, sodomy, and sapphism but did not provide a reason for omitting a history of masturbation crimes and the penalties for them, anal heterosexual sex, and heterosexual sex during the menstruation cycle, all of which are "crimes" according to his classification.

While examining the occurrence of these crimes in Arab history, Mursi specified that sodomy was "undoubtedly known to the [pre-Islam]

223. Ibid., 15
224. Ibid., 17.
225. Ibid., 17–18.

226. Ibid., chap. 1, 20–64.
227. Ibid., 33.

Arabs of *jahiliyyah* . . . It is likely that this vice started with the prisoners of war and among the slaves and then became widespread among *jahiliyyah* Arabs. The *jahiliyyah* Arabs used to purchase these deviants in the marketplace such as *Suq 'Uqaz* and *Dhi Majaz* [ancient markets in the Arabian Peninsula] and in other markets where concubines were sold and prostitutes offered"[228] Mursi's major bêtes noires are *zina* (adultery/ fornication) and sodomy, as, according to him, both have major religious, economic, social, and health ramifications.[229] The social ramifications include the destruction of the family,[230] while the health ramifications include the spread of venereal disease, including AIDS, which is caused by "adultery/fornication and other illicit sexual relations."[231]

Mursi also explored the psychological profiles of these criminals/deviants as well as criminological medical exams to ascertain their crimes. This included the physical trauma to women who were raped, as well as signs of resistance that left marks on the body and clothing of the male rapist. As for the crime of sodomy, it is common "in jails, and among soldiers in military camps, and among boarding school students."[232] As a criminologist, Mursi is precise in describing the situation of anal sex among men, whether consensual or not. He lavishes attention on the anus itself:

The sphincter muscle is more able to expand than the vagina, even in children. Moreover, there is nothing that resembles a hymen in the anus [whose tearing a physician could examine]. If a medium-size penis penetrated carefully and lightly or with the aid of lubricants, including saliva, Vaseline, or cream, and did so with the agreement of the crime victim [majni 'alayhi], the anus could expand sufficiently so that we could not find any traces of trauma to the anus or around it to indicate that the act had been committed. However, if sudden force were used in penetration, some traces would result and manifest in the following manner.[233]

Mursi then provided a list of possible physical signs of penetration. As far as the penetrator was concerned, "the accused should be examined seriously to find light skin scrapes and scratches on the penis, or traces of fecal matter or bloody spots on it."[234] As for "ubnah," Mursi tells us that "if a boy or girl were habituated to it since childhood, then this despicable habit would accompany him [*sic*] and he would become captive to it in many cases and it becomes impossible for the person to give it up regardless of what his age might be. It could [also] cause him

228. Ibid., 83–84.
229. Ibid., 117–21.
230. Ibid., 119, 136.
231. Ibid., 119 and 135.

232. Ibid., 238.
233. Ibid.
234. Ibid., 239.

scandals and humiliations. As for girls, the reason for the spread of this habit among them is partly related to their wish to preserve their hymen intact . . . or to grant the desires of the person she [sic] likes. Thus with the repetition of this act, the habit develops."[235]

The use of the term "ubnah" is noteworthy. "Ubnah" is a medieval Arabic medical term that was mentioned by medieval physicians and referred to a condition afflicting men only and manifesting in their seeking and enjoying penetration of their anus. The word initially referred to a "defect" in wood and came to apply to people metaphorically as "shame."[236] The ninth-century physicians 'Isa ibn Massah and Qusta ibn Luqa both cited Aristotle's *Physical Problems* and *Physiognomy* for their brief discussions of *ubnah*.[237] It was famed physician Abu Bakr al-Razi (died in A.D. 932 and known in English as Rhazes) who is said to have composed a brief and unknown treatise on the subject in which he diagnosed it as a congenital condition that might be incurable. Al-Razi associated "ubnah" with the male child having "weak testicles, drawn toward above." Also those afflicted with "ubnah" are said to have small penises. If the condition is "prolonged . . . it cannot be cured, in particular, if he is obviously feminine and loves to be like women. If it was intense and the person affected by it was not obviously effeminate and is not strongly inclined to pleasure but is repelled by it and would like to be free of it, it is possible for him to be treated."[238] Ibn Sina (Avicenna), who did not seem to know of al-Razi's obscure treatise, followed Aristotle's entries "with considerable distortion and change," and claimed it as a psychological condition, that should not be treated physiologically but with corporal discipline and even punishment.[239] Other medieval physicians like Al-Samu'al ibn Yahya questioned the advice given by other physicians who counseled "eminent men" that "sexual union with women leads more quickly to old age . . . and causes podagra and hemorrhoids, whereas relations with boys are less harmful."[240]

Mursi's uncharacteristic invoking of the term intends to hark back to this relatively unknown medieval medical engagement. While some

235. Ibid., 239.

236. See Muhammad bin Mukarram ibn Manzur, *Lisan al-ʿArab* (Beirut: Dar Sadir, 1990), vol. 13, 4.

237. See Franz Rosenthal, "Ar-Razi on the Hidden Illness," in Rosenthal, *Science and Medicine in Islam: A Collection of Essays* (Hampshire: Variorum, 1990), 48–49.

238. Rosenthal translated the treatise (*Science and Medicine in Islam,* 48–49). I am relying in my translation on the original text reproduced in Shihab al-Din Ahmad al-Tifashi, *Nuzhat al-Albab fima La Yuwjad fi Kitab* (London: Riyad al-Rayyis, 1992), 304–5.

239. Rosenthal, "Ar-Razi on the Hidden Illness," 49–50.

240. Cited in Danielle Jacquart and Claude Thomasset, *Sexuality and Medicine in the Middle Ages,* translated by Matthew Adamson (Princeton: Princeton University Press, 1988), 124. Ibn Yahya also dealt with the physiological causes of sapphism.

medical books, derivative of al-Razi and ibn Sina, continued to cite it as late as the seventeenth century,[241] the meaning of *ubnah* was not common outside the medical field, so much so that the famed thirteenth-century dictionary of ibn Manzur (1232–1311) did not cite its medical meaning, nor did the fourteenth-century al-Fayruzabadi (1329–1414), whose entry on "ma'bun" includes a reference to a man who suffers from excessive flatulence.[242] This is how Mursi described the modern condition: "For those who have been habituated to *ubnah* . . . it is notable that this group shows much daring and lack of modesty as well as effeminacy in speech and manners." Mursi then explored the "local signs on [their] genitals," which include intricate details about penetrated anuses:

The skin around the anus becomes smooth and thick; the sphincter loses its strength and resilience and does not contract quickly when the skin next to it is pinched or touched; the anus sinks to a deeper level than usual due to the absorption of fat resulting in a dent that looks like a funnel which pulls the skin on both sides and which in turn loosens the sphincter muscle making the anus open up and exposing a large section of the mucous membrane of the rectum which sometimes protrudes. Old scar tissue is often observed on it. Often, one observes in chronic *ubnah*, hemorrhoids and scrapes while the minute folds of the mucous membrane disappear, and [*sic*] the effeminate man in many cases decorates himself with women's clothing and his speech is uttered delicately as if he were a woman, and he wears all kind of jewelry which he thinks makes him look better and of higher status.[243]

In the case of sapphists, unfortunately for Mursi and other police criminologists, "there are no physical traces to be found that a pathologist can determine medically." In such cases "the search focuses on providing an opinion about the mental balance of the aggressor female, as often a masculine sadist transformation is evident in her manners and on her body."[244] Except in the case of heterosexual rape, the details for the other crimes are much less graphic and detailed, including the cases of adultery and fornication.

Mursi also provided police statistics for the occurrence of many sexually deviant crimes from 1952 to 1991, including adultery, rape and attempted rape of men and women, and prostitution. He discerned cli-

241. On Ottoman medical citations of *ubnah*, see the works cited in El-Rouayheb, *Before Homosexuality*, 19.
242. See ibn Manzur, *Lisan al-'Arab*, vol. 13, 4; and Muhammad bin Ya'qub al-Fayruzabadi, *Al-Qamus Al-Muhit* (Beirut: Dar Ihya' al-Turath al-'Arabi, 1997), vol. 2, 1544.
243. Mursi, *Al-Shudhudh al-Jinsi*, 240.
244. Ibid., 241.

matological and class causes in such occurrences, as they seemed to increase in summer months (his data in fact do not bear that out in most cases), and that the victims are uneducated and poor while the rapists are of working-class origins, peasants, or unemployed. The majority of victims are women (68 percent) and a minority are men (32 percent).[245]

Mursi, a man of the law, appears to heed the call issued a decade earlier by al-Barr as far as the need for juridical assistance to be rendered to physicians in combating the epidemic of sexual deviance. As consensual homosexual sex is not a crime in Egyptian law and thus does not appear in the police statistics that Mursi consulted, Mursi insisted that "in reality the crime of sodomy is the most widespread of these crimes and has begun to constitute a veritable danger to the youth and thus requires that all efforts be combined to confront it properly and effectively."[246] Mursi then proceeded to list the different kinds of sodomites "in the Egyptian street." These include "an active sodomite," "a passive sodomite," the "dual sodomite, active and passive" and the sodomite who only sleeps with foreigners (it is unclear if this sodomite is active, passive, or both).[247] Unlike other sexual criminals, those who commit the crime of sodomy come from all walks of life "without being exclusive to a specific social class, as it includes the professional and the artisan, the illiterate, the unlearned, and the educated. This peculiar trait of the crime of sodomy *is* the reason for its danger to society."[248] The danger that sodomy constitutes is contrasted with sapphism, which is "much less common in Egyptian society and is only found among certain groups . . . such as rich women or belly dancers and is seldom found among the poor and popular classes, as it is linked to luxury and opulence."[249]

Mursi's book is a guidebook to police work. It is not only interested in elaborating investigative methods that aim to locate, identify, prosecute, and punish sexual deviants but also a call to government and to legislators to aid in this effort. Indeed, Mursi is uniform in his views about sexual offenders of either gender. His advice for legal reform included a call to eliminate gender discrimination. While Egyptian laws on the books (like many European laws and U.S. state laws), for example, prosecute a male adulterer (but notably not fornicator, despite Mursi's refusal to make a distinction between the two), only if he commits adultery in his marital home, it prosecutes women adulterers regardless of where they committed adultery. Mursi exposes this discriminatory law and calls on

245. Ibid., 253–57.
246. Ibid., 271.
247. Ibid.

248. Ibid., 272.
249. Ibid., 273.

legislators to rectify it by prosecuting male adulterers regardless of where they committed adultery.[250] Similarly, he criticized the law for granting extenuating circumstances for husbands who murder their wives when they discover them in bed with another man while refusing to grant them to women in a similar situation, "although a woman feels the same anger upon discovering her husband's adultery, which may force her to avenge herself by murdering him."[251] Following al-Barr's prescriptions and those of other Islamists, the only way that such gaps in the law can be rectified, avers Mursi, is by "applying Islamic Shari'ah rulings."[252] As we will see, this will be key to achieving civilizational progress. Indeed the gaps that Mursi found

do not only relate to *zina* but extend to rape and attempted rape crimes, public exposure and disgraceful acts . . . for it is sufficient for us to state that there are many crimes of exhibitionism and sexual deviance that are not subject to criminalization [by Egyptian law], such as the practicing of sodomy, which has no prescribed punishment [in the law] as long as both partners practice it consensually and willingly. The legislator also has not criminalized bestiality or necrophilic practices unless they are related to other crimes, such as public exposure . . . We hope that such legislative gaps be rectified, as the cure is manifest, clear and easy, namely, the application of the noble shari'ah, which does not discriminate between men and women and includes a comprehensive unity of legislation and cure for the elimination of the germs and epidemics of sexual deviance and their burial in infancy and their elimination [*sic*] and the preservation of society, and the purification of souls from vice. In carrying this out, there will be elevation and progress for individuals and society alike.[253]

Issues of progress aside, other problems related to sodomy have to do with misconceptions that "poverty may be the direct cause." This proves inaccurate as "we have witnessed in many cases that opulence might be the reason for the commission of the crime and for delinquency, as the passive sodomite in many cases is well-to-do, which facilitates his spending money on his sexual practices and the facility with which he catches active sodomites. This does not mean that poverty is not related to the crime or to delinquency, rather that it is linked to it."[254]

Other causes include press coverage of criminals and deviants, including what the "press publishes about a world-famous singer who changes his facial features, and seeks to resemble women by bejeweling himself

250. Ibid., 335.
251. Ibid.
252. Ibid., 336

253. Ibid., 337.
254. Ibid., 362.

with gold and by applying makeup to his face, and [by publishing] accusations directed at him of raping a child; or, what the world press published about a famous tennis player who paid her female friend and partner in sexual delinquency (sapphism), three million dollars after she left her and replaced her with another, all of which gives the wrong impression about male and female delinquents."[255] Press publication of such stories also "presents some deviant delinquents as the elite of society and its role models, which is done unintentionally by publishing their news and news about their personal lives and financial fortunes, something that might influence children, the youth, and the illiterate [!] into thinking that this is the legitimate and quick way to wealth."[256]

In addition to the family unit, the state has an important role and mission to play in directing society away from such deviance and crimes. Mursi calls for the mobilizing of what Louis Althusser had dubbed the ideological state apparatus as well as the repressive state apparatus. Organs of the state that must be marshaled for the effort, according to Mursi, include schools, the media, cultural venues, the law[257] (as many Egyptian laws regarding adultery are derived from French law, and as Egyptian law does not include penalties for male or female "deviants," Mursi reiterates that Shari'ah would rectify the situation),[258] and the police. The surveillance ability of the police must be mobilized for the effort at hand: "We call upon the [police] to intensify their efforts to control the crimes of sexual deviance, such as sodomy and sapphism, despite the difficulty in catching them. However, policemen are able, through their capabilities and resources, to expose that type [of deviance] and to apprehend its practitioners. We foresee the launch of continuous consciousness-raising campaigns among those delinquents, as well as work to include the cases of sexual deviance under a unified statistical database instead of its being scattered [under different categories of crime], as we saw how

255. Ibid., 365–66.
256. Ibid., 366. Mursi is a strong feminist also when it comes to news coverage of sexual crimes. He assailed the press for publishing a story about an Egyptian young woman who was raped in a way that might incite people against the victim and in support of the rapist. The coverage showed the young woman "walking alone at a late hour of the night and that she was wearing immodest and revealing clothes that excite [sexual] instincts and other such descriptions of the circumstances [of the crime] and justifications which lead many to sympathize with the suspect and encourage others to commit similar crimes using similar justifications," ibid., 366. Having said that however does not mean that Mursi supports women wearing revealing clothes, as he insisted that the family, both mother and father, should exercise their "supervisory" role of not allowing their daughters to "go out wearing clothes that excite instincts and that the boy not be left with bad companions frequenting suspect places without supervision." Ibid., 375.
257. Ibid., 377–79.
258. Ibid., 379–81.

rape and attempted rape are crimes that are listed under the statistics of felonies and misdemeanors, while other crimes, such as public exposure and disgracing others are placed under a different statistical category."[259]

Mursi also called for the segregation of prisoners who committed crimes of sexual deviance from others so that they would not spread their crimes.[260] Police surveillance must also target the places where these deviants congregate, especially male deviants. Mursi enumerated many such places that must be subject to police surveillance, including public bathrooms.[261] Other places also include public baths in popular neighborhoods, public parks, five-star hotels, as well as popular-neighborhood restaurants and hotels, and at tourism and archeological sites.[262] Mursi's ideas about surveillance are not unlike what has been the practice of American police in targeting homosexuals, not only in the era before the rise of the gay movement and gay "liberation" but also after. Indeed as Mursi was making his recommendations for the Egyptian police, local police were entrapping gay men in public bathrooms in New York and other U.S. cities, a policy still in practice today.[263] Mursi finished his survey by presenting ten case studies of sex crimes, of which five were male sodomitic murders, one different-sex necrophilic rape, three adultery-related murders, and one rape and murder of a woman.[264] His calls to the police to apprehend deviants were not in vain, as the Cairo Queen Boat case and other minor ones were to prove a few years after his book came out. Indeed, it is surprising that no one saw the signs of the upcoming crackdown, as they could not have been broadcast any louder.

Deviance and "Islamic" Culture

The remaining area in which sexual debates were registered prominently had to do with popular books that invoke theological and medical implications of sexual deviance and the latter's influence on the cultural sphere. Islamist writers opted not to limit themselves to discussing Islam's views on sexuality in general and punishment of sodomy in particular, but also,

259. Ibid., 381.
260. Ibid., 382.
261. Ibid., 417.
262. Ibid., 272–73.
263. For a recent case of New York police entrapment of gay men at a public bathroom in 2004 for which they were sued, see Amnesty International, *United States of America Stonewalled: Police Abuse and Misconduct against Lesbian, Gay, Bisexual and Transgender People in the U.S.* (New York: Amnesty International, 2005), 38.
264. Mursi, *Al-Shudhudh al-Jinsi*, 410–70.

and following the secular nationalists, to write about "sexual deviance" in Arab history. Two such books appeared since 1999 to set the record— which is being corrupted by others—straight, al-Khatib al-ʿAdnani's *Adultery/Fornication* [Zina] *and Deviance in Arab History*, and Muntasir Mazhar's *The Forbidden Pleasure: Sodomy and Sapphism in Arab History*.[265] The cross-referencing of Islamist medical and jurisprudential books on the subject of sexual practices is readily apparent throughout. The persistent influence of Muhammad ʿAli al-Barr on Islamist writers is most apparent in al-Khatib al-ʿAdnani's book, which is peppered throughout with quotes from al-Barr. Al-ʿAdnani began with an overview of Islam's views of adultery, fornication, prostitution, and incest, and offered an extensive list of quotations attributed to the Prophet Muhammad, which he interpreted as predicting mortal diseases to those who commit such acts.[266] Al-ʿAdnani also provided examples from pre-Islamic and Islamic Arab history of closeted and open female prostitutes known to the public, and then discussed worldly and divine punishment that are meted out to sinners.[267] Lest this be taken as declaring open season on adulterers (including prostitutes), al-ʿAdnani was careful to warn against false accusations and defamation, listing the conditions for rightful accusation and reminding readers that harsh religious punishment is meted out to false accusers.[268] Al-ʿAdnani, citing al-Barr's views and echoing many others, expressed similar civilizational concerns and warned that the spread of adultery, fornication, and sodomy accounted for the fall of the Greeks, the Romans, and the Persians in the past.[269]

Al-ʿAdnani engaged existing literature on the topic. He cited, for example, al-Munajjid's claim that the reason for the spread of sodomy in the medieval Arab world was "the abundance of concubines."[270] He did not neglect to add, as nationalists and Orientalists had done before him, that "Arabized Persians had a big influence in the spread of sodomy and the love of boys in Arab countries, as the most famous sodomites in the Abbasid period were of Persian origins, especially the poets and ʿulamaʾ among them, such as Walibah bin al-Hubab, who corrupted Abu Nuwas and others, and Abu Nuwas himself, who corrupted numerous youthful

---

265. See Al-Khatib al-ʿAdnani, *Al-Zina wa al-Shudhudh fi al-Tarikh al-ʿArabi* [Adultery/Fornication and Deviance in Arab History] (Beirut: Muʾassassat al-Intishar al-ʿArabi, 1999); and Muntasir Mazhar, *Al-Mutʿah al-Muharramah, al-Liwat wa al-Suhaq fi al-Tarikh al-ʿArabi* [Prohibited Pleasure: Sodomy and Sapphism in Arab History] (Al-Dar al-ʿAlamiyyah lil-Kutub wa al-Nashr, n.p., 2001).
266. Al-ʿAdnani, *Al-Zina wa al-Shudhudh*, 25–34.
267. Ibid., 35–78.
268. Ibid., 81–101.
269. Ibid., 9.
270. Ibid., 108.

boys."[271] As for the kind of youthful boys that Arab men preferred, al-ʿAdnani provided meticulous details: "They preferred the slender youthful boy who has an upright posture, is soft-spoken, and is a superbeautiful adolescent with clear dark complexion containing a marvelous blush with large deep black eyes, rosy cheeks, a dazzling waist, clean teeth, combed locks, one who pulls his posterior back and forth, and shakes his sides."[272]

Al-ʿAdnani devoted a section to the epidemics and harms that sodomy causes. His concerns were not only confined to issues of civilizational decline but also to human extinction itself. He informs us that "sexual deviance is the biggest social deformation and epidemic, which leads to stopping human reproduction in the sense of its extermination and disfigurement and the robbery of its characteristics and abilities in both the doer/subject [faʿil] and the do-ee/object [mafʿul bihi]" of the act.[273] In addition to venereal diseases and epidemics, which affect both doer and do-ee, "femininity in males is harmful to health, as the do-ee/object continues to shuttle from one ailment to the next and from one dangerous disease to a more dangerous one . . . it harms mental abilities, moral traits and human characteristics."[274] He proceeded to provide a brief overview of Islam's indictment of male desires for other males and then moved to give a medical account of the causes of the disease of *ubnah* and argued that seminal fluid deposited in the anus produces infections that lead to an itch that requires penetration to alleviate it. The infection, however, can spread to the penis of the penetrator and then to his anus, rendering him also a passive homosexual.

If medical reasons do not convince penetrators that they risk becoming the penetrated themselves, al-ʿAdnani marshaled a saying attributed to the Prophet that states that "he who insists on mounting men will call on men [to mount him] before he dies."[275] It is unclear, however if the desire to mount men or for men to be mounted (at least for the first time prior to seminal fluid being deposited in their anuses) is natural or a result of low morals or rape. Indeed, al-ʿAdnani tells us that *ubnah* could occur naturally as a result of "sexual weakness," as does sapphism in females.[276]

As a physiological disease, *ubnah* has some unwanted social implications. Al-ʿAdnani asserts that "the disease of *ubnah* is more dangerous to those afflicted with it—in terms of the vileness, baseness, and contempt

271. Ibid., 108.
272. Ibid., 108.
273. Ibid., 110.

274. Ibid., 111.
275. Ibid., 111.
276. Ibid., 118–26.

it brings them—than all other anus-related diseases, like hemorrhoids, warts, and Vercularis Enterobis, as the latter diseases can be taken care of when seen by a physician and do not occasion humiliation or shame, which *ubnah* brings upon those who are afflicted with it."[277] Clearly aware of Western gay arguments that homosexuality is not a "choice," al-ʿAdnani has answers to offer. Lest someone claim *ubnah* as a disease that requires penetration for alleviation, al-ʿAdnani remains vigilant throughout:

Perhaps someone would say that if *ubnah* is a disease with which God afflicts those among his creation who have erred, then how would He have the right to torment those afflicted on Judgment Day. Such a person is clearly forced to do it [*sic*], and in cases of coercion, responsibility cannot be upheld . . . the answer is that the affliction of *ubnah* is not coercive such as fever or Jaundice, thus escaping responsibility and willfulness and rendering punishment not applicable to it. Rather, the maʾbun is the one who sought being afflicted with it and was led to it by his surrendering to those scoundrels [shuttar] to do abomination to him. It is more like a cancer that was caused by smoking or having a heart attack as a result of taking drugs.[278]

Moreover, unlike al-Razi, who only thought certain measures had a chance under certain conditions to cure *ubnah*, al-ʿAdnani's modern knowledge affirms that *ubnah* is not an incurable disease, but rather "is one of the easiest diseases to treat and the closest to a cure." He cited a few medieval cures, basing themselves on Hippocrates, and on a modern reference from 1925, including a dietary regimen, and certain herbs and oils that can be combined and wrapped around a stick and then "inserted in the anus where [the afflicted man] rubs against it momentarily and waits" until it kills the germs.[279]

Al-ʿAdnani was also concerned about the permissiveness of sodomy in Muslim history, especially with regards to a number of ʿulamaʾ (theologians) across the ages who regarded it as permissible under Islam. After presenting the fundamentalist Islamic position of prohibition of sodomy, he proceeded to review its history of permissiveness. Examples include the linguist ʿUbayda bin al-Muthanna, the judge Yahya bin Aktham, and ʿAbd al-Samad bin al-Muʿadhdhal, the tutor of the Umayyad caliphs. Casuistry on the part of these thinkers included (mis)interpretations, pace al-ʿAdnani, of the Qurʾanic verse "in people exist desires for women and boys [banin]" (admittedly, the word "banin," means boys as well as

277. Ibid., 126.
278. Ibid., 126.

279. Ibid., 127–28.

sons, children, or progeny, thus "people" have desires for "women and progeny" would be the conventional meaning). Other verses include one that refers to Heaven where "immortal boys will serve them. If you saw them you would say they are scattered pearls." Al-ʿAdnani had little patience with such "falsification, deception, and distortion . . . [misread] by scoundrels [shuttar] and deviants."[280] A most horrid misinterpretation is that of bin Aktham who protested to the imam Abi al-Hasan al-Hadi about the permissibility of sleeping with youthful boys by citing the Qurʾanic verse: "He will marry them to males and females." Al-ʿAdnani marveled at how God would have permitted this when he had cursed a whole nation, namely, the People of Lot, for such abomination: "what is meant by the verse is that God grants progeny and descendents 'females to those who want them, and males to those who want them, or He would pair them up' meaning that He would give to whomever of His worshippers progeny comprising both pairs males and females." The confusion related to the verb "zawwaja," which means to marry or to pair up.[281] In addition to Yahya bin Aktham, who received the lion's share of al-ʿAdnani's condemnation, there is the judge Shams al-Din ibn Khallikan, the poet Abu Nuwas, and seventeen others whose "infatuation with youthful boys" is explored.[282]

Al-ʿAdnani's historical overview reaches the present where he responded to the Gay International: "There are today groups who like this abomination (sodomy) and celebrate it, preferring coitus with youthful boys to coitus with women, supporting it and fighting those who prohibit and punish it, such as Dr. Laus Alerstam, the author of a book titled *Sexual Deviants (Al-Shadhdhun Jinsiyyan)* and another doctor who remained anonymous in his book *The Third Sex,* which he attributed to major scientists and physicians in Europe and America when it was all falsification and distortion aiming to popularize this abomination so that AIDS and other venereal diseases would spread."[283] Al-ʿAdnani would up the ante on Islamic prohibitions. He contended that Islam not only prohibited sodomy but also the incitement to practice it. This included, according to him, Islam's prohibition to look desirously at youthful boys, a boy sitting on a man's lap, embracing him or kissing him, as well as "Islam's" alleged prohibition for two men to sleep under the same blanket.[284]

It is not only the Western gay movement that is seen as an extension

---

280. Ibid., 135–36.
281. Ibid., 136.
282. Ibid., 137–52.

283. Ibid., 153.
284. Ibid., 153–57.

of the sins of the People of Lot, but, consistent with al-Barr, even AIDS proves to be an old disease. Al-ʿAdnani wrote that

the first appearance of AIDS was among the people of Lot and after that in Pharonic Egypt. It was also known during the Napoleonic campaign in Egypt . . . Early Muslims also discovered it and called it "the snake of adultery/fornication" and some physicians called it "the red fever." During the Napoleonic campaign in Egypt, he [Napoleon] tried to conquer Acre and amassed his troops by its walls and stayed for a long period during which they were overcome with lust and began to mount one another. As a result of this deviance and perversion among them, thousands contracted a disease that they called the "plague" although it was only AIDS. While the plague had a cure at the time, they tried to cure AIDS [in the same way] but failed. This is why Napoleon amassed those soldiers afflicted with AIDS in a stable and promised them that the physicians would be coming to cure them. When night fell, however, he lit a fire that burned them so as to avoid the spread of the disease and to prevent contagion.[285]

Al-ʿAdnani's coupling of AIDS with the plague was hardly original. He was invoking the authority of al-Barr's work on the subject. Like the latter, he also gave his interpretation of what the Islamic legal punishment was for those who practiced sodomy as well as the divine punishment awaiting them in the afterlife.[286]

Al-ʿAdnani's book was soon followed by another one of a similar caliber. Muntasir Mazhar's book is the first of its kind from an Islamist perspective that concentrates exclusively on sodomy and sapphism in Arab history rather than discuss them alongside adultery and other sexual prohibitions, as al-ʿAdnani had done. Mazhar quoted al-Munajjid's explanation for the "proliferation" of sodomy among Arabs, namely, "the abundance of concubines which caused men to be indisposed to them and to desire youthful boys."[287] His book simply reproduces earlier opinions, including al-Munajjid's, with little originality. Indeed he cop-

285. Ibid., 162–63.
286. Al-ʿAdnani's research was not concerned only with anal sex among men but also between men and women. He devoted a chapter about what he considered to be the Islamic prohibition on anal sex with women within marriage, as only vaginal coitus is considered legitimate. He also devoted a chapter to sapphism or what he called "the third sex," and provided a brief history of sapphism among the ancient and medieval Arabs, listing the diseases that result from this practice. They include the widening of the gap between the buttocks, sores, cancers, and anal pain, among others. It is not clear if this means that sapphism includes anal sex or not. He also provided environmental and hormonal causes for sapphism, which like in the case of sodomy, do not mitigate the effect of this abomination. Al-ʿAdnani listed the same punishments for women practicing sapphism as for men practicing sodomy. See ibid., 189–202.
287. Mazhar, Al-Mutʿah al-Muharramah, 62–63.

ied verbatim from Al-ʿAdnani, cannibalizing his book mostly without proper attribution.[288] He also cited Ahmad Amin on the Afghan and Khurasan origins of sodomy in the Abbasid period.[289]

Mazhar, who reviewed Islamic regulations punishing sodomy, whether with divine damnation or with stories of execution that some caliphs are said to have carried out in the first years of the Islamic state, regretted that such strict measures were relaxed soon afterward, which allowed for the existence of these practices among Muslims.[290] He pointed out that books and authors who speak of sodomy as having been widespread in these eras are mistaken, as the medieval books simply point to its "existence" and not to it being "widespread."[291] Mazhar even questioned the poems attributed to Abu Nuwas that speak of sodomy as a common practice, and he claimed that Jamal Jumʿah's account about Abu Nuwas was inaccurate, insisting that Jumʿah's account was taken from suspect sources that are not verifiable.[292] He further claimed that the so-called "prohibited poems" that Jumʿah edited and attributed to Abu Nuwas were "fabrications" and that a party who is

interested in disgracing our cultural heritage with deviance [was the one who] composed these lowly poems . . . [Such a party] is appalled that Arabs would hold on to their glorious past that Islam founded . . . they wanted to level this accusation of debauched deviance against our Arab nation so that we would be peeled off from our past and so that our past would not be looked at with respect. This would in turn facilitate their cultural attack on us and then we would follow them voluntarily.

Mazhar then provided a different biographical account of Abu Nuwas's life: he is said to have been imprisoned for drinking alcohol and was set free upon declaring his innocence. Mazhar wondered whether a system that jailed those who drank alcohol would not imprison Abu Nuwas for a much graver sexual offence. The fact that Abu Nuwas was never jailed for such an offence meant that many of the stories about his sexual life are Orientalist fabrications and thus untrue.[293] Mazhar did not seem to

288. Ibid., 64. For example, he reproduced the following statement verbatim from al-ʿAdnani without quotation marks or references: "Arabized Persians in Arab countries had the greatest influence on the spreading of sodomy and the love of youthful boys, which is why the most famous of sodomites [liwatiyyin] in the Abbasid period were of Persian origins, especially the poets and the ʿulamaʾ, such as Walibah bin al-Hubab, who corrupted Abu Nuwas, and Abu Nuwas, who corrupted an untold number of youthful boys." See al-ʿAdnani's original sentence in al-ʿAdnani, Al-Zina wa al-Shudhudh, 108.
289. Mazhar, Al-Mutʿh al-Muharramah, 117.
290. Ibid., 67.
291. Ibid., 68.
292. Ibid., 69–74.
293. Ibid., 76–79.

be familiar with arguments provided by the other authors we discussed, namely, that Abu Nuwas's practices hardly deviated from those of caliphs and other elite members of society, which was precisely the reason why he was never prosecuted for them. After discussing the views of monotheistic religions on sodomy, including Islam's, Mazhar railed against those who opposed capital punishment, as he viewed it as the best deterrent against the spreading of male and female sexual deviance, whose implementation would "extinguish this dirty habit."[294]

It is important to point out that the same year that Mazhar published his book, a project of publishing the collected poetry of Abu Nuwas was banned by the Egyptian Ministry of Culture. The four volumes of collected poems were going to be part of the series edited by Egyptian novelist Jamal al-Ghitani titled Al-Dhakha'ir, or Treasures, which reissued classics of Arabic culture. The series was published by the General Organization of the Cultural Palaces, which is an office of the Ministry of Culture that banned the book.[295]

Mazhar is up-to-date on Western celebrities who are lesbians and are out about their sexual orientation: "Although sapphism as a habit is disgusting to the balanced and healthy human spirit, we still find many women in the modern era who have fallen in this quagmire, and some of them possess . . . outstanding beauty, but despite this they came to practice sapphism in a public and unveiled way without being overcome with bashfulness, and have even become 'recruiters' for sapphism in our contemporary world." Examples include the tennis champion Martina Navratilova, "the queen of the female deviants," Brooke Shields, who "admitted" to lesbian encounters, and an unnamed Egyptian singer who was said to have been caught by the police having sex with another man. It is noteworthy that Mazhar was protective of the Egyptian singer's identity.[296] Other cases cited by Mazhar include a case of a murdered Egyptian ship captain as well as the case of designer Gianni Versace. The case of the famed Egyptian male-to-female transsexual, Sally (previously Sayyid), was also cited as well as an interview with her, where "she was asked about her favorite female star: he [sic] named the actress Samah Anwar. Then the newspaper [journalist] asked him, 'Who is your favorite male star?' he also answered Samah Anwar."[297] Mazhar immediately added that he was "not leveling any accusations against the actress Samah

294. Ibid., 109.
295. See the interview with Jamal al-Ghitani by Youssef Rakha in "The Crux of the Matter," Al-Ahram Weekly, 18–24 January 2001.
296. Ibid., 155–63.
297. Ibid., 176.

Anwar, but things have to be said [as they are]."[298] He also listed Egyptian films that dealt with lesbian affairs and male homosexual relations.[299]

Mazhar admonished the Egyptian state for not having laws that criminalized homosexuality, which is what happens to countries "that follow secularism and veer away from religiosity, although this dangerous epidemic [i.e., deviance] is far from natural human conduct."[300] He, uncharacteristically, was more horrified at lesbianism than at male homosexuality, which is exceptional in this literature. Indeed, he provided a medical description of how lesbians were different physiologically and psychologically from heterosexual women. Although the environment could have prevented the full-blown development of lesbianism (and male homosexuality), lesbians are said to lack maternal instincts, are controlling of their husbands, and like to emulate men. They also have thick skin that is conducive to acne, are susceptible to balding, are muscular and self-confident. They are aggressive and have an "active sexual instinct" [i.e., they like to penetrate other women], and dislike housework. He even cited phrenological markings on the heads of sapphists that can distinguish them.[301]

Responding to UN and other international conferences that uphold the agenda of the Gay International, Mazhar affirmed in conclusion that "as long as laws continue to be legislated in the interest of the deviants, and as long as whoring ['ahirah] conferences are convened under hollow titles like 'the rights of humans to their own bodies,' and like the population conferences that call for 'the destruction of the family order' and following 'the desires of the genitals'; and as long as satellite channels continue to broadcast their deviant poisons, and people remain silent in the face of all that, then [AIDS] will be the divine punishment."[302] Mazhar's book aimed to "put a limit to sexual deviance in all its forms, representations, and dimensions."[303] The concern again is not only civilizational but universal: "This book is a loud scream, if it found who would heed it, calling for the contribution [of people] and their effective cooperation in rescuing 'the boat of humanity,' which is about to sink."[304]

Identities or Practices?

While modern Arab intellectuals ushered in their debate about desire and sexual practices through exploring its literary and historical heri-

298. Ibid., 176.
299. Ibid., 176–79.
300. Ibid., 183–86.
301. Ibid., 186–87.

302. Ibid., 191.
303. Ibid., 198.
304. Ibid., 198.

tage from the seventh century onward, the nature of the debates and the very representation of desires changed as a result of a number of factors including positing such a heritage as a form of sexually liberating pedagogy to benefit present and future generations of Arabs, the emergence of new forms of identity politics in which local and international actors participated, and the explosion of the AIDS pandemic.

A puritanical Islamism (and secular conservatism, at times) borrowing most of its puritanism from Western Christianity and Western conservatism built up an unwitting alliance with the crusading Gay International in identifying people who practice certain forms of sex. The Gay International and the Islamists agreed that such practitioners must be identified. Where they disagreed was on whether they should be identified and endowed with rights and accorded the protection of the state, as the Gay International demands, or identified, repressed, and subjected to the punishment of the state, as the Islamists and other conservatives demand. In the history of Western homosexuality, as Michel Foucault noted, the discourses of power that produced and controlled "homosexuality" made "possible the formation of a 'reverse' discourse: homosexuality began to speak in its own behalf, to demand that its legitimacy or 'naturality' be acknowledged, often in the same vocabulary, using the same categories by which it was medically disqualified."[305] As we saw in this chapter, a similar operation was repeated in the Arab world when Islamists adopted the very same vocabulary and classifications of the Gay International to disqualify the very same gayness that the Gay International had been trying to legitimize. Making the state the arena where sexual practices are transformed into identities was indeed the novelty that the last two decades have fostered. In a context where the state has been the enforcer of repression of society at large, the Islamist call is consistent with such a role. What is ironic is that the state would be called upon by the Gay International, which is seeking liberation from repression but who claim it as the liberating organ.

It is in such a context that the London-based Arabic newspaper Al-Quds al-'Arabi reported that the U.S.-based anti-Arab British Iraqi writer Kanan Makiya, who consulted with the U.S. government in its plans to invade Iraq, demanded that the post-"liberation" Iraqi constitution must be "civilized like European constitutions" and that it must protect "human rights including the rights of homosexuals."[306] As he reportedly

305. Foucault, *The History of Sexuality*, vol. 1, 100.
306. "Mulasanat Athar Mutalabah bi-Huquq lil-Shawadh fi Dustur al-'Iraq al-Jadid" [Verbal Sparring Resulting from Demands for the Rights of Deviants in the New Iraqi Constitution], *Al-Quds al-'Arabi*, London, 18 December 2002, 1.

expressed such views at a U.S.-sponsored meeting of the Iraqi opposition groups in London, the reaction of these groups was swift. Islamist and tribal leaders were in the forefront of those who demanded that Makiya be expelled from the meeting.[307] Makiya insisted that he made no such demands at the reported meeting and that the reported story was not true (although he did not deny that he might have made such demands at other meetings of the opposition). I should note here that nobody had suggested that the new Iraqi constitution (any more than the one existing under Saddam Hussein) should condemn or criminalize homosexuality. At any rate, Makiya's denial led the newspaper to apologize to him and repudiate the story.[308] Yet others were not convinced. Prominent secular exile Iraqi poet Sa'di Yusuf cited Makiya's complete estrangement from Iraqi society and his immersion in U.S. society as the reason for his (alleged) fantastical demands that homosexuals be granted rights in post-Saddam Iraq. In a satirical column titled "Ayatullah Kan'an Makiyyah," commenting on Makiya's visit to the U.S.-occupied Iraqi city of Nasiriyah in April 2003, where Makiya suffered from lack of recognition by city residents, Yusuf had the following to say:

The calamity that afflicted Ayatullah Kan'an Makiyyah was that people in Nasiriyah did not respond to his call on behalf of the half-sodomites. I believe that the reason was that the number of women in the lands of Iraq is more than that of men, as all the wars have eliminated generation after generation [of men]. But the ayatollah would not have known this, as he has been constantly trekking between Washington and Tel Aviv. So, how would he know what was new in the [Iraqi] social structure? The man must be excused, as perhaps he imagined Nasiriyah to be close to [London's] Soho [neighborhood]![309]

It is unclear if these rumors about Makiya's alleged demands, whether true or not, had much to do with later developments. However, the renaming of the famed Abu Nuwas street in Baghdad in June 2003, three months after the U.S. invasion and occupation of the city, is perhaps a reaction to such rumors. It was initially reported that the street would be renamed "Imam al-Mahdi" Street by the new Islamist forces, released by the U.S. occupation authorities.[310] Abu Nuwas Street, which carried its

---

307. Ibid.

308. "Tawdih 'an Khabar Yakhuss Kan 'an Makiyyah" [A Clarification about a News Item Relating to Kanan Makiya], *Al-Quds al-'Arabi* (London), 28–29 December 2002, 3.

309. Sa'di Yusuf, "Ayatullah . . . Kan'an Makiyyah," *Al-Quds al-'Arabi* (London), 28 April 2003, 13.

310. "Baghdad Tughayyir Asma' Shawari'iha ba'da Shahrayn 'ala Itahat Saddam" [Baghdad Changes the Names of Its Streets Two Months after the Overthrow of Saddam), *Al-Hayah*, 11 June 2003, 2.

1 The statue of Abu Nuwas in Baghdad under American occupation and inaccessible to Iraqis.

name long before Saddam came to power and lies on the Tigris River in the heart of Baghdad, is famous for its bars and features a bronze statue of the great poet holding a wine glass made by renowned Iraqi artist Isma'il Fattah in 1972.[311] Its renaming after the awaited Shi'ite imam, al-Mahdi, who is yet to come to save the believers, indicates that only someone of the virtuous magnitude of the Mahdi could counteract the corrupting effects of Abu Nuwas and those seen as his modern followers. Soon, however, the new rulers of the streets of Baghdad realized that it would not be sufficient to name a street full of bars after the awaited imam of Shi'ism. Something even more potent was required. The street was then renamed the "Safinat al-Najah" Street, the "Rescue Boat" Street, or more literally the "Boat of Salvation" street.[312] "Safinat al-Najah" in fact is an expression that refers to the family of the Prophet Muhammad, all of whose members seem to be called upon to undo the vice of Abu Nuwas Street. Whether from Saddam or from sin, salvation was the operative theme of the renaming. It may not be long before the Gay International declares the renaming of the street as "homophobic oppression" and a

311. Palestinian novelist, art critic, and scholar of Iraqi art Jabra Ibrahim Jabra described the statue as resembling "a Gothic Christ." See Jabra I. Jabra, *The Grass Roots of Iraqi Art* (St. Helier: Wasit Graphic and Pub., 1983), 74.

312. "Shari' 'Arafat yatahawwal Shari' al-Mahdi wa Abu Nuwas Safinat al-Najah: Tabdil al-Asma' fi Baghdad Yuthir Makhawif min Hasasiyyat Ta'ifiyyah" [Arafat Street Becomes al-Mahdi Street and Abu Nuwas (Becomes) Safinat al-Najah: The Changing of Names in Baghdad Provokes Fear of Sectarian Sensitivities), *Al-Hayah*, 4 August 2003, 3.

sign of backwardness and before the Islamists demand the destruction of the statue of Abu Nuwas as a sign of "liberation" from debauchery and a step on the way to progress. Meanwhile, the street has been dying a slow death, as it has become part of the new security zone patrolled day and night by the U.S. occupation army, referred to as the "Green Zone."[313]

313. "Sayf Akhar Yazur Baghdad wa Shari' Abi Nuwas bila Ruwwad!" [Another Summer Visits Baghdad While Abu Nuwas Street Remains without Visitors!], *Al-Hayah*, 29 March 2005.

FIVE

Deviant Fictions

The central genre that represents modern and contemporary sexual practices is fiction, especially the novel. The novel form in Arabic, as in other languages, lends itself to function as a reading (and writing) of society that is most unintrusive in comparison with other genres of writing and investigation—sociological, psychological, criminological, medical, or anthropological—that claim to extract the "truth" and "nature" of experience. The early manifestations of the Arabic novel emerged in the late nineteenth century, but it did not constitute a genre as such until the twentieth century, and even then only established itself as a serious aesthetic form in midcentury. The most prominent among Arabic novelists, Nobel Laureate Naguib Mahfouz, was perhaps the best social and cultural historian of Egypt in the twentieth century. He has been joined by a number of first-class novelists writing in myriad styles who emerged on the scene since the 1950s. Among those are a number of innovative women novelists. While feminist writing (by men and women) goes back to the nineteenth century, a new wave of feminist novels written by women was inaugurated in the 1950s with authors like Lebanese Layla Baʿlabaki, and Syrian Colette Khuri, whose first novels rocked the literary establishment. Mahfouz himself engaged in much self-renewal, revolutionizing his own style every decade or so and raising the bar of his art higher each time.

The novel form is significant both in the type of labor it performs for social analysis and in its deployment of sexual allegories while representing social (and sexual) histories to address complex socioeconomic and political processes.

Short stories and plays also perform a similar function, albeit with certain limitations dictated by their genre. While deviant sex and homosexuality more specifically appear often in novels, short stories, and drama, they are not always represented in the same way or for the same purposes. Indeed, in most cases, they are used as sideshows or as enriching detail and not as social and national allegories. In this chapter and the next, I explore the history of such representations in Arabic novels, a number of short stories, and one play of the last half century precisely to show the wealth of styles and the complexity of representations that Arab novelists, short story writers, and playwrights have used in dealing with their societies. I explore how sexual desires and acts—especially of the nonnormative variety, which until the late 1960s, for the most part and with notable exceptions, added depth and detail to narrative—have been transformed into a quintessential social allegory to represent the state of society in the 1990s and beyond. Reading literature will help us to understand the processes through which subject formation occurs, particularly the subjective elements of subject formation.

I have elected to look closely in this chapter at five novels, a novella, and two short stories, as their engagement with desires deemed deviant is crucial to our topic, and more generally at a number of other novels and short stories that deploy related sexual allegories and narrate social and sexual histories. My readings are not meant to reduce these novels to their sexual representations. I aim to offer *specific* rather than limiting or reductivist readings of these novels, focusing on the sexual question, the concern of this book. Beginning with Naguib Mahfouz's *Midaq Alley* and Ra'if Khuri's *Dik Al-Jinn, The Devouring Love* (*Dik al-Jinn, Al-Hubb al-Muftaris*), both published in the late 1940s, and which will be discussed at length, I will briefly discuss other works of fiction published in the 1950s, 1960s, and 1970s, including, among others, Yusuf Idris's *The Black Cop* and Sunʿallah Ibrahim's *That Odor*. I will then move to Ismaʿil Waliy al-Din's *The Malatili Bathhouse,* Muhammad Shukri's *Plain Bread,* Jamal al-Ghitani's *The Events of Zaʿfarani Street,* Ghadah al-Samman's *Beirut '75,* and Yusuf Idris's novella *The Manliest of Men*. These works have had a considerable literary impact, perhaps on account of the remarkable ways in which they deployed and represented questions of desire and sex. In selecting these texts for discussion, I am of course ignoring a huge literary corpus that deals with matters of sexual desire. Every Arabic novel, short story, or play (indeed every novel, short story, or play) is steeped in questions of desire. Thus, it is not that I have only chosen these works because they address questions of desire (which they do in most interesting ways), but rather because they narrate social histories of desire and/or posit sexual desires and practices as a general socio-political allegory, which I believe represents a certain overall vision of how matters sexual are discussed and represented and additionally how the economy and society are allegorically posited in sexual terms. My readings of these literary works differ markedly from the critical reception they have received by literary critics. That previous readings have ignored the question of normative and deviant sexual desires as the organizing allegorical principle of these literary texts is itself a symptom of the epistemological complicity of the critics. In reading these texts in a way that addresses representations of same-sex desires, practices, deviance, and normativity as thoroughly central to what is being allegorized, I am insisting that they are nothing short of literary attempts to produce and repress, not merely to represent, the modern Arab subject.

I will make reference to other writings in the course of the discussion but will limit my analysis to these books whose representations will clarify much of what is at stake in the sexual debates in the Arab world of the post–World War II era, which closely coincides with the end of the colonial era and the beginning of the postcolonial age. Reading these writings will be most useful for our analysis in ways that laws, police reports, official histories, school textbooks, private letters, scholarly publications—the usual archive of the social and intellectual historian—are not. Fiction functions differently from laws and police reports, not only in terms of genre and form but also in terms of its impact on society. This is so, as the relation between the literary text and the historical context is not marred by direct reproduction and truth claims, and the authority that the fiction writer exercises is one over representation and not over people. Moreover, even were fiction to be imagined as a pedagogical tool, it is not one that is systematized through educational institutions, as are textbooks and scholarly publications. While the audience of a work of fiction is clearly not necessarily the audience of police reports (often inaccessible to the public) or of laws (often read by those who work within the judicial and legislative system and not by the public at large), it is a more general audience that need not be part of a scholarly community and whose only prerequisite is literacy. In the Arab world of the middle twentieth century, such a prerequisite excluded the majority of the population on account of illiteracy, while in the late twentieth century it did not (even though significant parts of the populations of some Arab countries remain illiterate). The sad reality remains, however, that even the literate elites remain illiterate where literary texts are concerned. The *direct* impact of novels and short stories in the contemporary Arab world is minimal outside intellectual circles, if compared to drama, television, and cinema. Their larger impact has been, however, in being turned into films and television serials (which has happened to many of the central novels of Mahfouz, to name the more prominent of novelists) that popularized them and their representations. Still, the ideas and representations that emerge in fictional writing generally reflect journalistic and political debates (just as much as television and cinema do) and indeed exercise considerable influence on these media. Rather than being a significant institutional player in the direct interpellation of subjects at the popular level, literature produces and represses subjects at an elite level that then proliferates, through its influence on other popular media forms, to a popular level. We will see here and in chapter 6 the strong lines connecting the fictional world with the nonfictional world that has been our concern so far.

There is also a central advantage to reading the novel, the short story, and the play, as they, being fictional accounts by definition, have more leeway in their modes of representation and their use of allegories than history books or police reports (the majority of which remain unavailable to researchers) or television or cinema, which remain more heavily censored. The kind of censorship exercised over writings with truth claims and over the visual entertainment industry do not operate in the same way on fiction, even though it faces its share of censorship. In this sense, fictional writing provides accounts of society that no other mode of representation has been able to provide during the colonial or postcolonial era. Its representations however should not be viewed only as reflections of what actually exists necessarily (although they are certainly that often), as much as critiques of what exists *and* of what does not exist. It is how the world of the novel, the short story, or the play is imagined and the uses to which desire and sexual practices are put in such writings that reveal more about reigning ideas in society than they do about the actual reality they purport to depict.

Thus, while in previous chapters, we explored academic, journalistic, popular, theological, medical, and criminological writings, none of them attempted to represent how desire, deviant or normative, is *lived* in contemporary Arab societies. Herein lies the importance of fiction for our analysis.

Deviant Desires

The first work of modern Arabic fiction to deal with the question of same-sex desire seriously is Naguib Mahfouz's *Zuqaq al-Midaq* (Midaq

Alley).[1] Published in 1947, *Midaq Alley* is one of the Egyptian novelist's earlier novels. Set in the early 1940s, while Egypt remained under British colonial rule and the confrontation between the Axis and the Allied powers was approaching at El-Alamein, the novel, a tragicomedy of sorts written in realist style, opens with a romantic rendition of the history of Midaq Alley:

It is a wonder of epochs past. It soared one day in the history of Cairo like a flashing star. Which Cairo, do I mean? That of the Fatimids, the Mamluks, or the Sultans? Only God and the archeologists know the answer to that, but at any rate, it is a relic, and a precious one at that. How could it be otherwise when its cobblestone road leads directly into Sanadiqiyyah Street? That historic cul-de-sac, and its famous café, known as Kirshah's Café . . . Although this alley lives in virtual isolation from what surrounds it, it still clamors with its own distinctive life, one that is connected in its depths to the roots of life as a whole while still preserving a good amount of the secrets of a world gone by.[2]

The novel tells of the transformation that the alley would undergo with the encroachment of colonial modernity, which had already enveloped much of Cairo over the previous century, but to which the alley had somehow remained immune.

As we will see, the change will not be only felt at the technological, economic, and political levels, but also at a deep social and ultimately epistemological level. The entry of Western epistemology is signaled in the novel by the appearance of certain words and concepts in English. It is in this realm that the opening scene in which a folk poet, who for the previous twenty years had worked at Kirshah's Café, playing the rababah (a one-string instrument played with a bow) and reciting folktales of olden days, was dismissed from his job by a popular demand among customers to be replaced by the radio. The Sufi ascetic Shaykh Darwish explains the

---

1. Mahfouz had indeed made a passing reference in an earlier novel, *Al-Qahirah al-Jadidah*, to a character who declares nonchalantly his desire for male youths and women simultaneously. The character, Salim al-Ikhshidi, who has a high position in government and is an old neighbor of the protagonist Mahjub, tells the latter, who sought him out for a job, and in an indication of his refusal to help that "you are not a hairless young man nor is your mother a charming coquette, so what am I to do?" in Najib Mahfuz, *Al-Qahirah Al-Jadidah* [The New Cairo] (1945; Cairo: Maktabat Misr, 1965), 86. In a reference to the frustrated sexual desire of Mahjub, who wonders about one blond Professor Irving, who teaches Latin at the university, and Miss Duriyyah, "the fat" and awkward young student: "Would it not have been fairer had he been created female and that Miss Duriyyah been created male?!" in ibid., 51.
2. Najib Mahfuz, *Zuqaq al-Midaq* [Midaq Alley] (1947; Cairo: Maktabat Misr, 1989?), 5. The novel is available in English as *Midaq Alley*, translated by Trevor Le Gassick (London: Heinemann Educational, 1975).

transformation: "Yes, everything has changed . . . the poet has gone and the radio has come. This is the way of God in his Creation. It was mentioned in ancient days in *tarikh* [history], which they call in English 'History' and is spelled 'H-i-s-t-o-r-y.'"[3] Presumably, the invocation of "History" as an "ancient" European concept is ironical in this context, given Mahfouz's enumeration of different historical periods through which Cairo passed long before Europe or the English language itself existed.

Shaykh Darwish had been an English teacher at one of the religiously endowed schools. He, like other employees, was let go when this traditional school system was placed under the control of the modern Ministry of Education, which required higher qualifications. He took up a job as a clerk in the Ministry of Religious Endowments with a lower salary, which made him so unhappy that he became notorious as the most stubborn complainer in the Ministry. News of his bad disposition reached his superiors who, though sympathetic, docked his pay a day or two. "One day he decided to write all his official correspondence in English, and would say that he was a technical employee, unlike other clerks." About to be fired, he requested to meet with the deputy minister and informed him that "God had chosen his man,"[4] referring to himself. He deserted his family and friends and began to roam the streets, wondering into "the world of God, as he calls it." He lost all his money and his house but seemed completely at peace. Everybody became his family. "If his gown wore out, someone would get him another one; if his necktie got torn, he would receive a new one too."[5] Shaykh Darwish, as he came to be known following Sufi tradition, was loved and considered blessed. "People feel that he brings them good luck and they say of him that he is a holy man of God who received Godly revelation in both Arabic and English."[6] It is noteworthy that while the march of the colonial modern state had already had its imprint on Darwish, wherein he taught English, a language that was not taught previously, the further entrenchment of the colonial state transformed Darwish's life at a deep institutional level, dismantling the school system of which he was part and erecting a new one. Unable to accept this modern transformation, which for him signaled *not* progress but regression in both his pay and in his rank as an employee (he was reduced from grade six to grade eight), he opted out of the whole affair and chose an alternative that was familiar to him, namely, that of Sufi asceticism. The alley and Kisrha's Café became his makeshift home.

3. Mahfuz, *Zuqaq al-Midaq*, 10, 12.
4. Ibid., 16.
5. Ibid., 16–17.
6. Ibid., 17.

Unlike Shaykh Darwish, Kirshah, the café owner, is of a different ilk altogether. A hashish dealer and user, he spent much money on his habit and on chasing after "his desires." Kirshah lived "in the embrace of the deviant life for so long that it seemed to him to be a normal life. As a narcotics dealer, he was used to working in the dark, a fugitive from normal life and a prey to deviance."[7] Kirshah resented the modern colonial government of the British Mandate and its local cronies, which "allows alcohol, which God has forbidden, and prohibits hashish, which God has permitted! It protects bars, which spread poison, but cracks down on hashish dens, which are a therapy to souls and minds . . . As for his other desire, he says with his traditional cough: 'You have your religion, I have mine!'"[8] Here Kirshah invokes the traditional tolerant impulse of folk Islam where each will be judged according to his/her religion or to his/her interpretation of religion. This metaphorical positing of sexual practice as tantamount to professing a religion is important in that it signals Kirshah's refusal of one uniform religious judgment of his sexual practice, and his refusal of one religious authority's right to pass such judgment.

While he had initially been private about his sexual practices with young men and would not invite them to frequent his café, "once his situation became known, and the scandal spread, he took the mask off his face and pursued his misdeed openly. Tragic scenes would take place between him and his wife that became fodder for scandalous gossip."[9] When his wife mobilized his son Husayn against him, Husayn was "not concerned with the misdeed [ithm] unto itself, but rather with the scandal that it engendered around them as well as the volley of curses and fighting it unleashed inside their home. The misdeed itself was utterly unimportant to him. Indeed the first time he was informed of it, he shook his shoulders and said indifferently: 'He is a man and nothing shames a man!' Then he condemned his father along with the others when he found his family's reputation in shreds by gossips."[10] Clearly, for Husayn, his father's sexual practices are not a cause of shame or embarrassment at all if they remain within the realm of the private and are not advertised publicly. People knowing what his father's practices are is one thing while his father becoming open about them is another. The issue is not that people in the neighborhood know that Kirshah fancies young men (which in itself causes no embarrassment), rather it is that Kirshah thinks he can openly court such young men before the

---

7. Ibid., 46.
8. Ibid.

9. Ibid., 54.
10. Ibid., 73.

eyes of the community without facing censure. It is the latter that the community rejects and that Husayn condemns. It is this kind of stark publicity of such private intimate practices that society condemns, not the practices themselves.

The novel is rich with characters derived from Cairene quotidian life. Take for example the character of Radwan al-Husayni. His biography is borrowed from the story of Job, as like the latter, he lost all his children but maintained his belief in God and His mercy and appeared always content. He was the one to whom Kirshah's wife, Umm Husayn, turned in order to pressure her husband to end his affair with an unnamed young boutique salesman whom she described as a "profligate [fajir]."[11] When he sent for her husband to have a word with him, Radwan thought to himself that this would be the first time he would allow a "dissolute" (fasiq) person to enter his room. Then, "he went on wondering about the devil's seduction of man, and how he makes him deviate from the proper nature that God gave him [fitrat Allah]."[12] Attempting to bring Kirshah back to the righteous path, Radwan asked him to let go of this "disreputable and profligate young man."[13] He then instructed him to "leave this man, for he is an abomination of Satan's handiwork."[14] It is interesting that Mahfouz has Radwan use this description, which is a direct Qur'anic quotation from a well-known verse. Ironically the Qur'anic verse has nothing to do with homosexuality, but rather with alcohol and gambling, among other things.[15] In the Qur'an, other abominations include eating pork, blood, or dead meat but not same-sex practice among men.[16] Undeterred, Kirshah answered back, "Man commits many bad deeds, of which this is only one; don't be angry with me, instead ask God to guide me, and accept my apology and my excuse. For what power does man possess over his soul?"[17] Kirshah's clever response to Radwan's Qur'anic reference marshals a modified Qur'anic verse about man's limited power to do good or harm to himself "except as God willeth,"[18] therefore exonerating Kirshah's own actions as predestined by God.

Radwan al-Husayni's failure in his mission on behalf of Kirshah's wife left her with no recourse but to confront both her husband and his boy

11. Ibid., 77.
12. Ibid., 91.
13. Ibid., 94.
14. Ibid., 95
15. See The Holy Qur'an, chap. 5, Al-Ma'idah [The Repast], verse 90.
16. See The Holy Qur'an, chap. 6, Al-An'am [The Cattle], verse 145.
17. Mahfuz, Zuqaq al-Midaq, 96.
18. See The Holy Qur'an, chap. 7, Al-A'raf [The Heights], verse 188, and chap. 10, Yunis [Jonah], verse 49.

lover. She marched one evening to the café and began to insult and beat up the young man, calling him a "son of a whore," and "a woman in man's clothing." When the shocked young man asked her what he had done to her, as he did not even know who she was, she answered him with ridicule that she was his "co-wife."[19] The bloodied young man slipped away in the mayhem of Umm Husayn's confrontation with Kirshah, who in turn was appalled at her audacity. Once the pious Radwan calmed her down and asked her to return home, despite her threats of walking out on her husband, Kirshah began to swear up and down that he "will not submit to a woman's will, for I am a man, free, I do as I like, let her leave the house if she wants."[20] Mistaking Kirshah's desire for young men as a substitute for, rather than a complement to, desiring women, the, evidently nonessentialist, Sufi Shaykh Darwish lifted his head and addressed Kirshah: "Your wife is strong, and has within her such manliness that is missing in many men. She is indeed a male, not a female, so why don't you like her?" Furious, Kirshah lashed back at Darwish to shut up and walked away. Shaykh Darwish proceeded to explain: "This is an old evil, which in English they call Homosexuality and is spelled, h-o-m-o-s-e-x-u-a-l-i-t-y, but it is not love. True love is only for the family and descendants of the Prophet."[21] For Darwish, the Sufi ascetic for whom love is always love of God and the Prophet, the opposite of homosexual love is not heterosexual love, but a much nobler kind.

Of all the English words that Shaykh Darwish utters in the novel, all the others have Arabic equivalents, except for homosexuality. This is important insofar as the other words—"history," "tragedy," "frog," "end," or even "viceroy" and "elopement" have either exact equivalent meanings in Arabic or common expressions that convey the same things, *except* homosexuality. While "tragedy," for example, is introduced to signal the sartorial effect of modernity on Egyptians—when Shaykh Darwish saw ʿAbbas walking in the strong sun bareheaded, without a fez, he told him that this would cause him to lose his mind, which would constitute a "maʾsah" or a "tragedy"[22]—"Viceroy" is introduced by Shaykh Darwish in response to ʿAbbas's volunteering to work for the British Occupation army, at which point Darwish told him "perhaps the English king will carve you up a little kingdom and appoint you the king's deputy, which in English they call 'Viceroy.'"[23] As for homosexuality, what is being

19. Mahfuz, *Zuqaq al-Midaq*, 97.
20. Ibid., 101.
21. Ibid.

22. Ibid., 45.
23. Ibid., 107.

introduced by Mahfouz is not only a word but also a new epistemology that seems to define such acts outside Midaq Alley, among the literati and those with English education, where the encroachment of colonial concepts was being felt more strongly. In the alley, the problem was not with Kirshah's desires for young men but his open sexual practice, which caused a minor scandal, one that ultimately had little social repercussions for him and affected more his wife, but no more and no less than had he taken a woman as a mistress and flaunted her in public. Mahfouz does not explore the situation from the vantage point of the young salesman whom Kirshah courted. The young man remains unnamed, an encroaching character that comes from outside Midaq Alley, who seems to have a small role to play and then disappears upon being beaten up by Umm Husayn. As the young man is unknown in Midaq Alley, there was no scandal for him. He simply disappears from the novel. The next time Kirshah's desires are expressed in the novel is when his own son Husayn moves back in accompanied by his young bride and her brother, whom Kirshah fancies.[24]

As far as the other English word "history," which has Greek origins, medieval Arabic adopted that very Greek term transforming it into "usturah" and endowed it with the meaning "myth" or "legend." Unlike the Greeks, who, it would seem, dabbled in myths masquerading as history, medieval Arabs had a full-fledged discipline of history that they called "tarikh." Homosexuality is another story altogether, as it is a combinational term with "homo" having Greek origins, and "sex" Latin origins (soon after its invention, Havelock Ellis and John Symonds called it "a barbarously hybrid term"[25]). In using an English term that has no Arabic equivalent, Mahfouz was instantiating an epistemological shift for his learned reader, a shift that the characters in the novel had not themselves undergone. It is important to note that although Mahfouz used the term *shudhudh* (deviance) to refer to Kirshah's sexual practices with men, that term was not limited to homosexual sex, but to all nonnormative sex, desires, excess, and general public conduct.[26] Indeed when Salim 'Alwan, the owner of a sales company in Midaq Alley, expresses his dissatisfaction with his wife's lack of responsiveness to his insistent sexual advances (he indulged in eating green toasted wheat with pi-

24. Ibid., 210.

25. Havelock Ellis and John Addington Symonds, *Sexual Inversion* (1898; New York: Arno Press, 1975), 3.

26. In a rushed reading of the novel, Nabil Matar mistakes "deviance" as an Islamic concept rather than a recent translation from European languages. See his "Homosexuality in the Early Novels of Negeeb Mahfouz," in the *Journal of Homosexuality* 26, no. 4 (1994): 78.

geons and much nutmeg baked and served in a pan, which he deemed an aphrodisiac and to which he attributed his virility), this is what the narrator tells us:

His wife did not welcome the baking pan at first, even when she was a young woman in the prime of her life. She had a healthy instinct [fitrah] but was repelled by *deviance* from nature; still, she bore what she had considered to be exhausting out of respect for her insatiable husband, and out of pity that she might unsettle his peace of mind.[27]

The novel however does naturalize heterosexual desire as that which is normative, insofar as the institution of marriage is linked to it definitionally. The declaration is made by Umm Hamidah, the alley's matchmaker, not only as a truism but also as an expression of economic necessity, for her livelihood depended on it. She stated that "men love marriage in their depths" and that "a man wants a woman even if paralysis had crippled him, for this is Our Lord's wisdom," and "this is why God created the world. He could have filled it with men only, but God created the male and the female, and he graced us with reason so that we understand his aim; there is no deviation [mahid] from marriage."[28]

Mahfouz spends much time on Kirshah in the novel, exploring his history, his inclinations, and his rationale for all that he does. Indeed, we are told that long before Kirshah entered the world of commerce, hashish, and deviant erotic practices, he had been involved in politics. "In his youth, he had acquired a reputation in the world of politics that rivals what he became reputed for later in other matters!"[29] Indeed Kirshah is said to have participated in the anti-British 1919 revolution as a fighter. He was also a hero in the violent battles of the revolt as well as an enthusiast for electoral battles in which he played an important role in 1924 and 1925. His last stint in politics was in 1936 when "he divorced it and married commerce." He continued to observe elections from a distance and became a partisan for whomever paid the most:

He would apologize for his desertion of politics by citing the corruption that had befallen political life . . . but corruption caught up with him personally, and he was overcome with absentmindedness, and became possessed by passionate desires, and

27. Mahfuz, *Zuqaq al-Midaq* 133. Emphasis added.
28. Ibid., 23.
29. Ibid., 147.

only a faint memory remained in his soul of those old revolutions, which he would fantasize about on occasion and mention out of pride in those serene hours when he was stoned around the coal brazier, but in his heart he had spurned all the values of an honest life and would no longer care for anything except hashish and the passions of the flesh, saying that everything else was pointless.[30]

Mahfouz's point is clear: Kirshah's disappointment in politics, having moved from nationalist revolutionism to the corruption of electoral politics, is what led him to enter the corrupt world of commerce, hashish, and sexual passions. It is almost a direct consequence of his realization that principles of social solidarity and nationalist politics in the context of colonialism are distorted by a collaborating native elite to the point of foreclosing the possibility of an "honest life," which turns out to be a sham. Having lost his enthusiasm for social responsibility, Kirshah, Mahfouz tells us, opted for an individualist project in commerce and bodily pleasures, which he now "married." If his new project, or "wife," did not constitute an "honest life," it seems at least to have made Kirshah honest in his pursuits of an individualism that he refused to couch in social terms, as would the collaborating native elite in charge of the Egyptian state under British colonialism. His "divorce" from politics signals the emergence of a kind of alienation, wherein disappointment in politics, the spread of dishonesty, the emergence of "deviance" and corruption under colonial rule came to be seen as normative. This sense of alienation will develop into a full-fledged nationalist ideology once the Egyptian Revolution overthrew the Royal regime in 1952, five years after the novel was published.

The other main narrative of *Midaq Alley,* the story of Hamidah, elaborates the transformations in a marriage plot. A beautiful but cantankerous woman of unknown paternity whose mother died when she was a baby, Hamidah was raised by a woman who lived in the neighborhood (Umm Hamidah). An ambitious woman who ventured out of the alley on daily walks, Hamidah wanted much for her future. Even though she reciprocated the advances of the alley's young barber, 'Abbas al-Hilu, and ultimately became engaged to him, she always felt that she deserved better. 'Abbas opted to close down the barbershop and leave the alley to go to work with the British army in al-Tall al-Kabir in order to make money that would enable him to marry Hamidah. He had been encouraged to do so all along by Husayn, Kirshah's son and his childhood friend. Husayn was also Hamidah's milk brother, which is why she could not

30. Ibid., 148.

marry him, even though she stressed that he was the only one among alley residents worthy of her. Husayn had already been working with the British and made good money. He hated the alley and always fantasized about leaving it. He expected, as many did, that World War II would last a long time and that therefore his employment with the British would continue to be a profitable enterprise. Husayn staked so much on this expectation that he had a fight with his parents in which he insisted on moving out of the alley and into an apartment with electricity and modern amenities. Kirshah became so angry that he told his son that he never wanted to see him again.

Once 'Abbas left the alley, Hamidah quickly forgot about him, especially as new offers began to come her way. Elderly Salim 'Alwan, whom we encountered earlier as having a "deviant" sexual appetite on account of its excess, which was made possible by the daily baking pan, asked for her hand in marriage, to which she quickly agreed, indifferent to her existing engagement to 'Abbas. Unfortunately, 'Alwan had a heart attack that same night after his marriage proposal was proffered and the matter was dropped. Soon, however, Hamidah would be approached by an outsider who began to stalk her. Titillated by the prospect of a new marriage proposal, she went along with the man's advances, which turned out to be less than honorable. Faraj Ibrahim, it turned out, was a pimp, and offered Hamidah the world if she would become a prostitute. In contrast to the kind of life she would have were she to get married and live in the alley—visualized in terms of pregnancy and breastfeeding on the streets with "flies hovering" all over—he offered her a world of luxury and bodily pleasure. Hamidah accepted and abandoned the alley as Husayn and 'Abbas had done before her. She was determined never to return.

Upon entering her new world in a lovely apartment in a tall building in the modern section of Cairo, Hamidah was transformed into another being. The change was commensurate with the male clientele she was expected to service, namely, British colonial, and other Allied, soldiers. The British soldiers were not only occupying the country, but they and Allied soldiers required the sexual services of Egyptian women, masquerading as relics from the time of the pharaohs. Aware of such predilections, Faraj decided to christen her "Titi," short for Nefertiti, "for this name is a relic that will charm the English and the Americans, and would be easily pronounced by their crooked tongues."[31] Hamidah also needed to receive instruction in English, she especially needed to learn

---

31. Ibid., 214.

the English names of body parts.[32] Her training and her virginity would yield much profit for Faraj. When in a hot moment of passion, Faraj came close to deflowering a willing Hamidah, he got up, "resisting a cunning smile" and said, "Slow down, slow down, an American officer would pay fifty pounds willingly as a price for a virgin."[33]

Hamidah's instruction also included belly dancing, Western dancing, applying makeup, and how to dress. Her belly-dancing instructor was an unfamiliar figure. Susu, as he was called, was "a young man in a silk lily white caftan with a dancing belt on his waist . . . he looked like he was in his late twenties, cross-eyed with vulgar features, his face made up with women's makeup, including eyeliner, lipstick, and blush, his curly hair glistening with Vaseline." Susu danced "like a viper, with such amazing lightness and flexibility that [Hamidah] thought him a body without bones or joints, or that he was a piece of electrified rubber."[34] When he asked Hamidah to disrobe to take a look at her body, he added: "Are you embarrassed, Titi? I am your sister, Susu! Did you not like my dancing?"[35]

While Susu was not identified as a "deviant" by the narrator, Hamidah certainly was on account of her finding pleasure in pain. Other prostitutes, we are told by the narrator, had little choice in their profession, but unlike them Hamidah had a choice. While the narrator recounts how Hamidah never regretted not marrying Faraj, but rather was impressed with his far-sightedness in guiding her to prostitution, the narrator (presumably standing in for Mahfouz), addresses the reader directly:

This aside, I warn you. You should not dare to imagine her as a lustful woman [shahwaniyyah] who is overcome by a tyrannical lust [shahwa]. She is far from being that! In fact, her deviance is not located in the intensity of her desire. She did not belong to that group of women who are overtaken by desire and who are humiliated on account of such desire that they sacrifice all that is dear to satisfy it. She was eager with soul and body to rise up, to control, and to fight. She was—even in the arms of the man whom she loved devotedly—feeling the fingers of love through the punches and slaps, and she started to be aware of this deviance in her emotions, or this lack in her nature, and this was the motivation for her general disdain and her going to extremes, and this was also one of the reasons for her attachment to her lover.[36]

32. Ibid., 218.
33. Ibid., 221.
34. Ibid., 215.

35. Ibid., 216.
36. Ibid., 255.

Deviance in fact seems to be the operative judgment not only of the sexual desires of Kirshah, Salim ʿAlwan, and Hamidah, but also of all socially unpleasant behavior. When Salim ʿAlwan returned to work weakened by his heart attack and deeply depressed, his hostility to his employees and the constant irritability that he now exhibited led them to conclude that he had become an "accursed deviant."[37] Faraj Ibrahim himself had once told Hamidah that if a beautiful woman like her walked down the streets without being followed by men, it would be a sort of "deviance that must be truly deplored, indeed if you walked and no one followed you, this would be a sign of the approach of the Day of Judgment."[38] While men's respectable behavior toward women on the streets is identified as "deviant" outside the alley, deviance is named only in reference to those characters who inhabit the alley. Literary critic Ghali Shukri surmised that what Mahfouz was exploring in *Midaq Alley* was "the ultimate development of social life in the shadow of [the World] war, [which] brings with it all kinds of deviances," but "is this to be considered deviance?" he wondered.[39] Shukri answered in the negative, especially as the postwar situation was such that Kirshah was unfazed by his deviance to the point of wondering why his wife bothered him about his affairs with young men: "He always saw himself in the right and wondered why she would stand in his way without justification! Is it not his right to do as he pleases? Is it not her duty to obey him and to be happy as long as her needs were met and her income abundant?"[40] Indeed, Salim ʿAlwan himself sought to legitimize what his wife thought of as his "deviant," because excessive, desires by marrying a second time. Shukri added that "even the change in Hamidah is not deviant at all, it is part of the natural cycle that began with need, then moved to want, and ended in the 'short road' to riches and the good life."[41]

While the old generation of alley residents were allowed to continue with much of their life and desires uninterrupted (the baker Jaʿdah and his wife Husniyyah who beats him daily but defends him when he is put down by others; the rich widow, Saniyyah ʿAfifi, whose sexual desires awaken and she marries a younger man; Kirshah's own predilection for handsome young men), except in those cases where the law is broken

37. Ibid. 239.
38. Ibid., 164.
39. Ghali Shukri, *Azmat al-Jins fi al-Qissah al-ʿArabiyyah* [The Crisis of Sex in the Arabic Novel] (1962; Cairo: Dar al-Shuruq, 1991), 103.
40. Mahfuz, *Zuqaq al-Midaq*, 75.
41. Shukri, *Azmat al-Jins fi al-Qissah al-ʿArabiyyah*, 104.

(Zita, a professional who manufactures artificial physical disabilities for those seeking to be convincing beggars, and Dr. Bushi, a self-taught dentist, are caught by the increased surveillance of the modern state while robbing gold dentures from the recently deceased at a local cemetery), the lives of the younger generation are changed forever. Husayn (whose own sister also was said to have run away from her husband with another man and was put in prison, presumably for prostitution) and Hamidah embraced modern life. In contrast, 'Abbas sought to benefit from it only financially while resisting its moral code (along the way he learned a few English words like "thank you"[42]). When he returned to Midaq Alley on vacation, having bought a necklace for Hamidah, and finding out that she had disappeared, he roamed the streets wondering what had become of his fiancée. Upon encountering her accidentally when riding in a carriage, he followed and confronted her. Hamidah opted to use him to get back at Faraj whom she now hated, as she was convinced that he only wanted to use her without having any emotional interest in her. When 'Abbas came unexpectedly early to the bar where she worked planning to kill Faraj, he was incensed to see her in the arms of scores of British soldiers. Mad with jealousy, 'Abbas threw a bottle at her, injuring her in the face. The colonial soldiers leapt to her defense and beat him to death. Clearly, for Mahfouz, this is an allegory about the collaboration between colonial soldiers and Egyptians previously thought to possess a sense of national loyalty (in this case 'Abbas's expectation of Hamidah's loyalty to him, which was dashed). That Mahfouz does so in sexual terms is intended to signal the historical changes and the epistemic shifts in sexual mores brought about by colonialism and the consequences of the traumas of war.

Unlike Hamidah or 'Abbas, Husayn had the deepest trust in the British and in the war as financially beneficial to him. When the war ended and he was dismissed from his job, he returned home emptyhanded and accompanied by his bride to beg his father to take him in. Still, Husayn had other plans. If exit from the alley to colonial Egypt failed, traveling to the heart of empire will not. He was deeply impressed with the lifestyle of British and American soldiers. Before 'Abbas was killed, Husayn (who watched him die, helpless to save him from the hands of the British soldiers) tried to convince him to emigrate:

Oh, how much I longed to be a fighting soldier! Imagine the life of a courageous soldier, fighting in the midst of war, moving from victory to victory, riding in fighter

42. Mahfuz, *Zuqaq al-Midaq,* 228.

jets and tanks, attacking, killing, taking fleeing women prisoner. A soldier on whom money is expended generously so that he can get drunk and debauch himself even above the law. This is life! Do you not wish you were a soldier?[43]

Husayn was so impressed with the British that he decided to emigrate to Britain and "take British nationality, for in the lands of the English, everyone is equal, there is no difference between a pasha and a garbage collector. It is not so far-fetched that a café busboy may become one day prime minister."[44] Indeed, at the beginning of the novel, Husayn spoke of how English soldiers "love and admire him" and that he was so much like them that one "Corporal Julian told me once that I only differ from the English in color!"[45] If he could pass as English in Egypt, Husayn surmised that he would have little trouble passing in England.

Exit from the alley meant death for those who resisted colonial morals and the deviance they ushered into the life of alley residents, and exit meant prostitution and financial loss for those who did not resist. There was still, however, one form of temporary exit that remained safe. The only character that left the alley and came back untouched by the transformations outside was Radwan al-Husayni, the Job of the novel. His destination was Mecca, where he had gone to perform the pilgrimage. It would seem that faith and religion emerge as the escape of last resort in the face of colonial modernity and the violence it wreaks on Midaq Alley. The emergence of faith and religious ritual as the only safe realms that lay inside and outside Midaq Alley is instructive here. While life in the alley was never going to be the same again, the new generation having joined the march of colonial modernity, faith and religious rituals are mobilized to defend against the imposed transformation. It is true that religious theology and religious law were undergoing different kinds of modernization projects outside the alley, but faith and ritual, ensconced in the realm of the personal, remained safe from the machinations of colonial and modern Western liberal thought, at least for a while longer. In this sense, the different available forms of religiosity, whether the formal pious form espoused by Radwan al-Husayni or the Sufi form espoused by Shaykh Darwish, provide ways of maintaining familiar forms of life that are ending for most other neighborhood residents. Perhaps the English word used by Shaykh Darwish in the final lines of the novel is revealing: "Does not everything have an end? Yes, everything has an end."[46] Unsurprisingly, the word "end" ends not only the novel but

---

43. Ibid., 246.
44. Ibid., 252.

45. Ibid., 35.
46. Ibid., 287.

also the era in which Midaq Alley existed before the final encroachment of colonial modernity, which the residents could not escape, backed as they were against an impasse (alley) that ultimately turned out to be *passable*. In this sense, the novel's opening words about Midaq Alley, that it "still preserves a good amount of the secrets of a world gone by,"[47] no longer hold, as the alley's secrets are now out for everyone to see, and the world preserved therein as late as the early-to-mid-1940s, had come to an "end."

Midaq Alley received critical acclaim by book reviewers of the period. Sayyid Qutb expressed his dissatisfaction with the novel on account of the abundance of "deviance" and "deviants" in it (understood as general social deviance). He proposed that Mahfouz reduce the number of deviant characters from five to two.[48] Nabil Matar, half a century later, misunderstood Qutb's reference to deviance and perversion as a reference to same-sex contact and attributed Qutb's dissatisfaction to those elements, which is a gross misinterpretation of Qutb and of the uses of the term "deviance" in the novel and by critics. Indeed, Matar strangely declares that the critics, Qutb included, received Midaq Alley with an "outcry against the novel's inclusion of homosexual characters."[49] Besides Qutb's review, Matar cites Lebanese critic Adib Muruwwah's review of the novel as another example of a critic objecting to homosexuality in the novel, merely because Muruwwah stated that "no one among writers has been able to depict these [popular] classes as they are, as Mr. Mahfuz has done. He was utterly realist and faithful, even though this reality might have contained that which would on occasion offend proper decorum (such as the sodomy of Kirshah, for example)." Matar also cites Muhammad Fahmi's review as another example, when all Fahmi stated was that he found "Kirshah's deviance . . . somewhat strange for [someone] like him; perhaps had Kamil, the sweets seller, been afflicted with it . . . it would have added an atmosphere of joy to the story." This is hardly an "outcry" against homosexual characters or anything remotely connected to it.[50] Contrast this with the reception that Gore Vidal's 1948 novel The City and the Pillar received in New York. The critical response was so violent that the New York Times refused to advertise the novel and, along with all major American magazines and newspapers, had a standing policy not to review any Vidal novels for the

47. Ibid., 5.
48. See Sayyid Qutb, Al-Fikr al-Jadid, 12 February 1948, 24–25, reproduced in ʿAli Shalash, Najib Mahfuz: Al-Tariq wa al-Sada [Najib Mahfuz: The Path and the Effect] (Beirut: Dar al-Adab, 1990), 181.
49. Matar, "Homosexuality in the Early Novels of Negeeb Mahfouz," 78.
50. See Muruwwah and Fahmi in Shalash, Najib Mahfuz, 182 and 178, respectively.

next six years merely because the novel depicted a homosexual encounter between two young, all-American athletic types, wherein one had an unrequited love for the other.[51] In contrast to Vidal, Mahfouz continued to be celebrated by the Arabic press for the rest of his career despite his continuing inclusion of characters who desire same-sex contact.

Mahfouz was the first to explore same-sex desire in Arabic novels with this amount of attention. His interest, however, was confined to the active male with penetrative desires who has an inner life worthy of exploration. Neither the unnamed salesman (produced as the passive partner of Kirshah) or Susu (whose sexual desires are implied, not stated) seem to have inner lives worthy of exploration. This will not be necessarily the case always for Mahfouz, the exception being the character of the young law-school student Radwan, an exceedingly handsome and elegant man that appears in the third part of Mahfouz's magnum opus, the Cairo Trilogy. In *Al-Sukkariyyah* (Sugar Street), published in 1957, a decade after *Midaq Alley,* and after the Egyptian Revolution had triumphed and colonialism was defeated, Mahfouz seemed to introduce male same-sex desire, not as social "deviance," as he had done in *Midaq Alley,* but as an "illness." This is a key shift, as the medical model of homosexuality had begun to be entrenched in the colonial North Atlantic world, where it remained contested in the forties and fifties by Kinsey and others. The story of the novel takes place in the early 1940s, around the same time that the story of *Midaq Alley* unfolded, yet *Sugar Street*'s representation of same-sex desire differs significantly. In *Midaq Alley,* it was the narrator who spoke of the deviance of Kirshah as the latter never thought of himself as "deviant" or non-normative—his desires led to sexual contact and not to an existential crisis. In contrast, Radwan of *Sugar Street,* for example, wondered, "Who divided humans into normal and deviant?" understanding himself as belonging to one of the two categories.[52] It is never made entirely clear in the novel whether Radwan was an active or passive deviant; what we do learn is that he desired men exclusively and was "disgusted" by women.[53] He refused to get married, just like the elderly statesman, the Pasha, with whom he had an implied sexual relationship, and who was also known to like young men.[54] Therefore, unlike Kirshah, they both remained outside the circuit

51. See Gore Vidal's preface to the recent edition of the novel in Gore Vidal, *The City and The Pillar, and Seven Early Stories* (New York: Random House, 1995), xvi.
52. Najib Mahfuz, *Al-Sukkariyyah* (1957; Cairo: Maktabat Misr, n.d), 136. For the English edition, see Naguib Mahfouz, *Sugar Street,* translated by William M. Hutchins and Angele Botros Samaan (New York: Doubleday, 1992).
53. Ibid., 304.
54. Ibid., 66.

of social reproduction in fairly literal ways. Upon Radwan's expression of disgust toward women and his statement that one could live without women "without a problem," the Pasha responded, "Humans [*sic*] can live without women, but it is a problem. You may not care about what people think, but what about what you think? You may say that women are disgusting, but why do they not disgust others? At that moment, you are overtaken by a feeling like an illness, an illness that has no remedy, so you give up the whole world and remain with it, and it [the illness] is the worst company during solitude. You might then feel ashamed of despising women even though you are obligated to continue to despise them."[55]

While for Kirshah desiring young men never meant a rejection of women, since his desires could accommodate a number of object choices that were not mutually exclusive, for Radwan and the Pasha the matter was different. The transformation of same-sex desire from one of many types of deviances found in society into an illness has much to do with the rejection of women and the social institution of marriage, which Kirshah, for example, never adopted. Kirshah clearly believed in marriage and family, loved his wife and never wanted to divorce her. He saw his attraction to young men as having nothing to do with these affective and social commitments. Kirshah's sexual desires are indeed class-specific and neighborhood-specific, as he (like most Egyptians) still lived in a neighborhood and belonged to a class that had not internalized modern European sexual categories. The more Westernized middle class and upwardly mobile Radwan and the elite aristocratic Pasha exhibit different desires, which register something new on account of their exclusivity. While Radwan and the Pasha were Royalist nationalists and sought the end of the British occupation under the collaborationist monarchy, on account of their class membership the two represent numerically but a minuscule part of Egyptians. The difference between their desires and the desires of Kirshah is precisely what accounts for the transformation of same-sex attraction from one of many existing and tolerated deviances among the lower middle classes and the poor in society into a medicalized condition among the rich and the upwardly mobile. Mahfouz's representation of Radwan as a self-declared deviant is intelligible to readers precisely because of the transformation of Arab society since the late nineteenth century, where the epistemic shifts instantiated by the Arab Renaissance project and the simultaneous European colonial project began to seep through to the interstices of society at large, to be

55. Ibid., 304.

internalized by new modern subjects, no longer remaining within the purview of the literati and colonial officers.

This situation was unfolding in the same period that saw the end of colonial modernity and the inauguration of nationalism's grand modernization projects. If for Kirshah his desires caused him some domestic problems with his wife, for Radwan and the Pasha their desires would constitute an identitarian self-questioning whether they fit in society at all and whether they were diseased. It is significant that the illness they seem to have suffered from was not the "illness" of desiring men but of desiring them exclusively while failing to desire women.

The influence of these two Mahfouz novels, as is the case with many others, was not confined to the reading public, but also to a mass viewing public, as both novels were made into popular films directed by Egyptian director Hasan al-Imam—*Midaq Alley* was released in 1963 under the title *Hamidah,* and *Sugar Street* a decade later in 1973.[56] Mahfouz's *Cairo Trilogy* was also made into a television series in the 1980s.

What is remarkable about reading *Midaq Alley* over half a century after it was published is the comic style that Mahfouz used to deal with matters of sexual desires and practices. While references to same-sex practices among men punctuate many of his novels, Mahfouz's style, reminiscent of Taha Husayn in a different register, was not necessarily moralist or tragic when he approached matters of sex and desire, the existential issues raised later in *Sugar Street* notwithstanding. As we will see in the rest of this chapter, many of the defining novels of the post-1960s period and particularly those published in the 1980s will have little room for a comedic approach and will be suffused with melodramas and tragedies that we have already encountered in nonfictional writings. In the meantime, however, novels were not only seen as a way to represent society as it exists but also to reconstruct the way it might have existed in the past. Indeed, Mahfouz himself had written a number of historical

---

56. More recently, *Midaq Alley* was also made into a popular and successful Mexican film in 1995 directed by Jorge Fons. The Mexican film, *Callejón de los Milagros* [Miracle Alley], received forty-nine international awards. *Hamidah* differed significantly from the novel on a number of counts. For example, Hamidah and Faraj are killed off at the end of the film, but not ʿAbbas as in the novel. Remarkably, Kirshah's sexual interest in young men is eliminated in the film and replaced puzzlingly by unexplained hatred that he felt for his wife. Susu the effeminate dance instructor does appear in the film, but is introduced as a European foreigner and addressed as "khawagah." In contrast, the film version of *Sugar Street* depicts clearly the homosexual practices of Radwan and the Pasha and is more explicit about their sexual roles. While the virile Pasha is depicted as the active homosexual, Radwan, identified as the "prettiest" among the grandchildren of the ʿAbd al-Jawwad family, is depicted as an effeminate who yells out "Mommie" in terror when the police accost a crowd at a political rally. Interestingly, the film presents Radwan's communist cousin as the one that was morally condemnatory of his sexual relations, and not the Islamist cousin.

novels, representing life in ancient Egypt in his early career, and among the medieval Arabs later. His novel *Layali Alf Laylah* (The Nights of a Thousand Nights)[57] was an attempt to read and write *A Thousand and One Nights* differently, in a novelistic style that strangely mimics the very style of that classic book written centuries before the novel form was invented. However, as genre is not just a literary form but also implies a range of attitudes and possibilities, the move from the comic to the melodramatic in representing matters sexual, and especially matters homosexual, marks perhaps a decrease in sexual sophistication and a puritanizing of sex, not to mention the infiltration of Western taxonomies and medical diagnostics. This is indeed ironic given the ostensible liberatory promises of modernity, which many later novels will register while shying away from the comic in favor of the melodramatic and the tragic.

Normalizing Past Desires

Naguib Mahfouz sought to register and represent actually existing desires and sexual practices. In contrast, Ra'if Khuri's novel *Dik al-Jinn: The Devouring Love,* sought to interrogate the veracity of certain medieval sexual desires and practices deemed deviant in *modern* times. His novel was published as part of a series of books that Beirut-based publisher Dar al-Makshuf had put out under the title The Most Famous Lovers. With the exception of *Dik al-Jinn,* the rest of the books were about love stories from the Western tradition (including Baudelaire, Edgar Allan Poe, Lady Hamilton, Madame de Pompadour, Pauline Borghese, the Empress Messalina, Pierre Abélard and Héloïse, and Lord Byron, who is identified as a "lover of himself"[58]). These were translations of books from French, one of which was indeed translated by Khuri about "Paganini, the Charmer of Women."[59] Khuri himself published another book in 1939 about the Umayyad poet 'Umar ibn Abi Rabi'ah, which was written in the tradition of medieval books of "akhbar" (anecdotes) that would include biographical anecdotes about a person. While his book about Dik al-

---

57. Najib Mahfuz, *Layali Alf Laylah* [The Nights of a Thousand Nights] (Cairo: Maktabat Misr, 1979). For the English version of the novel, see Naguib Mahfouz, *Arabian Nights and Days,* translated by Denys Johnson-Davies (Cairo: American University in Cairo Press, 1995).

58. André Moreau, *Al-Lurd Bayrun 'Ashiq Nafsihi* [Lord Byron, Lover of Himself], translated by Antun Ghattas Karam (Beirut: Dar al-Makshuf, 1948).

59. The series was published between 1947 and 1950. It is interesting to note that the editor of the book on *al-Mar'ah fi Hayat Idghar Bu* [The Woman in the Life of Edgar Poe] (Beirut: Dar Makshuf, 1949), is 'Abd al-Latif Shararah whom we encountered in an earlier chapter.

Jinn attempted to replicate the *akhbar* genre, it did so in a novelistic frame.[60]

In light of the major excavations of the heritage of the Arabs that had proceeded apace since the nineteenth century and of the precedent set by Jurji Zaydan's turn-of-the-century historical novels, Lebanese communist thinker, journalist, essayist, translator, and novelist Ra'if Khuri published in 1948 his historical novel about the medieval poet Dik al-Jinn al-Himsi (circa A.D. 777–849).[61] Little is known about Dik al-Jinn except for passing references about him and his poetry in medieval compendia and biographies. Dik al-Jinn, a contemporary of Abu Nuwas, wrote love poetry for women and youthful boys and is well known for his beautifully constructed and moving elegies. Born in Homs, Syria, where he also died, he never ventured geographically far from his hometown. Said to be of Persian origins, he was a Shi'ite. It is significant that Abu Nuwas was reported to have stopped in Homs en route to Cairo and visited Dik al-Jinn, having heard of his poetry while in Baghdad.[62]

Medieval accounts about Dik al-Jinn are not uniform and include stories that are not always corroborated and sometimes contradict one another. This is mainly the case in reference to Dik al-Jinn's most tragic double love story with his wife (or concubine) Ward, a Christian who converted and married him, and a beloved youthful boy named Bakr. The most coherent form of the story runs like this: Dik al-Jinn inherited money from his father and lived off his inheritance, writing poetry and pursuing carnal pleasure and drinking wine. He fell in love with Ward and with Bakr (and wrote love poems and later elegies about both of them).[63] Dik al-Jinn had a cousin who resented his "debauched" lifestyle and perhaps coveted Dik al-Jinn's inheritance, which he thought was being squandered. In retaliation, Dik-al-Jinn wrote a poem insulting his cousin. The cousin, intent on revenge, decided to rid Dik al-Jinn of both his beloveds. He concocted a story that he told to Dik al-Jinn, upon the latter's return from a brief trip to a neighboring town, namely, that Ward

60. Ra'if Khuri, *Wa Hal Yakhfa al-Qamar? 'Umar ibn Abi Rabi 'ah* [Can the Moon Hide?] (Beirut: Dar al-Makshuf, 1939).

61. Ra'if Khuri, *Dik al-Jinn, Al-Hubb al-Muftaris* [The Devouring Love] (Beirut: Dar al-Makshuf, 1948). The name "Dik al-Jinn," which was bestowed on the poet, means the rooster of the Jinn spirits, possibly on account of his heavy drinking.

62. For a good review of the medieval sources on Dik al-Jinn, see the introduction to his poetry collection by Ahmad Matlub and 'Abdullah al-Jaburi, editors, *Diwan Dik al-Jinn* (Beirut: Dar al-Thaqafah, 1964?), 5–21.

63. Ibn Khallikan claims that the name of the woman was Dunya and the youthful boy's Wasif. See Abu 'Abbas Shams al-Din Ahmad bin Muhammad bin Abi Bakr bin Khallikan, *Wafayat al-A'yan wa Anba' Abna' al-Zaman* [The Obituaries of Eminent Men and News about the Men of the Epoch], e.d. Ihsan 'Abbas (Beirut: Dar al-Thaqafah, 1970), vol. 3, 186.

and Bakr were having an affair with one another. Mad with jealousy, Dik al-Jinn killed them both. He later learned the truth of the deception and went into deep depression and uncontrolled bouts of crying.[64] He is said to have cremated their bodies and made two wine cups out of the ashes. He kept one wine cup on his right and the other on his left for the rest of his life. He would drink wine from them and kiss them as he recited poetry about his two beloveds.[65]

There are contradictory accounts in the medieval sources on two parts of the tragic love story, namely, whether it was indeed Dik al-Jinn at all who killed his wife due to deception and then wrote a famous poem about her, as that same poem is attributed to another unknown poet, al-Sulayk bin Mujammi',[66] and, granting that Dik al-Jinn did indeed kill his wife and the youthful boy, whether he had cremated their bodies and turned them into wine cups at all.[67]

The first modern reference to Dik al-Jinn in Arabic was in Jurji Zaydan's *The History of Arabic Literature*. Zaydan's multivolume study published between 1911 and 1914 included a short entry on the medieval poet, in which he identified him as "depraved and bawdy" (*khali' wa majin*), making mention of his love for youthful boys and his love affair with the concubine Ward. While Zaydan wrote of Dik al-Jinn's murder of Ward, he made no reference to Bakr.[68] It was Lebanese émigré belletrist Nasib 'Aridah who was the first modern Arab writer to provide a short fictionalized biography of Dik al-Jinn from his American exile in 1921.[69] For 'Aridah, the importance of Dik al-Jinn lay in his love for a Christian woman. The moral of the fictionalized biography that 'Aridah wrote had more to do with Arab Muslim and Arab Christian communal harmony and love, staged as romance, rather than with any unorthodox

64. See, for example, Al-Asfahani, Abu Faraj 'Ali bin al-Husayn, *Kitab al-Aghani* (The Book of Songs), ed. Ihsan 'Abbas, Ibrahim al-Sa'afin and Bakr 'Abbas (Beirut: Dar Sadir, 2002), vol. 14, 33–45.

65. See Dawud al-Antaki, *Tazyin al-Aswaq fi Akhbar al-'Ushshaq* [Decorating Markets with the News of Lovers] (Beirut: Dar wa Maktabat al-Hilal, 1994), vol. 1, 292–93. See also, Muhammad Baha' al-Din al-'Amili (1547–1621), *Al-Kashkul* (The Scrapbook) (Beirut: Dar al-Kitab al-Lubnani, 1983), 86.

66. See Al-Asfahani, vol. 14, 37; and Abu Muhammad Ja'far bin Ahmad bin al-Husayn al-Sarraj al-Qari' al-Baghdadi, *Masari' al-'Ushshaq* (The Death of Lovers), ed. Muhammad Hasan Isma'il (Beirut: Dar al-Kutub al-'Ilmiyyah, 1998), vol. 1, 75. Unlike al-Asfahani, al-Sarraj does not name the poet.

67. While al-Antaki, for example, mentions that part of the story, al-Asfahani does not.

68. Jurji Zaydan, *Tarikh Adab al-Lughah al-'Arabiyyah* (Cairo: Dar al-Hilal, 1956), vol. 2, 96–97. The four volumes were originally published in Egypt starting in 1911 and ending in 1914.

69. See Nasib 'Aridah, "Qissat Dik al-Jinn al-Himsi, Hikayat Gharam Sha'ir 'Arabi Qadim [The Story of Dik al-Jinn al-Himsi; A Love Story of an Ancient Arab Poet], published in 1921 in a collection of essays by Syrian and Lebanese immigrant writers in North America and reprinted *as Majmu'at al-Rabitah al-Qalamiyyah li-Sanat 1921* [The Collection of the Association of the Pen for the Year 1921] (Beirut: Dar Sadir, 1964), 117–51.

desires.[70] In fact, Bakr is presented throughout as Dik al-Jinn's best friend and companion without ever implying anything untoward. Jordanian literary historian Ya'qub al-'Udat, better known by his nom de plume, "al-Badawi al-Mulaththam," virtually copied 'Aridah's fictionalized biography of Dik al-Jinn in a book he published almost three decades later in 1948. Al-Mulaththam's book, like 'Aridah's, constructed a semifictional historical narrative woven around Dik-al Jinn's poems.[71] Like 'Aridah, al-Mulaththam was attuned to the morality of the age and reworked the part of the story relating to Bakr. While Bakr is initially identified as a young man with whom Dik al-Jinn was infatuated ("maftun"),[72] when the story of Ward is narrated, Bakr is miraculously transformed into Dik al-Jinn's best and most trusted "friend . . . since childhood."[73] Al-Mulaththam cited an incident from the medieval sources wherein the prudish young Bakr was taken for a promenade in Homs's most famous park of the time, the Mimas, by five other men who got him drunk and debauched him, to Dik al-Jinn's horror (the latter wrote a poem expressing his pain at the incident).[74] When it came to the tragic love story of Dik al-Jinn, however, no traces of passion or erotic love between Bakr and Dik al-Jinn are found. Indeed, Bakr is presented, as in 'Aridah's story, as Dik al-Jinn's "loyal and sincere brother."[75] Although al-Mulaththam reproduced the story of the wine cups, in his version Dik al-Jinn did not cremate the bodies but rather took earth from the graves of Ward and Bakr and had them molded into the cups. In this, al-Mulaththam copied 'Aridah's account. Like 'Aridah, al-Mulaththam reported that Ward's cup was kept on the right of Dik al-Jinn and Bakr's on the left, in accordance with medieval sources. Unlike the reports in the medieval sources, however, which spoke of Dik al-Jinn "kissing both [cups],"[76] both 'Aridah's and al-Mulaththam's Dik al-Jinn would only kiss Ward's cup "thinking that he was licking her lips," and would turn to Bakr's cup and simply cry.[77]

The insistence on renarrating Dik al-Jinn's tragic story as one of exclusive love for a woman had been picked up also by Palestinian-born

70. Ibid., 134.

71. Al-Badawi al-Mulaththam, *Dik al-Jinn al-Himsi* (Cairo: Al-Muqtataf Press, 1948), republished in a second edition by the Jordanian Ministry of Culture in Amman in 1991. All page references are to the second Jordanian edition.

72. Ibid., 51.

73. Ibid., 121.

74. Ibid., 52. For the poem, see al-Mulaththam, *Dik al-Jinn al-Himsi,* 53, and *Diwan Dik al-Jinn* (1964), 101–2.

75. Al-Mulaththam, *Dik al-Jinn al-Himsi,* 97.

76. See, for example, al-Antaki, *Tazyin al-Aswaq,* 292–93. Also see Shihab al-Din Ahmad ibn Hajlah, *Diwan al-Sababah* (Beirut: Dar wa Maktabat al-Hilal, 1984), 97.

77. Al-Mulaththam, *Dik al-Jin al-Himsi,* 123–24.

Syrian poet ʿUmar Abu Rishah. Anxious about Bakr's cup, Abu Rishah wrote in 1940 a poem about Dik al-Jinn and Ward in which Bakr was nowhere to be found. Abu Rishah prefaced his poem with a few lines about Dik al-Jinn's murder of Ward "out of love for her and of jealousy," and of his molding a wine cup out of her ashes, with no mention of Bakr or the alleged affair.[78] Indeed even Muhsin al-Amin al-Husayni al-ʿAmili (1865–1952), the Lebanese writer of a major modern compendium on Shiʾite personalities in history, questions the veracity of the cremation and the wine cups story, stating "that it must be a lie, as someone like him, with his abundant reason and well-reputed biography . . . could not have committed such absurdities."[79] While al-ʿAmili's compendium was written between 1935 and the time of his death in 1952, it was published posthumously in 1956, under the direction of his son who continued his father's work on the compendium. It is in the context of this literary revisionism that Raʾif Khuri wrote his novel. It is further interesting to note that the first modern collection of Dik al-Jinn's poems was not published until 1960,[80] with a more comprehensive collection published in 1964, another in 1987, and another, the most comprehensive yet, in 1990.[81]

Khuri's novel, published in 1948, begins, by way of justification, with an introductory dialogue between Khuri and Old Man History, in which Khuri interrogates History for leaving such a scanty account of the important poet, telling us little if anything about his personal life and upbringing, or about "his parents who bore him and raised him, or about his education and the factors that led him to this destination in life. You did not describe his looks or whether he bore a son, nor the reasons for his cousin Abu al-Tayyib's insistence on bothering him, or the year of his murder of the concubine and the youthful boy." Note the different ways in which "history" functions for Khuri and the way it functions for

78. For the text of the poem, see Jamil ʿAllush, ʿUmar Abu Rishah, Hayatuh wa Shiʿruh maʿ Nusus Mukhtarah [ʿUmar Abu Rishah: His Life and Poetry, including Selected Texts] (Beirut: al-Ruwwad, 1994), 192–94. Adonis does the same thing by citing Dik al-Jinn's murder of his female beloved with no mention of Bakr. See his Muqaddimah li al-Shiʿr al-ʿArabi [Introduction to Arabic Poetry] (Beirut: Dar al-ʿAwdah, 1983), 52–53.

79. See Muhsin al-Amin, Aʿyan al-Shiʿah [Shiite Notables] (Beirut: Matbaʿat al-Itqan, 1956), vol. 38, 30.

80. ʿAbd al-Muʿin al-Maluhi and Muhyi al-Din al-Darwish, editors, Diwan Dik al-Jinn al-Himsi [The Collected Poetry of Dik al-Jinn the Homsite] (Homs, Syria: Matabiʿ al-Fajr al-Jadid, 1960).

81. See Ahmad Matlub and ʿAbdullah al-Jaburi, editors., Diwan Dik al-Jinn [The Collected Poetry of Dik al-Jinn] (Beirut: Dar al-Thaqafah, 1964?); and Mazhar al-Hajji, editor, Diwan Dik al-Jinn al-Himsi (Damascus: Wizarat al-Thaqafah, 1987); ʿAbd al-Amir ʿAli Muhanna, editor, Diwan Dik al-Jinn, tabʿah jadidah tatadamman shiʿr yunshar li-awwal marrah [The Collected Poetry of Dik al-Jinn, a New Edition That Includes Poetry Published for the First Time] (Beirut:Dar al-Fikr al-Lubnani, 1990).

Mahfouz in *Midaq Alley*. For Mahfouz "history" recorded the past of the Alley and registered its transformation into the modern period, while for Khuri, "history" was an incomplete project whose completion was left to the novelist. If Mahfouz's novel simply recorded a history that unfolded outside its narrative confines, for Khuri, the novel form will be the agent of writing and rewriting history as an internal and conscious part of the novel itself. Take, for example, Khuri's continued interrogation of history within his novel about a matter of crucial importance to him:

> Did Dik al-Jinn indeed practice coitus with his youthful boy or was it visual enjoyment of all aspects of beauty? Was it ever clear whether Dik al-Jinn was indeed unjust toward the concubine and the youthful boy, and how? Or is it that he regretted his suspicions and jealousy and forgave them and lived on licking his burning wounds, bequeathed to him by his separation from the concubine forever? All these are questions that require answers.[82]

Unable to provide answers to Khuri's queries, Old Man History instructed him to weave a story about Dik al-Jinn from extant material and to pepper it with imagination. While this is indeed a task that the cultural historian engages in, it is noteworthy that Khuri thought the novel was the best form to do so. Unlike the cultural historian, Khuri seems to have the understanding that all history in the last instance is fictional. Old Man History cited the stories about Dik al-Jinn by the medieval author, Dawud al-Antaki, died 1600, (who in his book *Tazyin al-Aswaq*, confirmed the love story with the young man and the concubine[83]), referring to him as a "narrator who invented . . . tales about Dik al-Jinn."[84] Khuri set out to do just that. His novel seems to have the multiple tasks of rescuing Dik al-Jinn from oblivion and the neglect of official history, and to assimilate him, like al-ʿAmili, ʿAridah, al-Mulaththam, and Abu Rishah, to modern concerns about appropriate sexual and romantic conduct. In this sense, his novel is much less allegorical (except about harmonious Arab Christian–Muslim relations) and much more social historical, even a corrective history.

The fictional Dik al-Jinn that Khuri invented had lost his parents as a teenager and was raised by his cunning and clever grandmother, who was concerned that he might squander the fortune he had inherited

---

82. Khuri, *Dik al-Jinn*, 10–11.
83. See al-Antaki, *Tazyin al-Aswaq*, 86.
84. Khuri, *Dik al-Jinn*, 11.

on his debauched lifestyle. Determined to guide him, the grandmother told him tales and parables that she expected would sway him from being interested in chasing after women. The tales, however, seem to have another novelistic function, namely, the naturalization of the love of women and the denial of the love of youthful boys as an attractive alternative, even as substitution. The first tale, which is said to have taken place in ancient Arabia, is about a man who was conned by a young woman whom he encountered in the desert, having tarried behind her family's caravan. The woman tried to seduce him by disrobing and challenging him to disrobe as well (when questioned by her about what was more beautiful, a man's or a woman's nudity, the man told her that male nudity was more beautiful than female nudity, indeed that "a naked handsome man is unrivalled by any other beauty on Earth"[85]). The woman then stole his clothes and his camel, leaving him behind with hers. Naked, the young man had no choice but to don her clothes and rode her camel to rejoin her caravan. Discovered by her mother, he told her what had happened. The mother explained to him that her daughter had been on her way to be married to a wealthy older man, but that she loved another, younger man. Wanting to postpone the groom discovering the switch and the scandal this would cause, the mother dressed the young man in her daughter's wedding gown. When the bridegroom entered the room with his "huge body, which showed much strength and with eyes full of desire," the (presumably veiled) man-bride rejected him, going so far as wrestling with him to fend off his sexual advances. The groom finally gave up on his bride and left dejected; the young woman returned, having concluded that her groom would now dissolve the marriage. The man she tricked into serving as the bride departed on his way.[86] It seems that despite the young man's appreciation for naked young male beauty, he was not eager to see his older groom naked. More important, however, is how female sexual agency for Khuri can manifest itself only through a male proxy. This, as we will soon see, will be a key ploy that he will use to rewrite the desires of Dik al-Jinn.

The grandmother's parables seemed to have had the opposite effect on Dik al-Jinn. Her worst fears would soon be confirmed when Dik al-Jinn befriended a group of men of questionable conduct, who spent their time "reciting poetry, drinking wine, chasing women, and befriending youthful boys in a suspicious manner."[87] However, although Dik al-Jinn

---

85. Ibid., 15.
86. Ibid., 19.

87. Ibid., 29.

began to drink heavily, unlike his friends, when he "walked the city's neighborhoods or went out to Mimas [the promenade park], he would be prim and would not display vulgar manners in demanding women, and he would remain in the company of youthful boys as far as nature permitted and would not approach deviance [shudhudh] or corruption of manners."[88] Herein lies Khuri's interest. On the one hand, he wants to introduce a neglected poet to modern Arab readers, and on the other, he wants to preempt any condemnation of his sexual practices by insisting that they never took place. The preemption is set up within the narrative structure of the novel, wherein suspicions about Dik al-Jinn's desires are raised only to be dispelled.

Upon the sudden death of his grandmother, Dik al-Jinn is said to have recollected himself. Even though he continued to drink, he refused to dabble in carnal pleasures and remained celibate. His friends, however, suspected that he was in love with the youthful Bakr, as whenever they would attempt to make erotic references about him, Dik al-Jinn would become offended and would rebuff them. The issue would come up again ironically when Abu Nuwas passed through town and was invited to a banquet at Dik al-Jinn's. To Dik al-Jinn's consternation, his friends again began to make innuendos about Bakr. Abu Nuwas himself wondered if it was indeed jealousy that gave him offence. Denying the charge, Dik al-Jinn responded: "what would you know of what is between Bakr and me that you would call it jealousy?"[89] When the friends mentioned Ward, Dik al-Jinn launched into a lecture on how his love, unlike theirs, was not a love of the "flesh" for the flesh, or one of "leasing with money" a "beautiful or not-so-beautiful body." Indeed their love, Dik al-Jinn tells them, is an "instinctual" one, and that they are so impatient that they do not even wait for their instinct to be "excited naturally, for you insist on provoking it with liquor."[90] Unlike their crude objectification, "my love is radically different from all that. My love is the yearning of the soul before it becomes an instinct for the flesh. It is the call of a heart for another heart. On account of this, I felt jealousy." When queried by Abu Nuwas if he was then in love with both Ward and Bakr, he protested again. Although he affirmed his love interest in Ward, whom he had not yet officially met but had admired from afar, he defended himself against the implication about Bakr: "I repeat to you, my friend, what would you know, and what would people know, of what is between Bakr and me? If I am jealous that others may speak of him in an ill-mannered way, why

88. Ibid., 32.
89. Ibid., 60.

90. Ibid., 61.

would you conclude that I would permit myself to be ill-mannered with him?"[91] Here Khuri's Dik al-Jinn not only affirms good manners but is also affirming that he is no Abu Nuwas and that his desires should not be confused with those of the latter.[92] Indeed, what is transpiring here is a kind of reference to Socratic and Platonic ideas about boy love, which Oscar Wilde himself had resurrected at his trial in the 1890s.

Later Dik al-Jinn actively pursued the Christian Ward while on a picnic with her friends. The friends noticed him spying on them. Realizing that Ward also liked him, her friends intervened: "But he is not a man of our religion, sister, and has a reputation for profligacy, bawdiness, and deviance, so how would you feel safe opening your heart to him?"[93] Even though she had heard the same description of him from her own family, Ward could not help but fall in love with him.[94]

Having ascertained Dik al-Jinn's exclusive desires for women, Khuri moves on to his hardest task yet. His refusal to accept Dik al-Jinn's erotic love for Bakr leads him to concoct an incredible story to explain away the erotic love poems that Dik al-Jinn had written for Bakr. In the novel, Dik al-Jinn and Ward married, and she moved into his household, where Bakr also lived. Ward was suspicious of Bakr, especially after she had discovered and read the poems written for him by Dik al-Jinn. Overcome with jealousy and doubt, she confided in her favorite maid, Dalal, who dispelled her fears immediately, informing her that the poems were indeed written by Dik al-Jinn, but not on his own behalf, but rather on hers; for she was in love with Bakr and could not compose

91. Ibid., 62–63.

92. I should mention here that a later novel, namely, al-Tayyib Salih's *Mawsim al-Hijrah ila al-Shamal* [The Season of Migration to the North] (Beirut: Dar al-'Awda, 1969), has its protagonist recite the bacchic poems of Abu Nuwas to his English girlfriend, Anne Hammond, who was a sexual fetishist, enamored of the Abbasid period under the caliph al-Ma'mun. She would pretend that she was a concubine owned by the protagonist in the novel, Mustafa Sa'id, who played her master (145–48). Mustafa Sa'id met Anne at a lecture he was delivering at Oxford about Abu Nuwas in which he claimed that Abu Nuwas was a Sufi poet, wherein wine for him was a symbol for all his "spiritual yearnings." Mustafa Sa'id described his lecture about Abu Nuwas as composed of "made-up stories that have no basis in truth, but that night I felt inspired, I felt the lies pour forth from my mouth as if they were of transcendental significance. I felt ecstasy seep through from me to the audience; so I proceeded with my lies." (144). Salih was clearly aware of the Arab scholarly attempts to rehabilitate Abu Nuwas in accordance with Victorian morality which he was ridiculing. He, however, was only concerned with the rehabilitation of Abu Nuwas's bacchic poems (perhaps in response to Muhammad al-Nuwayhi's book about the poet, which was discussed in an earlier chapter), and opted to ignore the more active effort of rehabilitating or condemning Abu Nuwas's sexual desires and practices, to which *Mawsim al-Hijra ila al-Shammal* makes no reference. For the English edition, see Tayeb Salih, *Season of Migration to the North,* translated by Denys Johnson-Davies (London: Penguin, 2003).

93. Khuri, *Dik al-Jinn,* 70.

94. Ibid.

poems herself. Ward's heart was put at ease and she promised to help get the two hearts together.[95] Here, the grandmother's story of female sexual agency expressing itself through male proxy is repeated. Dalal's desire for Bakr can only be expressed through the mediation of a man. If in the grandmother's story, the proxy man, although infatuated with male beauty, had no desires for the bridegroom, Dik al-Jinn's poetry for Bakr is simply echoing the sentiments of the servant girl Dalal. It seems that for Khuri, for a man to love a man, he needs to ventriloquize a servant girl.

Unfortunately, it turned out that Bakr was not interested at all in Dalal and had his eye on Ward herself.[96] Even though Khuri represented Bakr as a narcissist, so much that "as manly as he is, he still possessed something of the nature of females who like to be the cause behind unfolding events,"[97] he lets the reader suspect along with Ward and Dik al-Jinn, the real object of Bakr's sexual desires well into the end of the novel. Khuri's ambivalent account about the character Bakr is demonstrated in his description of the latter's reaction when approached at a party by a desirous man who wanted to have his way with him. Bakr, to Dalal's and Dik al-Jinn's consternation, was not offended at all. His narcissism was indeed gratified by the attention.[98]

The story proceeds as expected. The trap is set by Dik al-Jinn's cousin, and the murderous deed is carried out. Dik al-Jinn, under the impression that Ward and Bakr were having an amorous affair, killed both of them, starting with Bakr, and then "forgetting to wipe the sword before he killed Ward, mixed their blood."[99] He was to find out soon from Dalal that they were both innocent. In complete shock and disbelief, he set out days later to unearth their buried bodies, cremated them, and had his ceramicist make him two wine cups from the ashes. The novel leaves the reader with the impression that the ashes of both, like their blood, were mixed in the crematorium. Thus when the cups were made, no distinction was made between them. While Dik al-Jinn placed one to his right and the other to his left, we do not learn whose cup is made of whose ashes. The narrator explains to readers that "since that day, he refused to drink wine except from them."[100]

Living in misery for the rest of his life, no longer seeking to be known as a poet, Dik al-Jinn, in Khuri's estimation, fell not only into deep sad-

95. Ibid., 75–81.
96. Ibid., 100.
97. Ibid., 83–84.

98. Ibid., 83.
99. Ibid., 118.
100. Ibid., 130.

ness, as the medieval accounts report, but also into deep self-questioning and moralizing (nowhere to be found in the medieval accounts), virtually "putting himself on trial"[101]:

And then, there was the question that Dik al-Jinn was running away from every time it posed itself—or was he running from himself? Was his love for Bakr a full love that included the desire of the flesh for the flesh?[102]

Dik al-Jinn's self-questioning is not unlike Radwan's in Mahfouz's *Sugar Street*. The novel ends leaving this key question unanswered. Clearly, for Khuri, if untoward sexual practices can be excised from the biography of Dik al-Jinn, the possibility of desire could not be eliminated altogether. If anything, it constituted the very tension driving the entire novel. While in the medieval accounts Dik al-Jinn's love and desire for Ward and Bakr is assumed and does not need explanation, for the modern Khuri, it is transformed into an existential quest for the ethical life. Gustav von Aschenbach's tormented passion for the young Polish boy Tadzio in Thomas Mann's *Death in Venice* brought about Aschenbach's own death rather than contamination of his love of beauty with the love of the flesh (Aschenbach's flesh becomes contaminated with cholera, leaving his love for Tadzio pure). Khuri, in line with Mann's strategy, eliminates the love object of Dik al-Jinn altogether from the picture, making sure that if there ever were such love, it would not have had a chance of being consummated, or more accurately, of being contaminated by the flesh. What Dik al-Jinn ended up doing with his life, Khuri tells us, amounted to nothing less than "his suicide."[103]

Khuri's commitment to interpreting Dik al-Jinn's infatuation with Bakr as a Platonic appreciation of beauty, which he announced at the outset of the novel in the dialogue with Old Man History, is not much unlike Mann's Aschenbach, who uses words from Plato's *Symposium* and *Phaedrus* and Plutarch's *Erotikos* throughout to express his love for Tadzio.[104] It is also reminiscent of Oscar Wilde's invocation during his trial of Greek male love as pure and intellectual as a rebuttal to the prosecutor's accusation that Wilde's relations with men were sexual. For Khuri as for Wilde, what was being invoked was a Platonic male love

---

101. Ibid., 142.

102. Ibid., 142–43.

103. Ibid., 142.

104. See David Luke, introduction, in Thomas Mann, *Death in Venice and Other Stories*, translated by David Luke (New York: Bantam Books, 1988), xxxvii, xliv. *Der Tog in Venedig* was first published in 1912.

viewed as the noblest of attachments, which if sullied with carnal practices would indeed be seen as base.[105]

For Khuri as for Mann, Dik al-Jinn's pain was necessary not only for his pleasure but also for his greatness, although ultimately it is this that brought upon his downfall (as it did Hamidah in Mahfouz's *Midaq Alley*). For Khuri, pleasure and pain are always coupled and intermingled, as he tells us in an essay on the topic. He offers an Aristotelian cautionary warning against "excess," which leads "to dysfunction and harm," and in favor of moderation.[106] Pain, for Khuri, "is the teacher of [morals], which it trains, and strengthens for struggle. Few great personalities who imposed themselves on history . . . were not educated at the hands of this great master."[107] In this vein, Khuri can be seen as one of the many modern Arab authors discussed in previous chapters who continued to be informed by modern European, and especially Victorian, ethics on the question of desire, and who insisted on rewriting the history of the past after filtering out desires and practices now considered objectionable. Their evaluation and assessments of these past desires and practices were thoroughly Victorian, as were their denials that such desires ever inhabited the hearts of great men (or women), then or now, and that if they ever did, few acted out on them.[108]

105. H. Montgomery Hyde, editor, *The Trials of Oscar Wilde* (Middlesex: Penguin, 1962), 245–52. Wilde, of course, was being insincere at the trial, using Plato as a cover for "feasting with panthers." On this, see Rupert Croft-Cooke, *Feasting with Panthers: A New Consideration of Some Late Victorian Writers* (London: W. H. Allen, 1967).

106. Ra'if Khuri, "Al-Ladhdhah wa al-Alam" [Pleasure and Pain], *Al-Duhur*, January 1934, reprinted in Ra'if Khuri, *Thawrat al-Fata al-'Arabi, 'A'mal Mukhtarah min Turath Ra'if Khuri* [The Revolt of the Young Arab Man; Selected Works from the Legacy of Ra'if Khuri] (Beirut: Dar al-Farabi, 1984), 88–89.

107. Ibid., 89.

108. Khuri's displeasure with representations of unorthodox desires led him to criticize Suhayl Idris's 1962 existentialist and autobiographical novel *Asabi'una allati Tahtariq* [Our Burning Fingers] for including a scene in which a woman makes sexual advances to another. For Khuri's review of the book, see Ra'if Khuri, *Al-Adab al-Mas'ul* [Responsible Literature] (Beirut: Dar al-Adab, 1968), 209. Scholarly, rather than fictional, interest in Dik al-Jinn was to be revived in the 1980s and beyond with a number of studies published about him and his poetry including Jurj Ghurayyib, *Dik al-Jinn al-Himsi* (Beirut: Dar al-Thaqafah, 1983), a competent account by Mazhar al-Hajji (who also compiled a new collection of Dik al-Jinn's poetry), *Dik al-Jinn al-Himsi, Dirasah fi Mukawwinat al-Sha'ir wa Madamin Shi'rih* [Dik al-Jinn al-Himsi, A Study of the Poet's Formation and the Content of His Poetry] (Damascus: Tlas lil-Dirasat wa al-Tarjamah wa al-Nashr, 1989), and a thorough comprehensive study by Khalid Halabuni, *Dik al-Jinn, al-Dhatiyyah wa al-Ibda'* [Dik al-Jinn, Selfness and Creativity] (Damascus: Al-Yamamah, 2001). See also Hasan Ja'far Nur al-Din, *Dik al-Jinn al-Himsi, 'Abd al-Salam bin Raghban, 'Asruh wa Hayatuh wa Fununuh al-Shi'riyyah* [Dik al-Jinn al-Himsi, 'Abd al-Salam bin Raghban, His Epoch, Life, and Poetic Arts] (Beirut: Dar al-Kutub al-'Ilmiyyah, 1990), and Salim Maja'is, *Dik al-Jinn Al-Himsi, Tahafut al-Ruwah wa Shafafiyyat al-Nass* [Dik Al-Jinn al-Himsi, The Incoherence of the Narrators and the Transparency of the Text] (Beirut: Dar Amwaj, 2000).

Deviance and Self-Abuse

But while Khuri attended to a Victorian ethic, Arab novelists in the next three decades would approach the matter of desire in a manner commensurate with the legacy of colonialism and the demands and limitations of national independence, as well as state sponsorship of modernization projects across the Arab world. Yusuf Idris's 1962 novella *The Black Cop* (*Al-'Askari al-Aswad*), explored how torture, including rape, of political prisoners in Egypt under the monarchy and the British in the late 1940s, in the wake of the Palestine War, led not only to the psychological breakdown of the tortured prisoner (one Dr. Shawqi, a student activist who was one of those tortured for demonstrating against colonialism in 1946 and the defeat in Palestine in 1948) but also of the torturer himself ('Abbas, aka "the black cop").[109] Not only did Dr. Shawqi dismiss the sexual component of the torture to his friend, telling him that "the black cop for us was something else, something other than the sexual things and nonsense you heard about, something else entirely,"[110] but even the friend-narrator, after speaking to other former political prisoners, found out "obscure" things about the matter. However, "despite their obscurity, they were sufficient to sketch out the general features of the role of the black cop in the life of Shawqi and his colleagues, that second, danger-fraught role that has no connection to the sexual rumors that some newspapers unleashed about him after his story was exposed following the end of the reign of terror and the beginning of the review of the crimes committed under its shadow."[111] 'Abbas "was not black, as the newspapers had dubbed him . . . , he only had a dark complexion and was from Upper Egypt."[112] 'Abbas had been discovered by the prime minister, who was full of admiration for him and "considered him the model of a perfect man. He would often send for him to be brought before his guests in the living room, especially the foreigners among them, to show him off to them. He would have him show off his physique and flex his muscles for them, showing much pride in the fact that he was his own discovery. Many moans would be uttered by the women present upon setting eyes on him."[113] Clearly, not only the women were moaning, as the male prime minister and the other men were enjoying a homoerotic spectacle that was presented equally for their benefit.

---

109. Yusuf Idris, *Al-'Askari al-Aswad wa Qisas Ukhra* [The Black Cop and Other Short Stories] (Cairo: Dar al-Ma'rifah, 1962).

110. Ibid., 28. 112. Ibid.

111. Ibid., 34. 113. Ibid., 41–42.

Idris was intent in his novella to detract from the sensationalism of rape, concentrating on the sadistic beatings of prisoners, which destroy them physically and mentally.[114] Although, we find out later that ʿAbbas was happily married, even though sterile and without children, he began to break down after he was "discovered" by the prime minister. He slowly withdrew from society, no longer approaching his wife sexually, and began to have nightmares. He finally fell into a catatonic state, barking like a dog. No longer able to destroy the flesh of his prisoners, he began to bite off his own flesh and chew it. When confronted by Dr. Shawqi, who coincidentally, was called in to diagnose him, ʿAbbas cowered in his bed in terror, not wanting to hear Shawqi's screaming condemnation upon his discovery of the identity of his patient, a scene reminiscent of how Shawqi and fellow prisoners used to cower under physical torture.

Idris's novella is important not only for its subsequent inspiration to those who criticized the Egyptian government's violent crackdown and torture of Islamist activists in the 1980s (a book on that torture was titled reminiscently *The Black Cop*[115]), but also for its lack of sensationalism regarding rape per se, except insofar as it was part of the overall sadistic torture of the bodies of prisoners. Idris's sober view, as we will later see, will be abandoned by those who would approach the matter in the 1980s and beyond.[116]

But if Idris tackled masculinity and the scene of torture as part of the ancien régime's reign of terror, Lebanese novelist and publisher Suhayl Idris (no relation to Yusuf) approached lesbian desire with horror, as unrestrained and misled Westernized feminism. In his semiautobio-

114. See his precise description of the scene of beating and its impact on the torturer and the prisoner in ibid., 35–38, 41.

115. Ayman Nur and Majdi Shandi, *Al-ʿAskari al-Aswad, Zaki Badr* [The Black Cop: Zaki Badr] (Cairo: al-Sharikah al-ʿArabiyyah al-Dawliyyah Lil-Nashr, 1990).

116. Bin Salim Himmish's classic novel *Majnun al-Hukm bi-Amr Allah, Riwayah fi al-Takhyil al-Tarikhi* [Crazy about Governing by God's Commands: A Novel about Historical Imagination] (London: Riyad al-Rayyis, 1990) and republished in 1998 in Rabat, Morocco, by Matbaʿat al-Maʿarif al-Jadidah, resurrects the historical story about the Fatimid caliph of Egypt in the eleventh century, al-Hakim bi Amr Allah, who suffered from bouts of manic melancholia. The caliph was said to have used a tall black slave with a large athletic body and a huge penis to rape cheating Cairo (male) merchants publicly and in full view of the caliph himself as punishment for cheating their customers. The slave, named Masʿud and dubbed "the machine/organ of sodomitic punishment" (alat al-ʿiqab al-liwati) by Himmish, would later be overcome by guilt and visions of bleeding anuses until he became impotent and could no longer perform his duties—not unlike the black cop of Idris's novella, which could have easily been inspired by this historical episode (45–85). The novel mixes history and fiction about a tyrannical medieval ruler deployed as an allegory of modern repressive Arab regimes. It is significant that Masʿud is also the name of the black slave with whom Shahrayar's wife is caught in the opening sequence of *A Thousand and One Nights*. See *The Arabian Nights*, translated by Husain Haddawy (New York: Norton, 1990), 5.

graphical novel also published in 1962, Idris recounted a minor incident about a lesbian relationship between a literary socialite and an up-
and-coming feminist novelist by the name of Salma ʿAkkawi who wrote
a book titled *Ana Hurrah* (I Am Free). Given the literary and political
battles of the period between Idris and ideological rivals on the Lebanese scene, some speculated that the reference in his novel might have
been to Lebanese feminist novelist Layla Baʿlabaki's (both the fictional
ʿAkkawi and the real Baʿlabaki's last names refer to Levantine cities),
who had recently published her first novel *Ana Ahya* (I Live), although
Idris never confirmed that this was the case.[117] In the novel, the socialite aggressively pursued the protagonist's wife and propositioned her
sexually. Horrified, the protagonist's wife, Ilham, kicked her out of her
house.[118]

Four decades later, Idris would comment in his memoir on the reason
for his distaste for lesbian desire, which apparently went back to his
childhood. In an exceedingly open and daring memoir, Idris spoke of
how much he "did not love" his father.

I used to feel that he lived in an air of hypocrisy. The time came when I realized that
my father lived two lives, one with his wife and children, and a second life with others. I discovered one day that he was accompanied by a handsome young man, with
blond hair, whom I used to see in the shop adjacent to my father's shop by the harbor.
He went with this young man into the living room of our house, which also had a second door that opened to the outside. I heard a bit later the inside door being closed
and the sound of the key turning in the lock. I called my older brother and told him.
He shook his head as if he'd understood what I meant. He then murmured a sentence
deploring [what our father was doing]. This incident would be repeated, and I began
to hate this duality in my father more and more . . . I believe that this incident left me
with a sense of repulsion toward deviant relationships [shadhdhah] despite the more
recent [scientific] justifications for them, in terms of the genetic and physical makeup
of humans. This is why I always avoided being with men alone, as I would discover in
their eyes, on occasion, suggestions of this deviance. This also applies to my repulsion
at homosexual [mithliyyah] relations among women, some of which I represented in
my novel, *Our Burning Fingers*.[119]

117. Egyptian (male) novelist Ihsan ʿAbd al-Quddus had in fact published a novel titled *Ana Hurrah* [I Am Free] (Cairo: Dar Ruz al-Yusuf, 1957), which was made into a popular film directed by Salah
Abu Sayf and released in 1959. However, it was clearly not the book to which Idris made reference.

118. Suhayl Idris, *Asabiʿuna allati Tahtariq* [Our Burning Fingers] (1962; Beirut: Dar al-Adab,
1998), 189–97. See also Layla Baʿlabaki, *Ana Ahya* [I Live] (Beirut: al-Maktab al-Tijari, 1958).

119. Suhayl Idris, *Dhikrayat al-Adab wa al-Hubb* [Memories of Literature and Love] (Beirut: Dar
al-Adab, 2002), part 1, 12–13.

It is noteworthy that Idris's father's liaison with a young man is registered as "deviance" while more recent lesbian relationships are described
as "homosexual." While both types of relationships are pathologized
through appeal to science and genetics, Idris seems to only substitute
one modern European term for another. As no one would have called his
father a "deviant" in the 1930s when this incident happened, any more
than any one (except perhaps Freud's translators) would have called the
socialite and the novelist "homosexual" in the late 1950s, the apparent
semantic difference and its attendant taxonomies are more a product of
2002, when the memoir was written. The encroachment of both terms,
"deviant" and "homosexual," from a Western register is what is being
historicized here and not their use in the Arab world.

All the same, few novelists created full-fledged characters who engaged in same-sex contact, although many would include minor characters who did. Sunʿallah Ibrahim's short story, *That Odor (Tilka al-Raʾihah)*,
a fictional autobiographical account of a just released political prisoner,
was the most daring in its depiction of male desires in the context of
masculine despair in the face of oppression and torture. The *Black Cop*
addressed imprisonment under the monarchy and British colonialism
and the impact it had on the torturer. In contrast, Ibrahim's book addresses the oppression of the postcolonial nationalist regime of Nasir
and its impact on those who are tortured. Upon publication in 1966, the
book was banned and its copies seized. It was republished in a censored
version in 1969 and was finally published in full in 1986.[120] The original
copy circulated underground until 1986. Ibrahim's interest in and depiction of male sexual desires can be found in all his subsequent work,
especially one of his later novels, *Sharaf,* discussed in chapter 6.

In *That Odor,* written in the first person, the protagonist witnessed
sexual acts with a teenage boy and with a woman prostitute without being able to participate. In a cell in which he was detained for one extra
night before being released, he witnessed how two common criminals
took turns buggering a detained teenager who consented to the act under a makeshift blanket. Once the second one finished with him, the
buggerer hogged the blanket leaving the teenager uncovered.[121] The protagonist observed the sexual act without intervening.[122] When his two

---

120. Sunʿallah Ibrahim, *Tilka al-Raʾihah* [That Odor] (Cairo: Maktab Yulyu, 1966). The 1969
incomplete edition was published by Dar al-Thaqafah al-Jadidah in Cairo. All references are to the
1986 complete edition published by Dar Shuhdi in Cairo. For the English version, see Sonallah
Ibrahim, *The Smell of It, and Other Stories,* translated by Denys Johnson-Davies (London: Heinemann
Educational, 1971).

121. Ibid., 27.

122. Jordanian novelist Ghalib Halasa, one of the best and most sensual of modern Arab novel-

friends brought a prostitute to his apartment after his release, they both had sex with her. When it was his turn, he failed to perform. Unable to gratify others sexually, whether boys or women, the only sexual act the protagonist was still capable of performing was autogratification.

In the story, the narrator recounts two incidents of masturbation, the first when he masturbated in the bathroom when his girlfriend, unresponsive to his sexual advances, fell asleep next to him, and the second when he masturbated one day when he was home alone. That latter scene became one of the better known scenes of male masturbation in modern Arabic literature, and was perhaps the reason for the initial banning of the story, on account of its "pornographic" nature. The protagonist, a writer, cleans his desk and holds his pen attempting to write but fails after repeated attempts. He closes his eyes and begins to fantasize about a naked woman he had seen from his window in the opposite building a few days earlier: "My hand reached for my leg. I began to play with my body. I finally sighed. I fell on the chair, tired, staring at the [blank] paper [on the desk] with an empty look. A little later, I got up and walked carefully around the remnants I had left on the tiled floor below the chair and went to the bathroom and washed my socks and my shirt and hung them on the window."[123] He would not clean the floor, yet he still noticed a few days later that "on the floor black spots appeared, which were the traces of my pleasure."[124] It is relevant to note the contempt that the protagonist showed toward the floor that was smudged with his semen in light of the contempt that the two cellmates felt toward the boy they buggered and in whom they deposited their semen (aside from taking the blanket from him, in the morning when the boy was taken to clean the hall, they ate their breakfast and saved nothing for him). The protagonist himself was so disgusted with the prostitute that he insisted on using a condom (this was still a time when condom use was not widely practiced) despite her assertions that she was "clean."[125] When she attempted to kiss him, he rebuffed her in disgust and failed to perform. This inability to deal with the object of desire except as degraded and reified was internalized by the protagonist, who at some

---

ists, depicted a similar scene in his novel *Al-Khamasin* [Khamasin Winds], 2nd ed. (1975; Beirut: Dar ibn Rushd lil-Tiba'ah wa al-Nashr, 1978), wherein a condemned mass murderer who was facing execution for his crimes the next morning "brought a juvenile from Room number 27, set aside for those under 16 years of age, took him into his cell and had intercourse with him [daja'ahu]. The boy was screaming. But everyone stood silent before the last desires of a man about to die," 69. It is significant that Halasa includes this story between parentheses.

123. Ibrahim, *Tilka al-Ra'ihah*, 45.
124. Ibid., 48.
125. Ibid., 49.

unconscious level seemed to identify with the boy and the prostitute as objects of contempt. Just like penetrated boys and prostitutes, through the mechanism of oppression, not only by the state but also by the social and family structure that is much elaborated in *That Odor,* penetrators of men are transformed into objects of contempt, into penetratees.

The protagonist seems not only to refuse biological and literary reproduction by insisting on spilling his seed *and* his ink, preventing it from joining with paper, thus squandering his literary potential, but he also seeks to refuse the social dimension of sex, limiting it to autoerotic activity. Even when he watched the two men having sex with the teenage boy in jail, or when he saw his female neighbor disrobe through her window in the opposite building, he did not show any excitement. It was later when he masturbated that he imagined her. His indifference to his spilled seed is an indifference to his future. Imprisonment and torture by the postcolonial state was such that the postcolonial citizen refuses to generate, indeed leaving himself open to *degeneration.* The protagonist himself seemed to have lost all respectability. When paying a visit to a friend who had not come home yet, the friend's wife ushers the protagonist into the living room where he is later joined by his friend's young daughter. He began to fart, to the displeasure of the child who kept complaining: "'There is a smell of poop.' I ignored her but she kept repeating, 'There is a smell of poop.' I began to sniff around me and told her 'Where,' until the odor disappeared."[126] It is only "that odor" that the protagonist was able to generate and that Ibrahim wanted society to smell, as oppression invariably smells like "poop."

The scene of masturbation was emblematic of the radicality of *That Odor* in its depiction of the impact of political oppression on masculinity (and on literary creativity). Ibrahim, however, was not the first to broach the subject. It had been visited a number of times by Arab intellectuals in their memoirs. Jurji Zaydan himself had described in his memoir about his early life (1861–81), how he had "fallen" into a "secret habit," when he was twelve years old, in 1873. Indeed the very term "al-ʿadah al-sirriyyah," meaning "secret habit" or "solitary practice,"[127] which would become the operative expression in Arab medical terminology in the twentieth century, was a translation of the modern Western term "secret habit," and its correlates "crime of solitude," "solitary vice," and "evil practice." The classical Arab medical term had always

---

126. Ibid., 35.
127. The term "ʿadah" in Arabic is derived from the verb "ʿada," meaning "to return to," and "aʿada" "to repeat," hence habit is always about repetition.

been "istimna²," literally "sperming," which was a term that applied to both sexes on account of the medieval Arab medical belief that both men and women produced sperm.[128]

While an apprentice at a shoemaker shop in Beirut learning how to make "western shoes," the young Zaydan became increasingly weak and sickly. The deterioration of his health was attributed to long hours of sitting down and infrequent mobility.

I do not deny that these two reasons have an impact on health, but there was another important reason, which is one of those secret reasons in which every boy and young man [ghulam] falls. I fell into this habit before I began to work with shoes, and found no pleasure in it due to how young I was. When I later befriended the rest of the working boys, they increased my desire for it, especially given the long hours I would spend sitting down [to make shoes]. All these reasons came together to weaken me. I remember that working at al-Dahik's shop had the biggest impact on my future, as I learned then the amount of harm that results from this habit. I learned it coinciden-tally, but it had the greatest impact on my heart. It happened that one of the sons of the notables of Beirut used to frequent al-Dahik's shop and was a friend of the two brothers who owned it . . . He once came and complained of degeneration [inhilal] and weakness. After he left, one of the brothers said to the other: "Poor fellow, do you know the cause of his weakness?" He said, "No." The other said, "The cause is that he plays with his hand." This was the first time I had heard this expression about this harmful habit. But I paid attention to him, and I pledged to myself that I would give it up. That I did, and I began to feel an overall improvement in my health. By then I had moved back to my father's hotel, which [also] helped to improve my health.[129]

The impact of Western medical ideas was already felt in Beirut, whose edu-cational system had become dominated by European missionary schools of all kinds. While there was little trace of ideas that masturbation caused bad health in Arab popular culture prior to the encroachment of the mis-sionary schools, *jald 'Umayrah* (flogging 'Umayrah, wherein 'Umayrah refers either to the hand, thus, hand flogging, or to the penis, thus, penis

---

128. For an account of masturbation in Western medical thought in the eighteenth and nine-teenth century and the terms used to designate it as a "secret habit," see Thomas Lacqueur, *Solitary Sex: A Cultural History of Masturbation* (New York: Zone Books, 2003), especially 222–27, and his *Mak-ing Sex: Body and Gender from the Greeks to Freud* (Cambridge: Harvard University Press, 1990), 227–30.

129. Jurji Zaydan, *Mudhakkarat Jurji Zaydan,* ed. Salah al-Din al-Munajjid (Beirut: Dar al-Kitab al-Jadid, 1968), 19–20. The memoirs were initially serialized in al-Hilal in 1954, in a highly censored edition. It was al-Munajjid who resurrected them and republished them verbatim. Indeed, in the index to the memoir, al-Munajjid, true to his liberal ideas about sex, has an entry about Zaydan's "affliction with the secret habit and his abandoning it," in ibid., 101.

flogging[130]), as the jovial colloquial reference to male masturbation had it since medieval times, would enter a new phase of cultural prohibition.

It is significant that most of those who wrote about masturbation, either as a practice that they or their family considered objectionable, are Arab Christians, to whom it might have constituted more of a problem on account of the larger impact of Western Christian ideas on them through missionary schooling. Indeed, as we saw in an earlier chapter, the radical Egyptian secularist Salamah Musa, who, like Zaydan, was Christian, wrote in the forties and fifties with utter horror at masturbation, reiterating Orientalist opinion that sexual segregation was the culprit. The 1930s and 1940s were seemingly decades of much anxiety about masturbation and other deviances, all of which attributable to what the West had diagnosed as the peculiar segregation of the sexes in Muslim societies. This anxiety also echoes the one that overtook social engineers in Europe from the eighteenth century on and which became a crisis for reform of all-boy schools in England in the late nineteenth century. Some parents, especially Christians, became worried about their young sons' immersion in such evil habits. Edward Said wrote in his memoir how as a teenager in the 1940s his parents were obsessed with his and his sisters' pubescent bodies and in the necessity of segregating him from them. "One chilly Sunday afternoon in late November 1949," when he had just turned fourteen and had already been the recipient of a number of lectures from his father on the harms of "self-abuse," which included becoming "useless" and a "failure," both the ultimate outcome of when "the degeneracy took final hold,"[131]

there was a loud knock on my bedroom door, followed immediately by a sternly authoritative wrenching of the handle. This was very far from a friendly paternal visit. Performed with unimpeachable rectitude "for your own good," it was *the* rigorous assault on my character that had been building to this climax for almost three years. My father stood near the door for a moment; in his right hand he clutched my pajama bottoms distastefully, which I despairingly remembered I had left in the bathroom that morning . . . When he was halfway into the room, just as he began to speak, I saw my mother's drawn face framed in the doorway several feet behind him. She said nothing but was present to give emotional weight to his prosecution of the case. "Your mother and I have noticed"—and he waved the pajama—"that you haven't had any wet dreams. That means you're abusing yourself."[132]

130. On *jald ʿumayrah,* see Muhammad bin Yaʿqub al-Fayruzabadi, *Al-Qamus al-Muhit* (Beirut: Dar Ihya' al-Turath al-ʿArabi, 1997), vol. 1, 622.
131. Edward W. Said, *Out of Place: A Memoir* (New York: Alfred A. Knopf, 1999), 71.
132. Ibid., 70.

The self-abusing Said had indeed learned the despicable habit at the country club, where one day in the locker room overlooking the swimming pool,

a gaggle of older boys, wet from swimming, burst in. They were led by Ehab, a very tall and thin boy with a deep voice that exuded confidence. Rich, secure, at home, and in place. "Come on, Ehab, do it," he was urged by others . . . Ehab lowered his trunks, stood on the bench, and while peering over the wall at the pool's designated sunbathing area, began to masturbate . . . We were all watching Ehab as he rubbed his penis slowly until, at last, he ejaculated, also slowly, at which point he started to laugh smugly, displaying his sticky fingers as if he had just won a trophy.[133]

It would seem that unlike the tortured young men that Salamah Musa portrayed in his memoir, Said and his peers were enjoying self-abuse, parental horror and missionary prohibitions notwithstanding. It is with this as social background that Sun'allah Ibrahim's *That Odor* caused a scandal to the cultural commissars who banned it. Although we are dealing here with different kinds of writings and different types of audiences—memoirs, pseudoscientific help books for the youth—and the different kinds of experiences they purport to represent, they were (except for Said's much later intervention, which was translated to Arabic) the only available literary representations of masturbation prior to Ibrahim's fictional intervention (indeed, even Zaydan's uncensored memoirs were published in book form two years after the first banned edition of *That Odor*). It is in this more general world of writing and texts that Ibrahim offered his graphic and fictional account.[134]

A New Trope of National Decline

A minor Egyptian novelist, Isma'il Waliy al-Din, who would become a well-known screenwriter of films and television series in the 1970s, pub-

133. Ibid., 73.
134. Novels and short stories would also begin to depict women's masturbation more explicitly by the 1970s. For a beautiful and sensitive description of a woman's fantasies and autoerotic pleasure, see, for example, Egyptian writer Alifah Rif'at's short story "'Alami al-Majhul" [My Unknown World] rendered in its English translation as "My World of the Unknown," in *Man Yakun al-Rajul?* [Who Is the Man?] (Cairo: Matabi' al-Hay'ah al-Misriyyah al-'Amah lil-Kitab, 1981), 45–68. For representations of male masturbation in movie theaters and in the privacy of one's home, see Ibrahim 'Abd al-Majid, *Bayt Al-Yasamin* [The House of Jasmine] (Cairo: Dar wa Matabi' Al-Mustaqbal, 1992). The novel was first published in 1986. 'Abd al-Majid depicts an alienated man who, while alone in his apartment, conjures up elaborate sexual fantasies that excite him so much that he ejaculates without even touching his penis (to which he refers as "my animal"), 85.

lished a novel in 1970 titled *Hammam al-Malatili* (The Malatili Bath-house). The novel, like many of Waliy al-Din's fictional writings, made little impact on the literary scene. Its effect however would be felt in cinematic form when famed director Salah Abu Sayf made it into a film in 1973.[135] *Hammam al-Malatili* was written in late 1969, when the ef-fects of the 1967 Arab-Israeli War continued to dominate Arab politi-cal and intellectual life. The setting of the novel and the film was the traditional bathhouse (in this case one that was built during the Mam-luk period for royalty), presented as the modern setting for criminal behavior—drug trafficking, gangsterism, and deviant sexual practice in the form of male prostitution. In the novel, the Malatili bathhouse was the address frequented by many elite men in society, Egyptians and Westerners, in pursuit of young penetrative and poor men of the un-derclass. In the film, only Egyptians frequent it. The novel is about de-generation and decadence that seem to have caused and resulted from national defeat in 1967. The major protagonist is a young twenty-year-old high school graduate, who, along with his family, is a refugee from the city of Ismailia whose civilian inhabitants were made refugees by unrelenting Israeli bombing during and after the war. Displaced in rural Egypt, the family dispatched the young Ahmad to Cairo in search of a job and university education. Running out of money and having no place to sleep, Ahmad finally comes upon the Malatili bathhouse, whose owner gives him a job as a bookkeeper. Ahmad would also sleep at the bathhouse.

The film, like the novel, included a portrayal of an upper-class painter named Ra'uf (played by famous actor Yusuf Sha'ban) who frequents the Malatili bathhouse in search of young men to paint and have sex with. It is there that he encounters Ahmad. While in the novel Ahmad is presented as a muscular, manly twenty-year-old and Ra'uf as a delicate sensitive and shy thirty-eight-year-old, the film has the opposite depic-tion. It is Ahmad who is young, clean-shaven, and boyish-looking while Ra'uf is physically manly and mustachioed. In the film, which follows the novel's text closely most of the time, Ra'uf invites Ahmad to his house in order to paint him bare-chested. That very day Ahmad had lost his virginity with a female prostitute, Na'imah, of whom he was growing fond. After a session of drinking and dancing to James Brown's "Like a Sex Machine" at the apartment, Ra'uf collapsed into bouts of laughter, followed by a soul-searching conversation with Ahmad about

---

135. Ismaʿil Waliy al-Din, *Hammam al-Malatili* [The Malatili Bathhouse] (Cairo: Kitabat Muʿasirah, 1970).

individual liberty. Faced with Ra'uf's escapism and despite his own economic woes and his family's displacement by war, Ahmad spoke insistently of patriotism and honest values. Ra'uf ridiculed his plans to get a job and support his family on a limited income, insensitively asserting, "Who knows when the war will be over?" and cited his own mother's example, who had emigrated to Australia, as "the only solution." This aspect of the film contrasts with the novel, where Ra'uf's family, who emigrated to Lebanon, not Australia, begs him to join them. He refuses on account of how much he loves Cairo.[136] The scene continues with Ra'uf mentioning the eighteenth–nineteenth-century Egyptian writer al-Jabarti, who chronicled the Napoleonic invasion of Egypt (and whom we encountered in the introduction), as someone who amazed him; for despite how much he had insulted and criticized political power (and the reference is to the ruler of Egypt at the time, Muhammad Ali), al-Jabarti's books remained available and widely read in the present. As Ahmad tried to answer, Ra'uf interrupted and explained that this was the case because "there used to be freedom and respect for the individual. Why can't one do what one wants, wear what one likes, grow one's hair long without anyone bothering him? Why not exchange our roles in life, why not break the tedium in our lives. Play an Indian chief one day." At this point the scene cuts *in medias res* and switches to a fantasy sequence with lively organ music, showing Ra'uf in (pseudo-) Native American garb and braided hair and tattoo walking in downtown Cairo raising eyebrows among passersby. The scene switches again to Ra'uf in an African shirt, and yet again to him wearing an animal-print shirt with most of the buttons open to expose his chest. It is significant that freedom for Ra'uf meant assuming the role not of Europeans, but of Africans and Native Americans, not to mention effeminacy, thus coupling the homosexual and the "primitive." Unlike the film, in the novel, Ra'uf does not specify Native American or African roles but rather that of an "unknown primitive chief or person."[137] The scene switches back to the apartment where Ra'uf flies into a rage, taking down his mother's portrait and throwing it on the floor. When Ahmad asked him why he would do such a thing, Ra'uf explained:

She is the one who did this to me. She kept indulging me until she got me lost. I got tired of medical treatment. When dad found out. He fled. He emigrated. He could not bear to see me like this. The psychiatrist told her that there was no use. We had to

136. Ibid., 57, 92.
137. Ibid., 93.

accept reality. My medicine is basically tranquilizer drugs. When she made sure that there was no use, she fled. She emigrated. She emigrated and left me to lose my way far from her.

Ra'uf collapses crying into Ahmad's loving embrace as the scene closes. After the implied sexual encounter, Ahmad walks aimlessly through the streets of Cairo for six days after which he runs into Na'imah. In the novel, Ahmad reacts normally to the encounter without soul-searching. We never see or hear of Ra'uf again in the film. In the novel, Ra'uf visits the bathhouse one more time and is arrested with other men for engaging in public sex and prostitution during a police raid looking for drugs at the bathhouse.[138]

Ahmad's loss of direction and of normative values coupled with his sexual precociousness led him to an affair with the wife of his boss, the same boss who had taken him in at the bathhouse and who trusted him. Eventually, Na'imah is killed by her uncle and cousin who come from the village to avenge their family's lost "honor." Ahmad collapses when he finds out she was murdered because he failed to protect her. She had been waiting to meet him when she was murdered, while he was having sex with his boss's wife. Ahmad's collapse signaled his realization that he failed in all his pursuits and that he had lost his values and succumbed to worldly temptation. The starry-eyed young man with whom the film starts is utterly destroyed at the end, crying by a saint's tomb in a mosque. In the novel, Ahmad announces that he is going back to rejoin his family.

The film includes an eccentric Sufi wanderer who punctuates the film and speaks the language of nationalism and Egyptian history, juxtaposing Ahmad's loss of his sense of direction, as well as Ra'uf's and Na'imah's, to Egypt having lost its way, which landed it in the defeat of the 1967 War. The novel and the film are thus an indictment of contemporary Egypt, which failed to protect its children who, in turn, failed to protect their mother, and a plea for the country and its people to restore past glories by finding the right path again. The film and the novel combine two accounts of homosexuality, one of blaming the biological mother and the other blaming the motherland for the decadence that leads to passive homosexuality, prostitution, drug trafficking, and delinquency. The nationalist dynamic, however, remains the connecting tissue of the story. The irony of Ahmad being introduced by the owner of the bathhouse as "one of our heroes from Ismailia" (an extranovelistic

138. Ibid., 118–19.

embellishment) and Ahmad's ultimate decadent reality constitutes the film's central tragic element of national decline.[139]

The Malatili Bathhouse was the first novelistic (and filmic) inversion of the homosexual encounter as being not between an older penetrative richer man and a younger effeminate poorer man, as in Mahfouz's *Midaq Alley,* but rather between a young penetrative poor man and an older rich man seeking to be penetrated. The film was more ambivalent than the novel about this representation, wherein despite the masculine exterior of the older man, he would act effeminately by seeking to have long hair, dress strangely, and dance. Also, the film's representation of Ahmad as having boyish physique did not deter it from presenting him as penetrative in his desires. Unlike in the novel, desire in the film did not seem to overlap with the gendered body necessarily. Moreover, although the novel couples passive homosexuality with national decline and decadence, it does so in the context of other elements, like the loss of women's honor, the loss of the values of the youth, delinquency, marital unfaithfulness, and criminality, as equally coupled with national decline. This ambivalence will soon be abandoned, as the novel/film would inaugurate a new trope that zeroes in on the passive homosexual (and passive homosexuality) as the most important element connected to national decline. Following Waliy al-Din's example, major writers and novelists, as we will see, would deploy this trope faithfully into the twenty-first century.

Orientalizing the Orient

Perhaps the most controversial of autobiographies was that of Moroccan writer Muhammad Shukri. Written in 1972 as a fictional autobiography that is immediately reminiscent of (and clearly influenced by) Jean Genet's *Journal du Voleur* (published in 1949), Shukri's *Al-Khubz al-Hafi* (Plain Bread) was published in French, English, and Spanish before coming out in Arabic in 1982.[140] He had been asked by Paul Bowles upon meeting

---

139. Garay Menicucci mistakes the film for a "plea for tolerance of sexual difference," and completely misses the nationalist dynamic, see Garay Menicucci, "Unlocking the Arab Celluloid Closet: Homosexuality in Egyptian Film," *Middle East Report* 206 (Spring 1998): 32–36. Menicucci's analysis, perhaps on account of his lack of Arabic literacy, misses key issues and misinterprets significant events in the films he covers.

140. Shukri in fact had met Genet in 1968 and would later write a memoir about the encounter in which he mentions that he had already read *The Thief's Journal.* See Muhammad Shukri, *Jan Junih fi Tanjah, Tinisi Wilyamz fi Tanjah* [Jean Genet in Tangiers, Tennessee Williams in Tangiers] (Cologne: Manshurat al-Jamal, 1993). William S. Burroughs wrote the introduction to Shukri's book.

him in Tangiers if he had written his memoirs. Shukri lied and said that he had and went away and immediately embarked on writing them.[141] Written sometimes in an ethnographic native informant style, the book became popular among Western readers while remaining unavailable in Arabic. Paul Bowles translated it to English after Shukri orally translated it to him from classical Arabic to Moroccan vernacular and to Spanish. Bowles' instigation is a much more direct and intimate kind of Western influence than, say, an Arab novelist reading a Western author. Bowles's intervention in the field of translating (some say outright writing) books attributed to North African authors (namely, Mohammed Mrabet and Larbi Layachi) is indeed a well-established one.[142] The book was most recently made into a feature film (2005) in a Moroccan-Italian-French production directed by Rachid Benhadj.

An illiterate young and poor man, Shukri learned to write as an adult.[143] In this frank autobiography, he recounted a variety of sexual experiences, including many masturbatory ones. One of the more shocking experiences to readers, Western and Arab alike, was when, as an early teen, Shukri forced a younger neighbor boy to submit to his sexual advances. Shukri's descriptions are not inhibited. He described the boy's resistance to his forceful violation, while speaking not only of buggering him but also of "touching his member with my hand; it became erect in my hand." The latter description, which would signify a declared desire for, or at least some sexual interest in, the boy's penis, and not only in the boy's orifices, is a rare admission in fictional or autobiographical writings of this sort, not to mention the admission of violent rape.[144]

---

141. See Sabri Hafiz, "Al-Bunyah al-Nassiyyah li-Sirat al-Taharrur min al-Qahr" [The Textual Structure of a Biography of Liberation from Oppression] published as an addendum to the second part of Shukri's autobiography *Al-Shuttar* (Beirut: Dar al-Saqi, 1992), 219–42.

142. See Greg Mullins, *Colonial Affairs: Bowles, Burroughs and Chester Write Tangiers* (Madison: University of Wisconsin Press, 2002), 111–34. See also Muhammad Shukri, *Bul Bulz wa 'Uzlat Tanjah* [Paul Bowles and the Isolation of Tangiers] (Cologne: Dar al-Jamal, 1997).

143. Muhammad Shukri, *Al-Khubz al-Hafi, Sirah Dhatiyyah Riwa'iyyah, 1935–1956* [Plain Bread, A Novelistic Autobiography, 1935–1956], fifth ed. (Beirut: Dar al-Saqi, 1995). For the English edition, see Mohamed Choukri, *For Bread Alone*, translated with an introduction by Paul Bowles (San Francisco: City Lights Books, 1987).

144. Ibid., 67. The rape of boys was visited by Egyptian writer Yahya Haqqi in a short story he published in 1967/1968. Haqqi's *Ka'anna* [As If] explores a man's identification with a suspect whose trial he read about in a newspaper and who is accused of raping and murdering scores of young boys and burying them in a cave. The unnamed protagonist, through identifying with the suspect, has an internal monologue, *as if* he were the suspect, narrating the background that led to the rapes and murders in a most empathic tone. For Haqqi, it is not sexual "deviance" and violence that is allegorized, but rather the intense sense of alienation that individuals feel due to societal and family oppression in the context of poverty leading the weak to prey on the weak. See Yahya Haqqi, *Ka'anna*, in Haqqi's collection *Al-Firash al-Shaghir wa Qisas Ukhra* [The Empty Bed and Other Stories], published as volume 19 of *Mu'allafat Yahya Haqqi* [The Collected works of Yahya Haqqi], ed. Fu'ad

Still, Shukri was aware that his sexual relationships with men, when it occurred, like his sexual relationships with women, meant mainly a relationship with their orifices in which his penis would be central. When as a child, he was asked by his French employer to wash her Italian husband's briefs: "I told her yes at first, a reluctant yes. When I placed the briefs in the water, I told myself, a man is not supposed to wash another man's underwear." He went back to his employer and refused to wash them. She acceded and asked it this was the custom in Morocco. He told her it was indeed a Moroccan custom when in fact, "I did not know whether this indeed was our custom or whether I made it up myself."[145] While clearly aware of the Western anthropological thirst for Oriental "customs," Shukri was self-conscious of the myths he was propagating. Expedience here was the operative criterion.

Shukri's desires were clearly polymorphous, accommodating a number of sexual objects: women, men, boys, girls, and animals.[146] He once described attractive dancing boys, and recounted how an older Spanish gentleman driving a car picked him up when he was a sixteen-year-old. "He must be a faggot [hassas], there is no doubt."[147] The older Spaniard began to

unbutton my fly slowly, button after button. He turned on the [car's] overhead light and went down on it, his breath warming it . . . I did not dare to look him in the face. "Bravo, bravo, macho" [the Spaniard said] . . . I fantasized that I was raping Asya in Tetouan. I ejaculated in his mouth. He moaned from pleasure like an animal . . . I buttoned my fly and crossed my arms around my chest as if nothing had happened. There are many women, why are humans sodomites? That's what I thought.[148]

While admittedly interested in buggering boys and women, Shukri still managed to marvel at those men who desired the penises of other men, forgetting his earlier interest in the penis of the boy he had raped. The incident with the Spaniard took place in the early 1950s, while Morocco was under French colonial rule and European colonials roamed its streets like they owned the place. Shukri wondered while still in the car with the older Spaniard: "Do all of those, who are like this old man, suck? This was a new profession [for me], that I can add to my other two, beg-

Dawarrah (Cairo: Al-Hay'ah al-Misriyyah al-'Ammah lil-Kitab, 1986), 275–306. The short story was initially serialized in the newspaper *Al-Masa'* between 18 December 1967 and 22 January 1968.

145. Shukri, *Al-Khubz al-Hafi*, 57–58.
146. Ibid., 36. He recounts how he fondled a cow and then sucked on its nipples.
147. Ibid., 106.
148. Ibid., 106.

ging and theft . . . My thing can also bring in money to help me live. It can also experience pleasure in the meantime. Does this old man find as much pleasure in sucking people's [sic] dicks as I do when I suck on women's breasts? It is still warm and sticky, dripping between my thighs. Is this how people become whores?"[149] He would wonder later about the world in which he was living, where "my sexual organ can be sold for fifty pesetas."[150] It is noteworthy that Shukri never compared the Spaniard's pleasure in sucking his penis (which rendered the Spaniard active) with the pleasure he himself had derived from having his penis sucked (rendering him passive). Shukri's comparison suggests identification and othering simultaneously. He and the Spaniard are both suckers of different part-objects attached to differently sexed humans. The comparison interestingly is about sexual object choice and *not* sexual aim, even though the sexual act that brought Shukri and the Spaniard together and that made the experience of pleasure possible for both of them was predicated primarily on their having different sexual aims. Indeed, Shukri's presumption is that the Spaniard would also find pleasure in having his own penis sucked, which is precisely why Shukri did not posit that experience as the mark of difference between them. Yet, it was Shukri's desire to have his penis sucked and the Spaniard's desire to suck his penis that made the encounter possible and pleasurable.

Throughout the book Shukri worried that he might be raped. Indeed, even his father was concerned about him.[151] One time he spent the night sleeping in a sitting position, rather than lying down, lest he be raped at an unsafe inn, where he slept in the animal barn.[152] His self-questioning about the penis-desiring male species, sacrificing their masculinity in the process, persisted. He understood his own masculinity in terms of preserving his own penis and in having a penetrative relationship to other men's anuses. The book is strewn with insults that he leveled against male rivals including, "I will spit in your anus,"[153] "I will urinate in your anus,"[154] in addition to the "I will feed you this" while clutching his penis over his trousers.[155] The last insult restores activity to the man whose penis is being sucked by claiming the act as one of feeding the sucker.

French colonialism was also seen in sexually symbolic terms. Upon hearing of the massacre of demonstrating Moroccans by French colonial soldiers, Shukri had a dream in which "there was a long row of naked men, in a big square, walking by three or four men who were also naked

149. Ibid., 107.
150. Ibid., 109.
151. Ibid., 30, 31, 97, 114.
152. Ibid., 111.

153. Ibid., 122.
154. Ibid., 207.
155. Ibid., 208.

like them and standing next to a table with medical instruments on it. They were excising their sexual organs and throwing them in a barrel. All around the square, which was fenced in with barricades, there were crowds of naked women crying for the men."[156] Such descriptions are not so unlike those uncovered by Frantz Fanon in *The Wretched of the Earth*, and that caused "mental disorders" in colonized men.[157]

Colonial castration aside, Shukri's anxiety about selling his penis, pleasure notwithstanding, was manifest. Upon finding a job as a porter that a skeptical friend offered him, he confided to himself, "I want to challenge my own strength and my age. Perhaps what makes him skeptical is how thin my body is. I thought that such a job is better for me than begging or stealing, better than to let my organ get sucked by an old man, and better than selling harirah [soup] and fried fish to Bedouins and workers in the outer market and at Hotel al-Shajarah, better than any job I ever had before."[158] In the second part of his autobiography, *Al-Shuttar*, Shukri would speak of being mostly attracted to girls who were "hermaphrodites. Perhaps, it was a latent sodomitic tendency that was still lodged in my depths. Boyish women [ghulamiyyat] are more active and attractive than feminine women . . . The latter's passivity . . . only inspires [a desire to] rape them."[159]

Shukri's *Plain Bread* still provokes scandals. It was suspended in 1999 from being taught in introductory courses of Arabic literature at the American University in Cairo (AUC) after parents complained that their children were reading pornographic material in a university course. Then Egyptian Minister of Higher Education Mufid Shihab vowed to ban the book from the curricula of all Egyptian universities. The Egyptian press jumped on the bandwagon, attacking Egyptian Professor Samia Mehrez for assigning the book in her course at AUC. *Al-Wafd* newspaper columnist Muhammad Mustafa Shirdi's article on the dispute argued: "Most or all of the works assigned in Mehrez's class attack society and deal with sex brazenly. It's obvious that the professor wishes to plant a particular, calculated view in the minds of students. When they find themselves confronted with so much negativity vis-à-vis their society, the honorable Dr. [Mehrez] has succeeded in sowing doubt in each of them, and we find an entire generation that renounces society, because it believes what AUC says is true and what society says is false, because they've

---

156. Ibid., 131.
157. See Frantz Fanon, *The Wretched of the Earth* (New York: Grove Press, 1963), especially the chapter titled "Colonial War and Mental Disorders," 249–310.
158. Shukri, *al-Khubz al-Hafi*, 156.
159. Shukri, *Al-Shuttar*, 172–73.

heard and read nothing but what the professor said and commented on."[160] Once more, sexual matters, even in fictional form, that are incongruent with what increasingly prudish cultural commissars believe should be taught, are identified as "foreign" to society.

If Shukri spoke of the illicit pleasures he had experienced in different types of sexual encounters, on the Egyptian front, there was a new genre of anthropological fiction writing produced in Cairo about that mystical land, Upper Egypt, where illicit sexual pleasure is represented as often leading to death. Upper Egypt has often functioned in Cairo-based writing as the Orient more generally does in European writing. Upper Egyptian writers contributed much to the increasing Cairene anxiety about that last bastion of feudal peasant culture whose traditions seemed to them to be so cruel and harsh, so "uncivilized." Perhaps some of the work of novelist Yahya al-Tahir ʿAbdullah exemplified native informant horror at the alleged practices of Upper Egyptians. His major novel *Al-Tawq wa al-Iswirah* (The Necklace and the Bracelet),[161] published in 1975, dealt with sexual repression of women and honor crimes, a theme visited decades earlier by Taha Husayn's *Duʿaʾ al-Karawan* (Call of the Curlew), which was published in 1934. Both novels were made into popular films by the Cairo-based cinema industry that contributed much to the exoticization of peasant Upper Egyptians. In addition to his novel, ʿAbdullah tells a horrific and far-fetched tale in one of his short stories about a father's murder of his young son after the latter was caught being buggered by an older boy. *Al-Raqsah al-Mubahah* (The Permitted Dance) is a favorite of ʿAbdullah fans precisely on account of the exotic fictional horror it recounts, often (mis)presented as anthropological observation.[162] Such interest in so-called "honor-crimes" made a comeback, especially for Western audiences, in stories emerging from Jordan in the 1990s (often circulated in the Jordanian English-language daily, the *Jordan Times,* a newspaper aimed not at Jordanians, but at Western expatriates). Such stories led to the publication and popularity of a book by one Norma Khuri that allegedly tells the story of a victim of honor crimes in Jordan.

160. *Al-Wafd,* 14 January 1999, quoted in Joseph Logan, "Morality Cops in the Classroom: AUC's Censorship Dilemma Prompts Hard-Line State Response," *Cairo Times* 3, issue. 2, 18–31 March 1999.

161. *Al-Tawq wa al-Iswirah* [The Necklace and the Bracelet], in Yahya al-Tahir ʿAbdullah *Al-Kitabat al-Kamilah* [Collected Works], 2nd ed. (Cairo, Dar al-Mustaqbal al-ʿArabi, 1994), 345–411.

162. *Al-Raqsah al-Mubahah* [The Permitted Dance], in Yahya al-Tahir ʿAbdullah, *Al-Kitabat al-Kamilah* [Collected Works], 2nd ed. (Cairo, Dar al-Mustaqbal al-ʿArabi, 1994), 224–31. The short story is cited by Frédéric Lagrange in his not very comprehensive survey of homosexuality in modern Arabic fiction, which misses many key texts. See his "Male Homosexuality in Modern Arabic Literature," in *Imagined Masculinities, Male Identity and Culture in the Modern Middle East,* ed. May Ghoussoub and Emma Sinclair-Webb (London: Dar al-Saqi, 2000), 181.

The book, called *Forbidden Love* in its Australian edition and *Honor Lost* in its U.S. edition, was revealed to be a sham only after it sold hundreds of thousands of copies around the world. Its author turned out to be an Arab American who never lived in Jordan and who had moved from the United States to Australia.[163] This is not to say that "honor crimes" do not occur, but rather that when they do occur (which, as indicated in the introduction, is a much more infrequent phenomenon than fatal crimes of passion in the West) they have much less to do with sexual puritanism and more so with a crisis of masculinity, as a number of the works to be discussed below will clarify.

Deviants in Power

In addition to memoirs and autobiographical writings, novels that included themes relating to sex of all kinds proliferated. In her first novel *Bayrut '75* (Beirut '75), published in 1975,[164] Syrian feminist novelist Ghadah al-Samman explored the transformation of two dreamy-eyed Syrians, one an aspiring writer called Yasminah, the other an aspiring singer called Farah. The two Syrians headed to Beirut to launch their careers. Yasminah became the mistress of the son of a Lebanese politician who would later discard her when an arranged marriage to the daughter of his father's rival was planned. Dejected, Yasminah sought out her brother, who knew of her affair but showed no disapproval as long as his sister gave him money. When she returned empty-handed, he beat her and then killed her to avenge his "honor." Farah was more successful in attaining his career goals only after he struck up a Faustian deal with Nishan, a distant family relation, now a powerful entertainment producer and public relations man in Beirut.[165] Nishan's sexual life was the topic of jokes in Lebanese high society, "as the frigidity of his wife, the daughter of an expatriate millionaire, led him to declare that he preferred sleeping with boys."[166]

The Faustian deal that Farah transacted with Nishan was spelled out in detail. One day while sunbathing, as per Nishan's orders (who was an onhand PR person), Nishan began to rub some lotion on Farah's back in such a way that Farah "understood." He explained that "in bed I was

---

163. Malcolm Knox, "Her Life as a Fake, Bestsellers' Lies Exposed," *Sydney Morning Herald*, 24 July 2004. See also David Fickling, "Bestseller on Honour Killing 'Is a Fake,'" *Guardian*, 26 July 2004.

164. Ghadah al-Samman, *Bayrut '75* (Beirut: Dar al-Adab, 1975). For the English edition, see Ghada Samman, *Beirut '75*, translated by Nancy N. Roberts (Fayetteville: University of Arkansas Press, 1995).

165. The deal is actually named a "Faustian" one in the novel. See ibid., 44–45.

166. Ibid., 52.

drunk and amazed simultaneously. While the whole thing was not pleasurable, it was not as bothersome as I had imagined it. For wealth, fame, and glory, and the accoutrements of the easy and free life, everything is permitted." As Nishan explained his lack of attraction to women and how much he enjoyed men, Farah "felt that he was trying to justify. I felt some tenderness toward him, but something inside me was breaking, breaking. I felt as if I no longer had possession of myself. I had sold it forever, to the devil!"[167] Farah had been launched by Nishan as the "singer of manliness" on account of his rugged good looks, as he had "the body of a stud with thick chest hair showing through his shirt opening, and such a husky peasant voice with no trace of affectation or deviance that the young women of Beirut fell in the trap. This young man began to excite in them all the possible hunger for an epoch of strong men . . . For in Beirut, Nishan said, there was a hunger for 'manly men.'"[168]

After his sexual encounter with Nishan, Farah was unable to have sex with women at all. He tried with a different woman every night but to no avail. When the last one closed the door on her way out, "he felt that the door between him and the world of women had been shut forever."[169] Unable to deal with the loss of his manhood that Nishan usurped, Farah began to drink and take prescription drugs nonstop and began to suffer from a nervous breakdown. His situation kept deteriorating to Nishan's horror, especially when Farah began to dress in women's clothing. He ultimately lost his fame and left Beirut.

For Ghadah al-Samman, the Lebanese ruling class was literally a bunch of fuckers penetrating dreamy-eyed youth, destroying them in the process. If active male homosexuality in al-Samman's novel resulted from female frigidity and wealthy decadence, and passive male homosexuality from ambition and greed, this was because manly masculinity was nothing less than a masquerade, just as femininity had always been.[170] Al-Samman's depiction is one wherein passive homosexual experiences not only render men impotent but also impel them to dress the part, wearing women's clothing and publicly declaring their womanly, and therefore unmanly, essence. As for those who continued to pose as manly men, her novel sought to remove the veil from them (Nishan, the early Farah, Yasminah's brother, as well as other male characters) in order to expose their unmanliness. Indeed, the attempt by Nishan

167. Ibid., 64–65.
168. Ibid., 63–64.
169. Ibid.
170. See Joan Riviere, "Womanliness as Masquerade," *International Journal of Psycho-Analysis* 10 (1929): 303–13.

to recreate the "epoch of manly men" was doomed to failure precisely because he lived in a world where castration dominated.

Egyptian novelist Jamal al-Ghitani would see the ruling class differently, mainly as desirous of being penetrated, not of penetrating. In this, he expands on *The Malatili Bathhouse*'s representation of Ra'uf. His novel *Waqa'i' Harat al-Za'farani* (The Events of Za'farani Street), published in 1976, would register impotence, which is presented as tantamount to castration, as the prevailing condition in the Arab world of the 1970s. His novel expressed the despair of intellectuals of the Nasirist generation who had believed in building socialism only to be faced with the reality of repression and the national security state.[171] The symbolic image that al-Ghitani used to express the usurpation of the power of citizens in that context was male impotence. His novel, written in a mélange of stream of consciousness, flashbacks, and police reports, is reminiscent of Mahfouz's *Zuqaq al-Midaq* in locating unfolding events in a street filled with myriad characters. If for Mahfouz, the street or the alley represented the other of the modern nation being formed by the colonial encounter, for al-Ghitani it represents the modern nation tout court.

The male residents of Za'farani Street are suddenly overcome with a case of incurable impotence, which turns out to be the result of a talisman conjured up by the Za'farani Street living saint, Shaykh 'Atiyyah, who begins to issue orders about when street residents should go to sleep, when they should wake up, what they should eat, that eating would be collective, that marriages and families must be dissolved in the interest of "freedom of choice," etc. Shaykh 'Atiyyah wanted to bring about equality and peace in a world lacking in both. Male impotence begins to spread everywhere inside the country and internationally. "Za'faranism," as the new philosophy of the Shaykh comes to be known, spreads to Paris, Buenos Aires, India, and many fictional countries around the globe. The Soviets issued denunciations of this new superstition in *Pravda,* asserting that equality and justice can only follow a natural progression sketched by Marx and cannot be altered by superstitions. Other countries closed down the borders and their airports in an attempt to control the spread of the impotence epidemic, but to no avail.

As background to the new epidemic, the novel tells of the emotional and sexual histories of most of the residents, men and women, as well as of the international economy of marriage and sex that prevailed. The

---

171. Jamal al-Ghitani, *Waqa'i' Harat al-Za'farani* [The Events of Za'farani Street] (1976; Baghdad, Dar al-Shu'un al-Thaqafiyyah al-'Amah, 1987). For the English edition, see Gamal Ghitany, *Incidents in Za'farani Alley,* translated by Peter O'Daniel, with an introduction by M. Enani (Cairo: General Egyptian Book Organization, 1986).

author in this sense is clear that the preimpotence period was not characterized by bliss, as we are told of the depredation of poverty, which forced families to marry their daughters off to rich foreigners, including in one case an elderly Libyan and in another a rich man "from one of the black countries." While the Libyan and his children from a previous marriage oppressed the young Egyptian wife until she fled back to her country, the rich black African "admired his beautiful white wife so much that one night his admiration increased to such a degree that he ate her."[172] Umm Suhayr, a Za'farani resident, commented that "this is the punishment of mothers who sell their daughters off."[173] Other foreigners, especially Gulf Arabs, would visit the country seeking prostitutes, including, Ikram, one of the street residents. In reality, many of these developments would come after the Nasirist period, in the 1970s and after, and did not occur in the 1940s, as the novel implies. But if capitalism led to the sale of Egyptian women to the highest foreign bidders, including African cannibals (itself a measure of the humiliation of poverty experienced by Egyptians) whose conjuring in such imaginings is informed by the racist trope that represents Black Africans as primitives, the native ruling class engaged in even more shocking practices, which al-Ghitani's novel exposes.

Such exposition occurs in the context of the sexual history of 'Uways, an Upper Egyptian peasant-turn-migrant worker who walks north to Cairo looking for work. After being fired from his first job as the Za'farani Street baker for sexually harassing a female customer, he was offered a position at a bathhouse where he would "become clean, eat meat on a daily basis, and live rent-free on condition that he spend the entire night at the bathhouse. He will receive a monthly salary, like government employees, and what he will perform is simple and pleasurable," consisting mainly of buggering a number of high-profile bathhouse customers on a nightly basis.[174] The customers "occupy high positions in society and control the destinies of many people. Some are famous and appear on television and are interviewed on radio, which renders their visits to the bathhouse top-secret." 'Uways agreed immediately. His first assignment involved a gentleman with "a light complexion and smooth skin, who did not utter a single word except for some harmonious moanings." 'Uways became the favorite of a high-ranking newspaper man who requested of the bathhouse owner that he only pleasure him and no one else. The owner as-

---

172. Al-Ghitani, *Waqa'i' Harat al-Za'farani*, 122.
173. Ibid.
174. Ibid., 39.

sured him that that would be the case, when in reality ʿUways was being called upon to perform his services seven times a night.[175] When alone with the "respectable gentlemen," ʿUways "would sleep with them and show them much respect, and when one of them asked him to beat him up and call him names, he did so as he would executing an order."[176]

Ghitani's novel is clearly inspired by *The Malatili Bathhouse* on a number of counts. Aside from the bathhouse setting and the class-age representation of same-sex practice, Ghitani has ʿUways, mutatis mutandis, play the role of Ahmad. It is interesting how for al-Ghitani, like for Waliy al-Din, powerful men in society and the media—though dominant and oppressive in every other way—seek to be dominated and buggered by the most disempowered members of the underclass. Society, it would seem, is being ruled not by penetrators but by penetratees. This theme is carried through to a number of female characters who for the most part seem to oppress their husbands, especially after the husbands became impotent. Al-Ghitani's use of sex appears more allegorical than representative in this novel, wherein these descriptions do not only or entirely describe actual practices as much as function as symbolic of wider political trends—homosexuality here is a metaphor more than anything else, standing in for other abominations and unnamable forces of anarchy infiltrating the social body and transforming the order of things.

When ʿUways was later approached by a Zaʿfarani Street woman, whom he had desired but who failed to arouse him, he was alarmed. He had not yet found out that Shaykh ʿAtiyyah's talismanic curse was behind his condition. He wondered: "Does his work prevent him from sleeping with women? He was scared. Would his life be turned upside down after a while and he will become like his customers?"[177] The next day, ʿUways realized that he could not even get aroused with his male customers, which led to his dismissal from his job. When he went to the Shaykh seeking help for his condition, he started by explaining, the narrator tells us, that "in the last few days, he has been overcome by a symptom . . . which equates him with women."[178]

ʿUways did seem to have at least one customer from Zaʿfarani Street who did not belong to the ruling class, a "young man called Samir who was the most debauched of all the men he slept with and the one who made the most [feminine] moves and uttered the most moans."[179] Samir, the younger of two brothers, appeared to everyone to be a polite and

175. Ibid., 40–41.
176. Ibid., 92.
177. Ibid., 40.

178. Ibid., 34.
179. Ibid., 41.

obedient teenage boy. His father, a low-ranking government employee, was a dreamy, traditional man who had grandiose plans for both his sons. Samir was on the honor roll and was, according to his father's plan, slated to become an engineer. When one day it came to the father's attention that Samir was not performing his daily prayers, he beat him and demanded an explanation. Samir claimed that "sometimes his clothes are . . ." and did not finish his sentence out of embarrassment. The father understood that the son must have been experiencing wet dreams, "but refused his excuse insisting that he bathe often. The next day, he went to Shaykh 'Atiyyah and asked him to make a talisman for his son Samir, as he thought that the evil eye must have struck him."[180] When Samir's father heard that Samir had been seen in another neighborhood with a

disreputable person named Mahdi, Samir cried for a long time and swore that he never met anyone by that name. The next day, his father bought two sets of underwear of different sizes . . . the shorter ones for Samir and the longer ones for Hassan. A week later he went to the kitchen, turned on the lights, and began to search through the dirty laundry in the hamper. He turned Samir's underwear over, exposed it to the light, and saw dry yellow smudges on it. He went to bed relieved and certain of his son's manliness.[181]

Samir, it would seem, had other sexual partners besides 'Uways and Mahdi. When Shaykh 'Atiyyah called for a meeting of street residents to announce his new regulations, Samir was terrified: "Maybe he [Shaykh 'Atiyyah] will tell his father about his relations with 'Atwah the falafel vendor and with Mabruk, the student at Al-Azhar University. Also 'Uways's presence there frightened him. He saw him once at the bathhouse. He limited himself that day to going into the bathtub. Does he remember him? He is careful not to look him in the eye."[182] Ultimately, appalled by the new regulations that Shaykh 'Atiyyah imposed and that his father wanted to enforce, especially regarding sleep and wake-up time, Samir challenged his father, disobeying him. The father beat him. Samir then fled the family home, never to be heard from again. The father, already showing signs of paranoia, lost his mind completely following his son's flight and began to hallucinate that he was a leader in the midst of battle and that his own son Samir had joined the enemy ranks against him. It would seem that on account of his desire to be penetrated, Samir

180. Ibid., 46.
181. Ibid., 49–50.
182. Ibid., 66.

did not belong among the working classes but rather among the ruling classes whom his father imagined him to have joined. In fact, it appears that the desire to be penetrated on the part of the upper classes was now trickling down to other classes.

Samir's literal flight from the scene was not incidental. Indeed, in accordance with Shaykh ʿAtiyyah's new regulations, street residents were instructed no longer to use greetings such as "good morning" and the like but substitute for all of them the expression "This is the time to flee" (hadha zaman al-farar). Several street residents besides Samir also fled, including the pimp Takrali and his wife Ikram, whose secret lives of prostitution were broadcast by the Shaykh. Faridah, wife of Abu Fijlah who fell in love with her daughter's private tutor, also fled and took her daughter along.

It is interesting that al-Ghitani does not explore female homosexuality in his novel. While most of the women of Zaʿfarani Street were full of passion and desires for men, which could no longer be fulfilled, none of them thought of having sex with other women. This is important, as the talismanic curse would render any man they would approach sexually beyond Zaʿfarani Street impotent as well. As the Shaykh sought equality among all humans, and given ʿUways's description of his condition as one which had rendered him "equal to women," it would seem that lesbian sex among all humans would be the most equitable form of sex among equals. Yet, surprisingly, that was not an option open to the characters. In fact, all desirous women in the novel either abandoned their husbands in the hope of finding men outside the perimeter of the street who would not be struck by the curse or lost all respect for them in those cases where they stayed with them. They thus fulfilled one of the maxims often used by Samir's father, that "the longer you stay with a woman, the less she should be trusted."

While one female character was allowed to masturbate,[183] no other sex seemed possible in a postmanly world. If men could penetrate men and women and some of the men could be penetrated by other men in the era when men existed, in a postmanly world full of women and their equals, no interhuman sex seemed possible at all, despite the persistence of women's desires for men and the persistence of men's desires for women *and* men. What is normative in a manly world remains normative in a postmanly world. It is nonphallic sex, not "deviant" sex, that is unimaginable by al-Ghitani's dystopic vision. Nonsex, for him, therefore is preferable to lesbian sex, which remains unthought. Al-Ghitani's

183. Ibid., 258–59.

point however is that the Nasirist system brought about equality among the citizenry through the castration of men. What is most interesting in this conceptualization is that as soon as the citizenry becomes equal, social and biological reproduction ceases. Here, the nonreproductive forms of sex that the ruling class and prostitutes engaged in become more generalized as nonsex. In this social context of sex as recreational and nonprocreative, equality leads to depopulation and decline, themes borrowed from post–French Revolution conservative English thinkers. We will see how the vision of Egypt as a country inhabited by biologically sexed women and by former men now socially sexed as women would occupy the thoughts of a number of Egyptian novelists for the next three decades. In this sense, following Fanon's views of colonialism and sexuality, the decolonizing nation inherits the colonial representative strategy of reading colonized men as castrated, while displacing the other colonial fantasy of the native man as hypervirilized on the internal native as local other, in this case, Upper Egyptian men. This is not to say that some Arab novelists did not address how the colonized man could liberate his country through sexual conquest of European women. Al-Tayyib Salih's classic novel, *The Season of Migration to the North* (Mawsim al-Hijrah ila al-Shamal) presented its main protagonist, the Sudanese Mustafa Sa'id, as such a man, as Sa'id was said to have declared, "I will liberate Africa with my . . . [sic]."[184]

But if Nasirism eliminated men from Egypt and at present consisted of a ruling class that enjoyed being mounted by poor peasant and working-class men, Yusuf Idris's novella *Abu al-Rijal* (The Manliest of Men, literally "The Father of Men") offered a different, albeit related, allegory. Published in 1987, a decade after Ghitani's novel and towards the end of Idris's life, the novella was most explicit in its sexual symbolism.[185] An allegory about President Nasir, to whom it alludes but never explicitly names, the novella is a cruel denouncement, not of Nasirism as such, but of Nasir himself. If the Nasirist experiment had rendered all Egyptian men "equal to women" in Ghitani's novel, for Yusuf Idris, it exposed Nasir himself as a "pseudoman" whose status everyone knew but could not say due to their "hypocritical manners." Sultan (which means "the one with authority"), the protagonist, who saw himself and was seen as "the manliest of men," was in reality a "pseudoman" who desired to

---

184. Al-Tayyib Salih, *Mawsim al-Hijrah ila al-Shamal*, 122.

185. Yusuf Idris, *Abu al-Rijal* [The Manliest of Men] was published as part of his collection of short stories *Al-'Atab 'ala al-Nazar* (Cairo: Markaz al-Ahram lil-Tarjamah wa al-Nashr, 1987), 69–99. The English translation appeared in a bilingual edition. See Youssef Idris, *A Leader of Men*, translated by Saad Elkhadem (Fredericton: York Press, 1988).

be mounted by manly men. The story opens and closes with the fifty-one-year-old Sultan—the approximate age at which Nasir (1918–70) died—a macho gangster who is married and has grown children, reflecting on his life and what led him recently to desire being mounted by other men, when he had been the manliest of men for much of his life. He looks at his reflection in the mirror, feeling alienated and overcome with an existential crisis, beginning to notice that he was losing the hair on his body, remembering how hair had functioned as his initiation into manhood when he was a fourteen-year-old boy, at which time the fair fluff on his body was transforming into coarse black hair.[186] Sultan realized that he desired one of his gangsters, whom he had christened "Bull." While Bull sits silently next to Sultan as Sultan revisits his entire life, in the final scene, Sultan acts out on his desire for Bull.

That evening, after noticing his disappearing hair and his aging body, Sultan called for Bull to join him on the balcony of his home. He did not speak to him, although he would look at him and size him up and fall back into deep thought. Bull was scared, not knowing what had befallen his boss. Sultan himself did not know what he wanted from him. The narrator recounts how Sultan was considering "the idea that he should surrender before that young man who is terrified of him, of his manliness and authority. One of the thoughts that occurred to him was that Bull was imagining the exact opposite situation, that he was trembling out of fear that Sultan would ask of him what the stronger asks of the weaker; for the requests of Sultan are sacred commands whose execution is inevitable and from which one cannot escape."[187] When he considered seeing a psychiatrist, he wondered what he would say. He refused the idea that he would have to "confess to the beginnings of strange desires, that take the form of attacks, initially infrequent, but later more frequent and closer to one another, so much so that his life and thoughts could revolve around nothing else."[188] As we revisit his earlier life, the narrator tells us that

When it came to the playfulness of boys, or precisely that phase in their age when boys invariably must touch one another, some responding with the pleasure of being the passive ones, while others with the pleasure of being the active ones, or both together, Sultan was extremely sensitive, refusing to submit. Indeed, he was so sensitive, and his desire to reach early manhood quickly was so strong that he would not let anyone touch him, and consequently, he would categorically refuse to touch

---

186. Idris, *Abu al-Rijal*, 71–72.   188. Ibid., 77.
187. Ibid., 83.

anybody else. He was a little man, who inherited his pride from his father, or rather he was proceeding with emulating his father or being like him—that father, whom he considered the manliest of all men, with the greatest stature. Indeed, he never felt and it never occurred to him that his father was a poor man. For those of his age, there were no rich and poor, there were only manly men, men who were halfmen, or those who were not men at all. The only difference among people was the difference between manly men and those men who were pseudomen.[189]

Sultan, who hailed from a poor rural family, was a smart and diligent student who attended university and was an activist seeking to help in the transformation of society. He joined the Arab Socialist Union, the only legal political party during the second decade of Nasir's rule. He was a double major in history and economics and studied at night and worked as a construction worker in the daytime and still managed to excel at his studies.

He was the pride of the university, and later all universities [in the country], a pride for his generation and the generations that followed. Indeed he was one of the prides of Egypt and its leap that had taken it from being an occupied country in an old and ugly world into a country that is a leader of liberation, and champion of peoples, exploder of revolts and of revolutions, until Sultan became a veritable sultan . . . He was the first youth leader with whom the Leader President had met, shook his hands, and who was granted a medal, and acquired status, the leader of a new school and direction, surrounded and accompanied by a small army of followers from among geniuses and admirers, and those who follow the followers.[190]

He neither sought "money or political ambition" but rather sought "justice" for the "oppressed." For him "a man is not such due to the thickness of his moustache and the intensity of his tyranny but rather the man is a man because he is chivalrous and generous, and courageous," and "the woman is a woman not on account of her femininity and her coquetry, but by her greater role, that she be the greatest mother for a more evolved humanity. Motherhood like manliness is not an adjective or a description; the two are rather values, high degrees of emotional and rational human conduct, even corporeal conduct. This is what makes humans unique and thanks to their guidance a human being reached the epitome of evolution rendering him the most paramount living thing in existence."[191]

189. Ibid., 79.
190. Ibid., 84.

191. Ibid., 85.

Sultan suspected that his mother might be the reason and the cause for the emergence of his sudden desires. Yet his "Upper Egyptian" mother never spoiled him nor was she harsh with him. She was unlike his friend's mother who always questioned her son's manhood whenever he came home late, accusing him, on account of his fair skin and blondish hair, that he was late "because he must have been with the other boys in the corn fields."[192]

It never happened that his [friend's] mother's prophesy came true, that he would become like that when he grew up, just like Shahin al-Tahhan. This Shahin al-Tahhan was one of the many phenomena that some rural villages specialize in, whether in Lower or Upper Egypt. He was a man in appearance and figure, with beard and moustache shaven; this aside, he was feminine in everything else, in the way he spoke, the way he walked, his attachment to womenfolk in the village, and even in his work. He used to sell butter, ghee, and cream and would seduce the young teenage boys of the village with the amount of money he would pay. He used to have an agent among the young loafers who would bring them to him in exchange for money. He was famous and well known to people in the village. He was deplored by many prudish and religious folks, but for normal people, and due to his long history and the fame of his habits, he was seen as one of those normal phenomena that were not condemned, but became an object of ridicule to some and used as an example by mothers to warn their sons of the consequences if they acted softly, or if they grew their hair long, or wore their skullcaps in a crooked way on their heads.[193]

His mother was not one of those, however, as she never impugned his masculinity. In fact, when she caught him mounting his uncle's she-donkey in the stable, she turned back quickly and said while walking away: "How could you ride your uncle's she-donkey without a saddle, you ass?"[194] Indeed, even when she caught him having sex with an older widow and beat him as punishment, he felt that she beat him because that was what she had to do, but that she was in fact "proud" of him.[195]

A decisive day came when he was called upon by a man to rescue him. Here, the analogy to Nasir and the plight of the Palestinian people is strongest. It was a plea to provide succor, "the call for succor that one knows will be heeded by the right man he had sought out," for that man was known for his "chivalry." Hundreds and thousands of Sultan's supporters came to help, but none of them could make the decision, as they

192. Ibid., 87.
193. Ibid., 87.
194. Ibid., 88.
195. Ibid.

all waited for him to make it.[196] Against all expectations, his deep and manly voice came out this time like the voice of a "hermaphrodite." He said: " 'I am of the opinion that we should let it pass this once and submit. We will later choose the time and place of the confrontation,' even though, everyone knew, and he, most of all, that this, this exact noon hour . . . is the most appropriate time, and mobilization for it at the moment would be the strongest mobilization. The only meaning for delay is not only missing an opportunity or postponing the battle, but also, and in all frankness, fear, retreat, and flight."[197] In this passage, Idris is clearly making reference to Nasir's refusal to open a battlefront with Israel, cautioning against letting the enemy decide the time of battle, until finally Israel attacked him in 1967.

Even rivals were in disbelief that Sultan retreated from the call of duty. "When the moment of truth and decision came challenging him in the heart of his home . . . he fled."[198] When Sultan later tried to explore within himself why he did what he did, he concluded that "he was not that powerful man around whom they drew a halo, nor that brave man that made souls tremble. It is this outside that makes him appear such, while on the inside, it was hollow all the time, empty, just a child who liked the way his father looked and liked his manliness and courage and went about emulating them."[199]

Things got worse. When Sultan retreated to his village, still acting as the strong courageous man that he was no longer, even though people pretended that he was, he demanded respect from everyone. Here the village is symbolic of Egypt, while the country stands in for the Arab world more generally. When Sultan ran into a young village peasant, Ahmad, reading a book and working the land, and the man did not greet him (the reference here is to the student movement that erupted in demonstrations in 1968 and was repressed by Nasir), he had him beaten up. Ahmad apologized upon being told who Sultan was. But that was not enough. When Sultan found out that this Ahmad's uncle was none other that Shahin al-Tahhan, he started to ridicule him and to ask him if he had done it with his uncle as the other boys had.[200] While Ahmad

196. Ibid., 89.
197. Ibid., 90.
198. Ibid., 90.
199. Ibid., 91.
200. An interesting short story in this regard was written by Egyptian writer Alifah Rifʿat. Titled "Badriyyah and her husband" [Badriyyah wa Zawjuha], the story tells of Badriyyah's husband who refuses to have sex with her after his release from prison. ʿUmar was a waiter in the neighborhood café and was popular and respected in the neighborhood, even though it turned out that everyone knew (except his wife) that he liked to be buggered by men so much so that "had he been a woman

initially did not respond to Sultan's taunts, Sultan tried to humiliate him publicly. The young man had had enough. He jumped Sultan, knocked him to the ground and put a sickle to his neck demanding that Sultan declare in front of the whole village, "I am a woman." No one could interfere to help him, as Ahmad was serious about killing him. Sultan chose life and uttered the declaration, to the horror of all the men. Sultan left the village after that day and became a gangster, surrounding himself with younger gangsters.

Having recollected his thoughts, with Bull still in the room full of anticipation and terror, Sultan finally made his move and had Bull mount him. "Everything ended. His sticky sweat was redolent with the smell of broken pride, torn-up dignity, and a degradation that he enjoyed and savored—smells that can only provoke nausea when combined together, but they never made him nauseous."[201] Rumors spread that he had become another Shahin al-Tahhan, who by then had died ("it is said that his nephew Ahmad had lured him to the dam and drowned him"[202]). Still he did not care, and no one dared tell him to his face that they knew. He proceeded to lead the gang, and all the gangsters, including Bull, remained around him, and "he remained the lion."[203]

For Idris, Nasir's defeat and refusal to initiate the battle with Israel for over a decade, his retreat from the Arab world to Egypt after 1967, and his repression of the student movement in 1968, insisting that he was still the leader, even though everyone saw him defeated, were all manifestations of an essential feminine cowardice whose truth lies in

---

he would have gotten pregnant by now." The interesting bit in this short story is that unlike al-Tahhan in Idris's story, 'Umar did not seem to suffer any social shame on account of his desires and sexual practices. What seems unexplainable in Rif'at's short story, however, is that although 'Umar liked getting buggered by men before he went to jail for theft, he still managed to have sex with his wife. No clear explanation is offered as to why he stopped having sex with his wife after his release from prison. The only possible explanation offered in the story is that after he came out of jail, it seemed that "jail time intensified his calamity." See Alifah Rif'at, *Fi Layl al-Shita' al-Tawil* [During the Long Night of Winter] (Cairo: Matba'at al-'Asimah, 1985), 53. I should note that this story was published first in English translation before it came out in Arabic leading to skepticism among some that it might have been written first in English. For the English edition, see Alifa Rifaat, *Distant View of a Minaret and Other Short Stories*, translated by Denys Johnson-Davies (London: Heinemann, 1983). The translator makes no mention that the translated stories had not been published in Arabic yet.

201. Idris, *Abu al-Rijal*, 98.

202. Ibid. There are many other novels and short stories in this period that feature characters that would engage in same sex contact with little moralizing. A notable example is Thani al-Suwaydi, a writer from the United Arab Emirates, who wrote a sensitive novella about a protagonist who narrates his story to a "mute friend" in a mixture of hallucinatory fantasy and reality, depicting his "feminine" desires to dress and sing like women and to be penetrated by men in *Al-Dizil* (Beirut: Dar al-Jadid, 1994).

203. Ibid., 99.

the body and its desires. It was not that Sultan had been a real manly man all along and then became a pseudoman, rather the opposite. Idris is a committed essentialist here, demonstrating that Sultan had always masqueraded as a man, when in reality he was never one. Indeed, when he finally declared that he was "a woman," he did so "as if he were breathing a sigh of relief."[204] It was after his inability to confront the enemy when called upon to do so, after he, out of cowardice, chose life as a woman, rather than death as a manly man that Sultan's desires fully exploded to the surface, insistent that they be satisfied, that Bull mount him and that he enjoy being mounted.

Rewriting the Nasirist experience in such terms in 1987, seventeen years after its demise, was not incidental. The figure of the passive deviant had become used consistently since the 1970s as a symbol of political and national defeat, in addition to its literal reference as a defeat of manhood itself. This is to be contrasted with earlier sexual allegories that dealt literally with castration rather than passive "deviance." Palestinian writer Ghassan Kanafani's classic novella *Rijal fi al-Shams* (Men in the Sun), published in 1963, had posited Abu al-Khayzaran, a character that stands in for Palestinian and Arab leaders, as literally castrated by a Zionist bomb during the 1948 war.[205] His impotence is what leads to the death of the three Palestinian refugees attempting to smuggle themselves into British-occupied Kuwait in search of work. The transformation of novelistic allegories from castration to impotence and to passive male homosexuality is significant. Indeed, locating desire in the body, which must be transformed in accordance with the nature of its desire, will be picked up by a number of novelists and playwrights in the 1990s. For Idris, the feminine catamite represented by Shahin al-Tahhan was indeed a normal feature of life, which should not be condemned. What was abnormal was that the manliest of men should be one. In such a context, we find out, like in al-Ghitani's novel, that there are no longer manly men, and that indeed the world is now divided between "pseudomen" and "those who were not men at all." As for Shahin al-Tahhan, he was killed on account of Sultan's coming out as a catamite while insisting on remaining "the manliest of men." If Nasirism rendered all Egyptian men into women, Idris revealed that it had also rendered Nasir himself into

204. Ibid., 96.
205. Ghassan Kanafani, *Rijal fi al-Shams*, in Ghassan Kanafani, *Al-Athar al-Kamilah, Al-Riwayat* [Collected Works, Novels] (Beirut: Mu'assassat al-Abhath al-'Arabiyyah, 1972), 29–152. For the English edition, see Ghassan Kanafani, *Men in the Sun, and Other Palestinian Stories*, translated by Hilary Kilpatrick (Washington, D.C.: Three Continents Press, 1978).

one. Abu al-Khayzaran's castration in Kanafani's novella resulted from colonial bombs, but Nasir's fictional passive deviance was the result of his own cowardice. Herein lies the centrality of Sultan's declaration that he *was* a "woman" to his *transformation* into one.

The novels of the 1940s and 1950s illustrated the impact of colonial modernization on existing sexual desires and practices (Mahfouz), or marshaled them in the service of transforming the desires and practices of ancient figures (Khuri). In contrast, the 1960s ushered in a new approach that depicted the distortion of desires and sex when it is deployed by the modern state machine of torture (Y. Idris and Ibrahim) or by new Western bourgeois feminism (S. Idris). The 1970s seemed to link male homosexuality to the local conditions of poverty and to European men during the colonial period (Shukri), or to poverty and bourgeois decadence in the postcolonial period (al-Samman). It is beginning in the 1970s that homosexuality begins to be deployed as political allegory that feminizes the ruling classes (Waliy al-Din and al-Ghitani) or the political leadership itself (Y. Idris), and where male homosexuality is depicted as a form of irreversible degeneration (Farah, Sultan, Ra'uf, and everyone in al-Ghitani's novel).

SIX

The Truth of Fictional Desires

Except for Yusuf Idris's *The Manliest of Men*, written at the cusp of political and social changes, all the novels and short stories we surveyed in the last chapter were written before the rise of Islamism and the Gay International. The relationship between masculinity and colonialism and their link to civilization make up a part of the allegorical representations in these novels, but the problem of degeneration was still not fully explicit in them, at least not in terms of focus on deviance as the most prominent feature of the epoch. Indeed, by the mid-1980s, "degeneration" in fictional writings had not yet partaken consciously of a Western epistemology and taxonomy of desires. Soon, however, this would change. The themes of civilization and primitivism, of liberal individual rights, and of degeneration as a racial, sexual, and territorial concept would become evident in a number of works of fiction. Sexual desire and "deviant" practices would become the organizing principle, nay, the axis, around which these questions are negotiated. This would coincide with the rise of the Gay International and the Islamist movement (AIDS remained absent from fiction entirely), as well as the advent of globalization.

In this chapter, I will discuss four major literary productions that exemplify this major turn, beginning with Hanan al-Shaykh's *The Deer's Musk* (1988), and Sa'dallah Wannus's very popular play *The Rites of Signs and Transformations* (1994), and then moving to Sun'allah Ibrahim's novel *Honor* (1997), and ending with 'Ala' Al-Aswani's much celebrated novel *The Yaʿqubyan Building* (2002). These four works of literature will be shown to be more conversant with Western liberal views of matters sexual, seeking not only to represent the contemporary sexual desires and practices of Arabs in light of Western norms but also to *steer* them in that direction.

A Tale of Degeneration

Hanan al-Shaykh's *Misk al-Ghazal* (published in 1988)[1] is a novel about civilization and primitivism, temporal concepts that in the novel have corresponding geographic designations. Lebanon and Britain designate civilization, although with some irony, while Saudi Arabia designates primitivism without any irony. Sexually this translates into questions of repression and inhibitions. Civilization in the novel seems to be a time and place when and where natural desires prosper while primitivism is a time and place when and where unnatural desires prosper. The novel tells the story of four women who live in an unnamed desert kingdom (all indications are that it is Saudi Arabia). The women have different backgrounds and nationalities. The major protagonist, Suha, like the novelist herself, is Lebanese. It is Suha's social circles that delimit the world of the novel. While Suha's story, told in the first person, opens the novel (and is the longest of the four accounts), the other three women, part of Suha's social network, follow suit one by one. Nur, native to the desert kingdom is followed by the American Suzanne, who is followed by Tamr, another desert native.

Suha moved to the unnamed desert country from Lebanon, accompanying her husband who obtained a job in the oil industry. She is quite unhappy in this new country, which, to her, feels extraterrestrial. The desert kingdom seems not only out of time but even out of place: "I opened the door and stood next to the elevated doorstep, looked around me, across the other wooden houses, painted in white, the few trees, the water tank, and the burning sun over the asphalt; they made me think as if I were on a space station."[2] On a good day, Suha would view the desert kingdom not as a static primitive place only but also as a space of transformation, a virtual evolutionary laboratory, where the more evolved species of humans can observe how the less evolved undergo this evolutionary process from primitivism into civilization. She

1. Hanan al-Shaykh, *Misk al-Ghazal* [The Deer's Musk] (Beirut: Dar al-Adab, 1988).
2. Ibid., 9.

did not fully believe that transformation was indeed taking place, but still pushed the line on her friends: "In my discussions with Arab and foreign women who hated living here, I also would drown in contradictions, pushing a line of argument to the limits of the unreasonable, even to the absurd. I told them that life here was ideal and that they were lucky, as they are seeing how cities are being established, and are witnessing the transformation of humans from nomadism to civilization [madaniyyah]"[3] It is not clear if what is "unreasonable" and "absurd" is that such transformation is possible at all, or that it is ideal.

Noting the contradictions between a highly equipped modern airport and its primitive surroundings, Suha grasps the logic of imperial pillage of natural resources and its impact on the native population through the prism of civilization:

Not much time had elapsed before I realized that I was deluded, as I was not completely in the desert, nor in the city. The desert is pure exploration, even living with its people, is like a tourist experience . . . the planes land, loaded with people and their different civilizations. There is no way to reject them, as it is they who know the secrets of the desert, as if they were born in its belly, and they know where the black liquid is, and how they can transform it into gold doorknobs and gold bathroom faucets.[4]

When she attended a private party where a well-known local singer was to perform, Suha's comparative referents were always derived from a European worldview. "When Ghusn [the singer] came out, she seemed like a heroine of African tribes, as if she had found her wig among the remnants left by Western missionaries, which she used to hide her Negro hair. She had a dark complexion, with Negro features, and wore a dress that was half black and half red, bunched up at the shoulders with ruffles that go down to the sleeves, gold chains and colored necklaces hanging from her neck, and many rings sparkling on her fingers."[5] When everyone joined the singer on stage to dance, they began to "jump in a primitive dance."[6] It is clear that no amount of Western veneer can hide the primitivism of the desert natives for Suha. The fact that Ghusn attempts to cover her negro hair with a fantasized Western wig left by Western missionaries clearly fails (ironically Western missionaries were never present in Arabia, although Western explorers were). Her naked primitivism remained visible to Suha throughout.

3. Ibid., 12.
4. Ibid., 30.

5. Ibid., 57.
6. Ibid., 61.

Suha is represented in the novel as a Western anthropologist observing "primitive Africans" in their "ritual" dancing. When she asks her desert woman friend, Nur, about one of the dance performances she witnesses, it is Nur who identifies the dance to her as an "authentic" one![7] The novelist's projection of Western categories onto the lexicon of natives is an interesting one here, as it corresponds to the systematic projection of Western anthropological, indeed, colonial notions onto the "primitives" being studied more generally. As Pierre Bourdieu has demonstrated, the native is made to say exactly what the anthropologist (or the colonist) wishes to hear.[8]

But Saudi Arabia is not only the terrain of anthropological observation for the sophisticated Suha, it is a dangerous laboratory where the observer, just like the more enlightened Western anthropologist, can easily slip into a participant role in the experiment at work. One should keep in mind that al-Shaykh herself had lived in Saudi Arabia for a period in her life. Suha's descriptions of the desert kingdom, one can safely assume, are heavily informed by al-Shaykh's own observations and experiences when she lived there.

While Suha resisted becoming a participant in the "primitive" dances she observed and tells the reader about, she opts to participate in other "primitive" practices of the carnal variety. Realizing that she had gone native and that the evolutionary laboratory that was advancing the natives to civilization might have degenerative effects on a civilized person like herself, Suha faces an existential crisis regarding her own identity as a civilized being. Fearing further degeneration and rejecting the "deviance" of primitivism in favor of civilized normativity, she will opt for the latter. In this vein, *The Deer's Musk* is not being innovative in expressing the fear of going native, as risk of "going native" is endemic to all colonial projects, including anthropology, and the colonial novel. In this context; Joseph Conrad's *Heart of Darkness* is the best expression of such anxiety.

"Deviant" sex appears throughout the novel and the different accounts provided by the four women. Suha, for example, comments on Ringo, the Sri Lankan servant of her American friend Suzanne. He walked "like a young woman who was aware of the beauty of her own body." When he served tea, "he seemed like an elegant hostess."[9] It is clear that

---

7. Ibid., 60.

8. On the structural position that makes the native speak what the anthropologist wants to hear, see Pierre Bourdieu, *An Outline of a Theory of Practice*, translated by Richard Nice (Cambridge: Cambridge University Press, 1977), 1–2.

9. Al-Shaykh, *Misk al-Ghazal*, 19.

Ringo's unnatural behavior was imported into Saudi Arabia, but the desert kingdom will soon expose its own brand of deviance. While visiting her native friend Nur, Suha is slowly and gradually courted by Nur, who appears experienced in what she is doing. "Suddenly, my heart pulsated in response to her warm breath, a certain feeling overtook me, and I became scared and I trembled. But I did not want to withdraw. I stayed in control of myself in order to remain frozen. . . . Before her arms embraced me and pulled me towards her, warmth overtook my neck. My entire body was overtaken by it, ignoring everything else. I said to myself, Nur is kissing me, and, still, I did not think that kisses, in reality, are between a man and a woman, but rather I wished for more, and every time Nur reached a spot on my body, she would awaken it and then leave it in a state of arousal."[10] Once the first sexual encounter was concluded, Suha felt "a beautiful rhythm that only *instinct* knows [emphasis added]." Soon, however, she would regain her senses. Fully alienated from her body, which experienced this "forbidden" pleasure, "I did not want to be one with my body, but rather I wanted to command it so that it can stand up and behave in the way I want. I wanted to dismiss my body, to open the door and kick it out."[11] The word "instinct" is interesting in terms of the slide from the primitive to the natural, which complicates the idea of deviance. It is unclear how, given this account, for al-Shaykh and for Suha, it is civilization that remains "natural." How this norm is grounded is organized in the novel around sexual desire and in appeals to Western bourgeois norms.

Rather than recognizing the sexual encounter she just had *as* an encounter, as a practice, Suha views it instead as having identitarian dimensions. Her conclusion is informed by the Western "civilized" values that the Lebanese *arriviste* culture she grew up in had adopted and internalized. Suha was able to calm herself and restore her sense of identity to avert an existential crisis through a solemn and conscious declaration of identity: "I am Suha. I am twenty-five-years old, my mother is Madame Widad and my father is Dr. 'Adnan. I am not a deviant like Sahar [presumably a Lebanese woman she knew in Lebanon], although I used to laugh and have fun and wink at boys with other girls. It's natural."[12] She proceeds to recount a heterosexual encounter she had (when she still lived in Lebanon) with her girlfriend's boyfriend to reassure herself that she was "natural." Still this was not sufficient to stop her degeneration. The instinctual rhythm she identified earlier continued to rise within

10. Ibid., 47.
11. Ibid.

12. Ibid., 49.

her, forcing her to seek more encounters with Nur, so much so that one day, when Nur visited her in her own bedroom, "only then did our relationship seem real . . . I no longer felt that I was a visitor or an observer this time"[13] Clearly, Suha's degeneration into a participant in deviant practices obliterated the boundaries she had maintained in observing the desert evolutionary laboratory. The evolutionary process that she "unreasonably" argued for when she first arrived seemed to be in reality a degenerative one. It was she, Suha, who was being transformed from civilization into nomadism and primitivism. Herein lies the "irrationality" and "absurdity" of her initial argument for the benefits of life in the desert kingdom. It is not that now she understood that the country was static but rather that it was dynamic in the wrong direction, at least as far as civilized beings were concerned.

Not only was Nur made to identify a local dance as "authentic," using Western anthropological terms, but the novelist seems at times also inexplicably at a loss as to what to make of Nur's sexual epistemology. While clearly seeing herself as normal and normative in her own society, Nur is still called upon by al-Shaykh (and by Suha) to identify Jalilah, the nanny of some aristocratic girls, who is dancing at the concert, as "scary, she must be a deviant . . . [Suha muses] I did not think about this word [deviant] until a while later."[14] It is interesting that Suha and al-Shaykh are unable to comprehend local sexual practices and their local epistemology except through Western categories. For Suha, if her Lebanese lesbian friend, Sahar, was a deviation from Lebanese normativity as she understood it, she clearly also understood that Nur and Jalilah acted *within* the realm of desert normativity. Yet al-Shaykh still slipped into the Lebanese categories of deviance that she had none other than Nur utter. Suha's musing that she only began to think about that word later is disingenuous, as this is a category that is meaningful *to her,* and much less so to Nur.

The novel seems to want to do two mutually exclusive things simultaneously: the desert kingdom is to be described and judged as a primitive place where uninhibited sexual desires of all varieties reign supreme, free from civilized regulation, thus approximating Western social Darwinist and Freudian descriptions of primitive and infantile sexuality, while simultaneously, desert sexuality could be subjected to a Western civilized taxonomy of normative and deviant sexuality. But if everyone locally, as can be discerned from the novel, engages in same-sex sexual practices, how is Jalilah to be identified as "deviant" at all? Who is she

13. Ibid., 54.
14. Ibid., 60.

deviating from within her society? How could Nur, the practitioner of same-sex contact, view Jalilah as deviating from her? The contradiction lies less in Nur and more with al-Shaykh's seeming confusion about the axis of civilization and primitivism around which she constructed her entire novel. For Suha, it seems that the only lesbian referent is that of the Lebanese Sahar whom she projects onto desert society.[15]

When Suha abandons Nur and decides that she could not allow her own degeneration into nativism, Nur is devastated. All of Nur's attempts to coax Suha back into the relationship fail. Kawkab, Nur's nanny and surrogate mother, intervenes and visits Suha in the hope of persuading her to "make up" with Nur. Immediately before Kawkab's unexpected arrival, we see Suha sitting alone reflecting on her canary, who, ever since he was heterosexually coupled, stopped singing. Suha interprets this as a longing for a loved one of the opposite sex. Her reflection on the canary, however, appears engineered to render heterosexuality as the natural order of things. After describing his courting ritual with his female mate, Suha tells us how "I realized that he needed a female when the frame of the mirror got dirty from the canary's excessive standing in front of it looking at himself; he approaches it and touches his image while bending his head, he plucks at his picture and sings. When she entered his life in feathers and blood, he no longer sang to complain about his solitude and yearning."[16] It is interesting that Suha does not consider or recognize that the canary's singing to his mirror reflection might signify narcissistic and/or homosexual attraction, which made him happy enough to continue to sing and that perhaps he stopped singing upon the introduction of the female canary to his life because it made him unhappy. At any rate, the canary story is designed to naturalize heterosexuality at the very moment when Kawkab interrupts Suha's reflections and introduces a new order of things, one in which heterosexuality is not the only natural sexual practice. And this Suha has experienced, as the novel tells us, at the level of "instinct."

Deep in her thoughts, Suha hears the doorbell ring: "I wondered. Who would not know how to open the front yard's gate? It was Kawkab."[17]

15. I should note here that a more extensive engagement with lesbianism in fiction is presented in a novel by Lebanese novelist Ilham Mansur, *Ana Hiya Anti* [I Am You] (Beirut: Riyad al-Rayyis lil-Kutub wa al-Nashr, 2000). The novel narrates the trials and tribulations of a young Lebanese woman, Siham, who pursues her same-sex desires, first in Paris, and later in Beirut, despite societal and maternal prohibitions. This poorly conceived novel registers many of the arguments of the Gay International and offers vernacular theories of same-sex and different-sex desires that masquerade as sociological.
16. Al-Shaykh, *Misk al-Ghazal*. 64.
17. Ibid., 65.

Indeed, Kawkab's entry registers almost like a clash of civilizations, or perhaps even a clash of two planets or heavenly objects—Kawkab's name conveniently means "star" (as in the European names "Stella" and "Esther") and "planet." This is how the story proceeds: Kawkab tries to convince Suha to go back with her to Nur's house and make up. Once in Nur's house, horrified, Suha tells Nur, "You sent your own mother?" Nur begins to scream hysterically. Her mother comes back in and begins to assail Suha for causing her daughter such pain. As Nur's mother's tone becomes more threatening and Nur's screams become louder, Suha's civilized response is to dehumanize both: "I could not help but think that Nur and her mother are vampires who have just found a prey and that I must flee at once."[18] Still unable to fathom that Nur's mother understands the real nature of her daughter's relationship to Suha, and thinking that she must not know the truth, Suha endeavors to explain: "What is between Nur and me is forbidden, it is not allowed."[19] Kawkab is quick to respond: "Forbidden! But adultery with a man is more forbidden, and you know Nur's situation with [her husband and] the father of her children."[20] Desperate to convince Suha to go back to Nur, Kawkab hands her a gold coin as possible payment for services to be rendered. Suha thinks, "This creature is from another continent."[21] Suha rushes home intent on going back to war-torn Lebanon. She starts to think of what she will tell her husband. One strategy was to tell him that "I cannot feel that I am just trying something new ["tajrubah," also means experimenting]. I am Arab. I should feel that I have a relationship to this [desert kingdom] civilization, but I do not feel that I have such a relationship. I am in one world and people here are in a different world."[22] Here, Suha's (and presumably al-Shaykh's) judgment is fully informed by the ideas of many anti-Gulf Arab writers who write in other genres, including Yasin al-Hafiz and George Antonius, whom we encountered in the introduction.

The Deer's Musk partakes of the same evolutionist framework of rescuing, this time, Lebanese Arabs from the European judgment of primitivism and projects it onto Gulf Arabs. This is not to say, however, that all Arabic novels that deal with Saudi Arabia or the Gulf more generally employ such evolutionist tropes. Egyptian novelist Ibrahim ʿAbd al-Majid's novel *The Other Town* (Al-Baldah al-Ukhra), for example, chronicles the life of an Egyptian labor migrant to Saudi Arabia with much sensitivity,

18. Ibid., 69.
19. Ibid.
20. Ibid., 70.

21. Ibid.
22. Ibid., 72.

not only to the Saudi natives but also to labor migrants of other nationalities living there without deploying a civilizational axis.[23]

This is how Suha works out this civilizational equation. Feeling that her words to her husband would not be persuasive, Suha fantasizes another conversation: "I want to live a normal and natural [tabi'iyyah] life."[24] It is unclear what normal life would be in a Lebanon drowning in civil war and foreign invasions. Lebanon, as a civilized place, seems ironically less repressed as far as violent desires are concerned, as clearly human violent inclinations are very well expressed there with little repression, while unnatural sexual desires may be repressed and considered deviant. The desert kingdom in contrast seems to be a place where violent tendencies are kept in check, but not unnatural and natural sexual desires, which seem to run amok.

At the airport, getting ready to leave the desert to Lebanon, Suha feels liberated. Her son 'Umar is beside her with his heterosexual canary in a cage. If her sexual encounter in the desert degenerated her body but not her mind, which rescued her, her departure from this evolutionary laboratory will reunify her body and soul on the evolutionary scale, putting them back in natural synch: "I feel that I am a natural human being. I am no longer Suha of the desert and Suha of the city."[25] This is in stark contrast to Suha's earlier reaction to her bodily pleasures. While she identified that pleasure as pure "instinct" and sought to separate her natural body from her social mind, Suha reworks social mores as that which is natural and "instinct" as that which is unnatural. Herein lies Suha's seeming confusion about the notion of civilization and the dichotomies it consecrates. Unaware of her contradiction, while on the flight home, Suha looks below and confirms the timelessness of the desert: "The desert appeared to me, as I had seen it the first time, sands and palm trees, a life whose axis is a human being without possessions and without extras. All his brain has to do is to invent what would make his heartbeat go fast or continue to beat regularly, that he look by himself for the buried brilliance, and know how to deal with two seasons instead of four."[26]

If Suha left the desert for civilization, the desert's primitivism and its evolutionary laboratory of locals, with their degenerative effects on civilized visitors proceeded apace. When Nur, as native informant, tells her story, she does not tell it as a local but as a Western projection,

23. Ibrahim 'Abd al-Majid, *Al-Baldah al-Ukhra* [The Other Town] (London: Riyad al-Rayyis lil-Kutub wa al-Nashr, 1991).
24. Al-Shaykh, *Misk al-Ghazal*, 72.
25. Ibid., 81.
26. Ibid., 82.

or more accurately as a Western anthropologist would. Here, her name "Nur," which means "light," is clarified, as she sheds light for Westerners on her native land. The novelist's inability to identify with Nur except through projection will also mar, as we will see later, her representation of the other native woman in the novel, Tamr. Nur, on her part, seems to be telling her story to an imaginary Western audience: "I am beautiful, I took the blackness of my hair and its length and my lightly dark complexion from the Orient. From the West, I took my clothes and all that surrounds me."[27] When she describes the young man she likes and enumerates the objects he admires, she details them, not as an *arriviste* herself, but rather as a cultured Westerner who ridicules the bizarre taste of third world nouveaux riches: "He loved hangings and all that civilization photographs—from the latest car makes to skiing gear, to 'Ali bin Abi Talib's Japanese-made stainless steel sword, to an antique Aubusson chair, to a new type of honey from the heights of Tibet to a briefcase made of ostrich skin."[28] It would seem that shopping and sexual desires function in the novel as the indices of civilizational worth.

Nur uncharacteristically marvels that "I did not know that Samir also likes his own sex except during one of our trips abroad.'[29] Her surprise notwithstanding, his desire for his own sex, just as in the modern West, seems to preclude him from actually desiring women—"I found myself discovering the fakeness of his desire for me when he slept with me, for it was a fantastical and continuous desire that most of the time subsided midway through."[30] Yet, Nur's, or perhaps al-Shaykh's, contradiction remains. Having told us that Samir's desire for women is cool, Nur states again and without any sense of irony that her husband "likes both sexes."[31] Still Samir divorces her and chooses his Moroccan male lover, Walid, over her. Even the American Suzanne fears the fate awaiting her American husband in Saudi Arabia's sexually degenerative world. She interprets his waning interest in her as evidence that he "likes men, or perhaps he has a relationship with [the servant] Ringo."[32] Ringo is clearly imagined as a penetratee, and certainly not a penetrator, not only by Suha who identified his femininity at the outset, but also by the American Suzanne and by her Saudi male lover. Ambivalence remains, however, as in the case of Nur's description of Samir. On the one hand, Ringo's sexual desires are identified within the desert world in terms of his sexual aim, namely, that he be penetrated by men, and not by sexual object choice

27. Ibid., 92–93.
28. Ibid., 93.
29. Ibid.

30. Ibid., 94.
31. Ibid.
32. Ibid., 148.

as such, namely, someone who desires men per se, regardless of what he may do with them. Yet, on the other hand, Ringo is assimilated, like Samir before him, into the agenda of the Gay International, where all same-sex desire must lead to the romantic telos of coupling, as it does among Western heterosexuals, which the Gay International seeks to emulate.

In an astute description of how modern civilized sexuality can be compatible with "primitive," polymorphously perverse, sexuality in a context of imperial pillage, Suzanne tells us the following:

> Ringo's admirers among the desert people are legion and he accepts all dates, explaining that he might perhaps meet the right person so that he could end all his other relationships and settle down. This, however, was not easy, as the desert was full of his likes. European companies began to prefer employing deviants and bringing them to the desert, for financial and practical reasons. As the companies save on expenditures and big houses, family transportation and kids' schools, as well as wife trouble and the problem of the wives' free time. Moreover, there is no missing women, no repression that might lead to neglecting work, or an inability to bear life in the desert and requests to go home, or even of a need for successive vacations.[33]

Suzanne's investment in Ringo's coupling aside, it is her Saudi married male lover Mu'adh, who, upon seeing London men in very tight trousers, which Ringo would love to wear, exclaims: "Where are you, Ringo? You will lose your mind." Mu'adh adds, while looking at a British young man: "By God, if this man walked down Nafurah Street, even a newly married man would jump him."[34] It is unclear why Mu'adh did not. Perhaps desire is geographically determined wherein it can erupt in Nafurah Street in ways that it cannot in South Kensington!

All these accounts, however, are invested in proceeding in the direction of evolution as a desirable telos. The subjects evolving seem often conscious of their evolution (or in Suha's case, degeneration). Some desire it (Tamr), others resist it (some men), and yet others want to be selective about it (Nur). Tamr, who was briefly befriended by Suha, is one of those who were desirous of reaching civilization through a process of learning. Tamr, for example, thanks Suha after Suha and her driver took her to obtain a license to open a shop.

> I got up to kiss Suha on both cheeks and said, "I don't know what I would have done without you. I want to thank you from my heart, dear." Suha thought I meant the

33. Ibid., 168–69.
34. Ibid., 153.

car and Saʿid [the driver], while I was actually grateful because through her I got to know the other life of the desert of which I was ignorant, beginning with colors and furniture all the way to civilization itself. I thanked God that I went to the association and that Suha was my teacher, and that I ate a slice of *gateau* [*sic*] in this white plate with flower drawings on it and drank tea with honey instead of sugar.[35]

But if Tamr learned about civilization through Suha, she and her aunt had much to learn when they traveled to London. It is there that they both receive a proper lesson in what civilization is all about. Their response will be selective acceptance of it:

My aunt listened and then remarked, "God bless Rashid and bless us. The children of the English are born strangers to their families and die as strangers. When the English doctor found out how we live and how we don't abandon our families and they don't abandon us, he said to me, 'You're more civilized than we are.'" I asked the English girl, Mariam [whose real name is Maria] . . . 'So what does the Doctor want?' Mariam explained to me in Arabic the meaning of the word civilization [hadarah]. It means the invention of airplanes, it means progress and modern life and machines. I told her to tell the doctor, 'I believe that airplanes exist because I rode in one and that steamships exist because I traveled in one, and that cars exist because I have been in them, but I don't believe that humans went to the moon even were I to see a million pictures. How could a man stand on it without falling when the moon is as big as a loaf of bread. Tell the doctor, 'I don't believe that the Earth rotates and that it looks like an apple, as, if it did, my bed would now be there and the table would be in its place.' Tell him that these are illusions, but lest he get upset tell him that my aunt believes in radio and television, as both entertain and are good. Indeed, the first time we heard the radio, we thought it was the devil, and then we saw television and we said this must be the devil's grandfather."[36]

This response to civilization is illuminating of the dynamic that al-Shaykh had set for the novel. While the English doctor appreciates the close kinship ties of the uncivilized and the uncivilized in turn appreciate the technology that civilization has brought forth, it is Suha and, indeed, al-Shaykh, who seem to have the benefits of both worlds. Here Lebanon's violence and civil war, just like Suha's internal contradictions and ambivalences, may very well be interpreted as a reaction to this in-betweenness that the novel constructs. Suha herself has a different view of radio and television. When she felt utterly alienated from the life of

35. Ibid., 198.
36. Ibid., 203.

the desert, she retreated to her house: "News of the world through radio and television seemed necessary. Listening to it, one feels that it speaks of human beings and of a life that one knows."[37] Suha's cosmopolitanism here may offer an explanation for why as an Arab, she could not relate to the desert kingdom but could relate to "world," read Western, news.

While the desert country (Saudi Arabia) remains in the novel a place where women continue to live and struggle, as women do everywhere, it is Suha who opts out and chooses modern uninhibited violence over uncivilized sensuality. Al-Shaykh's reconfiguration of her novel in the English translation, however, has caused concern to some. If in the original Arabic, Suha leaves the desert at the end of the first part of the novel, in the English version Suha's account is split in two, bracketing the novel, with one part at the beginning and the other at the very end.[38] The English version of the novel, titled *Women of Sand and Myrrh,* ends with Suha departing this unlivable uncivilized place, leaving the reader with the impression that exit from Saudi Arabia is the only way out (also the order of Nur's and Tamr's accounts are reversed, where Tamr's account is the second one after Suha's). The Arabic reader finishes the novel while still in the desert kingdom with Tamr. The English reader, in contrast, finishes the novel by exiting with Suha from that horror of a place.

Quite attuned to her Western readers, al-Shaykh and her novels have been welcomed by Western reviewers, who hailed the book as "memorable" for its depiction of life in "the great golden cage of the desert," as the *International Herald Tribune* described it.[39] Indeed, the U.S. edition of the novel has a more revealing description of the contents by the publisher on the back cover. The novel is not presented as descriptive of life in a desert kingdom but rather of "what life is like for contemporary Arab women living in the Middle East . . . a still-closed society." Jenine Abboushi has argued that *Misk al-Ghazal* is a novel written primarily for an English-speaking audience: "References [in the novel] specific to Western culture which would be unfamiliar to Arabs go unexplained, whereas references to customs or practices specific to Arab contexts are consistently accompanied by explanations."[40] While Suha's in-betweenness is obliterated in the U.S. edition's back-cover description, she remains the protagonist with which Western readers identify. Indeed, Western readers may very well identify with her more than with

37. Ibid., 37.
38. Hanan al-Shaykh, *Women of Sand and Myrrh* (New York: Doubleday, 1992).
39. Ibid., back cover.
40. Jenine Abboushi Dallal, "The Perils of Occidentalism: How Arab Novelists Are Driven to Write for Western Readers," *Times Literary Supplement,* 24 April 1998, 8.

the white American Suzanne, who fails to articulate, as Suha does, what is really at stake in the modern game of civilization and desires, even though, like Suha, she remains a participant in it.

There occurs in the novel a notable reversal of certain clichés about the sexual ideologies of modernity in the West. In many tradition-versus-modernity debates about life inside Europe, it is modernity that is the site of both prosperity and perversity—it is the city that is the seat of vice, the country, the home of virtue. In such debates, decadence, rather than deviance or degeneration, is the organizing trope. What the novel enacts, however, is the colonial pedigree of the tradition-versus-modernity clichés, where the reversal occurs and primitive non-Europe, which lacks urbanity and city life in such formulations, becomes the site of perversions and deviations from Europe's established civilized urban norms.[41]

While the deviant sexual desires of Gulf Arabs were dangerous because primitively seductive, one has a better chance of resisting them outside the territory of the Gulf. This is what Jamal al-Ghitani's *Risalat al-Basa'ir fi al-Masa'ir* (The Treatise of Insights into Fates), a book of fictional vignettes, wants to show. To do so, the novel puts Sadat's Egypt under the microscope.[42] As the country is being literally sold to Americans, Europeans, and Gulf Arabs, while Sadat makes a capitulationist peace with the enemy, the entire value system that had prevailed until then in Egypt is disappearing. Money now replaced ethics as the measure of success. It is in this context, described as such by al-Ghitani, that a young man, whose father had always hoped his son would obtain a diplomatic post in the foreign ministry when he grows up and graduates from university, ends up working at one of the new hotels that dot the Cairene landscape to service the new tourism economy overtaking the country. The young man. who is never named (all the characters in this vignette are unnamed) begins to realize that he is called upon by his Egyptian boss and the latter's American boss to perform tasks (for which he is handsomely paid) that he did not imagine would be part of his job description. These include becoming an escort, providing full sexual services to some hotel guests, including one European woman who works

---

41. This novel should be contrasted with a later novel by al-Shaykh in which the setting is London itself and which includes a Lebanese character, Samir, who is desirous of men. See Hanan al-Shaykh, *Innaha Landan Ya 'Azizi* [It Is London, My Dear] (Beirut: Dar al-Adab, 2001). For the English edition, see Hanan al-Shaykh, *Only in London*, translated by Catherine Cobham (London: Bloomsbury, 2001).

42. Jamal al-Ghitani, *Risalat al-Basa'ir fi al-Masa'ir* [The Treatise of Insights into Fates] (Cairo: Dar al-Hilal, 1989).

for a European airline, and an elderly American woman who only paid him for a conversation about Egypt in the privacy of her hotel room.

It was the third sexual task assigned him, however, that created a great deal of anxiety in him. When an elderly Gulf Arab man notices the young man and begins to flirt with him and gives him an expensive watch as a present, the young man refuses, on account of his inability to give back a gift of similar value. The Egyptian boss was furious with the young university graduate, explaining to him, as he had done before, how local and foreign investors had already invested sixteen million dollars in the hotel and want to see returns quickly. The young man finally confronts his boss: "Is it part of work that the elderly man would pinch my cheek and have a satisfied look on his face? Is it part of work that he should wink at him, could he accept such behavior?"[43] The Egyptian hotel manager laughs and begins to ridicule him as a boy pretending to be "honorable" and "chaste." He yells at him, telling him that he should cater to the elderly man from the Gulf "if not for the sake of the hotel, then for the sake of the country, as angering His Excellency may harm relations; plus, why is he scared anyway? Could [the elderly gentleman] take something from him that he does not want to give, by force? Never! And also, why does he assume what he is assuming, maybe His Excellency would be satisfied with a conversation and some flirtation . . . Who knows, perhaps he will be surprised when he goes up to his room to find him in a woman's nightgown."[44] Here al-Ghitani harks back to the ways he represented rich and powerful people in *Zaʿfarani Street* as desirous of being penetrated by those weaker than they.

The Egyptian manager proceeds to tell the young man that things are not always what they appear. He recounts to him the story of a young man who is "more handsome than you, as he is blond, while you have black hair," who ends up in jail. The prison officer worried about him being raped by the prisoners and put him in solitary confinement to protect him. He later moved him to the second floor where the prison's toughest prisoner lived, "a man three times the size of His Excellency the Shaykh." It turned out later and to the "surprise of the officers and soldiers that this young delicate man was the man, and the macho tough whom everyone feared took the female position in relation to him. So why should he be scared? Why should he be fearful? Moreover,

43. Ibid., 59.
44. Ibid.

this is plain stupidity. He is ruining his own chances for promotion and wealth." Indeed, the manager tells him that what he is being asked to do with the elderly Gulf man is no different from what he did with the young European woman and the elderly American, "it is all work."[45] Unlike ʿUways in al-Ghitani's *The Events of Zaʿfarani Street*, the young man only provides sexual services to foreign white women. When it came to the elderly rich Gulf Arab man, the young man chose honor and resigned under the manager's threats that he would pay his life as a price for "ruining what we are building here." Indeed, that night, the police arrested him on a trumped-up charge of murdering the female European hotel guest, ending his and his family's ambitions for a successful career.

This vignette has universal application as the young man and all the characters represent the state of things in Egypt under Sadat. That nobody is named in the story is because the characters stand in for Egyptians more generally; they could have a million Egyptian names. Sadat's new order was not only prostituting the new young generation of Egyptian men to European and American women, which is bad enough, but they are being sold off to Gulf oil money as well and the sexually deviant desires of elderly Gulf gentlemen. Yusuf Idris's "manliest of men" chose to live dishonored rather than die, but al-Ghitani's young man chooses an honorable death rather than be penetrated. It is unclear whether he would have been able to resist such deviance had he lived in the Gulf. If Hanan al-Shaykh's Suha could only resist deviance by escaping to a more evolved place like war-torn Beirut, Cairo, despite its degradation and decadence under Sadat's tourist economy, was still able to provide the requisite willpower to resist deviance, even if the cost is a ruined life. Reading fiction as a civilizational allegory, we will see later that Cairo will not be able to provide that willpower for much longer under the increasing pressure of globalization.

What we have in al-Ghitani's *The Treatise of Insights into Fates* is a capitalist cosmopolitan modernity as the agent of corruption as opposed to *The Deer's Musk's* articulation of desert primitivism as the agent of deviance. The confluence and contradictions in these representations of Gulf deviance are directly related. It is a capitalized oil industry that led the civilized to visit the primitive desert and experience its sexual deviance, just as the wealth generated by the oil industry has now allowed the desert deviants to visit civilization itself armed with capital to introduce their deviance unopposed.

45. Ibid., 60.

The Truth of Desire Lies in the Body

If many of the novels we analyzed sought to negotiate the state of things social and sexual in depicting contemporary life, Syrian playwright Sa'dallah Wannus's (1941–1997) play *Tuqus al-Isharat wa al-Tahawwulat* (The Rites of Signs and Transformations),[46] published in 1994, sought to do the same thing but at a temporal remove, namely, of a century or so in the past. The play is based, as Wannus tells us in the preface, on a story he read in the memoir of Syrian Arab nationalist activist Fakhri al-Barudi. Al-Barudi (1887–1966) published the first part of his memoir in 1951 (and the second part in 1952), which included a story told to him by an older mentor about an event in Damascus in the mid-1880s.[47] The story al-Barudi reports is about infighting between, on the one hand, the Mufti of the city, who was a highly learned man, and the Dean of the Syndicate of Nobles (Nobles, or "Ashraf," refers to those families who claim descent from the Prophet), who happened to be a highly unlearned man, and, on the other, between the police chief and the Dean of the Syndicate of Nobles. The police chief arranged to have the Dean followed and arrested while cavorting with his mistress in a Damascus garden. Upon hearing of this, the Mufti chided the police chief and intrigued with the jailer and with the wife of the Dean to have the mistress switched with the wife without anyone knowing of the switch. Then the Mufti proceeded to mobilize the community of Nobles to go to the Ottoman governor, or Wali, and denounce the police chief for making them unsafe in their own city to the point of arresting their Dean with his own wife. Having ascertained, after the switch was completed, that indeed the jailed woman was the wife, and not the mistress, the Wali ordered the release of the Dean and his wife, and the police chief was jailed in their stead. The Mufti then persuaded the Dean to "forgive" the police chief and ask the Wali to release him. The Mufti then moved to ask for payback from the Dean himself, forcing him to resign his position, which he had sullied by his untoward behavior, upon which his long-standing enmity with the Mufti would end.[48]

For al-Barudi, the story is about nationalism, friendship, and loyalty, wherein the solidarity shown by these three elite Damascene personalities, despite their deep differences and enmities, testified to a sense of

46. Sa'dallah Wannus, *Tuqus al-Isharat wa al-Tahawwulat* (Beirut: Dar al-Adab, 1994).
47. Fakhri al-Barudi, *Mudhakkarat al-Barudi, Sittun Sannah Tatakallam,* vol. 1 (Beirut and Damascus: Dar al-Hayat, 1951).
48. Ibid., 114–17.

identity and common interest against the "foreign" Ottoman Wali. Indeed, al-Barudi begins his story, which appears under the heading "The solidarity of Damascenes," by affirming that "it is known that Damascenes in that period were united, obedient to their leaders, and supportive of one another against the foreigner . . . unlike in these days where friendship and loyalty are scarce."[49] To affirm such solidarity, al-Barudi concluded that the Ottoman Wali, Rashid Nashid Pasha, who ruled Damascus twice, the first for eight months in 1876 and the second for more than three years starting in 1884, "witnessed throughout his tenure the solidarity among the leaders and the religious scholars, and their unified word, so much so that when he left Damascus and people went out to bid him farewell . . . he cried. Someone asked him, 'Why do you cry, Your Excellency, is it because you will miss Damascus?' He answered, 'No. I cry because throughout my sojourn in the city I was unable to create divisions between any two of its residents!'" Al-Barudi concluded that "from this story we learn of the amount of cohesiveness among the Damascenes of that period."[50]

Wannus's *Tuqus* has in fact very little to do with the nineteenth century and much more to do with the present. He acknowledges as much in the preface: "Perhaps, it is necessary for me to point out that the place, Damascus, and the time, the second half of the nineteenth century, are only conventional in this play. My concern was not to provide a work on the overall conditions, or an approach to the social and historical realities, of the second half of the nineteenth century."[51] The plot, while much related to the story narrated by al-Barudi, differs from it in significant ways. The play actually uses the story of enmity between the police chief and the Mufti on one side and the Dean of the Syndicate of Nobles on the other as the event that triggers the dissolution of public order as it existed.

Attempting to ingratiate himself to the Mufti, the police chief (hereafter 'Izzat Bek, as he is named in the play) acts on information provided to him by one of the Mufti's virile toughs, al-'Afsah, to follow and arrest the Dean (hereafter 'Abdullah) with his mistress Wardah while on a picnic in one of 'Abdullah's private gardens. News of the arrests is announced to the Mufti by his two toughs: "Al-'Afsah: we saw your enemy chained and naked but for his underwear, with his slut donning his 'imamah [head covering] on her head and wearing his clothes."[52] Note

49. Ibid., 114.
50. Ibid., 117.

51. Wannus, *Tuqus al-Isharat*, 5.
52. Ibid., 18.

the importance of the sartorial switch, both of gender and social station, as a *sign* of scandal, humiliation, and *transformation*. When the Mufti affects horror, al-ʿAfsah and ʿAbbas explain:

AL-ʿAFSAH: We are telling you what we saw. ʿIzzat Bek made them ride on a mule, which he pulled through the neighborhoods and alleyways in front of onlookers.
ʿABBAS: Astounded, people stared at them. A hail of whistles, spittle, and curses poured on your enemy.
AL-ʿAFSAH: They are now in prison continuing their affair, and the rest of it.[53]

The Mufti, who was holding a public audience with Damascene merchants, waxed honorable: "The Dean of the Syndicate of Nobles is not an enemy. There may be differences in interpretation [ijtihad] and in opinion between us, but these are disagreements and don't amount to enmity. Our enemy now, my enemy and the enemy of the Nobles, and your enemy too, are those who attempt to debase your elders and insult your Nobles. They want all of us to bow our heads [in shame] and allow the lowly to disrespect the elders and the scoundrels to disrespect the notables. Do you approve of this?"[54] It is interesting to note here that unlike al-Barudi's Mufti, the Mufti in Wannus's play is interested not in national solidarity but rather in class solidarity. It is not the foreign Ottoman Wali who needs to witness the unity of Damascenes, as in al-Barudi's narration, rather it is the lower classes that must know that the elite of the city will always stand unified and that their internal differences cannot be exploited by the lower classes or by the state. In Wannus's play, the Mufti is the invidious mover and shaker of all that unfolds. He is a power monger who intrigues with everyone, allies and enemies, to rid himself of them and run the city as his personal fiefdom. Unlike the Mufti of al-Barudi's story, the Mufti of the play sacrifices the police chief and refuses to save him, leaving him to rot in jail.

The play is essentially about elite maintenance of a public system of morals that contradicts private conduct. In some ways, the play is reminiscent of, and perhaps inspired by, Shakespeare's *Measure for Measure* in its use of multiple substitutions and disguises of characters and in terms of the centrality of desire and public sexual conduct (including prostitution) to the plot. Unlike *Measure for Measure*, a comedy concerned with lax sexual mores and the prevalence of brothels in Vienna (a substitute

53. Ibid., 18.
54. Ibid., 19.

for Shakespeare's London), which ends in multiple marriages that render illicit sex licit and restores honor to dishonored women, *The Rites of Signs and Transformations* is a bona fide tragedy that has no facile resolution in sight. The play is about an unholy alliance between religious clerics, the state, the aristocracy of nobles, and the merchants to maintain a public order based on what Wannus considers hypocrisy. It is about the preservation of the chasm between what must remain "latent" and what has to be "manifest." The terrain of this struggle is not the monetary economy, nor the exploitation of the poorer classes by the richer classes, but rather that of the body and its desires, in short, the social economy of patriarchal masculinist rule. This struggle unfolds in two parallel stories that structure the entire play, that of Mu'minah (which means "believer"), the learned aristocratic wife of 'Abdullah, Dean of the Syndicate of Nobles, and of al-'Afsah, the macho tough of the Mufti. It is their transformation from respectable to contemptible social personalities that exposes the fakeness of Damascene society within which they live. Indeed, their transformation brings about the transformation of every major character in the play (except the servants and the merchants), whose latent private conduct is exposed and made manifest for everyone to see. Indeed, like in *Measure for Measure,* the transformation of the Mufti from the figure who upholds public morals into someone who violates them is parallel to the transformation of Angelo (the substitute Duke of Vienna) from an upholder of sexual mores into a fornicator.

Let us begin with al-'Afsah and his transformation. Upon being publicly chastised by the Mufti for reporting the news of the arrests, al-'Afsah and his colleague 'Abbas are privately rewarded by the Mufti's assistant 'Abduh, who communicates to them the Mufti's apology for chastising them, which was only for the benefit of his merchant guests. Both men set out to the bank of the River Barada where they sit to chat and to sip arak (the Syrian alcoholic drink made of grapes and anise, also known metaphorically as "the milk of lion cubs" on account of its milky color once ice and/or water are added to it). Al-'Afsah was assuaged by the Mufti's apology but not 'Abbas. Al-'Afsah tries to placate him but without much success—"Brother, this is my nature. I like everything to be straight. My soul does not like detours and evasions nor ambiguity."[55] 'Abbas, however, was mollified upon seeing Simsim, "an effeminate young man who walks in a depraved [khali'ah] manner," pass them by.[56]

55. Ibid., 28.
56. Ibid., 29.

He calls up to Simsim (a derogatory feminine name meaning "sesame") and invites him to join them:

ʿABBAS: Take . . . drink the milk of cubs.
SIMSIM: I'd die for your moustache. I'm ready to give up all the cubs for a taste of your milk.
ʿABBAS: It seems that you're quite horny.
SIMSIM: Oh, Aba Fahd [ʿAbbas's nickname[57]], I can only be satisfied with a stab from your dagger. Don't you remember that one orphan time! By God, [when you took it out,] it was as if you pulled my soul out of my body.
ʿABBAS: Come on, Sus [a diminutive feminization of Simsim]. Manners dictate that you respect the feelings of those present and that you distribute your love equally among them.[58]

Al-ʿAfsah, who had referred to Simsim initially as an "impurity [naja-sah]," is appalled and objects to ʿAbbas's invitation to Simsim to join them.[59] As he begins to insult Simsim, the latter retreats behind ʿAbbas in terror: "Why are you picking a fight with me? Did I talk or expose a secret?"[60] Al-ʿAfsah, shaken, stands up and moves to slug Simsim and calls him "the slut of the cemeteries."[61] ʿAbbas interferes to stop al-ʿAfsah and inquires of Simsim as to the cause of al-ʿAfsah's displeasure:

SIMSIM: Well, we tried him, only to find out that what he had is like [a grain of] rice, or a twining of cloth, and we found out that what he has is like what we have, and what itches us itches him.
ʿABBAS: (Suppressing his laughter) Now go and don't look behind you, and if you repeat what you just said, you will die.[62]

It is not entirely clear if the reference to rice and twining is to the size of al-ʿAfsah's penis, his possible impotence, or both, and if so, whether there is a correlation between penis size or potency/impotence and the desire to penetrate or be penetrated.[63] At any rate, ʿAbbas gets the point.

---

57. Aba Fahd literally means "father of Fahd." Fahd is a proper male name, which also means "leopard."

58. Wannus, *Tuqus al-Isharat*, 30.

59. Ibid.

60. Ibid., 31.

61. Ibid., 31. I should note here that when the Mufti was accused of dispatching al-ʿAfsah to inform on ʿAbdullah to the police chief, he dissociated himself from him and referred to him as "a hyena of cemeteries who makes his living by slandering people, inciting discord and gossip, and I cannot employ someone like him among my men and assistants" (22).

62. Ibid., 31.

63. Al-ʿAfsah's name means an oak apple or a nonfertilizing seed, which oak trees produce in certain years instead of acorns, and very well may be a reference to the possible small size of al-

AL-ʿAFSAH: (*defeated*) Have I lost your respect? [literally, have I fallen from your eye?]

ʿABBAS: I swear . . . I had my doubts. No . . . , you are now my beloved [in the feminine], and I shall protect and care for you ["I shall put you inside my eye"]. Drink up!

AL-ʿAFSAH: (*Drinks an abundant gulp*) Such words injure me [in reference to the feminine form of "beloved"].

ʿABBAS: You've been exposed before me just like my wife would [halali].[64] There's no need to feign shyness.

AL-ʿAFSAH: (*Holds ʿAbbas's hand and kisses it [a gesture of abject imploration]*). I beseech you, don't expose me publicly.

ʿABBAS: (*Puts his own hand on his neck [in a gesture of swearing on his honor]*) What! Would one expose one's wife [halal] publicly!

AL-ʿAFSAH: (*Caressing his face on ʿAbbas's hand*) Do you promise that everything will remain as it is on the surface?

ʿABBAS: (*Touching him playfully*) So we will have latent and manifest sides?

AL-ʿAFSAH: Like everyone else, ʿAbbas, like everyone else . . . Oh! I have suffered and been tormented much in order to hide this matter. It was like an abscess festering inside me.

ʿABBAS: And now the abscess has burst and you can rest . . . You shall remain as you are and you will not suffer after today.[65]

The question of the latent and the manifest has much to do with the parallel characters that the play presents. Al-ʿAfsah's manifest manliness and his latent desire to be penetrated are contrasted with Simsim's manifest effeminacy and open expression of his desire to be penetrated.[66] It is this contrast and comparability between what is latent and what is manifest that, as we will see, forms the axis of the play's events.

Let us turn to the story of Muʾminah, ʿAbdullah's wife. Muʾminah is introduced to us as part of the Mufti's ploy to free ʿAbdullah. She is visited by the Mufti, who asks her to be part of his scheme.[67] Surprised by his attempt to substitute the prostitute with the wife, even though everyone had seen the prostitute, she asserts: "Is the difference between the wife and the prostitute so slight?"[68] The Mufti ignores her crucial question. But she insists that as a result of what he is proposing, the

---

ʿAfsah's penis or to his impotency. "ʿAfsah," however, also refers to the pungent quality of the taste of an oak apple.

64. "Halali" literally means those who are lawful for the speaker to marry, and in this context a reference to one's wife.

65. Wannus, *Tuqus al-Isharat*, 32–33.

66. I should note here Simsim's name may also be comparable to al-ʿAfsah, as it also refers to the tiny sesame seed.

67. In al-Barudi's version, she is called upon to visit the Mufti's wife.

68. Wannus, *Tuqus al-Isharat*, 36.

wife will be accused of being caught, all made up, with her husband in a compromising situation in open space, while in reality she was "confined to her home reading *A Thousand and One Nights.*"[69] Mu'minah is appalled that she should be mistaken for exhibiting her body publicly but has little problem exhibiting her intellectual prowess. She informs the Mufti that she is a well-educated woman, having read theology and popular literature: "Would it amaze you to know that I have read all of my father's library and the library of the Dean of the Syndicate of Nobles!"[70] He *was* amazed. Here, Wannus is presenting Mu'minah explicitly as a nineteenth-century version of Shahrazad who is first described in *A Thousand and One Nights* as "the older daughter [of the vizier], Shahrazad, had read the books of literature, philosophy, and medicine. She knew poetry by heart, had studied historical reports, and was acquainted with the sayings of men and the maxims of sages and kings. She was intelligent, knowledgeable, wise, and refined."[71]

Mu'minah resisted the Mufti, insisting that she could not help him, as what he wanted her to do was "to play the role of a prostitute." The Mufti insisted that that was not the case and that his plan was to "dismiss the prostitute so that the companionship would be revealed to be with the wife." Mu'minah countered: "The wife-prostitute, the prostitute-wife. This is nice manipulation and a dangerous one too. No . . . You're pushing me onto a bumpy road, and I don't know where it will lead me . . . What you're asking of me is a terrifying gamble, to walk on the edge of the precipice, and, of seduction . . . The precipice shakes me at the roots. Falling terrifies me, but it also seduces me at the same time."[72] The Mufti showed even more amazement at her speech. Mu'minah's feminist consciousness appears at its most astute at this point: "It never occurred to you that I might be alive and that I have my own inclinations and thoughts . . . I do not believe that you thought of me except as an obedient tool, or as a thing among the property [of my husband] . . . But I refuse because I resist entering the charm of seduction. If I accept, I will slip into the place of fragility—my fragility and the fragility of our conditions. I shall be at the edge of the precipice, and I fear this time that I shall heed the call of the precipice."[73] She finally agrees to the Mufti's scheme but on one condition, namely, that after the whole affair is over and her husband is set free, she wants the Mufti to guarantee to her

69. Ibid.
70. Ibid.
71. *The Arabian Nights,* translated by Husain Haddawy (New York: Norton, 1990), 11.
72. Wannus, *Tuqus al-Isharat,* 37.
73. Ibid., 38.

that her husband would divorce her.[74] As for the precipice, Mu'minah's approach of it constitutes the very condition of society itself. Society, it would seem, was at the edge of the precipice, and the violation of the privacy of 'Abdullah and Wardah, as we will see, sent it tumbling over.

For Mu'minah, transformation begins at the moment she is conflated with the prostitute. The moment of the physical switch in the prison is also a moment of sartorial switch between the now made-up wife, Mu'minah, and the prostitute, Wardah. Upon being divorced from her husband, Mu'minah sets out to visit Wardah (which means Rose) and asks that the latter teach her how to become a prostitute. In utter disbelief, Wardah thinks that Mu'minah is ridiculing her. Once she realizes Mu'minah is sincere, Wardah is overcome by a sense of schadenfreude and tells Mu'minah that she'd been a servant in Mu'minah's household as a young girl where Mu'minah's father abused and raped her, even before she was old enough to menstruate. The shock strengthens Mu'minah's resolve to transform herself into a prostitute. Her transformation is almost magical, reminiscent of a character in *A Thousand and One Nights,* a book, as we saw, that is dear to her heart. When the Mufti, appalled by her transformation, for which he felt responsible, offers her marriage in front of her father as a way out of her errant ways, she refuses. In a semidelirious state, she speaks of her transformation, her liberation from tradition:

It seems to me that at the moment of my fall [into the precipice], colored feathers will grow in my follicles . . . and I will soar like a bird, like a breeze, like a ray of sun. I want to cut out the coarse fibrous cords that dig deep into my flesh, repress my body—cords that are braided with terror and diffidence, chastity and feelings of dirtiness and filth, of sermons, verses and warnings, of maxims and the commandments of the ancestors. . . . I want to manumit my body . . . and untie those ropes that suck its blood, in order that it be free to stay in the orbit for which it was created . . . I dream of reaching myself, of becoming transparent like glass. What eyes see of me is my innermost secret, and my innermost secret is what eyes see of me.[75]

Mu'minah here seems to conflate the body and its desires. She seems to posit that the truth of the body is that of desire. Her insistence on becoming a prostitute, as she tells the Mufti, is unrelated to anger at her husband's infidelity, the latter having provided her the opportunity to make the latent manifest. In undertaking her project of manumitting

74. Ibid., 40–41.
75. Ibid., 100–1.

her body as part of the liberation of her repressed desire, a contradiction arises in Mu'minah's logic (and in the logic of Wannus). If the play stresses the quest for individuality and individualism in a society that represses both, then desire cannot be the foundation of such a quest.[76] As desire is always already social and not part of the individualist economy, how is Mu'minah's quest to release her desires from the shackles of traditional repression, and even oppression, to enter the social economy of carnal pleasure, a quest for modern individualism? Wannus seems to posit Mu'minah's quest as a Hegelian one, of transforming the being-in-itself into the being-for-itself and the being-for-another. But the Hegelian story is not only about the journey of self-consciousness into individualist self-realization but also that of the journey of self-consciousness into sociality, of being "in the world," as Edward Said, echoing Heidegger, put it. When in response to her father's horror at her sullying the family name and its honor by her action she responds that "what I do is no concern to anyone but me,"[77] she is insisting on deploying the individualist project and exiting from society. Indeed, no less an authority than the Qur'an is marshaled to the cause of individualism by Mu'minah: "In the last instance, do we not know that no one carries the burden of others, and that each soul receives *every good that it earns, and it suffers every ill that it earns* [emphasis added]."[78] How is desire, which presupposes sociality, liberated in an asocial individualist world? As we will see, the play provides inadequate answers at best to the very questions it raises.

While still beholden to the Qur'an as an ethical reference (which is not unlike the Duke's invocation of the biblical verse of "a measure for measure" in Shakespeare's play), Mu'minah ("believer") needed a new name to go with her manumitted body. If Mu'minah *believed* in that which is most precious for the afterlife, her new name "Almasah" (diamond) transformed her into that which is most precious in this one. Soon she would outdo her teacher Wardah and corner the prostitution market. Even Wardah's own female servant (present in the opening scene exchanging words of love with 'Abdullah's male servant at the moment the arrests take place in the garden) switches mistresses, becoming Almasah's servant.

76. For a learned and interesting discussion about the individualism of the play, see Mahmud Nasim, "Tuqus wa Isharat, Su'ud al-Fardiyyah am Inkisaruha? Wa Madha ba'da al-Haffah?" [Rites and Signs, the Rise of Individualism or Its Defeat? And, What Comes after the Precipice?], in *Al-Tariq*, January–February 1996, no. 1, 166–77.

77. Wannus, *Tuqus al-Isharat*, 95.

78. Ibid., 97. The italicized part of the sentence is a direct quote from the Qur'an, chap. 2, "Al-Baqarah" [The Heifer], verse 286.

As Mu'minah leaves the life of ascetic respectability and transforms herself into a provider and consumer of carnal pleasure, her ex-husband 'Abdullah is transformed by the scandal into an ascetic Sufi who exchanges the world of carnality for the world of the spirit, and roams the streets of Damascus praising God. The police chief also is transformed. He begins to show signs of losing his mind by the prison experience and the Mufti's volte-face against him. When his state of disbelief persists, concerning the fact that it was Warda, not Mu'minah, with whom he caught 'Abdullah, the Mufti tells his assistant Abdu: "Did you not tell him that truth is established through consensus?"[79]

The corporeal transformation of Mu'minah into Almasah, whose body can now soar with birds, is parallel to the transformation that al-'Afsah's body will experience later in the play. If Mu'minah felt the need to transform the latent into the manifest by externalizing her desire, which she saw as the *truth* of her body (which is now differently dressed, groomed, made up, and moves sinuously), al-'Afsah will follow a similar path. Feeling dejected by the increasing inattention of 'Abbas since the latter left the Mufti and took up his new job as the bodyguard of Almasah, al-'Afsah takes drastic action. He shaves his moustache, has his entire body waxed, and begins to affect effeminacy in his physical behavior and speech. His body transformed, he visits 'Abbas, who receives him with horror and "repulsion":

AL-'AFSAH: Don't make me cry. I wanted to be pretty in your eyes. I noticed that your passion had decreased, and that you were slipping away from me, so I was overcome with panic . . . It occurred to me to give you the most precious thing I possess and the last thing that distinguishes me in people's eyes . . . Take Aba Fahd, this is my present to you . . .

'ABBAS: . . . Is this your moustache?

AL-'AFSAH: Yes it is. I bestow it upon you. You can declare throughout the city that Al-'Afsah's moustache is mine, and that all of al-'Afsah is mine.

'ABBAS: God help me! What has befallen you, man? . . . Didn't you seek confidentiality and fear defamation?

AL-'AFSAH: I didn't know then the tyranny and madness of passion . . .

'ABBAS: . . . Do you think you will make me happy if you become effeminate?

AL-'AFSAH: Well, what makes you happy, then? Do you not prefer me smooth and tender?

'ABBAS: You repel me. You're nothing but a catamite training for bawdiness (mujun).

AL-'AFSAH: I am *your* catamite. I wanted you to know that I have been transformed, and that I have the courage to declare my transformation and to face people with it. Tell me, how do you want me to be?

79. Wannus, *Tuqus al-Isharat*, 73.

ʿABBAS: I wanted you to remain a man beside me . . . [but] with this exposed effemi-nacy, I am embarrassed of you being next to me and am embarrassed that anyone would know that I have any connection to you. Looking like this, you are but another Simsim.[80]

Al-ʿAfsah's transformation was a coming to terms with what he consid-ered to be his inner truth, for which a public confession was a necessity. It is only through these public confessionals that the unification of the latent and the manifest is possible, al-ʿAfsah insisted. This is how he explains his actions to ʿAbbas:

AL-ʿAFSAH: You know that what I did is very costly for me . . . I cannot bear you casting me aside after I had changed my constitution. I've become like water in its purity and clarity. No matter how you look at me, you'll find me one and the same. *What I look like is my innermost secret and my innermost secret is what I look like.* Didn't you say that you were repelled by those who have an outward appearance that is different from their intrinsic truth? What I did is to expose my intrinsic truth, for I no longer have anything to suppress or conceal. I wanted to . . . confess without equivocation or hiding that I am infatuated with you. This passion is what made me dare to challenge other people and my own self, and it is what provides me with courage and life.[81]

The investment in public exposure for both Almasah and al-ʿAfsah is clearly based on their insistence on obliterating the division between the latent and the manifest, the "innermost" truth of their being and their public persona, a sort of ultimate Hegelian immediate unity of the being-in-itself, the being-for-itself, and the being-for-another. While previously he was one of the manliest men in the city, affecting and performing masculinity in all its public details, al-ʿAfsah's passion for being penetrated by another man signified to him a requisite feminiza-tion of physical appearance and gendered conduct in the public sphere. Like Almasah, he seems to think that his desire is located in the body, that it is the *truth* of the body. Although he resisted the similarity to Simsim, which the latter insisted was the case ("what itches us itches him"), and almost killed him for suggesting it, by now he accepted its logic. Unable to see same-sex desire among men except in heterosexual terms, al-ʿAfsah misidentifies ʿAbbas's desire to penetrate men as a desire for what is *different,* not for what is the *same.* The fact that ʿAbbas enjoys coitus with women, effeminate men, and manly men did not signify to

80. Ibid., 85–87.
81. Ibid., 87. Emphasis added.

al-ʿAfsah that ʿAbbas's desire is organized primarily around sexual aim (being the penetrator) and can accommodate a variety of penetrable object choices. Al-ʿAfsah also failed to see that affective relationships are not necessarily the telos of sexual desire, a clear projection by Wannus from his own time period, the 1990s, onto the 1880s.

ʿAbbas, after all, like Simsim and Wardah, was transparent in his desires. He was in his innermost truth and in his outward appearance a penetrator, and experienced no embarrassment in seeking the services of female prostitutes or of Simsim, any more than Simsim and Wardah were embarrassed about their desires or about soliciting penetrative men to satisfy them. The secrecy that ʿAbbas kept regarding his penetration of al-ʿAfsah was to protect the latter from public scandal, and an expression of his friendship toward him. This misrecognition on the part of al-ʿAfsah would cost him dearly. ʿAbbas's response to him came as a shock:

ʿABBAS: What is this nonsense that you pour into my ear. You're speaking like a whore who is ulcerous from passion and deprivation.

AL-ʿAFSAH: I am speaking as a lover does.

ʿABBAS: You speak of love and nonsense! There is no passion or infatuation between men.

AL-ʿAFSAH: Then what was between us?

ʿABBAS: You want the truth?

AL-ʿAFSAH: Yes, it is time for the truth, even it leads to my death.

ʿABBAS: What was between us was desire, which disappears after being satisfied. It gave me pleasure to mount a man who was counted among the virile, and to see his stature break and get smaller between my thighs. But now, what kind of pleasure will I obtain from mounting a foolish [raqiʾ] effeminate?[82]

ʿAbbas's expression of a desire for the same (he also desired what is different), his *homosexual* desire, eluded al-ʿAfsah, who himself had desired ʿAbbas because he *was the same,* and failed to desire Simsim who *was different.* If, as in all masculinist societies, women and effeminate men are always already conquered a priori by the social position accorded them, then the real and only conquest for men, sexual and otherwise, in such societies (and indeed this is the condition of all existing societies) is of manly men. The fact that such conquest is rare to achieve makes it a more titillating object of desire for manly men, as ʿAbbas clearly understood.

Al-ʿAfsah's failure to understand the law of desire in his society is hard to explain, given his own manifest and latent desires. Surely he un-

82. Ibid., 87–88.

derstood, as ʿAbbas and everyone else had, that the telos of sexual desire is consummation and not romantic love, and that this is the case even if the desire is between men and women, something Almasah insisted on when she rejected the Mufti's marriage proposal. ʿAbbas, on his part, had not fallen in love with Almasah or with Simsim, any more than he did with al-ʿAfsah, whom he did love as a friend. The projection of romantic love onto sexual desire between men and the endorsement of "coming out" as a courageous act of honesty to oneself and to society at large, which the play enacts, owes more to contemporary Western notions than to Arab society, whether of the nineteenth or the twentieth century. Indeed, the internal logic of al-ʿAfsah's insistence on coming out is that of a late twentieth-century America. Oscar Wilde, whose trial would take place a decade after the purported story of the play took place, had never sought to "out" himself and indeed sued Lord Alfred Douglas's father, the Marquess of Queensberry, for suggesting that he "posed" as a "Somdomite" (sic). Wilde was subsequently "outed" by the universalizing impulse of the Western gay movement seeking to assimilate all same-sex desire historically and geographically into an image of itself. Wilde's love and desire for his wife and other women fall by the wayside in such accounts in the interest of a uniform desire, expressing his "inner truth" that the transhistorical Gay (and Straight) International now insist on. Al-ʿAfsah's assertion that his coming out is "in our country . . . like death or worse than death" is more in tune with the claims of the Gay International and not the reality of the nineteenth- or twentieth-century Arab world. In fact, this is belied by the world of the play itself, where Simsim roams the streets turning tricks unmolested.

I should mention here that although al-Barudi's narration of the original story does not include same-sex desire, al-Barudi's memoirs do mention the openness with which effeminate men were accepted. While traveling to France in early 1911, the twenty-three-year-old al-Barudi took the train to Haifa where he spent an evening at a an all-male theater-café and attended a show: "A female dancer with a slender build came out and performed brilliantly to the point of getting everyone's attention. Once the curtain dropped, she came out to mingle and collect tips. People started to flirt with her, but she turned out to be a young man with a low voice who imitated women's dancing and wore a wig. I understood that [unlike in Damascus and other cities in Palestine] female dancers are not allowed to appear on stage [in Haifa] on the orders of the [Ottoman] governor and that [instead] it is permitted for men to imitate women. This [imitation by men of women] was well known and popular in the Ottoman provinces; and the Turks call a man who plays the role of girls 'Zinah.'"[83] Such state and societal sanctioning is hardly tantamount to death or anything like it except in fantastical projections that have no basis in reality. Indeed, we also know of men who imitated women in their songs as being quite popular in Cairo through the 1920s and 1930s. Singer 'Abd al-Latif al-Banna (1884–1969) did much of that in the 1920s. He had begun his career reciting the Qur'an in 1908 and on the eve of World War I gave up his caftan and turban and began to sing feminine songs that were recorded by the famed record company Baidaphon. The only male singer at the time without a moustache, he sang seductive songs like "Ih ra'yak fi khafafti" (Do you not find me cute), recorded in 1930, in which he would compare himself to women, insisting that he was better looking and that he should win more favor with men than his female competitors. He gave up his career in the 1930s and moved back to his village in 1939 and got married.[84] Even in more recent times, as late as the 1970s and early 1980s, Syrian television and film actor Anwar al-Baba played only his signature role, that of the older woman Umm Kamil, on television and cinema, to the delight of viewers who celebrated him without a hint of excoriation.

Al-'Afsah manages a last act before he lets 'Abbas off the hook. He insists that 'Abbas grant him a last wish, namely, to arm-wrestle him.

'ABBAS: Do you want to test the strength of my arm!

AL-'AFSAH: I know the strength of your arm. I just want to know if there's any strength left in mine.

'ABBAS: Save yourself the humiliation.

AL-'AFSAH: This humiliation is my last wish. Don't let me down.

'ABBAS: I will pulverize you.

'AL-'AFSAH: You've already pulverized what is more important than my arm. I won't feel more pain if you pulverize my arm also. Come on!

(They sit around the table. Their fists grip one another, and each of them begins to press to bend the arm of the other. They last a long time and 'Abbas remains unsuccessful in bending al-'Afsah's arm. He turns red with anger.)

AL-'AFSAH: Shall we continue?

'ABBAS: (Frustrated) No . . . This is enough.

AL-'AFSAH: (Before he lets go of 'Abbas's fist, bows gently and kisses it). Now, I bid you farewell, 'Abbas . . .

83. Fakhri Al-Barudi, *Mudhakkarat al-Barudi, Sittun Sannah Tatakallam* [The Memoir of al-Barudi, Sixty Years Speak] (Damascus: n.p., 1952), vol. 2, 28.

84. See the text by Frédéric Lagrange in "Les Archives de la Musiqe Arabe, Cafés Chantants du Caire," vol. 1, Compact Disc released by Club du Disque Arabe, Montreuil, 1994, 4–5.

(*Exit al-ʿAfsah.*)

ʿABBAS: What happened to me? Where did he get this strength from? This effeminate almost bent my arm. God damn him, he ruined my mood.[85]

The last masculine stand that al-ʿAfsah took was clearly designed to show that what was manifest was not what was latent at all, that he was indeed a manly man in his "innermost truth" and only behaved outwardly as an effeminate catamite. Here al-ʿAfsah sees clearly that the truth of his body is that of a manly man and is separate from his desire to be penetrated, that the two are not one and the same nor necessary conditions for one another. Alas, this is a lesson that he refused to learn and insisted that others unlearn. ʿAbbas, falling in the trap of the theatricality of al-ʿAfsah's declaration that his essence and his appearance had been unified, failed to see that it was al-ʿAfsah's femininity that was a conscious masquerade, and not his masculinity, which was clearly internalized. It is this trap that explains why ʿAbbas wonders about where al-ʿAfsah obtained his strength, the very same strength that ʿAbbas had always recognized as the basis of his own desire to penetrate al-ʿAfsah.

What the play and Wannus insist on is that everyone recognize desire as embedded in the body, as the truth of the body, and that it can only be freed in an individualist project of liberation through public confessionals. Those, who like ʿAbbas, resisted this conflation and understood that Almasah, Simsim, and al-ʿAfsah had different bodies but that they all had a desire to be penetrated, were finally taken in. But unable to be recognized for what he claimed to be, al-ʿAfsah (unlike Hegel's consciousness, which killed the other as a measure of its material effect on the world around it, thus denying itself the possibility of being recognized by that other), realizing that recognition was not forthcoming at all and that the other refuses to enter his economy of signs, opts to kill the self instead:

AL-ʿAFSAH: There are no more hopes or pleas . . . I have lost my status in people's eyes. And he, for whom I exposed my secret, cast me aside and called me shameful. What do I have left before me? It is an obligatory step, and I must take it. What a strange world this is. If you suppress and conceal, you can live and be honored. If you are honest and you expose, they ostracize and banish you. I did not know how to express to him that I was braver than him. He loved me when I was a bunch of lies and artifice, and then he had contempt for me and cast me aside when I came to him as pure as crystal without lies or artifice. He is the lies and he is cowardice. He did not understand the courage that I had nor the torments I suffered to make peace with myself

85. Ibid., 89–90.

and to become transparent. I cannot regret what I did, nor can I retreat from it or advance beyond it. Doors have been shut. This is an unjust world in which only the liar and the forger can live . . . God, I am ashamed of calling out to you and do not know how I will meet you. God, you are the just and the merciful, fix my heart, grant my mother patience, and forgive me.[86]

With these words, al-ʿAfsah hangs himself, literally and metaphorically. His individualist project was in contradiction with the social basis of desire and the organization of social mores. His rejection of the basis of ʿAbbas's desire for him (namely, that he was a manly man who possessed the body of a manly man but also desired to be penetrated) insisting that ʿAbbas desire to penetrate him as an effeminate man, and that this desire must be consummated as a public event, a public declaration of passion, and no longer in the private, was in contradiction with his quest for sociality. He sought to integrate into society at the moment that he insisted on exiting from it. The contradiction was not that of society, which was willing to accommodate another Simsim in its midst, but rather in his insistence that by being Simsim, he is also *not* Simsim, that he can arm wrestle manly men and win. Simism, like ʿAbbas, Wardah, and Almasah, clearly understood that desire is desire and not romantic love. Al-ʿAfsah's refusal to accept this has no explanation within the world of the play, and seems to have an external source, one that is also external to the time and place in which he lived. His refusal was Wannus's refusal. Wannus, who is clearly thoroughly imbued by the contemporary Western ethos characterized by what Michel Foucault identified as the "repressive hypothesis," seemed to espouse the contradictory notions that on the one hand the Freudian notion that civilization, or to use a different word, the social, is constituted through repression and, on the other hand, the liberal notion that society is the forum through which individual freedom, however defined, can be achieved. Having read French Marxism, the structuralists, and the poststructuralists, Wannus surprisingly continued to confuse these categories, as would American-style liberals, in that he would view society as both the repressive mechanism of individuality while maintaining that individual expression can only be achieved within society. Such a contradiction remains unexplored in the play and proves to be its major conceptual failing.[87]

86. Ibid., 109.
87. See Sabhah Ahmad ʿAlqam, *Al-Masrah al-Siyasi ʿind Saʿdallah Wannus* [The Political Theater of Saʿdallah Wannus] (Amman: Wizarat al-Thaqafah, 2001).

We know of al-ʿAfsah's funeral because of the merchant Hamid, who, in the tradition of Arab chroniclers of the premodern era, is writing a chronicle of Damascus:

And in these days, Damascus was hit by a number of quakes, which we are not used to and the likes of which we had never seen before . . . A few days ago, al-ʿAfsah hanged himself in his home after God had revealed his secret, and it turned out that he was a catamite, who got sodomized [yulatu bihi], and he possessed only the image of manhood. What is quite amazing is that the above mentioned was counted among the virile men [of the city], and was counted as a man among men. His funeral was a public defamation the likes of which never happened before. The mean-spirited and the insolent gathered behind the dead man's procession and began to sing impudent and salacious songs and did not respect the sanctity of death. Even a poor man would say that the sanctity of death is necessary, even if the dead man does not deserve mercy. At the end of this public defamation, they threw him in a hole, and no one prayed for his soul. No one shed a tear for him [either], except his old mother who had remained at home wailing.[88]

It is important to point out here that Simsim and Wardah are not presented as part of the calamities that hit Damascus. They were rather seen as part of the natural order of things and not an affront to it. The importance of al-ʿAfsah's story for the chronicler is precisely the discrepancy between the latent and the manifest, which defined al-ʿAfsah's own internal struggle. The fact that al-ʿAfsah lived in a society that for the most part respected the private (a violation of which, in fact, set the entire plot of the play in motion and almost brought about society's dissolution) and did not condemn what it did not know, was unsatisfactory. Simsim therefore can remain part of the order of the comic. But in the world of "sexual freedom," where the sexual "self" is conceived as the "true" and "authentic" self, sexuality becomes tragic.

In describing al-ʿAfsah's funeral, Wannus is echoing the funeral of the famed medieval poet Bashshar bin Burd who lived at the end of the Umayyad dynasty and the beginning of the Abbasid (c. 714–784). Bashshar, of Persian origins, was blind and reportedly physically hideous. He was an atheist and wrote much erotic poetry for women. He is said to have boasted of his sexual prowess and of being irresistible to women, both in his poetry and in reported stories about him, and that he was a hateful, despicable misanthrope who was hated by many for his nasti-

88. Wannus, *Tuqus al-Isharat*, 130.

ness and unattractiveness. Taha Husayn did not seem to like him much, and few modern critics appreciated him.[89] Muhammad al-Nuwayhi, the sympathetic critic of Abu Nuwas, was one of the first to write a study of Bashshar's personality in an attempt to dispel many of these strongly held negative opinions about the medieval poet.[90] Indeed, in his 1951 book about the poet, al-Nuwayhi defends him against the accusation that he had been so mean that he insulted his own friend, the poet Hammad ʿAjrad, in poetry. Al-Nuwayhi reveals that Hammad had done the same to Bashshar, and that "our" sympathies should be more with Bashshar, who, despite all his other negative qualities, including those of bawdiness and recklessness, unlike Hammad, did not engage during his life in one important "vice," which Hammad engaged in, namely, "sodomy."[91]

The importance of Bashshar here relates to his death and funeral. At the age of seventy, the poet was flogged to death on the orders of the Abbasid caliph al-Mahdi. The accepted conventional reason for his execution is said to be his atheism and/or his debauchery, although this is not proven, as sources are contradictory on this matter.[92] It is said that the people of his city of Basra congratulated each other upon hearing of his death, and that they thanked the Lord and gave alms. "When his funeral set forth, no one followed it except his black Sindi foreign maid who did not speak Arabic. I saw her marching in his funeral yelling, "Oh, master! Oh, master!'"[93] Al-Nuwayhi, who declared Bashshar "the first martyr in the history of Islamic thought,"[94] marvels about his funeral procession: "Where were his friends when he died, that no one among them marched in his funeral procession? Did cowardice stop them that they did not dare challenge people's feelings? Or did they all die before he did?"[95] Perhaps, Wannus wants his readers to ask the same question about al-ʿAfsah's friends. For him, it seems, al-ʿAfsah was not the first Arab fictional martyr of a universalizing Western imperial im-

89. See Taha Husayn, *Hadith al-Arbiʿaʾ* (Cairo: Dar al-Maʿarif bi-Misr, 1964), vol. 2, 188–211.

90. See Muhammad al-Nuwayhi, *Shakhsiyyat Bashshar* [Bashshar's Personality] (Beirut: Dar al-Fikr, 1971). This is the second and revised edition of the book, which was originally published in 1951.

91. Ibid., 121.

92. Ibid., 137–46. For an account of his death, see Al-Asfahani, Abu Faraj ʿAli bin al-Husayn, *Kitab al-Aghani* [The Book of Songs], ed. Ihsan Abbas, Ibrahim al-Saʿafin, and Bakr ʿAbbas (Beirut: Dar Sadir, 2002), vol. 3, 166–75. This multivolume classic was written in the tenth century. It is interesting to note that Dik al-Jinn's grandmother, in Raʾif Khuri's novel, had told Dik al-Jinn that Bashshar bin Burd had been flogged to death for political reasons and that only his "black maid" walked in his funeral," in Khuri, *Dik al-Jinn*, 41.

93. Al-Asfahani, *Kitab al-Aghani*, vol. 3, 174.

94. Al-Nuwayhi, *Shakhsiyyat Bashshar*, 146.

95. Ibid., 119.

position of sexual identities and their commensurate social telos of love and coupling, but rather of the intolerance of his own fake and hypocritical society. True, Bashshar, unlike al-ʿAfsah, was not a penetratee, although people sometimes insulted him as one. If ʿAbbas penetrated al-ʿAfsah, Bashshar was imagined as being penetrated by an ape. When a painter he engaged to make a drawing for him on a silver bowl shows up with the finished product, Bashshar was unhappy with the drawing as described by the painter and thought him trying to take advantage of his blindness. When he threatened to write a poem defaming him, the painter threatened back: "If you do so, you will regret it . . . I will paint you on my front door as your ugly self and place behind you an ape fucking you, so that all passersby would see you." Fearful, Bashshar relented.[96] While Bashshar feared public exposure of an act he did not engage in, al-ʿAfsah sought it out as a route to liberation. That this route led to his ultimate demise is a warning that remains unheeded by the purveyors of Western gayness and its liberation strategies, just as the real repression of alleged homosexuals in the Queen Boat case in Cairo was no deterrent.

Al-ʿAfsah's fate however should be contrasted with that of Almasah. Almasah, who by now had become the most attractive and sought after prostitute in Damascus, excited the desire of many, including the Mufti himself, who, after she rejects his marriage proposal, cannot get her out of his mind. He did try to sway her away from the life of vice but to no avail:

There is something in your tone and in your insistence that makes my hair stand on end. You stretch your hand to vice with such rashness as no woman had done before in this city. I know that there are violent desires residing within you, but can I leave you to continue on this path? A woman with your strength and power of speech can corrupt a kingdom of women. You are overturning what is familiar in our lives, in our established order, and in our future. No, no I cannot permit you.[97]

He was not alone in his concerns. The city's top merchants were also concerned. Ibrahim, one of the merchants, feared that "our life is coming upon disorder and madness . . . I think this is part of the effects of foreigners [Ottomans?]. We are entering into a disorder whose end no one knows."[98] Hamid, the merchant chronicler, agreed and added that "this calamity has a strange smell." As he finishes his sentence, "Simsim

96. Cited in ibid., 27.
97. Ibid., 102.

98. Ibid., 104–5.

369

appears in the street walking coquettishly."[99] Asked by a pedestrian in a tone of ridicule about how work was going, Simsim lashes back:

Go and apply henna to your ass [a common expression indicating schadenfreude]. As a result of the abundance of shops, we had to close ours down. (He stops near Hamid and Ibrahim) Oh, people of Islam, is what is happening acceptable? I used to have a small trading business the size of this (and he smacks himself on the buttocks) preponderant one. But people begrudged me even that! Virile men have been opened up from the back, and aristocrats have been opened from the front. Tell me, people, does commerce not get spoiled when there is too much merchandise?

Ibrahim asks him, "Has competition become so heavy in the prostitution market?" "It is like a fever," answers Simsim. "And if I am not saved by a virtuous man like yourself, whose Godly reward awaits him, spiders will make a home in my shop and in my soul." Furious Hamid curses him, and Simsim insults him back. Hamid turns to Ibrahim: "How did we remain quiet about the likes of him? Did they not spill the blood of people like him?" Ibrahim answers, "That was before the likes of him filled the palaces of the Sultans and those in authority."[100] It is important here to note that it is the coming out of al-ʿAfsah (a privileged and respected man) that has precipitated the call to kill Simsim who until then, as I pointed out earlier, was at worst an object of ridicule and not a target for religious- or state-sanctioned extermination. While al-ʿAfsah opted for exit through suicide, his act would now embolden and mobilize the state against those weaker than he, whom the state and the religious authorities had left unmolested before. This is not so unlike what has recently transpired in Egypt with the Queen Boat case, as discussed in chapter 3. It is upper- and middle-class Westernized men who seek publicity for their newly acquired sexual identities, who are able to exit Egypt, while those poorer members of society who do not possess the choice of exit remain to bear the brunt of the state's repression and that of the religious authorities, which was precipitated to begin with by those who possess social and class power.

When visited by the city's merchants (including Hamid, the chronicler) asking that he intervene to stop what had befallen the city, the Mufti decides to issue a religious decree (fatwa) calling for the execution of all *prostitutes* [baghaya], whether men or women, specifically nam-

---

99. Ibid., 105.
100. Ibid., 105–6.

ing Almasah as the biggest culprit who had disseminated a culture of "vice that corrupted the hearts of men."[101] Here again, Wardah, who had been left to work fairly unmolested (her arrest with ʿAbdullah was more about ʿAbdullah's enmity with the Mufti rather than the latter's horror at prostitution per se) was now to face repression once Almasah made the choice of becoming a prostitute. Wardah had explained to Muʾminah early on that she had had no choice: "This profession is never chosen by any of us except under duress, out of necessity, and as a result of becoming downtrodden. That a woman who possesses everything and has no other motive except predilection and desires, chooses it, she insults us all, and defrauds us of all the suffering we bore."[102] Wardah and Simsim were not the only ones affected by the decree. The Mufti decides to add other items to be banned, including alcohol and lewd books, like *A Thousand and One Nights*. The merchants object that he may be going too far and worry that commerce will be affected by such "excess." They beg him to limit the decree to prostitution. He refuses.

The Mufti's decree was stopped by the Ottoman Wali, upset at the ban of alcohol and at the endangerment of Almasah, whose services he clearly appreciated. The Wali insisted that the decree be approved in the imperial capital of Constantinople before being promulgated into law, a clear stratagem to nullify it without a public showdown with the Mufti. The Mufti himself would violate his own decree out of his obsession with Almasah, whom he finally visits. Almasah, insistent that she will not marry him, offers him her sexual services, which he finally, in utter abjection, accepts. Thus the transformation of the main protagonists had come full circle. If the play opened with the sexual excesses of ʿAbdullah that the Mufti wanted stopped, his scheme to rid himself of ʿAbdullah transforms him into another ʿAbdullah at the very moment that it transforms ʿAbdullah into an ascetic man. The Mufti clearly was defeated by the very desires that he sought to suppress in ʿAbdullah and in Almasah. Having succumbed to his fate (the second part of the play is significantly titled "Fates"), Almasah awaited hers.

Enter Almasah's brothers. Her father, a religious cleric, who had disowned her after her transformation, for fear that she would reveal his sexual excesses publicly if he hurt her ("I fear that she would create for us a larger scandal in death than in life"[103]), was confronted by his younger son Safwan. Unlike his elder brother, ʿAbd al-Rahman, who is seen as a manly man and who saw the matter as his father did, Safwan is described

---

101. Wannus, *Tuqus al-Isharat*, 117.   103. Ibid., 113.
102. Ibid., 80.

as a sweet and tender man who "faint[s] when he sees a chicken slaugh-
tered or blood dripping from a wound."[104] His father, in fact, chastised
him for being spoiled by his mother and by being ill-mannered for challenging his (the father's) decision. Safwan, feeling defamed by his sister
and by his father's disrespect for him for not being a manly man, decides
to *transform* himself and thus takes matters into his own hands. He goes
to his sister's house and embarks on stabbing her with his dagger. Fear-
less, Almasah eggs him on. Before he kills her, however, she tells him of
her historic import in a final speech, which sounds more like a sermon:

I, Safwan, am a tale, and a tale cannot be killed. I am an obsession, a yearning, a
seduction, and daggers cannot kill an obsession, a yearning, or a seduction . . . (*as
she collapses*) O my brother . . . you have done nothing. My tale will blossom like
the gardens of Ghuta [the name of the fertile oasis on the south side of Damascus]
after a rainy winter. Almasah is getting larger and is spreading. She is spreading with
thoughts, obsessions, and tales; tales, ta . . .[105]

As Almasah undergoes a second transformation by metamorphosing
into a tale told by Wannus, Safwan is transformed by his honor killing
into a man. As he "regains his wits" he says, "I killed her . . . with my
own dagger I killed her . . . I am a man . . . I am a man . . . look, Father . . .
I am the [real] man among you . . . I am the man among you."[106]

Safwan might have become a man, but the transformation of society
had become complete. Whether the representative of state order, the
police chief, the representative of nobility, ʿAbdullah, or the representatives of religiosity and religious scholarship, Muʾminah's father and
the Mufti, the ruling class was compromised. Only the foreign Ottoman
Wali remained in control. It was now up to those who were not transformed to take control. ʿAbdu, the Mufti's secretary, and ʿAbbas were
obvious candidates. ʿAbbas and ʿAbdu, as virile men protecting the ruling class, decide to save them from themselves. ʿAbdu suggests that the
ruling class become instruments for their power.

Listen to me, ʿAbbas. The situation of the notables of this city has been corrupted,
and their status has been degraded. They will not be notables [again] except upon
our shoulders. Our fists and our strong arms are what upholds their status and ensures
obedience to it. We are the virile men, the men with the canes, the pillars on which
the structure stands. And now, look, after the notables came apart and they began to

104. Ibid., 114.
105. Ibid., 150.

106. Ibid.

stink, no one but we shall preserve order and protect values . . . What I am aiming at is clear. If we don't stop this deterioration, the country is going to slip into dissolution [or degeneration] and chaos. No status will be respected, and manhood will not be appreciated. The entire structure will collapse on us all . . . We must form a fraternity of men in order to preserve security and order and to apply the decrees issued by the Mufti before his fall and degradation . . . We shall expose the notables and make them only a front without power. We are the men, Aba Fahd, and the country now needs men and manliness. We must stop corruption and restore awe to order. I am certain that the Wali will not mind and that the state itself will bless our initiative.[107]

As the enforcers of manhood and order plot to take their rightful position as the upholders of the class system (here they are standing in for the modern military and its history of coups d'état in Syria), transforming themselves from instruments of aristocratic rule into rulers who use the aristocracy as their instrument, the merchants and the servants remained what they were at the beginning of the play. The only notable exception concerns the issue of love and marriage among them. ʿAbdullah's male servant and Wardah's (now Almasah's) female servant, who, unlike the merchants, are never named in the play, had found true romantic love whose telos was indeed marriage. When the female servant asks her beloved to speak to her words of love, as the Mufti spoke to Almasah, he tells her that "we live love, what need have we for words?" He then decides to parody love talk: "Listen to me then. My flesh loves your flesh, and my blood loves your blood, you are my half and I am your half. These are all the words I have." She answers, "I am not asking for more. I am your half and you are mine." Her husband quips back, "Is this not love?" "It is," she affirms, "as long as it satisfies us and makes us happy."[108] While for the unnamed and perhaps unnamable poor, love and desire, as the manifest and the latent, are unified in a perfect reflection of society's claims, for the rest of society, the latent and the manifest will remain divided in the interest of safeguarding the hypocrisy of the ruling classes and those who serve them. As the poor seem to have no individuality and no names, their existence in society is not problematic. For those who seek the liberationist project of individuality, society will prove to be the wrong place for them.

Wannus's Western liberal project (although he had been politically a Marxist throughout much of his career) intends to scandalize Arab society for its repression and hypocrisy. That he uses Orientalist and Western facile notions about individualism and sociality as the prism through

---

107. Ibid., 145–46.
108. Ibid., 143–44.

which he conducts his project did not seem to unsettle many of the critics. In his preface to the play, Wannus warns readers not to read the characters as stand-ins or as "simplifying symbols of institutions that they represent," but as "individuals who possess their own selves and their individual and personal suffering."[109] Having himself been transformed, like many Arab intellectuals, following the Gulf War of 1990–91, from nationalist Marxism to Western-style neoliberalism and self-Orientalization, he spoke of his adoption of the individualist project in an interview:

I used to have illusions on all levels, illusions on the human level. *For the first time I feel that writing is freedom,* as in the past I used to impose on myself a kind of self-censorship. An internal censorship whose foundation, as I used to delude myself, *was marginalizing what is secondary for the benefit of what I thought of as important causes.* For the first time I feel that *writing is pleasure.* I used to feel that personal suffering or individual particularities are nonessential superficial "bourgeois" matters that can be set aside. My interest was focused on consciousness of history. This is why I considered, mistakenly, that interest in the movement of history must transcend individual particularities and the traps of bourgeois writing.[110]

Indeed, in revising his erstwhile Stalinized Marxist analysis, which ignored the individual at the behest of society in favor of the new liberal one that emphasizes the individual whose enemy is declared to be society, Wannus remarked that "I should have also discovered that the national project, in all that it means of liberation, progress, and modernity, does not require that we cancel ourselves as individuals with our own desires [ahwaʾuna], tendencies, compulsions, and insistent needs for freedom and to declare the 'I' without embarrassment (God forbid we should say 'I'), but rather the contrary, that this national project cannot succeed and be achieved unless this 'I' blossoms and practices its freedom, unless this 'I' speaks itself without embarrassment, incontestably and without apology."[111] For Wannus, the critique of the state that he used to believe was primary was no longer sufficient. After his transformation, the critique of "society" becomes paramount, trying to move it out of its immersion in "myth."[112]

The play, produced in two successful productions (one Lebanese, the other Egyptian) that toured Arab countries, was welcomed by most

109. Ibid., 6.
110. Interview with Saʿdallah Wannus conducted by Dr. Mari Ilyas, *Al-Tariq,* January–February 1996, no. 1, 99. Emphases in the original.
111. Ibid., 104.
112. Ibid., 99.

critics, many of whom emphasized its feminist impulse (while ignoring the parallel gay liberationist motif).[113] The post-1990s Arab liberal internalization of facile Western notions of liberation, as we saw in the last chapter, has become endemic to the secular intelligentsia. Perhaps, Wannus consciously or unconsciously sought to implicate the popular and nationalist Fakhri al-Barudi himself in his project by implicitly trying to out him. Al-Barudi was a descendant of an aristocratic Damascene family. His great-grandfather arrived in Damascus from Acre in the late eighteenth century while his mother's ancestry is from Jerusalem. A fervent Arab nationalist who was at odds with French and British colonialism (he fled the former for some years to neighboring Transjordan), al-Barudi was not the favorite of colonial officials. Rumors in colonial and some native circles had it that al-Barudi, who was married, had a predilection for youthful boys, something Wannus must have heard about.[114] Whether the rumors were part of colonial propaganda or true is not at issue here. What is noteworthy is that Wannus might have been seeking to out an icon of Arab nationalism, both for the scandalous effects this would have and to assimilate him into a 1990s agenda, just like the Gay International had assimilated Oscar Wilde into its own project. Wannus never does so explicitly, but the association is hardly innocent of conscious or unconscious processes.

While Wannus's efforts to criticize contemporary Arab societies is admirable and courageous, his espousal of ready-made and uninterrogated Western formulae is not. In this sense, Wannus, not unlike, Syrian author Ibrahim Mahmud, whom we encountered in chapter 4, espouses a sexual rights agenda that has led to much repression and oppression in the contemporary Arab world and not to the liberation that they, and the Gay International with them, seek. The fact that they and their Islamist detractors share an epistemology of rights, liberation, and progress is something to which they remain oblivious. This is what characterizes the political and epistemological impasse facing contemporary Arab intellectuals, secular or religious.

113. On the Lebanese and Egyptian productions, see Ahmad Sakhsukh, *Ughniyyat al-Rahil al-Wannusiyyah, Dirasah fi Masrah Sa'dallah Wannus* [The Wannusite Songs of Departing, A Study of the Theater of Sa'dallah Wannus] (Cairo: Al-Dar al-Misriyyah al-Lubnaniyyah, 1998). On critical assessments of his work, including *Tuqus,* see the special issue of the Beirut-based journal *Al-Tariq,* January-February 1996, no. 1, 94–207. The main exception among the critics is Mahmud Nasim, "Su'ud al-Fardiyyah," in *Al-Tariq,* 166–77, who discusses seriously both Mu'minah *and* al-'Afsah.

114. See Philip S. Khoury, *Syria and the French Mandate: The Politics of Arab Nationalism, 1920–1945* (Princeton: Princeton University Press, 1987), 275. Khoury cites Sir Richard Beaumont as his source. Beaumont was a political officer at the British consulate in Damascus in the early 1940s and "was well acquainted with Barudi" (275n). The rumors about al-Barudi are hardly out of tune with what was standard sexual practices in the British public school system of which Beaumont and others were a product.

Al-'Afsah's and Mu'minah's quest, like that of Wannus and the Gay International, is to obliterate the space of the private by making all desires and sexual practices public. Wannus's condemnation of Arab society, like that of the Gay International, is due to society's insistence on preserving the private realm and punishing practices and desires only when they insist on entering discourse by invading public space and when they demand public rights as identities. While previously, male and female prostitutes existed mostly unmolested by the state and the clerics, and men and women practiced all kinds of sex deemed illicit by the clerics and the state, the insistence by those who assume Western sexual identities on obliterating the division between the private and the public as a route to "liberation," who insist that the Wardahs and Simsims of the world are not truly liberated unless they out themselves to the state and its religious authorities as Almasah and al-'Afsah had done, has precipitated a repressive onslaught not only targeting them (and they are but a tiny minority) but targeting those who until recently were left alone by state and religious authority and suffered only different forms of social shame. The point here is not that the Wardahs and Simsims of the world lived in some prediscursive bliss but rather that their entry into discourse, their insertion into a discourse of liberation, identities, and rights have made their lives much worse, if not altogether impossible, as the play amply demonstrates. Indeed this new situation may very well bring about their social and physical death from which the Gay International claims it is trying to save them in the first place.

In this sense, and contra Wannus's stated intentions, *The Rites of Signs and Transformations* should be read as a cautionary tale, a veritable warning, to those who think liberation lies in following the agenda of the Gay International. The individualist project of the play failed and caused the death of their two purveyors, not only because society is retrograde and must be changed, but also because "individualism" as conceived by Wannus and others fails to deliver on its stated aims. In this sense, the play registers most of all the transformation of Wannus himself into a Western liberal, offering itself both as a rite and as a sign of such transformation.

Dishonoring Men: Sun'allah Ibrahim's *Sharaf*

If Hanan al-Shaykh's *Misk al-Ghazal* and Sa'dallah Wannus's play pushed a civilizational model of desires and individualism, respectively, partaking of dominant Western modes of representation and being, Sun'allah Ibrahim continued the theme of castration he had deployed in *That*

Odor and his other novels. His latest novel (published in 1997) to deal explicitly with matters of deviant sex and its civilizational implications is *Sharaf* (Honor).[115] The attempted rape of a young man called Sharaf by an Australian (who turns out to be English[116]) blond man named John, sets the novel in motion. The attempted rape, which was thwarted by Sharaf's accidental murder of the Englishman while resisting his advances and defending his "honor," functions as the symbolic "rape" of Egypt, which is the central theme of the novel. Egypt and its men (and women) are not only being raped by Englishmen, who stand in for international capital, but also by international capital's local Egyptian agents. In a globalized world, being buggered, or as the euphemism used in the novel avers, "yatasakhmat" (more on this later), becomes the only fate awaiting all oppressed men, including the majority of Egyptian men.

The novel is the journey of one oppressed Egyptian man, nicknamed Honor[117] (his real name, Ashraf, means "the more honorable one") from his belief that his "honor" is worth defending to his later understanding that his "honor" is always already lost.[118] This is a bildungsroman of the education and coming to consciousness of Sharaf, who had initially believed that he had a socially sanctioned duty to defend his "honor" from being sullied by an Englishman, or any other man for that matter, to his final grasp of the tragic truth, on the final page of the novel, that his fate, as is the fate of all men like him, is that they are always already buggered, and that he must acquiesce in this fate and stop fighting it, for being sexually buggered (physically) may be less detrimental than being buggered economically, politically, socially, and psychologically. This cathartic realization is described by Sharaf while serving his sentence in an Egyptian jail, after a potential buggerer, Salim, offers him a razor to shave his beard. It is significant that while the razor is made by Gillette, the blades had no name brand printed on them, except for "Made in Israel."[119] Having finished shaving, Sharaf duly returns the razor:

"Why don't you keep it? You might as well remove all the excess hair on your body" [Salim tells him] . . . I carried my undershirt, my towel, and the Palmolive shaving

---

115. Sun'allah Ibrahim, *Sharaf* (Cairo: Dar al-Hilal, 1997).

116. Ibid., 25.

117. I should note here that unlike the English proper name "Honor" or the French "Honoré," "sharaf" is a very uncommon first name in Arabic, although derivations of it are, such as "Sharif" and "Sharifah" (masculine and feminine names meaning the honorable one), and "Ashraf."

118. For the circumstances and the controversy surrounding the publication of the novel, see Samia Mehrez, "Dr. Ramzy and Mr. Sharaf: Sonallah Ibrahim and the Duplicity of the Literary Field," in *Literature and Social Transformations*, ed. Wael Hallaq (Leiden: Brill, 2000), 262–83.

119. Ibrahim, *Sharaf*, 535–36.

cream. He went ahead of me to the bathroom and filled a big bucket with hot water, which I then carried with me to the last stall. I drew the curtain, took my clothes off and hung them on the wooden edge. I put the soap on my leg and rubbed it well with a brush until a sizeable lather formed. I lifted my leg up and grabbed the razor, placing it at the top of my thigh, and then I began to remove the hair.[120]

In the world of the novel, this assured yet dreaded fate awaiting all oppressed men is epigrammatically summarized in an anecdote told by a fellow prisoner as part of the script for an audience-interactive puppet show he directs in prison. The context of the epigrammatic story in Dr. Ramzi's tendentiously didactic script is the difference between U.S. and European exploitation of Egypt and the Arab world in the context of the unfolding Arab/Israeli "peace process":

Audience Member 1: A story has just occurred to me that fits our topic. Its protagonists are two compatriots of ours. One is a Bahrawi [from the coastal area], while the other, as expected, is an Upper Egyptian [a peasant from southern Egypt whose inhabitants are viewed in Egyptian lore as "conservative" and committed to virile manliness].The two men's search for livelihood took them to the African jungle where they were captured by a savage tribe. The tribal chief was a very nice man who offered them two possible fates: The first is "Honga," and the second is "death." From the gestures of his hands, they both understood what was meant by "Honga." At once, the Upper Egyptian, who values his honor more than his life, declared that he chooses death. The Bahrawi had another point of view. After a bit of assessment, he said: "Honga." The tribal chief stared at them for a long time and then gave the orders to his followers: "Both should get Honga, even the one who chose death!"[121]

As the Honga versus death joke is an old racist one, known in a number of colonial contexts to show how sexually depraved and mendacious Africans are, it very well may mark the repression of cross-racial male homosexual fantasies. It also partakes of the already mentioned colonial trope of hypervirilizing African natives while presenting Egyptian colonized men as castrated. It is noteworthy that the verb "Honga" in Swahili, a language spoken in a number of African countries south of Egypt, means to pay tribute or toll, to corrupt, or to bribe. Although he never investigates the meaning of "Honga," which is thrown around as a generic "African" term, it is the function of "Honga" as tribute or toll

120. Ibid., 543.
121. Ibid., 439–40.

and as corruption that Sunʿallah Ibrahim seems to want to emphasize in the novel.

The moral of the story was picked up by the prison audience at the end of the show, as they all began to holler: "Honga, even for the one who chose death!"[122] Clearly this anecdote seeks to show how barbaric international capitalism and imperialism are turning civilized Egypt, indeed reducing it, to a primitive "African jungle," a "savage" place where people await their savage fate of paying tribute to the new imperium by being "Honga'd," whether they choose life or death. In fact, the two unemployed Egyptian men travel outside civilization to the African jungle seeking work. But the humiliating search led to even more humiliation. Being Honga'd has unified the realms of life and death and the realms of the savage and the civilized worlds under a new globalized order. That Ibrahim chooses the colloquial Egyptian term "yatasakhmat" (and "asakhmatu"), which is one of a number of vernacular words used as a metaphor for buggery, to indicate being buggered or to bugger another man, is hardly incidental. "Yatasakhmat" is derived from the word "sukhmah," meaning blackness, and "sukham," meaning coal or soot. The classical verb "sakhkhama" means to blacken. The Egyptian colloquial verb "sakhmata" is the colloquial rendering of "sakhkhama," which means blacken as well as other related vernacular meanings indicative of "messing someone up" or getting "messed up" and the like. Thus being "Honga'd" and "yatasakhmat" ensure that men are rendered black and penetratees in one stroke.

This sexual dichotomy of civilization and barbarism is part of an imperialist episteme, which it seems, in relation to Africa, the novel accepts and reproduces uncritically. The measure of the humiliation and oppression of the world is clearly signified by the inability of any oppressed man (the majority of the men of the world) to escape paying tribute by being "Honga'd," even if he chooses death, as the latter has ceased to be an alternative to being Honga'd. Uncivilized Africans aside, the fact that it is an American razor equipped with Israeli blades that shaves the remaining masculinity of Egyptian men is most significant throughout the novel.

Sunʿallah Ibrahim vacillates in the novel between an ironic presentation of the world of the novel, where being buggered is considered by all the male characters as the worst fate awaiting men under globalization, and the real world of economic exploitation, which leads to a fate much worse than buggery, namely, severe poverty, loss of national resources

122. Ibid., 457.

and national independence, and loss of local cultures to the new culture of consumerism (he is at pains to show how important name brands and Western consumer products have become to local Egyptian consumers). However, the very traps that Ibrahim sees his characters fall into are traps which he cannot avoid himself. The metaphor of rape and male honor, which structures the entire novel, beginning with its title and ending with the final scene of feminization of men, is not interrogated at all, but rather confirmed throughout. Ibrahim's objection is to the literalization of buggery in the mind of his characters and their inability to see its metaphorical forms, which have more detrimental material consequences for their lives. Where Ibrahim seemingly agrees with his characters is that the crisis precipitated by globalization is a crisis of Arab masculinity.

While the novel allows for homoerotic love of the Platonic variety or of a sexual variety that restrains itself from consummation (such an example includes Sharaf's relationship to another prisoner from Upper Egypt, 'Abd al-Fattah, which has a physical dimension that includes holding hands,[123] a warm hug,[124] a kiss on the mouth,[125] but is not necessarily consciously sexual), it presents all manifestly sexual relationships among men that are consummated as violent rape. After Sharaf tells his story to 'Abd al-Fattah, the latter in solidarity (and perhaps due to his being stereotypically Upper Egyptian in the view of the novelist) affirms to him that one could bear the violation of "everything except one's honor."[126] As indicated earlier, in many of these novels, the Upper Egyptian, the Gulf Arab, or the African seem to occupy the internal native against whom modern civilized Arabs are defined, or whom they must repudiate as the condition of being "civilized."

To sustain the men's masculine physical integrity from attack and certain degeneration into femininity, *Sharaf* offers us the ostensibly marginal figure of 'Azizah, who proves to be central, in his/her standing in for the horrifying future of all oppressed men after they get Honga'd. This is how 'Azizah is introduced by Sharaf who encounters her/him in jail:

I heard a feminine laugh approaching me, so I turned around toward the sound. I saw a young man in prison uniform sitting next to the wall with a number of prisoners. He was telling them something while gesturing with his fingers in front of his mouth just

123. Ibid., 182.
124. Ibid., 157.

125. Ibid., 198.
126. Ibid., 155.

like the women of the popular neighborhoods do. I also noticed that his fingers were decorated with gold rings.[127]

'Azizah makes a few other appearances in the novel. One occurs when Sharaf and 'Abd al-Fattah were walking hand in hand in the jail court-yard (a common gesture of homosocial friendship with no conscious sexual connotations). 'Abd al-Fattah

saw the prisoner who distributes the incoming mail. He let go of my hand and rushed toward him. I went next to the wall and stood against it. A group of prisoners passed me by. They included the prisoner who decorates his fingers with rings. He was known as 'Azizah and walked in a scandalous way, swaying like a woman. He saw me look at him. He winked at me and hollered: "Where is your other half?" . . . I turned my head away, ignoring him. He was not the first to refer to me and to 'Abd al-Fattah as each other's half. Our closeness had become the object of envy of many.[128]

When later on in the novel, a convicted Israeli spy offers Sharaf's new friend and protector Salim (a serial killer) a pack of Egyptian-made Cleopatra cigarettes in exchange for buggering Sharaf (an offer Salim categorically rejects), the narrator tells us that Sharaf was "shocked by the news, not because he had become the object of negotiations between outside forces, nor because of the nature of the service to be rendered, but because of the cheap price that was offered, which placed him on a par with a prisoner of the status of 'Azizah who charges a similar packet for a fast round during daytime and several times that price if the matter involved a whole night."[129] Ibrahim is not necessarily endorsing Sharaf's comparative grid but is rather questioning it. The intended irony here for Ibrahim is not that 'Azizah is an honorable character, but rather that he/she is not the lowliest character in the novel. For Ibrahim, what Sharaf and the rest of the male prisoners are blind to is that they are all already 'Azizahs.

Other necessary representations of men who get Honga'd (such male characters have the central function of consolidating the identity of non-Hongable men in the novel) occur in jokes. This one was told by Batsha, a cellmate of Sharaf's, who later tried to rape him:

Two of those wanted to be cured, so they went to the doctor. A month later, they ran into each other. One of them saw the other peeling a sugarcane stick and then cutting

---

127. Ibid., 147.
128. Ibid., 183–84.

129. Ibid., 518.

it into small equal strips, the size of a finger . . . so he yelled at him: "Didn't we say we were going to give it up?" The other answered him: "Well, the doctor's cure did not bode well with me, so I decided to try herbal medicine instead." The cell shook with laughter and Batsha looked at us with pride.[130]

It is interesting that the novel does not leave the matter of active male homosexual desire untheorized. Toward the end of the novel, a full-fledged theory is offered, whose intent, as we will see, is to naturalize heterosexuality, wherein men who like to bugger other men are redeemed, and only Hongable men, like ʿAzizah, are left out of the deal. ʿAzizah is the figure that represents the real and imaginary reality of all oppressed men in the novel, one that they can never accept. They, like Sharaf, seem not to mind the economic exploitation and social denigration to which they are subjected by international capital and its local agents. This is evidenced, on the one hand, by their attempts to shut Dr. Ramzi up when he explains to them the detailed workings of their economic oppression, and, on the other, by their persistent chanting the fateful epigram "Honga, even for the one who chooses death." The men are flexible on "everything except honor," as ʿAbd al-Fattah had succinctly put it. The novel's theory of active male homosexuality is articulated by Salim, the serial killer friend and protector of Sharaf. Salim offers his theory in the context of being caught in flagrante delicto when Sharaf awoke one night to find Salim's hand inside his (Sharaf's) trousers. Salim retracts his hand and they both ignore the incident, which produces much tension between them. In order to alleviate the situation, Salim, by way of apology, offers the following explanation:

I don't want you to misunderstand me. What happened was against my will. Don't think that this is what I want from you. I can easily take care of my needs. You know this well. But I can never find a friend. Listen, I've been in jail for more than twenty years. What do you think is the thing I need most?" I didn't answer, so he continued. "Do you think I didn't need someone next to me? Someone who would pat me on the back and whom I would pat on the back? Someone to hug me and for me to hug? Do you know what it means to sit around for twenty years without touching another human being? With no one to love you? This doesn't mean that you want to do something with him. That's not necessary. There's something called friendship. That there is someone next to you who knows what you're thinking and what you mean when you say something. Someone who'd understand you, appreciate you, hold you dear

130. Ibid., 115–16.

THE TRUTH OF FICTIONAL DESIRES

to himself, worry about you, help you, and stand by you in times of need." I suddenly said: "My father never hugged me."[131]

This interruptive intimate moment does not deter Salim from elaborating his theory. Having explained his emotional and physical motivations, Salim proceeds to explain the sexual element of these needs:

As for the [sexual] drive, this is entirely natural. It is prison that is not natural. The world here is entirely delinquent. Do you think I don't know the difference between a man and a woman? *It is impossible for a man to ever take the place of a woman, even if he lies on his back.* But look around. Do you see many women around? So what should one do? Sometimes I feel like I am going to go crazy. No matter what I do not to think of it, I can't. Not one day passes without something reminding you of it—a picture in a magazine, a song, a gesture. Some people here pretend not to care about this at all. But they're simply scared of what might happen. They're scared of getting buggered [yata-sakhmatu]. No one here likes to be a deviant. Deviants are always despised and people treat them as weaklings and give them no consideration. So what should one do?[132]

Salim follows his theory with a story of someone he knows who was raped by three men. On a later occasion, this fellow beat up a seventeen-year-old boy and then raped him. He initially hated himself because he remembered his inability to resist when he was raped. He later "admitted that he enjoyed raping the boy. Not the physical element, but, as he put it, because 'he was on top, not on the bottom.'"[133] Indeed Salim himself pities his own state. When he first arrived in prison, he used to fantasize about "naked women with big tits." Now he fantasizes about Idku, a guard, whom he sees in his fantasy crying: "I grab him by the hair and shake him in front of the other prisoners and tell him to undo his pants. He begs me not to kill him for his kids' sake. After he lowers his pants, I have him bend over and I bugger him [asakhmatu]. I then find my self holding a knife and stabbing him in the back. It's a terrible thing, isn't it?"[134]

This theory of substitutive homosexuality and of eroticized power does not account for everything, nor is it intended to. Does ʿAzizah, for example, get buggered because he wants to or because he has to? Do men bugger other men and enjoy it because they are on top? Do they enjoy vaginal sex with women for other reasons? Why do women, and men who are "deviant," like to be buggered? Because they are on the

131. Ibid., 534–35.
132. Ibid., 535. Emphasis added.

133. Ibid., 536.
134. Ibid., 537.

bottom? Is there a place for physical pleasure at all in this narrative? While we are treated in the novel to many of Sharaf's masturbatory heterosexual fantasies, it is not clear if the pleasure he feels is "physical" or because he is "on top."

A theory of eroticized power unfolds everywhere in the narrative. What is difficult to grasp however is whether eroticism can escape compulsion at all within a male homosexual matrix that is consummated (a theory not unlike that propounded by Adrienne Rich with regards to heterosexual coitus[135]). The Honga metaphor of defeat and oppression is a classic misogynist trope that is not exclusive to *Sharaf*. As Sun'allah Ibrahim seems somehow aware of being implicated in such misogyny, he makes a feeble attempt to interrogate it. While the narrator reminisces about the torture of communist prisoners under the Nasir regime in the 1960s, he recounts the following incident: "[the torturer] continued to beat up one of them (a textile worker) with a thick stick on his head until he would say that he was a woman, but [the worker] refused. When his arms were tired and the detainee's head was on the verge of being split open, he stopped and asked him about the secret of his intransigence. He answered that he found nothing offensive in being a woman because he believes in full equality between the two sexes, but that he would not say it except according to his own will."[136] It seems unlikely that the textile worker would have withstood equal torture if he were asked to declare that he was a tree, for example, insisting that he had nothing against trees but that he would not declare that he was one except according to his own will. We should contrast this scene with a much earlier one when Sharaf himself was being tortured and beaten up by the police so that he would confess his crime. "I felt very sick and then I heard one [of the torturers] curse me and question my manhood. I could not control myself and I yelled back at him, "I am manlier than you are."[137] Subjected to more torture, one of the officers tells him to choose the name of a woman so that they can call him by it. Sharaf continues to resist until they threaten to bring his sister and rape her. Only then, he collapses and confesses the false crime of which he was accused.[138] It is unclear if Sharaf's refusal to be called by a woman's name is also based, like the communist textile worker, on his belief in complete equality of the sexes or due to his contempt for the Hongable species of humans.

135. See Adrienne Rich's classic, "Compulsory Heterosexuality and Lesbian Existence," *Signs* (Summer 1980): 631–60.
136. Ibrahim, *Sharaf*, 462.
137. Ibid., 32.
138. Ibid., 33.

The mark of femininity functions throughout the novel as the mark of Hongability (as corruption). This is what distinguishes real men from the other human species of either sex. The horror of globalization in the novel is that of eliminating the masculine gender completely and transforming all humans into a Hongable species, thus doing away with their "honor." It is this feminine condition to which all oppressed masculine men will be reduced by globalization that seems to stir the emotions of most of the male characters in the novel, even Dr. Ramzi, who volunteered the "African jungle" story. *Sharaf* perhaps could be read as Ibrahim's plea to his readers that they change their notion of honor and grasp the implication of globalization on their economic and social lives, which he deems much more detrimental to them than a literal sexual notion of honor and manhood. After all, for Ibrahim, it seems that the very humanity of these men in the third world is what is at stake, not only their manhood. Their dehumanization in the context of the prison, itself a metaphor for globalized Egypt as the larger prison, is, to him, what should be at stake; that this should be the condition which they must reject rather than hold on to some notion of manliness as supreme in a world that takes their humanity even though it maintains the masquerade of manliness intact. But if Ibrahim is removing the mask of manliness to show these men that they are always already *Hongable* under globalization, what is the moral of his novel? For, if the worst thing about globalization is its rendering all men "Hongable," then it will have no direct impact on women and Hongable men, who in turn should not resist it at all. If anything, through Ibrahim's representation of it, globalization functions in *Sharaf* like "Za'faranism" does in al-Ghitani's novel, namely, as an equalizer of citizens, all of whom are now equally Hongable. Ibrahim may very well be asking of his readers that they question the male characters' value system, and that they be outraged by it; that they should ask why should all exploitation and oppression be bearable except for sexual violation even though the former is a graver violation at all levels. That he continues to insist on metaphorical sexual violation as the predominant image and as the quintessential allegory, however, fully implicates him in the very value system that his characters espouse and that he wants to criticize. If earlier metaphors had it that colonialism was rape, there was a slight shift now to a new, yet related, metaphor of globalization as sodomy/castration.

The irony for Ibrahim and *Sharaf* is that all the characters, whether buggerers or buggerees, are always already buggered by globalization and that the physical sexual act that they fear has already happened to them at much deeper levels. Sharaf, who wandered the streets at the beginning of the novel looking at consumer goods he could not afford, whose very future had little or no prospects, had already been buggered by globalization long before the Englishman tried to literalize that sexual metaphor. Indeed it is this realization on the part of Sharaf (and Ibrahim), that he had already been buggered that allows him at the end of the novel to ready himself for the sexual act, which he finally understands as submitting to a feminization that was not at all different from his actual status.

While Ibrahim, unlike his male characters, sees buggery as a metaphor for dehumanization, which for him is a form of feminization, like his characters, he is committed to a notion of manhood that should be safeguarded from "Hongability." That being buggered, and thus feminized, is a horrible fate is an attitude that Ibrahim shares with his male characters. While for him, 'Azizah is the most manifest form of that degradation, his/her condition hardly differs from the rest of the characters. That globalization will not civilize Egyptians but rather render them all Hongable, a notion Ibrahim couples with primitivism and degeneration into the "African jungle," is hardly incidental to the structure of the novel. That Egyptian men may be raped by Englishmen is only the rhetorical ruse that opens the novel. The ultimate degradation and degeneration is that primitive Africans will now also bugger the erstwhile civilized Egyptians, which is the form of tribute/corruption ("Honga") required by globalization. It remains a mystery why, in the context of the continuing ravaging and pillaging of Africa by global capital, the African chief and his men are immune to the buggering dynamic of globalization and are exempted from paying the necessary "Honga."

Ibrahim's attempt to play with the metaphor of buggery and its linkage to questions of civilization and degeneration as the central allegory of his novel reveals as much about his own moral system as it does his characters'. Still, his novel is one of the more provocative novels in recent years that couples political economy with libidinal economy. Indeed *Sharaf* insists that the political and libidinal economies are the same economy and that power in all forms is always already eroticized. If Hanan al-Shaykh's *Misk al-Ghazal* saw international capital as leading to an interrelationship between Western gay men seeking to be penetrated by native desert men who are uninhibited by their polymorphous sexual perversity, Ibrahim begs to differ. For him, what international capital seems to be doing is penetrating national economies and the bodies of laboring classes, not least among them Egyptian men.

Degeneracy and Decadence

We find in this period notable exceptions of fictional writings that refuse to deploy same-sex contact allegorically and posit it more in the realm of personal and social history. A prominent example is Egyptian novelist Muhammad al-Bisati's beautifully written fictionalized memoir *Wa Ya'ti al-Qitar* (And the Train Comes).[139] Al-Bisati's childhood memoir, which includes incidents of same-sex contact among boys and between boys and men in an Egyptian village (and anal sex between rich men and their unmarried maids as well as sex between animals), does not seek to posit this as allegorical or as moralistic and exotic, but rather as part of normal village life. When al-Bisati's father, for example, is visited by 'Abduh, who tells him that the young al-Bisati and four other boys raped his son while playing in the irrigation canal, al-Bisati overhears the conversation and gets angry, as he and the other boys did not rape 'Abduh's son. It was the latter "who wanted it and sought it out. He thought he would make us happy so that we would include him in our games. When [afterwards] we included him, he was overjoyed, diving and doing summersaults in the water, showing off his swimming skills. When he saw us getting annoyed at the ruckus he made, he offered himself to us a second time."[140] Al-Bisati's father would ignore him as a form of punishment and delegated many of his normal duties to his younger brother. Unlike in Yahya al-Tahir 'Abdullah's *Al-Raqsah al-Mubahah,* to which I referred earlier, the distraught 'Abduh did not kill his son.

Al-Bisati also reminisces about a middle-aged, short, pudgy, one-eyed man, picked up by a young student (about seventeen years old and in his last year of secondary school) on a train and invited him to the village, where the student and two friends of his would regularly have active sex with him. He would give them cigarettes and buy them dinner. The younger students (who were about thirteen at the time), including al-Bisati, were jealous and wanted to share in the pleasures. They would wait for him at the train station when he arrived and would later follow the older boys to the fields where they would engage in sex with the man. The older students would throw stones at them to deter them from pursuing. The man would come to the village regularly for the next four years, and every year the three graduating students would change (as the ones from the previous year would have gone to college and gotten

139. Muhammad al-Bisati, *Wa Ya'ti al-Qitar* [And the Train Comes] (Cairo: Dar Al-Hilal, 1999).
140. Ibid., 21.

jobs elsewhere). Al-Bisati and his friends figured that they would have to wait for five years before their turn came and opted to look for other sexual venues. By the time they came of age, the man did not return to the village any more.[141]

Such fictional depictions, which shy away from sensationalism and contemporary political agendas, are not much noted in the Arabic tabloid press, nor is there a rush to translate them into foreign languages. Al-Bisati's matter-of-fact approach should be contrasted with another novel that exploded on the Egyptian scene three years later, namely, *'Imarat Ya'qubyan* (The Ya'qubyan Building), and which received much critical acclaim in literary magazines and the tabloid press and was indeed translated to English in 2004.[142]

If Naguib Mahfouz's *Midaq Alley* aimed to portray the final overtaking of Egypt by colonial modernity through the story of an alley, then 'Ala' al-Aswani's *'Imarat Ya'qubyan* (The Ya'qubyan Building), written over half a century later, aimed to show the decadence, degeneracy, and misery to which Egyptian society succumbed as a result of the postcolonial state. This he demonstrates in the context of a tall apartment building and the inhabitants therein. Published in 2002 as its author's first novel (he had published short stories before), the book became a bestseller, going into multiple editions. Written in realist style, the novel, as its back cover describes it, "uncovers all that is hidden about downtown society as well as its secrets. Its author delves into all that is banned and socially circumscribed to reach the truth. He describes for us sex, deviance, corruption, repression, and the infrastructure of the city's downtown, which is ignored by all as miserable attempts to beautify it proceed; the author presents to us the society of marginals who live in tin rooms on the roofs of tall buildings and uncovers the intimate liaisons of those miserable people."[143] It is not clear what is meant by the "truth." Is it the truth of downtown life that is to be contrasted with existing lies or cover-ups that the author uncovers? If so, "we" do not know who is doing the covering up of the "secrets" and the facts that are "hidden" from public view? Is it the state, a subservient media, society at large? As much of what the novel uncovers seems to be known about Cairo's downtown life, whether in the media, in Islamist opposition discourse, in government discourse, or at the societal level at large, as we have already seen in nonfictional accounts in earlier chapters, and to which the novel itself, as we will see,

141. Ibid., 75–78.

142. Alaa Al Aswany, *The Yacoubian Building* (Cairo: American University in Cairo Press, 2004).

143. 'Ala' al-Aswani, *'Imarat Ya'qubyan* [The Ya'qubyan Building] (Cairo: Mirit Lil-Nashr wa al-Ma'lumat, 2002), back cover.

attests, it remains a mystery why the author (and perhaps the publisher) thinks that the novel's major function and service was to render visible and audible that which has been hidden and muted. There is an obvious need here to sensationalize, to tell what is already known as if it were new in order to induce moral panic. We will see how this panic will unfold.

The Ya'qubyan Building is about the current residents of an old Cairene building located downtown built in 1934 in grand European style during the colonial period and under the Egyptian monarchy, and the transformation the building has undergone since the anticolonial revolt triumphed in 1952 Egypt, ushering in the age of postcolonial republicanism. Like Mahfouz's Midaq Alley, the novel tells of the lives of a number of building residents, whether living in its proper apartments or in the tin storage rooms-cum-apartments located on its roof and inhabited by displaced peasants and the urban poor. Built by an Armenian millionaire, the head of the Armenian community in Egypt at the time, the building was designed by an Italian architectural office he had engaged for the project: "Ten floors high in classical luxurious European style, its balconies decorated with statues with Greek faces sculpted in the stone. The columns, the steps, and the hallways are all built with natural marble, and the elevator, of Schinder make, was of the latest style. It took two years to build after which it appeared as an architectural gem beyond all expectations, so much so that the owner asked that the Italian architect etch his name "Ya'qubyan" on its door from the inside in big Roman letters lit up at night with neon lights as if he was immortalizing his name and affirming his ownership of this marvelous building."[144]

The Ya'qubyan Building, as we will see, not only continues the recent trends we observed in fiction since the late 1980s in deploying tropes of degeneration and decadence that it links to sexual deviance, but goes further to make not sexual deviance, but a community of sexual deviants, the manifest sign of postcolonial degeneration. The writings we have surveyed in this chapter narrate the difficulties facing the emergence of the postcolonial modern Arab male subject as a self-sustaining, self-respecting, rational, autonomous, because masculine, man. Al-Aswani's novel will insist, through its deployment of sexual desires in contemporary Cairo as representative social history and as allegory, that the postcolonial male subject is *stillborn* and that the only kind of subject that emerges through colonial and postcolonial violence (physical, social, economic, and epistemic) is the degenerate, the corrupt, and the sexual deviant.

144. Ibid., 20–21.

The novel tells the stories of a number of building residents who either live in its apartments, have offices there, own shops on its ground floor, or live in the tin-roof storage rooms on the rooftop. The five main male characters and the three female characters associated with them are characterized by one main fate that they all share in this period of Cairene history, namely, that they are all either biologically unreproductive or prevented from being so in one way or another. Al-Hajj ʿAzzam, a pious and wealthy businessman, a postrevolutionary nouveau riche, who had started out his life polishing shoes for a living, now owns companies and shops, one of which is located on the ground floor of the Yaʿqubyan Building. Even though ʿAzzam had been reproductive during the Nasirist period, having had two sons with his first wife, at this point in his life he was interested in business and political ambitions (which, to him, are the same). These ambitions occurring, as they did, in his middle age, seem to have excited his long latent sexual desires, manifesting in persistent wet dreams. ʿAzzam, who did not want to offend his first wife nor become a subject of gossip, opted to marry a young widow from Alexandria on condition that the marriage remain secret, that she leave her young son behind in Alexandria, and that she not conceive any children for him.

The young wife, Suʿad, was set up in an apartment in the Yaʿqubyan Building and the newly contracted marriage seemed to go very well for ʿAzzam, whose political (and pleasurable) life was taking off. He ran for parliamentary elections (which provided al-Aswani with the occasion to discuss in gory details the corruption of the political process in Egypt) and won. His money was multiplying but with limits, as the corrupt connections that helped him win the elections wanted a large share of all profits he would accrue from his new position. He resisted and then had to submit to the profit sharing arrangement with an elusive character known as the Big Man. When Suʿad decided to create a fait accompli by becoming pregnant, ʿAzzam was furious and insisted that she abort. This she refused while recognizing that she was in violation of their contract. She was prepared for divorce but nothing worse. ʿAzzam as revenge arranged to have her kidnapped, drugged, and undergo an abortion against her will, after which he sent her her divorce papers and kicked her out of the apartment.

Taha, another resident of the building, is the young teenage son of the doorman. A smart young man who is graduating high school, Taha seeks to exit his base world of nonrespectability and ascend the social ladder by becoming a respected police officer, but his application for cadet school was rejected due to the class bias of an examining officer. Disappointed,

Taha applied and was accepted at university, where he met Islamist students who offered him new solutions to his class anxiety. Taha was in love with Buthayna, a young woman who was the main financial supporter of her mother and siblings following her father's death, and lived with them in one of the tin-roof storage rooms on the rooftop of Ya'qubyan. An honest and hardworking young woman, Buthayna suffered from sexual harassment from every male boss for whom she worked. Refusing to yield to sexual advances, Buthayna would be periodically fired from jobs, until she finally realized (or was made to realize) that she, like other young women in her position, would have to accept her situation and yield to the sexual advances of her bosses. Her entry into the pragmatic yet tragic life of poor working women coincided with Taha's entry into the world of the Islamists, mostly as an idealist. Buthayna broke off her relationship with the increasingly restrictive and jealous Taha soon after.

Zaki al-Disuqi is another main character. Son of a major prerevolutionary Wafdist politician and living with his sister Dawlat in an apartment his father had left him, he owned an office in the Ya'qubyan building. Dawlat is a widow whose two children had immigrated to Europe and the United States, never to return. Zaki had never married, having pursued women much of his life. He spent his life lamenting an aristocratic future he could have had, had it not been for the 1952 Revolution. Zaki would patronize seedy downtown bars in search of cheap hookers whom he would invite to his office. After the last hooker robbed him and stole his sister Dawlat's expensive diamond ring, Dawlat kicked him out of his own apartment, and he moved into his office at Ya'qubyan. His assistant (an unattractive Coptic character whose profile is borrowed from the underworld of Charles Dickens's *Oliver Twist*) procured Buthayna for him, now used to being paid for sexual services that did not compromise her virginity. Their relationship becomes more than sexual, and begins to be defined as a love affair.

The fourth male character is Hatim Rashid, the editor of a Cairo-based French-language Egyptian newspaper, *Le Caire*, to which he added an Arabic section. He comes from an aristocratic family and is the son of a famous Egyptian jurist and the dean of the law faculty at Cairo University in the 1950s, and of a French woman of low class origins.[145] In fact, Hatim knew all along that his mother was a bartender whom his father had picked up in the Latin Quarter and moved to Egypt where she treated Egyptians with contempt.[146] Hatim is identified as a "sexual

145. Ibid., 55 and 105.
146. Ibid., 257.

deviant," the etiology of whose "affliction" is fully presented in the novel. Like Zaki and Taha and contemporary ʿAzzam, he is biologically unreproductive.

Although ʿAbduh, the fifth character, did not live in the building initially, he and his wife and their infant son would move there later, living in a tin-roof apartment on the rooftop. ʿAbduh, a conscript whom Hatim picked up, became Hatim's lover and kept man. Playing the "active" sexual role with Hatim, ʿAbduh resisted the emotional and domestic demands of Hatim, who wanted to transform him from a sexual partner into a romantic steady boyfriend or spouse. When ʿAbduh finished his military service, Hatim bought him a kiosk shop to provide him with a steady income, and sent for his wife and son to move to Cairo where Hatim rented for them a roof apartment in Yaʿqubyan, to make sure ʿAbduh remained near.

The ensuing engine of the story is the way the sexual desires of the rich older male protagonists unfold and how the worldly desires of the poor young male and female characters express themselves, namely, in the cases of Buthayna, Suʿad, ʿAbduh, and Taha, who seem to desire mainly a better life, with sexuality being a medium through which to reach it but not necessarily as a teleological pleasure in itself. Other characters live a decadent if not a degenerate life. Dawlat, the older woman and sister of Zaki, who lives alone, abandoned by her children and without class status, manifests disgust at her brother's sexual life and calls the police on him in order to better her economic situation, while Christine, the Greek Egyptian restaurant owner and ex-flame of Zaki, is past her prime and is no longer a sexual object.

This is a story of degeneration and decadence and generational disconnect. Zaki and Hatim (and Christine) represent the old aristocratic classes that are mostly unreproductive, biologically and socially. Zaki tries to make amends at the end of the novel and marries Buthayna, the poor young woman who is antirevolutionary just like him, thus indicating that the old rich and the new young poor may be new allies against a corrupt revolution. Hatim is killed off by ʿAbduh who saw him as leading him to temptation and "sin" to the point of incurring God's wrath on him, manifesting in the sudden illness and death of ʿAbduh's only son. ʿAbduh's murder of Hatim signals the final death of aristocratic decadence, while Zaki's wedding to Buthayna (after she tells him he must stop drinking) signals the inauguration of a new social alliance, especially as the remaining alliance between the aristocracy itself had faltered, evidenced by the warfare that Dawlat, Zaki's sister, launched against him when she kicked him out of his own home and called the police on him while in bed with Buthayna. The humiliation of Zaki and Buthayna equally at the hands of the new regime's police signals their ultimate equality, making their marriage possible, especially, as they plan on moving to France. Thus, even were they to be reproductive, which the novel leaves unclear, they would do so abroad, outside the nation that had been transformed into a space of decadence and degeneration. In this, al-Aswani's novel is on a par with *The Events of Za'farani Street,* except that impotence would spread from Za'farani to the rest of the world, leaving no exit.[147]

On the one hand there seems to be an unbridgeable gap between the prerevolutionary generation—the aristocracy, which was overthrown, and the middle class who assumed power—and the children of the revolution, even though, except for middle-class beneficiaries, the aristocracy and the children of the revolution were disappointed by a revolution that only serves the few and the corrupt. On the other hand, it is precisely members of this prerevolutionary generation (whether beneficiaries or victims of the revolution) who desire the children of the revolution, who in turn sell their sexual services to them in order to survive. As the marriage between the lower-middle-class Su'ad and the rich 'Azzam, the beneficiary of revolutionary corruption, was unreproductive by design and therefore faltered, the Hollywood ending of the novel where an alliance is struck between the aristocratic Zaki and the poor Buthayna seems at best silly and at worst untenable given the parameters that the novel sets throughout.

The novelty in al-Aswani is his representation of what he terms "sexual deviants." If our encounter with same-sex practice moved from the character of Kirsha in *Midaq Alley,* whose sexual practices were not captured by either the English term "homosexuality" or by the term "deviant," we later observed the invention of the sexual deviant (male or female) as a mark of degeneration (especially in al-Shaykh's novel). Later still, the figure of the passive male sexual "deviant" becomes the primary allegory of defeat in novels in the 1990s like *Sharaf,* or one of two primary figures (the other being the sexually liberated woman) whose gain or loss of individual rights signals society's enlightenment or darkness, as in the play *The Rites of Signs and Transformations.* What *The Ya'qubyan Building* registers however is something altogether different from its predecessors, namely, the invention of the homosexual deviant as a fully articulated social and communitarian identity. It is here where, to borrow

147. Jamal al-Ghitani praised the novel, which he had serialized initially in the magazine *Akhbar al-Adab,* which he edits. His review (and the reviews of others) are reproduced in subsequent editions of the novel. See 'Ala' al-Aswani, *'Imarat Ya'qubyan,* 4th ed. (Cairo: Maktabat Madbuli, 2004), 350–51.

from Michel Foucault, the homosexual becomes a species, a notion that is fully complicit with the agenda of the Gay International that seeks this very "development" that mirrors its own. In al-Aswani's novel, as we will see, sexual deviance functions both as part of social history and as national allegory.

Discussion of matters deviant begins in the novel with the description of a downtown bar called Chez Nous, which ironically is akin to an English pub in design. The bar, seemingly like the clientele that patronizes it, is located "several steps below street level," and has "dim lights."[148] When one enters it, one is overcome with the feeling that one is "hiding from daily life in some sense; this feeling of privacy is what most distinguishes Chez Nous, which has become well known as a meeting place for sexual deviants (and it has been presented as such in more than one Western tourist guidebook)."[149] The bar owner, an Egyptian by the name of ʿAziz, "known as the Englishman" on account of his blond hair and blue eyes, is

afflicted with deviance and is said to have been the companion of the older Greek foreigner who used to own the bar and bequeathed it to him after his death. They also say that he organizes orgiastic [majinah] parties during which he introduces devi- ants to Gulf tourists and that the prostitution of deviants earns him huge profits from which he pays off bribes—which has made him completely safe from police harass- ment. He has a strong presence and is very tactful. Under his sponsorship and his care deviants meet in Chez Nous where they start friendships and are liberated from social pressures that prevent them from declaring their predilections. The meeting places of deviants are like Hashish dens and gambling joints. The patrons belong to different social backgrounds and different ages. You would find among them artisans and pro- fessionals, young and old men, all unified by deviance. Moreover, the deviants are like pickpockets and muggers and all groups who lie outside the law and accepted con- ventions in that they make up their own special language that enables them to speak in ways that only they understand. They call the passive deviant "Kudyana," and refer to him by a feminine name by which he would be known among them, like Suʿad, Inji, Fatimah, etc. They call the active deviant "barghal" and if he is an ignorant simple man they would call him a "dry barghal." They call deviant intercourse "waslah" [lit- erally and in classical Arabic "attachment," while in the vernacular it means an artistic "performance" by a singer or belly-dancer].[150]

Note that Chez Nous, like the Yaʿqubyan Building itself, was originally owned by a "foreigner" and is now managed by Egyptians. Moreover, not

148. Ibid., 51.
149. Ibid., 52.

150. Ibid., 52–53.

only does Chez Nous function as a hideout from nondeviant others but it also constitutes itself as a deviant "us"—"at our place," Chez Nous. It is with this communitarian background that Hatim Rashid is introduced as a "Kudyana."[151] Al-Aswani, like the Gay International, seems intent on outing this community of "passive deviants" by making its "secret" language known to all. In this, he fulfils the same role as police major ʿAbd al-Wahid Imam Mursi does in his criminological book *Sexual Deviance and Murder Crimes,* discussed in chapter 4.[152] Al-Aswani also does not seem to grasp that actually the so-called secret language of "deviants" 'is not theirs at all, but rather a mobile language borrowed from popular belly dancers or "ʿawalim" (hence "waslah," "kudyana," which used to refer to the madam of a brothel and is derived from *kudyah,* the title of the Sufi woman who leads Sufi rituals, known as "Zar," and *barghal,* which referred to a brothel patron and is probably derived from the English "bugger," itself an Orientalist derivation from "Bulgarian"[153]), which seems to have been exported to a new marginalized group.

As for Hatim, he is "a conservative deviant (if the expression permits) . . . He does not use makeup on his face and does not prance around in a seductive way, as many *kudyana*s do. In his outer appearance and conduct, he stands always and with skill between delicate elegance and effeminateness."[154] Hatim is elegant and in shape "with precise French features like those of a successful film star except for the wrinkles that a boisterous life left on his face and that hateful, obscure, and miserable ashen look that always envelops the faces of deviants."[155] His description of the ashen look aside, al-Aswani provides a social, *not* a genetic or physiological, etiology for Hatim's "affliction" with deviance. It seems that when Hatim was a child, on account of his father being busy with his legal career and his mother busy with her work as a translator at the French embassy, he was often left alone: "In addition to his painful solitude, there was a sense of alienation and mental confusion from which children of mixed marriages suffer."[156] It was in this state that Hatim loved the Nubian Egyptian butler Idris, with whom he would spend most of his time. Idris would soon start to kiss Hatim on the face and neck and tell him how "beautiful" he looked and how much he "loved" him. When Hatim was nine,

---

151. Ibid., 55.
152. ʿAbd al-Wahid Imam Mursi, *Al-Shudhudh al-Jinsi wa Jaraʾim al-Qatl* [Sexual Deviance and Lethal Crimes] (Cairo: n.p., 1995).
153. "Barghal" is also the Egyptian colloquial rendering of the classical Arabic word "barjal," meaning compass, as in the geometric instrument used to draw arcs and circles.
154. Al-Aswani, *ʿImarat Yaʿqubyan,* 55.
155. Ibid., 55–56.
156. Ibid., 106.

Idris asked him to disrobe and then had intercourse with him. Despite Idris's overwhelming desire and pleasure, he "penetrated Hatim's body with care and caution and asked him to let him know if he felt the least amount of pain." Hatim apparently felt none.[157] When Hatim's father died of an aneurism seven or eight years later and his mother had to let Idris go, his departure "affected Hatim's emotional state so much that he got a low grade point average on his school graduation exams. He threw himself after that into his boisterous deviant life. His mother died two years ago, which liberated him from the last obstacle to his pleasure."[158]

Here al-Aswani seems to posit an antiessentialist theory of "passive deviance." It is in learning to enjoy being penetrated as a child that Hatim developed into an adult seeker of this type of pleasure. It is not made clear what the etiology of Idris's sexual enjoyment was, except in its subtextual appeal to existing Cairene stereotypes that Nubian men are active sodomites by nature, perhaps even biological nature. This is especially so as Idris could not have learned to penetrate boys from his social circles, as we are told that he was taken away from his family as a child and brought to work as a servant in Cairo.[159] Sex is presented in the novel as a sort of habit: "Hatim knew many men and left them for many reasons but his sinful and buried desire remained attached to Idris the butler. As a man looks in all the women he meets for the image of the first woman he loved and knew pleasure with for the first time, Hatim looks for Idris in all the men he meets, that primitive uncouth man that civilization has not refined in all that he represents of toughness, coarseness, and vigor. He never stops thinking about Idris and often recalls with striking and pleasurable nostalgia the feelings he felt as he lay on his stomach on his bedroom floor looking at the etched Persian designs on the rug while Idris's hot and overfilled body mixed with his, squeezing and melting him."[160] Hatim thus seems to fit Freud's postulate that finding a love object is always the refinding of it. Moreover, as a degenerate, he prefers primitive rather than "civilized" men.

Male deviants who are always passive and, with the exception of Idris who is never identified as a "deviant," seduce normal men rendering them active deviants in the process seem to have a predilection for certain kinds of jobs:

Sexual deviants are usually skilled at those types of jobs that require communication with people, like public relations, acting, brokerage, or as lawyers, and it is said that

157. Ibid., 107.
158. Ibid., 109.
159. Ibid., 106.
160. Ibid., 109.

THE TRUTH OF FICTIONAL DESIRES

their success in these professions is attributable to their being rid of shyness and embarrassment, which deprives others of these opportunities for success. Their deviant life, which is full of diverse and unfamiliar human experiences, makes them better understand the nature of people and more able to influence them. Deviants are also skilled in the professions that deal with good taste and imagination, such as interior decorating and fashion design. It is well known that the most famous fashion designers in the world are deviants because their dual sexual nature makes them able to design women's fashions that are seductive of men and vice versa.[161]

The question of seduction of normal men seems easy, as all they are required to do is perform the same sexual functions they perform with women. Thus it is not their sexual aim that is being corrupted but rather their sexual object choice, which is not supplanted by a new object choice but rather multiplied to include both sexes. Thus, they are not deviants although they are led to practice "deviant" sex. This arrangement is what is implied throughout al-Aswani's novel. Al-Aswani seems to posit either a combinational theory of nature and nurture to explain sexual deviants, or is confused, as is the Gay International, about what causes this "affliction." If it is being exposed to penetrative sex in a passive mode as a child that accounts for a man's desires to be penetrated for the rest of his life, then what is the role of a "dual sexual nature" in the matter? Could it be that nurture affects nature, which is malleable and not essentialist? If so, then nature is not nature at all if it can be redefined constantly by nurture. If this is the case, when a man becomes a passive deviant, his sexual nature changes and becomes a "dual" one rather than a unitary one, which is what it presumably was in the first place. It would seem that "active sexual deviants," like normal men, do not have this dual nature. Sexual nature seems to be linked in al-Aswani's account not to sexual object choice but decidedly to one's sexual aim.

But sexual aim is also gendered, even and precisely when it accommodates both sexes. Here al-Aswani echoes the history of the social constructionist versus essentialist Western debates around homosexual identity, which is where Michel Foucault located his intervention. If for Foucault homosexuality was an effect of medical and juridical discourses of power that produced it as a deviant pathological identity and then sought to police it in the interest of normalizing and disciplining modern subjects and consolidating the category of "normal," for al-Aswani passive sexual deviance is the effect of colonial violence and the postcolonial state, which is but a continuation of it. Indeed, social deviance

161. Ibid., 181–82.

more generally constitutes all the characters that inhabit the novel and the Ya'qubyan Building, whether in the dissolution of family ties (Dawlat and Zaki, Hatim and his parents, Dawlat and her children, 'Azzam and Su'ad, Su'ad and her son), of chaste versus unchaste love (Buthayna and Taha versus Buthayna and Zaki), and of honest business relations (Buthayna and her bosses, 'Azzam and his racketeering state sponsors). Deviance, sexual and otherwise, is then the only effect and social product of colonial violence, which the postcolonial state has spread across the surface of society and in its interstices.

We learn this when we are introduced to 'Abduh, a young Upper Egyptian conscript doing his military service in Cairo. One night, a drunk Hatim picked up 'Abduh, "who looks very much like Idris."[162] Hatim took him in his car,

> gave him money and kept flirting with him until he succeeded in seducing him. Following this encounter, 'Abd Rabbuh tried many times violently to extricate himself from this relationship with Hatim, who used to know, due to his long experience in deviant passion, that a beginner deviant (barghal) like 'Abd Rabbuh is usually overtaken with a huge amount of sinfulness that quickly transforms into bitterness and black hatred towards the deviant (kudyana) who had seduced him. He also knows that the deviant experience, through repetition and the tasting of its pleasure, gradually transforms into a genuine desire on the part of the deviant *barghal* no matter how much he hated it or was repelled by it at the beginning.[163]

It would seem that Hatim was correct in his assumptions. The narrator tells us later that "what is amazing is that 'Abduh, despite his youth and ignorance, was understanding of Hatim's feelings [towards him] and became much more accepting of their relationship. The initial repulsion was gone and was replaced by a delicious and sinful yearning."[164] According to this account, men's desire to penetrate other men and to be penetrated by them is not an inherent desire but develops by force of habit. This is not so unlike what Salamah Musa proposed in his own writings. If habit is addiction to repetition, to an iteration of sorts, then its very repetitiveness as practice is what transforms it into desire. This certainly seems to be the case for both Hatim and 'Abduh. It is unclear, though, who taught Idris to enjoy penetrating the young Hatim, as the stereotype of the Nubian sodomite is never cited in the novel. Does same-sex practice among men reproduce itself simply as a practice that

162. Ibid., 109.
163. Ibid.

164. Ibid., 183.

only later leads to desire? If Idris introduced Hatim to a pleasure that Hatim did not know and Hatim introduced ʿAbduh to a pleasure ʿAbduh did not know, then is it simply that if the cycle is broken, the practice and the pleasure would disappear? Is this how deviant sex reproduces itself in a society where biological reproduction is interrupted? It appears that in the novel, the failure of procreation both represents and is part of a wider failure to imagine a future for the Yaʿqubyan Building, itself a microcosm of Egypt in a globalized world. One could argue that a place like Chez Nous could represent another model for social reproduction—one working through *affiliation* rather than *filiation*—but one that cannot be allegorized as the nation except in failure. The reasons for this are elaborated in describing the deviant as the new national subject.

The novel explores how the signs of some deviant desires manifest physically. All passive deviants are not only inwardly but also outwardly feminine, even though they have different degrees of femininity, while active "deviants" are as manly as nondeviant men. Indeed, Hatim, who does not apply creams and other facial products to his face and does not present himself in the "common feminine way" that others do, in that he does not wear "negligees" nor does he don "artificial breasts," "does make a great effort with expert touches to bring forth his beauty as an effeminate: he dons diaphanous *galabiyyahs* embroidered with beautiful colors on his naked body and shaves his beard completely, plucks his eyebrows the right calculated amount, and puts some eyeliner lightly and then combs his fine hair to the back letting some tresses fall on his forehead. This is how he always tries in his makeup to become the model handsome youth [ghulam] of olden eras. With the same sensitive taste, Hatim bought his companion new clothes: tight trousers that show off the strength of his muscles [and presumably his endowment], dress shirts and T-shirts in light colors to light up his dark complexion; the open collars always show the neck muscles and the thick chest hair."[165] Thus in contemporary Cairo, not only do the impious masquerade as pious and the corrupt as virtuous, but masculinity and femininity too become a masquerade in a place like Chez Nous.

In contrast to passive sexual deviants who revel in being buggered, the novel provides a counterexample of manhood, one that prefers death to being feminized in this manner. The novel offers Taha as the model of manly self-respect.[166] A short while after Taha begins to be-

---

165. Ibid., 182.

166. Novelistic representations of Islamists do not always present them in this manner. Egyptian writer ʿAbd al-Hakim Qasim's 1984 novella *Al-Mahdi*, for example, sympathetically narrates a sexually charged love scene between Saʿid, a leading figure in the Muslim Brothers, and a young ef-

come active in Islamist politics, he starts attending Islamist sermons and participating in leafleting and demonstrations. At one of the sermons he attended, the Islamist Imam explained to the faithful that "our rulers claim to apply the Islamic Shariʿah while they confirm that they are ruling us democratically. God knows that they are liars in the former and the latter. The Islamic Shariʿah is suspended in our disastrous country and we are being governed by a secular French law that permits drunkenness, adultery, and deviance as long as it is practiced with the consent of the two parties."[167] Soon after, the police began to crack down on the Islamists, and the novice Taha was arrested. If Taha initially longed to join the ranks of police officers to ensure his future, it is the police now who would destroy his. While under arrest, Taha was subjected to physical and sexual torture as well as humiliation and ridicule. The officers torturing him removed his underwear and pinned him to the ground: "A pair of huge hands grabbed and separated his buttocks, and he felt a hard object penetrate his behind cutting through his internal tissue. He started to scream. He screamed as hard as he could. He screamed until he felt his throat tearing."[168] After his release, Taha was overcome with the need to avenge himself. He is perhaps most reminiscent of the character of Dov Landau in Leon Uris's *Exodus,* which was also made into a film. Landau, who was an Auschwitz survivor, is depicted in the novel as having witnessed the rape of young men and women by Nazi soldiers, and in the film version admits that the soldiers "used me like you use a woman," something that impels him to become a fanatical Zionist and join the terrorist Irgun organization in order to blow up the British and the Arabs in Palestine as the way to restore his manhood.[169] Taha, in contrast, seemed less committed to Islamism and no longer committed to a professional future. Abandoned by Buthayna earlier on, all he thought about was revenge. His Islamist mentor tried to sway him from such thinking by citing the Prophet's own forgiveness of those who had oppressed him before they converted to Islam. Taha would have none of it. He would insist: "I am not a prophet. I cannot forget what these criminals did to me. What happened to me chases me every second. I am unable to sleep. I have not gone to the university since I was released, and I don't think that I'll go back. I spend the entire day

---

feminate recruit named Subhi, which leads to an ongoing liaison and camaraderie. See his *Al-Mahdi* [The Guided One] (Damascus: Dar al-Mada, 2002), 98, 110.

167. Al-Aswani, *'Imarat Yaʿqubyan,* 134.

168. Ibid., 216.

169. Leon Uris, *Exodus* (New York: Doubleday, 1958). The film, directed by Otto Preminger, was released in 1960.

in my room and don't speak to anyone. I sometimes feel that I'm losing my mind."[170] When his mentor counseled him to return to university, Taha countered:

"That is impossible, how can I face people after . . ."
Taha fell suddenly silent, his face contracted and he exhaled violently.
"They violated my honor, sir."
"Quiet down."
"They violated my honor ten times, sir, ten times."
"I told you to shut up, Taha."[171]

Taha would not. His obsession led him to use the Islamist insurgency against the regime to avenge himself. He began to insist on being sent on antiregime military operations. When counseled by his mentor that this would be dangerous and that "they will kill you in the first confrontation," Taha seemed unfazed: "I am already dead now. They killed me in the detention center. When they violate your honor while laughing, when they call you by a woman's name and force you to respond to your new name, and you are forced to respond as a result of the cruelty of torture. They called me Fawziyyah. They would beat me every day until I would say to them, 'I am a woman and my name is Fawziyyah.' You want me to forget all this and live?!"[172]

Taha was married off by his Islamist superiors, almost under duress, to the wife of an Islamist martyr killed in action by the police. His new wife and her child from her first husband (the only child that seems to survive the unreproductive order of the novel, exiled as he was to a desert camp outside Egyptian towns and cities) did not distract him from his quest for revenge. Finally Taha joined an assassination party charged with assassinating a high-ranking police officer for his role in torturing Islamists. Taha later found out that it was the same officer who had supervised his torture. He killed him and hollered "God is Great," and waited, against instructions, to see him die and then ran back to the getaway car. Before reaching the car, Taha was shot. As he lay on the ground dying, "he felt a strange sense of overwhelming comfort envelop him and carry him in its folds."[173]

We never learn if the police who sodomized Taha were sexual deviants or normal men. What we clearly know is that some men (Idris and

170. Al-Aswani, 'Imarat Ya'qubyan, 238.
171. Ibid., 238–39.
172. Ibid., 268. See also page 289.
173. Ibid., 343.

the police officers) seek out men to sodomize them voluntarily or to rape them, but men like Taha prefer death to life as sodomites, a decision that saves him from the charge of sexual deviance. Taha's decision to leave the world of Ya'qubyan, and therefore his social station, cost him his manhood, which he only restored by losing his life. He died childless at the hands of the postcolonial state, never having had a chance to reproduce. Islamism's allure was in offering a possible restoration of virility, a remasculating in the face of the emasculation produced by the corruption of the postcolonial state. On that count, however, Islamism failed to deliver completely, unless we consider martyrdom a form of remasculation. If sexual deviance can reproduce itself through habit and recruitment of normal men, normal masculinity is killed off before it can reproduce socially or biologically.

As for Hatim, the narrator tells us that at the newspaper he edited, all the employees knew of his "deviance," as did his neighbors at Ya'qubyan who saw 'Abduh, now living with his wife and son on the roof, spend the night at Hatim's twice a week. 'Abduh himself seemed to be transformed fully into an active "deviant," as he began to think about Hatim while having intercourse with his wife. "He would sleep with his wife violently to prevent her from thinking, as if he was raping her as punishment for her knowledge of his deviance."[174] 'Abduh would fantasize that he and his wife would have an open conversation about the nature of his relationship to Hatim so that he could tell her "that he cannot give up Hatim because he needs the money."[175] What is certain in the history (or is it etiology?) of 'Abduh's desire to penetrate Hatim is that the corruption and degeneration of society and of sexual practices has reached the inner psyche, where sexual desire seems to be located. Even though 'Abduh would only recognize the economic factor as what motivated his sexual relations with Hatim, through habit as repetition, he came to desire Hatim even while having sex with his primary object choice, a woman. His desire was degenerating according to a code of heteronormative masculine conduct tied into idealized forms of national and religious autonomy and respect. Here al-Aswani echoes some of the Islamist writers we encountered in chapter 4 who sought to warn men who engage in active homosexual sex with other men (an act that does not carry the same kind of social disdain that passive homosexual sex carries) of the consequences at the level of desire. For the Islamist writers, such men would eventually be biologically infected with passive sexual

174. Ibid., 219.
175. Ibid.

deviance and would begin to desire to be penetrated themselves. In the case of al-Aswani, such men penetrated passive deviants as substitutes for unavailable women. These penetrative acts would degenerate their primary sexual object choice, rendering women the real substitutes for the passive male deviants that these men became habituated to penetrating.

As for Hatim's work environment, despite the knowledge of employees, no one ever noticed any untoward behavior on his part, especially "because he is serious and tough, perhaps more than he should be."[176] This however had not prevented the "base occurrences" he encountered while at the newspaper. In one case, a lazy journalist, who was reproached by Hatim, decided to embarrass him during an editorial meeting by proposing that the newspaper publish an investigative report "on sexual deviance in Egypt." After a deadly silence, Hatim responded calmly, "I do not think that this is a topic of interest to our readers." The journalist countered back, "It interests them a great deal, especially as there is a great increase in the number of deviants, some of whom occupy leading positions in the country. Scientific studies confirm that the deviant is not psychologically equipped to be in leadership positions in any organization due to the psychological deformations caused by his sexual deviance."[177] The narrator describes the encounter as "a cruel and devastating attack," but Hatim decided to respond "violently." He said, "Your traditional way of thinking is the reason for your journalistic failure." The journalist countered, "Has sexual deviance become progressive behavior?" Hatim retorted, "No, but it is not the national problem in our country, either. As an educated man, you should know that Egypt has not gone backward because of sexual deviance but as a result of corruption, dictatorship, and social injustice. Moreover, spying on people's private lives is a reprehensible conduct that is not becoming of a great newspaper like *Le Caire*."[178] Note that Hatim, like the general tenor of the novel, seems to agree that Egypt is degenerating by going "backward," except that he attributes the cause of degeneration to political matters. In this, Hatim misses what is at stake in these postulations. For the main proposition of the novel is not that "sexual deviance" is the cause of degeneration but rather that it is the primary mark of its occurrence. It is this that al-Aswani's novel wants to highlight.

Other "occurrences" include an instance when a training editor harassed Hatim by approaching him from behind and pressing against him. Hatim threatened him with dismissal. The narrator does not tell us

176. Ibid., 252.
177. Ibid., 252.

178. Ibid., 253.

if the harassing editor is a normal man with a plurality of object choices or a deviant, as the harassment act is not presented as compromising the harassing editor as a deviant but rather as compromising Hatim as such.[179] The narrator, however, is quick to tell us that "Hatim Rashid is not merely an effeminate, he is a talented diligent person [note that he does not describe him as a man]" and that he is a socialist and a personal friend of the most well-known Egyptian socialists, to such an extent that he was once called in for interrogation by the intelligence services.[180] Hatim is presented as living a bifurcated life.

> He lives his daily life as a journalist and a official in a leading position and at night he practices his pleasure for a few hours in bed and tells himself that most men in the world have special passions that lighten the pressures of life and that he knows personalities that occupy the highest positions: doctors, political advisors, university professors, who are addicted to alcohol, hashish, women, or gambling, and this has not lessened their successes or self-respect. He convinces himself that his deviance is something similar, simply a different passion. He likes this idea because it comforts him and restores his equilibrium and grants him respect.[181]

When after a night of passion, 'Abduh (whose full name, 'Abd Rabbuh, as it is pronounced colloquially, means "worshipper of his Lord") confided in Hatim that he is scared of God: "I am fearful He may punish us for what we are doing . . . I have believed in God all my life . . . I always prayed in the mosque and fasted Ramadan and followed all the commandments until I met you and I changed." Hatim comforted him by telling him to resume his prayers. 'Abduh retorted: "How can I pray when I drink alcohol every night and I sleep with you? I feel that God is angry with me and wants to punish me." When Hatim asked if "God wants to punish us because we love one another," 'Abduh interrupted: "God prohibited this kind of love. This is a very big sin. We used to have a cleric in the village . . . who told us during Friday sermons: 'Stay away from sodomy, for it is a great sin to which God's throne shakes in anger.'"[182] An exasperated Hatim explained that "God is great and has real mercy, unlike the words of ignorant clerics in your village. There are many people who pray and fast but who steal and harm others; God will punish them. As for us, God will forgive us because we hurt no one, we only love one another."[183] Indeed, Hatim would later push 'Abduh

---

179. Ibid., 253–54.
180. Ibid., 254.
181. Ibid., 255.

182. Ibid., 185–86.
183. Ibid., 187.

to get a university education and explained to him how class oppression worked: "Education and health care and work are natural rights for all citizens all over the world but the Egyptian regime intentionally leaves the poor, like you, ignorant so that it can rob them . . . had you been educated, you would never accept to work in Central Security under the worst circumstances for pennies while the big folks steal millions daily from people's livelihoods."[184]

It is noteworthy that although Zaki and Hatim are presented as anti-Revolution, they are also presented as socialists who support democracy and social justice. 'Abduh's blaming Hatim or their "deviant sex" for the later death of his young son is important in this regard. While Hatim explains to 'Abduh that certainly God is not punishing all those whose sons die, 'Abduh is unconvinced. In fact, it seems that despite the horrid poverty that 'Abduh lives in and from which Hatim was rescuing him, the illness of his infant son and the lack of immediate care given to him, as the novel makes clear, were very much on account of the lack of education and heath care available in the country for the poor. When Hatim accompanied 'Abduh and his wife, Hadiyyah, and their baby to the hospital, it was Hatim's intervention that guaranteed the best possible medical care that ended up being offered to the child. All the other people and children left unattended in the emergency room surely died, too, but the novel leaves it unclear if lack of medical care or divine punishment for sexual deviance was the reason, as the novel does not let Hatim use that example as an explanation to 'Abduh.

Indeed, when upon his son's death, 'Abduh took Hadiyyah and left Ya'qubyan without a forwarding address, leaving behind the keys to the kiosk Hatim had bought him, the narrator tells us that "had Hatim been a believer in God, he would have thought that his crisis was divine punishment for sodomy. But he knows at least ten sodomites who enjoy a calm and peaceful life with their lovers."[185] Hatim looked everywhere for 'Abduh and finally found him at a well-known café for Upper Egyptian workers. 'Abduh accepted to go back for one final night of passion with Hatim in return for a substantial check and possible employment, as his economic situation and that of his wife since he had left Ya'qubyan was dismal. 'Abduh carried Hatim 'like a child" to bed and threw him on it: "[H]e took off his trousers and threw himself on top of him. He had sex with him violently; he ravished him as he had not done before so much that Hatim yelled out loudly more than once on account of the

184. Ibid., 259.
185. Ibid., 315.

excess of pleasure and pain. ['Abduh] quenched his desire in his body three times in less than one hour."[186] When 'Abduh got dressed to leave, Hatim hugged him and asked him to spend the night until morning. 'Abduh pushed him to the floor. When a shocked Hatim reminded him that the agreement was that he spend the night, 'Abduh retorted that he had already carried out his part of the deal. The ensuing conversation consisted of a desperate Hatim insulting 'Abduh as "just a barefoot ignorant Upper Egyptian. I picked you up from the street, cleaned you up, and made you human." When Hatim clung to him as he opened the door, 'Abduh slapped him. "You slap your master, you servant, son of a bitch." Hatim threatened to stop payment on the check and withdrew his promises of finding a job for 'Abduh. Groaning like a "savage animal," 'Abduh attacked Hatim, beating and kicking him; finally he held him by the neck and began to ram his head against the wall until he died. The neighbors told the police that they had heard screams at four in the morning coming out of Hatim's apartment, but they "did not interfere as they knew the nature of his private life."[187] Privacy is spectacularly double-edged here; it initially protects Hatim but then allows him to be killed.

The novelist, who is adept at inhabiting his characters, fails in producing a convincing character in Hatim by endowing him with inexplicable inconsistencies. Why would a dejected, educated, socialist aristocrat who is full of sympathy for the poor choose to insult 'Abduh as an Upper Egyptian servant? Could his anger not have been expressed differently, telling 'Abduh how he is blaming him for the failure of the state and the capitalist system, that he is blaming him for a certain scapegoating of sexual pleasure? While on an earlier occasion, as we saw, Hatim did articulate ideas about how it is not really so sinful to have sex with men, as they are not hurting anyone, he could have easily reminded 'Abduh how adultery with a woman has many more Qur'anic verses condemning them and specifying punishment for them, than for sodomy (liwat), which has no specified punishment at all in the Qur'an and is mentioned sparingly. It is interesting that such verses are never cited in the novel in relation to the fornication of Buthayna and Zaki.

As far as reproduction is concerned, clearly not only did Hatim die childless, but even 'Abduh was rendered unreproductive with the death of his son and his implied imprisonment following his murder of Hatim. Reproduction is a critical trope for the novel, not only because it links

186. Ibid., 231.
187. Ibid., 234.

the present to the future and because its absence severs the present from any possible future, but also because the condition of postcolonial degeneration and decadence is such that little reproduction, if at all, takes place. The elite beneficiaries of the revolution, just like the aristocracy they supplanted and the massive population who is ill served by it, are living parasitically in contemporary Cairo, which seems to reproduce only deviants (Chez Nous), and has become the place where normal men engaged in resisting this deviant state of affairs are sodomized and killed for daring to challenge it. It is true that not only are normal men killed, but so are sexual deviants as well. However, the former are killed for resisting degeneration while the latter for inhabiting it.

The novel seems particularly interested in the question of Islamist and clerical interpretations of Islamic regulations of sexuality and reproduction and the kinds of casuistry that can be exercised by state-sponsored Islam. While it allows both sides (although the Islamist voice is louder in the novel) to express some of their opinions on the matter, the narrator offers no third alternative. Nowhere do we hear the narrator, who challenges the self-justification of the characters (especially Hatim but also Zaki and Buthayna, among others) challenge the accepted wisdom of Islamist or clerical declarations. The popular saying about the throne of God shaking every time a sodomitic act is committed, is not only a weak saying attributed to the Prophet, many Muslim theologians, including Muhammad Jalal Kishk (discussed in an earlier chapter), have dismissed it as an inauthentic hadith.[188] As for the ban on abortion in Islam, which was introduced in the nineteenth century after contact with the West (before that, most jurisprudential schools in Islam allowed abortion, some up to the third month of pregnancy), the narrator presents this as the casuistry of a government cleric.[189] The argument is introduced when 'Azzam invited the state's major cleric to convince Su'ad of the permissibility of abortion in Islam. While clearly the cleric was resurrecting the Islamic tradition (against existing state law and Islamist interpretations) in a casuistic move, the reality of the matter is that he was indeed speaking the truth. The cleric says: "Abortion is banned of course but some trusted jurisprudential opinions confirm that getting rid of a pregnancy in the first two months is not abortion, as the fetus is not ensouled until the third month." When Su'ad asked who said such a thing and the cleric assured her that it was "major theologians," she

---

188. Muhammad Jalal Kishk, *Khawatir Muslim fi al-Mas'aslah al-Jinsiyyah* [A Muslim's Thoughts on the Sexual Question], 3rd ed. (Cairo: Maktab al-Turath al-Islami, 1992), 196.

189. See Basim Musallam, *Sex and Society in Islam: Birth Control before the Nineteenth Century* (Cambridge: Cambridge University Press, 1983).

retorts: "[T]hey must be American clerics."[190] That abortion and sexual deviance become the normative state of affairs and major modern sins, adultery, and fornication mostly class sins (with no Qur'anic or hadith quotes provided by the novelist about their sinfulness), as is corruption and exploitation, is more telling of the novelist's own agenda than the social reality he wants to depict. Here it seems that it is Taha who most deviates from the behavior of all other characters, which is why he must be killed. The colonial and postcolonial condition has rendered otherwise "normal" Taha the deviant while making deviance normative throughout. That Hatim is also killed is tragic not for him but for his killer, 'Abduh, whose murderous act while attempting to extricate himself from sexual deviance consolidates his social deviance further. Whatever ambivalence *The Ya'qubyan Building* has about Hatim, whom it allows to rebut common social arguments against "sexual deviance," it resolves at the end by killing him off and keeping Zaki alive.

The Ya'qubyan Building wants to register the effects of the aristocracy in postrepublican Egypt as well as the effect of degenerating foreigners, whether Christine, the French-speaking and French-singing Greek Egyptian owner of a restaurant bar called Maxim, the original Greek owner of Chez Nous, or the Armenian Ya'qubyan family who built and still owns the building, even though they live in Europe and have deputized an Egyptian native to attend to their business. The building survived the overthrow of the aristocratic monarchy and British colonialism, for whose comfort it was built, and it continues to frame the lives of its Egyptian residents despite the many metamorphoses it underwent. If the Ya'qubyan Building is indeed the modern Egyptian state, or even Egypt itself, designed by a foreign architect and owned by a foreigner who might have left after the revolution but continues to have agents to run the show for him (just as 'Aziz the Egyptian, known as the "Englishman," still runs Chez Nous), then perhaps all that is left to do is to destroy that building altogether (as well as Chez Nous), as all it contains today is the decadence and degeneracy of the *ancienne* aristocracy, as well as that of the republican nouveaux riches, the decadent and the degenerate deviants, and the misery of the poor Egyptians floating on the surface like oil refusing to mix with the water-building. While 'Abduh's mixing with Hatim destroyed both their lives, the wedding of Zaki and Buthayna is not a successful counterexample except at the individual level. That Buthayna ended up marrying Zaki did not bridge the gap, as their plan was to leave the country altogether, to France, and exit the Ya'qubyan Build-

190. Al-Aswani, *'Imarat Ya'qubyan*, 245.

ing. Indeed, the wedding took place in the foreign-owned cosmopolitan Maxim and not in Egyptian-owned national space.

Midaq Alley was a sort of last bastion against the march of colonial modernity, but the Ya'qubyan Building is its sturdy structure that nothing seems to shake. While familiar forms of life constituted some escape for Shaykh Darwish and Radwan al-Husayni, no such familiar forms of life remained possible in Ya'qubyan. Even 'Abduh, who insisted that an Upper Egyptian would always go back to the Upper Egyptian café in Cairo regardless of how far he ventures out (and in that he is not unlike 'Uways in al-Ghitani's *The Events of Za'farani Street*), he had nothing left to go back to except poverty and misery. Sharaf killed the Englishman for attempting to rape him and ended up becoming feminized and readied himself for his new reality as a catamite, and 'Abduh tried to bugger his catamite Hatim to death. Indeed, he "quenched" his desire in him three times violently, perhaps as a dress rehearsal, before he killed him and evicted him from life altogether.

Zaki, in contrast, was saved from degeneration and rescued by the youthful love of poor Buthayna, whom he seduced by his aristocratic manners and money. The deviant Hatim, however, could never use such attributes to rescue himself from the fate of death. In this, Hatim is like Tahiyya Kariyuka in the popular 1956 Egyptian film *Shabab Imra'ah* (The Youth of a Woman), directed by Salah Abu Sayf. The desirous middle-aged woman, who seduces a young Upper Egyptian university student who rented a room at a boarding house she owns, is killed off at the end of the film for her evil desire and designs, just as Hatim was.

The novel insists that nationalism, like colonialism, is just another oppressive system that resides in the Ya'qubyan Building. Even though he is most sympathetic to the Islamists, al-Aswani seems at times to discuss the corruption of Islamism as well, especially when he addresses how *hijab* clothing as fashion was another capitalist conspiracy marketed by shop owners. The book reaches an impasse at the end, describing Su'ad's defeat and expulsion from Ya'qubyan, Taha's death, 'Abduh's transformation into a criminal, Hatim's death, 'Azzam's subservience to the "BIG MAN," and Zaki and Buthayna's emigration. All that is left are the dying Dawlat, the degenerating aristocrat, and the degenerating foreigner Christine, as well as 'Azzam's sons who are as complicit with the corruption of the revolution as is their father; in addition to them, there exists "below street level" the decadent and degenerate passive sexual deviants on the prowl in Cairo's streets seeking to transform poor manly men into active sexual deviants. Those who escape the deviants' seduction would be sodomized by the police who rule the streets of Cairo and are paid off by the deviants.

The failure to imagine viable social/national reproduction is something that the novel not only describes but also shares. *The Ya'qubyan Building* appears to be caught somewhere between description and critique—the sexual deviant is a figure who represents degeneration but also appears as a kind of scapegoat for national failure, a stand-in for the combined forces of international capital and the comprador bourgeoisie, which the novel cannot represent directly in their full horror. The interests and values of Hatim, 'Abduh, Su'ad, Buthayna, and Taha are represented as inevitably competing in the failure of a state and economic system that cannot imagine allowing them equal protection. There is a kind of equality in death for some of them, but the sensationalism of the novel compromises the political critique it wants to offer.

This is made most explicit in the recent film version of *The Ya'qubyan Building,* released in 2006, wherein Hatim is represented as more consciously *affiliating* with the Gay International than in the novel. He insists to 'Abduh that "you think it is only you and me who are like this. Oh no, we are many. We are here, in Europe, in America, in the Gulf, all over the world." Indeed, upon reflecting on his "deviance" and blaming it on his parents' neglect, Hatim takes down their portraits and throws them out (an extranovelistic embellishment reminiscent of Ra'uf's destruction of his mother's portrait in *The Malatili Bathhouse*). In doing so, Hatim is ending his filiation, especially and specifically because he is now affiliated with a worldwide community of "deviants." Hatim is depicted in much more negative terms in the film version than he is in the novel, while 'Abduh is depicted as his passive victim who disappears after his son's death never to be heard from again. Upon discovering 'Abduh's departure, Hatim is devastated, but only momentarily. In contrast to the novel, Hatim proceeds with the dirty business of seducing other young men. He soon picks up a new trick, who turns out to be a criminal. It is not 'Abduh who kills Hatim as in the novel, rather it is the trick who kills and then robs Hatim without even having sex with him. While Hatim is killed off, the community with which he affiliated continues to thrive. The Egyptian nation, however, having failed its children (as Buthayna describes this failed filiation in the film version) comes undone.[191]

191. The film project was engulfed in a controversy regarding who would play the Hatim character. Famed actor Faruq al-Fishawi refused to play the role incurring the condemnation of the megastar 'Adil Imam (who plays the role of Zaki), who declared at a press conference that people are not going to "chase the actor down the street were he to play such a role." See Muhammad 'Abd al-Rahman, "Al-Mithliyyah al-Jinsiyyah wa al-Sinama al-Misriyyah" [Homosexuality and Egyptian Cinema], *Elaph,* online newspaper, 22 December 2004 (http://www.elaph.com). Khalid al-Sawi, a competent if less known actor, accepted the role. The film, directed by young director Marwan Ha-

In *Midaq Alley,* Mahfouz explored the inner life of Kirsha as a penetrative man who fancied young men. Although Waliy al-Din was the first to allow a penetrated man to explain the etiology of his "deviance" in his *The Malatili Bathhouse,* al-Aswani is the first Arab novelist to present a penetratee who fancied young men as a main protagonist, attempting to explore his inner life with depth albeit inconsistently (a deep exploration of al-'Afsah's inner life, in contrast with Mu'minah's, was absent in Wannus).[192] The only other medium through which a penetrated man spoke, as we saw earlier, was cinema and even then rarely.

mid, was released in February 2006 to European and American film festivals. The film has the largest budget of any film in the history of Egyptian cinema and was released in Egypt in June 2006.

192. In the same year al-Aswani's novel was published, Egyptian novelist Hamdi Abu Julayyil's novel *Lusus Mutaqa'idun* [Retired Thieves] (Cairo: Dar Mirit, 2002) included a character of a young man called Sayf, identified by his brothers and the whole neighborhood as an "effeminate or better yet a 'faggot' [khawal]," 29. To my knowledge, this is the second time that the word "khawal" is used in an Egyptian novel in reference to a man who practices passive same-sex contact. The first novelist who ever used it is Ibrahim 'Isa in his banned novel *Maqtal al-Rajul al-Kabir* [The Murder of the Big Man], wherein the fictional president (presumably of Egypt) and his prime minister discuss a change in the cabinet during which they want to decide who should become the new minister of culture. The president affirms that "these cultured folks need a decisive and tough minister [to control them]. They need a real man . . . just like the minister we have now. It is true that he is a faggot [khawal], but he is worth sixty men." The prime minister explains that he is nominating a major intellectual for the position. The president asks him: "Is he a faggot too?" Confused and hesitant, the prime minister asks: "Would your Excellency want him to be a faggot or not?" "Does it matter?" retorts the president. Finally, the president suggests that a decision be postponed in this matter "until we decide if we want him to be a faggot or not." See Ibrahim 'Isa, *Maqtal al-Rajul al-Kabir* [The Murder of the Big Man] (Cairo: n.p., 1999) 56–57. 'Isa, who is the editor-in-chief of the Egyptian opposition weekly *Al-Dustur,* began to serialize his banned novel in October 2005 (for the first episode, see *Al-Dustur,* "Maqtal al-Rajul al-Kabir," 5 October 2005, 7). In Abu Julayyil's novel, the married protagonist and Sayf (the "faggot") ultimately play a game wherein Sayf pretends that he is arranging for the protagonist and Zannubah, a female neighbor, to meet for sex, only for him to play the role of Zanubbah and visit his neighbor under the cover of night, ascertaining that the lights were turned off. The protagonist penetrates her/him from behind ("perhaps this is the ideal position for her," 106) knowing that it is Sayf and not Zanubbah. The two pretend that Sayf is only the facilitator of the pseudoheterosexual encounter and speak of their adventure as if it involves Zannubah and not the two of them (103–7). What is odd about the representation of Sayf is that while most men who practice passive same-sex contact are normally married and practice (and are expected to practice) their heterosexual conjugal duties, the novelist marvels at how Sayf's bride (he was married off after being released from a psychiatric hospital) got pregnant: "But from whom?" (88). Unlike in al-Aswani's novel, Sayf is neither a stereotype nor an allegory but an individual character among a panoply of others. The only precedent to al-Aswani is perhaps Lebanese Huda Barakat's *Hajar al-Dahiq* [The Stone of Laughter], whose protagonist, Khalil, is tormented by his desires for men—desires that he never consummates. Khalil interestingly seems to inhabit the Western stereotype of the misogynist homosexual whose hatred of women and adoration of men, masculinity (despite his horror at masculine violence manifesting in the Lebanese civil war), and narcissism are most apparent throughout the novel. Khalil is so misogynistic that at the end of the novel, after much torment and alienation from the violence of the Lebanese civil war, in which he persistently refused to participate, succumbs to the very masculinity that attracted and repelled him all along by joining its ranks. His last act in the novel is to rape his female neighbor, which registers his break with the female novelist on the last page of the novel where she also registers her loss of control over him and ends her novel. See Huda Barakat, *Hajar al-Dahiq* (London: Riyad al-Rayyis, 1990), 250. It is never made entirely clear in the novel if Khalil wants to penetrate men or be penetrated by

While representation of same-sex contact and effeminate men, read as "deviants," can be found in many Arab films since the 1960s and in a number of cases earlier,[193] there is only one other film beside *The Malatili Bathhouse* in which male characters explain why they desire to be penetrated by other men. This more recent Egyptian film, *Dayl al-Samakah* (The Tail of the Fish), directed by Samir Sayf and released in 2003, tells the story of a young man who obtains a job as the electric company meter man. His job takes him to poor and rich neighborhoods, entering households to check the electric meters and encountering people from all walks of life. In one such encounter in an upper-class area of Cairo, the young man, named Ahmad and played by 'Amr Wakid, goes into the posh condominium of an elderly man dressed in his *robe de chambre* without trousers. The man had just been disappointed by a sexual companion who could not come to see him despite his pleading with him on the telephone. When Ahmad comes into the apartment, the elderly man invites him to a lavish lunch, already prepared by the cook. He also gives him a Viagra pill, telling him it was a vitamin pill that would provide him with much energy during his physically taxing daily routine. Feeling energized and erect, Ahmad asks whether the pill has

---

them or both. For the English edition, see Hoda Barakat, *The Stone of Laughter*, translated by Sophie Bennett (New York: Interlink Books, 1995). The latest novel addressing questions homosexual is Omani Hasan al-Lawati's first novel *Al-Bahth 'an al-Dhat* [The Search for the Self]. Al-Lawati's novel addresses itself to the question of homosexuality, which it refers to intermittently as *mithliyyah* and *shudhudh* (deviance). Written as an internal monologue of the protagonist Tahir (the pure one) over eight "journeys," which is how the chapter headings are titled, the novel presents Tahir as torn by guilt and repentance toward God and religion for acting out on his sexual desires for men, whom he mostly meets through the Internet. The novel quickly shifts to the effect that a friend of the protagonist, Basil (the brave one), would have on Tahir. Basil, also torn by his same-sex desires, leaves his Arab homeland to an unidentified English-speaking Western country to escape his life's contradictions and seeks to help people in need through the mechanism of a philanthropic non-governmental organization (something Westerners stereotypically do but not Arabs!). His search for his *self* leads him to realize that the contradictions he felt at home persisted in exile where he met Western gay men and that the only solution to the dilemma of his desires is to return home and resume his journey on the path of God. The novel presents homosexual desire as either a learned behavior/medical condition, which men can choose to act out on, repress or seek medical treatment for (a view identified by the novelist with Islamic teachings), or a congenital condition with which one is born and over which one exercises little choice (identified as Western medical opinion). The protagonist wishes that this latter "Western ideology not impose itself on our societies lest we fall in the very same trap [in which it fell] and render permissible what God has prohibited" (53). Confused and unsure of itself just like its protagonists, the novel, although sympathetic to the suffering of its characters, rests at the end of its journeys on pushing what it identifies as the religious solution of self-denial. The novel is clear that the "purity of life derives from the purity of souls, and that the decadence of a people begins with the decadence of their souls" (117). See Hasan al-Lawati, *Al-Bahth 'an al-Dhat* (Amman: Dar al-Azminah, 2004).

193. For a discussion of homoerotics in the films of Egyptian director Youssef Chahine, see Joseph Massad, "Art and Politics in the Cinema of Youssef Chahine," *Journal of Palestine Studies* 110 (Winter 1999): 77–93.

side effects. The elderly man assures him that it does not and becomes increasingly pushy. He exposes his chest and legs and places his hand on Ahmad's thigh, close to his crotch. Realizing what was happening, Ahmad asks him to cut to the chase. The man explains that they should go to the bedroom and enjoy themselves. When Ahmad says, "What if I say no," he is surprised by the answer he gets. The elderly man explains that it has to be with Ahmad's consent and based on mutual pleasure, otherwise it would be rape. Ahmad refuses the offer calmly and gets up to leave. It is then that the elderly man feels the need to explain himself. He declares with broken pride that he is a respectable man. Ahmad responds that he had "no authority" over him and that this is "your [own personal] freedom." The elderly man commends Ahmad for being such a "civilized man" and proceeds to ask him if he had had a choice about what his name was, who his family was, what kind of a job he had. When Ahmad answers in the negative, the elderly man explains that it is the same for him: "I did not choose to be like this. Do you understand?" Ahmad nods and leaves.

Unlike *The Malatili Bathhouse* and *The Ya'qubyan Building*, *The Tail of the Fish* presents the elderly man as a slice of life in contemporary Cairo that is (must be?) tolerated. It can do so by deploying liberal notions of personal freedom as a civilizational value but with a twist. If liberalism calls for the tolerance of personal choice, the liberalism that *The Tail of the Fish* deploys is that of tolerating that which is *not* chosen. Unlike *The Malatili Bathhouse* and *The Ya'qubyan Building* (and *The Events of Za'farani Street*), *The Tail of the Fish* presents a missed sexual encounter and a failed seduction. Like them, however, it represents the homosexual encounter as class- and age-differentiated, with the passive partner being the older richer man, and the active partner, the poorer younger man. The penetratee is invariably ashamed of what he does, or, more accurately, of what he lets other men do to him, and must provide explanations and justifications, if not apologies. Such representation is an inversion of stereotypical representations of same-sex encounters, whether in classical or Ottoman Arab history or in Classical Greece as well as a departure from Mahfouz's representation of Kirsha in *Midaq Alley* and of al-Samman's representation of Nishan, neither of whom ever expresses shame or feels the need to provide justification.

The new modern Arab subject that modern Arabic literature imagines is a proper, middle-class, heterosexual, enlightened citizen, but what much of modern Arabic literature records is the failure of the emergence of this modern subject as a result of colonial and postcolonial nationalist violence and more recently, since the late 1980s, that of globalization and Islamism, which become the running theme of these writings. Ultimately, then what is being recorded is the failure of the emergence of the modern Arab male subject, who has remained in gestation for far too long, and his replacement with the deviant and decadent. It is this state of affairs that these writings record and lament simultaneously. Indeed, in 1970, the passive homosexual was introduced in *Hammam al-Malatili* as one of many marks of decadence and degeneration; in the present moment, however, the major mark of this state of decadence and degeneration *has become* the emergence of a community of "passive deviants" that meets in colonial establishments, like Chez Nous, conveniently located below street level. While al-Aswani and the Gay International want to out this new affiliative "community" as a degenerate or oppressed community, respectively, they both endow its practices with a social Darwinist narrative of progress and degeneration.

Conclusion

In the era before the Gay International, academic and scholarly debates among Arab intellectuals analyzed the past and less often the present. They were followed by highly charged interventions of the secular and Islamist varieties in the post–Gay International period, which pushed an agenda of what should or should not exist in contemporary society as well as in past history. In contrast, recent literature—in the formal sense of fictional aesthetic writing—has sought to represent and allegorize desire and has done so mostly without making truth claims, although, on occasion, it would offer sermons on the matter. What this literature registers, intentionally and unintentionally, are not only the views of an author but also the dominant views in society, which is precisely what makes a work of fiction intelligible. The fiction we surveyed is in direct dialogue with other realms of writing. Ra'if Khuri's rewriting of the past, for example, is not unlike Jurji Zaydan before him or Salah al-Din al-Munajjid after him; and Sunʿallah Ibrahim's, Jamal al-Ghitani's, and Hanan al-Shaykh's writings are also conversant with nonfictional writings such as the Islamist concern about deviance coming from the West or some of the Marxist Arab writers, like Yasin al-Hafiz, who criticize the influence of Arab Gulf oil money on cultural production and sexual mores in the rest of the Arab world. Other examples abound. Saʿdallah Wannus's play inhabits the same discursive field as Ibrahim Mahmud's works and that of the Gay International more generally even though many of the play's undiscerning critics failed to make the connection. This also applies to ʿAlaʾ al-Aswani's novel. It is this dialogue that makes these novels, stories, and plays familiar and popular, anchoring them in a hegemonic cultural idiom, which they in turn help to anchor.

This dialogue, however, does not necessarily replicate the same arguments or the same format extant in nonfictional writing. What it does is make arguments and present pretexts that are congruent with the larger debate enveloping society. Naguib Mahfouz's novels are perhaps best at reflecting these debates in a most undidactic form—this is especially the case as he takes the novel form seriously as an aesthetic product. A few novelists have tried to employ the novel form as a medium for ideological posturing of the most parochial variety. What is most interesting, however, for our purposes is how literature has become in the twentieth-century Arab world a central (if not necessarily the most popular) forum through which matters of sexual desire and its connections to civilization and its antonyms are negotiated and how matters political and economic are allegorized through appeals to the sexual and to the realm of desires. What is revealed in this undertaking is precisely what we saw in other realms of writing—namely that cultural production as a whole has been marshaled, consciously and unconsciously, toward a teleological end that accords with nineteenth- and twentieth-century European Orientalist ideas of shaming non-Europe into assimilation. This is most obvious in the preoccupation with the figure of the medieval *majin*, or bawdy person, by intellectual and literary historians from the 1890s to the 1950s (in reaction to Orientalist representations) and his transformation into the pathological figure of the deviant (in full concordance with prevailing Western psychiatric and sociological categories), which was fully consolidated in the 1950s (although glimmers of that transformation are evident in the 1940s) in the novel as well as in multiple genres of writing. In the post-1980s period to the present, we are witnessing the rendering of the deviant into not only a scholarly and literary concern as before but also as a major public and policy concern for the Islamists and for the Gay International at large, and increasingly, and as a result, for the state and its instruments of repression *and* production. This is unfolding, as we saw in chapter 3, as an effect of the serious ongoing attempts by the Gay International and their adherents to impose their own sexual taxonomy and transform the medically and sociologically marginal figure of the "deviant" (itself a European invention) into the "homosexual" (mithli), a juridical subject endowed with legal rights (another more recent European invention), and then posit the existence of homosexuality as a communitarian societal group category.

The novel and other forms of literary writing, despite much evident resistance to hegemonic views contained within them, have been central to this assimilationist project of rewriting not only the Arab past but also the Arab present in accordance with European concepts of civilization and culture, with the goal of demonstrating that desiring Arabs are no different from desiring Europeans—except that many Europeans seem to resist this evident similarity. The struggle of modern Arabs, as far as the archive we surveyed indicates, is to prove to all Arabs and all Europeans that Arabs (or at least those among them not inhabiting the Gulf) are just like Europeans in civilizational and cultural terms, even though Europeans insist on treating Arabs as lesser than they. The fact that this message is informed by a European epistemology and taxonomy of civilizations and cultures and is contained in aesthetic forms that are thoroughly European is a demonstration of how deep this assimilationist impulse reaches within modern Arab cultural production. Yet given the messiness of fiction—its engagement with the idiosyncratic and the subjective—it is not necessarily *only* ideological. While sex between men is a powerful allegory of national decline in *The Ya'qubyan Building* and can be seen as a powerful argument for the last gasp of local resistance to the imposed subjectifying and sexual norms of colonial power in *Midaq Alley,* there may be something excessive in representations of sexual desire which inevitably elicits a new incitement to discourse. This incitement however need not take the forms deployed by Islamism and the Gay International, and its object need not only be sex and desire. Perhaps another discourse that takes for its object the very incitement to discourse about sexual identities and practices *can* invoke older forms, identities, and practices in the service of a future that is *not just* social reproduction or degeneration.

Desiring Arabs opens up an archive for such a project. In creating and constituting this archive, I have not merely been interested in recording important debates and representations in modern Arab intellectual history, but also in gesturing towards their importance for an undetermined future yet to come, indeed to resist the attempts by a number of forces to *determine and script* that future a priori. I understand, in line with Jacques Derrida, that the act of archiving "produces as much as it records the event," and that it "determines the structure of the *archivable* content in its very coming into existence and in its relationship to the future."[1] As the debates I reproduced in this book were repressed,

---

1. Jacques Derrida, *Archive Fever: A Freudian Impression* (Chicago: University of Chicago Press, 1996), 17.

in the psychoanalytic sense, bringing them back to consciousness can check the forces of current and future repression. There is, as we have seen, a rich and spectacularly diverse (in terms of ideology, genre, and intellectual discipline) literature on sex produced in the Arab world in the twentieth century. It is true that much of it is compromised by an unavoidable engagement with Western imperial endeavors from Orientalism to the ostensibly "benign" ethnocentrism of human rights. Close attention to these works, however, confounds the repressed/licentious binary imposed on the sexual desires and practices of Arabs (dubbed "Arab sexuality") by the spectrum of Western commentators. While Arab intellectuals, following Orientalism and the colonial encounter, came to perceive the existence of the Arabs principally in terms of civilization and culture, there emerges in the literature they produced an elaboration and an occasional contestation of the place of sexual desires in wider discourses and practices of modernity. It is at these rarer moments when the imposition and seduction of Western norms fail that the possibility of different conceptions of desires, politics, and subjectivities emerges. My hope is that the critique that *Desiring Arabs* offers marks an instance of that possibility.

Works Cited

Arabic-Language Works

'Abd al-'Aziz, Muhammad Kamal. *Limadha Harram Allah Hadhih al-Ashya'? Lahm al-Khanzir, al-Maytah, al-Damm, al-Zina, al-Liwat, al-Shudhudh al-Jinsi, al-Khamr, Nazrah Tibiyyah fi al-Muharramat al-Qur'aniyyah* [Why Has God Prohibited These Things?]. Cairo: Maktabat al-Qur'an, 1987.

'Abd al-Ghani, Mustafa. *Al-Mufakkir wa al-Amir: Taha Husayn wa al-Sultah fi Misr, 1919-1973* [The Thinker and the Prince: Taha Husayn and Political Authority in Egypt, 1919-1973]. Cairo-Al-Hay'ah al-Misriyyah al-'Ammah lil-Kitab, 1997.

'Abd al-Majid, Ibrahim. *Al-Baldah al-Ukhra* [The Other Town]. London: Riyad al-Rayyis lil-Kutub wa al-Nashr, 1991.

————. *Bayt Al-Yasamin* [The House of Jasmine]. Cairo: Dar wa Matabi' Al-Mustaqbal, 1992.

'Abd al-Quddus, Ihsan. *Ana Hurrah* [I Am Free]. Cairo: Dar Ruz al-Yusuf, 1957.

'Abd al-Raziq, 'Ali. *Al-Islam wa-Usul al-Hukm: Bahth fi al-Khilafah wa al-Hukumah* [Islam and the Bases of Governance: An Inquiry into Succession and Government in Islam]. Cairo: Matba'at Misr, 1925.

'Abduh, Muhammad. *Al-A'mal al-Kamilah lil-Imam Muhmmad 'Abduh* [The Complete Works of Imam Muhammad 'Abduh]. Edited and collected by Muhammad 'Imarah. Beirut: al-Mu'assassah al-'Arabiyyah lil-Dirasat wa al-Nashr, 1972-74.

'Abdullah, Yahya al-Tahir. *Al-Kitabat al-Kamilah* [Collected Works]. Cairo: Dar al-Mustaqbal al-'Arabi, 1994.

Abi Hiffan, 'Abdullah bin Ahmad bin Harb al-Mihzami. *Akhbar Abi Nuwas* [The News of Abu Nuwas]. Edited by 'Abd al-Sattar Ahmad Farraj. Cairo: Maktabat Misr, 1957?

Abu Fakhr, Saqr. "Al-Jins ʿind al-ʿArab" [Sex among the Arabs]. *Al-Hayah al-Jadidah (Beirut)* 5 (1981). Republished in Manshurat al-Jamal, *Al-Jins ʿind al-ʿArab* [Sex among the Arabs], 39–64. Cologne: Manshurat al-Jamal, 1991.

Abu Nuwas, al-Hasan bin Haniʾ. *Diwan Abu Nuwas* [The Collected Poetry of Abu Nuwas]. Cairo: Iskandar Asaf, Al-Matbaʿah al-ʿUmumiyyah bi-Misr, 1898.

———. *Al-Fukahah wa al-Iʾtinas fi Mujun Abi Nuwas wa baʿd Naqaʾidih maʿ al-Shuʿaraʾ* [Humor and Sociability in the Bawdiness of Abu Nuwas]. Edited by Mansur ʿAbd al-Mutaʿali and Husayn Ashraf. Cairo: A.H. 1316 [A.D.1898].

———. *Abu Nuwas, al-Nusus al-Muharramah* [Abu Nuwas: The Forbidden Texts]. London: Riyad al-Rayyis, 1994.

Abu Julayyil, Hamdi. *Lusus Mutaqaʿidun* [Retired Thieves]. Cairo: Dar Mirit, 2002.

Al-ʿAdawi, Muhammad Quttah, editor. *Alf Laylah wa Laylah* [A Thousand and One Nights]. Facimile edition of the Bulaq edition published in Cairo in A.H. 1252 (A.D. 1836). Beirut: Dar Sadir, n.d.

Al-ʿAdnani, Al-Khatib. *Al-Zina wa al-Shudhudh fi al-Tarikh al-ʿArabi* [Adultery/Fornication and Deviance in Arab History]. Beirut: Muʾassassat al-Intishar al-ʿArabi, 1999.

Adunis. *Muqaddimah lil-Shiʿr al-ʿArabi* [Introduction to Arab Poetry]. Beirut: Dar al-ʿAwda, 1983.

Al-Afghani, Jamal al-Din. *Al-Radd ʿala al-Dahriyyin* [Response to the Materialists]. Translated from the Persian by Muhammad ʿAbduh. Cairo: Al-Salam al-ʿAlamiyyah lil-Tabʿ wa al-Nashr wa al-Tawziʿ, 1983.

Alf Laylah wa Laylah [A Thousand and One Nights]. Cairo: al-Matbaʿah al-Saʿidiyya wa Maktabatuha, A.H. 1348 [A.D. 1930].

ʿAllush, Jamil. *ʿUmar Abu Rishah, Hayatuh wa Shiʿruh maʿ Nusus Mukhtarah* [ʿUmar Abu Rishah: His Life and Poetry, including Selected Texts]. Beirut: Al-Ruwwad, 1994.

ʿAlqam, Sabhah Ahmad. *Al-Masrah al-Siyasi ʿind Saʿdallah Wannus* [The Political Theater of Saʿdallah Wannus]. Amman: Wizarat al-Thaqafah, 2001.

ʿAmil, Mahdi. *Azmat al-Hadarah al-ʿArabiyyah Am Azmat al-Burjuwaziyyat al-ʿArabiyyah* [The Crisis of Arab Civilization; or, The Crisis of the Arab Bourgeoisies]. Beirut: Dar al-Farabi, 1985.

Al-ʿAmili, Muhsin al-Amin al-Husayni. *Abu Nuwas, al-Hasan bin Haniʾ al-Hikami al-Sha ʿir al-Mashhur* [Abu Nuwas: The Renowned Poet]. Damascus: Matbaʿat al-Itqan, 1947.

Amin, Ahmad. *Duha al-Islam* [The Forenoon of Islam]. Cairo: Matbaʿat Lajnat al-Taʾlif wa al-Tarjamah wa al-Nashr, 1933.

———. *Zuhr al-Islam* [The Noon of Islam]. Cairo: Matbaʿat Lajnat al-Taʾlif wa al-Tarjamah wa al-Nashr, 1945.

———. *Hayati* [My Life]. Cairo: Lajnat al-Taʾlif wa al-Tarjamah wa al-Nashr, 1950.

Al-Amin, Muhsin. *Aʿyan al-Shiʿah* [Shiite Notables]. Beirut: Matbaʿat al-Itqan, 1956.

Amin, Qasim. *Tahrir al-Mar'ah* [The Liberation of Women]. In *Qasim Amin, al-A'mal al-Kamilah,* edited by Muhammad 'Imarah. 1899. Cairo: Dar al-Shuruq, 1989.

'Ammar, 'Abbas Mustafa. *Abu Nuwas, Hayatuh wa Shi'ruh* [Abu Nuwas: His Life and Poetry]. Cairo: Matba 'at Wadi al-Muluk, 1929–1930.

Al-'Ani, Suhayl al-Sayyid Najm. *Hukm al-Muqsitin 'ala Kitab Wu''az al-Salatin* [The Judgment of the Just of *The Sultans' Preachers*]. Baghdad: Matba'at al-'Ani, 1954.

Al-Antaki, Dawud. *Tazyin al-Aswaq fi Akhbar al-'Ushshaq* [Decorating Markets with the News of Lovers]. Beirut: Dar wa Maktabat al-Hilal, 1994.

Al-'Aqqad, 'Abbas Mahmud. *Abu Nuwas, al-Hasan Bin Hani', Dirasah fi al-Tahlil al-Nafsani wa al-Naqd al-Tarikhi* [A Study in Psychoanalysis and Historical Criticism]. Cairo: Kitab al-Hilal, 1960.

'Aridah, Nasib. "Qissat Dik al-Jinn al-Himsi, Hikayat Gharam Sha'ir 'Arabi Qadim" [The Story of Dik al-Jinn al-Himsi: A Love Story of an Ancient Arab Poet]. In *Majmu'at al-Rabitah al-Qalamiyyah li-Sanat 1921* [The Collection of the Association of the Pen for the Year 1921], 117–151. Beirut: Dar Sadir, 1964.

Arsalan, Shakib. *Limadha Ta'akhkhara al-Muslimun wa Limadha Taqaddama Ghayruhum* [Why Were the Arabs Delayed and Why Did Others Advance]. Beirut: Al-Hayat, 1975.

Al-Asfahani, Abu Faraj 'Ali bin al-Husayn. *Al-Qiyan* [The Singing Girls]. Edited by Jalal 'Atiyyah. London: Riyad al-Rayyis lil-Kutub wa al-Nashr, 1989.

———. *Kitab al-Aghani* [The Book of Songs]. Edited by Ihsan 'Abbas, Ibrahim al-Sa'afin, and Bakr 'Abbas. Beirut: Dar Sadir, 2002.

Al-'Askari, Murtada. *Ma' al-Duktur al-Wardi fi Kitabihi Wu' 'az al-Salatin* [With Dr. al-Wardi in His Book *The Sultans' Preachers*]. Qum: Kulliyat Usul al-Din, 1997.

Al-Aswani, 'Ala'. *'Imarat Ya'qubyan* [The Ya'qubyan Building]. Cairo: Mirit Lil-Nashr wa al-Ma'lumat, 2002.

———. *'Imarat Ya'qubyan.* Fourth edition. Cairo: Maktabat Madbuli, 2004.

Al-'Atiyyah, Jalal. "Muqadimmat al-Tahqiq" [Introduction], to Muhammad bin Ahmad al-Tijani, *Tuhfat al-'Arus wa Mut'at al-Nufus.* London: Riyad al-Rayyis lil-Kutub wa al-Nashr, 1992.

Al-Azhari, Muhammad ibn Ahmad. *Tahdhib al-Lughah.* Edited by 'Abd al-Karim al-Gharbawi and Muhammad 'Ali al-Najjar. Cairo: al-Dar al-Misriyyah lil-Ta'lif wa al-Tarjamah, 1964.

al-'Azm, Sadiq Jalal. *Fi al-Hubb wa al-Hubb al-'Udhri* [On Love and on Virginal Love]. Beirut: Manshurat Nizar Qabbani, 1968.

Al-'Azmah, 'Aziz. *Al-Asalah Aw Siyasat al-Hurub min al-Waqi'* [Authenticity or the Politics of Flight from Reality]. Beirut: Dar al-Saqi, 1992.

———. "Al-Turath wa al-'Awlamah" [Heritage and Globalization]. In *Dunya al-Din fi Hadir al-'Arab* [The World of Religion in the Present of the Arabs]. Beirut: Dar al-Tali'ah, 1996.

Ba'labaki, Layla. *Ana Ahya* [I Live]. Beirut: al-Maktab al-Tijari, 1958.

Al-Baghdadi, al-Khatib. *Tarikh Baghdad* [History of Baghdad]. Beirut: Dar al-Kitab al-'Arabi, 1966.

Bakkar, Yusuf Husayn. *Ittijahat al-Ghazal fi al-Qarn al-Thani al-Hijri* [The Directions of Love Poetry in the Second Century A.H.]. Cairo: Dar al-Ma'arif bi-Misr, 1971.

Barakat, Huda. *Hajar al-Dahiq*. London: Riyad al-Rayyis, 1990.

Al-Barr, Muhammad. 'Ali, *Al-Amrad al-Jinisyyah: Asbabuha wa 'Ilajuha* [Venereal Diseases: Its Causes and Treatment]. Jiddah: Dar al-Manarah, 1986.

Al-Barudi, Fakhri. *Mudhakkarat al-Barudi, Sittun Sannah Tatakallam*. Part 1. Beirut and Damascus: Dar al-Hayat, 1951.

———. *Mudhakkarat al-Barudi, Sittun Sannah Tatakallam* [The Memoir of al-Barudi: Sixty Years Speak]. Volume 2. Damascus: n.p., 1952.

Basha, Ahmad Taymur. *Al-Hubb 'ind al-'Arab* [Love among the Arabs]. Cairo: Dar al-Afaq al-'Arabiyyah, 2000.

Al-Bisati, Muhammad. *Wa Ya'ti al-Qitar* [And the Train Comes]. Cairo: Dar Al-Hilal, 1999.

Brukilman, Karl. *Tarikh al-Adab al-'Arabi* [History of Arabic Literature]. Ten volumes. Cairo: al-Hay'ah al-Misriyyah lil-Kitab, 1993.

Bu Hudaybah, 'Abd al-Wahhab. *Al-Islam wa al-Jins*. Translated by Halah al-'Uri. Cairo: Maktabat Madbuli, 1986.

———. *Al-Islam wa al-Jins*. Translated by Halah al-'Uri. Beirut: Riyad al-Rayyis lil-Kutub wa al-Nashr, 2001.

Al-Bustani, Butrus, *Da'irat al-Ma'arif, Encyclopedie Arabe, wa huwa qamus 'am li-kul fann wa matlab* [The Compendium of Knowledges: Arab Encycloped, Which Is a General Dictionary of Every Art and Question]. Beirut: Matba'at al-Ma'arif, 1877.

———. *Muhit al-Muhit, Qamus Mutawwal Lil-Lughah al-'Arabiyyah*. Beirut: Maktabat Lubnan Nashirun, 1987.

———. "Khitab fi Ta'lim al-Nisa'" [A Speech on the Education of Women, 1852]. Reproduced in Majid Fakhri, *Al-Harakat al-Fikriyyah wa Ruwwaduha al-Lubnaniyyun fi 'Asr al-Nahdah, 1800–1922* [The Intellectual Movements and Their Lebanese Pioneers in the Age of the Renaissance, 1800–1922], 183–197. Beirut: Dar al-Nahar Lil-Nashr, 1992.

———. "Khutbah fi Adab al-'Arab" [A Speech on the Literature of the Arabs]. Beirut, 1859. Reproduced in Majid Fakhri, *Al-Harakat al-Fikriyyah wa Ruwwaduha al-Lubnaniyyun fi 'Asr al-Nahdah, 1800–1922* [The Intellectual Movements and Their Lebanese Pioneers in the Age of the Renaissance, 1800–1922], 155–181. Beirut: Dar al-Nahar Lil-Nashr, 1992.

Al-Bustani, Butrus. *Udaba' al-'Arab fi al-A'sur al-'Abasiyyah, hayatuhum, atharuhum, naqd atharihim* [Arabic Belletrists in the Abbasid Epochs: Their Lives, Their Work, and Criticism of Their Work]. Third edition. Beirut: Maktabat Sadir, 1947.

Dayf, Shawqi. "Taqdim al-Kitab" [Introduction to the book]. In Jurji Zaydan, *Tarikh Adab al-Lughah al-'Arabiyyah*. Volume 1. Cairo: Dar al-Hilal, 1956.

———. *Al-ʿAsr al-ʿAbbasi al-Awwal* [The First Abbasid Era]. Cairo: Dar al-Maʿarif 1966.

Ibn Durayd, Abu Bakr Muhammad bin al-Hasan. *Al-Ishtiqaq* [Etymology]. Edited by ʿAbd al-Salam Muhammad Harun. Cairo: Muʾassassat al-Khanji, 1958.

Fakhri, Majid. *Al-Harakat al-Fikriyyah wa Ruwwaduha al-Lubnaniyyun fi ʿAsr al-Nahdah, 1800–1922* [The Intellectual Movements and Their Lebanese Pioneers in the Age of the Renaissance, 1800–1922]. Beirut: Dar al-Nahar Lil-Nashr, 1992.

Farid, Mahmud Kamil, editor. *Diwan Abi Nuwas, Tarikhuh, Raʾy al-Shuʿaraʾ fih, Nawadiruh, Shiʿruh* [The Collected Poetry of Abu Nuwas: His History, Poets' Evaluation of Him, His Anecdotes, and His Poetry]. Cairo: Al-Maktabah al-Tijariyyah al-Kubra, 1937.

Farrukh, ʿUmar. *Abu Nuwas, Shaʿir Harun al-Rashid wa Muhammad al-Amin, Al-Qism al-Awwal, Dirasah wa Naqd* [Abu Nuwas: The Poet of Harun al-Rashid and al-Amin]. Beirut: Maktabat al-Kashshaf, 1932.

———. *ʿAbu Nuwas, Shaʿir Harun al-Rashid wa Muhammad al-Amin* [Abu Nuwas: The Poet of Harun al-Rashid and al-Amin]. Revised edition. Beirut: Dar al-Kitab al-ʿArabi, 1988.

Fawzi, Ibrahim. *Tadwin al-Sunnah* [Recording Sunnah]. London: Riyad-Rayyis lil-Kutub wa-al-Nashr, 1994.

Al-Fayruzabadi, Muhammad bin Yaʿqub. *Al-Qamus Al-Muhit*. Beirut: Dar Ihyaʾ al-Turath al-ʿArabi, 1997.

Fayyad, Muna. *Fakhkh al-Jasad, Tajalliyyat, Nazawat, wa Asrar* [The Body Trap: Transfigurations, Caprices, and Secrets]. Beirut: Riyad al-Rayyis lil-Kutub wa al-Nashr, 2000).

Fruyd, Sighmund. *Tafsir al-Ahlam*. Translated by Mustafa Safwan. Cairo: Dar al-Maʿarif Bi Misr, 1969.

———. *Thalathat Mabahith Fi Nazariyyat al-Jins*. Translated by Jurj Tarabishi. Beirut: Dar al-Taliʿah, 1981.

Fuku, Mishil. *Iradat al-Maʿrifah, Al-Juzʾ al-Awwal min Tarikh al-Jinsaniyya*. Edited and translated by Mutaʿ Safadi and Jurj Abi Salih. Beirut: Markaz al-Inmaʾ al-Qawmi, 1990.

Al-Ghadhdhami, ʿAbdallah Muhammad. *Al-Marʾah wa al-Lughah 2, Thaqafat al-Wahm, Muqarabat hawl al-Marʾah wa al-Jasad wa al-Lughah* [The Culture of Illusion: Approaches to Women, the Body, and Language]. Beirut: Al-Markaz al-Thaqafi al-ʿArabi, 2002.

Al-Ghamri al-Wasiti, Shams al-din Muhammad bin ʿUmar. *Al-Hukm al-Madbut fi Tahrim Fiʾl Qawm Lut* [The Exact Ruling in the Prohibition of the Act of the People of Lot]. Edited by ʿUbayd Allah al-Misri al-Athari. Tanta: Dar al-Sahabah lil-Turath, 1988.

Al-Ghitani, Jamal. *Waqaʾiʿ Harat al-Zaʿfarani* [The Events of Zaʿfarani Street]. Baghdad: Dar al-Shuʾun al-Thaqafiyyah al-ʿAmah, 1987.

———. *Risalat al-Basaʾir fi al-Masaʾir* [The Treatise of Insights into Fates]. Cairo: Dar al-Hilal, 1989.

Ghurayyib, Jurj. *Dik al-Jinn al-Himsi*. Beirut: Dar al-Thaqafah, 1983.

Hafiz, Sabri. "Al-Bunyah al-Nassiyyah li-Sirat al-Taharrur min al-Qahr" [The Textual Structure of a Biography of Liberation from Oppression]. Addendum to Shukri, *Al-Shuttar*, 219–242. Beirut: Dar al-Saqi, 1992.

Al-Hafiz, Yasin, *Al-Hazimah wa al-Aydiyulujiyyah al-Mahzumah* [Defeat and the Defeated Ideology]. Beirut: Maʿhad al-Inmaʾ al-ʿArabi, 1990.

Al-Haj, Faʾiz Muhammad ʿAli. *Al-Inhirafat al-Jinsiyyah wa Amraduha* [Sexual Perversions and Their Diseases]. Beirut: Al-Maktab al-Islami, 1983.

Al-Hajji, Mazhar, editor. *Diwan Dik al-Jinn al-Himsi*. Damascus: Wizarat al-Thaqafah, 1987.

———. *Dik al-Jinn al-Himsi, Dirasah fi Mukawwinat al-Shaʿir wa Madamin Shiʿrihi* [Dik al-Jinn al-Himsi: A Study of the Poet's Formation and the Content of His Poetry]. Damascuss: Tlas lil-Dirasat wa al-Tarjamah wa al-Nashr, 1989.

Hajlah, Shihab al-Din Ahmad ibn. *Diwan al-Sababah*. Beirut: Dar wa Maktabat al-Hilal, 1984.

Halabuni, Khalid. *Dik al-Jinn, al-Dhatiyyah wa al-Ibdaʿ* [Dik al-Jinn: Selfness and Creativity]. Damascus: Al-Yamamah, 2001.

Halasa, Ghalib. *Al-Khamasin* [Khamasin Winds]. Beirut: Dar ibn Rushd lil-Tibaʿah wa al-Nashr, 1978.

———. *Al-ʿAlam, Maddah wa Harakah, Dirasat fi al-Falsafah al-ʿArabiyyah al-Islamiyyah* [The World, Matter and Movement: Studies in Arab-Islamic Philosophy]. Beirut: Dar al-Kalimah, 1984.

———. "Buʾs al-ʿAql al-Nahdawi" [The Poverty of Renaissance Reason]. In Ghalib Halasa, *al-Haribun min al-Hurriyyah* [Fugitives from Freedom], 205–225. Damascus: Dar al-Mada, 2001.

Hamzah, ʿAli ʿAbd al-Halim. *Al-Qamus al-Jinsi ʿind al-ʿArab* [The Sexual Dictionary of the Arabs]. Beirut: Riyad al-Rayyis lil-Kutub wa al-Nashr, 2002.

Haqqi, Yahya. *Kaʾanna*. In *Al-Firash al-Shaghir wa Qisas Ukhra* [The Empty Bed and Other Stories], vol. 19 of *Muʾallafat Yahya Haqqi* [The Collected Works of Yahya Haqqi], edited by Fuʾad Dawarrah, 275–306. Cairo: Al-Hayʾah al-Misriyyah al-ʿAmmah lil-Kitab, 1986.

Harb, ʿAli. *Mudakhalat, Mabahith Naqdiyyah Hawl Aʿmal: Muhammad ʿAbid al-Jabiri, Husayn Muruwwah, Hisham Juʿayt, ʿAbd al-Salam bin ʿAbid al-ʿAli, Saʿid bin Saʿid* [Interventions: Critical Studies on the World of Muhammad ʿAbid al-Jabiri, Husayn Muruwwah, Hisham Juʿayt, ʿAbd al-Salam bin ʿAbid al-ʿAli, Saʿid bin Saʿid]. Beirut: Dar al-Hadathah, 1985.

———. *Al-Hubb wa al-Fanaʾ, Taʾammulat fi al-Marʾah wa al-ʿIshq wa al-Wujud* [Love and Evanescence: Meditations on Women, Erotic Love, and Existence]. Beirut: Dar al-Manahil, 1990.

Harun, ʿAbd al-Salam Muhammad, editor. *Rasaʾil al-Jahiz* [The Treatises of al-Jahiz]. Beirut: Dar al-Jil, 1991.

Himmish, Bin Salim. *Majnun al-Hukm bi-Amr Allah, Riwayah fi al-Takhyil al-Tarikhi* [Crazy about Governing by Godʾs Commands: A Novel about Historical Imagination]. London: Riyad al-Rayyis, 1990.

Huraytani, Sulayman, *Al-Jawari wa al-Qiyan wa Zahirat Intishar Andiyyat wa Manazil al-Muqayyinin fi al-Mujtama' al-'Arabi al-Islami* [Concubines and Singing Girls and the Phenomenon of the Proliferation of Clubs and the Inns of the Owners of Singing-Girls in Arab-Muslim Society]. Damascus: Dar al-Hasad, 1997.

Husayn, Taha. *Hadith al-Arbi'a'* [Wednesday Talk]. Three volumes. Cairo: al-Matba'ah al-Tijariyyah al-Kubra, 1925.

———. *Adib* [Belletrist]. Cairo: Dar al-Ma'arif, 1930.

———. *Hadith al-Arbi'a'* [Wednesday Talk]. Three volumes. Cairo: Dar al-Ma'arif bi-Misr, 1964.

———. *Khisam wa Naqd* [Disputation and Critique]. In *Al-Majmu'ah al-Kamilah li-Mu'allafat al-Duktur Taha Husayn* [The Complete Collected Works of Dr. Taha Husayn]. Volume 11, part 2. Beirut: Dar al-Kitab al-Lubnani, 1974.

———. *Al-Ayyam* [The Days]. Three volumes. Cairo: Dar al-Ma'arif, 1978.

———. *Mustaqbal al-Thaqafah fi Misr* [The Future of Culture in Egypt]. Cairo: Dar al-Ma'arif, 1993.

———. *Fi al-Shi'r al-Jahili* [On Jahiliyyah Poetry]. Cairo: Dar al-Nahr lil-Nashr wa al-Tawzi', 1996.

Ibrahim, Sun'allah. *Tilka al-Ra'ihah* [That Odor]. Cairo: Dar Shuhdi, 1986.

———. *Sharaf*. Cairo: Dar al-Hilal, 1997.

Idris, Suhayl. *Asabi'una allati Tahtariq* [Our Burning Fingers]. Beirut: Dar al-Adab, 1998.

———. *Dhikrayat al-Adab wa al-Hubb* [Memories of Literature and Love]. Part 1. Beirut: Dar al-Adab, 2002.

Idris, Yusuf. *Al-'Askari al-Aswad wa Qisas Ukhra* [The Black Cop and Other Short Stories]. Cairo: Dar al-Ma'rifah, 1962.

———. *Abu al-Rijal* [The Manliest of Men]. In *Al-'Atab 'ala al-Nazar*. Cairo: Markaz al-Ahram lil-Tarjamah wa al-Nashr, 1987.

Ikhwan al-Safa'. *Rasa'il Ikhwan al-Safa'* [The Treatises of Ikhwan al-Safa']. Beirut: Dar Sadir, 1957.

'Isa, Ibrahim, *Al-Jins wa 'Ulama' al-Islam, Kalam fi Muharramat al-Tatarruf wa Rijal al-Din* [Sex and the Theologians of Islam: A Discussion of the Taboos of Extremism and about the Men of Religion]. Cairo: Madbuli al-Saghir, 1994.

———. *Maqtal al-Rajul al-Kabir* [The Murder of the Big Man]. Cairo: n.p., 1999.

Al-Jabiri, Muhammad 'Abid. *Takwin al-'Aql al-'Arabi*. Volume 1 of *Naqd al-'Aql al-'Arabi* [The Formation of Arab Reason. Volume 1 of The Critique of Arab Reason]. Beirut: Markaz Dirasat al-Wihdah al-'Arabiyyah, 1984.

———. "Ishkaliyyat al-Asalah wa al-Mu'asarah fi al-Fikr al-'Arabi al-Hadith wa al-Mu'asir: Sira' Tabaqi am Mushkil Thaqafi?" [The Problematic of Authenticity and Contemporariness in Modern and Contemporary Arab Thought: A Class Struggle or a Cultural Problem?]. In *Al-Turath wa Tahadiyyat al-'Asr fi al-Watan al-'Arabi (al-Asalah wa al-Mu'asarah)*, Buhuth wa Munaqashat al-Nadwah al-Fikriyyah allati Nazzamaha Markaz Dirasat al-Wihdah al-'Arabiyyah. Beirut: Markaz Dirasat al-Wihdah al-'Arabiyyah, 1985.

———. *Al-Turath wa al-Hadathah, Dirasat wa Munaqashat* [Heritage and Modernity: Studies and Debates]. Beirut: Markaz Dirasat al-Wihdah al-ʿArabiyyah, 1991.

———. *Nahnu wa al-Turath, Qiraʾat Muʿasirah fi Turathina al-Falsafi* [We and Heritage: Contemporary Readings in Our Philosphical Heritage]. Beirut: al-Markaz al-Thaqafi al-ʿArabi, 1993.

———. *Al-Khitab al-ʿArabi al-Muʿasir, Dirasah Tahliliyyah Naqdiyyah* [Contemporary Arab Discourse: A Critical and Analytic Study]. Fifth printing. Beirut: Markaz Dirasat al-Wihdah al-ʿArabiyyah, 1994.

Al-Jiddawi, ʿAbd al-Munʿim, *Al-Jins wa al-Jarimah* [Sex and Crime]. Cairo: Dar al-Hilal, 1973.

Jiha, Shafiq. *Darwin wa Azmat 1882 bi al-Daʾirah al-Tibiyyah wa Awwal Thawrah Tulabiyyah fi al-ʿAlam al-ʿArabi bi al-Kulliyyah al-Suriyyah al-Injiliyyah (Al-An: Al-Jamiʿah al-Amrikiyyah fi Bayrut)* [Darwin and the Crisis of 1882 in the Medical Department and the First Student Revolt in the Arab World in the Syrian Protestant College (Now the American University of Beirut)]. N.p.: n.p., 1991.

Jumʿah, Jamal. "Al-Irutikiyyah al-ʿArabiyyah, al-Sath wa al-Qaʿ" [Arab Eroticism, the Surface and the Bottom]. In Shihab al-Din Ahmad al-Tifashi, *Nuzhat al-Albab fima La Yuwjad fi Kitab* [A Promenade of the Hearts in What Does Not Exist in a Book]. London: Riyad al-Rayyis, 1992.

———. "Faqih al-Hurumat" [The Jurisprudent of What Is Forbidden]. In *Abu Nuwas, al-Nusus al-Muharramah* [Abu Nuwas: The Forbidden Texts]. London: Riyad al-Rayyis, 1994.

Al-Kahil, Dr. ʿAbd al-Wahhab, *Al-Jarimah wa al-Jins, Al-Adab al-Qurʾaniyyah li-Nashr Qisas al-Jarimah fi al-Sahafah* [Crime and Sex: Qurʾanic Manners for the Publication of Crime Stories in the Press]. Cairo: Maktabat al-Turath al-Islami, 1991.

Kanafani, Ghassan. *Rijal fi al-Shams,* in Ghassan Kanafani, *Al-Athar al-Kamilah, Al-Riwayat.* Beirut: Muʾassassat al-Abhath al-ʿArabiyyah, 1972.

Khallikan, Abu ʿAbbas Shams al-Din Ahmad bin Muhammad bin Abi Bakr bin. *Wafayat al-Aʿyan wa Anbaʾ Abnaʾ al-Zaman* [The Obituaries of Eminent Men and News about the Men of the Epoch]. Edited by Ihsan ʿAbbas. Beirut: Dar al-Thaqafah, 1970.

Kilani, Dr. Najib. *Qissat al-Ids* [The Story of AIDS]. Beirut: Muʾassassat al-Risalah, 1986.

Al-Khalidi, Salah ʿAbd al-Fattah, editor. *Amrika min al-Dakhil bi-Minzar Sayyid Qutb* [America from the Inside, through the Eyes of Sayyid Qutb]. Jiddah: Dar al-Manarah, 1986.

Khulayf, Yusuf. *Al-Hubb al-Mithali ʿind al-ʿArab* [Ideal Love among the Arabs]. Cairo: Dar al-Maʿarif, 1961.

Khuri, Fuʾad Ishaq. *Aydiyulujiyyat al-Jasad, Rumuziyyat al-Taharah wa al-Najasah* [The Ideology of the Body]. Beirut: Dar al-Saqi, 1997.

Khuri, Ra'if. *Wa Hal Yakhfa al-Qamar? 'Umar Ibn Abi Rabi'ah* [Can the Moon Hide?]. Beirut: Dar al-Makshuf, 1939.

——. *Dik Al-Jinn, Al-Hubb al-Muftaris* [The Devouring Love]. Beirut: Dar al-Makshuf, 1948.

——. *Al-Adab al-Mas'ul* [Responsible Literature]. Beirut: Dar al-Adab, 1968.

——. "Al-Ladhdhah wa al-Alam" [Pleasure and Pain]. Reprinted in Ra'if Khuri, *Thawrat al-Fata al-'Arabi, 'A'mal Mukhtarah min Turath Ra'if Khuri* [The Revolt of the Young Arab Man: Selected Works from the Legacy of Ra'if Khuri]. Beirut: Dar al-Farabi, 1984.

Kishk, Muhammad Jalal. *Khawatir Muslim fi al-Mas'alah al-Jinsiyyah* [A Muslim's Thoughts on the Sexual Question]. Beirut and Cairo: Dar al-Jil and Maktabat al-Turath al-Islami, 1992.

Kurayyim, Samih. *Taha Husayn fi Ma'arikihi al-Adabiyyah wa al-Fikriyyah* [Taha Husayn in His Literary and Intellectual Battles]. Cairo: Kitab al-Idha'ah wa al-Tilifizyun, 1974.

Al-Labwani, Muhhamad Kamal. *Al-Hubb wa al-Jins 'ind al-Salafiyyah wa al-Imbiryaliyyah* [Love and Sex in Fundamentalism and Imperialism]. London: Riyad al-Rayyis, 1994.

Al-Lawati, Hasan. *Al-Bahth 'an al-Dhat* [The Search for the Self]. Amman: Dar al-Azminah, 2004.

Mahfuz, Najib. *Al-Qahirah Al-Jadidah.* Cairo: Maktabat Misr, 1965.

——. *Layali Alf Laylah* [The Nights of A Thousand Nights]. Cairo: Maktabat Misr, 1979.

——. *Zuqaq al-Midaq* [Midaq Alley]. Cairo: Maktabat Misr, 1989?

——. *Al-Sukkariyyah* [Sugar Street]. Cairo: Maktabat Misr, n.d.

Mahmud, Ibrahim. *Al-Jins fi al-Qur'an* [Sex in the Qur'an]. Beirut: Riyad al-Rayyis Lil-Kutub wa al-Nashr, 1994.

——. *Jughrafiyyat al-Maladhdhat, al-Jins fi al-Jannah* [The Geography of Pleasures: Sex in Paradise]. Beirut: Riyad al-Rayyis lil-Kutub wa al-Nashr, 1998.

——. *Al-Mut'ah al-Mahzurah, Al-Shudhudh al-Jinsi fi Tarikh al-'Arab* [The Forbidden Pleasure: Sexual Deviance in the History of the Arabs]. Beirut: Riyad al-Rayyis lil-Kutib wa al-Nashr, 2000.

——. *Al-Shabaq al-Muharram, Antuluyia al-Nusus al-Mamnu'ah* [Forbidden Lust: Anthology of Banned Texts]. Beirut: Riyad al-Rayyis, 2002.

Maja'is, Salim. *Dik al-Jinn Al-Himsi, Tahafut al-Ruwah wa Shafafiyyat al-Nass* [Dik Al-Jinn al-Himsi: The Incoherence of the Narrators and the Transparency of the Text]. Beirut, Dar Amwaj, 2000.

Al-Maktab al-'Alami lil-Buhuth. *Al-Hubb 'ind al-'Arab* [Love among the Arabs]. Beirut: Dar Maktabat al-Hayah, n.d. 1980?

Al-Maluhi, 'Abd al-Mu'in, and Al-Darwish, Muhyi al-Din, editors. *Diwan Dik al-Jinn al-Himsi* [The Collected Poetry of Dik al-Jinn the Homsite]. Homs: Matabi' al-Fajr al-Jadid, 1960.

Mansur, Anis. *Min Awwal Nazrah, Fi al-Jins, wa al-Hubb wa al-Zawaj* [At First Sight: On Love, Sex, and Marriage]. Cairo: Dar al-Shuruq, 2001.

———. *Fi Salun al-ʿAqqad Kanat lana Ayyam* [We Had Many a Day in Al-ʿAqqad's Salon]. Cairo: Dar al-Shuruq, 2005.

Mansur, Ilham. *Ana Hiya Anti* [I Am You]. Beirut: Riyad al-Rayyis lil-Kutub wa al-Nashr, 2000.

Manzur, Muhammad bin Mukarram Ibn. *Akhbar Abi Nuwas, Tarikhuh, Nawadiruh, Shiʿruh, Mujunuh* [The Stories of Abu Nuwas, His History, His Anecdotes, His Poetry, and His Bawdiness]. Edited by Muhammad ʿAbd al-Rasul Ibrahim and ʿAbbas al-Sharbini. Cairo: Matbaʿat al-Iʿtimad, 1924.

———. *Lisan al-ʿArab*. Beirut: Dar Sadir, 1990.

Al-Marnisi, Fatimah. *Al-Hubb fi Hadaratina al-Islamiyyah*. Beirut: al-Dar al-ʿAlamiyyah lil-Tibaʿah wa al-Nashr wa al-Tawziʿ, 1984.

Matlub, Ahmad, and al-Jaburi, ʿAbdullah, editors. *Diwan Dik al-Jinn*. Beirut: Dar al-Thaqafah, 1964?

Mazhar, Ismaʿil. *Asl al-Anwaʿ wa Nushuʾuha bi al-Intikhab al-Tabiʿi wa Hifz al-Sufuf al-Ghalibah fi al-Tanahur ʿala al-Baqaʾ* [Origin of the Species and Its Emergence through Natural Selection and the Preservation of Dominant Classes in the Struggle for Survival]. Cairo: Dar al-ʿAsr lil-Tabʿ wa al-Nashr, 1928.

Mazhar, Muntasir, *Al-Mutʿah al-Muharramah, al-Liwat wa al-Suhaq fi al-Tarikh al-ʿArabi* [Prohibited Pleasure: Sodomy and Sapphism in Arab History]. Al-Dar al-ʿAlamiyyah lil-Kutub wa al-Nashr: n.p., 2001.

Moreau, André. *Al-Lurd Bayrun ʿAshiq Nafsihi* [Lord Byron, Lover of Himself]. Translated by Antun Ghattas Karam. Beirut: Dar al-Makshuf, 1948.

Mubarak, Zaki. *Al-Muwazanah bayna al-Shuʿaraʾ* [Comparing Poets]. Cairo: Dar al-Katib al-ʿArabi lil-Tibaʿah wa al-Nashr, 1968.

———. *Madamiʿ al-ʿUshshaq* [The Sources of Tears of Lovers]. Beirut: Dar al-Jil, 1993.

Muhanna, ʿAbd al-Amir ʿAli, editor. *Diwan Dik al-Jinn, Tabʿah Jadidah Tatadammanu Shiʿran Yunshar li-Awwal Marrah* [The Collected Poetry of Dik al-Jinn, a New Edition That Includes Poetry Published for the First Time]. Beirut: Dar al-Fikr al-Lubnani, 1990.

Muhyi al-Din, ʿAbd al-Razzaq. *Diwan al-Qasaʾid* [Collected Poems]. Edited by Dr. Muhammad Husayn ʿAli al-Saghir. Amman: Dar Usamah lil-Nashr wa al-Tawziʿ, 2000.

Al-Mulaththam, Al-Badawi. *Dik al-Jinn al-Himsi*. Cairo: Al-Muqtataf Press, 1948.

Al-Munajjid, Salah al-Din. *Fi Qusur al-Khulafaʾ* [In the Palaces of the Caliphs]. Beirut: Dar al-Makshuf, 1944.

———. *Al-Hayah al-Jinsiyyah ʿind al-ʿArab, min al-Jahiliyyah ila Awakhir al-Qarn al-Rabiʿ al-Hijri* [The Sexual Life of the Arabs: Since Jahiliyyah until the End of the Fourth Century A.H.]. Beirut: Dar al-Kitab al-Jadid, 1975.

———. *Nisaʾ ʿAshiqat* [Women in Love]. Damascus: Manshurat Asdiqaʾ al-Kitab, 1945.

———. *Jamal al-Mar'ah 'ind al-'Arab* [Women's Beauty among the Arabs]. Beirut: Dar al-Kitab al-Jadid, 1969.

———. *Al-Zurafa' wa al-Shahhadhun fi Baghdad wa Baris* [Charmers and Beggars in Baghdad and Paris]. Beirut: Dar al-Kitab al-Jadid, 1969.

Al-Muntasir, Khalid. *Al-Hubb wa al-Jasad, Dirasah 'Atifiyyah fi al-Jins* [Love and the Flesh: A Romantic Study of Sex]. Cairo: Dar al-Khayyal, 1996.

Mursi, 'Abd al-Wahid Imam, *Al-Shudhudh al-Jinsi wa Jara'im al-Qatl* [Sexual Deviance and Lethal Crimes]. Cairo: n.p., 1995.

Muruwwah, Husayn. *Dirasat Naqdiyyah, fi Du' al-Manhaj al-Waqi'i* [Critical Studies in the Light of the Realist Method]. Beirut: Maktabat al-Ma'arif, 1965.

———. *Al-Naza'at al-Madiyyah fi al-Falsafah al-'Arabiyyah al-Islamiyyah* [Materialist Tendencies in Arab-Islamic Philosophy]. Beirut: Dar al-Farabi, 1979.

———. *Turathuna, Kayfa Na'irifuh* [Our Heritage: How Do We Know It?]. Beirut: Mu'assassat al-Abhath al-'Arabiyyah, 1985.

Musa, Salamah. *Al-Hubb fi al-Tarikh* [Love in History]. Cairo: Salamah Musa lil-Nashr wa al-Tawzi', 1946.

———. *Muhawalat Saykulujiyyah* [Endeavors in Psychology]. Cairo: Maktabat al-Khanji, 1953.

———. *Al-Adab Lil-Sha'b* [Literature Is for the People]. Cairo: Salamah Musa Lil-Nashr wa al-Tawzi', 1956.

———. *Muqaddimmat al-Subirman* [Introduction to the Superman]. Cairo: Salamah Musa lil-Nashr wa al-Tawzi', 1962.

———. *Tarbiyat Salamah Musa* [The Education/Upbringing of Salamah Musa]. Cairo: Mu'assasat al-Khanji, 1962.

———. *Tariq al-Majd lil-Shabab* [The Path of Glory for the Youth]. Cairo: Matba'at al-Khanji, 1964.

———. *Al-Balaghah al-'Asriyyah wa al-Lughah al-'Arabiyyah* [Contemporary Rhetoric and the Arabic Language]. Cairo: Salamah Musa lil-Nashr wa al-Tawzi', 1964.

———. *Ahadith ila al-Shabab* [Sayings for the Youth]. Cairo: Salamah Musa lil-Nashr wa al-Tawzi', n.d.

———. *Asrar al-Nafs* [The Secrets of the Heart]. Cairo: Salamah Musa lil-Nashr wa al-Tawzi', n.d.

———. *Dirasat Saykulujiyyah* [Psychological Studies]. Cairo: Salamah Musa Lil Nashr wa al-Tawzi', n.d.

———. *Al-Mar'ah laysat Lu'bat al-Rajul* [Woman Is Not Man's Plaything]. Cairo: Salamah Musa Lil-Nashr wa al-Tawzi', n.d.

———. *Al-Shakhsiyyah al-Naji'ah* [The Efficient Personality]. Cairo: Salamah Musa lil-Nashr wa al-Tawzi', n.d.

al-Mu'tazz, 'Abdullah ibn. *Tabaqat al-Shu'ara'* [The Ranks of Poets]. Cairo: Dar al-Ma'arif fi Misr, 1956.

Al-Nafzawi, al-Shaykh al-'Arif Abu 'Abdullah Muhammad bin Abi Bakr bin 'Ali. *Al-Rawd al-'Atir fi Nuzhat al-Khatir* [The Perfumed Garden in the Promenade of the Mind]. Edited by Jamal Jum'ah. London: Riyad al-Rayyis Lil-Kutub wa al-Nashr, 1990.

———. *Al-Rawd al-'Atir fi Nuzhat al-Khatir*, in *Al-Jins 'ind al-'Arab*. Volume 2. Cologne: Manshurat al-Jamal, 1991.

Nasim, Mahmud. "Tuqus wa Isharat, Su'ud al-Fardiyyah am Inkisaruha? Wa Madha ba'da al-Haffah?" [Rites and Signs, the Rise of Individualism or Its Defeat? And, What Comes after the Precipice?]. *Al-Tariq* 1 (Jan.–Feb. 1996): 166–177.

Nur, Ayman, and Shandi, Majdi. *Al-'Askari al-Aswad, Zaki Badr* [The Black Cop, Zaki Badr]. Cairo: al-Sharikah al-'Arabiyyah al-Dawliyyah Lil-Nashr, 1990.

Nur al-Din, Hasan Ja'far. *Dik al-Jinn al-Himsi, 'Abd al-Salam bin Raghban, 'Asruh wa Hayatuh wa Fununuh al-Shi'riyyah* [Dik al-Jinn al-Himsi, 'Abd al-Salam bin Raghban, His Epoch, Life and Poetic Arts]. Beirut: Dar al-Kutub al-'Ilmiyyah, 1990.

Al-Nuwayhi, Muhammad. *Nafsiyyat Abi Nuwas* [The Psychology of Abu Nuwas]. Cairo: Dar al-Fikr, 1970.

———. *Shakhsiyyat Bashshar* [Bashshar's Personality]. Beirut: Dar al-Fikr, 1971.

Qanawati, Shihatah. "Athar al-Ma'dubah aw al-Hubb al-Aflatuni fi al-'Alam al-Islami" [The Influence of the Sympoisum; or, Platonic Love on the Islamic World]. In *Al-Ma'dubah aw fi al-Hubb li-Aflatun* [The Symposium; or, On Love by Plato]. Translated and edited by 'Ali Sami al-Nashshar, Jurj Shihatah Qanawati, and 'Abbas Ahmad al-Sharbini. Alexandria: Dar al-Kutub al-Jami'iyyah, 1970.

Qasim, 'Abd al-Hakim. *Al-Mahdi* [The Guided One]. Damascus: Dar al-Mada, 2002.

Al-Qudah, 'Abd al-Hamid. *Al-Amrad al-Jinsiyyah, 'Uqubah Ilahiyyah* [Venereal Diseases, Divine Punishment]. London: Medical Publications, 1985.

———. *Al-Ids, Hasad al-Shudhudh* [AIDS, the Harvest of Deviance]. Beirut: Dar Ibn Qudamah lil-Tab' wa al-Nashr, 1986.

Qutb, Muhammad 'Ali. *Al-Hubb wa al-Jins min Manzur Islami* [Love and Sex from an Islamic Perspective]. Cairo: Maktabat al-Qur'an, 1984.

Qutb, Sayyid. *Al-Naqd al-Adabi, Usuluh wa Manahijuh* [Literary Criticism: Its Bases and Methods]. Beirut: Dar al-Kutub al-'Arabiyyah, 1965.

———. *Fi Zilal al-Qur'an* [In the Shadow of the Qur'an]. Volume 2. Cairo: Dar al-Shuruq, 1996.

Al-Rafi'i, Mustafa Sadiq. *Tarikh Adab al-'Arab* [The History of the Literature of the Arabs). Beirut: Dar al-Kitab al-'Arabi, 1974.

Al-Rifa'i, Ahmad Farid. *'Asr al-Ma'mun* [The Epoch of al-Ma'mun]. Cairo: Matba'at Dar al-Kutub al-Misriyyah, 1928.

Alifah Rif'at. *Man Yakun al-Rajul?* [Who Is the Man?]. Cairo: Matabi' al-Hay'ah al-Misriyyah al-'Amah lil-Kitab, 1981.

———. *Fi Layl al-Shita' al-Tawil* [During the Long Night of Winter]. Cairo: Matba'at al-'Asimah, 1985.

Al-Sa'dawi, Nawal. *Dirasat 'an al-Mar'ah wa al-Rajul fi al-Mujtama' al-'Arabi* [Studies about Women and Men in Arab Society]. Beirut: al-Mu'assassah al-'Arabiyyah lil Dirasat wa al-Nashr, 1986.

Sadiq, 'Abd al-Rida. *Sufista'iyyah lil-Bay'*, *Manhaj al-Duktur 'Ali al-Wardi wa Tafkiruh* [Sophistry for Sale: The Method and Thinking of Dr. 'Ali al-Wardi]. Baghdad: Dar al-Hadith, 1956.

Al-Saffar, Al-Shaykh Muhammad bin 'Abdullah. *Al-Rihlah al-Titwaniyyah ila al-Diyar al-Firansiyyah 1845–1846* [The Tetouanite Journey to the Country of the French, 1845–1846]. Edited by Umm Salma. Titwan: Matba'at al-Haddad Yusuf Ikhwan, 1995.

Salih, Al-Tayyib. *Mawsim al-Hijrah ila al-Shamal* [The Season of Migration to the North]. Beirut: Dar al-'Awda, 1969.

Al-Samman, Ghadah. *Bayrut 75*. Beirut: Dar al-Adab, 1975.

al-Sarraj al-Qari' al-Baghdadi, Abu Muhammad Ja'far bin Ahmad bin al-Husayn. *Masari' al-'Ushshaq* [The Death of Lovers], edited by Muhammad Hasan Isma'il. Beirut: Dar al-Kutub al-'Ilmiyyah, 1998.

Sidqi, 'Abd al-Rahman. *Alhan al-Han, Abu Nuwas fi Hayatih al-Lahiyyah* [The Melodies of the Tavern: Abu Nuwas in His Whimsical Life]. Cairo: Dar al-Ma'arif al-Misriyyah, 1957.

———. *Abu Nuwas, Qissat Hayatih wa Shi'ruh* [Abu Nuwas: His Life Story and His Poetry]. Cairo: Dar Ihya' al-Kutub al-'Arabiyyah, 1944.

al-Sha''ar, al-Shaykh Marwan Muhammad. *Al-'Ilaqat al-Jinsiyyah fi al-Islam* [Sexual Relations in Islam]. Beirut: Dar al-Nafa'is, 1990.

Shalash, 'Ali. *Najib Mahfuz: Al-Tariq wa al-Sada* [Najib Mahfuz: The Path and the Effect]. Beirut: Dar al-Adab, 1990.

Sakhsukh, Ahmad. *Ughniyyat al-Rahil al-Wannusiyyah, Dirasah fi Masrah Sa'dallah Wannus* [The Wannusite Songs of Departing, A Study of the Theater of Sa'dallah Wannus]. Cairo: Al-Dar al-Misriyyah al-Lubnaniyyah, 1998.

Shararah, 'Abd al-Latif. *Falsafat al-Hubb 'ind al-'Arab* [The Arabs' Philosophy of Love]. Beirut, Dar Maktabat al-Hayah, 1960.

———. *Al-Janib al-Thaqafi min al-Qawmiyyah al-'Arabiyyah* [The Cultural Dimension of Arab Nationaliam]. Beirut: Dar al-'Ilm lil-Malayin, 1961.

Al-Shaykh, Hanan. *Misk al-Ghazal* [The Deer's Musk]. Beirut: Dar al-Adab, 1988.

———. *Innaha Landan Ya 'Azizi* [It Is London, My Dear]. Beirut: Dar al-Adab, 2001.

Al-Shinnawi, Kamil. *I'tirafat Abi Nuwas*. Cairo: Dar al-Ma'arif bi-Misr, 1968.

Shukri, Ghali. *Azmat al-Jins fi al-Qissah al-'Arabaiyyah* [The Crisis of Sex in the Arab Novel]. Beirut: Dar al-Adab, 1962.

———. *Salamah Musa wa Azmat al-Damir al-'Arabi* [Salamah Musa and the Crisis of Arab Conscience]. Cairo: Maktab al-Khanji, 1962.

———. *Azmat al-Jins fi al-Qissah al-'Arabiyyah* [The Crisis of Sex in the Arabic Novel]. Cairo: Dar al-Shuruq, 1991.

Shukri, Muhammad. *Al-Shuttar*. Beirut: Dar al-Saqi, 1992.

———. *Jan Junih fi Tanjah, Tinisi Wilyamz fi Tanjah* [Jean Genet in Tangiers, Tenessee Williams in Tangiers]. Cologne: Manshurat al-Jamal, 1993.

———. *Al-Khubz al-Hafi, Sirah Dhatiyyah Riwa'iyyah, 1935–1956,* [Plain Bread: A Novelistic Autobiography, 1935–1956]. Beirut: Dar al-Saqi, 1995.

———. *Bul Bulz wa 'Uzlat Tanjah* [Paul Bowles and the Isolation of Tangiers]. Cologne: Dar al-Jamal, 1997.

Shulir, Ghrighur (Gregor Schoeler), editor. *Diwan Abu Nuwas.* Vol. 4. Damascus: Dar al-Mada, 2003.

Shumayyil, Shibli. *Falsafat al-Nushu' wa al-Irtiqa'* [The Philosophy of Evolution and Ascent]. Cairo: Matba'at al-Muqtataf, 1910.

Sulayman, Musa. *Al-Hubb al-'Udhri* [Virginal Love]. Beirut: Dar al-Thaqafah, 1954.

Al-Suwaydi, Thani. *Al-Dizil.* Beirut: Dar al-Jadid, 1994.

Al-Suyuti, al-Hafiz Jalal al-Din. *Tarikh al-Khulafa'* [The History of the Caliphs]. Beirut: Dar al-Kutub al-'Ilmiyyah, 1988.

Al-Tahtawi, Rifa'ah. *Takhlis al-Ibriz fi Talkhis Bariz Aw Al-Diwan al-Nafis bi-Iwan Bariz* [The Extrication of Gold in Summarizing Paris; or, The Valuable Collection in the Drawing Room of Paris]. In *Al-A'mal al-Kamilah li-Rifa'ah al-Tahtawi,* edited by Muhammad 'Imarah. Volume 2. Beirut: al-Mu'assassah al-'Arabiyyah lil-Dirasat wa al-Nashr, 1973.

Al-Tawil, Nabil Subhi. *Al-Amrad al-Jinsiyyah* [Venereal Diseases]. Beirut: Mu'assassat al-Risalah, 1986.

Al-Tawili, Ahmad. *Kutub al-Hubb 'ind al-'Arab* [Books about Love among the Arabs]. Beirut: Riyad al-Rayyis lil-Kutub wa al-Nashr, 2001.

Tarabishi, Jurj. *Al-Muthaqqafun al-'Arab wa al-Turath: Al-Tahlil al-Nafsi Li-'Usab Jama'i* [Arab Intellectuals and Heritage: A Psychoanalysis of Collective Neurosis]. London: Riyad al-Rayyis, 1991.

———. *Fi Thaqafat al-Dimuqratiyyah* [On Democratic Culture]. Beirut: Dar al-Tali'ah, 1998.

———. *Masa'ir al-Falsafah Bayna al-Masihiyyah wa al-Islam* [Philosophy's Destinies between Christianity and Islam]. Beirut: Dar al-Saqi, 1998.

Al-Tifashi, Shihab al-Din Ahmad, *Nuzhat al-Albab Fima La Yuwjad Fi Kitab* [A Promenade of the Hearts in What Does Not Exist in a Book]. London: Riyad al-Rayyis, 1992.

Al-Tijani, Muhammad bin Ahmad. *Tuhfat al-'Arus wa Mut'at al-Nufus* [The Gift of the Bride and the Pleasure of the Souls]. London: Riyad al-Rayyis lil-Kutub wa al-Nashr, 1992.

Tizini, Tayyib. *Min al-Turath ila al-Thawra* [From Heritage to Revolution]. Beirut: Dar ibn Khaldun, 1978.

Al-Turk, Niqula. *Dhikr Tamalluk Jumhur al-Faransawiyyah al-Aqtar al-Misriyyah wa al-Bilad al-Shamiyyah* [A Chronicle of the French Republic's Occupation of the Lands of Egypt and Syria]. Beirut: Dar al-Farabi, 1990.

Waliy al-Din, Isma'il. *Hammam al-Malatili* [The Malatili Bathhouse]. Cairo: Kitabat Mu'asirah, 1970.

Wannus, Sa'dallah. *Tuqus al-Isharat wa al-Tahawwulat.* Beirut: Dar al-Adab, 1994.

Al-Wardi, ʿAli, *Wuʿ ʿaz al-Salatin, Raʾy Sarih fi Tarikh al-Fikr al-Islami fi Duʾ al-Mantiq al-Hadith* [The Sultans' Preachers: An Honest Opinion about the History of Islamic Thought in the Light of Modern Logic]. London: Dar Kufan, 1995.

———. *Usturat al-Adab al-Rafiʿ* [The Legend of Refined Literature]. London: Dar Kufan, 1994.

Wasil, ʿAbd al-Rahman. *Mushkilat al-Shabab al-Jinsiyyah wa al-ʿAtifiyyah taht Adwaʾ Al-Shariʿah al-Islamiyyah* [The Sexual and Romantic Problems of Young People under the Gaze of Islamic Shariʿah]. Cairo: Maktabat Wahbab, 1984.

Yasin, Buʿali. *Al-Thaluth al-Muharram, Dirasah fi al-Din, wa al-Jins, wa al-Siraʿ al-Tabaqi* [The Prohibited Trinity: A Study in Religion, Sex, and Class Struggle]. Beirut: Dar al-Kunuz al-Adabiyyah, 1999.

Yasin, Najman. *Al-Islam wa al-Jins fi al-Qarn al-Awwal al-Hijri* [Islam and Sex in the First Century A.H.]. Beirut: Dar ʿAtiyyah Lil-Nashr, 1997.

Al-Zahi, Farid. *Al-Jasad wa al-Surah wa al-Muqaddas fi al-Islam* [The Body, the Image and the Sacred in Islam]. Casablanca: Afriqya al-Sharq, 1999.

Zaydan, Jurji. *Tarikh al-Tamaddun al-Islami* [History of Islamic Civilization]. Volume 5. Cairo: Matbaʿat al-Hilal, 1906.

———. *Al-ʿAbbasah Ukht al-Rashid* [Al-ʿAbbasah, the sister of al-Rashid]. Cairo: Matbaʿat al-Hilal, 1911.

———. *Al-Amin wa al-Maʾmun* [Al-Amin and al-Maʾmun]. Cairo: Matbaʿat al-Hilal, 1911.

———. *Tarikh Adab al-Lughah al-ʿArabiyyah* [The History of the Literature of the Arabic Peoples]. Cairo: Dar al-Hilal, 1956.

———. *Mudhakkarat Jurji Zaydan* [The Memoirs of Jurji Zaydan]. Edited by Salah al-Din al-Munajjid. Beirut: Dar al-Kitab al-Jadid, 1968.

Al-Zayyat, Ahmad Hasan. *Tarikh al-Adab al-ʿArabi, lil-Madaris al-Thanawiyyah wa al-ʿUlya* [The History of Arabic Literature for Secondary and High Schools]. Beirut: Dar al-Thaqafah, 1978.

Al-Zayyat, Habib. "Al-Marʾah al-Ghulamiyyah fi al-Islam" [The Boyish Woman in Islam]. *Al-Mashriq* (March–April 1956): 153–192.

Zuʿaytar, Akram, editor. *Wathaʾiq al-Harakah al-Wataniyyah al-Filastiniyyah, 1918–1939* [The Documents of the Palestinian National Movement, 1918–1939]. Beirut: Muʾassassat al-Dirasat al-Filastiniyyah, 1979.

Other Sources

AbuKhalil, Asʿad. "New Arab Ideology? The Rejuvenation of Arab Nationalism." *Middle East Journal* 46, no. 1 (winter 1992): 22–36.

———. "A Note on the Study of Homosexuality in the Arab/Islamic Civilization." *Arab Studies Journal* (Fall 1993): 32–34, 48.

Abu-Lughod, Ibrahim. *Arab Rediscovery of Europe: A Study in Cultural Encounters.* Princeton: Princeton University Press, 1963.

Al-Afghani, Jamal al-Din. "Answer of Jamal al-Din al-Afghani to Renan." 1883. Reproduced in A. M. Goichon, editor and translator, *Réfutation des Matérialistes.* Paris: Paul Geuthner, 1942.

———. *The Truth about the Neicheri Sect and an Explanation of the Neicheris.* In Nikki Keddie, *An Islamic Response to Imperialism, Political and Religious Writings of Sayyid Jamal ad-Din al-Afghani.* Berkely: University of California Press, 1968.

———. "Answer of Jamal al-Din al-Afghani to Renan." 1883. Reproduced in Nikki Keddie, *An Islamic Response to Imperialism, Political and Religious Writings of Sayyid Jamal ad-Din al-Afghani.* Berkeley: University of California Press, 1983.

Ahlwardt, W. *Diwan des Abu Nowas nach der Weiner und Berliner handschrift, mit Benutzung anderer Handschriften herausgegeben.* Volume 1, *Die Weinlieder.* Greifswald, 1861.

Amin, Qasim. *Les Égyptiens, réponse à M. le duc d'Harcourt.* Cairo: Jules Barbier, 1894.

Amnesty International. *United States of America Stonewalled: Police Abuse and Misconduct against Lesbian, Gay, Bisexual and Transgender People in the U.S.* New York: Amnesty International, 2005.

Antonius, George. *The Arab Awakening.* New York: Capricorn Books, 1965.

Arguelles, Lourdes, and B. Ruby Rich. "Homosexuality, Homophobia, and Revolution: Notes toward an Understanding of the Cuban Lesbian and Gay Male Experience, Part I." *Signs* (Summer 1984): 683–699.

———. "Homosexuality, Homophobia, and Revolution: Notes toward an Understanding of the Cuban Lesbian and Gay Male Experience, Part II." *Signs* (Fall 1985): 120–135.

Asad, Talal. *Formations of the Secular, Christianity, Islam, Modernity.* Stanford: Stanford University Press, 2003.

Assfar, Akhadar. "Jordan." In Rachel Rosenbloom, *Unspoken Rules, Sexual Orientation and Women's Human Rights.* New York: Cassell, 1996.

Aswany, Alaa al. *The Yacoubian Building.* Cairo: American University in Cairo Press, 2004.

Barakat, Hoda. *The Stone of Laughter.* Translated by Sophie Bennett. New York: Interlink Books, 1995.

Bencheikh, Jamel Eddine. "Poésie bachiques d'Abu Nuwas, thèmes et personnages." *Bulletin d'Études Orientales* (Damascus) 18 (1963–1964): 1–84.

———. "Khamriyyat." In *The Encyclopaedia of Islam.* Leiden: Brill Academic Publishers, 2001.

Benedict, Ruth. *The Chrysanthemum and the Sword: Patterns of Japanese Culture.* Boston: Houghton Mifflin Company, 1946.

Benjamin, Walter. "Theses on the Philosophy of History." In *Illuminations: Essays and Reflections.* Edited by Hannah Arendt. New York: Schocken Books, 1969.

Berque, Jacques. *The Arabs: Their History and Future.* New York: Praeger Publishers, 1964.

Bieber, Irving. *Homosexuality: A Psychoanalytic Study.* New York: Basic Books, 1962.

Bieber, Irving, and Laud Humphreys. *Tearoom Trade: Impersonal Sex in Public Places*. Chicago: Aldine Pub. Co., 1970.

Bleys, Rudi. *The Geography of Perversion: Male-to-Male Sexual Behaviour outside the West and the Ethnographic Imagination 1750–1918*. New York: New York University Press, 1995.

Boone, Joseph. "Vacation Cruises; or, The Homoerotics of Orientalism." *PMLA* 110 (1995): 89–107.

Boswell, John. *Christianity, Social Tolerance, and Homosexuality: Gay People in Western Europe from the Beginning of the Christian Era to the Fourteenth Century*. Chicago: University of Chicago Press, 1980.

Bouhdiba, Abdelwahab. *La sexualité en Islam*. Paris: Presses universitaires de France, 1975.

———. *Sexuality in Islam*. Translated by Alan Sheridan. London: Routledge and Kegan Paul, 1985.

Bourdieu, Pierre. *An Outline of a Theory of Practice*. Translated by Richard Nice. Cambridge: Cambrdige University Press, 1977.

Brunschvig, R., and G. E., von Grunebaum, editors. *Classicisme et Déclin Culturel dans l'histoire de l'Islam , actes du symposium international d'histoire de la civilisation musulmane, Bordeaux 25–29 juin 1956*. Paris: Besson, Chantemerle, 1957.

Burton, Richard F. "Terminal Essay." In *The Book of the Thousand Nights and a Night: A Plain and Literal Translation of the Arab Nights Entertainments*. Translated and annotated by Richard F. Burton. Volume 10. London: The Burton Club, 1886.

Butler, Judith. *Undoing Gender*. New York: Routledge, 2004.

Calasso, Roberto. *The Marriage of Cadmus and Harmony*. Translated from the Italian by Tim Parks. London: Vintage, 1994.

Choukri, Mohamed. *For Bread Alone*. Translated with an introduction by Paul Bowles. San Francisco: City Lights Books, c1987.

Croft-Cooke, Rupert. *Feasting with Panthers: A New Consideration of Some Late Victorian Writers*. London: W. H. Allen, 1967.

D'Emilio, John. *Sexual Politics, Sexual Communities: The Making of a Homosexual Minority in the United States, 1940–1970*. Second edition. Chicago: University of Chicago Press, 1998.

Derrida, Jacques. "Cogito and the History of Madness." In Jacques Derrida, *Writing and Difference*. Chicago: University of Chicago Press, 1978.

———. *Archive Fever: A Freudian Impression*. Chicago: University of Chicago Press, 1996.

Dunne, Bruce. "Homosexuality in the Middle East: An Agenda for Historical Research." *Arab Studies Quarterly* 12, nos. 3–4 (Summer–Fall 1990): 55–82.

———. "Power and Sexuality in the Middle East." *Middle East Report* 206 (Spring 1998): 8–11, 37.

Duran, Khalid. "Homosexuality and Islam." In *Homosexuality and World Religions*, edited by Arlene Swidler. Valley Forge, PA: Trinity Press International, 1993.

Egger, Vernon. *A Fabian in Egypt: Salamah Musa and the Rise of the Professional Classes in Egypt, 1909–1939.* London: University Press of America, 1986.

Ellis, Havelock, and John Addington Symonds. *Sexual Inversion.* New York: Arno Press, 1975.

El-Rouayheb, Khaled. *Before Homosexuality in the Arab-Islamic World, 1500–1800.* Chicago: University of Chicago Press, 2005.

———."The Love of Boys in Arabic Poetry of the Early Ottoman Period, 1500–1800." *Middle Eastern Literatures* 8, no.1 (2005): 3–22.

Fanon, Frantz. *The Wretched of the Earth.* New York: Grove Press, 1963.

Fink, Amir Sumaka'i, and Jacob Press, editors. *Independence Park: The Lives of Gay Men in Israel.* Stanford: Stanford University Press, 1999.

Foucault, Michel. *The History of Sexuality.* Volume 1, *An Introduction.* Translated by Robert Hurley. New York: Vintage Books, 1980.

———. *The History of Sexuality.* Volume 2, *The Use of Pleasures.* New York: Vintage, 1984.

Fuss, Diana. *Identification Papers.* London: Routledge, 1995.

Ghitany, Gamal. *Incidents in Za'farani Alley.* Translated by Peter O'Daniel, with an introduction by M. Enani. Cairo: General Egyptian Book Organization, 1986.

Gibb, H. A. R. *Arabic Literature: An Introduction.* London: Oxford University Press, 1926.

Gollain, Francoise. "Bisexuality in the Arab World." In *Bisexual Horizons, Politics, Histories, Lives,* edited by Sharon Rose and Chris Stevens. London: Lawrence and Wishart, 1996.

Guha, Ranajit. *Dominance without Hegemony: History and Power in Colonial India.* Cambridge: Harvard University Press, 1997.

Haddawi, Husain, trans. *The Arabian Nights.* New York: Norton, 1990.

Hasso, Frances S. "Problems and Promise in Middle East and North Africa Gender Research." *Feminist Studies* 31, no. 3 (fall 2005): 653–78.

Hendriks, Aart, Rob Tielman, and Evert van der Veen. *The Third Pink Book: A Global View of Lesbian and Gay Liberation and Oppression.* Buffalo, N.Y.: Prometheus, 1993.

Hersh, Seymour M. "The Gray Zone." *New Yorker,* 24 May 2004.

Hoad, Neville. "Wild(e) Men and Savages: The Homosexual and the Primitive in Darwin, Wilde, and Freud." Ph.D. diss., Columbia University, 1998.

———. "Between the White Man's Burden and the White Man's Disease: Tracking Lesbian and Gay Human Rights in Southern Africa." *GLQ* 5, no. 4 (1999): 559–84.

———. "Arrested Development; or, The Queerness of Savages." *Postcolonial Studies: Culture, Politics, Economy* 3, no. 2 (2000): 133–158.

———. "Homosexuality, Africa, Neoliberalism and the African Church: The Lambeth Conference of African Bishops, 1998." In *Studies on Religion in Africa* 26 (2004): 54–79.

Horkheimer, Max, and Theodor Adorno. *The Dialectic of Enlightenment.* New York: Continuum, 1972.

Human Rights Watch. *In a Time of Torture: The Assault on Justice in Egypt's Crackdown on Homosexual Conduct*. New York: Human Rights Watch, 2004.

Husayn, Taha. *The Days*. Translated by E. H. Paxton, Hilary Wayment, and Kenneth Cragg. Cairo: American University in Cairo Press, 1997.

Hyde, H. Montgomery, editor. *The Trials of Oscar Wilde*. Middlesex, Penguin, 1962.

Ibrahim, Sonallah. *The Smell of It, and Other Stories*. Translated from the Arabic by Denys Johnson-Davies. London, Heinemann Educational, 1971.

Idris, Youssef. *A Leader of Men*. Translated by Saad Elkhadem. Fredericton: York Press, 1988.

Ingrams, Doreen. *The Awakened: Women in Iraq*. London: Third World Centre, 1983.

Ingrams, W. H. *Zanzibar: Its History and Its People*. London: H. F. & G. Witherby, 1931.

———. *Abu Nuwas in Life and in Legend*. Port-Louis, Mauritius: Privately published, 1933.

———. *A Report on the Social, Economic, and Political Condition of the Hadhramaut*. London: H. M. Stationery office, 1937.

International Lesbian and Gay Association. *The Second ILGA Pink Book: A Global View of Lesbian and Gay Liberation and Oppression*. Utrecht: Interfacultaire Werkgroep Homostudies, 1988.

Irigaray, Luce. *This Sex which Is Not One*. Translated by Catherine Porter. Ithaca: Cornell University Press, 1985.

Al-Jabarti, ʿAbd al-Rahman. *Tarikh Muddat al-Faransis bi-Misr, Muharram-Rajab 1213 H*. (June 15–December 1798). Translated as *Al-Jabarti's Chronicle of the First Seven Months of the French Occupation of Egypt*, edited and translated by S. Moreh. Bilingual edition. Leiden: E. J. Brill, 1975.

Jabra, Jabra I. *The Grass Roots of Iraqi Art*. St. Helier, 1983.

Jakobi, Patricia L. "Medical Science, Christian Fundamentalism and the Etiology of AIDS." *AIDS and Public Policy Journal* 5, no. 2 (Spring 1990): 89–93.

JanMohamed, Abdul R. "Humanism and Minority Literature: Toward a Definition of Counter-Hegemonic Discourse," *Boundary 2* 12–13 (Spring–Fall 1984): 281–99.

Jacquart, Danielle, and Claude Thomasset. *Sexuality and Medicine in the Middle Ages*. Translated by Matthew Adamson. Princeton: Princeton University Press, 1988.

Kanafani, Ghassan, *Men in the Sun, and Other Palestinian Stories*. Translated by Hilary Kilpatrick. Washington, D.C.: Three Continents Press, 1978.

Kaplan, Danny. *Brothers and Others in Arms, The Making of Love and War in Israeli Combat Units*. New York: Harrington Park Press, 2003.

Khoury, Philip S. *Syria and the French Mandate: The Politics of Arab Nationalism, 1920–1945*. Princeton: Princeton University Press, 1987.

Kraft-Ebing, Richard von. *Psychopathia Sexualis*. London: Velvet Publications, 1997.

Lacey, Edward. English translator's introduction to Ahmad al-Tifashi, *The Delight of Hearts; or, What You Will Not Find in Any Book*. San Francisco: Gay Sunshine Press, 1988.

Lacqueur, Thomas. *Making Sex: Body and Gender from the Greeks to Freud*. Cambridge: Harvard University Press, 1990.

———. *Solitary Sex: A Cultural History of Masturbation*. New York: Zone Books, 2003.

Lagrange, Frédéric. "Male Homosexuality in Modern Arabic Literature." In *Imagined Masculinities, Male Identity and Culture in the Modern Middle East*, edited by May Ghoussoub and Emma Sinclair-Webb, 169–198. London: Dar al-Saqi, 2000.

Laroui, Abdallah. *L'idéologie arabe contemporaine*. Paris: François Maspero, 1967.

———. *The Crisis of the Arab Intellectual: Traditionalism or Historicism?* Berkeley: University of California Press, 1974.

Lazreg, Marnia. "Feminism and Difference: The Perils of Writing as a Woman on Women in Algeria." *Feminist Studies* 14, no. 1 (spring 1988): 81–107.

Long, Scott. "The Trials of Culture: Sex and Security in Egypt." *Middle East Report* 230 (Spring 2004): 12–20.

Mahfouz, Naguib. *Midaq Alley*. Translated by Trevor Le Gassick. London: Heinemann Educational, 1975.

———. *Sugar Street*. Translated by William M. Hutchins and Angele Botros Samaan. New York: Doubleday, 1992.

———. *Arabian Nights and Days*. Translated by Denys Johnson-Davies. Cairo: American University in Cairo Press, 1995.

Mann, Thomas. *Death in Venice and Other Stories*. Translated by David Luke. New York: Bantam Books, 1988.

Marx, Karl. *Capital*. Volume 1, *A Critical Analysis of Capitalist Production*. Edited by Frederick Engels. New York: International Publishers 1967.

Massad, Joseph A. "Art and Politics in the Cinema of Youssef Chahine." *Journal of Palestine Studies* 110 (winter 1999): 77–93.

———. *Colonial Effects: The Making of National Identity in Jordan*. New York: Columbia University Press, 2001.

———. "The Intransigence of Orientalist Desires: A Reply to Arno Schmitt." *Public Culture* 15 (Fall 2003): 593–594

———. *The Persistence of the Palestinian Question: Essays on Zionism and the Palestinians*. New York: Routledge, 2006.

Matar, Nabil. "Homosexuality in the Early Novels of Negeeb Mahfouz." *Journal of Homosexuality* 26, no. 4 (1994): 77–90.

———. *Turks, Moors, and Englishmen in the Age of Discovery*. New York: Columbia University Press, 1999.

Mehrez, Samia. "Dr. Ramzy and Mr. Sharaf: Sonallah Ibrahim and the Duplicity of the Literary Field." In *Literature and Social Transformations*, edited by Wael Hallaq, 262–283. Leiden: Brill, 2000.

Menicucci, Garay. "Unlocking the Arab Celluloid Closet: Homosexuality in Egyptian Film." *Middle East Report* 206 (Spring 1998): 32–36.

Merabet, Sofian. "Disavowed Homosexualities in Beirut." *Middle East Report* 230 (Spring 2004): 30–33.

Mercer, Kobena, and Isaac Julien. "Race, Sexual Politics and Black Masculinity: A Dossier." In *Male Order, Unwrapping Masculinity*, edited by Rowena Chapman and Jonathan Rutherford. London: Lawrence and Wishart, 1988.

Mernissi, Fatima. *Beyond the Veil: Male-Female Dynamics in Modern Muslim Society* Cambridge: Schenkman Publishing Company, 1975.

———. *Beyond the Veil: Male-Female Dynamics in Modern Muslim Society*. Revised edition. Bloomington: Indiana University Press, 1987.

Mez, Adam. *The Renaissance of Islam*. Translated by Salahuddun Khuda Bakhsh and D. S. Margoliouth. Patna: Jubilee Printing and Publishing House, 1937.

Mullins, Greg. *Colonial Affairs: Bowles, Burroughs and Chester Write Tangier*. Madison: University of Wisconsin Press, 2002.

Murray, Stephen O., and Will Roscoe, editors. *Islamic Homosexualities: Culture, History, and Literature*. New York: New York University Press, 1997.

Musa, Salama. *The Education of Salama Musa*. Translated from the Arabic by L. O. Schuman. Leiden: Brill, 1961.

Musallam, Basim. *Sex and Society in Islam: Birth Control before the Nineteenth Century* New York: Cambridge University Press, 1983.

Nicholson, Reynold A. *A Literary History of the Arabs*. Cambridge: Cambridge University Press, 1966.

Nordau, Max. *Degeneration*. New York: Howard Fertig, 1968.

Orton, Joe. *The Orton Diaries*. Edited by John Lahr. New York: Perennial Harper, 1986.

Patai, Raphael. *The Arab Mind*. New York: Charles Scribner's Sons, 1976.

Poovey, Mary. *The Proper Lady and the Woman Writer: Ideology as Style in the Works of Mary Wollstonecraft, Mary Shelley, and Jane Austen*. Chicago: University of Chicago Press, 1984.

Povinelli, Elizabeth. *The Cunning of Recognition: Indigenous Alterities and the Making of Australian Multiculturalism*. Durham: Duke University Press, 2002.

Praz, Mario. *The Romantic Agony*. Translated by Angus Davidson. Second edition Oxford: Oxford University Press, 1970.

Reich, Wilhelm. *The Sexual Revolution: Toward a Self-Regulating Character Structure* New York: Farrar, Straus and Giroux, 1974.

Renan, Ernest. "Islamism and Science." Reproduced in *Orientalism: Early Sources*, volume 1, *Readings in Orientalism*, edited by Bryan S. Turner. London: Routledge, 2000.

Rich, Adrienne. "Compulsory Heterosexuality and Lesbian Existence." *Signs* 5, no. 4 (Summer 1980): 631–660.

Rifaat, Alifa. *Distant View of a Minaret and Other Short Stories*. Translated by Denys Johnson-Davies. London: Heinemann, 1983.

Riviere, Joan. "Womanliness as Masquerade." *International Journal of Psycho-Analysis* 10 (1929): 303–13.

Rousseau, Jean-Jacques. *On the Social Contract*. In Jean-Jacques Rousseau, *On the Social Contract, Discourse on the Origin of Inequality, and Discourse on Political Economy*. Indianapolis, Hackett Publishing Company, 1983.

Rowson, Everett K. "The Categorization of Gender and Sexual Irregularity in Medieval Arabic Vice Lists." In *Body Guards: The Cultural Politics of Gender Ambiguity*, edited by Julia Epstein and Kristina Straub, 50–70. New York: Routledge, 1991.

Rosenthal, Franz. "Ar-Razi on the Hidden Illness." In Franz Rosenthal, *Science and Medicine in Islam: A Collection of Essays*. Hampshire: Variorum, 1990.

Sabbah, Fatna A. *Woman in the Muslim Unconscious*. New York: Pergamon Press, 1984.

Said, Edward W. *Orientalism*. New York: Vintage, 1978.

———. "Orientalism Reconsidered." *Cultural Critique*, 1 (Fall 1985): 89–107.

———. *Culture and Imperialism*. New York: Alfred Knopf, 1993.

———. *Out of Place: A Memoir*. New York: Alfred A. Knopf, 1999.

Salih, Tayeb. *Season of Migration to the North*. Translated by Denys Johnson-Davies. London: Penguin, 2003.

Samman, Ghada. *Beirut '75*. Translated by Nancy N. Roberts. Fayetteville: University of Arkansas Press, 1995.

Saunders, J. J. "The Problem of Islamic Decadence." *Journal of World History 7*, no. 3 (1963): 701–720.

Schulze, Reinhard. "Mass Culture and Islamic Cultural Production in the 19th Century Middle East." In *Mass Culture, Popular Culture, and Social Life in the Middle East*, edited by Georg Stauth and Sami Zubaida, 189–222. Boulder: Westview Press, 1987.

Schmitt, Arno. "Gay Rights versus Human Rights: A Response to Joseph Massad." *Public Culture* 15 (Fall 2003): 587–592.

Schmitt, Arno, and Jehoeda Sofer, editors. *Sexuality and Eroticism among Males in Moslem Societies*. New York: Harrington Park Press, 1992.

Al-Shaykh, Hanan. *Women of Sand and Myrrh*. New York: Doubleday, 1992.

———. *Only in London*. Translated by Catherine Cobham. London: Bloomsbury, 2001.

Spivak, Gayatri Chakravorty. *A Critique of Post-Colonial Reason: Towards a History of the Vanishing Present*. Cambridge: Harvard University Press, 1999.

———. "Righting Wrongs." *South Atlantic Quarterly* 103, nos. 2–3 (Spring–Summer 2004): 523–81.

Stoler, Ann Laura. *Race and the Education of Desire: Foucault's History of Sexuality and the Colonial Order of Things*. Durham: Duke University Press, 1995.

Tardieu, August Ambroise. *Étude médico-légale sur les attentats aux moeurs*. Paris: Bailliére, 1857.

Uris, Leon. *Exodus*. New York: Doubleday, 1958.

U.S. Department of Justice, Bureau of Justice Statistics. *Violence by Intimates: Analysis of Data on Crimes by Current or Former Spouses, Boyfriends, and Girlfriends*. Edited by Lawrence Greenfeld et al. Publication no. NCJ167237. Washington, DC: U.S. Department of Justice, Office of Justice Programs, Bureau of Justice Statistics, 1988.

———. *Violence against Women: A National Crime Victimization Survey Report.* Edited by Ronet Bachman. Washington, DC: Department of Justice, Office of Justice Programs, Bureau of Justice Statistics, 1994.

Vidal, Gore. *The City and The Pillar, and Seven Early Stories.* New York: Random House, 1995.

Warner, Michael, editor. *Fear of a Queer Planet: Queer Politics and Social Theory.* Minneapolis: University of Minnesota Press, 1993.

Whitaker, Brian. *Unspeakable Love: Gay and Lesbian Life in the Middle East.* London: Dar al-Saqi, 2006.

Williams, Raymond. *The Country and the City.* Oxford: Oxford University Press, 1973.

———. *Marxism and Literature.* Oxford: Oxford University Press, 1977.

———. *Culture and Society, 1780–1950.* New York: Columbia University Press, 1983.

———. *Keywords, Vocabulary of Culture and Society.* Revised edition. Oxford: Oxford University Press, 1983.

Wollstonecraft, Mary. *A Vindication of the Rights of Woman.* New York: Dover, 1996.

Wockner, Rex. "Homosexuality in the Arab and Moslem World." In *Coming Out: an Anthology of International Gay and Lesbian Writings.* Edited by Stephen Likosky. New York: Pantheon Books, 1992.

Ziadat, Adel A. *Western Science in the Arab World: The Impact of Darwinism, 1860–1930.* New York: St. Martin's Press, 1986.

Name Index

Subject Index

Abbasids, 55, 58–61, 63, 66, 70, 72–77, 85, 86, 92–93, 97–98, 101, 103–104, 106–120, 121n, 123, 145, 151, 154, 192, 195–199, 232, 234, 236, 242–243, 257, 262, 298n, 367, 368
Abu Ghraib Prison, 44–45
Abu Hassan (opera), 54n
Abu Tartur, 67
adab, 61–62, 62n, 65,
adab al-ghilman, 198
Afghanistan, 10, 108, 177
Africans, sexual representations of, 11n, 177, 312, 323, 337, 338, 378–379, 380, 385, 386
AIDS, 174, 177, 187, 192, 206, 212–223, 241, 246, 250, 260–261, 264, 265, 335,
American University of Beirut, 58
Amnesty International, 161, 183, 256n
anal sex, 109, 137n, 175, 200, 230, 232, 249, 250, 261n, 387, 411n
Anglican Church, 175, 204
anus, 93, 148–149, 231, 249, 250, 251, 252, 258, 259, 303n, 317
Arab nationalism, 8,25, 47, 51, 53, 108, 112, 144, 193, 375
Arabian Nights. See Thousand and One Nights, A
Arabic novel, 269–272
arrested development, 86–87, 97, 154
Al-Azhar University, 6, 31, 66, 67, 73, 141, 222, 325

Bacchic poems. *See* khamriyyat
backwardness, 8, 11, 17, 18, 20, 21, 22, 23, 25, 26, 28, 37, 47, 53, 110, 194, 195, 209, 210, 216, 243, 268, 403
barghal, 394, 395, 395n, 398
bathhouses, 33–34, 256, 311, 323, 324
bawdiness. *See* Mujun
bawdy poets. *See* mujjan poets
buttocks, 125, 150, 258, 261n, 370, 400

Christian fundamentalists, 194, 207, 213, 215, 220, 221, 222,
Christianity, 13, 14, 52, 165, 171, 175, 201, 202, 205, 218, 219, 237, 265
civilization, x, 1–8, 13–16, 17, 20, 22, 28, 36, 47, 49, 50, 52–98, 99–144, 151, 157–159, 191–196, 199, 202–204, 207, 208, 213, 215, 217, 219, 223, 235, 239, 248, 254, 257, 258, 264, 335, 336–350, 366, 376, 377, 379, 386, 396, 413, 416–418
class analysis, 34, 39, 72, 92, 119, 135, 166, 182, 196, 197, 198, 238–240, 241–243, 253, 288, 321–323, 327, 353, 370, 405, 408
colonialism, 1–2, 5, 7–9, 17, 20, 22, 38–39, 46, 55, 78, 79, 100, 161, 177, 189n, 271–275, 278, 280, 281, 284–286, 287, 288–289,